J. Camp.
Feb. 1915

The Times

HISTORY

OF

THE WAR

VOL. II.

PRINTING HOUSE SQUARE.

PRINTED AND PUBLISHED BY "THE TIMES,"
PRINTING HOUSE SQUARE, LONDON.

1915.

201806

CONTENTS OF VOL. II.

CHAPTER XXX.

THE FIRST THREE MONTHS OF NAVAL WAR.

INTRODUCTION — THE NATURE OF NAVAL SUPREMACY — AN UNSEEN DOMINATION —PROTECTION OF TRANSPORTS — SECURITY OF COMMERCE AND SUPPLIES — ECONOMIC PRESSURE ON THE ENEMY — THE NEW MATÉRIEL — MINES — SUBMARINES — AIRCRAFT — A BRILLIANT RECORD — THE KING'S MESSAGE — ADMIRAL JELLICOE'S COMMAND — INITIAL OPERATIONS — THE NORTH SEA AREA — GERMAN STRATEGY — MINE-LAYING — LOSS OF THE "AMPHION" — THE "BIRMINGHAM'S" SUCCESS — MINE-SWEEPING — A SWEEP OF THE GERMAN COAST — VICTORY OFF HELIGOLAND — A BRILLIANT ENGAGEMENT — SUBMARINE RECONNAISSANCE — GAINS AND LOSSES — BRITISH MINE-FIELD IN THE NORTH SEA — LOSS OF "ABOUKIR," "HOGUE," AND "CRESSY" — FOUR GERMAN DESTROYERS SUNK — THE MEDITERRANEAN — FRENCH NAVAL POLICY — ESCAPE OF THE "GOEBEN" AND "BRESLAU" — THE BALTIC — BRITISH MONITORS ON THE FRENCH COAST.

THREE months of war shed light upon the conduct of naval operations in modern conditions, and threw into strong relief alike the efficiency and the predominance of the British Navy. In his memorable interview with the British Ambassador in Berlin, Sir E. Goschen, on August 4, the German Imperial Chancellor for a moment revealed his real convictions. The idea of British intervention was, he said, "terrible to a degree." The conjectures of the eager experts, who laboured to make their countrymen believe that naval supremacy no longer counted as in the past, and that modern weapons, combined with steam and speed, had imposed heavy disabilities upon the superior fleet, were soon brought to the test and proved unfounded. To Germany the might of the British Navy showed itself "terrible to a degree."

In the broad sense it can be said that the old lessons of naval war were strikingly re-affirmed, and that those who had strongly maintained that the many startling changes of *matériel* had not impaired the potency of the

superior fleet. or prevented our Navy from discharging its vitally important functions in war, were amply justified. In 1804 the positions of the British battle squadrons and the nature of the duties they were carrying on were almost unknown to the public. Yet, as Admiral Mahan has pointed out, "while bodily present before Brest, Rochefort and Toulon, strategically the British squadrons lay in the Straits of Dover barring the way against the Army of Invasion." More than this could be said of the British Grand Fleet after three months of war. Unseen since the war began it dominated the Western Campaign in the strategic sense. If it had not existed or had been overwhelmed, the sea-board of France would have been at the mercy of the enemy. Large forces might have been landed, which would have gravely embarrassed the French Armies. No British troops would have been available to stem the first German onset and—steadily reinforced—to have co-operated powerfully in hurling back the invaders and holding them fast at a long distance from their objective—Paris. British and French trade

1

FIRST AND SECOND SQUADRONS AT SEA,   [*Cribb, Southsea.*
Headed by the "Iron Duke" and the "Marlborough."

would have been paralysed, and no oversea possession of either would have been secure. England would have been daily expecting invasion, with an unemployed population clamouring for food. Now, as in the great wars of the past, the better fleet proved not only the "sure shield" of the nation, but the firm basis of offensive action. The British Navy set free the whole military forces of the Empire and enabled them to be brought to

bear upon the needs of the land campaign. More than 350,000 men were transported across the seas without a single mishap. German shipping was either captured or driven to seek refuge in neutral ports, with the result of economic pressure upon Germany that was certain to increase with every month of war. The attack upon British commerce, elaborately planned and supported by measures taken before the outbreak of war, proved far less serious than had been expected. The Admiralty was able to point out in October that only 1 per cent. "out of 4,000 British ships engaged in foreign trade" had been sunk, and that the rate of insurance for cargoes, originally fixed at 5 per cent., had "been reduced to two guineas per cent. without injury to the solvency of the fund." Moreover, a portion of the relatively small losses—that caused by the Emden especially—was due in part to the preoccupation of the ships of war in convoying troops, while "a large number" of these losses was "caused by merchant vessels taking everything for granted and proceeding without due precautions." Lastly, as at the battle of the Alma, but with infinitely greater effect, British ships had directly co-operated with military forces and powerfully aided in defeating violent attacks on the left of the line of the Allies in Flanders.

While thus, in the strategic sense, the effect of changed *matériel* had been to extend the power of the superior Navy, and to enable that power to be exerted in a shorter time than formerly, the new conditions had led to significant results. The large use of mines by the

[*Russell, Southsea.*
REAR-ADMIRAL C. E. MADDEN,
Chief of the Staff.

Germans, in direct violation of accepted restrictions, caused the Admiralty to adopt similar measures, and ultimately to proclaim the North Sea a "military area." German naval activity at the outset was practically confined to mine-laying and to the employment of submarines; but our losses in ships of war relatively to our strength were small compared with those of the Japanese in 1904. We had to deplore the deaths of too many gallant men, deprived by the new methods of warfare of the chance of striking a blow; but our naval strength was not sensibly reduced, and our means of carrying on the war remained unimpaired, and were in some respects increased.

Of the powers of submarines we learned many valuable lessons. They proved to be dangerous antagonists, as was expected. They also showed their disabilities during the action off Heligoland on August 27. Vice-Admiral Beatty states that several attacks by submarines were made; but "our high speed," "rapid manœuvring," and "the use of the helm," combined with a smooth sea, effectually frustrated them. On the other hand, when continued patrolling at slow speed without destroyers in company, or when slowing down to search craft which may have been decoys, was resorted to, we paid the penalty. Of the work of our own submarines, as described by Commodore Keyes, it is impossible to speak too highly. For reconnoitring purposes they, from the first days of war, proved invaluable. Their officers showed skill and daring beyond all praise, and that their successes were fewer than those of the Germans was wholly due to the fact that the number of enemy ships at sea was trivial compared with our own. British destroyers were able to sink only one ship with the torpedo; but their varied and strenuous work was supremely valuable, and as a deterrent to the submarine they showed their importance. The prompt action of the Commander of the Badger is significant, and we learned that the submarines must always be attacked, and that "low visibility and a calm sea" are "the most unfavourable conditions" for their activity. Finally, in the new arm, the Navy gave proof of the highest efficiency and boldness. The raids on Düsseldorf and Cologne rank among the finest instances of the successful and legitimate use of aircraft.

Such were the achievements of the Royal Navy in three months, and the history of naval war records none equal in importance, or so far-reaching in scope, within such a period. No great fleet action was fought, which was in accordance with the teaching of the past; but the unseen battle fleet controlled that of

SUNDAY SERVICE ON BOARD H.M.S. "NEPTUNE." [*Cribb, Sou'hsea.*

A DREADNOUGHT STEAMING THROUGH A ROUGH SEA.   [*Cribb, Southsea.*]

the enemy, provided the support upon which the whole of the British naval operations depended, and thus brought enormous weight to bear upon the cause of the Allies. British naval strength was growing. The one defect—the paucity of light cruisers, due to five years' neglect of this valuable type of vessel—was being gradually remedied. The Empire and its Allies could continue to repose the fullest confidence in the " tremendous weapon " of British sea-power.

" At this grave moment in our national history I send to you, and through you to the officers and men of the fleets of which you have assumed command, the assurance of my confidence that under your direction they will revive and renew the old glories of the Royal Navy, and prove·once again the sure shield of Britain and of her Empire in the hour of trial.

" GEORGE, R.I."

The above message was communicated to the senior naval officers on all stations outside of home waters, and published on August 5.

The Admiralty at the same time issued the following :

" With the approval of His Majesty the King, Admiral Sir John R. Jellicoe, K.C.B., K.C.V.O., has assumed supreme command of the Home Fleets, with the acting rank of Admiral, and Rear-Admiral Charles E. Madden, C.V.O., has been appointed to be his Chief of the Staff."

On Monday, August 3, 1914, in a supplement to the *London Gazette* the following proclamation was published :

1. Men of the Royal Naval Reserve and Royal Fleet Reserve, and officers and men of the Royal Naval Volunteer Reserve, are called out " into actual service."

2. Officers of the Royal Naval Reserve are called out " for actual service."

3. The term of service of time-expired men in the Royal Navy is extended for five years should their services be so long required.

4. The Admiralty may requisition for use as transports and for similar purposes any British ship or British vessel within the British Isles " or the waters adjacent thereto " ; payment on terms to be arranged afterwards to be made for such use.

This was followed by a supplementary proclamation, " For extending the services of time-expired men in the Royal Navy." An Admiralty notice calling out the Reserves had been published in *The Times* on the previous day.

" Three hours after the outbreak of war, Submarines E6, Lieutenant-Commander Cecil

P. Talbot, and E8, Lieutenant-Commander Francis H. H. Goodhart, proceeded unaccompanied to carry out a reconnaissance in the Heligoland Bight. These two vessels returned with useful information and had the privilege of being the pioneers on a service which is attended with some risk." This sentence is extracted from the despatch dated October 17 of Commodore Roger Keyes, and demonstrates that no weed accumulated on the bottoms of the ships of His Majesty's Navy while they were waiting to attack the foe.

War on the sea, no less than war on the land, is influenced by the area in which it is waged ; and although all the seven seas are open as a battle-ground for the opposing fleets, as a matter of practical fact the struggle—which matters—has to be fought out in the North Sea, "and the waters adjacent thereto," as is set down in the proclamation already quoted.

If we draw a line across the North Sea due west from Hantsholmer Light on the coast of Denmark, we shall strike the coast of Scotland at Girdleness, just to the southward of Aberdeen ; and it is roughly 380 miles from one point to the other. From Hantsholmer to the Elbe the coast runs nearly due south, then turning sharply to the west, it creeps through sand and shoal to Terschelling ; here it trends south-south-west to the Texel and on in the same general direction to Blankenberg and Ostend through the maze of shoals off Rotterdam and Antwerp. From the mouth of the Scheldt it turns sharply to the westward, the lie of the land to Grisnez, near Calais, being west-south-west ; here is the narrowest portion

of the sea known as Dover Straits or the Pas de Calais. Our own coast trends in a south-westerly direction from Girdleness to the Forth and then south by east to the Wash ; then south to Winterton, Haisborough, and Lowestoft, afterwards in a generally south-westerly direction to Dover Straits. The course from Dover Straits clearing all obstructions to the Hantsholmer-Girdleness line would be about north-east by north. The area thus defined may be conceived to be the southern manœuvring area in the North Sea for battle fleets in time of war. It is 380 miles wide at the north, it is 21 miles wide at the south ; a clear run through it is 360 miles ; but we have yet to observe how this area is further circumscribed.

The North Sea is of all seas the most shallow, and from the Hantsholmer-Girdleness line to the Dover Straits you may seek long for a depth of 60 fathoms—and then in all probability you will not find it—while in a line from Great Grimsby to Terschelling—which is where the absolute definite contraction of the coast begins, and which is some 180 miles in length from east to west—you will be hard put to it to find 20 fathoms. If we study the chart to the southward of a line thus drawn and consider it as a manœuvring area for the deep-draught ships of modern navies we shall see how constricted it is ; as from Dover Straits to the Grimsby-Terschelling line a fleet to have open water must stand outside the Goodwins, the Galloper, and the Outer Gabbard. There is then, from Orford-ness to Scheveningen, an area which is clear

H.M.S. "BADGER," [*Symonds, Portsmouth.*
Which rammed and sank a German submarine off the Dutch coast.

MINES.　　[*Cribb, Southsea.*
Photograph to illustrate the position of mines and ship.

of shoals, that begin again at Smith's Knoll on the west and the Texel on the east. It is from Dover Straits to the Grimsby-Terschelling line some 170 miles; from Smith's Knoll to the Texel about 85 miles. The area is small indeed, and owing to the speed of modern battleships, opposing fleets in this area would in all probability not be long before they met; especially having in view their heavy draught, which precludes any close approach to the shore. England has access to the sea from scores of magnificent ports; Germany by means of infinite labour and appalling expense has driven channels through the sands by which she is surrounded to enable her heavy-draught battleships to reach such open ocean as is provided by the North Sea. West from Terschelling to the Elbe, and north from the Elbe again to the Horn reefs on the coast of Denmark, the coast is a seaman's nightmare. That such a littoral should shelter the second greatest naval Power of the day is a measure of the stern activity, of the resolute determination, displayed by these seekers for the sea.

It may be asked why this point has been dwelt upon. The answer is that it is here, in the area described, that must be fought out the battle for the mastery of the sea. It was not for us to cherish delusions that the High Sea Fleet of Germany was going to remain in port for ever. Naval strategy, no less than that of the land, decrees the waiting for the right moment to strike. In the past many people were misled by "frantic boast and foolish word" of the self-appointed champions of German sea expansion; and were intensely surprised that the lightning-like "hussar stroke," which was to follow immediately on the declaration of war, was not attempted. But however much the gallant officers and men of the High Sea Fleet might be longing to get at their enemy, it was certain that they would not be loosed on their mission until a favourable opportunity occurred. In the meanwhile the policy of attrition on the military side, and the destruction of mercantile shipping on the commercial side, was being worked for all that it was worth. Also, " in spite of spite," we have to admit that the German Navy did well. Both their torpedo attacks and their raids on our merchantmen were attended with far more success than we cared to contemplate; and we could salute those brave and enterprising officers who had deserved so well of their service and their country.

In the past we heard that war if it came would most certainly be at " Germany's selected moment "; that the programme she had mapped out for herself would be carried out, and that before war had been declared half an hour determined and desperate attacks by torpedo craft would have seriously impaired the fighting efficiency of our fleet. As we all know, this did not happen; England was ready and there was no chance for the surprise attack. What, then, was left for the weaker combatant to accomplish? We were not left long in doubt; with an utter disregard of the rights of neutrals, mines were laid wherever the mine-layers could succeed in dropping their deadly cargoes near by the waters of the United Kingdom. On Wednesday, August 5, H.M.S. Amphion and the third destroyer flotilla fell in with the Königin Luise some forty miles from Antwerp; this vessel, a Hamburg-Amerika liner of about 2,000 tons, had been converted into a minelayer, and probably carried four to five hundred mines. What her destination was is unknown, but it is likely to have been the mouth of the Thames, where, had she succeeded in her mission, the destruction wrought would certainly have been considerable. Summoned to surrender after a chase which lasted some hours, she declined, and was accordingly sunk by gun fire ; twenty-eight wounded men from her crew were brought into Harwich and landed from the destroyers. We had not long to wait for an indication of the deadliness of the mine as a passive instrument of warfare, as on the following day H.M.S. Amphion struck a mine and foundered almost immediately. She was a new ship of 3,440 tons and had cost some £280,000 ; in her case, fortunately, a considerable proportion of the crew, including her commanding officer, Captain Cecil H. Fox, were saved. On Sunday, August 9, an attack was made by German submarines on the first light cruiser squadron ; this was quite in accordance with the " attrition " tactics of the foe, but it ended unfortunately for him, as one German submarine was sunk, the U15. Subsequently the First Lord of the Admiralty telegraphed to the Lord Mayor of Birmingham as follows : " Birmingham will be proud to learn that the first German submarine destroyed in the war was sunk by H.M.S. Birmingham."

Whenever and wherever it was possible the enemy laid his mines, and had it not been for the counter measures of the British Admiralty the narrow seas by a very early date in the course of hostilities would have been closed to navigation altogether ; save at a risk that few mariners would have cared to undertake. An antidote was provided in the shape of a special section of the Royal Naval Reserve, which was employed in mine sweeping. At the beginning of the war there were 142 officers and 1,136 men employed in this duty, and the numbers both of men and craft employed were afterwards considerably augmented. The craft were trawlers, the men fishermen, brave men, almost

SINKING OF H.M.S. "AMPHION." [*Beckett.*
This photograph was taken 30 seconds after the magazine had exploded.

H.M.S. "PATHFINDER."   [*Cribb, Southsea.*
Sunk by a German submarine on the East Coast.

unimaginably hardy, and who knew the North
Sea as intimately as the landsman knows the
inside of his bedroom. Their method of conducting their special business was with a
weighted steel hawser between two trawlers,
which, going ahead abreast of one another, in
this manner sweep the bed of the ocean. When
the hawser strikes the mooring of a mine, the
mine is brought to the surface and rendered
harmless by being exploded by a shot from an
accompanying destroyer.

On August 19 the British Admiralty,
through the Press Bureau, announced that
" a certain liveliness " was noticeable in
the North Sea ; that enemy vessels had
made their appearance : destroyers, scouting
cruisers, and suchlike *poussière navale*, as
the French call their subsidiary units ; but
although some long-range shots were exchanged,
and although cruisers were invited to come out
from the coast and to destroy destroyers flying
the White Ensign, which were moving with
somewhat suspicious slowness towards sister
vessels tucked away beneath the distant blue-
grey horizon line, the net was spread idly in
the sight of a bird too wideawake to be thus
decoyed. The "liveliness" announced by the
Press Bureau did not extend itself to the main
fleet of Admiral von Ingenohl.

During the third week in August a sweep had
been made of the waters between the British

and the German coasts, but the naval forces of
the German Empire were still apparently
stowed away in the Kiel Canal, or in the well-
protected waters adjacent to that strategical
waterway.

Then at last came an action in the Heligoland
Bight. Both strategically and tactically this
action was full of instruction. It was also the best
of omens for subsequent battles afloat, as the
insight displayed by the higher command was
no less admirable than the tactical dispositions
carried out, and the gallantry of the officers
and men employed in the action. " The Saucy
Arethusa " added another wreath to that
chaplet of fame which has ever surrounded the
name of the famous frigate that captured the
Belle Poule. In what manner it was discovered
that the enemy was on the move, that cruisers,
submarines, and destroyers were " showing a
certain liveliness," we have not been told ;
but from the despatch of Vice-Admiral Sir
David Beatty it is easy to see that the fleet
did not reach a certain rendezvous merely to
take part in another sweeping movement ; in
fact this theory is disposed of by Rear-Admiral
Christian, H.M.S. Euryalus, who speaks of " a
reconnaissance in force with the object of
attacking the enemy's light cruisers and
destroyers." The disposition of force seems
to have been as follows : Outside of all were
the battle cruisers which were " watchfully

waiting"; then the cruiser force, waiting also "watchfully" to intercept any enemy vessels chased to the westward; and lastly the Arethusa and Fearless, accompanied by the first and third flotillas of destroyers, which flotillas were short of four ships—the Hornet, Tigress, Hydra and Loyal.

On August 21, while the cruiser force was coaling, a message was received from a light cruiser by wireless, "Am being chased by enemy's cruisers," followed a few minutes afterwards by "Am engaging enemy's cruisers."

Great is the discipline of the Navy; but it is to be feared that the busy silence of coaling ship on this occasion was broken by many whispered conversations; to be exchanged for a subdued cheer when through the coherers of the wireless came the message, "Proceed at once to the assistance of Fearless." The colliers were immediately cast off and the five cruisers swept out to sea like greyhounds slipped from the leash. But in the end disappointment awaited them. The elusive, tantalising, well-named Fearless had drawn the enemy away from his coasts—near enough even to shell the audacious fleeing twenty-seven-knot light cruiser.

But the ecstasy of combat for which they yearned was not long to be denied to them; for at 3.30 a.m. on Friday, August 28, the Fearless and Arethusa, the latter vessel the pioneer ship of a new class and less than three days out of the builders' hands, escorted by some twenty destroyers, were advancing in a

[*Heath, Plymouth.*

COMMODORE TYRWHITT,
H.M.S. "Arethusa."

south-westerly direction at twenty knots, on a course that would bring them to a point some six miles south and three miles west of Heligoland. Before we proceed with the story of the action it is well to draw attention to the Arethusa and the conditions in which she went into battle. Whenever a ship is commissioned

H.M.S. "BERWICK," [*London News Agency.*
Which captured a German armed merchant cruiser and two colliers in Atlantic waters.

[Speaight.

VICE-ADMIRAL SIR DAVID BEATTY,
In command of the First Battle Cruiser Squadron.

it naturally takes her some time to shake down ; for the officers to know their men ; for the men to know their officers. There are naturally a thousand and one things to be done before she attains to the status of a well-ordered man-of-war. None of these things had been done, none of them could have been done ; save and except the assignment of the company to their stations. They had never worked together ; they were strangers in all to one another ; strangers save for that cord which bound them indissolubly.

The day on which the battle occurred was brilliantly fine but extremely hazy, while the sea was so smooth that Admiral Beatty reports the track of a torpedo fired could easily be traced by the wake of bubbles that these fearsome instruments of war leave upon the surface of the water. At 8 o'clock dim shadows became visible through the mist to the reconnoitring English ships ; these were soon discovered to be six German destroyers. Course was altered six points to port and orders given to engage as soon as possible. At 8.30 a.m. fire was opened by the Arethusa and some of the destroyers, and at 8.45 a.m. the course was altered again, bringing the rest of the destroyers into the fight.

At the same time three German cruisers of the same class as the British " Town "

cruisers were sighted. (The " Town " class, of which at the outbreak of war there were fifteen in the British Navy, are light cruisers ranging from 4,800 to 5,400 tons). These ships came into action and the fight became general. The German fire was fairly well directed on the whole, though many of the shots fell short and exploded on striking the water. In spite of this the Arethusa came in for severe handling between 9 a.m. and 9.45, and at 10 o'clock she had to haul out temporarily, as only her foremost 6-inch gun was capable of continuing to fire. Why at this juncture the German cruisers did not close in and complete her destruction only the commanders of those vessels could explain. The fact remains, however, that they did not follow up what was an undoubted success, and after 55 minutes' strenuous work on board of the British light cruiser she steamed into action again. In Commodore Tyrwhitt's official report he states :

Two cruisers with four and two funnels respectively were sighted on the port bow at 7.57 a.m., the nearest of which was engaged. Arethusa received a heavy fire from both cruisers and several destroyers until 8.15, when the four-funnelled cruiser transferred her fire to Fearless. Close action was continued with the two-funnelled cruiser on converging courses until 8.25, when a 6-inch projectile from Arethusa wrecked the forebridge of the enemy, who at once turned away in the direction of Heligoland, which was sighted slightly on the starboard bow at the same time. All ships were at once ordered to turn to the westward, and shortly afterwards speed was reduced to 20 knots. During this action Arethusa had

[Symonas, Portsmouth.

COMMODORE W. E. GOODENOUGH,
Who took part in the action in the Heligoland Bight.

H.M.S. "CUMBERLAND." [*London News Agency.*

This cruiser made many captures off the Cameron River.

been hit many times and was considerably damaged : only one 6-inch gun remained in action, all other guns and torpedo tubes having been temporarily disabled.

By this time the German formation had become very ragged and several of their destroyers were out of the fight, apparently fully occupied in attempting to keep themselves afloat. As the struggle progressed, the Arethusa continued to monopolise most of the enemy fire, and a shell which damaged her feed tank materially reduced her speed. She was, notwithstanding, able to continue, and it soon was evident that one of the German cruisers was in a bad way : two of her funnels had gone, also her mainmast, and she was blazing furiously amidships ; she continued, nevertheless, to keep up a spirited fire from her foremost and after guns.

A comparison between the Arethusa and the Mainz may be appropriate here. The British ship launched in 1913 was 3,520 tons ; 30,000 horse-power ; speed, 29 knots. She was armed with two 6-inch and six 4-inch guns and four above-water torpedo tubes that discharged the 21-inch torpedo. The German cruiser was launched in 1909 and was 4,350 tons ; horse-power (designed), 20,000 ; speed, 25·5 knots. Armament, twelve 4·1-inch guns ; two machine ; and two under-water

torpedo tubes firing the 18-inch torpedo. It will be seen that the British cruiser design was much superior to the German. The smaller vessel was 3·5 knots the faster. The British 6-inch gun fired a 100 lb. projectile, the British 4-inch gun fired a 25 lb. shot, the German 4·1 one of 31 lbs.

So far the battle had been waged by the light cruisers and destroyers alone on our side ; out to seaward, however, enemy submarines were engaged in attacking the Battle Cruiser Squadron ; the water was smooth, the submarines were detected in time, and Admiral Beatty, manœuvring at high speed, had no difficulty in avoiding these unpleasant attentions. Meanwhile all ears were strained on board the big ships listening to the sounds of the distant firing. No doubt many impatient comments were passed at not being allowed to have a hand in the game. But at last their time came. The official report from Admiral Beatty runs :—

At 12.15 Fearless and First Flotilla were sighted retiring west. At the same time the Light Cruiser Squadron was observed to be engaging an enemy ship ahead. They appeared to have her beat. I then steered N.E. to sounds of firing ahead, and at 12.30 p.m. sighted Arethusa and Third Flotilla retiring to the westward engaging a cruiser of the Kolberg class on our port bow. I steered to cut her off from Heligoland, and

[Heath, Plymouth.

COMMODORE ROGER KEYES,
Commanding Submarine Flotilla.

at 12.37 opened fire. At 12.42 the enemy turned to the
N.E., and we chased at 27 knots. At 12.56 p.m. sighted
and engaged a two-funnelled cruiser ahead. Lion fired
two salvoes at her, which took effect, and she disappeared
into the mist burning furiously and in a sinking condition. In view of the mist and that she was steering at
high speed at right angles to the Lion, who was steaming
at 28 knots, the Lion's firing was very creditable.

It would appear that only the Lion among the
big ships actually fired, the remainder arriving
on the scene to see the German cruiser Mainz
lying on her beam ends with only a propeller
and her starboard quarter showing, while a
heap of wreckage marked the spot where the
Köln had gone down; and a dim ruddy glare
in the haze showed where the third cruiser
was drifting away, her hull a blazing furnace.

The account of the action issued through the
Press Bureau speaks thus of the destroyers
engaged :—

Although only two of the enemy destroyers were
actually observed to sink, most of the eighteen or twenty
boats rounded up and attacked were well punished, and
only saved themselves by scattered flight. The superior
gun power and strength of the British destroyers, ship
for ship, was conclusively demonstrated. The destroyers
themselves did not hesitate to engage the enemy cruisers,
both with gun and torpedoes, with hardihood, and two
of them, the Laurel and Liberty, got knocked about in
the process. Intercepted German signals and other
information from German sources confirms the report of
Vice-Admiral Beatty as to the sinking of the third
German cruiser, which now appears to have been the
Ariadne. . . . The complements of the five German
vessels known to have been sunk aggregated about
1,200 officers and men, all of whom, with the exception of
some 330 wounded and unwounded prisoners, perished.

Besides this there is the loss, which must have been
severe, on board the German torpedo boats (the Germans
never use the term " destroyers ") and other cruisers
which did not sink in the action. The total British
casualties amounted to 69 killed and wounded, among
whom must, however, be included two officers of exceptional merit—Lieutenant-Commander Nigel K. W.
Barttelot and Lieutenant Eric W. P. Westmacott. All
the British ships will be fit for service in a week or ten
days. The success of this operation was due, in the first
instance, to the information brought to the Admiralty
by the submarine officers, who have during the past
three weeks showed extraordinary daring and enterprise
in penetrating the enemy's waters.

A remarkable description of this action
was given in a letter of an officer to the *Morning
Post* :—

The Mainz was immensely gallant. The last I saw
of her, absolutely wrecked alow and aloft, her whole
midships a fuming inferno. She had one gun forward
and one aft still spitting forth fury and defiance, " like a
wild cat mad with wounds." Our own four-funnelled
friend recommenced at this juncture with a couple of
salvoes, but rather half-heartedly ; and we really did not
care a damn, for there straight ahead of us in lordly
procession, like elephants walking through a pack of
pi-dogs, came the Lion, Queen Mary, Invincible, and
New Zealand, our battle cruisers. Great and grim and
uncouth as some antediluvian monsters, how solid they
looked, how utterly earth-quaking ! We pointed out our
latest aggressor to them, whom they could not see from
where they were, and they passed down the field of
battle with the little destroyers on their left and the
destroyed on their right, and we went west while they
went east, and turned north between poor four-funnels
and her home, and just a little later we heard the
thunder of their guns for a space, then all silence, and we
knew. Then wireless—Lion to all ships and destroyers
—" Retire."

That was all. Remains only little details, only one of
which I will tell you. The most romantic, dramatic and
piquant episode that modern war can ever show. The
Defender, having sunk an enemy, lowered a whaler to
pick up her swimming survivors ; before the whaler got
back an enemy's cruiser came up and chased the Defender,
and thus she abandoned her whaler. Imagine their
feelings : alone in an open boat without food, 25 miles

[Central News.

REAR-ADMIRAL A. H. CHRISTIAN,
H.M.S " Euryalus."

THE SINKING OF THE "MAINZ."

Sketch, constructed from authoritative sources, depicting the last moments of the "Mainz," which was finished off by the "Fearless," and Commodore Goodenough's Light Cruiser Squadron.   (*See page 12.*)

from the nearest land, and that land the enemy's fortress, with nothing but fog and foes around them. Suddenly a swirl alongside, and up, if you please, pops His Britannic Majesty's submarine E4, opens his conning tower, takes them all on board, shuts up again, dives, and brings them home 250 miles ! Is not that magnificent ? No novel would dare face the critics with an episode like that in it, except, perhaps, Jules Verne ; and all true.

At the time of the action it was widely reported that German officers had fired on their men while in the water. This, however, appears not to have been the case. What happened was that the men in the Mainz, seeing the approach of the battle cruisers, were seized with panic and were deserting their guns. Then it was that the officers fired upon them as they fled across the deck and flung themselves overboard. Out-generalled, out-manœuvred and out-fought, we can still give every credit to the German officers ; they fought their ships till they sank beneath them, and more than this no man can do.

It is perhaps somewhat difficult to take a perfectly calm and judicial survey of a success-

ful feat of arms performed by one's own countrymen ; nevertheless, restraining all enthusiasm, let us look at it from four points of view. These are (1) reconnaissance, (2) strategy, (3) tactics, (4) discipline and training as exemplified in the actual fighting.

In all military operations efficient reconnaissance must precede action. From August 5 until August 28, the date of the Heligoland action, the enemy must have been kept under constant surveillance by the submarines.

The doings of the enemy were faithfully and accurately reported to the higher command. In their hands lay the decision when, where, and at what time to attack ; also to decide what force was necessary. Here, again, nothing was left to chance, and that first principle of having an overwhelming force at the right place and at the right time was carried out with success. The question arises very naturally, what would have happened had the main German fleet sallied forth, as it might very well have done, in support of its lighter craft ? In that case would not the whole operation have been seriously endangered ? The answer to this is that though we know Vice-Admiral Beatty and his Battle Cruiser Squadron were in support, and that they came into action exactly as it were to time-table, we are not told what ships were held in reserve behind his force. Had the enemy battle fleet elected to come out, no doubt they also would have found as warm a welcome as did their sisters, the cruisers and destroyers. Tactically the battle left nothing to be desired. With the screen of cruisers for " cripple stopping," with the support of the battle cruisers, the light cruisers and flotillas went gaily about their work. There were moments of peril for some, as we have seen in the case of the Arethusa, also in the Laurel, the leader of the third flotilla, which came upon the German cruisers unsupported by any of our vessels of that class. Being in action with two destroyers and a cruiser at the same time, she was badly knocked about, and was only saved by the timely appearance of the British cruisers when only three rounds of ammunition remained in her lockers. But there must be critical moments in any battle either by land or sea.

Fine and gallant as was the action in the

Heligoland Bight, it was still, as an operation of war, of comparatively minor importance from the point of view of the number of enemy ships destroyed and of officers and men put out of action. Where its real importance lies is as a test case of capacity from the Commander-in-Chief in his flagship down to the boy on the lower deck. The nation was entitled to draw from this brilliant little affair the highest hopes for the future.

Continuing our record chronologically we next come to the loss of the Speedy, a gunboat, which struck a mine and foundered, her bottom blown out by one of those contrivances with which the North Sea had been strewn by the enemy. She was an old vessel of small fighting capacity and the casualties were few in number. It was noticed at this time that in nearly every case the locality in which the mines were laid was some thirty miles from the shore, and almost opposite to the commercial harbours on the East coast.

The loss of the Speedy occurred on September 3, and on Saturday, September 5, the nation had to mourn the loss of the Pathfinder, a light cruiser of 2,940 tons, and a complement of 268 officers and men ; unfortunately in her case there was considerable loss of life. This vessel was sunk off May Island, Firth of Forth,

AN ENGLISH MINE READY TO BE PUT OVERBOARD.　　*[Record Press.*

A SUBMARINE MINE EXPLOSION.   [*Sport and General.*

by a German submarine. There was some question at first if she had not struck a mine, but the statements of the survivors are quite clear that the periscope of their assailant was seen. The survivors were rescued by the destroyer Stag after being in the water for an hour and seventeen minutes. On September 15 the Hela, a German light cruiser, was sunk by Submarine E9 six miles south of Heligoland. She was a vessel of 2,040 tons, with a complement of 178, and was of small fighting value.

During September an order was issued by the Admiralty to the effect that, as it had become obvious that minelaying was still going on, also that no ship dared to show a German flag in the North Sea, the mines must be laid by vessels under a neutral flag. Consequently it was the duty of all ships, while observing due courtesy to neutral countries, to stop and search every vessel that hove in sight. Such an order as this is much easier to give than to obey, as the North Sea compared to other highways of the ocean is as the Strand at midday to a sleepy country lane. On the Dogger Bank, and in the shallows between the Maas Light and Terschelling, fishing boats alone are often to be counted by the score; and active agents of the enemy no doubt frequently received most valuable information as to the movements of British men-of-war from perfectly well-meaning and unsuspicious fishermen. It is the opinion of many persons

that it was this that led directly to the misfortune which happened on September 22.

For weeks after the outbreak of war calms and fogs and smooth seas prevailed in the North Sea. On September 11 a complete change came in the weather, and for the next ten days, right up to the morning of the 22nd, it blew furiously with a high short steep sea, characteristic of these waters, and the wind was accompanied by frequent blinding deluges of rain. The line of the patrol was moved something further along to the north, and was, for the most part, carried out without the accompanying destroyers, the weather being far too bad for these small craft to keep the sea. This weather culminated in a whole gale on September 18, in which the force of the wind was quite exceptional for northern latitudes, and almost paralleled that of the cyclone or the typhoon. On the 21st, the wind having moderated somewhat, arrangements were made for the destroyers to come out of harbour on the morning of the 22nd and to join the Aboukir, the Hogue, and the Cressy about 10 a.m. The morning broke cloudless with no haze, a brisk northerly wind and a short choppy sea. The cruisers had just separated out to their day patrol stations, three miles apart, when a few minutes before 6.30 a.m. the Aboukir was seen to reel violently and then settle down with a list to port. The Aboukir had been struck by a torpedo.

H.M.S. "ABOUKIR,"

Sunk by a German submarine in the North Sea.   The "Hogue" and "Cressy" were of the same class.

We will now quote the words of an eye-witness of the disaster :

There was only one explosion, and most of the onlookers were of opinion that she (the Aboukir) had struck a mine, and following their first and strongest impulse, both the Cressy and Hogue closed in at once to save life. At 6.55 a.m. the Hogue was within a quarter of a mile of the Aboukir on her starboard bow, with the Cressy a similar distance away on the other side. The Aboukir had started to lower her starboard seaboat, but the list had become so great that she stuck and could not be got away. The sun was shining very brightly, and the red glow of her copper bottom with the pink naked bodies of the men as they climbed down her sides made a picture that will never be forgotten.

Some jumped in, others sat down and slid, still others contented themselves with walking a few paces as the vessel heeled over. Suddenly, with two tremendous crashes, one immediately after the other, the Hogue was struck, both torpedoes exploding in the same place, just aft of the starboard after bridge. The ship leapt up like a rowelled horse (she is a vessel of 12,000 tons, so this gives some idea of the violence of the explosion); and quivered all over, just as a steel spring will quiver when firmly held at one end and sharply struck at the other. Looking over the side the twin lines of bubbles made by the torpedoes were plainly visible and led the eye at once to the first sight of the submarine's periscope. The Hogue's two seaboats had been got away, together with the launch, in aid of the Aboukir, and the latter with a number of saved was close to on the port bow. When the Hogue was struck she stood off a few yards and waited. Meanwhile another party were busy throwing overboard several planks and baulks of timber whic⁴ had been used for the construction of targets. The rest of the men stood quietly by waiting for the order to jump, and passing the time in slipping off their clothes. After a few minutes the order came and the men went in. Unfortunately, obeying a natural impulse, by far the greater majority went off the port bow close

to where the launch lay, and as the Hogue disappeared about six minutes after she had been struck scores of them clung to the gunwales of the launch until she was unable to stand the strain and fell to pieces, precipitating her own crew and those unfortunates already saved from the Aboukir. What followed is best left to the imagination, suffice it to say that nearly all those from the Hogue who were lost perished here.

By something like a miracle, as the Hogue went down, she partially righted, with the result that the steam picket boat and steam pinnace both floated off her undamaged, and in this manner many of the survivors were saved. At this juncture the Cressy came up, and—says the narrative—" opened fire with both batteries on the submarines (sic)." She continued the work of rescue until she herself was struck amidships by two torpedoes and sank almost at once. The Flora, of Ymuiden, and a Lowestoft trawler did noble work in rescuing those still floating about in the water when they arrived on the scene, also the Titan, of Rotterdam. The men from the boats were taken on board the steamers, and when it became clear that no more survivors could be picked up each left for its own port. As the Flora steamed away eye-witnesses stated positively that three conning towers of submarines were sighted, yet the German account declared that only one was engaged in this action, so disastrous in its loss of life to the British Navy.

Judged by modern standards the fighting powers of the sunken cruisers was not great, and, as a purely material loss, the deduction from our sea strength was insignificant. Part of the official comment issued by the Secretary of the Admiralty runs thus :

The loss of nearly 60 officers and 1,400 men would not have been grudged if it had been brought about by gunfire in an open action, but it is particularly dis-. tressing under the conditions that prevailed. The absence of any of the ardour and excitement of an engagement did not, however, prevent the display of discipline, cheerful courage, and ready self-sacrifice among all ranks and ratings exposed to the ordeal.

We cannot close this episode in the history of the war without recording the noble sympathy, the practical goodness, the whole-hearted compassion shown to the British sailors by the Dutch people of all ranks and classes. Their true philanthropy was one of the brightest spots in the almost unrelieved gloom of a terrible sea tragedy.

On October 3 the Secretary of the Admiralty communicated the following :

The German policy of minelaying, combined with their submarine activities, makes it necessary on military grounds for the Admiralty to adopt counter measures. His Majesty's Government have therefore authorised a mine-laying policy in certain areas, and a system of mine-fields has been established and is being developed upon a considerable scale.

In order to reduce risks to non-combatants, the Admiralty announce that it is dangerous henceforward for ships to cross the area between
   Latitude 51° 15′ N. and 51° 40′ N. and
   Longitude 1° 35′ E. and 3° E.

In this connection it must be remembered that the southern limit of the German mine field is Latitude 52° N. Although these limits are assigned to the danger area, it must not be supposed that navigation is safe in any part of the southern waters of the North Sea.

Instructions have been issued to His Majesty's ships to warn east-going vessels of the presence of this new mine field.

On October 15 H.M.S. Hawke, a cruiser of 7,350 tons, was torpedoed and sunk " in the Northern waters of the North Sea." Her complement was normally 544 officers and men ; of these three officers and 49 men were landed at Aberdeen fish market by the steam trawler Ben Rinnes, and subsequently one officer and twenty men were saved from a raft. H.M.S. Theseus, a sister ship to the Hawke, was also attacked at the same time, but was un-damaged. The Hawke was an old ship of the 1890-91 programme.

We now come to the next act in this tremendous drama which, on October 17, resulted in the sinking of the four German destroyers S115, S117, S118 and S119 off the Dutch coast. The official report ran :

The new light cruiser Undaunted (Captain Cecil H. Fox), accompanied by the destroyers Lance (Commander W. de M. Egerton), Legion (Lieutenant C. F. Allsup), and Loyal (Lieutenant F. Burges Watson), engaged four German destroyers off the Dutch coast yesterday afternoon. All the enemy's destroyers were sunk. The British loss in the destroyer action yesterday was one officer and four men wounded. The damage to the British destroyers was slight. There are 31 German survivors prisoners of war.

An interesting circumstance in connexion with this lively and successful little action is the fact that the senior officer present in the light cruiser Undaunted was Captain Cecil H.

H.M.S. ' HAWKE,"   [*Record Press.*
Sunk by a German submarine in the North Sea.

H.M.S. "LION" SINKING THE "KÖLN." (*See page 12.*)

Fox. This officer took part in the first action of the war when, in the Amphion, he was instrumental in the destruction of the mine-layer Königin Luise; his next adventure was when the Amphion was sent to the bottom by a mine, and he himself had a marvellous escape. The explosion of the first mine knocked him insensible. He recovered, and was able to leave the ship three minutes before she went down under the shock of a second explosion, when he saw a 6-inch gun belonging to his wrecked command turning over and over in the air like a baby's toy. He was then appointed to the new destroyer leader Faulkner, which was building in this country for Chile when war was declared. Only a few days before the action he was transferred to the Undaunted, the second light cruiser of a new class to be commissioned, the first having been

the Arethusa. The destroyers of the "L" class were part of the 1911-12 programme. They were formidable vessels of 35-knot speed, armed with three 4-inch guns and four torpedo tubes—in pairs—discharging 21-inch torpedoes.

The German destroyers were older boats, carrying only two 23-pounder guns, and not only were they slower, but there was absolutely no comparison between the accuracy of their shooting and that of the British craft engaged.

The destruction of the Hawke took place on October 15, and by the sinking of the four German destroyers two days afterwards the balance as between the two navies was more than satisfactorily adjusted from our point of view. The loss of life, some 300 men in each case, was about the same, but the value of an obsolescent cruiser like the Hawke was far less serious to England than that of four destroyers to Germany.

In less than two hours the whole affair was over. In one account of the fight it was said that firing began at a range of from four to five miles. Whatever the distance may have been, the result was never in doubt for a moment owing to the superior accuracy of the fire of the British destroyers. On the return of the Undaunted and the four destroyers that had been engaged they were given a warm reception by the warships in Harwich, by the general public, and particularly by the wounded soldiers in the hospital who were strong enough to get to the windows and cheer.

On or about October 18 we had to mourn the loss of submarine E3. What her exact fate was, how she came by her end, even the British Admiralty did not seem to know. Her fate, no less than that of the ships lost on both sides, demonstrated how costly in human life modern naval warfare had become. Not only was it a fight to a finish—as it had always been—but he who lost the battle lost his life also, almost automatically, as the steel shells, the hulls of the warships, were no match for the steel shells from the guns.

In war, as Admiral Mahan has said with so much point, " It is no good snapping at the heels, one must strike straight at the heart." The stroke at the heart had to be delivered in the waters of the North Sea, but there was one subsidiary theatre of enormous importance, even when compared with the northern area— the Mediterranean. By agreement with France, Great Britain, in the event of war, charged herself with the entire range of the northern waters—she was also to lend assistance in the southern. The result of this compact was that the French Battle Fleet was at the outbreak of hostilities in the Mediterranean, and here the Republic was supported by the British Mediterranean Fleet.

Those who had studied war in time of peace knew that one of the principal preoccupations of the French General Staff had been for years the question of how, in the event of collision between the Triple Alliance and the Triple Entente, the French armies in Algeria, numbering 120,000 first-line troops, were to be ferried across the tideless sea from Algeria to the Midi. Most of the manœuvres undertaken by the French Navy of late years had had this problem as one of the underlying ideas of their work, and much ingenuity had gone to

its solution. Italy, however, having refused to come in and wage a war of pure aggression that was none of her business, and for the waging of which she was not even consulted, the problem was reduced to elemental simplicity. In the Mediterranean there only remained the weak Austrian Fleet, which, imitating the example of " the predominant partner " elected to remain " stowed away up a drain." This is not meant as any reflection on the gallant seamen of Austria. To come out was merely to invite destruction at the hands of overwhelming superiority of force. Alone among the conscript navies of the world our allies, the French, had to their hands a large supply of seamen upon whom to draw for the manning of " l'Armée de la Mer." And the French " loup de mer " is a fine fellow, as our seamen could testify who fought with him so many tough battles from the day of Sluys, in the year 1340, down to the end of *that* " great war " that had its apotheosis in Trafalgar. At the head of the sea forces of France was Admiral Boué de Lapeyrère, in whom England, no less than France, had supreme confidence. No politician, even although he had held the position of Minister of Marine in

A GERMAN FLOATING MINE.

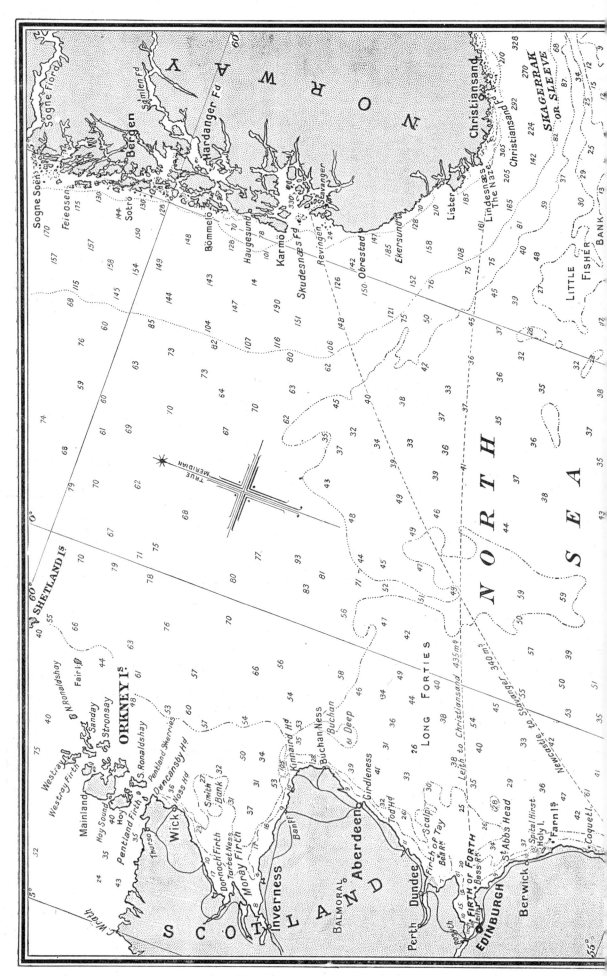

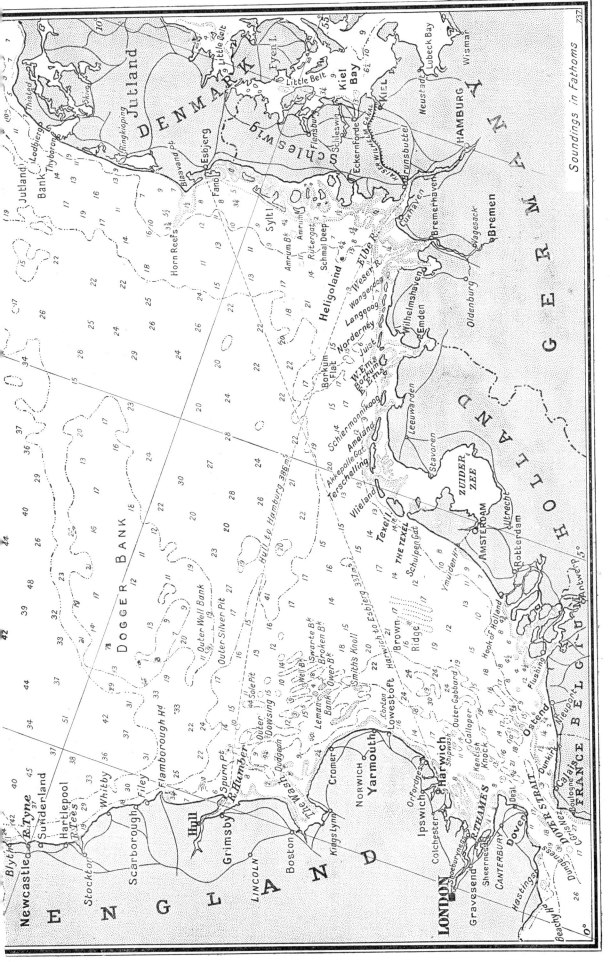

CHART OF THE NORTH SEA.

BELGIAN FISHERMEN WATCH A BRITISH MONITOR SHELL THE GERMAN TRENCHES.

Paris, no respecter of persons, all through his career this great seaman had but one ideal, the greater glory and the higher efficiency of the service.

It would be the height of ingratitude on our part to undervalue the priceless service that France was to render to us on the sea. It was by the action of Boué de Lapeyrère and the fine fleet that he commanded that the Mediterranean was a French and English lake ; also that the Grand Fleet could keep intact that iron ring which was drawn around the sea forces and the sea communications of the enemy. Also let it not be forgotten that France was also rendering assistance in the Northern area of conflict, where she had a squadron of armoured cruisers, as well as quite a considerable number of those small craft, such as destroyers and submarines, which, as has been said, the Navy of the Republic designate as *poussière navale.* Early in the war *La Vie Maritime et Fluviale* published a conversation between " un ancien commissaire " and its editor, Monsieur Charles Bos, once " rapporteur du budget de la marine."

The " ancien commissaire," like a good many other people, had observed that no action had been fought between the French Fleet and that of the enemy, and asked the question, " À

quoi bon désormais entretenir des escadres aussi nombreuses ? " the point of his argument being, that, as the Navy was not fighting, it would be much better for the ships to return into port and utilise the mariners in the fighting line on shore. Driven into a corner, and being made to admit that it was some use to allow the merchant ships of France and England to proceed without let or hindrance, the commissaire returned to the charge with the demand to know why Cattaro had been bombarded by the Fleet ?

The answer to this was fairly comprehensive :

He (that is to say, Admiral Boué de Lapeyrère) has done that which was imperative. He has seized upon Lissa as a base of operations. He has thus blockaded from a distance all the Austrian ports from Trieste as far as Pola. He bombarded Cattaro to facilitate the action of Montenegro ; and lying in wait in front of Pola, after having cleared the minefields with which the sea was strewn, he awaits the time when the Austrians shall issue from their ports . . . what he has done, in effect, is what the English Admiral has done in the North, who has blockaded Wilhelmshaven, Cuxhaven, and, in consequence, Bremen and Hamburg and also the Cattegat, with the result that the German fleet dares not come out into the open. I would ask you also to observe that at this moment German and Austro-Hungarian commerce is ruined. Surrounded as they are by enemies nothing can reach their countries.

At the outbreak of war the German battle cruiser Goeben and the cruiser Breslau were in the Mediterranean. On August 6 it was reported that these two ships had been driven into Messina by British cruisers after an exciting chase, and on August 8 it was further reported that they had left Messina for an unknown destination. That destination was the Dardanelles. A plucky attempt was made by the light cruiser Gloucester to prevent the escape of the German ships. After a farcical sale of them to the Turkish authorities, German crews and officers were sent to Constantinople, nominally to man other ships of the Turkish Fleet. Finally, under the stimulus of his German friends, Enver Pasha induced his unhappy country to declare war on the Allies.

Otherwise, nothing of first-class importance from the naval point of view happened, or seemed likely to happen, in the Mediterranean. This is easily explained by reference to the opposing forces afloat in the middle sea.

The Austrian forces consisted of three Dreadnought battleships, the Viribus Unitis, Tegetthoff, and Prinz Eugen ; six smaller so-called battle-ships, of which the Zrinyi was sunk, and two armoured cruisers, besides small craft. To oppose this force the French had eight first-class Dreadnoughts in their first Battle

[*Topical*

THE BRITISH MONITOR "SEVERN."
In the operations off the Belgian Coast the British monitors fired on the Germans with great effect.

Squadron, five pre-Dreadnought ships in their Second Squadron, six reserve battleships, six armoured cruisers, and a number of older vessels, no doubt put into commission after the war began. The English Mediterranean Fleet at the beginning of hostilities consisted of three battle cruisers, four armoured cruisers, and four light cruisers, besides small craft. When Turkey had been drawn into the war we had to reckon with her fleet, such as it was ; but apart from those modern units the Goeben and the Breslau, the remainder of this sea force consisted of obsolescent vessels, and the service was informed throughout with an inefficiency and a slackness on which German methods of hustle were likely to produce a confusion worse confounded. Since the days when the Ottoman emerged from the back of beyond in Asia Minor in 1453, down through the time of Soliman the Magnificent—when Turkey was at her apogee—to the present day, the Turk had been a useless person on the sea.

Before leaving the subject of the Mediterranean it is necessary to touch on a notification issued by the British Government to the representatives of foreign maritime powers in London concerning the Suez Canal. It appeared that, contrary to all right and precedent, certain enemy merchant ships were using the Canal

as a sanctuary or refuge from capture. The conclusion of the notification of our Government runs thus :

His Majesty's Government do not admit that the conventional right of free access to and use of the Canal enjoyed by merchant vessels implies any right to make use of the Canal and its ports of access for an indefinite time to escape capture, since the obvious result of permitting any such course must be greatly to incommode and even to block the use of the ports and Canal by other ships, and they are consequently of opinion that the Egyptian Government are fully justified in the steps that they are taking to remove from the Canal all enemy ships which have been long enough in the Canal ports to show clearly that they have no intention of departing in the ordinary way, and that they are putting the Canal and its ports to a use which is inconsistent with the use of the Canal in the ordinary way with other shipping.

One answer to the question why the German High Sea Fleet did not leave the security of its harbours is to be found in the fact that on Germany's flank was another "fleet in being," in the shape of the sea forces of Russia. It is true that, measured by the modern standard, these were not very formidable, but Russia had a considerable number of cruisers, and in the interests of Germany Russia had to be watched closely in the Baltic, lest she should embark in transports some of those troops that were bound for Berlin. To leave the Baltic altogether unguarded by sea would be to invite the landing of Russian troops on the then abso-

[*Record Press.*

THE "GOEBEN" FLYING THE TURKISH FLAG.

lutely defenceless littoral. It is true that the Russian Fleet was static while her army was dynamic, but to release this static force, by the advance of all her available naval power into the North Sea, was a thing that Germany could not and dared not do.

Early in the war the Germans lost their fine new cruiser Magdeburg, a sister ship to the Breslau, in the Baltic. She was of the 1911 programme, and was 4,550 tons displacement. It was reported that she ran on shore in a fog and was blown up by her crew as a superior Russian force was approaching. *The Times* naval correspondent, commenting on this, said, " It seems more probable that the Russian ships engaged the enemy vessel, and that she was run ashore in the course of the action, and that the fight and her violent beaching accounted for the heavy casualty list." On September 4 the Admiralty issued the statement that " seven German destroyers and torpedo boats have arrived at Kiel in a damaged condition " ; adding that, " it is understood that several others have been sunk in the vicinity of the Canal." At the time no explanation was given as to who was the enemy on this occasion. *The Times* published the following despatch from Petrograd on September 16 :

The news of a disaster to the German fleet in the Baltic, already reported abroad, is confirmed by information received here. There appears to be no doubt whatever that the German warships fired on each other. All rumours of an engagement with the Russian fleet in the Baltic are untrue. I gather from trustworthy information that a fairly numerous flotilla, attended by cruisers, while engaged in hunting down passenger steamers, mistook their own for enemy ships and engaged in a lively battle. The number of vessels crippled is unknown, but I have ascertained that several

cruisers and destroyers entered Kiel badly mauled and riddled by shot and shell, and that many wounded were conveyed ashore.

On October 10 the Russian armoured cruisers Admiral Makaroff, Pallada and Bayan, were on patrol duty in the Baltic. That morning the Admiral Makaroff was attacked by an enemy submarine as she was in the act of searching a sailing ship that she had stopped. Several torpedoes were fired at her, but happily none took effect. On October 11, at 2 o'clock in the afternoon, the enemy's submarines again attacked the Bayan and the Pallada. A lively fire was kept up by the cruisers, but in spite of this, one of the submarines got home on the Pallada with a torpedo ; an explosion followed—the Pallada having probably been struck under her magazine—and the ship sank, carrying all her ill-fated crew with her. The Pallada, an armoured cruiser of 7,775 tons, was built in 1906.

On October 22 the Secretary of the Admiralty made the following announcement :

The monitors Severn, Commander Eric J. A. Fullerton ; Humber, Commander Arthur L. Snagge ; and Mersey, Lieutenant-Commander Robert A. Wilson, have recently been engaged in operations on the Belgian coast, firing on the right flank of the German army. Owing to their light draught they have been able to contribute materially to the success of the operations in the district, and have already abundantly justified their acquisition on the outbreak of war. In addition, detachments with machine guns have been landed from these vessels to assist in the defence of Nieuport, where they performed meritorious service.

With this announcement, of great importance for the operations in France, we close this phase of naval operations in the North Sea, Baltic, and Mediterranean.

CHAPTER XXXI.

THE NAVY'S WORK IN THE OUTER SEAS.

THE NAVY'S TASK—PROTECTION OF BRITISH TRADE AND SUPPLIES—DESTRUCTION OF THE ENEMY'S COMMERCE—INTERNATIONAL LAW—THE DECLARATION OF PARIS—CRITICISMS—THE HAGUE CONFERENCES—THE RIGHT OF CAPTURE—THE DECLARATION OF LONDON—GERMAN FORCES IN THE OUTER SEAS—ARMED LINERS—PRIZES AND PRIZE MONEY—THE "EMDEN" AND HER SUCCESSES—THE "HIGHFLYER"—A NAVAL DUEL—WORK OF BRITISH CRUISERS—GERMAN ACTIVITY IN THE ATLANTIC—ATTACKS ON GERMAN COLONIES—WIRELESS TELEGRAPHY AND ITS IMPORTANCE—GERMAN EAST AFRICA—SAMOA—THE BISMARCK ARCHIPELAGO—THE AUSTRALIAN NAVY AT WORK—JAPAN AND KIAO-CHAU—INLAND FIGHTING IN AFRICA—GAINS AND LOSSES.

MORE than a century had elapsed since Britain had been engaged in a war which seriously affected her maritime interests. Her mercantile marine had meanwhile increased enormously, and she was more than ever dependent upon over-sea supplies for her very existence. Food of almost every description, supplies of material to feed her huge factories, and a host of other things which, if they cannot be regarded as necessaries, nevertheless play a not unimportant part in the round of barter—for all these she relied to an increasing extent upon sea-carriage ; to such an extent, indeed, that anything approaching complete stoppage would involve disaster, and possible conquest.

Germany had also, during recent years, developed a large mercantile marine, and had maintained persistent competition with Britain all over the world, both in freight and passenger services. Although the entire closing of the seas to her would not involve consequences so immediately disastrous as in our case, it would nevertheless occasion a fatal stagnation of her industries which could not fail very seriously to hamper her resources.

It is an axiom, maintained by all the highest authorities, and sanctioned by history, that the power of destroying or driving off the seas the commerce of the enemy, while preserving one's own more or less intact, is the sure road to ultimate victory, even against a vastly superior military State. It was this power which, in the years following Trafalgar, slowly but surely tilted the scale in our favour. It is as though one should block the main arteries of the body, leaving the heart to pulsate fruitlessly, until it becomes atrophied, flaccid and powerless through continued futile effort. While armies furiously contend on land, the persistent, silent, and relatively humane pressure of the stronger afloat is steadily achieving ultimate victory, by sapping the commercial resources of the other.

These pregnant facts, of such paramount importance to Britain, had not been lost sight of, despite our long immunity from peril afloat. The subject had formed the basis of many arguments, in the Press and in Parliament, and had called forth exhortation, and occasionally denunciation, from naval officers and others of high repute. " Cruisers, cruisers, and

[Elliott and Fry.

REAR-ADMIRAL A. G. H. W. MOORE,
Who took part in the action in the Heligoland Bight.

yet more cruisers ! " This was their cry. The
enormous extent of our trade routes could not
be covered in war time save by lavish expenditure in this direction in time of peace. It was
almost a truism, but the actual provision necessary to secure adequate protection remained,
after all, more or less a matter of opinion.
The Admiralty had done a good deal, more
especially in the years immediately preceding
the war, both in shipbuilding and in organization ; but the verdict must be that it had not
done quite enough.

For years we had been told of the elaborate
preparations in progress by Germany for
preying upon our commerce, more especially
by means of fast merchant vessels converted
into warships ; and it had come to be regarded
as at least a possibility that, in the event of
war, we should immediately be plunged into a
condition of semi-famine, with prices rising to
a figure prohibitive except to the wealthy.

The consideration of the matter of attack
and defence of commerce lands us at once in
the quagmire of Maritime International Law.
Quot homines, tot sententiæ. It is related that
one of the delegates at the Geneva arbitration
on the Alabama claims declared : " There is *no*
International Law ! " Perhaps, like David,
he said it in his haste ; and, also in common

with the psalmist, he enunciated a half truth.
Up to the time of the Crimean War certain
standing laws, or traditions, based upon
ancient maritime law and centuries of usage,
had been universally recognized—

1. The right to supplement the fleet by
means of " private armed ships " ; that is to
say, ships which were owned by private individuals or companies, but were licensed by a
commission from the Government to be armed
and to attack and capture the enemy's ships.
The owners provided the ship and her whole
outfit, and paid the crew ; and the value of the
prize, when duly ascertained, went almost
entirely to the owners and the crew, in pre-
arranged proportions. As will be readily
imagined, it was sometimes a very paying business, and in the wars of the eighteenth and
early nineteenth centuries privateers swarmed
upon the seas.* Some of the commanders
were, however, very great rascals, and got the
business into disrepute by their piratical
practices. Nelson was very much down upon
them, as well as other naval officers of repute,
because, the privateer owners alleged, they
were deprived of some of their prize money !
Who shall say ? However, there was the
practice, permitted by the consent of all
nations.

2. The right to capture enemy merchant
ships and their cargoes. This had always been
recognized as a natural condition of warfare ;
but there was a proviso, dating from a considerable time back, that cargoes owned by
neutrals, even in an enemy ship, should be
immune, unless they were contraband of war.

3. The right to seize the property of persons
of enemy nationality, even though carried in a
ship under a neutral flag, involving, of course,
the right to board and search neutral ships.
This, as will be realized upon the smallest consideration, was an eminently reasonable stipu-
lation, and of very great value to a maritime
power at war with another—and yet it was the
first to be thrown overboard !

In 1856, after the Peace of Paris had been
concluded, a document, entitled the Declaration
of Paris, drawn up by the Peace Plenipotentiaries, was offered for the acceptance and
recognition of all the Powers.

---

* As an instance, the privateers Duke and Prince Frederick
captured, in 1745, three French ships bound from Lima to St.
Malo, and a *seaman's* share of prize money was £850, the officers',
of course larger according to rank, while the owners pocketed
£700,000, which they patriotically—or prudently—offered as a
loan to Government to assist in dealing with " the '45 " rebellion.

[*Cribb, Sou'hsea.*

**A 12-INCH PROJECTILE BEING HOISTED
ABOARD.**

**In the later pattern this missile is sent to its mark by
a 307 lb. charge of cordite.**

It embodied some drastic alterations in
Maritime Law ; the four effective clauses being
as follows :

1. Privateering is and remains abolished.

2. The neutral flag covers enemy's merchandise, with the exception of contraband of
war.

3. Neutral merchandise, with the exception of
contraband of war, is not capturable under the
enemy's flag.

4. Blockades, in order to be obligatory,
must be effective.

The third clause, as will be realised, is in
accordance with ancient usage. The subject
of blockade need not here be entered upon.
Probably there will never be another blockade
on the old lines ; modern conditions of naval
warfare do not lend themselves to the process.
Blockades had, in some instances, been
effective in the past, and in others had been
rather of the nature of a fiasco.

The first two clauses of the Declaration,
however, demand attention ; and it is remarkable that they had been anticipated by Britain
at the commencement of the war—in 1854
an announcement having appeared in the

London Gazette, March 28, in the form of a
declaration by the Queen, to the effect that,
being " desirous of rendering the war as little
onerous as possible to the Powers with whom
she is at peace," she will, while reserving the
right of seizing contraband of war, and preventing neutrals from carrying despatches or
breaking blockades, " waive the right of seizing
enemy's property laden on board a neutral
vessel unless it be contraband of war " ; and,
finally, the Queen declares that " it is not her
present intention to issue letters of marque for
the commissioning of privateers."

This voluntary abnegation of important
rights was, it is true, labelled as a temporary
or tentative measure, by the occurrence in the
preamble of the words, " for the present " ;
but in the Declaration of Paris, of course, it
bears no such stamp.

This declaration stands upon very infirm
ground. It is decidedly doubtful, to start with,
whether the Peace Plenipotentiaries, having
performed the task for which plenary powers
had been conferred upon them, were competent, without further authority, to transact
international business of such weighty nature ;
and the bestowal of such authority by the
Sovereign is not in evidence : indeed, there is

[*Cribb, Southsea.*

WAITING FOR THE GERMANS.
**A pile of 6-inch projectiles, each weighing
100 pounds.**

H.M.S. "DREADNOUGHT"   [*Cribb, Southsea.*
Cleared for action.

ground for strong presumption that it was never conferred.

Finally, as Mr. Gibson Bowles puts it, " It has never received, either from the Sovereign, from the Privy Council, or from Parliament, that subsequent formal sanction which alone could suffice to give a semblance of adequate authority to an alteration in the rules of warfare so tremendous, a surrender of maritime rights so unprecedented."*

Spain and the United States of America declined to subscribe to the Declaration, while Russia repudiated the privateering clause ; so, when all was said and done, there remained material for drastic differences in case of war with any of these Powers.

There ensued a long period free from any further tampering with maritime law ; but at the second Peace Conference, held at The Hague in 1907, some effort was made at international agreement upon several points. The most important of these, from our present point of view, was the question of the conversion of merchant ships and warships, upon which certain rules were agreed to—

* " The Declaration of Paris of 1856," p. 132.

1. Such a ship must be under the direct authority and responsibility of the Power whose flag it flies.

2. It must bear the external marks which distinguish the warships of its nationality.

3. The commander must be a genuine naval officer, his name appearing in the Navy List.

4. The crew must be subject to military discipline.

5. The ship must observe the laws and customs of war.

6. The conversion of the ship must be announced as soon as possible by the belligerent in the list of its warships.

These rules, however, were prefaced by the statement that the delegates had been unable to come to any agreement as to whether the conversion of a merchant ship into a warship might take place upon the high seas. Germany stoutly maintained the right, England as stoutly opposed it ; result : the right remains, for those who elect to make use of it.

Probably all such conferences as this are predoomed to futility. To quote the concluding words of an article on the subject in the *Edinburgh Review* for January, 1908 : " A Peace

Conference which is forbidden to discuss expenditure upon armaments, and from which the rules of naval warfare have admittedly to be withdrawn, a world congress which the world treats with silence or with ridicule, an assembly in which diplomacy and law confound each other, does not justify itself. It provides opportunities for political demonstrations, but to Powers which do not make use of those opportunities it brings little but humiliations which are unrequited by any sense of lasting service done to the cause of peace."

Concurrently with the assembly of The Hague Conference, though initiated previously, in 1905, at the conclusion of the Russo-Japanese war, an agitation was being carried on for the abolition of the right of capture of enemy merchant ships and cargoes at sea. Private property, it was alleged, was immune in land warfare. Why not at sea ? The allegation of the immunity of private property on land was certainly liable to liberal discount, even before the war of 1914. A humane general will certainly spare " household gods," but he will seize any property, private or otherwise, which will serve to further his ends. It has always been done, and always will be done, and the seizure of enemy ships and their cargoes serves a most vital end to a belligerent.

The proposal was strongly supported by Sir Robert Reid (afterwards known, by his title of Lord Loreburn, as Lord High Chancellor) in a long letter to *The Times* of October 14, 1905, and by other persons of influence, but the arguments in favour of it would not stand the test of history and common sense, and the agitation came to nothing. Our acquiescence in such an arrangement would certainly have been throwing away a trump card.

Then followed the Declaration of London, of 1909, the outcome of a conference of the representatives of all the great Powers, at the invitation of the British Government. On this occasion, as at The Hague Conference, the question of converting merchant ships into warships on the high seas was ignored. There were long lists of "absolute" and "conditional" contraband of war ; it would serve no good purpose to transcribe them ; as a matter of fact, belligerents usually make their own lists, and what is contraband in one war is permissible in the next. Definition is almost futile.

The main object of the London Naval Conference, as set forth in the final protocol, was to establish a code of International Law, with the further view of setting up an international Prize Court, as proposed at The Hague Peace Conference ; but the Declaration of London was never ratified, nor was the International Prize Court established before the war broke out.

H.M.A.S. "AUSTRALIA." [*Cribb, Southsea.*

FIRING A TORPEDO FROM A DESTROYER.   [Cribb, Southsea.

The Navy was thus left bound by the Declaration of Paris, but the Government, immediately after war was declared, intimated that the Declaration of London was to form the basis of naval procedure, as though it had been ratified ; and this would concede the right to search neutral ships, and, under certain conditions, to condemn their cargoes, or even to destroy the ships.   The clauses which dealt with these matters were, however, far more favourable to a military State than to Great Britain.

What, then, were the circumstances, with regard to the attack and defence of commerce afloat, when war was declared ?

The German main fleet, through the prompt action of the British Admiralty, was locked up, its movements confined to Kiel Harbour, a portion of the Baltic, the Kiel Canal, and the estuary of the Elbe, unless it should elect to come out and risk encounter with a vastly superior force.

The outlying British squadrons available were pretty nearly as follows :

China : One battleship, four cruisers, six smaller vessels, eight destroyers, four torpedo boats, three submarines.

East Indies : One battleship, two cruisers, four smaller craft.

Cape : Three cruisers.

New Zealand : Three cruisers, one sloop.

West Coast of Africa : Three sloops.

West Coast of America : Three sloops.

East Coast of South America : One cruiser.

Australian Navy : One battle cruiser, three light cruisers, three destroyers, two submarines.

The Fourth Cruiser Squadron, consisting of five ships, was on the point of returning from Mexico and the West Atlantic.

This, however, does not represent the total force available for the defence and destruction of commerce, for a number of fast liners were immediately put in commission under naval commanders. These were, of course, genuine warships, flying the White Ensign, without any attempt at disguise.

Furthermore, a certain number of merchant steamers were, at the request of the owners, provided with guns, mounted only astern, for the purposes of defence in the event of being chased. The status of an " armed merchant ship," as distinguished from a warship or a privateer, had always been recognised. Such a vessel is permitted to use her guns only in self-defence, and must not initiate an action. If, however, she should prove strong enough to overcome and capture her assailant, such capture is recognised, and the enemy ship is " good prize " ; a trifle paradoxical, perhaps, but not unreasonable. Instances of such captures were by no means lacking in the old wars; as witness the case of the Ellen, of Bristol, which, in 1780, brought into Port Royal, Jamaica, as prize a Spanish sloop of war.

Against us there were known to be some eight or nine German cruisers abroad, all efficient for commerce-destroying purposes, and several with very high speed, which it was recognised would require a great deal of catching.

As to the number of armed liners which would be opposed to us, this was, of course, at first mere matter of conjecture. Germany, as we have seen, had asserted her right to convert merchant ships into men-of-war—or, in reality, privateers—at a moment's notice, on the seas, or even in a neutral port; and it was well known that some of these vessels carried their war equipment below decks, in readiness for mounting; also, it was said, the captains and superior officers held naval commissions, to come into force upon the declaration of war. These matters had been discussed in the Press at intervals, and even in Parliament, it being urged by many persons that some similar move should be made by Britain to safeguard our interests. The danger was considerably exaggerated, as was proved upon the declaration of war; the number of German converted liners available was obviously small, and a couple were accounted for by our ships before the war had been many weeks in progress.

As in every instance of maritime war, there were merchant vessels of either side in enemy ports, and these, of course, were liable to seizure; while our cruisers were speedily busy picking up prizes all over the world, and the Prize Courts had work cut out for many weeks.

It had been notified, however, by the Admiralty that there was to be no prize money for British naval officers. The motive of such a novel regulation was somewhat obscure; it did not appear to be covered by the rare possible instances in which a naval commander might be tempted to subordinate his duty to his pocket; nor was it, indeed, very complimentary to the cloth to assume that such temptation would prevail. Some years previously, during the agitation before alluded to, for the abolition of the capture of private property at sea, it had been suggested by some interested quasi-humanitarians that the opposition of naval officers was based upon an avaricious greed of gain—a hypothesis which was very warmly and justly repudiated by Mr. Julian Corbett in the *Nineteenth Century* of June, 1907.

The German commerce destroyers displayed no lack of enterprise; their raids and captures were soon reported from various quarters of the globe. This was, indeed, to be expected, for our merchant vessels are ubiquitous; nor was the rounding up of these cruisers an easy task. Landsmen, perhaps, scarcely realise how minute is the ground covered on a large-scale chart by the limit of vision, even in bright daylight; how immense is the area of, say, the Bay of Bengal, when it comes to hunting down a single vessel—a vessel, moreover, which is provided with wireless apparatus, and is thus in direct communication with a friendly base, whence she can sometimes be warned of danger.

The thing cuts both ways, of course, and any number of possible prizes may, and do, escape from the same cause. The captures of our ships were, indeed, trivial compared with the number which our cruisers brought in, but they were sufficient in some quarters to occasion indignant enquiries as to when the Navy was going to put a stop to them.

The Bay of Bengal has been mentioned above as a sample of an extensive expanse in

[Cribb, Southsea.

COALING A WARSHIP AT SEA.

[*Topical.*

" CAP TRAFALGAR."
Sunk in the famous duel with the " Carmania."

which the running down of a single enemy cruiser might be a difficult task, and the selection is apposite, for it was in this region that a German cruiser, the Emden, commanded by Captain Karl Von Müller, particularly distinguished herself.

The Emden was a small vessel of some 3,500 tons, with a speed of about 25 knots—quite fast enough to overhaul any British steamer she was likely to encounter, and fast enough also to run away if necessary.

The exploits of the enterprising commander of this vessel recalled those of Robert Surcouf, the famous French privateersman, in the same quarter, over one hundred years previously. Like the Confiance, Surcouf's swift, rakish craft, the Emden was generally heard of where she was least expected, and, after reaping her harvest of merchantmen, as unaccountably disappeared. In something under six weeks she had captured nearly twenty steamers, always contriving to pick up a collier among them, so that she was able to keep her bunkers replenished. It was her captain's invariable practice to sink his prizes, reserving one in which to send all the crews and passengers into port ; indeed, it is not easy to see what else he could have done, as he could not have hoped to take them into any friendly port, nor could he cumber his own ship with the crews.*

As a variety of adventure, the Emden steamed one evening into Madras roads, and threw shell into the outskirts of the town for

* It was urged at the time that the destruction of these vessels was contrary to International Law, and that Britain should make reprisals. It is, however, and always has been quite within the captor's right to destroy enemy property at sea ; a neutral vessel captured is upon a different footing, and must not be destroyed save under exceptional circumstances.

the space of half an hour or so—some oil tanks were set ablaze, and two or three natives killed ; Fort George returned the fire—probably without effect—and the Emden retired.

It may be assumed that the German captain received information by wireless of the probable approach of colliers or other vessels as he was so very much on the spot ; in any case he was a very courageous and enterprising man, and a good sportsman ; but we wanted very badly to catch him. There are so many holes and corners in that part of the world, where a vessel may lie for a time with little chance of detection, and the Emden's speed would have enabled her to reach some such refuge very quickly.

It was alleged against the Emden, and some other German ships, that they approached under British or French colours in order to get within range, a proceeding strongly condemned as " not playing the game." It may not be very admirable, but it has always been considered admissible, so long as no *hostile act* is committed ; a vessel which fires upon another under a false flag is guilty of an act of piracy.

Towards the end of August there arrived intelligence of the destruction of one of the most formidable of Germany's converted commerce raiders. This was the Kaiser Wilhelm der Grosse, a liner of 14,000 tons and 22 knots speed, armed with ten 4-inch guns. She had made good her escape from Bremerhaven soon after war was declared, and was probably one of those vessels already provided with guns, etc., converted, quite irregularly, according to our notions, into a man-of-war or privateer after leaving port as an ordinary merchant ship. It was this ship which was supposed to have sunk the British vessel Hyades, off Pernambuco; thence she had crossed the Atlantic and haunted the route of our Cape steamers, holding up on one occasion the mail steamer Galician, which, however, she left in peace, and hurried away—possibly warned by wireless of the proximity of a British cruiser.

She was not permitted a long respite ; on August 27 she was sighted by the Highflyer, a cruiser of 5,600 tons, carrying 6-inch guns, but not as fast as the German ship by two knots or more. The latter had a couple of colliers in company, one alongside coaling her, and the Highflyer was within range before she could get fairly under way.

There was a fight, but it was not of long duration, the liner being clearly outclassed in the matter of ordnance. She hit the cruiser

H.M.S. "PEGASUS." [*London News Agency.*

Completely disabled in Zanzibar Harbour by the German cruiser "Königsberg."

with a shot or two, killing one man and wounding five, but her doom was sealed, and she shortly went down, her crew being rescued by the colliers.

This was a very good score for us, as the German ship might have been very troublesome on that route. The fight took place somewhere off the round of the coast of Africa, north of the Cape Verde Islands, near the Rio de Oro.

The Highflyer had been commissioned in the previous year as a training ship for the " Public School " naval cadets, a new institution for the recruiting of naval executive officers ; probably some of these young gentlemen were on board at the time, and were thus brought face to face with the realities of naval service at this early period of their career.

Another incident which aroused immense interest was a duel between the Carmania, one of our converted liners, commanded by Captain Noel Grant, and a German ship of like nature and about equal force, the Cap Trafalgar.

These two antagonists encountered on September 14 off the east coast of South America, and there was a stubborn fight. For an hour and three-quarters they engaged fiercely, exchanging hard knocks. It was a revival of the old duels in wars of the past ; with the difference, however, that these almost invariably involved the capture of the vanquished vessel, very often by boarding. In the war of 1914 boarding was, of course, out of the question ; actions were fought at anything from 3,000 to 10,000 yards, and they banged away until one or the other went down with colours flying.

THE "CARMANIA." [*Central News.*

"KAISER WILHELM DER GROSSE."   [*Topical.*

Used by the Germans as an armoured cruiser.   Sunk by H.M.S. "Highflyer" off Rio de Oro.

So it was in this instance ; the Carmania commenced the action at 9,000 yards, and a lively mutual fire was maintained at various ranges, but never within 3,000 yards. The British gunners, however, proved themselves the superior marksmen, getting their hits in on the hull at or near the water-line, while the German projectiles mostly crashed into the boats and upper works ; moreover, from the account of an eye-witness, Captain Grant appears to have manœuvred his ship more cleverly, often contriving to present her end-on to the enemy, and using his guns ahead or astern with fatal effect upon the huge target presented by the Cap Trafalgar, broadside on.

There was no blenching, however ; the German commander took his gruelling like a man, and the survivors of his crew got away in the collier, thanks to the approach of a German cruiser, with which the Cap Trafalgar was in wireless communication during the action. She did not heave in sight, but Captain Grant, having picked up the wireless message, thought it was time to be off. The Carmania had nine men killed and twenty-six wounded ; the German, which was repeatedly hulled, must have suffered a far heavier loss ; she was in flames before the action had been half an hour in progress, and capsized before she sank.

Meanwhile our regular cruisers had not been

THE GERMAN CRUISER "EMDEN."   [*Central News.*

idle. The Berwick, Captain Lewis C. Baker, captured in the North Atlantic the Hamburg-Amerika liner Spreewald, which was known to be fitted as an armed cruiser ; also two colliers with about 6,000 tons of coal, 180 tons of provisions, destined for the enemy's cruisers—a very useful haul. The Berwick also captured an American ship laden with ammunition, and a Norwegian with coal, and the French cruiser Condè made a similar capture.

On the east coast of Africa the small British cruiser Pegasus met an untimely fate. She had done some useful work, including the destruction of Dar-es-Salaam, in German East Africa, with its wireless station, the sinking of a gunboat and of a floating dock. On September 20, while she was lying at Zanzibar, giving her engines and boilers a necessary overhaul, the German cruiser Königsberg appeared and attacked her. The Pegasus, thus taken at a disadvantage by a vessel carrying more up-to-date ordnance and outranging hers, had no chance. She was terribly battered, and had eventually to be beached, with 25 killed and 80 wounded out of a crew of 234—a very heavy loss. The Königsberg steamed away, and her damages are not known.

The Yarmouth, Captain Henry Cochrane, in the East Indies, captured and sunk the Hamburg-Amerika liner Markomania, and the Greek steamer Pontoporos, with coal, which latter was taken into harbour.*

On the west coast of Africa the cruiser Cumberland, Captain Cyril Fuller, made an excellent haul in the middle of September at the German port of Cameroon (Kamerun), in the Bight of Biafra, destroying two small river steamers laden with ammunition, appropriating the gunboat Soden for our own use, and capturing no fewer than nine merchant steamers, all in good condition, of a total of over 30,000 tonnage. This was a good off-set against the Emden's achievements, with a decided balance in our favour ; for, thanks to our command of the sea, we were not compelled to sink our prizes, and these vessels, with their coal, etc., were probably worth some £400,000.

Another German cruiser had been busy, however, in the Atlantic, and exacted a pretty heavy toll. This was the Karlsruhe, which intercepted and destroyed no fewer than thirteen steamers in the course of a week or two.

* The owners of the Pontoporos protested that, if she was coaling the German ship, it was by compulsion, though it had previously been reported that she was acting as collier for the Emden.

[*Record Press*

CAPTAIN KARL VON MÜLLER,
Commander of the " Emden."

In the Pacific the Leipzig and Nürnberg had some success. The Dresden, Strassburg, and Bremen were also known to be at large in the Atlantic.

On September 22 the two cruisers Scharnhorst and Gneisenau arrived off Papeeta, the chief town of Tahiti, in the Society Islands, a French colony, entirely unprotected. They sunk a small and harmless disarmed gunboat, and then proceeded to shell the open town. This cruel and absolutely useless proceeding was on a par with many other incidents, apparently the outcome of wanton mischievousness.

The end of October came with a further exploit on the part of the Emden, which, disguised by an extra dummy funnel, and flying the Japanese colours as she approached, contrived to torpedo a small Russian cruiser and a destroyer in the British harbour of Penang. At last, on November 10, came the welcome news that the Emden had been caught at Keeling Cocos Island by His Majesty's Australian ship Sydney, and driven ashore and burned.

Such was the position at the end of three months' war. So far from suffering from famine prices and shortage of food, the people

[*Cribb, Southsea.*

THE NAVAL BRIGADE HAULING THEIR 4·7 GUN ASHORE.

of these islands were able to live much as usual, with a slight rise on some commodities— thanks to the silent pressure of our sea-power, at home and abroad.

Despite her complaints to the contrary, Germany possessed, at the opening of the war, a good number of " places in the sun "— colonies scattered about in various warm quarters of the globe ; to wit, German East Africa, German South West Africa, Cameroon, and Togoland ; in the Pacific, German New Guinea, the Bismarck Archipelago, one of the largest of the Solomon Islands, the Caroline, Ladrone, Pellew and Marshall Islands ; and further east the Samoa Islands, or at least the chief portion of them. All these possessions were accessible from seaward, and consequently fitting objects for the attentions of the British Navy ; and there was one very important particular in which they were worthy of notice— namely, that every one of them was probably fitted with a wireless telegraphy installation.

The remarkable development in wireless telegraphy which had occurred during the ten or twelve years previous to the war had been exploited by Germany with characteristic energy, and it is not easy to over-rate the importance of this somewhat uncanny means of communication. Like many other very admirable and useful inventions, it has its drawbacks during time of war ; enemy messages may be intercepted and utilised to his disadvantage, and a code will not always avail to

ensure immunity from this ; but on the whole it is the most valuable medium of communication ever invented.

Realizing the importance of this new factor in warfare, Germany had, in 1906, erected at Nauen, about five-and-twenty miles from Berlin, an experimental wireless station on a grand scale, and had there gradually developed apparatus of immense range and power ; while, at the same time, wireless installations were set up in all her chief dependencies ; indeed, it was not known in what quarter they might not exist, for they need not have been confined to German territory. It is not absolutely necessary to set up a great mast or tower in order to establish, at least, an effective receiving station ; an unobtrusive arrangement at a window will serve very well, and may remain altogether unnoticed ; and it is certain that such means were employed in this instance.

The range of modern wireless telegraphy is immense ; more than two years before the war the Nauen station covered a circle of some 3,500 miles radius, and this had been increased, until it was certain that German cruisers and others on the coast of South America, over the whole of German Africa and in the East Indies could be reached from Berlin ; in fact, with reinforcement by powerful intermediate stations, the whole world was practically covered.

The fact was not overlooked by British soldiers and seamen ; and wherever a German station could be successfully attacked the first business was to locate and destroy the wireless station.

The cruiser Pegasus was busy, quite early in the war, in German East Africa, and was responsible for the destruction of the wireless apparatus at Dar-es-Salaam, a little north of Zanzibar ; unhappily, as previously recorded, she was caught at a disadvantage and put out of action before she could perform other valuable service.

Early in August an expedition was planned from New Zealand to capture Samoa Islands, and it was very ably carried out, under Rear-Admiral Sir George Patey. Samoa had been the scene of much international wrangling in past years—Britain, Germany and America all having a finger in the pie. It was one of the resulting crises which caused the squadron of men-of-war to be assembled at Apia in 1889, when every ship in the harbour was wrecked in a furious cyclone, except the British cruiser Calliope, commanded by Captain H. C. Kane, who, with a combination of skill and resolution which evoked enthusiastic admiration on the spot and at home, took his ship out through the reefs in the teeth of the storm. Eventually, in 1899, a solution of the difficult international problem was arrived at—Germany retaining the principal islands, America the others, while Britain retired from the scene with certain compensations, including the possession of the greater part of the Solomon Islands, and

also the Tonga Islands. On March 1, 1900, the German flag was hoisted with due ceremony at Samoa ; it was now, with a dramatic absence of ceremony, to be hauled down again.

The expedition left Wellington, New Zealand, on August 15, bound for the French island New Caledonia, it being considered prudent to pursue an indirect course, in view of possible interference from two large German cruisers, the Scharnhorst and Gneisenau, which were known to be about in the Pacific. At an appointed rendezvous the British cruisers Psyche, Pyramus and Philomel met and took charge of the expedition.

Arriving at New Caledonia on August 20, the British vessels left again on the 23rd, strengthened by the addition of the French cruiser Montcalm, and subsequently by the battle cruiser Australia and the cruiser Melbourne, of the Australian Navy—the former flying the flag of Rear-Admiral Sir George Patey. After a call at Fiji Islands, the expedition arrived off Samoa on August 30, and steered for Apia, on Upolu Island, the headquarters of the German government. After some preliminary precautions to ascertain that there were no mines about, the Psyche steamed in under a flag of truce, and conveyed to the authorities the demand of the British Admiral for the surrender of the Island.

The Germans were considerably taken aback, as they had been expecting some of their own warships ; but they had no force available

SAMOA.
The Harbour of Apia.

HARBOUR AND FLOATING
Surrendered to the

which was capable of offering any effectual resistance, so there was nothing for it but to yield. The surrender being made known by signal, the squadron immediately steamed in and anchored, armed parties of bluejackets were quickly landed, and took charge of the

[*Record Press.*

ADMIRAL MEYER WALDECK,
German Governor of Kiau Tschau.

chief streets and bridges, &c., while the main body was disembarked. The government buildings were seized, the plugs in the telephone exchange pulled out to prevent any inconvenient conversations among the residents, and an armed party started out to seize the wireless station, conspicuous by its tall, latticed iron-work mast, some three or four miles distant. Meantime the German flag had been unceremoniously hauled down by a soldier, the Germans ruefully saluting it before it was carried out of sight.

On the following morning at eight o'clock the British flag was slowly and solemnly hoisted, to a salute of twenty-one guns from the Psyche, reaching the summit of the staff with the final report: the troops gave the " Royal Salute," and the ceremony ended with the National Anthem, and three rousing cheers for the King.

It was very well done, and there were no unnecessary and aggravating international controversies to detract from the success of a perfectly legitimate and humane operation. The Germans, since the declaration of war, had treated the British and French residents with courtesy, and received, it is needless to say, similar treatment at our hands; the Governor was sent to New Zealand for detention, but was treated as a distinguished guest.

The largest island in the Bismarck Archipelago, to the North of New Guinea, is Neu Pommern (New Pomerania, formerly New

DOCK OF TSINGTAU.
Allies, November 7, 1914

Britain); the centre of government is at Herbertshöhe, at the north-east end of the island, upon what is known as the Gazelle Peninsula. It was known that there was a wireless station in this vicinity, and an attempt had been made early in August to reach it, but it had only been found possible to destroy the post office. On September 11, however, a naval landing party, under Commander J. A. H. Beresford, managed to get on shore at daybreak unobserved—presumably at some distance from the town—and at seven o'clock presented themselves to the astonished residents, and proceeded, without opposition, to hoist the British Flag. They then set out to destroy the wireless station, but here they encountered considerable opposition, and having reason to suspect that the road was mined and ambushed, they fought their way through the bush for four miles, with very little loss ; the Germans in charge of the station surrendered, and on the following day guns were landed, and the place formally occupied ; two German officers and five non-commissioned officers were made prisoners, also thirty native police.

The German governor had retired to the island of Bougaiville, in the Solomon Islands, and two days later our forces paid a visit there ; they met with but little resistance, and after a parley the governor surrendered.

Wilhelmshaven, in German New Guinea, was occupied on September 24, without resistance.

The Australian squadron, in conjunction with the local military, thus performed excellent service, accounting eventually for pretty well all the German wireless stations in the Pacific. It was reported from Sydney in October that those on Yap (or Uap) in the Caroline Islands, and Pleasant (or Nauru) Island had been destroyed. Pleasant Island is a very small bit of terra firma, lying to the south-west of the Gilbert Islands, and really forming practically one of that group, which is British ; it is included, however, with the Caroline Islands in the German sphere.

These satisfactory operations were to be balanced by a sad misfortune, involving the loss of two officers and thirty-two seamen. The submarine A.E.1, built only in the previous year for the Australian navy, a most valuable and up-to-date craft of her class, was unaccountably lost—that is to say, she dived on September 14 and never reappeared. Her loss was attributed to accident. She and her sister vessel had made the voyage to Australia under their own power, by far the longest voyage then undertaken by a submarine.

Meanwhile Japan had taken a hand in the war by sending an ultimatum to Germany, on August 15, demanding the surrender of Kio-chau. This was a very fine harbour, on the south side of the Shantung Peninsula, which Germany had acquired, on a ninety-nine years' " lease " from China, as an offset against Britain's acquisition of Wei-hai-Wei, facing

Port Arthur. A certain amount of territory inland was included in the lease, and the Germans proceeded to fortify the town and harbour, which had many natural advantages.

The Japanese Government declared that the possession by Germany of this place was a source of irritation and possible mischief in the Far East, and on the refusal of Germany to give it up, commenced combined naval and military operations against it, in which some of our warships took part; the Kennet, destroyer,·chasing a German destroyer into the entrance to the harbour, came under the fire of the shore batteries, and sustained some damage, with several casualties. The affair developed a more military than naval side, and the Germans offered a stubborn resistance. Tsingtau, however, fell at the beginning of November.

The Japanese navy rendered good service by the capture of Jaluit, or Bonham Island, in the Marshall Group, where the Germans had considerable supplies and a wireless station. The island is of considerable size, and has good anchorage within the coral reefs, with a clear wide entrance on one side.

In Africa there was some inland naval fighting—paradoxical as it may appear at first sight—on the great Nyassa Lake, the northern portion of which runs into German East Africa, while the whole western shore is in British Central Africa.

On this inland sea Britain and Germany had each some small armed steamers, and these naturally came into conflict on some occasions, the Gwendolen, British, capturing a German craft in August. The Gwendolen was a vessel of about 350 tons, and was built on the Clyde, taken out in sections to Central Africa, and commenced her genuine aquatic existence when launched on the lake in 1898. These minor operations, however, could have no weight in the matter of the conquest of German East Africa, which was essentially a military work.

As an offset against the capture of Samoa, and consequent loss of a wireless station, a German cruiser, probably the Nürnberg, o ı September 9, visited Fanning Island, the intermediate station of the Fiji and Britis Columbia submarine telegraph, and subsequently cut the cable. Fanning Island is of a somewhat scattered group of small islan in lat. 4° N, long. 160° W; it was annexe with the others, by Great Britain in 1888.

Thanks chiefly to the enterprise of th Australian squadron, a great deal had be done by the end of October towards the co plete interruption of Germany's chain o ı wireless communication; but there remained the mighty sweep from Nauen, which could not be controlled, and which was doubtless being used with effect over its vast radius.

CHAPTER XXXII.

THE BATTLES OF THE MARNE.

END OF THE GREAT RETREAT—THE ARMIES MANŒUVRE FOR POSITION—VITAL EFFECTS OF THREE EVENTS WHICH OCCURRED ON AUGUST 22—SAARBURG DETERMINES THE EASTERN FRONT—CHARLEROI DETERMINES THE NORTHERN FRONT—GUMBRINNEN DETERMINES GERMAN STRATEGY—THE GREAT RETREAT DETERMINES MORAL FACTORS—*MORAL* OF FRANCE, OF PARIS, OF THE ARMY—NUMBERS ENGAGED AT THE MARNE—OBJECTIVES OF THE RIVAL ARMIES—CHOICE OF THE GERMAN OBJECTIVE —THE SCENE OF CONFLICT—TACTICAL ISSUES AT STAKE—DISPOSITIONS OF THE RIVAL ARMIES— VON KLUCK UNDERESTIMATES BRITISH ARMY—GERMAN RIGHT BREAKS—GERMAN LINE GIVES WAY—ALLIES' LEFT REACHES THE AISNE—CRITICISM OF LEADERS AND TROOPS—EFFECT OF THE VICTORY ON FRANCE—THE BATTLE OF THE OURCQ—THE BRITISH ADVANCE.

"THURSDAY, September 3," said the British official report, " marked the end of our Army's long retirement from the Belgian frontier through Northern France." For the next few days there was a lull in the fighting, which had been continuous since the first collisions on the frontier.

On September 3 (said Sir John French) the British forces were in position south of the Marne between Lagny and Signy-Signets. Up to this time I had been requested by General Joffre to defend the passages of the river as long as possible, and to blow up the bridges in my front. After I had made the necessary dispositions, and the destruction of the bridges had been effected, I was asked by the French Commander-in-Chief to continue my retirement to a point some 12 miles in rear of the position I then occupied, with a view to taking up a second position behind the Seine. This retirement was duly carried out. In the meantime the enemy had thrown bridges and crossed the Marne in considerable force, and was threatening the Allies all along the line of the British Forces and the 5th and 9th French Armies. Consequently several small outpost actions took place.

Air reconnaissances revealed to the Allies that the columns of the German First Army had turned south-eastward.

That army since the battle near Mons had been playing its part in the colossal strategic endeavour to create a Sedan for the Allies by outflanking and enveloping the left of their whole line so as to encircle and drive both British and French to the south. There was now a change in its objective ; and it was observed that the German forces opposite the British were beginning to move in a south-easterly direction instead of continuing south-west on to the capital.

Leaving a strong rearguard along the line of the River Ourcq (which flows south and joins the Marne at Lizy-sur-Ourcq) to keep off the French 6th Army, which by then had been formed and was to the north-west of Paris, they were evidently executing what amounted to a flank march diagonally across our front.

I met the French Commander-in-Chief at his request (continued Sir John French) and he informed me of his intention to take the offensive forthwith by wheeling up the left flank of the 6th Army, pivoting on the Marne, and directing it to move on the Ourcq ; cross and attack the flank of the 1st German Army, which was then moving in a south-easterly direction east of that river.

He requested me to effect a change of front to my right—my left resting on the Marne and my right on the 5th Army—to fill the gap between that army and the 6th. I was then to advance against the enemy in my front and join in the general offensive movement. . . . German troops, which were observed moving south-east up the left bank of the Ourcq on the 4th were now reported to be halted and facing that river. Heads of the enemy's columns were seen crossing at Changis, La Ferté, Nogent, Château Thierry, and Mezy.

Considerable German columns ot all arms were seen to be converging on Montmirail, whilst before sunset large bivouacs of the enemy were located in the neigh-

[Otto, Paris.

GENERAL SARRAIL.

bourhood of Coulommiers, south of Rebais, La Ferté-Gaucher, and Dagny.

There was considerable fighting with the 5th French Army, which fell back from its position south of the Marne towards the Seine.

These combined movements practically commenced on Sunday, September 6, at sunrise ; and on that day it may be said that a great battle opened on a front extending from Ermenonville, which was just in front of the left flank of the 6th French Army, through Lizy on the Marne, Mauperthuis, which was about the British centre, Courtecon, which was the left of the 5th French Army, to Esternay and Charleville, the left of the 9th Army under General Foch, and so along the front of the 9th, 4th and 3rd French Armies to a point north of the fortress of Verdun. . .

The dispositions of the rival armies on the front Paris-Verdun-Belfort were the direct outcome of three events which happened many hundred miles apart on August 22.

The factor of time required that the French Army should not be merely dispersed—for an army dispersed in its own country has every chance of rallying further back—but disabled. For this reason the Germans had evolved a plan of strategical deployment leading up to a battle formation consisting of a comparatively thin centre with enormously strong wings. The former was to engage the enemy closely and keep him pinned to his ground while the latter should swing around his flanks, completely envelop him, and produce the " super-Sedan " so confidently anticipated by German theorists. The great strength of the French fortifications

along the frontier common to the two nations induced the Germans to apply their plan to the French frontier north of Verdun, i.e., through neutral territory. Here the gap between Thionville and the Ardennes would permit the passage of the Left-Attack. The rugged region of the Ardennes, traversed by few roads and railways, was allotted to the Centre. North of the Ardennes the Belgian plain, covered by a network of roads, railways and canals, was an ideal theatre of operations for the Right-Attack.*

On August 16, while the Right-Attack was still endeavouring to burst its way through Belgium, the French 15th Corps from Lunéville reached Saarburg, cut the railway between Metz and Strassburg and threatened the flank and rear of the German Left-Attack. On August 22 a powerful German detachment—perhaps four Corps—hurled the French out of Lorraine with heavy loss in men and guns. Thus the French offensive in the lost provinces ended in tactical defeat, but it proved that there was no strong German force south of Metz, and it induced the enemy to make such a powerful detachment, afterwards reinforced to two complete Armies—the 6th and 7th—as amounted to the diversion of his whole Left-Attack into the lost provinces, where, during the Battles of the Marne, they found themselves faced by that very barrier of French fortresses which the German plan of campaign had proposed to ignore.

The whole of this incident is very interesting as being the first suggestion of divided counsels in the German Headquarters. Purely strategical reasons required that the Germans should send a force only just strong enough to *check* the French advance in Lorraine. The success of the Left-Attack would automatically clear the enemy out of their lost provinces. To detach sufficient troops to

* That this was really the German intention is indicated by four things :—

1. It was in consonance with oft-declared German theory.

2. The situation of the fortified line Verdun-Toul and the rugged Ardennes, coupled with the factor of time, practically compelled the Germans to restrict themselves to a demonstration against the line Verdun-Belfort, pass their main masses through the two gaps, Luxemburg and the Belgian Plain, and connect them by a thin centre passing through the Ardennes.

3. The known positions of German Corps at noon on August 10, as published in *The Times* of August 12 and 16.

4. Of the twenty-four Army Corps Regions into which Germany is divided, at least seven lie south of a line drawn east and west through Metz. If there had been any intention to deploy a large force in Alsace-Lorraine these Corps would have been railed and marched straight to their front—viz., due west ; but the French offensive in the lost provinces proved that, up to August 22, there was no large German force south of Metz.

smash the hostile force at Saarburg was to cripple the Left-Attack, to preclude the prospect of breaking the French line opposite Luxemburg, to abandon the hope of a new and greater Sedan, to abort the whole plan of campaign at its very inception. It meant ascribing to the Left Wing a defensive instead of an offensive rôle—just when the Right Wing had lost several precious days before Liége—and the adoption of a new plan of campaign at the very moment when the main army was about to seek a decisive result. The other line of argument was this : After the Zabern incident, General von Falkenhayn had declared that Alsace-Lorraine might as well be an enemy's country. The French had now been conducting offensive operations in their lost provinces for a fortnight. If

this state of affairs were allowed to continue much longer, it might result in an insurrection, which, of course, would have a terrible effect on friends and foes and neutral powers. It was necessary to make such an example of the presumptuous enemy as would impress all beholders. Even on military grounds there was something to be said for this line of action. Thirteen years before, the world had been startled to learn from the evidence given in the Dreyfus trial that, in the event of war with Germany, the French would take the offensive in their lost provinces. It was, therefore, quite possible that the French Corps at Saarburg was not the main body, but the advanced guard of a very powerful offensive. Every plan of campaign is necessarily liable to modification as the result of the first collisions. It

EARLY MORNING AT THE FRONT. *[Photo press.*
French Dragoons and British soldiers in the foreground.

FRENCH MARCHING TO THE FIGHTING LINE. *[Photo press*

was true that the Right-Attack had experienced some delay, but it had now burst its way through Belgian opposition and was about to fall upon the enemy's main army with about twice the numbers he was expecting. There could be no doubt that it would annihilate his flank and roll up his line.

On this same day—August 22—the French 5th Army was defeated at Charleroi. The French troops which had formed for battle along the Meuse and Sambre had been organised into five " Field Armies," numbered from right to left. When the 5th Army was driven back from the Sambre, the British and 4th French Armies found their flanks uncovered and were obliged to conform. In the same way the retreat of the 4th Army necessitated that of the 3rd. The right flank of the latter, however, was protected by the great fortress of Verdun. One of Napoleon's four strategical maxims was " always manœuvre about a fixed point," and there can be no doubt that Verdun was General Joffre's " fixed point." Verdun was the centre on which the whole forces north of it pivoted as they fell back through an angle of 90 degrees until the British on the left of the line had reached the northern outworks of Paris. Meanwhile, a new 6th Army, which had been secretly concentrated in Paris, was brought up on the British left ; and a new 9th Army was formed and brought up into the French

battle-front between their 4th and 5th Armies. Thus did the Battle of Charleroi influence the position of the Franco-British line between Paris and Verdun during the Battle of the Marne.

Again, on this same day—August 22— the Russian covering troops on the Niemen defeated the Prussian covering troops near Gumbinnen and Insterburg. Three days later the Russian left wing advancing westwards through Galicia, met the Austrian Second Army at Lemberg in the first *great* battle of the eastern theatre of war. By August 28 or 29 the Russians in East Prussia had laid siege to Königsburg and pushed on to Osterode. The inhabitants—having a lively recollection of the Cossacks of a century back, and being, perhaps, not altogether ignorant of German methods in Belgium—incontinently fled for Berlin, where they filled the capital with panic and the ears of their King with cries for rescue. We may be sure that we have here another instance of divided counsels at the German Headquarters. It has been laid down that " concentration of superior force at the decisive point is the grand rule of war," for " success at the decisive point is success everywhere." It is also an axiom in strategy that there is not any place or district the possession of which is decisive in any campaign— not even the fall of Paris will be decisive.

There is only one thing which is decisive, and that is the destruction of the enemy's main field armies, not a detachment. The Russian forces in East Prussia may have amounted to a few hundred thousands, but it was not a question of hundreds of thousands but of millions. Therefore no victory in East Prussia could be decisive, nor could any conceivable pursuit carried out from East Prussia bring the Germans to any point of real importance to them or to the Russians. If reinforcements were to be sent to any place in the eastern theatre of war, it would be better to send them to Lemberg, because Germany could not afford to see her ally smashed up. A little arithmetical calculation would suffice to show that the *main* Russian Army could not be up for a long time yet. The Russians may have had enough men to smash the Austrian Second Army, *if given the chance*; but they must not be given the chance. It was the business of the Second Army to fight falling back continually till joined by the First Army on the line of the San ; and it was the business of the combined Austrian Armies to fight falling back continually until the Germans could come up *after* they had decisively defeated the French. The *decisive* point, therefore, was in France ; and it was

[Otto, Paris.

GENERAL FRANCHET D'ESPERAY.

here and at once that the Germans should " concentrate superior force." To weaken themselves at the decisive point at this moment would be a fatal mistake. What could the Russians do to injure permanently Germany or their ally ? Those that were in East Prussia could not possibly force the impregnable line of the Vistula ; those that were in Galicia could not cross the Carpathians into Hungary to the south leaving undefeated armies on their flank—they must advance westwards against those armies. Those armies had a succession of excellent defensive positions, such as the San, the Wistoka, the Donajee. The Russians could not exercise any material pressure on their enemies until they should reach the rich industrial region of Silesia. They were now at Lemberg—250 miles from Silesia. If the Austrians could reduce the rate of the enemy's advance to five miles a day, he would not reach Silesia for seven or eight weeks. It is true that by then they would have lost the whole province of Galicia *for a time*, but it was better to lose it for a time than to lose it, and much else, for ever. In seven weeks the Germans would join them, having accomplished the complete defeat of the French. In seven weeks in 1866 the

[Otto, Paris.

GENERAL FOCH.

15—2

A BRITISH COLUMN HALTS BY THE WAY.   [L.N.A.

Germans had broken the Army of Austria to pieces, in less than eight weeks in 1870 they had destroyed the whole Regular army of France. When the French advanced beyond the Moselle in 1870, von Moltke detrained on the Rhine instead of on the Saar, and thus, apparently, abandoned ninety miles of country to the enemy. In that crisis the Germans had kept their heads, and, in these exactly similar circumstances it behoved their sons to keep theirs. On the other hand it might be objected that the continued occupation of East Prussia and Galicia by the Russians could not fail to have a terrible effect on friends and foes and hesitating neutrals. East Prussia must be cleared of the enemy and the Austrians must stand their ground at Lemberg. The Army in the East must be reinforced by troops from the West. The French and the British had been hunted from pillar to post. What guarantee was there that they would not continue to retire indefinitely ? If they should decide to stand their ground now, who could doubt the issue ? The Germans might be at some slight disadvantage in point of numbers in the whole field, but, since the initiative lay with them, they would naturally spread a screen along the enemy's entire front, hurl overwhelming forces against a selected point and smash up all opposition.

" Success at the decisive point is success everywhere," not only in strategy but in tactics also. If the French could be beaten at the decisive point they would be beaten everywhere.

The distracted Kaiser compromised : no troops were transferred from France, but all the troops on the eastern frontier of Germany were sent to East Prussia—not to Lemberg— and the Kaiser could not bring himself to advise the retreat of the Austrians until too late. Von Hindenburg inflicted a heavy defeat on Samsonoff at Osterode (or Tannenberg) on the last day of August, but this was a very poor set-off for the utter *débâcle* of the Austrians two days later at Lemberg, where they were said to have lost 130,000 men—killed, wounded, and captured—and 200 guns. Four or five German Army Corps were immediately hurried from the western to the eastern front—again too late, for the Russians caught the Austrian First Army at Tomasow on September 5 and drove it westwards. Thus, by the time that the fighting began in the basin of the Marne, the whole Austrian Army was in full retreat on Cracow, and the Germans were advancing to the decisive battle of the west with the numerical odds somewhere about 100 to 85 against them. Moreover, and most serious of all, the German plan of campaign had been

changed twice : first, when the Left-Attack
was changed into a Left-Defence ; and,
secondly, when troops were transferred from
the western to the eastern front before a decisive
issue had been obtained in France, which obliged
the Germans to turn their Right-Attack into
a Right-Defence. The net result, as far as the
struggles on the Marne were concerned, was to
substitute an attempt to *break* the Allies'
front for the attempt to envelop their flanks
or flank. Thus did the battles of the east
influence the numbers and dispositions of the
Germans in the decisive battles of the west.

It was on the last day of July, 1914, that the
Kaiser and his advisers took the step which
flung the fate of man into the melting pot of
war. Just about a month later they took
this other step of transferring troops from the
western to the eastern front, which decided
the issue, for within the octave, the fiery
flood of German invasion which had swept
across the fields of France and Belgium,
burning and blotting out like molten lava,
burst in thunder on the steel-bound barrier of
the Franco-British Army at bay—*and recoiled !*

The Marne was no ordinary battle. History
records a score or more of so-called " decisive
battles," each of which in its turn has stood

[*Otto, Paris.*

GENERAL MANNOURY.

like a mighty rock to divert the fortunes of the
human race into this channel or that ; and
there is hardly one of these which has not been
more immediately decisive in itself and, therefore, more apparently decisive in its effects
upon history than the " Battle of the Marne " ;
but the more we appreciate the issues at stake
and the really final character of the decision
determined in the basin of the Marne, the more
we shall be convinced that the importance of
that tremendous trial was as much greater than
that of any previous conflict as the population
and prosperity of the world to-day exceeds
those of times past. The tide of Teutonic
invasion here reached its pitch. For months
the rollers continued to hurl themselves upon
the breakwater, but the barrier did not break—
the tide was on the ebb.

" The moral," said Napoleon, " is to the
physical factor as three is to one." " There is
a force in war," says Henderson, " more potent
than mere numbers." Of all the factors which
went to determine the issue in the basin of the
Marne, there was, we may be sure, none so
decisive as *moral*. As was inevitable, the Great
Retreat had profoundly affected the issue of
the whole campaign—not only in its material
results, but more particularly in its moral
results. It had settled for a generation to

[*Otto, Paris.*

GENERAL DE LANGLE DE CARY.

come the estimation in which the fighting man on each side would regard his opponent. The British soldier had formed a very definite appreciation of his antagonist, as a soldier and as a man. As a soldier he admired the German's courage, but he marvelled at his poor shooting, his mass-tactics, his lack of initiative and intelligence, and the way in which he permitted himself to be herded and driven into action by his officers. He was, of course, not able to appraise correctly German higher leadership and staff work, but he was a first-class judge of matters within his competence. He conceived a profound contempt for the German company officer and his utter want of consideration for his soldiers and the inhabitants of the country through which he passed. As a man he considered the German both a bully and a brute who had no notion of "playing the game." At Mons and after he had had some opportunity of witnessing German atrocities. The extracts given below from letters written and statements made by British officers and men are typical of those which must be within the knowledge of every English citizen.

Never was attack made with more reckless courage nor pressed with such relentless ferocity. And never was defence conducted with greater heroism. Every mile has been contested with stubborn gallantry, British and French retiring with their faces to the foe. . . . Their numbers were overwhelming. They gave us no rest. Night and day they hammered away, coming on like great waves. The gaps we made were filled instantly. Their artillery, which is well handled, played upon us incessantly. Their cavalry swept down upon us with amazing recklessness. . . . Column after column, squadron after squadron, mass after mass, the enemy came on like a battering ram crushing everything in its way. Shattered to fragments by shot and shell, the hordes of the enemy seemed instantly to renew themselves ; they swarmed on all sides. Nothing but the sheer pluck, the stedfast courage and the unflinching determination of our soldiers saved the Army from annihilation.

The losses inflicted on the enemy must have been enormous. They attacked in solid formation, and whole brigades of infantry were decimated by the fire of our rifles and guns. No army of civilised men can endure such devastation as was wrought amongst the Germans in this long battle over scores of miles.

A private soldier says :

They come up like a football crowd leaving Hampstead Park. They come marching up in droves, firing their rifles from their right hips. They have absolutely no idea of aim. If their rifle fire is bad, there is no doubt about the accuracy of their work with the machine guns and heavy artillery. The aeroplanes gave them great help in finding the range, and most of our soldiers were injured by the shrapnel.

Private Whittaker, of the Coldstream Guards, writes :

The Germans rushed at us like a crowd streaming from a cup-tie at the Crystal Palace. You could not miss them. Our bullets ploughed into them, but still on they came. I was well entrenched, and my rifle got so hot I could hardly hold it.

Sir Robert Edgcumbe, of Newquay, received a letter from his son, Lieut. O. P. Edgcumbe, 1st Battalion D.C.L.I., on the staff of General Haking, in which the following passages occur :

My regiment has had a bad time, and I am dreadfully afraid that they have been badly cut up, although I

SOME OF OUR MEN RESTING IN CAMP.　　　*[Newspaper Illustrations.*

[*Underwood & Underwood.*

A MORNING TOILET ON THE RAILWAY LINE.

can as yet get no details. They were caught in a village by Germans in the houses, who had managed to get there by wearing our uniforms. Never again shall I respect the Germans. They have no code of honour, and there have been several cases of their wearing French and British uniforms, which is, of course, against the Geneva Convention.

The following is from an officer of the Royal Field Artillery :

One night we had a great attack on us from a wood near our camp. Over 800 Germans were counted next morning. They attacked shouting, "Vive l'Angleterre," headed by men dressed as peasants in French uniforms.

A sergeant, wounded in the action near Mons says that :

As he lay helpless on the ground the German infantry swept by. He could hear from the imploring cries of the wounded in his front that they were being ruthlessly put to death by their savage foes. Closing his eyes and simulating death, the wounded sergeant lay perfectly still. As the Germans passed him he received a violent blow in the chest from the butt end of a rifle which broke one of his ribs.

It is only fair to state that the Germans were not always brutal and callous.

H. G. W. Irwin, of the South Lancashire Regiment, writes that after three days' hard fighting, in which the men behaved splendidly against overwhelming odds, he was wounded by shrapnel. Owing to the darkness he and other wounded were overlooked, and were left lying all night in a turnip field. Eventually the Germans discovered him and offered the kindest treatment to him and other wounded. A German soldier brought him a bundle of hay to lie on, and later he was taken by stretcher bearers to a temporary hospital where he lay for a fortnight. He was then taken to Valenciennes, and by the kindness of the German commandant was permitted to write to his friends, the letter being forwarded through Germany.

Lieut. Irwin says the hospital was left to the Germans when the Allies retired. All the French doctors and nurses remained on duty and the wounded prisoners received every consideration from the German officials.

And what of France and the French, upon whom the brunt of the fighting and losses in men and material were bound to fall—at first, at all events ?

The Germans had advanced from Mons to near Luzarches with a venom never surpassed and a vigour never equalled in history. On August 31 they were as near Notre Dame as Tilbury or Staines, Hertford or Reigate is to St. Paul's. The Military Governor of Paris, wishing to be rid of " les bouches inutiles," had invited the citizens to leave, and nearly a third of the population had departed and the Government had withdrawn to Bordeaux. Those who remained were calm. The German airmen who had sought to terrorise the people by a

[Newspaper Illustrations.

FRENCH OFFICERS TAKING A HURRIED MEAL UNDER CANVAS.

daily shower of bombs had achieved nothing more than the murder and mutilation of a few elderly men and little girls. Even this had practically ceased, since half a dozen French airmen had been detailed to attack the German aeronauts at sight.

In 1871 the advocates of uncompromising national defence were the object of merciless attacks at the hands of vindictive political opponents ; 43 years later no voice was raised in captious criticism of the statesmen or strategists responsible for the national safety.

The defence of the great city had been completely thought out and calmly prepared. Hundreds of civil engineers, masons, and other artisans had volunteered to clear the fields of fire around the outer and inner rings of forts and to connect up the forts themselves and to block or cover all roads leading into Paris with entrenchments, barbed wire entanglements, *chevaux de frise* and abattis. Aeroplanes armed with mitrailleuses continually circled in the sky. Immense quantities of food and munitions of war had been concentrated in and about the city. Cattle, sheep and milch cows in tens of thousands were corralled on almost every green space within the defensive peri-meter of 90 miles. The Bois de Boulogne was one vast stockyard. Thousands of soldiers were encamped at such places as Versailles and Fontainebleau on the outskirts.

Myriads of refugees had poured into Paris from all the country to the north and east. In

many townships in the track of the advancing Germans even the authorities had fled to avoid the certainty of being arrested as hostages and the probability of being shot on any pretext. Everywhere, however, the curé stood his ground, the father of his flock, the comforter of the bereaved, the mayor, the village constable, and the general factotum of the neighbourhood. He often paid for his fidelity with his life, but he never flinched from his post. Hundreds of thousands of people had been induced to move on from Paris by the offer of free fares on the railway. Many refugees left by road. Inter-minable files of ox-wagons, tradesmen's carts, horse-carriages and motor-cars stretched along all the roads leading southwards from Paris, and everywhere might be seen broken-down vehicles, jettisoned luggage and stranded way-farers.

But Paris herself—and France like Paris— awaited the stroke of impending fate, quietly and hopefully prepared to resist to the death, and comforted with the thought that, if the worst *should* come to the worst, the fall of Paris would not again involve the fall of France. As Bernhardi had pointed out, the fall of a fortress —even that of Paris herself—would not again necessarily decide the issue of a campaign.

It was estimated before the war that Germany would mobilize some 25 Army Corps (3 Divisions each) of First Line troops and a like number of " Reserve " Army Corps (2 Divisions each) of Second Line troops. It was expected, and the event went to show, that Germany would allocate a fifth of her forces to a defensive campaign against Russia, while with 100 German and 36 Italian Divisions she overwhelmed the 90 or 100 First and Second Line Divisions which, it was thought, France might be able to put in the field. The defection of Italy and the accession of Britain and Belgium to the side of the Dual Alliance brought the odds about level. Germany, however, designed to gain time as well as to save it. She, therefore, commenced her mobilization secretly some days before her prospective adversaries, and it is probable that on August 22 there were 100 German Divisions against, perhaps, 75 French, British and Belgian Divisions. During the next fortnight the Franco-British Army must have been raised to about 95 Divisions, while, as we have seen, the Germans were reduced to, perhaps, 80 Divisions by the transference of troops from the western to the eastern front and the necessity of providing a garrison for Belgium and the lines of communication. Allowing 20,000 men to a Division, and adding Staffs, Cavalry, Army Troops, &c., there must have been rather more than two million French and British and rather less than that number of Germans extended on the front Paris-Verdun-Belfort. Of combatants actually engaged there might have been about three millions altogether.

On September 4, as we have seen, it became known to the Allies that the columns of von Kluck's German First Army which had pursued the British from Mons south-westwards to the outworks of Paris had suddenly turned sharp to their left—*i.e.*, south-eastwards. At the time, and for some time afterwards, the reason for this sudden change of objective, which clearly indicated a change of plan, was much debated; but it is now certain that it was due mainly to the transference of German troops from the western to the eastern front, which necessitated a closing in towards the left. This move of the 1st German Army to its left was a bold and most perilous operation, for it required von Kluck to execute a "flank march" along the front of the British and 6th French Armies and exposed his right flank to attack by those Armies. Everything now depended on which belligerent could attain his object first. Could the French Centre, possibly dispirited by retreat, withstand the rush of the victorious Teutons? Could the British, exhausted by their long retreat and possibly by their losses, participate effectively in the counter-attack; and, if so, could the German First Army, after all its immense exertions, support the impact of a determined counter-stroke? It was obvious that if the Allies were to achieve success that success would not be complete unless the 6th French Army could make itself master of the railway by which the First German Army was supplied.

The question arose, "What point will the Germans select for their attempt?" It was obvious that they would strike as near to the

[*Newspaper Illustrations.*

FRENCH SOLDIERS CARRYING A MACHINE GUN.
Each man has a section.

[Newspaper Illustrations.

**OUR MEN ARE GREAT FAVOURITES
WITH THE VILLAGE CHILDREN.**

line of the French fortresses as possible, because
success in this direction would enable them to
drive the Allies' centre and left away from the
resources of the rich south and the great pen-
tagon of ring-fortresses (Belfort, Epinal, Langres, Dijon, Besançon) especially designed to
shelter beaten armies ; to cut off the French
frontier fortresses and eastern armies ; and
reduce those fortresses and thus open a shorter
and better line of supply with Germany. But,
not only was the line of the Meuse heavily
fortified, but the adjacent country was very
hilly, covered with forests separated by strips
of pasture land studded with spinneys and
copses, traversed by hedges and broken by
ravines. Running north and south parallel
with the terrain of the Meuse, and separated
from it by a comparatively narrow and broken
valley, was the long forest-clad hill-barrier of
the Argonne ending at Triaucourt and continued southwards by a line of lakes and vast
forests. In all these regions the population was
comparatively sparse, supplies scanty, roads
and railways few and far between, which
prohibited the operations and supply of a large
force, and nothing but a large force could hope
to break the French line.

West of the difficult country of the Meuse and
the Argonne stretched the interminable plain
of the Champagne-Pouilleuse, the plain of
Châlons, the Aldershot of France, a hundred
miles and more from north to south and

some forty miles in width. A bare, open
undulating country of alternate heath and
plough, scarred here and there by lines of
small newly planted firs. A lonely, lost,
depressing region, but sacred to Gaul and Frank
as the ground on which from time immemorial
they have repulsed invasions from the east.
Here and there amid these endless wastes there
is to be found some place of interest—the field
of Valmy and the tomb of Kellerman, the
house where Joan of Arc was born, the spot
where Goethe stood and wondered if this were
the beginning of a new world, the home of
Danton, the " Camp of Attila "—a huge oval
bank, several hundred yards in length, towering
massive and lonely above the desolate rolling
plain. Here, then, was the ideal terrain for the
German effort. History was about to repeat
herself. Once more the fate of France would be
decided on the field of Châlons.

On the west of the plain of Champagne lies
the Plateau of Sézanne. If we imagine that
plain and plateau were once on the same general
level, that a long irregular fissure running
roughly north and south suddenly appeared
between the two, and that the plain then sank
some 300 ft., we should have the line of bluffs
in which the plateau falls to the plain under the
name of " Les Falaises de Champagne." At
the foot of these " cliffs " runs the road from
La Fère-Champenoise to Rheims. Some fifty
miles west, in the neighbourhood of Meaux,
the plateau sinks into the Plain of Paris.

Linking plain and plateau lies the Marne.
It rises near Langres and flows northward
through hilly and thickly wooded country to
St. Dizier, north-westward across the Plain of
Champagne, past Vitry-le-François and Châlons,
and westward through the Plateau of Sézanne,
by Epernay, Château Thierry, La Ferté-sous-
Jouarre and Meaux, to join the Seine south of
Paris. In the neighbourhood of Meaux the
Marne receives three tributaries—the Ourcq,
from the north, and the Grand Morin and the
Petit Morin, from the east. Towards the eastern
borders of the Plateau of Sézanne lie Les Marais
de St. Gond—ten miles long from east to west
and a mile or two broad—the source of the Petit
Morin, which has been converted into a drain
to carry off the waters of the marshes now in
process of reclamation.

The right half of the Allies' line was based on
the fortified line Belfort-Verdun. The left
half of their line extended from Verdun and the
difficult country of the Argonne and the

BRITISH, FRENCH, AND MOROCCAN TROOPS AT THE FRONT.

[Newspaper Illustrations.

FRENCH AEROPLANE BEING REPAIRED ON THE FIELD.

Meuse to Paris—the greatest fortress in the world. Therefore both flanks were secure from being turned, and the Germans were reduced to the attempt to break the centre, while their right was exposed to an attack in flank. Their troops in this direction had made such enormous exertions during the last three weeks and their losses had been so heavy that they must have been brought perilously near exhaustion. Their lines of communication, stretching over 200 miles to Brussels, must have presented many difficulties and many anxieties. Their whole Army was committed to a tactical effort abhorred of German theorists. From Frederick the Great, who declared that above all things it was necessary for the Prussians to throw their greatest weight on their adversaries' wings, down to von Schlieffen, who points out that the effort against the Austrians at Sadowa was futile, the envelopment of an enemy's flank or flanks, not the breaking of his line, had been the aim of German tacticians—Sedan, not Ligny, had been their ideal. Moreover, in this particular instance success against the Allies' centre would not necessarily have been decisive. The Germans would still have Paris upon one flank and the French frontier fortresses and armies upon the other flank ; and the Allies' lines of retreat across the Seine were all open and offered the means of rallying further back. But for the Germans defeat must inevitably mean that downfall which

General von Bernhardi said must follow the failure of her bid for world-power.

The Allies can face defeats. For Germany a single defeat in a battle on the grand scale must now mean final failure. She fights with every civilized nation praying for her downfall, and for the obliteration of the perverse ambitions which have led her to plunge the world into strife. . . . We note that the Crown Prince's Army is believed to be near Châlons, a place of evil omen for any Attila or his offspring. . . . Here Attila was overwhelmed and here prophets innumerable have declared that some day Armageddon would be fought. It is being waged upon the very ground where Napoleon conducted his campaign of 1814, which still remains a masterpiece of defensive strategy. Fère-Champenoise . . . was the scene of the famous resistance of a French force which refused to surrender to the Allies even when its general had delivered up his sword. The whole region is full of inspiration for the Army of France. (*The Times,* September 9.)

The higher command on both sides took their soldiery into their confidence. The French officers were directed to explain to their men that the retreat from the Belgian frontier had been a strategical movement designed to gain time ; that the plans of the Great General Staff had now matured, and that the moment had arrived for decisive action.

On September 6 General Joffre, the Commander-in-Chief, issued an order to all the French troops in the following terms :—

At the moment when a battle on which the welfare of the country depends is about to begin, I feel it incumbent upon me to remind you all that this is no longer the time to look behind. All our efforts must be directed towards attacking and driving back the enemy. An Army which can no longer advance must at all costs keep the ground it has won, and allow itself to be killed on the spot rather than give way. In the present circumstances no faltering can be tolerated.

On the same date Sir John French issued the following Special Army Order to the British troops :—

After a most trying series of operations, mostly in retirement, which have been rendered necessary by the general strategic plan of the Allied Armies, the British forces stand to-day formed in line with their French comrades, ready to attack the enemy. Foiled in their attempt to invest Paris, the Germans have been driven to move in an easterly and south-easterly direction, with the apparent intention of falling in strength on the 5th French Army. In this operation they are exposing their right flank and their line of communications to an attack from the combined 6th French Army and the British forces.

I call upon the British Army in France to now show the enemy its power, and to push on vigorously to the attack beside the 6th French Army.

I am sure I shall not call upon them in vain, but that, on the contrary, by another manifestation of the magnificent spirit which they have shown in the past fortnight, they will fall on the enemy's flank with all their strength, and in unison with their Allies drive them back.

On the entry of the victorious French into Vitry-le-François there was found in the house that had been occupied by the staff of the 8th German Army Corps the following order signed by Lieut.-General Tülff von Tschepe und Weidenbach :—

Vitry-le-François, Sept. 7, 10.30 p.m.

The object of our long and arduous marches has been achieved. The principal French troops have been forced to accept battle after having been continually forced back. The great decision is undoubtedly at hand. To-morrow, therefore, the whole strength of the German Army, as well as all that of our Army Corps, are bound to be engaged all along the line from Paris to Verdun. To save the welfare and honour of Germany I expect every officer and man, notwithstanding the hard and heroic fights of the last few days, to do his duty unswervingly and to the last breath. Everything depends on the result of to-morrow.

Both Armies—the German and the French— were numbered from the right. By the morning of Sunday, September 6, the French 1st and 2nd Armies, based on the line Belfort-Verdun, were facing the German 7th (von Heeringen) and 6th (Crown Prince of Bavaria) Armies in Alsace and Lorraine. The extreme right of the French still clung to a corner of Alsace, and their centre to Nancy, while the left of the 2nd Army lay east and north of Verdun.

During the Battle of the Marne these German Armies attacked the French Armies opposed to them. At Nancy, in particular, these attacks were of a desperate nature. There was a great unfortified gap between the fortresses of Toul and Epinal, and the object of this attack on Nancy was to penetrate behind the main French Army, so that a success on the Plain of Châlons would enable the Germans to cut off the 2nd, 3rd, and part of the 4th French Armies, together with the fortified line Verdun-Toul with its garrisons.

MEAUX.   [*Topical*

The Pont du Moulin, destroyed by French Engineers.

THE BRIDGE AT PONTOISE.

[*Newspaper Illustrations.*]

General Sarrail's 3rd French Army was based on Verdun and the Meuse Heights. His right extended to a point north of Verdun and his left towards Bar-le-Duc. Thus he faced west and stood back to back with the 2nd French Army. The 3rd German Army (Crown Prince) which had poured westwards through Luxemburg and turned south through the Argonne, now faced to attack the 3rd French Army, with the object of breaking the French fortified line Verdun-Toul at Fort Troyon and thus complete the investment of Verdun.

A glance at the map of the districts adjacent to the frontiers common to Germany and France will show that all the railways which cross this frontier are led through the great French frontier fortresses and diverge again on both sides.

General de Langle's 4th French Army was south of Vitry-le-François, facing north. It stretched across almost the whole plain of Châlons, which had been selected by the Germans for their principal effort, and it had for its chief opponents the 4th German Army (Prince of Würtemberg).

The 3rd German Army (von Hausen's Saxon Army) seems to have been much reduced by this date. Most of its units reappeared later on the eastern front. The gap thus created in the German strategical line had been filled by von Bülow closing in to his left and by von Kluck turning sharp to his left when almost in touch with the outer defences of Paris, so as to close in on von Bülow.

General Foch's newly formed 9th French

Army had just been brought up between the 4th and 5th Armies. According to *Le Temps* of September 5 it held the line Camp de Mailly Sézanne, but it is probable that its left flank extended further west. Its principal opponent was the 2nd German Army (von Bülow).

General d'Espérey's 5th French Army held the line Esternay-Courtecon with Conneau's Cavalry on its left flank, while General Pau's 6th French Army, advancing from the north of Paris, pushed eastward with its right on the Marne, near Meaux, and its left towards Betz. These two French Armies had for their chief opponent the 1st German Army (von Kluck). The latter proceeded to act as if he had only these two armies to deal with. He left the 2nd and 4th Reserve Corps on the east side of the Ourcq, between La Ferté Milon and the Marne, facing west, to hold off the 6th French Army, while with the 4th, 3rd and 7th Corps he advanced to Coulommiers, Rébais, La Ferté Gaucher, and points between that place and Montmirail, with the apparent intention of attacking the centre and left of the 5th French Army. It is difficult to understand how any German General could have come to consider the British Army a negligible quantity. It is true that for more than a generation the Germans had been engaged in persuading their fellow-countrymen, particularly their troops, that their own Army was very much superior to any other in the world. Being driven by necessity to adopt universal service, with a very *short* Colour-Service, they had sought to establish the great superiority of the new system by decrying the old. The volunteer *long*-service Army of Britain was to them a relic of the Dark Ages, and they never lost any opportunity of declaring that its officers were a sport-loving band of amateurs and its rank and file a mob of " mercenaries " recruited by crime and hunger from the dregs of the population. It is related that when someone suggested to Bismarck that the British Army might be landed in Germany, he very quietly replied : " If it does, I shall ring for the police and have it locked up." We have related how a general order issued by the Kaiser in August had described it as " contemptible." It had been forced to retreat from its position at Mons and had been driven back for nearly a fortnight. Taking one consideration with another, the German authorities seem to have concluded that the British Army really could be ruled out of the immediate problem. Anyone who has been in touch with German thought for the last generation must have observed in them the peculiarly Chinese characteristic of deciding that a thing must be so because they wish it to be so. On this occasion it was very inconvenient for the Germans that the British Army should be able to intervene in the approaching struggle, and, therefore, of course, it could not

[*Underwood & Underwood*

LIVE SHELLS LEFT ON THE BATTLE-FIELD BY THE GERMANS IN THEIR RETREAT.

do so. The only other possible explanation is that the Germans had to " chance it." There was a gap between the 5th and 6th French Armies, and the Germans proposed to hold off the latter while they enveloped the

[*Sport & General.*

GUN TRENCH AND SHELL CASES ABANDONED BY THE GERMANS.

left wing of the former, but the troops engaged in the latter operation would themselves be liable to an attack in flank by any troops which might come up in the interval between the two French Armies. As a matter of fact at this moment the British Army, to the extent of five strong Divisions, with five Cavalry Brigades, was lying concealed by the Forest of Crécy from Villeneuve-le-Comte to Jouy-le-Chateau. That von Kluck thought that there was at least a remote possibility of the intervention of the British is suggested by the fact that he despatched his 2nd Cavalry Division towards Coulommiers, and his 9th Cavalry Division to a point west of Crécy. Thus placed, the German horsemen should be able to notify the approach of any hostile troops from the south-west.

The battle may be said to have commenced with the advance of the 6th French Army against the Ourcq. The Germans consisted of three First Line Divisions of the 2nd Corps and two Second Line Divisions of the 4th Reserve Corps. They held the plateau on the east bank of the Ourcq, which here runs in a deep trench or ravine. They held most of the villages on the plateau west of the Ourcq as advanced posts. The 6th French Army consisted of three " Active " and four Second Line Divisions, and had to capture the villages on the west bank of the Ourcq before they could proceed to the attack of the enemy's main position across the river. The fighting resolved itself into as many separate combats as there were villages held by the Germans, who, on being obliged to evacuate any point held by them, proceeded to set it on fire to postpone the enemy's occupation, and to permanently deny to him any shelter it might afford. The other French Armies all became engaged in a series of furious, but practically stationary, combats, in which neither side made any progress except on the right of the 3rd French Army, which was gradually pushed southwards along the heights of the Meuse.

It was at this moment that the British contingent entered the fight and created a situation which was both dramatic and almost immediately decisive. It was organized in three Army Corps.* The First and Second consisted of the 1st and 2nd, 3rd and 5th Divisions, all of which had fought at Mons. The

---

* Lieut.-General W. P. Pulteney took over the command of the 3rd Corps just before the commencement of the Battle of the Marne.

GERMAN SOLDIERS IN THEIR TRENCHES.
In the foreground is an Officer superintending the sighting of a machine gun.

[Underwood & Underwood.

FRENCH ZOUAVES BURYING THE DEAD AFTER BATTLE.

so-called 3rd Army Corps consisted of the
4th Division, most of which had been engaged
on August 26, and the 19th Brigade, which
had been formed of battalions on the lines of
communication and rushed up to the front
when it was discovered that the enemy's forces
opposed to the British at Mons were very much
larger than had been anticipated. Thus the
British Army may be put down at five Divisions
with five Brigades of Cavalry. These Divisions
broke up from their billets and bivouacs at
dawn on Sunday, September 6, and advancing
north-eastwards through the Forest of Crécy,
drove in the enemy's Cavalry Divisions and
Infantry Advance Guards. By nightfall they
had established themselves on the line Dagny-
Coulommiers-Maison. " I should conceive it
to have been about noon on September 6," says
Sir John French, " that the enemy realized the
powerful threat that was being made against
the flank of his columns moving south-east."

On September 7 the British Army continued
to drive the enemy in front of it, and by nightfall had reached the line of the Grand Morin ;
and it may be noted that five British Cavalry
Brigades (45 Squadrons) engaged and defeated
the 2nd, 9th, and Guard (German) Cavalry
Divisions (72 Squadrons).

The enforced retreat of the enemy's Corps on
the west uncovered the west flank of the troops
operating against the 5th French Army, and
obliged them to retreat, so that by nightfall the
5th French Army had advanced up to the Grand
Morin between Esternay and La Ferté Gaucher.

On September 7 (says Sir John French) both the 5th
and 6th French Armies were heavily engaged on our
flank. The 2nd and 4th Reserve German Corps on the
Ourcq vigorously opposed the advance of the French
towards that river, but did not prevent the 6th Army
from gaining some headway, the Germans themselves
suffering serious losses. The French 5th Army threw
the enemy back to the line of the Grand Morin River
after inflicting severe losses upon them. . .
The enemy retreated before our advance, covered by
his 2nd and 9th and Guard Cavalry Divisions, which
suffered severely.
Our Cavalry acted with great vigour, especially
General De Lisle's Brigade with the 9th Lancers and
18th Hussars.
On Monday, the 7th (says the Press Bureau), the
Germans commenced to retire towards the north-east.
This was the first time that these troops had turned back
since their attack at Mons a fortnight before, and, from
reports received, the order to retreat when so close to
Paris was a bitter disappointment. From letters found
on the dead there is no doubt that there was a general
impression amongst the enemy's troops that they were
about to enter Paris.

The fighting further east was everywhere
furious. The battle swayed backwards and
forwards with " charge, counter-charge, and
rally," but with little definite result, except that
a succession of determined assaults in the
neighbourhood of Nancy were repulsed with
heavy loss under the eyes of the Kaiser, and
the right of the 3rd French Army was pushed
sufficiently south to enable the Crown Prince
to bombard Fort Troyon. Maubeuge is reported to have fallen this day, and a number of
German troops were set free to reinforce their
field armies ; but the defence of the place had
obstructed the main line of railway required
for the supply of von Kluck's Army, and its
capture had only been effected with enormous
losses.

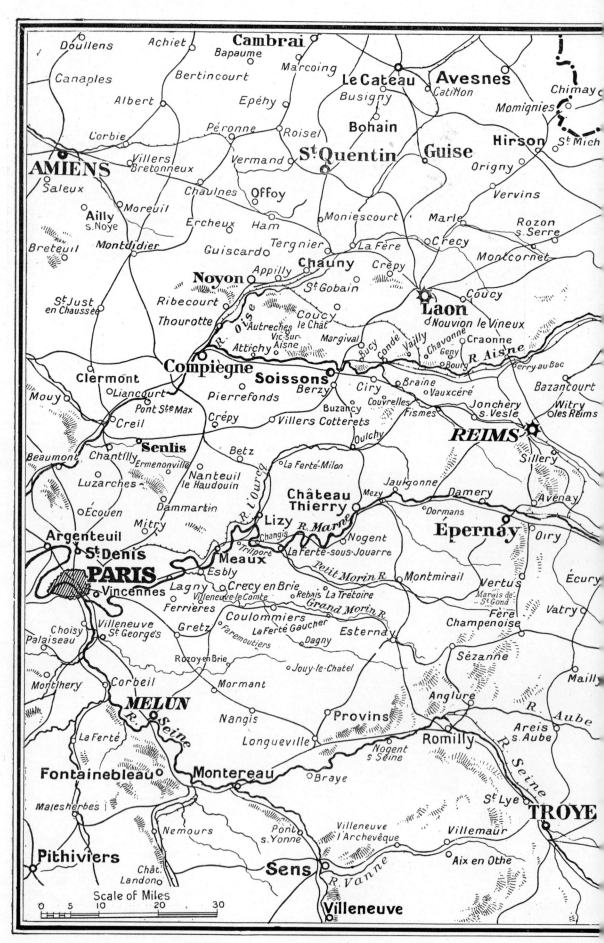

THE MARN

[*Newspaper Illustrations.*

BRITISH ARTILLERY PASSING THROUGH A VILLAGE.

On September 8 the French 6th Army got to grips with the German Flank Guard on the Ourcq, and the fighting became of the most sanguinary character.

The British fought their way to the line of the Marne and Petit Morin from near Trilport to near La Trétoire.

The 1st Army Corps encountered stubborn resistance at La Trétoire (north of Rebais). The enemy occupied a strong position with infantry and guns on the northern bank of the Petit Morin River ; they were dislodged with considerable loss. Several machine guns and many prisoners were captured, and upwards of two hundred German dead were left on the ground.

The forcing of the Petit Morin at this point was much assisted by the Cavalry and the 1st Division, which crossed higher up the stream. Later in the day a counter-attack by the enemy was well repulsed by the 1st Army Corps, a great many prisoners and some guns again falling into our hands. . . . The 2nd Army Corps encountered considerable opposition, but drove back the enemy at all points with great loss, making considerable captures.

The 3rd Army Corps also drove back considerable bodies of the enemy's infantry and made some captures. —SIR JOHN FRENCH.

The 5th French Army, greatly assisted by the British operations, attacked the enemy fiercely, stormed Montmirail and two other villages by hand-to-hand fighting, and established itself on the Petit Morin. The flank of the 2nd German Army being now uncovered, was obliged to withdraw, and the 9th French

Army was enabled to advance its left and centre to the line of the Petit Morin.

On September 9 the enemy had resigned himself to the idea of a general retreat. He therefore held La Ferté-sous-Jouarre strongly, reinforced his Flank Guard on the Ourcq, delivered a number of furious counter-attacks on the 6th French Army, and under cover of these demonstrations withdrew the whole of his west flank. The 6th French Army was now in full possession of the west bank. The fighting was of a peculiarly desperate character, but the French hold upon the positions they had won was unshaken. At one spot the Germans tried all day to complete a pontoon bridge. The French allowed the Germans nearly to complete this, and then opened on it with their guns and destroyed it. The weather which up to now had been perfect, in fact, too hot, changed, and rain fell in torrents, accompanied by a terrific wind.

The 3rd Army Corps on the British left was unable to bridge the river at La Ferté-sous-Jouarre in the face of a strong rearguard with machine-guns, and, therefore, did not get across here until after nightfall, but it pushed a party across near Changis which established itself on the north bank in the afternoon. The 1st and

2nd Army Corps had little difficulty in driving in the enemy's rearguards on the Petit Morin, whence they advanced upon Charly and Château Thierry, where they forced the passages of the river and established themselves some miles to the north.

The advance of the 1st and 2nd British Army Corps had driven a wedge between the Germans on the Ourcq and von Bülow's west flank, and the German Armies found themselves constrained to give way in sections commencing from the west.   Sir John French says :—

> During the day's pursuit the enemy suffered heavy loss in killed and wounded, some hundreds of prisoners fell into our hands and a battery of eight machine guns was captured by the 2nd Division. . . .
> The left of the 5th French Army reached the neighbourhood of Château Thierry after the most severe fighting, having driven the enemy completely north of the river with great loss.
> The fighting of this Army in the neighbourhood of Montmirail was very severe.

As an example of the spirit which inspired our Allies the following translation of the Ordre du Jour published on September 9 after the battle of Montmirail by the Commander of the French 5th Army is given :

> Soldiers,—Upon the memorable fields of Montmirail, of Vauchamps, of Champaubert, which a century ago witnessed the victories of our ancestors over Blücher's Prussians, your vigorous offensive has triumphed over the resistance of the Germans. Held on his flanks, his centre broken, the enemy is now retreating towards east and north by forced marches. The most renowned army corps of Old Prussia, the contingents of Westphalia, of Hanover, of Brandenburg, have retired in haste before you.
> This first success is no more than a prelude. The enemy is shaken, but not yet decisively beaten.
> You have still to undergo severe hardships, to make long marches, to fight hard battles.
> May the image of our country, soiled by barbarians, always remain before your eyes. Never was it more necessary to sacrifice all for her.
> Saluting the heroes who have fallen in the fighting of the last few days, my thoughts turn towards you—the victors in the next battle.
> Forward, soldiers, for France !
>
> > Montmirail, September 9, 1914.
> > General Commanding the Vth Army,
> > FRANCHET D'ESPEREY.

The 3rd French Army, attacked in front, flank, and rear, was very hard pressed this day, but managed to hold out. On the French right (or east face) a number of assaults delivered by the Germans were repulsed, and some slight advance was made. We may suspect that the German attacks in these parts were designed to conceal the transference of troops from Alsace-Lorraine to the west flank. Here, also, were concentrated the troops set free by the fall of Maubeuge and others which had hitherto been holding such places as Amiens and Arras.

On Thursday, the 10th, the 1st German Army beat a hasty retreat, which obliged their 2nd Army to conform. The British Army led the pursuit in echelon from the right—that is to say, the 1st Army Corps from Château Thierry

FRENCH OUTPOSTS.   *[Newspaper Illustrations.*
This Photograph is typical of the Plain of Champagne.

was the most advanced, while the 2nd Army Corps followed to the left rear of the 1st, and the 3rd Army Corps from La Ferté-sous-Jouarre followed to the left rear of the 2nd.

The advance was resumed at daybreak on the 10th up to the line of the Ourcq (which here runs east and west), opposed by strong rearguards of all arms. The 1st and 2nd Corps, assisted by the Cavalry Division on the right, the 3rd and 5th Cavalry Brigades on the left, drove the enemy northwards. Thirteen guns, seven machine guns, about 2,000 prisoners, and quantities of transport fell into our hands. The enemy left many dead on the field. On this day the French 5th and 6th Armies had little opposition.—SIR JOHN FRENCH.

It was raining in torrents and the roads were bad going. The Germans had got their heavy guns away the evening before, but even so it is wonderful that they should have succeeded in saving them.

The retreat of the Germans on the 9th had evidently been carefully prepared, and the last of their infantry escorting their guns were hurried away in motor cars.

The 6th French Army, and what had been von Kluck's flank guard, moved rapidly towards the line Compiègne-Soissons; the 5th French Army reached the Marne from Château Thierry to Dormans. By nightfall the left of the 9th French Army had followed in echelon to the right rear of the 5th Army, and the centre of the 9th French Army had driven the Prussian Guard Corps into the marshes of St. Gond, while its right was still engaged in a furious, but practically stationary, combat between Fère-Champenoise and Mailly-le-Camp.

The unfortunate Prussian Guard set out to retreat across the swamps by the four tracks which lead across them northwards, but just at this time it came on to rain, and men, horses and guns were said to have been en-

gulfed in considerable numbers. This *corps d'élite* had suffered heavily, and achieved little during the whole campaign. It is true that they broke the French line on the Sambre on August 22, but they here encountered the formidable Algerian Corps, and, like their opponents, suffered terribly. On August 26 they were employed against the British at Le Cateau, and were decimated. Three days later they were assailed by the 5th French Army and flung back at Guise. By the time they emerged from the slough of St. Gond they were little but the wrecks of the proud Corps which had left Berlin five weeks before with such confident anticipations of adding to its laurels.

On the plain to the east a violent engagement raged, in which, however, the French made little progress. Here both sides sought to advance, each in turn attacking the other's trenches at the point of the bayonet. Backwards and forwards swayed this deadly, hand-to-hand conflict, in which an observer estimates the Germans lost from 15,000 to 20,000 dead alone.

Many of the enemy were killed and wounded, and the numerous thick woods which dot the country north of the Marne are filled with German stragglers. Most of them appear to have been without food for at least two days. Indeed, in this area of operations the Germans seem to be demoralized and inclined to surrender in small parties, and the general situation appears to be most favourable to the Allies.

Much brutal and senseless damage has been done in the villages occupied by the enemy. Property has been wantonly destroyed, pictures in the châteaux have been ripped up, and the houses generally pillaged. It is stated on unimpeachable authority, also, that the inhabitants have been much ill-treated.

Interesting incidents have occurred during the fighting. On the 10th, part of our 2nd Army Corps advancing north found itself marching parallel with another infantry force at some little distance away. At first it was thought that this was another British unit.

REMAINS OF A GERMAN ENTRENCHMENT NEAR THE MARNE.

THE MARNE.
"We harried them before the crossing and drowned them during it."
(*See page 77.*)

After some time, however, it was discovered that it was a body of Germans retreating. Measures were promptly taken to head off the enemy, who were surrounded and trapped in a sunken road, where over 400 men surrendered.

On the 10th a small party of French under a non-commissioned officer was cut off and surrounded. After a desperate resistance it was decided to go on fighting to the end. Finally the n.c.o. and one man only were left, both being wounded. The Germans came up and shouted to them to lay down their arms. The German commander, however, signed to them to keep their arms, and then asked for permission to shake hands with the wounded non-commissioned officer, who was carried off on his stretcher with his rifle by his side.

The arrival of the reinforcements and the continued advance have delighted the troops, who are full of zeal and anxious to press on.

Quite one of the features of the campaign, on our side, has been the success attained by the Royal Flying Corps. In regard to the collection of information it is impossible either to award too much praise to our aviators for the way they have carried out their duties or to over-estimate the value of the intelligence collected, more especially during the recent advance. In due course, certain examples of what has been effected may be specified and the far-reaching nature of the results fully explained, but that time has not yet arrived. That the services of our Flying Corps, which has really

been on trial, are fully appreciated by our Allies is shown by the following message from the Commander-in-Chief of the French Armies received on the night of September 9 by Field-Marshal Sir John French :

" Please express most particularly to Marshal French my thanks for services rendered on every day by the English Flying Corps. The precision, exactitude, and regularity of the news brought in by its members are evidence of their perfect organization and also of the perfect training of pilots and observers."

To give a rough idea of the amount of work carried out it is sufficient to mention that, during a period of 20 days up to September 10, a daily average of more than nine reconnaissance flights of over 100 miles each has been maintained.

The constant object of our aviators has been to effect the accurate location of the enemy's forces, and, incidentally—since the operations cover so large an area—of our own units. Nevertheless, the tactics adopted for dealing with hostile aircraft are to attack them instantly with one or more British machines. This has been so far successful that in five cases German pilots or observers have been shot in the air and their machines brought to the ground. As a consequence, the British Flying Corps has succeeded in establishing an individual ascendancy which is as serviceable to us as it is damaging to the enemy. How far it is due to this cause it is not possible at present to ascertain definitely, but the fact remains that the enemy have recently become much

BRITISH SOLDIERS CUTTING UP RATIONS AND COOKING. [*Photo Press.*]

less enterprising in their flights. Something in the direction of the mastery of the air has already been gained.

In pursuance of the principle that the main object of military aviators is the collection of information bomb-dropping has not been indulged in to any great extent. On one occasion a petrol bomb was successfully exploded in a German bivouac at night, while, from a diary found on a dead German cavalry soldier, it has been discovered that a high explosive bomb thrown at a cavalry column from one of our aeroplanes struck an ammunition wagon. The resulting explosion killed 15 of the enemy.—An "EYE-WITNESS" on Sir J. French's Staff.

As the 1st and 2nd German Armies were now in full retreat, this evening marks the end of the battle which practically commenced on the morning of the 6th instant ; and it is at this point in the operations that I am concluding the present dispatch.

Although I deeply regret to have had to report heavy losses in killed and wounded throughout these operations, I do not think they have been excessive in view of the magnitude of the great fight, the outlines of which I have only been able very briefly to describe, and the demoralization and loss in killed and wounded which are known to have been caused to the enemy by the vigour and severity of the pursuit.

In concluding this dispatch I must call your Lordship's special attention to the fact that from Sunday, August 23, up to the present date (September 17), from Mons back almost to the Seine, and from the Seine to the Aisne, the Army under my command has been ceaselessly engaged without one single day's halt or rest of any kind.—SIR JOHN FRENCH.

The Ourcq flows from east to west as far as La Ferté Milon, and thence south. It was along this north and south stretch that von Kluck's flank guard had stood. "In the early morning of the 11th," says Sir John French, "the further pursuit of the enemy was commenced ; and the three Corps crossed the Ourcq practically unopposed, the Cavalry reaching the line of the Aisne River ; the 3rd

and 5th Brigades south of Soissons, the 1st, 2nd, and 4th on the high ground at Couvrelles and Cirseuil."

From the Ourcq to the Aisne the British pursuit was so hot that the enemy found it all he could do to keep ahead of it, and that any attempt at resistance meant annihilation or capture ; and it is here in particular that an acknowledgment is due to the Air Service. It would often have been impossible to say whether a position was or was not held in strength ; in which case, under ordinary circumstances, it would have been necessary to halt and make some sort of reconnaissance, or take some action to force the enemy to show his hand ; but as our airmen kept our leaders constantly informed of what they had in front of them, it was always safe to rush any position which the airmen reported was not held in force. An acknowledgment must also be made to the Army Service Corps ; its work throughout the operations was really wonderful, for the men were kept fully supplied, and that, as we know, goes such a long way towards keeping up the efficiency of troops ; in fact, both these branches of the British Service commanded the unbounded admiration of our Allies.

On Friday, the 11th, but little opposition was met with by us along any part of our front, and the direction of advance was, for the purpose of cooperating with our Allies, turned slightly to the north-east. The day was spent in pushing forward and in gathering in various hostile detachments, and by nightfall our forces had reached a line to the north of the Ourcq extending from Oulchy-le-Château to Long Pont. On this day there was also a general advance on the part of the French along their whole line, which ended in substantial success, in one portion of the field Duke Albrecht of Würtemberg's Fourth Army being driven back across the Saulx, and elsewhere the whole of the corps artillery of a German corps being captured. Several German colours also were taken.

It was only on this day that the full extent of the victory gained by the Allies on the 8th was appreciated by them, and the moral effect of this success has been enormous. . . .

It seems probable that the Germans not only expected to find that the British Army was beyond the power of assuming the offensive for some time, but counted on the French having been driven back on to the line of the Seine ; and that, though surprised to find the latter moving forward against them after they had crossed the Marne, they were in no wise deterred from making a great effort.—" Eyewitness " on Sir J. French's Staff.

Since the 10th the whole of the German right wing has fallen back in considerable disorder, closely followed by the French and British troops. Six thousand prisoners and 15 guns were captured on the 10th and 11th, and the enemy is reported to be continuing his retirement rapidly over the Aisne, evacuating the Soissons region. . .

While the German right wing has thus been driven back and thrown into disorder, the French Armies further to the east have been strongly engaged with the German centre, which had pushed forward as far as Vitry. Between the 8th and 10th our Allies were unable to make much impression west of Vitry. On the 11th, however, this portion of the German Army began to give way, and eventually abandoned Vitry, where the enemy's line of battle was forming a salient under the impulse of French troops between the upper Marne and the Meuse. The French troops are following up the enemy and are driving portion of his forces northwards towards the Argonne forest country.—PRESS BUREAU.

The 6th French and British Armies reached the Aisne west and east of Soissons on the 12th, followed by the 5th, 9th, 4th, and 3rd French Armies in echelon from the left. The official *communiqué* issued at Paris at midnight said :

In the centre the German Armies are continuing their movement of retreat. We have crossed the Marne between Epernay and Vitry-le-François.

On our right wing also the enemy began to retire to-day, and have abandoned the country round Nancy. We have re-occupied Lunéville.

In spite of the fatigue caused by five days' incessant fighting, our troops are strenuously pursuing the enemy in their general retreat, which appears to be more rapid than their advance. At certain points it was so precipitate that our troops have collected in the German headquarters, notably at Montmirail, maps, documents, and personal papers abandoned by the enemy, as well as parcels and letters received or ready for posting.

Everywhere, particularly around Fromentières, the enemy has abandoned batteries of howitzers and numbers of ammunition wagons.

The prisoners give a strong impression of starvation, overwork, and depression. The horses are particularly exhausted.

The enforced retreat of the Crown Prince's Army came just in time to save Fort Troyon, and perhaps Verdun as well. It was afterwards ascertained that Fort Troyon was *in extremis*. The fort itself had been reduced to a heap of ruins, and its garrison to 44 men with four serviceable guns. With the instance of St. Mihiel before us, it seems probable that if the Germans had succeeded in breaking through at Fort Troyon, and in cutting off Verdun, they would have maintained their position ; in which case, of course, Verdun would have fallen, the whole problem of supplying the German Armies

LA FÈRE CHAMPENOISE.   [*Newspaper Illustrations,*
German dead—evidently killed whilst charging.

FRENCH TROOPS.
An hour's respite.

would have been immensely simplified, and a pivot of manœuvre *which might yet prove invaluable*—not to mention the large numbers of men that would have been captured—would have been lost to the Allies. There was no real victory until all danger to the frontier fortresses had been eliminated.

On this day the French had the great satisfaction of retaking Lunéville, a town of 26,000 inhabitants near the German frontier, which had been occupied by the Germans since August 22. In fairness to the Germans it should be stated that they had neither bombarded the place nor ill-treated the inhabitants.

The recapture of Lunéville goes further to suggest that German troops were being withdrawn from this wing to reinforce the German right, and there is no doubt that all the German troops that could be spared from Belgium were hastening south. This fact was discovered by King Albert, who made a sortie from Antwerp, which considerably alarmed the Germans for the safety of their communications.

Thus ended the Battles of the Marne. The German offensive had failed, and with it all prospects of final success, for, as von Caemmerer said a generation before the war, " an offensive which has to retrace its steps before the gates of Paris, or cannot even reach them, means a complete fiasco of the whole enterprise."

In many instances the German higher leading

had proved itself really brilliant. For instance, the conception, organization, energy, and execution of the advance to, and the retirement from, the Marne, compel our admiration ; but these things leave us all the more astonished at the palpable blunders which the Kaiser's chiefs committed in other directions. Those which preceded the battle have been mentioned already—to them we may add the adoption of too many tactical objectives in the battle itself. Thus, at one and the same time, they tried to turn the left flank of the 5th French Army, and to break through at Vitry-le-François, at Fort Troyon, and at Nancy. In tactics as in strategy they attempted too much at once, with the result that they were stronger at Nancy and in the direction of Fort Troyon than was necessary to pin the enemy in those parts of the field to his ground, and not strong enough either towards Coulommiers (where it was necessary that they should maintain their position) or towards Vitry-le-François (where they desired to break the enemy's line). The fact is they excelled in dealing with material factors, but they lacked inspiration. They could neither gauge the spirit of the enemy's troops nor penetrate the mind of the enemy's general. The word " Grand Tactics " had no meaning for them. Their training seems to have made their minds as precise, but also as wooden, as their manœuvres.

Some day, when criticism of the Allied operations becomes permissible, critics will suggest that General Joffre lacked enterprise. They will say that he should have retired still further—perhaps even to the line Orleans-Nevers-Dijon-Langres-Epinal—in order to impose upon the enemy longer marches and longer communications ; to induce the enemy to weaken himself by sending detachments to attack Paris and the fortress group Verdun-Toul ; and to give the Allies time to develop their resources. They will also suggest that the force which he allotted to his counter-stroke at the Marne—the 6th French Army—was too weak to achieve much—they will say it would have been better to have placed the 9th French Army with the 6th. The first criticism assumes that a prolonged retreat would have had no very serious effect upon the Allied Armies and upon France, her friends and those neutrals who were waiting " to rush to the rescue of the conqueror." It forgets, too, that the fall of the frontier fortresses must have ensued and would have opened shorter and better railway communications with Germany and would have immensely simplified the supply problem of the German Army. The second criticism loses sight of the fact that to have weakened the Allied line in order to strengthen its decisive counter-attack would have been to take the serious risk of the Allies' line being pierced. Since it was the Germans and not the Allies who were pressed for time, it was General Joffre's business not to run any considerable risks in the effort to gain considerable successes. If he could gain time he would gain all. That he achieved his object is now clear.

As for the troops themselves, a comparison is easily instituted. At Mons four British Divisions beat off the attacks of eight German Divisions. At Coulommiers and La Ferté Gaucher four German Divisions were immediately crumpled up by the onslaught of five British Divisions—comment is superfluous.

In a letter found on a dead German officer occurs the remark, " German infantry and cavalry will not attack English infantry and cavalry at close quarters. Their fire is murderous. The only way to attack them is with artillery."

As for the French, " the immediate interest to us," said the Military Correspondent of *The Times* on October 7, " is the proof which this battle affords of the capacity of the French leading, and of the resolution of the French troops. For a fortnight the French Armies had been in retreat. No Army likes to retreat, and a French Army least of all. Yet directly General Joffre called upon his lieutenants they responded nobly, and the leading of the various Armies by their commanders is deserving of the highest praise. The German Armies in their full career of victory were immediately checked, stubbornly fought, and rapidly driven back with heavy loss. . . . The Germans hoped to obtain a decisive victory. They suffered, on the contrary, a severe defeat.

" The French Armies, in the battle of the Marne, performed prodigies of valour, and changed the aspect of the campaign. The French staff and commands gave to the world a convincing proof of their worth and competence. The cavalry were active and audacious. The famous ' 75 ' shattered the German infantry and overwhelmed the German guns. The French infantry fought with all their legendary dash, and were not to be denied with the bayonet. All the German Armies in France were in line and bent upon victory. It was a fair field with no favour. The good ordering of the battle, its methodical conduct by the French Army commanders, and the self-

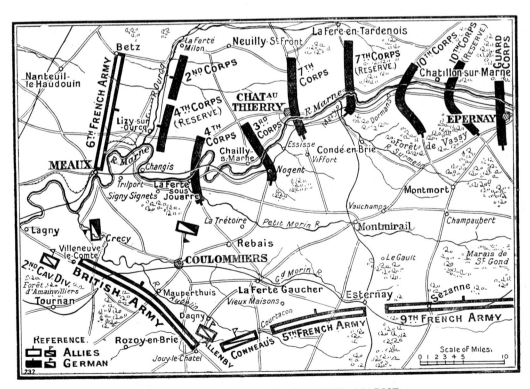

THE GERMAN RIGHT AT THE MARNE.

[Topical.
TURCOS BRINGING IN GERMAN ACCOUTREMENTS FROM THE BATTLEFIELD.

sacrificing of France's gallant soldiers brought victory to the French standards. France has every reason to be proud of the splendid valour of her sons."

The effect of the news of the victory on the French population cannot be better described than by the following extracts from *The Times* Special Correspondent on " the extreme right of the French Army," dated Dijon, September 12 :—

We reached Paris . . . on Thursday (Sept. 10) morning . . . started again at midnight, and did not get to Dijon till 12.30 next day (Friday, Sept. 11) . . . Between Paris and Dijon we stopped at practically every station. The train, which was just about half a kilometre (550 yards) in length, was packed. . . .

We were not at heart a cheerful crowd. Many of us had come long distances, some even from America. . . . Except in the deserted streets of Paris . . . I have never seen such uniform sadness on so many faces at once. The women especially, bravely as they tried to face their griefs and their anxieties, kind and helpful as they were to one another and the tiny babies that some of them had with them, were indescribably pathetic.

These people were not refugees like the trainloads one had seen lately in Belgium and Holland. They were going to the scene of the war instead of away from it. Most of them were reservists and their wives and children, bound for their old homes near the various headquarters to which the men had been called up. Some of them were nurses of the Croix Rouge, middle-aged women and quite young girls ; some were on their way to visit wounded relations. Each and all carried the same heavy burden. Not one but many of those near and dear to them were at the front. They knew in some cases that they were already among the dead or wounded or missing. Generally they knew nothing except that, if they were still alive, they were there

somewhere on one of the many battlefields on the long line of the Allies' front, face to face with the enemy and death.

We made many friends of different conditions in life during the slow hours between dawn and midday, and all had the same story to tell. But there was no need to ask. It was written in their faces. The natural vivacity of these sorrowing women of France was gone. They talked, when they did talk, quietly and sadly, and of only one subject. More often they sat with unseeing eyes, looking far off into the darkness of the unknown future, fearful of the fate that waited for the men by their sides, and of the ruin and suffering that threatened their homes and their children. The tragedy that has brought sorrow to the women of half the world had come upon them with the suddenness of a bomb from a Taube, and some of them were wounded and all were stunned by its effect.

That was when we were still in the dark about the result of the great battle that had begun to rage on the left wing near Paris, before the German retreat began. On the second day of our stay in Dijon there was a sudden change in the emotional atmosphere. Directly I left the hotel in the evening I felt that good news had come. Relief and happiness were in the air. In the newspaper offices, where the daily news of the war is posted up, the look of the people was absolutely different. For the moment personal griefs and losses were forgotten. General Joffre's general order of September 11 had been published to the troops, and from them the news had spread so quickly that in half an hour everyone seemed to know what had happened.

It was the first real success of the war, the first time since its very early days that the French had begun to lose the feeling of apprehension produced in their minds by the steady retreat of the Allied troops from the Belgian frontier, after the battles of Charleroi and Mons. Even the officers at Dijon were affected by it. Up till then, though they spoke confidently enough of eventual success, the subject uppermost in their minds and their conversation was the wonderful perfection of the German organization. That was a nightmare which they had not so far been able to shake off. Now suddenly it was gone. In a day it had become evident that France and England had their organization as well as the common enemy, and that the strategy of the Allied forces was beginning at last to tell. And the really hopeful sign of it all was . . . the . . . way in which Dijon and France received the good news. . . . There was no . . . hysterical excitement, but only a more determined resolution to see the thing through to the end, a strengthening of the national spirit of unity and a fuller realization of the value and sincerity of the alliance with England and the fine fighting qualities of our troops. . . They are taking the ups and downs of the war with a quiet and level-headed resolution that surprises even their own critics. . . . That, as well as their valour and fighting skill, makes them an ally in whom we may have double confidence. The French are friends worth having.

The incidents of the battle which have come to our knowledge are so disconnected, and so very much fuller of some parts of the struggle than of others, that to include them in any general description of the conflict is not only to overload the narrative with detail, but to present a very distorted impression of the fighting as a whole. And yet these details permit us a peep behind the scenes ; they bring us more in touch with the human side of war ; and give us a sense of a more intimate knowledge of the sort of thing modern fighting really is. The incidents in the Battle of the Ourcq and in the British Advance described here are compiled from the narratives of eye-witnesses.

General Pau's 6th Army advanced eastwards against the Ourcq, with its right on the Marne, and its left towards Betz. The German guns

were in action across the river, some miles to the French front. Their shells were falling in the field just beyond Meaux. From the rise that overhangs the little town looking towards the valley, white puffs of smoke in the air betrayed the bursting shrapnel. Tremendous explosions of high-explosive shells, followed by clouds of greasy black smoke, flung fountains of mud to the sky, devastated the farmhouses, and set the haystacks in flames.

In one part of the field a French battery set a sugar refinery on fire. The unfortunate German garrison was trapped, and the men, attempting to jump out of the windows, were shot down by the French infantry, which had got within close range. It is said that scarcely 200 of the 2,000 Germans in and about the building escaped. The French infantry, lying close in its trenches, probably suffered little.

Elsewhere, wide open country spread before the French in gentle undulations, covered with green fields and stubble, interspersed with farmhouses and copses of big trees. Field glasses revealed the figures of French soldiers moving across the open—disappearing and reappearing. Here and there a cloud of oily, yellowish smoke betrayed the bursting of a big shell. Haystacks were burning in the French lines. Away on the horizon, towards the German artillery position, a big farmhouse, or

[*Topical.*

WOUNDED AND DYING FRENCH AND GERMAN SOLDIERS IN A CHURCH NEAR MEAUX.

CHOISY AU BAC.   [*Topical.*
Bridge destroyed by French Engineers.

perhaps it was a whole village, was burning brightly. The landscape was dotted by burning homesteads and hayricks.

The town of Meaux itself was a scene of ruin—houses wrecked, the bridge destroyed. Shells were bursting overhead and aeroplanes were circling in the blue. The road to the east was strewn with the bodies of Zouaves, Turcos, French riflemen, grey-clad Germans, and slaughtered horses.

Some four miles east of Meaux the ground rises steeply to the north, and is covered with trees. Beyond the woods were broad, undulating stretches of cultivation, dotted with farmsteads; under the screen of the trees the Germans had levelled gun-platforms. Near the crests of the rises were the trenches, extending for nearly a mile parallel with the edge of the wood. The position was skilfully chosen, with a good field of fire to front and flanks. The French had attacked these trenches from the north-west, scourging the enemy's lines with shrapnel. Covered by this fire the infantry advanced against the trenches, but it was not till late on Sunday that the resistance began to weaken.

On Monday, September 7, the fighting on the Ourcq was again extremely severe. There was a great deal of bayonet work, and the colours of the Magdeburg (German) Regiment were captured in a terrible mêlée, in which the lieutenant colour-bearer was killed, to-

gether with a number of men who had attempted to defend the flag.

The fighting was from village to village, the Zouaves and the Turcos having their fill of bayonet work. The whole landscape was full of burning villages, farms, and haystacks, from which columns of smoke and flying sparks rose up and spread out in a dense dark pall over the blue sky. Everywhere the ground was strewn with German wounded and dead; in some places they lay in heaps. But the enemy's machine guns took a heavy toll of the French—their fire was held to the last, and then opened with annihilating effect. The French losses appear to have been especially heavy at Brégy and Penchard, where there was some very heavy fighting The French infantry was located by a German airman, and came under a very severe fire of all sorts.

When darkness fell each night the country-side was lit by burning villages flaming more furiously at every puff of wind. It was during these hours, and by the light of burning homesteads, that the Germans collected their dead, piled them into great heaps on pyres of wood, saturated them with paraffin, covered them with straw, and cremated them.

On Tuesday, September 8, the English left, with some heavy batteries, came up to the help of the French near Meaux and shelled the high ground west of the junction of the Ourcq and the Marne. The road here is lined with particularly large Lombardy poplars; and the country beyond consists of orchards and copses and acres of rolling wheat land studded with patches of potatoes and maize. The position soon became an indescribable scene of mangled bodies, shattered guns, and splintered and uprooted trees.

On the 9th, near Meaux, a French battery was shelling the enemy across the river. The scene is thus described in *The Times* of September 12 :—

Smack, smack, smack, smack go the French guns; and then, a few seconds later, four white mushrooms of smoke spring up over the far woods and slowly the pop, pop, pop, pop of the distant explosions comes back to you. But now it is the German gunners' turn. Bang go his guns two miles away ; there is a moment of eerie and uncomfortable silence—uncomfortable because there is just a chance they might have altered their range—and then, quite close by, over the wood where the battery is, come the crashes of the bursting shells. They sound like a Titan's blows on a gigantic kettle filled with tons of old iron.

. . . What we saw to-day was the German guns covering the retirement of their right wing, with the

French artillery replying and the French infantry advancing to keep the retreating enemy on the move.

Meaux was still a town of blank shutters and empty streets when we got there this morning, but the French sappers had thrown a plank gangway across the gap in the ruined old bridge, built in A.D. 800, that had survived all the wars of France since the 16th century, only to perish at last in this one.

At Trilport there is a yawning gap, where one arch of the railway bridge used to be, with a solitary bent rail still lying across it. And among the wreckage of the bridge below, lying on its side and more than half beneath the water, is the smashed and splintered ruin of a closed motor-car.

" Three Germans were in it," explains a French sentry —" two soldiers and an officer; they did not know the bridge had been blown up, and they came down this road last night at top speed, going towards Meaux, until suddenly, when they got here——" and a wave of his hand indicated the probable trajectory of the car through the air to the bed of the river below. " It was a nice little surprise for them."

Beyond the town was a ridge on which the French batteries were posted. We could see the ammunition wagons parked on the reverse slope of the hill. More were moving up to join them.

The village beyond—Penchard—was thronged with troops and blocked with ambulance wagons and ammunition carts. . . . Through the rank grass at the side came tramping a long file of dusty, sweating, wearied men. They carried long spades and picks as well as their rifles. They had come out of the firing line, and were going back to Penchard for food. And from the next ridge we really see a firing line at last. The hill slopes steeply down to the hamlet of Chambéry, just below us. The battery of which I spoke just now is in the wood on this side of it to our right. The Zouaves' firing line is lying flat on the hillside a little way beyond the village, and behind them, farther down the hill, are thick lines of supports in the cover of entrenchments. It is a spectacle entirely typical of a modern battle, for there is scarcely anything to see at all. If it were not for those shells being tossed to and fro on the right there, and an occasional splutter of rifle fire, one might easily suppose that the lines of blue-coated men lying about on the stubble were all dozing in the hot afternoon sun.

Even when some of them move they seem to do it lazily, to saunter rather than to walk. . . . It is only in the kinematograph or on the comparatively rare occasions of close fighting at short range that men rush dramatically about. For one thing, they are too tired to hurry ; and anyhow, what is the use of running when a shell may burst any minute anywhere in the square mile you happen to be on ?

We talked with the company officers who were planning a fresh advance, map in hand. They had gained the village in which we were that same morning, but at tremendous loss. " Out of my company of 220," said one captain, " there are only 100 left. Of our four officers two are wounded and one dead. I am left alone in command." It was the same story—the German machine guns. " Their fire simply clears the ground like a razor," said the captain. " You just can't understand how anyone gets away alive. I had men fall at my right hand and at my left. You can't look anywhere as you advance without seeing men dropping."

All round us and for two miles back of Chambéry the bodies lay. Germans and French mingled, dead men among the cornstooks, dead on the stubble, dead in the turnip fields, in the ditches, in the woods. Horses, too, everywhere, lying with a hind leg thrust out stiffly into the air ; cows torn open by the shells. The whole fair countryside, radiant under the golden harvest sun, sent up the sickening stench of death.

The British communications ran through their left flank to Paris. At Lagny both bridges over the Marne had been demolished by the British on Thursday, September 3. They lay half submerged in the water, the windows of neighbouring houses had been shattered by the explosion, the streets in the vicinity were strewn with glass, telegraph and telephone wires hung down in festoons from the positions on the water's edge, and all the boats in the vicinity were sunk. The road from Lagny, along the British front, runs

[*Topical.*

WOUNDED GERMAN PRISONERS OUTSIDE A CHURCH NEAR MEAUX.

WOUNDED TURCOS BEING CARRIED IN BY FRENCH HUSSARS. [Topical

through a beautiful wooded country, now utterly silent and desolate; every home shuttered and deserted.

The British started from their bivouacs and billets on Sunday, September 6, just as a perfect summer's day was dawning. Réveillé called the men from their slumbers, and produced an immediate bustle, in which, however, there was no sign of confusion. A meal of biscuits and hot coffee was succeeded by the fall-in, and in an incredibly short time the troops were on the white roads running north-east from Pontcarré, Tournan, and Rosny, through the green forests of Crécy. A whisper had run through the ranks that at last they should take the offensive against the enemy, and the men stepped out with a will which had lately been lacking in their stride. Hour after hour the beat of marching feet resounded on every road to the front. Every now and then someone would start to whistle or sing some popular air, and would soon be joined in chorus by all who were within hearing. At first the country round was gay with golden corn; little farmhouses, amid their bright flower gardens and heavily-laden orchards, completed a scene of peace. Old men and women, girls and fresh-faced children waved to the troops as they passed.

By noon the heat was tremendous, so that the halt for a much-needed rest and a meal was very welcome. As the afternoon wore on,

signs of the enemy's recent presence began to multiply. Acres of corn land were now mere stretches of ashes and dust. The humble homes of the hard-working peasantry were wrecked and burnt. Here and there some more pretentious dwelling had been pillaged and gutted by fire. Broken picture frames, marble statuettes, crockery, children's toys, furniture, and goods and chattels of all sorts— once the treasures of departed households— now littered the floors indoors, or were flung broadcast over the ground outside. The village church had been burnt, the flowers that fond hands had placed upon the graves had been trampled flat; crosses had been trodden underfoot and tombstones smashed.

When the march was resumed there was a distinct change in the bearing of the men; there was no more whistling, singing, or chaff. It had gone home to them that this might be their own country, and the rumble of the guns in the distance reminded them that they would soon have the opportunity of striking a blow for their own hearths and homes, and of those of the poor people through whose country they were passing.

Beyond the forests spread some open country, where a belt of timber marked the enemy's position. The woods were alive with armed men; beyond the woods were his guns. Suddenly from the distance came the "thud-ud" of a heavy gun, and a shell passing overhead, with a long-drawn wail, burst with a tremendous roar just behind the extended lines. The whole of the enemy's artillery quickly joined in chorus, and it was not long before the British guns took up the challenge. The ear was stunned with the sound of roaring guns, flying projectiles and bursting shells. The infantry advanced, and ere long little spurts of dust and the zip-zipping of flying lead showed that they were coming under rifle fire from the woods in front.

Presently the enemy attempted a counter-attack, and at last the British infantry commenced to fire. A few seconds sufficed to dash the enemy back to cover. After a couple of hours' fighting, the infantry was close up to the enemy's position. Above the rattle of the rifles rang the order to charge, and "with that stern appalling shout—which no enemy every heard unmoved," the British dashed upon the foeman and drove him headlong from his position. The trenches were full of dead and dying men; the ground around was covered by wounded horses and wrecked guns, and was pitted with great holes where high explosive shells had burst, or was pock-marked by the British shrapnel.

On Monday, September 7, the British continued their advance in touch with the French Armies on both flanks. In the small hours of the morning the roads leading north from Coulommiers were filled with long columns of retreating Germans of all arms. The heads of the English columns reached the village at 5 a.m. From here the battle rolled on to La Ferté Gaucher and the marshes of St. Gond.

The following extracts from a letter written by a German officer, which appeared in the *Intelligenzblatt* of Berne, and afterwards in *Le Temps*, are interesting :

We were obliged to retreat as the English were attempting a turning movement, which was discovered by our airmen. During the last two hours we were continually exposed to the fire of the enemy's artillery, for our artillery had all been either put out of action or had retreated and had ceased to fire. The enemy's airmen flew above us describing two circles, which means : " There is infantry here." Then hell was let loose. The enemy's artillery "mowed" the ground with its fire. In one minute's time I counted 40 shells. The shrapnel exploded nearer and nearer ; at last it reached our ranks. I quickly hugged a knapsack to my stomach in order to protect myself as best I could. The shrieks of the wounded rang out on all sides. Tears came to my eyes when I heard the poor devils moaning with pain. The dust. the smoke and the stench of the powder were suffocating.

An order rang out, and bending as low as possible we started up. We had to pass right in the line of the enemy's fire. The men began to fall like ninepins. God be thanked that I was able to run as I did. I thought my heart would burst, and was about to throw

WRECKED CHÂTEAUX.

On the left the remains of the Manor House, at La Ferté Gaucher, and on the right the remains of President Poincaré's Château.

myself on the ground, unable to continue, when your image and that of Bolli rose before my eyes, and I ran on.

At last we reached our batteries. Three guns were smashed to pieces and the gun carriages were burnt. We halted for a few seconds to take breath. And all the time that whistling and banging of the shells continued. It is a wonder one is not driven mad.

When the British advanced on the morning of Tuesday, September 8, the sky was already full of aeroplanes and the air full of the humming of their engines. On the south side of La Ferté Gaucher stands a manor-house, from which the enemy was driven. It had been mercilessly pillaged. The dining-room table was heaped with the wreckage of a drunken meal. The floor was strewn with bottles ; all the drawers, cupboards, wardrobes, and presses had been forced open and their contents thrown about the rooms. Beds, telephone instrument, gramophones, and records were smashed to pieces.

The fighting here between the British and the 5th French Army against the Germans began at dawn, and was of a most sanguinary character. The British artillery got into action about 5 a.m. The German guns at La Ferté Gaucher were posted on the heights beyond the Grand Morin. The line of battle extended right away to Sézanne and Vitry-le-François. All along their position the Germans had heavy guns in action among their lighter field pieces, and their fire was extremely heavy, but fortunately not very accurate. The guns of the Allies, lighter and better in quality and better handled, covered the advance of their infantry with excellent effect. It was not long before the latter were loosed from the leash. All that afternoon a furious struggle raged along the British right and the left and centre of the 5th French Army, but towards night the German resistance began to weaken. Their infantry was pushed across the Grand Morin and across the plateau of Sézanne. The battle, however, never ceased.

West of La Ferté Gaucher the engagement continued towards Coulommiers and Rébais. Here British cavalry were pressing eagerly forward. Everywhere the British found that the poorest of the poor had been robbed of all the money and food they had, with the result that the British gave away half their rations and more to the destitute peasantry.

The fighting was very fierce by La Trétoire, where the British guns were in action against the Germans across the Petit Morin. The country here is covered with fruit trees and the

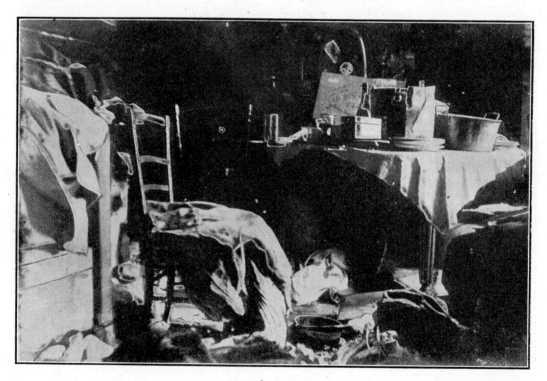

LA FERTÉ GAUCHER.   [Newspaper Illustrations.

A German officer's cap lies on the floor, amidst the scattered contents of drawers and cupboards, emphasizing the enemy's hurried retreat.

GERMAN PRISONERS ON THE ROAD TO PARIS GUARDED BY CUIRASSIERS.

open roads are lined with the pears and apples. Under cover of artillery fire, the infantry fought its way steadily through the orchards and across the corn fields, where the unharvested sheaves still stood. Wherever they were checked or halted to fire, they quickly found or extemporised some sort of cover, behind which they lay down, rising again sharply when the order to advance was given, for the advance was steadily pressed and the British not to be denied. In widely extended lines they swept across the terrain under a fire from guns, machine guns, and rifles, which would have made a holocaust of troops in close formations. Taking advantage of all cover—farmsteads, hayricks, undulations, trees, rocks, hedges, and ditches—they closed steadily with the enemy, pouring on from point to point until at last the welcome order to fix bayonets was received, and with a roar they burst upon the Germans and drove them headlong from their lines.

In *The Times* of September 15 it is stated that

At Coulommiers, on Tuesday morning . . . General Smith-Dorrien . . . who was seated in a high-powered car, called a group of young officers fresh from England to him. They had been marching all night until 2 a.m. with British reinforcements. It was now about 7.45 a.m. The sun had been up two hours, and the heat was already great and the roads dusty. General Smith-Dorrien said to these officers :

" You have done some splendid marching, but I want

you to push on another nine miles to the fighting. The Germans are on the run, and we hope to keep them going. If you do these nine miles your men will get a clasp. There will be great fighting to-night or to-morrow morning."

The officers saluted and were delighted with their orders. Their men, when met later the same day near the end of their march were still cheerful and looking eagerly for a fight.

From Doue my informant made his visit to the fighting line towards the Petit Morin River. It was getting dark, and the Germans were making desperate efforts to cross the river by the bridge, retreating before our shell fire. Our artillery was on the right and had the range of the bridge perfectly, dropping shells on it as soon as a wagon attempted to cross. German artillery from the far side was replying without much effect. One shell burst close to a group of our men. The men laughed. Only three or four were hit, and they showed torn putties and coats.

A private in the 1st Lincolns states :

During the German retreat the British were held up on a ridge by a battery. Two companies of us made a detour on the right, marched down a valley out of sight of the German gunners, and entered a wood on the enemy's left. The German battery, about 200 yards away, were busy with their work in front, not dreaming that we were on their flank. In extended order we took steady aim, and at the first round every man of the German battery fell. That was all we fired. Our artillery continued firing on the guns and smashed four. The other two were taken.

On Wednesday, September 9, the enemy were driven across the Marne closely pursued by the British, one of whom said of the crossing : " We harried them before the crossing and drowned them during it " (*Times*, September 14), for the river was filled with German dead. The German artillery came into action

GERMAN TROOPS PASSING RED CROSS WAGONS WITH WOUNDED RETURNING
FROM THE BATTLEFIELD.

again from the heights across the river, and there was a certain amount of hand-to-hand fighting with small bodies of German troops who had been unable to cross in time. By Tuesday night the British were in possession of La Ferté-sous-Jouarre, Charly, and Château Thierry.

Near Château Thierry there was more fighting. The road runs straight across the Plain of Chezy before it plunges into the dark shadows of the Grande Fôret. As soon as the British infantry entered the woods it could be no longer supported by their artillery, and the fighting developed into an immense hunt, in which the British pursued the Germans from tree to tree, capturing them in little blocks every here and there, and making a rather larger haul of a number of the enemy who were cut off by the marshes of Hotisseaux and Bergis.

Just beyond Château Thierry itself the Germans had left a considerable rearguard with a few large guns on the heights above the town. As the British approached they came first under the fire of these heavy guns. Some of them pushed into Château Thierry itself, with the result that many of the houses were destroyed by shell fire. The fronts of the houses on the road towards Soissons were furrowed deep by flying shot and shell; their

sides in many cases presented gaping holes; the tall trees which lined the road had been stripped of their leaves, and often topped and lopped by shell fire; the beautiful country around was burnt and charred. Every here and there individuals or groups of Germans were forced to surrender—often under circumstances which suggested that they had been left without much hope of avoiding capture, in order to secure the safe retirement of their main body.

The following "from an English Officer's diary" appeared in the Paris edition of the *New York Herald*:

My regiment has crossed the important River X (evidently the Marne near its junction with the Ourcq). The bridge was blown up by the Germans, but was replaced by pontoons. In front of us the British field guns are pouring a hail of shot against the German batteries posted on hills to the north. Above our heads "old cow guns" supported the advanced batteries. We were ordered to occupy the hill south of a mill round which the Germans were strongly entrenched.

Lying flat on the ground I could see through my glasses an extraordinary spectacle. The mill was three or four miles away, the roof seriously damaged by the French 75mm. guns. For two hours the German position was bombarded; then some of the enemy's infantry tried to flee from their trenches, but were forced to return at the point of their officers' revolvers. For another hour the relentless French artillery poured shrapnel on the position, which resisted stoutly until suddenly a dozen white flags waved above the trenches. A section of Zouaves, carried away by excitement, at once rushed forward. Forgetting that they had surrendered, about 100 German infantrymen ran away, and they were allowed to escape, while the Zouaves took possession of the trenches, in which only 115 men were found alive, starving, covered with mud and glad to be taken prisoners.

The fighting at La Ferté-sous-Jouarre is thus described by *The Times* own correspondent :

An eye-witness has given me a description of the fight at Ferté-sous-Jouarre on the night of September 10 (? 9). The Germans crossed the river, blowing up the bridge between them and the English on the other bank.*

Immediately after the firing had ceased, my informant entered the town. A weird effect was created by the houses burning in the night, and to these sights was added the sounds of a hand-to-hand encounter in the streets.

The English passed over the Marne on a pontoon bridge, which they had thrown across in two hours. Over this construction numbers of French troops also passed. The swiftness of everything surprised the observer. In the morning there was no sign of the pontoon bridge. The English and the enemy had cleared off. It was difficult to realize that the town had been the scene of a fierce fight in the night, for beyond the gaunt walls of a burnt-out or half-demolished house there was no sign of war.

When the British transport was on the road, a hundred Germans, with about a dozen officers, suddenly emerged from a wood and held up their hands. Accustomed to the enemy's wiles, the Army Service Corps men grasped their rifles ; but they soon discovered that the enemy were anxious to give themselves up. They were utterly starved and worn out and had no more fight left in them ; they ate dry bread ravenously.

* This is said to have happened at 4 p.m. The Germans left a party with two Maxims to command the passage.

An officer writes :

The other day, Thursday (September 10) I think it was, we, a battery of the X division, were marching along the road towards —— River. The day before there had been a small advance guard action and we were expecting a peaceful march. However, as we neared the river the battery was ordered to trot and I guessed something was on. Soon we passed through a small village and saw some dead and wounded lying about, also we heard the rattle of Maxims. The major had ridden on with me and showed me where the battery was to come into action. I sent back word and selected a position, which was soon taken up. We fired a few rounds and very shortly after I was ordered to take my section on down the hill towards the river. Well, I found that the road was blocked by a section of another battery. I stopped my section and tried to find out the situation.

The Germans were holding the opposite bank, a very steep bluff, with a battalion of the Jaegers and eight machine guns. These guns were trained on the road where it was fully exposed for about 100 yards, and nothing could cross. The section of the other battery were trying to locate them and knock them out. So I took my section up the hill behind these and waited for any targets to appear. The advance guard had been working well. By taking cover of the woods they had managed to get down into the river bed and round the flanks. From there they opened a hot fire on to the German machine guns.

From my position I could see a portion of the road on the opposite bank. I had just got the range to this when a machine gun came galloping up. I fired two rounds at it. The first was over and just behind ; the second

[*Sport & General.*

FRENCH AND BRITISH SOLDIERS TOASTING THEIR COUNTRIES.

short. However, I had never seen anything move quicker than that gun. By now our infantry had forced the Jaegers back, and we had orders for a general advance. As we crossed the bridge I heard that seven of their machine guns had been captured. We wound up and up, and on all sides saw evidences of our fire. In one place an ammunition wagon had been hit. Both horses were blown over into the ditch. A bit higher up was a young boy hit in the back. All that we could do was to give him water. He told me that his orders had been to stay till shot or captured. These German infantry are a brave lot.

Well, we went on into the village at the top of the hill and came into action again. Our job there was to shell retiring infantry. We soon got a target and started away. Everything was working like a well-oiled machine. Suddenly I saw spurts of dust in and about my section and also heard the unpleasant noise of Mauser bullets round my head. Some one was firing at my section from a wood 150 yards on the right front. I promptly switched my two guns half-right and fired at 300 yards into the wood. Also our spare gunners turned up with rifles and fired. After about five rounds, out came what I thought was a French officer and two Germans. I ran out with two gunners to take them over, but on nearing them saw they were all three Germans. However, they were very much more frightened than I, and put their hands up.

Soon after about eight more came out. I interrogated them, and they said that they were lost and had been wandering about for two days. I got a revolver off one, and a young horse, thoroughbred, four years old. This was brought in by one of the men, and had belonged to one of their officers, who had got away. In the holsters I found a large bottle of eau de Cologne, sweets, and a box of matches. While this excitement was going on the other two sections had also been busy, one firing at German infantry and one at a German battery. The total capture that day was 300 Germans and seven guns. Not bad for advanced guard action. Still, they had held up our Division for a day and done their job well and bravely.

The following letter from a Major, R.F.A., gives an account of a wild exploit, in which nine men and a trumpeter captured 50 Germans and two Maxim guns :—

SEPTEMBER 14.

We got the order to go off and join a battery under Colonel Carey's orders. We came *en route* under heavy shrapnel fire on the road. I gave the order to walk as the horses had hardly had any food for a couple of days, and also I wanted to steady the show. I can't say I quite enjoyed the "swank" of walking along at the head with old —— behind me, especially when six shrapnel burst right in front of us. . . . We got there just in time, rushed into action, and opened fire on a German counter-attack at short range, destroying the lot as far as I could see. We then moved slightly to another position to take on a valley, down which they were attacking, and were at it the whole day, firing about 900 rounds into quantities of German attacks and counter-attacks. They cannot stand the shrapnel, and the moment I got one on them they turned and bolted back to the wood. I got on to their trenches, one shell dropped in. I was enfilading them and they tore out of the trenches, and so on, each trench in turn, and fell in hundreds. Also through the rangefinder Cox saw I'd hit a machine-gun and they had abandoned it and another. So it went on all day, shell and bullets humming round, but only one of my staff horses hit. Our

infantry advancing and retiring—others advancing and coming back—Germans doing likewise, a hellish din of shell fire, and me pouring in fire wherever I could see them.

At last I got six shrapnel into a wood and cleared a heap of them out and got into them with shrapnel. It is awful. The sergeant-major put his hand up to his head and said : "Oh, sir, it's terrible." That seemed to settle them, and at last we saw the infantry advancing to their position without resistance. Now was my chance. I determined to get those machine-guns if I could, as otherwise the infantry would. So I left —— to command and got the trumpeter, sergeant-major, and six men with six rifles, and went forward "to reconnoitre," as I reported to the Gen. by ——, after I had gone. It was a weird ride, through thick black woods, holding my revolver ready, going in front with the little trumpeter behind and the others following some way in rear. We passed some very bad sights, and knew the woods were full of Germans, who were afraid to get away on account of the dreaded shell fire. We got in front of our infantry, who were going to fire at us ; but I shouted just in time.

At last we came to the edge of the wood, and in front of us, about 200 yards away, was a little cup-shaped copse, and the enemy's trenches with machine-guns a little farther on. I felt sure this wood was full of Germans, as I had seen them go in earlier. I started to gallop for it, and the others followed. Suddenly about 50 Germans bolted out firing at us. I loosed off my revolver as fast as I could, and —— loosed off his rifle from the saddle. They must have thought we were a regiment of cavalry, for except a few they suddenly yelled and bolted. I stopped and dismounted my lot to fire at them to make sure they didn't change their minds. I held the horses, as I couldn't shoot them like that myself. I then suddenly saw there were more in the copse—so I mounted the party and galloped at it, yelling, with my revolver held out.

As we came to it I saw it was full of Germans, so I yelled "hands up" and pointed the revolver at them. They all chucked down their rifles and put their hands up. Three officers and over 40 men to 10 of us with six rifles and a revolver. I herded them away from their rifles and handed them over to the Welsh Regiment behind us. I tore on with the trumpeter and the sergeant-major to the machine-guns. At that moment the enemy's shrapnel, the German infantry who'd got away, and our own howitzers, thinking we were hostile cavalry, opened fire on us. We couldn't move the beastly things, and it was too hot altogether, so we galloped back to the cup wood and they hailed shrapnel on us there. I waited for a lull, and mounted all my lot behind the bushes and made them sprint as I gave the word to gallop for cover to the woods where the Welsh company was. There I got —— who understands them, and an infantryman who volunteered to help, and —— and ran up to the Maxims, and took out the breech mechanism of both and one of the belts and carried away one whole Maxim. We couldn't manage the other. The Welsh asked what cavalry we were. I told them we were the staff of the —— Battery and they cheered us, but said we were mad. We got back very slowly on account of the gun and the men wild with excitement, and we have got the one gun complete and the mechanism and belt of the other. The funniest thing was the little trumpeter, who swept a German's helmet off his head and waved it in the air shouting "I've got it," wild with excitement. He is an extraordinarily brave boy.

CHAPTER XXXIII.

THE DEFENCE AND FALL OF ANTWERP.

The Fortifications and Plan of Defence—Position during the German "Advance on Paris"—Capitulation of Ghent—Belgian Army Retires on Antwerp—Sortie in Force—Fresh German Proposals to Belgium Made and Rejected—German Strategy—Bombardment of Malines—Antwerp Forts Shelled—Outer Forts Fall—Situation in the City—German Proclamation—Government Prepares to Depart—British Reinforcements—Reasons for the British Expedition—Criticisms and Explanations—Work of Naval Brigades—Relief Too Late—Germans Cross the River—Government and Legations Depart—General Exodus—The Belgian Army's Escape—Costly German Delays—The Bombardment of the City—Plight of the Population—A Dreadful Pilgrimage—Dutch Hospitality—Fire and Destruction in Antwerp—The Formal Surrender—Fate of the Naval Brigades—Germany's Empty Triumph and Military Disappointment—Belgian Heroism.

ANTWERP, with its elaborate defences evolved through 30 years of addition to and improvement of Brialmont's original plans, was designed to be the great stronghold of Belgium : " the base of the field army and final keep of the kingdom." To this rôle it seemed to be admirably adapted by nature, with access to the sea on one side, and to landwards being practically encircled at an advantageous distance by the rivers Scheldt, Rupel and Nèthe. The fortifications, with their successive developments, have already been fully described in a former chapter of this History.* It will only be necessary now to recall that the " old " or inner ring of forts, placed at regular intervals of 2,200 yards at an average distance of about 3,500 yards outside the enceinte of the city itself, were planned, and mostly built, before the year 1869. The first of the " new " or outer forts (Rupelmonde, Waelhem, Lierre, Schooten and Berendrecht) were designed by Brialmont in 1879 ; while the final forts and redoubts of this series were

* See Chapter VI. (Part 3) on " The Army and the Fortresses of Belgium," pp. 103-120.

only completed as recently as the end of November, 1913. The inner forts, like the defences of the enceinte itself, were excellently planned to resist the assaults of an enemy armed with the weapons of the period in which they were built—namely, half a century ago. Properly held (as the Belgians could have been relied upon to hold them), they would have rendered Antwerp impregnable to direct infantry attack or to bombardment by the field guns of those days. The more modern outer forts, with the line of the rivers, would have similarly furnished a complete defence against any artillery that had been recognized as employable in field or siege operations up to the outbreak of the present war. Military authorities were entirely justified in believing Antwerp to be a position of practically incomparable strength. But the large German—or Austrian—howitzers, with a range exceeding any pieces which had heretofore been regarded as mobile, and far exceeding that of any guns mounted in the Antwerp forts, and with the extreme destructiveness of their projectiles, introduced a new element into the situation.

[Ortmans, Antwerp.

LIEUTENANT-GENERAL DEGUISE.
The gallant defender of Antwerp.

Against them even the holding of the line of the rivers Rupel and Nèthe, which had seemed so valuable a feature of the defensive works, was useless for the protection of the city. The average distance of the rivers from Antwerp itself is about 6 miles. The 28 cm. guns have an effective range of over 7½ miles, with an extreme range of some 2 miles more. As soon as the enemy could approach his guns, therefore, to the further side of the river, the town was at his mercy. So that all that stood between him and the capture of Antwerp was in fact the guns of the outer forts. And these themselves, as we have seen, would be helpless as soon as the enemy had placed his big guns in position against them.

This, then, was the actual condition of Antwerp as a defensible position when, towards the end of September, 1914, it began to be evident that the Germans meditated a serious attack upon it. But before proceeding to the narrative of that attack it will be necessary to give a brief survey of the events which had been going on in Belgium since the gallant defence of Liége, the fall of Namur, and the German occupation of Brussels, though some outstanding incidents of that period have already been touched upon.

As the mass of the German army swept southward in what was to have been the triumphant dash on Paris, there remained in possession of the Belgians as much of their country as lies between the sea coast and the line made by the river Scheldt from Antwerp to Ghent and thence by the river Lys to Deynze, thence to Roulers, Ypres, Poperinghe and the French frontier. To south and east of this line was a strip of debatable territory, which the Germans made no attempt to occupy with any permanent force, but which continued to be the scene of desultory fighting throughout the latter part of August and the whole of September. Some of the more conspicuous incidents which disgraced the German arms in the course of this fighting have been already mentioned, as the repeated and wanton burnings of Termonde and the dropping of bombs on the Convent at Deynze and other defenceless places. The Belgian forces throughout this period at any point along this line were insignificant. The army as a whole had been withdrawn within the fortified area of Antwerp, and the holding of this long front, even of the important lines of communication by rail, road and water, between Ghent and Ostend, Bruges, Zeebrugge and other points, as well as the defence of the towns themselves, was largely left to the Civic Guards and the Gendarmerie. It was immensely to the credit of the vigilance and valour of these small, and often untrained, forces that the Germans, in whatever strength they sought to penetrate this front, never failed to find their opponents ready for them. This strength, it should be said, was rarely considerable. The chief object of the Germans was now to pour all the troops which they could send down to the main battle front in France, where unexpected difficulties had arisen. They evidently hoped that their methods of "frightfulness" had sufficiently terrorized the Belgians, so that they would not venture to provoke them to further "reprisals" by interfering with this process and, on those terms, they were for the present content to leave this unviolated portion of Belgium territory in Belgian hands.

Meanwhile fencing and petty skirmishes went on along the whole line. At one time (on August 26) a mixed force of a few hundred German infantry and cavalry approached to within five miles of Ostend, where, at a small engagement at Snaeskerke, they were pluckily driven off, with the loss of a material portion of their numbers in wounded and prisoners, by the gendarmes. Later (on September 25) an airship dropped bombs on Ostend itself, without causing any loss of life, and doing but insignificant damage to property. There were continual minor affairs at a score of different points, and in the early part of September these were so frequent and occurred simultaneously at so many points that there is reason to believe that the story told by Uhlans who were captured was true—namely, that a force of 1,200 Uhlans had been sent out with instructions to break up into smaller parties and, at all hazards, to get to the coast and find out what, if any, reinforcements of French or British troops had been, or were being, landed at Zeebrugge or Ostend. The prisoners added that all members of the force who got back alive bringing any trustworthy information were to be decorated with the Iron Cross. It is certain that none earned the decoration ; but for a week or so there was a very lively time at villages, cross-roads and railway crossings all up and down the front.

More serious was the demonstration against Ghent on September 6, when General von Boehn, in command of large reinforcements for the southern army, appeared at Oordeghem, some 12 miles south-east of Ghent, and sent on an advance force of some 5,000 infantry with machine guns towards the city with a view, presumably, to occupying it if it was found undefended. This force, however, found the Belgians well entrenched in a strong position between the river Scheldt and the line of the railway embankment at Melle, where a lively action took place. The Belgian loss, owing to superiority of position, was slight, amounting to less than a dozen killed and only a score of wounded. The wreckage of their machine guns left by the roadside and the size of the trenches in which the Germans buried their dead (two officers being buried in separate graves) showed that their loss was much heavier. They, as usual, burned, with the fusees which they carried for the purpose, every house in that portion of the long, straggling village which they were permitted to reach ; then, under cover of night, they retired on the main army.

On the following day General von Boehn sent the Burgomaster of Ghent a summons to surrender under threat of bombardment of the city. The destruction of Ghent, just 100 years after the famous Treaty of Peace between Great Britain and the United States had been signed within its walls, would have been a crime which would have shocked the world even more than did the destruction of Louvain or Rheims Cathedral. The Germans were un-

Swaine

SIR CECIL HERTSLET.
British Consul-General at Antwerp.

doubtedly willing to perpetrate the crime, and to avert it the Burgomaster visited the German General at Oordeghem on the following morning, when a convention was entered into which provided that, on the one hand, the city should not be bombarded nor should any German armed force enter it ; while, on the part of the Belgians, any soldiers that were in the town should be withdrawn and the Civic Guard disarmed, and, in addition, certain supplies of grain and fodder, petrol and cigars should be furnished by the city to the German troops.

As the Burgomaster was a civic officer, the Belgian military authorities were afterwards disinclined to regard the convention as binding upon them. But it was, on the whole, sufficiently observed by both parties, and it undoubtedly saved the city of Ghent from, at least, partial demolition. And it was followed by other consequences.

The whole episode served to advertise the fact that large German reinforcements were on their way south. The supplies requisitioned from the city of Ghent were, according to the convention, not to be delivered at Oordeghem, but at different points on each of the next two days ; on the second day, as far south as at Beirlegem, a village nearly 20 miles by road south-west of Oordeghem, and only about nine miles north-east of Audenarde. This sufficiently indicated the route which General von

A JOYOUS SCENE.
German prisoners passing through Antwerp, before the siege, on their way to England.

Boehn's force was taking. In fact, it did go as far as Audenarde, where it divided into two columns, and followed the same two roads to the French frontier as had been used by the first advancing German army. But the whole force did not get far upon these roads.

When the Belgian Army retired on Antwerp the King of the Belgians is believed to have declared that it should not again act as a field army in operations on a large scale. Its losses had been terrible in the early fighting, and the sacrifices, not only among the rank and file but among the officers, drawn from the first and oldest families of Belgium, had deeply touched his Majesty's heart. He decided not to permit their repetition : a decision as honourable to the King as it was complimentary to the heroism of his troops. When, however, it was known that General von Boehn with his large force was on his way south an immediate sortie in force from Antwerp was determined upon.

Advancing from Termonde and Lierre the Belgian left recaptured Alost and pushed its way to and beyond Aerschot ; on the right, issuing by Waelhem, it reoccupied Malines and penetrated to Nosseghem and Cortenberg between Louvain and Brussels. The connected story of the week's fighting which followed has

not, and probably never will be, told, but it was undoubtedly the heaviest which took place in all this phase of the war in Belgium. The Belgian casualties were large. Antwerp alone, by the end of the week, contained 8,000 wounded, and many also were taken to Ghent, Bruges, and other places. But the German losses were greater. For some days it looked as if they would be compelled, and intended, to evacuate Brussels, and—the real object of the sortie—a great part of General von Boehn's force which had reached the other side of Audenarde hurried back over the road it had so recently travelled to help to repel the threat against the German position in Belgium. It was presumably this manifestation of what the Belgian Army in Antwerp was still capable of doing that decided the Kaiser to order an immediate attack upon that place.

It was characteristic of him, however, and it showed how little he understood the Belgian temperament, that, before facing the losses which the taking of Antwerp must involve, he should have ordered that another attempt be made to induce the King of the Belgians, even at this date, to consent to observe a species of neutrality. Direct negotiations were opened with the King in Antwerp. The intermediary selected was an eminent Belgian, resident in

Brussels, well known in civil life. He was approached by General von der Goltz and asked if he would undertake to carry overtures to the Belgian Government suggesting that, in return for an engagement on the part of the Germans not to molest Antwerp, the Belgian army on its side would remain quiet within the defences and refrain from harassing the Germans in their occupation of the country or from interfering with their communications with the main battle line in France.

The gentleman in question undertook the mission, while frankly declaring his conviction of its hopelessness. Hopeless, indeed, it was. Neither the King nor his Ministers gave the dishonourable proposal a moment's consideration, and the message which the intermediary took back to Brussels was terse and unmistakable in its tenour.

It is not easy to understand the strategy which determined upon a direct attack on Antwerp without any vigorous attempt first to isolate it, at least to the extent of severing its communications with the coast at Ostend and Zeebrugge. So long as the roads and railway lines to those places were intact the way remained open both for the receipt of reinforcements and, if need be, for retreat. Whether the Germans failed to appreciate until too late the importance of those communications, or whether they were deceived as to the strength in which they were held (which is unlikely,

seeing that Belgium throughout all these weeks was swarming with German spies, who were continually being arrested in all sorts of queer and ingenious disguises, as priests, as Belgian soldiers, as rural postmen and a woman), or whatever the reason was, no serious attempt was made to cut the Belgian line anywhere west of Termonde ; a fact for which the Allies had cause in time to be abundantly grateful.

Simultaneously with the beginning of the attack on Antwerp, indeed, a demonstration of some seriousness was made on poor, stricken Termonde itself, resulting in fairly heavy fighting to the immediate south of that town on September 26 and 27. The fighting of the former day is known as the battle of Audegem, from the village two or three miles to the south-west of Termonde, which formed the centre of the engagement. In the early part of the day a force of some 700 Belgian infantry, without any guns, was attacked at Audegem by a much superior German force, which bombarded the village (especially, as usual, battering the church to bits) and succeeded in driving the Belgians out, inflicting on them a loss of about one-third of their total strength. The Belgians fought with extreme stubbornness, however, giving way only, as it were, by inches until early in the afternoon, when, being reinforced, they counter-attacked and drove the enemy headlong down the road towards Alost. In this latter part of the action the German

THE NAVAL BRIGADE'S ARMED MOTOR CARS.

BEFORE THE SIEGE.
Removing Rubens' masterpiece, " The Descent from the Cross," to a place of safety.

losses were heavy and the Belgians took 117 prisoners.*

The Battle of Lebbekke (from another village, lying to the south-east of Termonde) on the 27th followed much the same course, commencing with the surprise of an inferior Belgian force in the early morning, followed by the arrival of reinforcements and the complete rout of the enemy, who were driven back as far as Maxenzee and Merchtem, on the roads to Brussels, by the middle of the afternoon. A very considerable Belgian force had by this time been massed about Termonde and Grembergen, on the north side of the river, and the

* In one batch of these prisoners, 47 in number, which the Special Correspondent of *The Times* saw at Grembergen, on the morning after their capture, there were 4 who wore the Red Cross. The correspondent was informed that they had been armed both with rifles and revolvers and, before their capture, had been seen to take part in the fighting, so he obtained leave of the Belgian commandant in charge to interview them. The first question asked of them was : Why, when they wore the Red Cross, had they taken part in the fighting ? The prisoner addressed replied immediately : " Because our officers would have shot us if we had not." When asked if this was not un-usual, he replied with warmth that it certainly was not, but that the Red Cross contingent was always counted in the fighting strength of a battalion. The others agreed with him and spoke in all sincerity, evidently quite ignorant of the larger bearing of what they were saying. They knew only the orders to which they were individually obedient. Reports of similar cases were so frequent in the fighting in Belgium that it was impossible not to believe that the conditions which they indicated were general in, at least, a large part of the German troops engaged.

Germans gave up the attempt to force a crossing at that point.

Simultaneously with the fighting at Termonde, minor attempts to cross the river were made at other points, from Schellebelle, on the west, to Baesrode, on the east. They were made by small parties of Germans and were in each case repelled. All this activity may only have been intended to distract the attention of the Belgian army from the attack which was being prepared on Antwerp itself ; but the earnestness of the two days' fighting at Termonde indicated at least a willingness to get across the river, so as to approach Antwerp from the west as well as from the south, if it could be achieved without too heavy sacrifice. The futility of the endeavour, however, was soon evident and the real attack on Antwerp was developed. The Allies were well aware of what was in progress, and the Belgian army within the defences made all possible arrange-ments to meet the attack.

By referring again to the map of the fortifi-cations of Antwerp, published on an earlier page, it will be seen that the rivers Rupel (from its junction with the Scheldt) and Nèthe, make a rough semicircle round the southern and south-eastern sides of the city at an average distance of about 6 miles from the walls of the town. Outside the line of the rivers, in this section, were, besides various minor defence works, the forts (counting from the west) of Bornhem, Liezel, Breendonck, Waelhem, Wavre Ste. Catherine, Koningshoyckt, Lierre, and Kessel. It was on these forts (though the first-named and the last were not at once engaged) that the initial attack was delivered, com-mencing on September 28.

On the preceding day, being Sunday, the Germans had advanced as far as Malines and had subjected the now defenceless town to a new bombardment. Characteristically, they selected the hour when the people were assem-bling for worship as the time for opening fire and the Cathedral as their immediate target. The only possible justification for the attack was that the civil population was compelled to flee northwards to Antwerp, where its coming might embarrass the defenders. If this was the object, the citizens could as easily have been driven out of the town by mere occupation and proclamation, without the gratuitous cruelty of bombardment.

On the following day, Monday, September 28, as has been said, the German guns advanced

A ZEPPELIN IN FLIGHT.   [*Drawn by Joseph Pennell.*

beyond Malines could reach the southernmost of the Antwerp forts, and it was on these—on Waelhem and Wavre Ste. Catherine—that the brunt of the initial attack fell.

The actual forces which the German commander, General von Beseler, had in hand for the attack on Antwerp is not known. The Special Correspondent of *The Times*, who was in Antwerp during the siege and had access to the best information available, placed the number at 125,000 men. After the fall of the place there was a disposition to minimize the force used, and it was placed as low as 60,000. Against this, however, is to be set the semi-official statement made in Berlin, in the exultation of victory, that the fall of Antwerp released 200,000 troops for use in the main theatre of war. However many were at any

BRITISH NAVAL BRIGADE WAITING ORDERS TO LEAVE FOR THE TRENCHES.

time actually engaged, it is probable that 125,000 is not an overestimate of the force which was ready to be used. As a matter of fact, however, the decisive factor was not the weight of men but the calibre of the guns. No guns in any of the Antwerp forts or defences could range with the German 28 cm. howitzers. The inner forts in particular are believed to have been armed with nothing more formidable than 4-inch guns of an obsolete pattern, firing black powder.

Throughout the day and night of September 28, and on the following day, Forts Waelhem and Wavre Ste. Catherine were subjected to a truly terrific bombardment. The guns in the forts were backed by field batteries, which were skilfully masked in the intervals between the forts and at various points on the other side of the Nèthe, and, putting the big howitzers out of the question, there was no evidence that the Belgian artillery was not fully able to hold its own against that of the enemy. It was, indeed, curious how little damage the German fire did, except, in these first days, to the forts themselves and, later, to the various villages which they successively bombarded and to the men in open trenches. On the other hand, there were occasions when the Belgian fire was conspicuously effective. But no skill or gallantry could long delay the end against the superior weapons.

Wavre Ste. Catherine was the first fort to be silenced, on September 29. It had been badly battered by the big howitzer shells, which smashed concrete and steel cupolas alike, and half its guns were out of action, when the final catastrophe came in the explosion of the magazine. It is uncertain whether the explosion was caused by a projectile of the enemy or by the premature bursting of one of its own shells. Apart from the wreckage to the structure wrought by the explosion, the galleries were filled with fumes so that (or so it was consistently reported at the time) many of the garrison lost their lives and most of the rest, including the commander, were dragged out of the ruins, as had occurred also at Liége, half asphyxiated. New men were put into the fort, the gallant commander, it is said, insisting on returning with them ; but it was found that no gun could be effectively used, and Wavre Ste. Catherine was abandoned.

The German attack was now concentrated on Forts Waelhem and Lierre, especially on the former. Not far in the rear of Waelhem were the main waterworks of Antwerp, and on September 30 the enemy succeeded in destroying the waterworks and bursting the great reservoir. One of the curious sights of the bombardment was said to be that of a 28 cm. shell falling in the middle of the reservoir, with the enormous column of water which it threw up to an almost incredible distance. The bursting of the reservoir had two results. In the first place it flooded certain of the Belgian trenches, nearly drowned out some of the field guns, and made the carrying of supplies and ammunition to parts of the defence works very difficult. Second, it cut off the city's water supply.

Antwerp had, indeed, an auxiliary supply from artesian wells ; but this was quite inadequate to the needs of the population. All water for domestic uses had after this date to be carried from central points in pails and buckets, and the poorer parts of the town especially suffered severely. As there was no water in the pipes, the danger of fire was very great, and even more serious was the threat of epidemic diseases arising from insanitary conditions.

By the night of September 30 Waelhem Fort was badly crippled, but it continued to reply to the enemy's fire with such guns as could be worked throughout October 1. The defence of Waelhem, indeed, longer continued, was characterized by the same tenacious courage as had been shown in Wavre Ste. Catherine. When the remnant of its garrison was finally compelled to relinquish it they left behind them little more than a shapeless heap of tumbled earth and steel and masses of concrete. They themselves had difficulty in getting away, one by one, by a ladder which made a temporary bridge across the moat. On the same day Forts Koningshoyckt and Lierre were silenced after three days of almost continuous bombardment, and part of Lierre village was set on fire

by shells, the great column of smoke rising from it in the still air being visible from the whole circuit of the fortifications.

There is some uncertainty as to the size of the guns used against the Antwerp forts. In Antwerp at the time, among the Belgian troops in the forts and in the trenches, it was universally believed that the Germans had two or more 42 cm. howitzers in action. Colour was given to this by the undoubted fact that four of these great pieces had, shortly before, been laboriously brought back from Maubeuge northwards after that place had fallen. Their progress had been noted across the plain of Waterloo as far as Brussels, and it was generally opined that they were being brought for use against Antwerp. But it is difficult to get positive evidence that they were in use there. The 28 cm. shell is such a formidable projectile— it spreads such havoc when it falls effectively— that it was easy for those who witnessed its effects for the first time to believe that it belonged to one of the very largest pieces. That the 28 cm. howitzers were employed against Waelhem, Wavre Ste. Catherine, Koningshoyckt, Lierre and Kessel—all the forts of the southern section—is certain ; and even before the fall of these forts occasional shells were thrown from the howitzers among the trenches and batteries well across the river. The normal range at which they were used against the forts appeared to be 12,000 metres (7½ miles), but the time-fuse of one which was thrown a mile or so across the river, and failed

SOME OF THE BELGIAN GARRISON.

THE BRIDGE OF BOATS OVER THE SCHELDT.   [L.N.A.

to explode, was said to have been set for 15,200 metres, or 9½ miles.   This is a materially longer range than the 28 cm. gun is commonly credited with being capable of, and it is possible that the Germans had in use some pieces intermediate in size between 28 and 42 cm.

With the fall of these outer forts—that is, from October 1—the situation of Antwerp became practically hopeless.   The way of the attacking force was still barred by the line of the river Nèthe, on the holding of which the defence was now concentrated, the Belgian troops withdrawing across the river on October 2, destroying the bridges behind them.   But, as has already been said, it would not in fact have been necessary for the enemy to advance their heavy guns further than to within a mile or two of the river to be able to pound the city to pieces.

The people of Antwerp in the mass had no way of gauging the seriousness of the situation. The firing was still so distant that, from the streets, it was only occasionally faintly audible in the stillness of the night.   In the day nothing could be heard.   But all day great crowds surged about the main thoroughfares of the town—the Avenue de Keyser, the Place de Meir, in the Place Verte and along the

quays—while all manner of contradictory rumours flew abroad.   The local Press was, by authority, studiously and persistently sanguine, and the only evidences of the nearness of the enemy which the populace in general possessed were the abiding inconvenience of the shortage of water, the continued dashing of military motor-cars through the streets and the daily circling of aeroplanes—generally friendly—in the sky for purposes of observation. These, from their height, were commonly visible from all parts of the city.

The visiting aircraft was not, however, always friendly.   Early in the morning of October 1 an aviator circled over the outskirts of the town and dropped bombs without doing any harm in the neighbourhood of Broechem and Schilde.   On October 2 a Taube flew over the city and let fall quantities of copies of a proclamation from the German commander of the attacking army to the Belgian soldiers. This document, translated, ran as follows :—

PROCLAMATION.
BRUSSELS : October 1, 1914.

BELGIAN SOLDIERS !

It is not to your beloved country that you are giving your blood and your very lives ; on the contrary, you are serving only the interests of Russia, a country which is only seeking to increase its already enormous power, and, above all, the interests of England, whose perfidious avarice is the cause of this cruel and unheard-of war. From the beginning your newspapers, corrupted by French and English bribes, have never ceased to deceive you and to tell you falsehoods about the origin of the war and about the course of it ; and this they continue to do from day to day. Here is one of your army orders which proves it anew ! Mark what it contains !

You are told that your comrades who are prisoners in Germany are forced to march against Russia, side by side with our soldiers. Surely your good sense must tell you that that would be an utter impossibility ! The day will come when your comrades, now prisoners, returned to their native land, will tell you with how much kindness they have been treated. Their words will make you blush for your newspapers and for your officers who have dared to deceive you in such incredible fashion. Every day that you continue to resist only subjects you to irreparable losses, while after Antwerp has capitulated your troubles will be at an end.

Belgian soldiers ! You have fought long enough in the interest of the Russian princes and the capitalists of perfidious Albion ! Your situation is desperate. Germany, who fights only for her own existence, has destroyed two Russian armies. To-day there is not a Russian to be found on German soil. In France our troops are setting themselves to overcome the last efforts at resistance.

If you wish to rejoin your wives and children, if you long to return to your work, in a word, if you would have peace, stop this useless strife which is only working your ruin. Then you will soon enjoy the blessings of a happy and perfect peace !

> Von Beseler,
> *Commandant in Chief of the Besieging Army.*

The proclamation is worth publishing in full as a characteristic example of German fatuousness (in that General von Beseler should hope, after Germany's treatment of Belgium, that anything that he could say would influence the enemy's gallant troops) and German tactlessness, in the sneers at the patriotic Belgian press and the officers of the army who had shown such devoted courage and possessed the entire confidence and affection of their men. One sentence only of the docu-

ment was, perhaps, approximately near the truth, namely, that which said that the situation of Antwerp was desperate. But the mass of the people and the rank and file of the army were very far from believing it.

In official circles, however, the seriousness of the outlook was recognised. On the afternoon of Friday, October 2, it was decided that the Government should leave Antwerp for Ostend. Two boats were ready at the Quai du Rhin. It was arranged that one of these should sail for Ostend at 10 o'clock on Saturday morning, having on board the members of the Government and the foreign legations. On the second the British and French Consuls-General, Sir Cecil Hertslet and M. Crozier, were to invite the members of their respective colonies to be on board by 5 o'clock on the Saturday evening, with a view to leaving for England either that night or early on Sunday morning. It was understood that this was a

THE ROYAL NAVAL DIVISION IN THE TRENCHES.

prelude to the evacuation and surrender of the city.

This, as has been said, was the plan on Friday night. Many of the Government officials and others slept that night on board, where nearly all their luggage was also taken during the night. By nine o'clock on Saturday morning (October 3) cabs and motor-cars were already leaving for the boat, carrying the passengers with their personal belongings, when suddenly there came a dramatic change of plan. The Government would not leave. The sailing of the earlier boat was countermanded, and it was given out that it had been determined to defend Antwerp to the last. The second boat, containing the majority of the French and British colonies (though without Sir Cecil Hertslet and M. Crozier, who stayed behind), left according to programme.

It was soon known that the cause of the sudden change of plan was the receipt of news that British reinforcements were on their way.

Not much of the foregoing facts was known to the people of Antwerp in general. None the less, a suspicion spread that the outlook was sufficiently gloomy, and from this date onwards there was a constant trickling away of the population, especially of the more well-to-do, chiefly by railway to Ghent, Bruges and Ostend. As for the soldiers, whatever they may have thought, they maintained the same gallant and cheery optimism as was characteristic

of the Belgian troops through all the trials to which in the first months of the war they were subjected. Their courageousness and gaiety were the admiration of all who saw them.

One most important fact was that the Belgian soldier (as did the British, French and Russian soldiers no less) early acquired confidence that he was individually a better man than his enemy. This conviction, born of experience, was too universal in all the allied armies to be without foundation. However devastating the German artillery might be, and for all that the German massed troops would come heroically again and again to almost certain death, British, French, Belgian and Russian soldiers alike soon learned that, when it came to work at close quarters with the rifle or, still more, at even closer quarters with bayonet, lance or sabre, they were always more than a match for an equal number of the enemy. How much the moral strength created by this confidence counted for in the success with which, on countless occasions, the Allies in almost absurdly inferior numbers held and drove back bodies of the enemy which should have overwhelmed them, it is impossible to say. That it counted enormously is certain.

It is said that in the Revolutionary War in America the great importance of the Battle of Bunker Hill was that it taught the Colonists that, untrained as they were, their levies could

MARINES MARCHING TO THE TRENCHES.

[*Newspaper Illustrations.*

AN ARMOURED TRAIN WITH BRITISH NAVAL GUNS IN ACTION.

fairly hold their own in open fight against the trained British troops, with their world-wide reputation ; and that discovery was calculated to be equivalent to a multiplying of the American armies by four or five fold. Something similar to this happened in this war. The Allies soon learned that, so far as infantry attacks were concerned, they had nothing to fear from much superior numbers of Germans. In Antwerp, as elsewhere, the result was that the Belgian soldier went daily to the front and to his place in the trenches lightheartedly, filled with a certain gay contempt for his opponent, only desiring to have a chance to get at him, serenely assured that at anything like reasonable odds he would have the best of it.

None the less, there had never been a time when the Belgian army had not been acutely aware of its hopeless numerical inferiority. It knew that the odds against it were not reasonable. And there had been no time when it had not earnestly longed for reinforcements, especially British reinforcements. It has been explained in an earlier chapter why the hope of the Belgians in the very first stages of the war that Great Britain would at once throw all her strength into Belgium itself had of necessity

to be disappointed. In Antwerp this hope had grown again. Antwerp was easily accessible from Great Britain, and it seemed to the Belgian army and people that here was an occasion, when a definite fortified position was being desperately defended against immense odds, where British reinforcements, even in such numbers as could be easily spared from the main theatre of war, could render a vital service to Belgium and to the Allied cause. At last the Belgian Government made a direct appeal to the British Government for reinforcements. In an official statement issued on October 11, Mr. Winston Churchill, Secretary of the Admiralty, said :

" In response to an appeal by the Belgian Government, a Marine Brigade and two Naval Brigades, together with some heavy naval guns, manned by a detachment of the Royal Navy, the whole under the command of General Paris, R.M.A., were sent by His Majesty's Government to participate in the defence of Antwerp during the last week of the attack."

Mr. Churchill himself accompanied the expedition, remaining in Antwerp nearly to the end, and on more than one occasion going under fire and visiting the men in the trenches.

16—3

THE NAVAL BRIGADE AT ANTWERP.
Men of the Royal Naval Division carrying ammunition into the trenches.

As a result of these facts, coupled with the purely naval character of the force, there was a tendency in England to represent the expedition, after Antwerp had fallen, as in the nature of a personal adventure on the part of the Secretary of the Admiralty, and there was a good deal of criticism of " amphibious warfare." Point and bitterness were lent to this criticism of Mr. Churchill by the fact that a large proportion of the Naval Brigades consisted of very young men who had so recently joined and were so untrained that some of them literally did not know how to use a rifle. In not a few details the equipment also was sadly inadequate. It is evident, however, that such action could not have been taken without the approval of the Cabinet as a whole or the consent of the War Office The reason why those particular troops were employed was explained in a message sent by Mr. Churchill to the Royal Naval Division on October 17, which, besides being a message of congratulation to the Division, was also in a measure a reply to the criticisms which had been made. He said :

" They (the Naval Brigades) were chosen because the need for them was urgent and bitter ; because mobile troops could not be spared for fortress duties ; because they were nearest, and could be embarked the quickest ; and because their training, although incomplete, was as far advanced as that of a large portion not only of the forces defending Antwerp, but of the enemy forces attacking."

After arriving at Antwerp General Paris's command was, of course, under the direction of General Deguise, the officer commanding the defending army.

The first detachment of British troops reached Antwerp late in the evening of Saturday, October 3, and the effect on the people of the city and on the Belgian soldiers was electrical. Not only were the khaki-clad companies received with the greatest enthusiasm by the people, but " for the first time since I have been here," wrote the Special Correspondent of *The Times* in Antwerp on October 4, " I have heard the Belgian soldiers singing triumphantly as they marched ; not a few or a single regiment, but every troop that passed through the streets swung along joyously singing. And for the first time since I have been here everywhere the crowds rushed to cheer them. I sincerely believe that it is no exaggeration to say that every Belgian soldier in the trenches to-day is worth three of what he was yesterday."

The melancholy fact had soon to be recognized, however, that British help had come too late. Whether the number of troops that were actually sent, with the guns that they had, would at any time have been of material assistance is another question. It has been said that "with five times the number of men and ten times the number of guns sent a fortnight earlier, Antwerp could have been held indefinitely." That is probably true. Mr. Churchill has stated that "the Naval Division was sent to Antwerp, not as an isolated incident, but as part of a large operation for the relief of the city. Other and more powerful considerations prevented this from being carried through." In Antwerp itself it was believed by high military authorities until as late as October 6 that British troops, largely regulars, sufficient to bring the British contingent there up to a total of 35,000 men were close at hand. Precisely what troops and how many had been "earmarked" for dispatch to Antwerp, and

exactly what the "other and more powerful considerations" were which prevented their being sent, has never been disclosed. All that arrived seem to have been the Marine and Naval Brigades mentioned, or about 8,000 men in all, and "some" naval guns. It has never been stated that more than six of the guns were ever in action, two being mounted on an armoured train, and four of 6·5 in the neighbourhood of forts 3 and 4 of the inner ring. Arriving as late as they did it is very doubtful if a much stronger force could have been successful in materially delaying the inevitable end, except at the cost of the prolonged bombardment and wrecking of the city.

On October 2, as we have seen, the Belgian forces in the south-eastern section had been withdrawn to the right bank of the Nèthe. As the outer forts had been silenced, the German guns were pushed up nearer to the river, and by October 3 their shells were searching the country as far on the road to Antwerp as the villages of Waerloos and Linth, and an extremely heavy fire was poured upon the Belgian

A MAGAZINE OUTSIDE ANTWERP EXPLODED BY GERMAN HOWITZER SHELLS.

trenches nearest to the river. Under cover o
this fire the Germans made determined efforts
to cross the river at Waelhem, and desperate
fighting occurred there through the night of
October 3 and the early morning of October 4,
but the attempt to force a passage entirely
failed. At one time in the night the enemy
had succeeded in getting a pontoon across the
river, and troops in solid masses hurried to
cross it. Before any had reached the right
bank the pontoon was blown to bits by the
Belgian fire, and it is believed that in the losses
suffered by the masses of German troops as they
advanced to cross occurred the heaviest
casualties suffered by either side in any individual incident of the attack on Antwerp.

Apparently discouraged by the experiences
of the night, the Germans withdrew from their
attempt to make a crossing at Waelhem, and
turned their attention further east, to between
Duffel and Lierre. Throughout the night of
October 4 and the day and night of October 5
the battle raged about Lierre with great
severity, British marines having now relieved
the Belgians in some of the most advanced
trenches at this point. These trenches were
not of a character to afford much protection

against shell fire, and the position in which
our untrained troops were placed was one
which would have tested tried veterans. But
British and Belgians alike did all that was
possible. In the afternoon of October 5 the
casualties from shrapnel fire, to which the men
had no chance of replying, were so heavy that
it was decided to be too costly to endeavour
to hold any longer the line of trenches nearest
to the river, and these were evacuated in favour
of a line a few hundred yards further back and
less exposed. During that evening and night
the enemy made repeated attempts to cross
the river, only to be beaten back by machine
gun and rifle fire. More than once small
parties succeeded in reaching the right bank,
only to be shot down, and it was not until
4 a.m. of October 6 that the Germans made
good their footing across the river. According
to the official report of the British Admiralty,
the circumstances in which the crossing was
effected were that " the Belgian forces on
the right of the Marines were forced by a heavy
German attack, covered by very powerful
artillery, to retire, and in consequence the
whole line of the defence was withdrawn to the
inner line of forts."

BELGIAN SOLDIERS ENTRENCHED BY THE RAILWAY.
Pieces of exploded shells may be seen on the lines.

LIERRE.
Here the British Naval Brigade erected a barricade with wagons and sandbags.

The inner line of forts, however, old as they were, even when supported by the British naval guns referred to, were quite incapable of resisting for any length of time the assault of such artillery as the Germans could bring against them. They could doubtless have held out for some days—perhaps for a good many days—and any advance of infantry, through the barbed wire entanglements and other obstacles, could have been made very costly. But it would only have been delaying the inevitable for a comparatively short space of time ; and it must have been at the price of many lives, the probable surrender of either the whole or a large part of the defending force, and the more or less complete destruction by bombardment of the city of Antwerp. It was decided not to make any more prolonged resistance than would suffice to cover the retreat of as many as possible of the Allied troops.

Arrangements were made for the immediate departure of the Government and Legations of the Allied Powers for Ostend. Since the earlier abortive plan for the transfer of the Government, two packet boats—the Amsterdam and the Brussels—had been kept in constant readiness with steam up. On the evening of October 6 the Ministers and other official passengers went on board the Amsterdam, and

the remaining members of the French and British colonies on board the Brussels, and both sailed early in the morning of the 7th.

On October 5, while the struggle for the Nèthe still hung in the balance, the City Council of Antwerp had adopted a fine and spirited resolution, bidding the general commanding the defence to be guided solely by military considerations without regard to property interests in the city, and pledging him the support of the civil population. On the same day, however, both the Burgomaster and the general commanding issued proclamations, advising the citizens to leave Antwerp, and warning them as to the course they must pursue in case either of the bombardment or the entry of the enemy into the city. The public rightly accepted these as ominous of the serious situation of the city, and from October 6 onward great numbers of fugitives passed all day across the ferry which led to the Gare Waes and the railway lines to Ghent, and not a few left also by vehicle or on foot along the road to the Dutch frontier.

During the night of October 6, also, the Belgian army began to be withdrawn. That evening and continuously thereafter there was a constant succession of troops of cavalry and carabineer cyclists and auto-mitrailleuses passing through the city, not, as heretofore.

towards the Porte de Malines and the front, but in the reverse direction—towards the bridge of boats which crossed the Scheldt close beside the ferry to the Gare Waes. The significance of this, however, was perhaps only partly understood, even by the soldiers themselves. Persistent reports of the nearness of the remainder of the 35,000 British troops continued to circulate, and in the army it seemed to be generally believed that the reason why they did not appear in the city was only because a great surprise was being prepared for the enemy. Instead of being brought to Antwerp, the reinforcements were engaged in a great enveloping movement on the German left, from the direction of St. Nicolas towards Malines, which would isolate the army besieging Antwerp and crush it against the defences of the city. Whether such a manœuvre was truly in contemplation will only be known, if at all, when all the secret history of the war comes to light. Certainly it was believed in high military circles in Antwerp. Perhaps it was only interrupted by those " other and more powerful considerations " of which Mr. Churchill spoke. At least, the belief in it sustained the spirits of those who witnessed the last phases of the struggle for Antwerp with the hope that the nearer the besieging force approached to the city the more certain would be its destruction when caught between the guns of the inner forts and the assault of the enveloping troops.

If the plan had been in contemplation, however, it must have been abandoned before October 6. The Belgian troops, who on that day began to be withdrawn, were not detained to take part in any enveloping movement, but with some exceptions, as will be noted later on, were moved steadily, by road and railway, towards Ghent and on towards Ostend. The actual evacuation had indeed begun. Already all the larger German ships lying in the Antwerp docks—some 30 in number—had been rendered useless for immediate service by blowing up the machinery with dynamite. It was generally reported in the Press at the time, and appears not to have been contradicted, that the ships were sunk. This was not true. What was done was that charges of dynamite were exploded in the cylinders and boilers of the engines, necessitating long and difficult repairs before they could be made serviceable. On October 7 also, the oil tanks on the west side of the Scheldt were set on fire. Antwerp was the

oil depot not only for Belgium, but for much of Holland and the northern part of France, and immense stocks were stored there which it was plainly undesirable to allow to fall into the enemy's hands. At first the tanks were tapped and the contents allowed to run off ; but this was seen to be too slow a process, and in the night of October 6–7 the tanks were fired.

So on the morning of Wednesday, October 7, with the Government, the Legations, and all the members of the French and British colonies departed ; the civil population, though not yet in any panic, prudently withdrawing in continually increasing numbers ; the defending troops coming in from the fighting line and steadily passing westward out of the city, and with the work of destruction of property which might be useful to the enemy already going on, it was evident that the end was near. Near, too, were the enemy's guns to the doomed city.

With his heaviest artillery, as we have seen, the enemy could indeed have reached the city without ever crossing the Nèthe. It does not appear, however, that the 28 cm. howitzers were brought into advanced positions after they had done their work in battering the outer forts to pieces. The German official reports explicitly denied that these weapons were used against the city itself, and there is every reason to believe that this is true. Meanwhile the fire of the other heavy artillery drew daily closer to the inner defences. As early as October 2 the village of Waerloos had been under fire. In the afternoon of October 4 the first shrapnel shells burst over Contich (about half way between the river and the gates of the city), driving the householders in panic through the streets. The 5th of the month was occupied with the desperate fighting for the river between Duffel and Lierre, but on that day and on the 6th Contich suffered severely, and the villages of Hove, Linth and Vieux Dieu were all subjected to heavy bombardment. The village of Mortsel also was practically obliterated, not by German shells but by Belgian troops clearing the field of fire of the guns in the inner forts.

This is a fact which must be taken into consideration in subsequent calculation of the ruin wrought by the German advance. Not all the destruction visible was caused by German guns. It is said that, in preparation for the defence, within the whole fortified position of Antwerp (a radius of, perhaps, 15 or 20 miles from the city itself) no less than 10,000 buildings

TYPICAL BRITISH MARINES AND OFFICERS AT ANTWERP.

were levelled by the Belgians. It was evidence of the heroic spirit in which the civil population faced the hardships of the war that the officers who had charge of the work of demolition declared that in no single case did they receive any protest or complaint from those whose houses were destroyed. It was enough that the sacrifice was demanded for the welfare of their country.

Whether the destruction was wrought by friend or enemy, however, the effect on the inhabitants of farms and villages was equally to leave them homeless and to drive them into Antwerp for shelter. It has been said that this was the effect on the people of Malines when that place was bombarded at the very commencement of the operations. Every day since then the stream of refugees into the city had increased in volume. By the night of October 6 practically the whole district from Malines to the walls of Antwerp had been swept bare of inhabitants, all of whom, who had not been killed, had fled into the city for refuge. Even before the end of September a great number of refugees had come to Antwerp, but in the 10 days from September 27 to October 6 the influx had increased until the population was swelled by certainly not less

than 100,000 extra people. These counter-balanced the exodus of the real residents of the city who, in their turn, when the danger of bombardment began to be imminent, sought some place of greater safety, so that until the very last days Antwerp continued to be fully populated, and the crowds in the streets—especially along the quays and in the region of the Cathedral and Place Verte—remained as dense as ever. On the night of October 6 and the morning of the 7th the exodus of the civil population, however, began in earnest. The defending forces, as we have seen, had fallen back within the ring of the inner or second line of forts, some of which commenced firing that night. It was no longer possible to go out of the city on the roads to Contich or Vieux Dieu any distance beyond the line of these forts.

On the morning of October 7 the streets of Antwerp presented an extraordinary spectacle. It was known that the city now lay at the mercy of the enemy's guns. Somehow a rumour had got abroad that bombardment was to begin at 10 o'clock in the morning, as if it were some new and portentous kind of theatrical entertainment. Notification of the intention to bombard the city if it was not surrendered had been sent

MARINES IN THEIR IMPROVISED SHELTER.
Our men sustained their reputation for cheerfulness in spite of hardships.

BRITISH AND BELGIANS JOIN HANDS IN WORKING THE GUNS.

to the defenders on October 6, and General Deguise had replied refusing to surrender and accepting the consequences. A request was also made by the German commander for a map of the city with the situation of the chief architectural and artistic treasures, as well as of the hospitals, marked upon it, when it would be endeavoured to respect them as far as was consistent with the conditions of present-day artillery fire. Such a map was taken to him by the American Vice-Consul, and copies are said to have been placed in the hands of each artillery officer. The Correspondent of *The Times* in the city wrote that it was significant of the amount of confidence that was placed in German promises that, after these pourparlers, it was the general opinion in Antwerp that perhaps the most dangerous spot in the city was likely to be the immediate neighbourhood of the Cathedral.

Up to October 6 the newspapers of Antwerp had continued to endeavour to encourage the people, and even the editions of that evening declared in large type that " La Situation est bonne," and held out hopes of a speedy hurling of the invaders back beyond the river Nèthe. On October 7 it was no longer possible to ignore

the gravity of the crisis. *Le Matin* that morning declared that it intended to continue publication until the last possible moment, but announced that some of the second line of forts had, on the preceding night, come into action, and that the Administration had arranged for a special service of boats to leave for Ostend at 1 o'clock, on which, as there would be no restaurant facilities, passengers were advised to take their own provisions. " Whatever the future may have in store," wrote the editor of that paper, " all our people have behaved worthily and like heroes. We must now prepare to face the time of trial which we have to go through. Whatever bitterness it may contain, Belgium will emerge from it greater than ever." Similarly *La Métropole*, in an article " Sous la Menace du Bombardement," acknowledged the critical nature of the situation and, while congratulating the people of Antwerp on their sang-froid, which enabled them to " contemplate with a certain amusement the precipitate departure of a large number of their fellow-citizens," recounted the steps which the people were taking for their personal security ; how the majority had stored food, candles and fuel in their cellars,

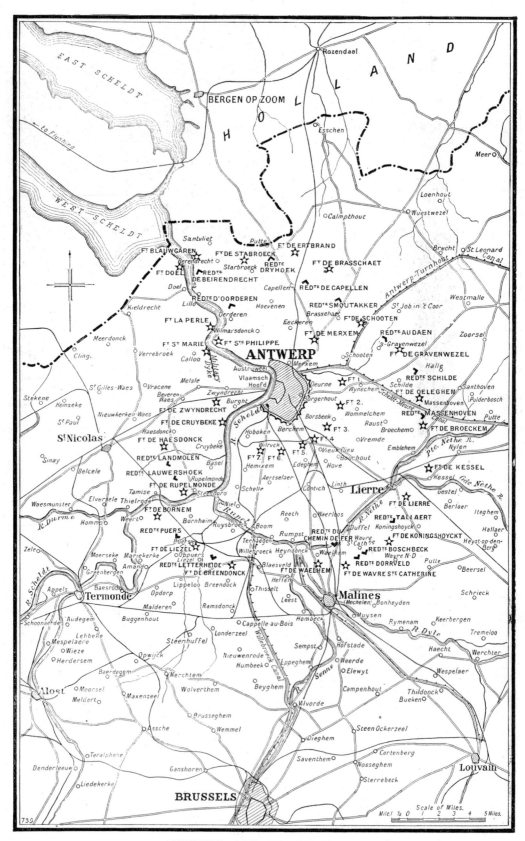

ANTWERP AND ITS ENVIRONS.

A HAVEN OF REFUGE. [*Newspaper Illustrations.*]
Belgian families arriving at Dover Harbour in a fishing smack.

and not a few had banked the openings into the cellars with earth from their gardens or other material. But " although there is evident recognition of the gravity of the hour, nowhere does one see any sign of depression. . . . Antwerp awaits events with serenity and in confidence."

These were the last newspapers to be published in Antwerp. The bombardment did not begin at the appointed hour, and throughout the day the city waited in anxious suspense. In the morning the streets were crowded with people hurrying to take passage on the boats which were leaving or to the railway station. Vehicles and porters to carry luggage being equally unobtainable, the spectacle was seen of well-dressed and evidently well-circumstanced men and women dragging trunks along the pavements or bearing portmanteaux on their shoulders. By noon the chief streets were curiously empty. The post offices and most of the public bureaux were closed. The majority of the leading hotels, including those which had been occupied by the members of foreign Legations, Government officials and so forth, had shut their doors. A great proportion of the shops, restaurants and cafés, especially in the more fashionable parts of the city, were barred and shuttered. There was an almost total absence of vehicular traffic, except as an occasional military or Red Cross motor-car dashed by. In the course of the day the Correspondent of *The Times* visited the famous Zoological Gardens and found the keepers at work with carbines killing all the dangerous animals, lest the cages should be broken by shells and the beasts escape into the streets. In one great grave lay the bodies of two magnificent lions and two lionesses. So everywhere the shadow of its coming doom hung over the city ; and all day long there was a constant defiling of Belgian troops along the quays and over the bridge of boats which led to the roads westward.

This withdrawal of the troops, however, was skilfully screened, not only by the fire from the forts in the inner line most directly in the line of attack and from batteries dispersed behind various kinds of cover at points before the town, but also by the continued holding of some of the advanced trenches well beyond Contich and not far from the river. The troops who held these advanced trenches until the last, suffering heavy casualties and running evident risk of being either annihilated or captured, were both British and Belgian, and they clung to their dangerous work with equal courage. One must presume that the German commander was completely deceived. It is true that the Belgian artillery was, as always, admirably handled, and that the inner line of forts would have made a direct attack in force by infantry very costly. But it is also true that if General von Beseler, after he had made good his footing on the north side of the river at daybreak of October 6, had pressed his advantage at once, he must, whatever his own loss might be, have taken a very much larger number of prisoners from the enemy, besides a great quantity of guns and supplies. As it was, he was content to spend two days in searching the intervening country with his artillery, making no effective attack upon the trenches beyond the constant harassing of them with shrapnel, causing not a few casualties, indeed, but by no means forcing their evacuation. Perhaps he had difficulty in getting guns across the river. In any event,

nearly 48 hours elapsed after the forcing of the crossing of the Nèthe before the first shells fell on Antwerp ; and with every hour his prize was melting away from his grasp.

It was not until three or four minutes before midnight of October 7 that the actual bombardment of the city began. It has already been said that the Germans did not bring up their heaviest guns against the city itself. From the first until the end, though high-explosive shells were also employed, the great majority of the projectiles used were shrapnel, which generally burst above the roofs. The actual destruction of the fabric of buildings, therefore, was at no time large in proportion to the severity of the bombardment. The object of the attacking force was evidently to terrorise and to kill, rather than to destroy buildings. And from the first the fire was distributed with curious impartiality all over the city. This had, indeed, been the German plan throughout the approach to the city. So long as the outer forts had presented a definite and stationary

BRIDGE AT LIERRE,
Blown up by the British Marines.

[*Farringdon Photo Co.*

ANTWERP REFUGEES CROWD THE QUAY AT OSTEND.

objective, fire had been concentrated on one or another until the big howitzers had battered it to pieces. Thereafter the way in which the Belgian guns and trenches were scattered ove. a large area made any concentration of fire in the attack difficult. At moments there was evident a definite aiming at a village, a captive balloon, a certain section of the trenches, a railway bridge, or the supposed whereabouts of an armoured train. But for the most part the fire was extraordinarily diffused : a general searching of the country without, apparently, any particular objective, the result being that in proportion to the ammunition expended the casualties were few, except in those trenches immediately confronting the points (first at Waelhem and later near Lierre) where the attempts were made to cross the river.

So it was in the city. A lively controversy afterwards developed as to which part of Antwerp had the honour of receiving the first shells ; and half a dozen different localities claimed the distinction with equal confidence. In fact, even the first half-dozen shells—which came in rapid succession—were widely scattered, and shells which burst over the roof-tops seem in the silence of midnight very close to all parts of a wide area.

For many nights before the end Antwerp had been going to bed early. The streets were

in darkness after 8 o'clock, and from that hour no restaurant or hotel was permitted to serve food, nor was any light allowed to shine from a window into the street. Beginning with the evening of October 6, the regulations were even more strict. No street lamps were lighted at all, and the tramway service ceased at 6 o'clock. No illumination, visible from without, was permitted after dusk. As the obscurity of night settled down, therefore, Antwerp was as dark as the heart of a forest. There was hardly a vehicle or a footfall in the streets, and indoors the larger proportion of the population withdrew at evening to—if it had not spent the day in—its cellars. Few people probably slept in their beds on that night of October 7, and fewer still slept at all after midnight. By far the greater number spent the last hours of darkness, while the shells crashed outside, in gathering together such household goods as it was possible to carry away, and with the dawn began that amazing outpouring of the population of the city which will probably live in history as one of the pathetic incidents of all time.

It has been explained why, in spite of the emigration of a considerable proportion of the more affluent classes of the citizens, in spite of the departure of the British and French residents and the Government officials, and of the commencement of the withdrawal of the troops,

ELECTRIFIED BARBED WIRE ENTANGLEMENT OUTSIDE THE CITY.

Antwerp was still populous. It had received the immense influx of refugees who came to it for safety and were reluctant to go further. On October 7 there were probably still 400,000 or 500,000 people in the city. By nightfall of October 8 there remained only a few hundred. By far the greater portion of this immense population left the town between daylight and the middle of the afternoon of that day by a single high-road and mostly on foot. Like the population of any other large city, it included people of all walks in life, of both sexes and all ages, and it had the usual proportion of very old and very young, of sick and infirm. Obviously also, the fact that so large a number were refugees who had already fled from other places, coupled with the further fact that all had been under peculiar mental strain for some days and practically all had spent at least one sleepless night, made them in the mass more than ordinarily unfitted to face the hardships of the journey. Nearly all carried burdens, of food or bedding or household effects, to the limit of their strength.

From early morning on October 8 an immense mass of people, estimated at one time to number over 100,000, crowded the Steen and the Quai Van Dyck, waiting for the ferry-boat to take them across the river to the railway. Close by, over the bridge of boats, pressed an uninterrupted stream of soldiers, military motor-cars, and transport wagons. All along the Quai Jordaens and about the docks people swarmed

on to craft of every kind : packets, tugs, cargo boats—later in the day coal barges and lighters —anything that would float was pressed into service for the urgent need of the moment— namely, to get the fugitives away from Antwerp. The destination was immaterial. Flushing, Folkestone, Tilbury, Ostend, Zeebrugge, Lillo, Terneuzen, Rotterdam ; it did not matter so long as the boat would go somewhere away from the Germans.

By these various channels it may be that 150,000 to 200,000 people made their escape ; but the outstanding episode of the exodus was the pitiable procession which poured out by road by Wilmansdonck and Eeckeren to the Dutch frontier. Probably not less than a quarter of a million people took that route.

" Moving at a foot's pace went every conceivable kind of vehicle ; great timber wagons, heaped with household goods topped with mattresses and bedding, drawn by one or two slow-moving stout Flemish horses, many of the wagons having, piled upon the bedding, as many as 30 people of all ages ; carts of lesser degree of every kind from the delivery vans of fashionable shops to farm vehicles and wagons from the docks ; private carriages and hired cabs ; occasional motor-cars, doomed to the same pace as the farm team ; dog-carts drawn by anything from one to four of those plucky Belgian dogs, the prevailing type of which looks almost like pure dingo ; hand-trucks, push-carts, wheelbarrows, perambulators, and bicycles ; everything loaded as it had never been loaded before and all alike creeping along in one solid un-ending mass, converting the long white roads into dark ribands, 20 miles long, of animals and humanity.

"Between and around and filling all the gaps among these vehicles went the foot pas-sengers, each also loaded with bundles and burdens of every kind, clothes and household goods, string bags filled with great round loaves of bread and other provisions for the road, children's toys, and whatever possessions were most prized. Men and women, young and old, hale and infirm, lame men limping, blind led by little children, countless women with babies in their arms, many children carrying others not much smaller than themselves ; frail and delicate girls staggering under burdens that a strong man might shrink from carrying a mile ; well-dressed women with dressing bags in one hand and a pet dog led with the other ; aged men bending double over their crutched sticks.

"Mixed up with the vehicles and the people were cattle, black and white Flemish cows, singly or in bunches of three or four tied abreast with ropes, lounging with swinging heads amid the throng. Now and again one saw goats. Innumerable dogs ran in and out of the crowd,

trying in bewilderment to keep in touch with their masters. On carts were crates of poultry and chickens, and baskets containing cats. Men, women and children carried cages with parrots, canaries, and other birds ; and, peep-ing out of bundles and string bags—generally carried by the elder members of the families— were Teddy bears, golliwogs, and children's rocking-horses. It was impossible not to be touched by the tenderness which made these wretched folk, already overburdened, struggle to take with them their pets and their children's playthings.

"From Antwerp to the Dutch frontier, whether at Putte or by Santvliet and Ossen-drecht, is about 10 miles. But the actual frontier was only a half-way stage on the journey. There on Thursday and Friday nights there was a huge and pathetic encampment. Some hundreds of tramcars had been run down to the terminus of the line at the frontier, and gave sleeping quarters to thousands of the refugees ; but the great majority slept, of course, in the open air.

"As a means of conveyance the tramways could not accommodate more than a very small percentage of the crowd, the volume of which poured on almost without diminution over

GERMANS REJOICE OVER CAPTURE OF BELGIAN GUN.

GERMAN TROOPS PREPARING TO CROSS THE SCHELDT.

the roads to Bergen-op-Zoom or Roosendaal, whence trains of immense length, loaded to the last inch of standing room, carried the fugitives to Rotterdam, to Flushing, and other places. Only a small proportion of the mass of people, burdened as they were and in the congested condition of the roads, covered the 20 miles from Antwerp to Bergen or Roosendaal in one day. To the vast majority it was a two-days-long tramp under most distressing and arduous conditions before the railway was reached."*

Of course, the dreadful pilgrimage had its individual tragedies. Here were the sick, no matter what their disease or how critical its stage, on wagons, in wheelbarrows and hand-carts, being carried on improvised stretchers or hobbling on their feet as best they could. In such a concourse, also, it was inevitable that there should be mothers who had just been confined, with babies, in some cases, only a day or two days old. Babies also were born upon the road. There were some deaths by the wayside ; more in the succeeding days as a result of the shock and exposure of the journey. Happily. however, the weather throughout the

time was beautiful, with bright autumn sun-shine, not too hot, during the days, and crisp, cool nights. Happily, too, the road lay through an almost perfectly flat country.

Here, also, mention should be made of the extreme kindness and hospitality of the Dutch people. It is said that in all over 1,500,000 refugees from Belgium sought safety in Holland in the months of August, September and October. Probably not less than half a million crossed the frontier in the course of the three days from the 7th to the 10th of October, for, besides the stream which poured from Antwerp, minor streams flowed into Holland, wherever there was a road, from all the towns and villages along the north of Belgium, and these streams continued to flow until the beginning of Novem-ber, as the population fled from one place after another in all the country from Antwerp to Ostend. At the time of the fall of Antwerp the chief volume of this incoming tide bore heaviest upon the town of Bergen-op-Zoom. With a total population in ordinary times of about 16,000, it had suddenly thrown upon it, in the course of two or three days, over 300,000 people. Every effort was made to get them out by railway as fast as possible to Roosendaal. whence they could be distributed to other parts of Holland. But it was not possible to pass them out as fast as they came in, and for

* From the correspondent of *The Times* (*The Times*, October 13, 1914), who witnessed the exodus from Antwerp on the morning of October 8, and accompanied the fugitives for a few miles along the road, then rejoined the procession on the afternoon of October 9, and walked with—and as part of—it as far as Bergen-op-Zoom.

several days Bergen fed and cared for a refugee population of upwards of 100,000. The problem of feeding them was a very serious one. Five or six days passed before supplies in sufficient quantities could be brought in from other towns—which were also feeling the strain upon their stores—and during those days the regular residents of Bergen suffered no little privation. A month afterwards 20,000 Belgians, more than doubling the population of the town, remained either distributed among the private houses or quartered in two large camps, being supported at the public expense. But though, perhaps, the burden fell more heavily on Bergen-op-Zoom than on any other town, nothing could exceed the universal kindliness and ungrudging generosity with which the " vluchtelingen " were treated throughout Holland, by the Government and by all classes of the people.

As soon as the fugitives had fairly left the city of Antwerp behind they were beyond the reach of the German guns ; but it was curious that no shells fell at any time among the crowds as they were struggling through the streets.

Shells reached the quays and fell in the river— one narrowly missing a crowded Ostend boat as it put out—and wrecked, later in the day, some of the structures by the riverside ; but nowhere, during those perilous hours, did one fall anywhere among the massed people. Towards noon, as the procession struggled along the road to Holland, a German aeroplane circled overhead, apparently studying what was going on below, and was fired upon by guns from the forts on the west side of the Scheldt. All day long—also on the west of the Scheldt—there rose into the air, steadily increasing in volume, the great triple column of black smoke from the burning oil tanks.

The bombardment, which had begun at midnight on October 7, continued with varying severity throughout the 8th. As the Germans drew nearer to the city all the inner forts on the south and east sides of the ring took part in replying to their cannonade. Some of these forts —notably Forts 2, 3, 4 and 5—were badly battered, but with the guns posted between and before them, continued to answer vigorously the

ON THE OUTSKIRTS.
Germans pause to regard the work of their shells.

enemy's fire, while trenches two miles in advance were still held by both British and Belgian troops. The Germans made no attempt to rush these trenches or the zone of barbed wire entanglements which would have to be crossed to reach the city; but contented themselves with pouring shell fire upon the trenches, the forts, and the city itself from beyond the reach of rifles.

Shelling the city, however, after noon of October 8 could do little good; for Antwerp was no longer a city but only the husk of one. All the streets, usually so busy and so gay, were shuttered, silent and deserted. By the shells as they continued to fall—now chipping the corner off a building, now crashing through a wall or falling harmlessly in an empty square or garden—there was hardly a human being to be either hurt or frightened. Devoted nurses and doctors there were struggling to get their wounded patients to places of safety.* Craft of various kinds was still passing out of the dock basins into the Scheldt, and in the immediate vicinity of the wharves a few cabarets kept open. Two or three hotels, in

safer positions in the city, with much-reduced staffs, also did not close up. With these exceptions, the nurses and their wounded, the military, some city officials, half a dozen British newspaper correspondents, and a certain number of dubious citizens who had good reason to know that they had nothing to fear from falling into German hands, represented practically the whole population of Antwerp. In the shuttered and desolate streets not a vehicle moved. Now and again a solitary figure hurried along, stopping to shelter in a doorway as a shell screamed overhead. Otherwise Antwerp, which yesterday had held half a million people, was like a city of the dead.

As dusk fell a detail of Belgian soldiers sank by rifle fire a number of lighters in the channel from the outer to the inner dock basin, so closing the last exit by water; and then followed a night which offered, to those few who witnessed it, what was perhaps one of the most terrible spectacles that the world has seen.

Across the river still rose into the sky the great triple pillar of smoke from the burning oil tanks. The air was windless and the thick vapour rose straight upwards for some hundreds of feet. There it apparently encountered a light breeze, for, very slowly, still black and solid as a pall, it drifted steadily but almost

---

* Three British hospitals in Antwerp continued to operate until noon of October 8 and all succeeded in getting their patients away, namely, the English Colony Hospital, under Nurse Edith Ward, the British Field Hospital, and Mrs. St. Clair Strobart's British Women's Hospital.

A LONDON MOTOR OMNIBUS TAKEN IN ANTWERP BY THE ENEMY.
Motor Omnibuses have done excellent service in the transport of troops and supplies.

ADMIRAL VON SCHROEDER,
German Governor of Antwerp.

[*Underwood & Underwood.*]

imperceptibly north-eastwards, spreading out till it covered half the sky. By nightfall this heavy curtain overlay the greater part of the city and stretched away into the distance. In the darkness the blaze of the burning oil became visible, tossing into the air and throwing off great masses of flame to float away like individual clouds of fire. The red glow from below lighted up the whole underside of the black canopy, making such a scene as a man might dream of in visions of the Inferno.

Resting almost stationary overhead, so slow was its drift to east and north, this cloud left below it to the south-east a strip of clear starlit sky, ringing one-third of the horizon. Against this, looking from the quays or the river, the outline of Antwerp was silhouetted : the stately spire of the cathedral, the noble tower of St. Jacque, the dome of the Central Station, and other conspicuous buildings being clearly distinguishable above the dark mass of the body of the town. Then, as the night wore on, out of this mass rose other fires—one, two, three, six, ten, fifteen—making almost a continuous ring round the southern and eastern sides of the city. Some of these fires were burning dwelling-houses which had been set on fire by shells ; others had been caused on purpose by the Allies, who were destroying whatever stores might be of comfort to the enemy.

All these—the flames of the burning oil and of all the lesser fires—threw their glow upwards on the pall overhead, caught the points of all the buildings in the city with flame, and were again reflected in the water of the Scheldt, until, above and below, heaven and earth and water were all blood-red—the inside of a hideous furnace, the lid of which was the terrible black cloud of smoke. And inside that furnace, adding immeasurably to the horror, the guns roared, the shells bursting in little lightning flashes of quick spurts of white flame against the black and red.

Intermittent and desultory—perhaps not more than one shot to the second—for the earlier part of the night, about half-past ten the cannonade became truly terrific, by far the heaviest that had occurred at any stage of the siege. In the continuous and deafening uproar it was no longer possible to distinguish the screaming of the shrapnel, the bursting of the high-explosive shells, or the hurtling of the projectiles from the long naval guns, but all blended into one great roll of thunder. It was Chaos come again. Antwerp was in its last agony ; and never surely did great city have a more terrific passing.

Before the first grey of dawn the clamour subsided. Cannonading went on in desultory fashion. But the morning had a terror

From the oil painting by J. Snijders.]   *[In the possession of H. Perry Robinson, Esq.*

"ANTWERP, OCTOBER 8, 1914."

This painting by the Dutch artist was made immediately after the fall of Antwerp, from notes and sketches furnished to him by the Special Correspondent of *The Times* who spent the night of October 8 on board a lighter anchored in the Scheldt at a spot which would be in the immediate foreground of the picture of its own, for the black pall still shrouded the sky. No longer illumined with the flames— for the oil had burned itself out—it hung a leaden shield between the sun and half the city and all the country to the north, so that the day could not break, but until an hour or two of noon twilight prevailed. It truly seemed as if the day itself mourned for fallen Antwerp.

For Antwerp had fallen. Nothing but the necessary formal preliminaries stood between the Germans and their entry into the town. Under cover of the tremendous artillery duel of the night most of the remaining infantry, Belgian and British, had been brought in and passed through the city on the long tramp to the bridge of boats across the Scheldt. In the early hours of the morning the garrisons began to retire from the forts. Several, not already rendered useless, were blown up; guns which could not be taken away were rendered worthless and quantities of ammunition were destroyed, much of it being thrown into the Scheldt. By seven o'clock in the morning of Friday, October 9, the last of the defending troops was believed to have crossed the river, and the bridge of boats, which had done such good service, was, prematurely as it proved, destroyed. Between 8 and 9 o'clock the Burgomaster went out to meet the German commander and make formal surrender of the city. At noon the Germans entered the city by the Porte de Malines.

The actual damage done to Antwerp by the bombardment was comparatively slight. Though a certain number of high-explosive shells were used, by far the greater proportion of the projectiles, as has been said, were shrapnel, which generally burst well over the roofs. Neither the Cathedral nor any of the most precious historic buildings in the city were damaged, though all had narrow escapes, as was inevitable in a bombardment so promiscuous and diffused as this was. The most notable building which suffered—but that not very seriously—was the Palais de Justice. All parts of the city bore traces of its experience. There was considerable miscellaneous wreckage about the Place Verte and in the business section of the town, notably in the Marche aux Souliers; but the chief injury was to private houses about the Boulevard Leopold and the rich residential quarters on the north-east side of the city.

Attention has already been drawn to the doubtful quality of the German strategy which directed the attack on Antwerp while leaving uninterrupted the communications between the city and the seacoast at Zeebrugge and Ostend. We have seen how these communications were used for bringing to Antwerp the reinforcements of British troops and guns while the siege was in progress. What was even more important, the route still lay open for the retirement of the evacuating army.

It will be remembered that simultaneously with the preparations for the attack on Antwerp serious fighting took place around Termonde, in the battles of Audegem and Lebbekke, on September 26 and 27. If the Germans hoped thus to force an easy passage of the Scheldt at that point, they were disappointed. The fighting on these two days ended distinctly in favour of the Belgians; but the repulse which the Germans suffered there by no means ended their efforts to get across the river. Throughout the days of the attack on the city, indeed, there was almost constant pressure on the whole line of the Scheldt from Baesrode, to the east of Termonde, as far almost as Melle, in the vicinity of Ghent. At Termonde itself, at Schoonaerde, and at Wetteren the attacks were at times pushed with great violence, and it was estimated that a minimum of 30,000 men, with a great number of guns, were employed in these operations. From what we know of the forces which were present in this western theatre of action at the time when the main besieging army was entering Antwerp, it is evident that this estimate is not too large.

Interest during these days was so concentrated on Antwerp itself that few details are known of this fighting which went on along the river, but for several days the thin screen of Belgian troops succeeded in holding back the German attacks at each critical point. On October 6 and 7, however, the Germans at last succeeded in forcing a crossing at three points—namely, at Termonde, Schoonaerde, and Wetteren. At Termonde, under cover of heavy artillery fire, they managed to repair the often-wrecked bridge sufficiently to make it once more serviceable. At Schoonaerde the crossing was made, similarly protected by great superiority in weight of artillery, by pontoons. It was evident that the advance of the enemy north of the river would seriously threaten the retreat of the troops defending Antwerp unless it was checked.

Recurring to the narrative of the attack on Antwerp, it will be remembered that on the

GERMAN MARINES ON A TRAIN
Which did not reach its advertised destination.

night of October 6–7 certain troops began to be withdrawn from the city, especially cavalry, carabineer cyclists and mitrailleuses mounted on armoured cars. These constituted in themselves a mobile and useful force. And it soon proved its usefulness. To it was entrusted the task of checking and holding the German advance until the main Allied forces could get away. This function it performed admirably, successfully holding the roads northward against much larger forces for two days, in the course of which sharp fighting occurred at several points, notably at Zele and around Overmeire. Thanks to the obstruction offered by these troops, it was not until the evening of October 9 that the Germans penetrated as far as the railway line at Lokeren. By that time the main body of the retiring Belgian and British armies had already passed westwards. Had General von Beseler succeeded in striking the railway twenty-four hours earlier, it is probable that, instead of the mere husk of Antwerp, which is all that fell into his hands, he would either have captured or would have driven into Holland the whole Belgian army, together with the British contingent. He had neglected what seemed an obviously necessary measure until too late.

Not that the retirement of the defending army was effected without mishap. According to the official statement of the Secretary of the Admiralty issued on October 16 : "After a long night march to St. Gilles the three Naval Brigades entrained. Two out of the three have arrived safely at Ostend, but, owing to circumstances which are not yet fully known, the greater part of the 1st Naval Brigade was cut off by the German attack north of Lokeren, and 2,000 officers and men entered Dutch territory in the neighbourhood of Hulst and laid down their arms, in accordance with the laws of neutrality." In a later *communiqué* the Secretary of the Admiralty spoke of the loss of these men as having occurred "through a mistake." It is to be feared that neither of these statements tells the whole story. The actual number of British troops who then came to be interned in Holland seems to have been 1,560. In addition, the official casualty lists showed a total of 967 members of the Royal Naval Division "missing," of whom 200 were reported to be prisoners of war in Germany. The number of killed was given as 32, and of wounded as 189.

Out of many fragmentary and sometimes

conflicting reports it is not easy to tell what happened. The initial "mistake" seems to have been that some of our men in certain of the inner forts and the neighbouring trenches were forgotten, or, at least, that the message telling them to withdraw never reached them.

In the final disposition of the Royal Naval Division on this last night, the second Brigade was on the right of the road from the Porte de Malines towards Vieux Dieu (in and about forts 5, 6, and 7), and the First Brigade was on the left of the road (in and about forts 1, 2, 3, and 4). The Second Brigade received the order for retirement in proper season. The order was also given to fort 4 (the nearest fort on the left of the road), which was occupied by the Drake Battalion of the First Brigade. This battalion made its retreat without mishap.

But, by whose fault cannot be stated, the order never penetrated to the Hawke, Collingwood and Benbow Battalions, which held the line further to the left. They retired from the position, which they had held with great gallantry, of their own accord when they found that they were practically deserted. Some of them arrived, after many difficulties, at the bank of the Scheldt, but the bridge was already destroyed in the rear of the army which had gone. They managed to get across the river on barges, and found a train which took them as far as Lokeren. There they learned that the Germans were already in possession of the railway line ahead of them, and, detraining, they made their way, not without some rear-guard fighting on the road, to the Dutch frontier.

Another and later party similarly succeeded in crossing the river, and attempted to make their escape on a train already partly loaded with civilian refugees ; but the train failed to get as far as St. Nicolas. It seems that it arrived unsignalled and unexpected (it is presumed that the men were running the train themselves without assistance from the railway staff) at the station of Nieuwkerken, east of St. Nicolas, when it was already in German hands. The train was deflected on to a side-track, so that some of the carriages left the rails, and it was captured. The Germans began firing on the train and, in order to save the refugees, the officer in command surrendered. Eye-witnesses estimated the number of British troops on board at between 500 and 600. Part of the occupants of that train were undoubtedly the 200 members of the Naval Division who were reported to be prisoners of war in Germany ; but more is needed to explain the whole number of 967 "missing." An authoritative account of what occurred will probably not be forthcoming until after their release. What is certain is that the First Brigade of the Royal Naval Division arrived at Antwerp (after leaving some 700 of the most recently joined recruits behind in Walmer) a trifle over 3,000 strong. The Drake Battalion, which numbered

STABROECK FORT.
Destroyed by the Belgians before leaving Antwerp.

[*Alfieri.*

about 800 returned, practically complete. Of the Benbow Battalion less than 70 members returned, and only about 20 and 30 respectively of the Collingwood and Hawke Battalions. A few stragglers came in later; but practically the whole of those three battalions were lost. Besides the British troops, some 20,000 Belgians also crossed the Dutch frontier and were interned.

It is unfortunate that these mishaps marred the withdrawal of the defending forces from Antwerp. But, even as it was, the fact that the Belgian army as a whole succeeded in getting away caused unconcealed disappointment in Germany, and converted the capture of the place into a barren and unsubstantial victory. In so far as the sending of the British reinforcements delayed the surrender of the city by some five or six days and helped to screen the retirement of the Belgian forces, the adventure which was so much criticised had justification.

That that justification was an extraordinary piece of good luck need not be denied. It has already been seen that a more vigorous and masterful commander in General von Beseler's place would probably not have allowed his prey to escape him. And the same failure to grasp the fruits of his success characterized the German commander's subsequent movements. He appears to have wasted precious days in the occupation of the city and the ostentatious parading of the empty streets. Though Antwerp was entered at noon of October 9, Ghent was not occupied until the 12th, nor Bruges until the 15th. The value of the week thus given to the Allies cannot be overestimated, allowing them, as it did, to withdraw unharassed beyond Ostend to consolidate their position upon the Yser. There the Belgian army surprised the world by the spirit and courage with which it once more turned to face its enemy.

And with the Belgian army, now as always since the war began, was its King. Few things in the early part of the war were more remarkable than the ascendancy which King Albert, in the very first weeks, came to exercise over the minds and hearts of his people. Of his personal courage he gave repeated proofs. During the siege of Antwerp and, later, on the Yser he was frequently under fire in the trenches, where he went to encourage his men. Of even greater value were the larger soldierly qualities which he displayed, the fortitude, the clearness of vision, and the strength of character which

BRITISH MARINES UNDER ESCORT OF DUTCH GUARDS.

THE RUSH FOR THE BOATS
At the Ferry to the Gare Waes. The bridge of boats is seen beyond.

won for him the sincere respect and admiration of all—especially the military officers of experience—who came in immediate contact with him. It was not a little thing for Belgium that at such a moment she had such a King.

A NOTE ON THE HISTORY OF ANTWERP.

In 1914 there were still among us some whose personal memories of Antwerp went back to that sinister autumn of 1870, when Prussia had just beaten unhappy France to her knees and the Empress and the Prince Imperial were fugitives in England. The stately city on the Scheldt had no premonitions then of the grim series of events which were destined to bring upon her, too, all the horrors and sufferings of Paris. She was at that moment *en fête*, celebrating the fortieth anniversary of Belgian independence.

In Antwerp itself the revolution which had freed Belgium from the domination of the House of Orange did not become effective until after two years of desperate fighting, during which the Dutch General Chassé, holding the old Citadel, gave the sturdy burghers a foretaste

of modern German methods : for on October 27, 1830, he bombarded the helpless town " with red-hot balls and shells, setting it on fire in many places and doing immense mischief." His day of reckoning came, however, two years later when a French army of 50,000 men under Marshal Gérard bombarded him in turn and, after reducing the interior of the Citadel to a heap of ruins, forced him to capitulate. Antwerp was then formally handed over to the Belgians by the French, thus completing the revolution of 1830, which by the irony of history the city was celebrating at the moment when France herself was in the grip of the Prussian invader. And in 1914, after almost the same period, we could read in retrospect the same irony of history : for another autumn had come, when helpless Antwerp, bombarded and in flames, again turned her despairing eyes westward for that help from France which was almost her only hope.

Not necessarily French help, for during the last grim hours of Antwerp's defence against overwhelming odds she actually received an earnest of Britain's immediate desire and ultimate power to succour : and it had been reliance upon this help in need which even in 1870 had made the British so welcome, merely because they were British, at the commemorative *fêtes* of Belgian independence.

It was a new sensation for the Briton landing on foreign soil, perhaps for the first time, at Antwerp in those days to find that, provided his credentials were in order, he was honoured wherever he went as a guest of the city. On the first evening at his hotel arrived invitations from the various *cercles*—social, musical and artistic—to their pending functions, and his British nationality seemed the only passport needed to free admission wherever he desired to go. For, although it was to a French army that in 1832 Antwerp had owed her final release from Orange domination, it was British influence, British protection and British example which had inspired her progress during those forty years of wonderful prosperity which culminated with the epoch of the great Franco-Prussian war.

Thereafter, although the prosperity of Belgium, and especially of Antwerp, continued, not only unabated but with the steadily increasing flow of a stronger current, new forces were at work. While shattered France was feverishly reorganising her forces, the new German Empire, strong in the pride of conquest, was extending its influence with sleepless activity in every direction, and in none more energetically than in the regions that lay between its ambitions and the North Sea. Not until Antwerp had witnessed in 1914 the exodus of Germans after the outbreak of the war to Dutch territory, where they waited to return with the victorious German troops, did the citizens realize how great a part of their civic and commercial life had filtered into German hands during the forty years which had elapsed since the defeat of France by Prussia.

Another potent factor in creating this new situation had been the changed relations between Britain and Belgium. While the great war of 1870–71 had opened the eyes of Queen Victoria's advisers to the necessity for maintaining the defences of the Empire in a state of efficiency, economy was always their guiding-star : and the one thing dreaded above all others was the "entangling alliance." So whenever policy offered two alternatives, that one was almost always chosen which involved the less responsibility in Continental affairs ; and thus, although Britain never failed in her readiness to stand by engagements which had been deliberately undertaken, the tendency of

THE FLIGHT INTO HOLLAND.   [*Underwood & Underwood.*
Refugees crossing the border. Note the Dutch flag and Dutch soldiers.

THE DUTCH FRONTIER.
Dutch soldiers behind a barrier of barbed wire and revolving spikes.

British policy from 1871 onwards was to withdraw more and more from the risk of European complications.

Belgium on her part, with neutrality guaranteed by all the Powers, was also drifting away from her old position of reliance upon British friendship. National and dynastic ambitions were pursued, especially in Africa, in a manner which did not always commend itself to British ideas. The very wealth which Antwerp, with its strong leaven of German enterprise, was amassing tended more and more to come into direct competition with British trade. So there was some justification for the confidence with which Germany laid her plans for the Teutonisation of Antwerp as soon as the word should be given for the occupation of Belgium at the beginning of the war. Had those plans prospered and had Germany thus quietly succeeded in obtaining command of Antwerp's clustered waterways commodiously opening toward the sea, respect for the neutrality of Holland would hardly have restrained her from the navigation of the Scheldt.

But events in the early stages of the war dislocated the German plans ; and those desperate weeks when the heroic Belgians drenched their fields with their own and German blood so changed the position of affairs at Antwerp that it was only as returning exiles in the rear of the conquering German hosts that the German colony were able to re-establish themselves, instead of, as had been hoped, themselves inducting the new rulers into the City of the Wharves.

It is this aspect of Antwerp—in Flemish " Antwerpen," meaning " on the wharf "—which most strongly strikes every visitor who penetrates ever so little in almost any direction beyond the usual routes of city traffic. Wharves and canals, canals and wharves, bales of merchandize and ships loading and unloading—these seem to confront you at every turn. But this is probably one of the less familiar aspects of the many-sided city to the ordinary visitor.

The first and strongest impression upon the mind of the newcomer to Antwerp must undoubtedly be that produced by the fairy-like structure of the Cathedral spire, with its flying buttresses, rising high above the expanse of the city, in such strong contrast to the low horizon fringed with poplar trees—like rows of round-headed pins—which, with windmills, are the characteristic features of the Scheldt landscape. And as the delicate magnificence of the Cathedral is the first impression which one receives of Antwerp, so it remained the last, even on that awful night of October 8, 1914, when its dainty masonry was silhouetted against the blazing sky under the black pall of smoke. At frequent intervals during each hour of day and night the Cathedral with the music of its carillon of 99 bells always dominates the newcomer's thoughts of Antwerp, especially if, as is probably the case, his bedroom in one of the hotels hard by vibrates to the sonorous harmony. Very soon the habit is acquired of hearing the chimes without hearing them, so to speak ; and one becomes immersed in the absorbing interests of life in the quaint old city, a veritable Museum of Musées. Gallery upon gallery of the Old Masters await inspection. Libraries, societies, and clubs invite your visits, and Antwerp also has its spacious edifices and fine boulevards, with a magnificence of open spaces all the more striking by contrast with the artistic jumble of the fifteenth-century Flemish streets in the central town. If the genius of an Old Master had been set to the modern pastime of city-planning, he could not have evolved better pictures in brick and stone than Bruges for artistic beauty and Antwerp for contrasts.

Two of the world's most famous painters, Quentin Matsys and Rubens, belonged especially to Antwerp ; and nowhere else could you find such array of their masterpieces, the Cathedral itself rightly keeping Rubens' two greatest works for the safety of which—with characteristic Flemish devotion to art even in war—the defenders of Antwerp seemed almost equally concerned with that of the fortress itself. But it is, of course, in the world-famed Picture Gallery, more important even than the Cathedral, that Antwerp's pride in the genius of its

own Rubens has been most rightly justified and most amply displayed.

The records of Antwerp as a place of note go back to A.D. 517, more than five centuries before the British King Harold was killed near Hastings by the invading Normans ; and from the seventh century onwards for several hundred years it was admittedly the first commercial town of Europe. But in those days, as in these, the owners of wealth always suffered when warlike ambitions were let loose, and during the conflicts of the sixteenth century the prosperity of Antwerp dwindled, until in 1648 it seemed to have received the *coup de grâce* by the Treaty of Münster, when the Scheldt was closed to traffic. Early in the eighteenth century Antwerp surrendered to Marlborough, and forty years later was taken by Marshal Saxe ; but the close of the century saw it in the possession of the French. Then came the stormy period of its possession by Holland, which was ended, as already narrated, by the French bombardment in 1832, when it was annexed to the kingdom of Belgium, under international guarantees. From that time, still rich in treasures of architecture and painting, it became richer still in the world's goods from year to year ; and, in spite of the burning of the beautiful old Exchange in 1858, its career of continuous prosperity knew no check until in 1914 it unfortunately barred the way of German aggression.

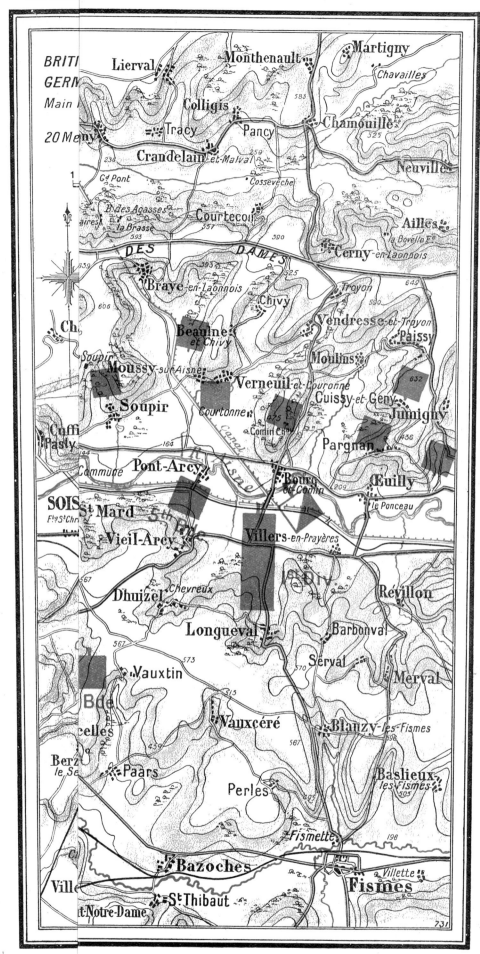

CHAPTER XXXIV.

THE BATTLES OF THE AISNE.

GERMANS MAKE FRESH STAND AFTER RETREAT FROM THE MARNE—THE POSITION ON THE AISNE—
THREE SECTIONS DESCRIBED—THEIR STRENGTH AND WEAKNESS—DISLOCATION OF GERMAN PLANS
—PASSAGE OF THE AISNE—LINES OF ADVANCE—POSITION OF BRITISH DIVISIONS—THE FRENCH
ADVANCE—STRATEGY OF THE ALLIES—THE GERMAN FRONT—EFFECT OF FALL OF MAUBEUGE—
FURIOUS GERMAN ASSAULTS—DIARY OF THE OPERATIONS—THE "HELL IN THE TRENCHES"—
GERMAN LETTERS AND ADMISSIONS—THE AISNE BATTLE AND THE LESSONS OF MANCHURIA—
EFFECT OF GERMAN REINFORCEMENTS—SITUATION UP TO SEPTEMBER 24—LIFE IN THE BRITISH
LINES DESCRIBED—SNIPING—BOMBARDMENTS—TRIALS OF TRENCH LIFE—THE SECOND LINE.

THE war with France had been long prepared, the possibility of checks clearly realised, every position from which a reverse might be retrieved carefully studied, and the plans for holding it patiently elaborated.

When the Kaiser sanctioned the step of transferring troops from the western to the eastern front before he had achieved a decisive result in France, the German Headquarter Staff must have foreseen the possibility of a reverse and the necessity for some position in which they could shelter their discomfited hosts until such time as they could spring upon their enemies still one more of those "little surprises" which had been prepared in long years of peace. That Germany had quite as many able-bodied untrained men as she had trained men was well known, but that she would venture to use vast masses of untrained men; that, in the short space of two months, she could train them sufficiently to act by Divisions and Army Corps; and that she could find the officers, staffs, guns, stores, equipment, transport and subsidiary services required, does

not seem to have entered into the calculations of military experts. This, however, is just what she had secretly prepared to do, and the Germans retiring from the Marne, pivoting still upon the left flank of their 5th Army (Crown Prince), fell back through an angle of some 30 degrees, and turned to bay in a carefully-prepared position to gain the time required for putting in the field those great masses of untrained men with whom they proposed to resume the offensive and the march on Paris.

This position was perhaps as strong as any to be found between the Urals and the Bay of Biscay. It extended from a point on the "Heights of the Meuse" north of Verdun westwards across the Argonne and the Plain of Champagne to Reims, where it turned north-west along (and including) the Forts de la Pompelle, Nogent l'Abesse, Berru, and Brimont, and across the Aisne near its confluence with the Suippe to Craonne, whence it ran westwards along the heights of the Aisne to the Forêt de l'Aigle, north of Compiègne. This position falls into three very different sections. The heavily wooded, contorted country of the Meuse

BEHIND A BRITISH TRENCH.
Showing the entrance to the dug-out covered with wire netting.

and the Argonne and the open rolling plam of the Champagne-Pouilleuse, which formed the eastern and central sections, have already been described, and we need only pause to note that the German centre stretched south of and parallel to the railway from Bazancourt to Grand Pré, by which the defenders of this section were supplied.

The western section, from near Craonne to Compiègne, lay along the crest of the main ridge from three to five miles north of the Aisne. From the crest the ground sloped gently southwards until it reached a line a mile or two from the river, when it fell steeply for some 300 or 400 feet to the meadows which border the stream. The gently-sloping plateau above the meadows offered an excellent field of fire, but the steep slopes referred to provided a belt of dead ground, that is ground which could not be hit by rifle or shell fire from positions to the north of it. Moreover, the plateau was every-where eroded by a number of short, deep, heavily-wooded ravines which met to form still deeper ravines running southwards to the Aisne. These ravines broke up the southern portion of the plateau into a number of rounded spurs and re-entrants. A notable feature about these spurs is that the crest lines were very gently

rounded. Trenches on the actual crests would appear on the "sky-line" to an enemy approaching from the south and would present too good a mark to him. It was, therefore, necessary to retire them ; but concealment was gained at the price of restricting the field of fire from the trenches. On the other hand, the assailants must necessarily cross the ridges, where they would find their advance obstructed by barbed wire entanglements under a close and terrible fire from the trenches beyond. It was, therefore, natural that the assailants should dig themselves in as near as they could to the trenches to await a more favourable opportunity of attacking them. And thus it came about that the opponents on the heights of the Aisne were often separated only by very narrow strips of neutral territory, across which there raged for weeks an interminable and deadly series of charge and counter-charge.

The south side of the Aisne—that which provided the 6th French and British Armies with a base of supplies and positions for their heavy artillery—partook of the general character of the terrain on the north bank. The valley bottom was flat meadow land, 800 to 3,000 yards wide, through which the placid stream—some 60 to 70 yards in width and 15 feet in depth—took its tortuous course to the west. The whole terrain was open downland, entirely unenclosed except for occasional ditches and the walls and fences in and about inhabited localities. The ground was interspersed with patches of lucerne, wheat or beetroot, studded with compact little villages, farmhouses, châteaux and woods; and intersected by straight unfenced roads, lined by poplars, fruit trees and tall white telegraph posts. The patches of woodland, often enclosed by high rabbit netting supported by strong iron stanchions, provided the Germans with little natural fortresses and served to screen their troops and guns. The trees which lined the roads served to conceal columns moving along them, but also betrayed the positions of the roads themselves. The villages and buildings which nestled in the valleys and hollows and the cave-dwellings which honeycombed the steeper slopes afforded shelter and accommodation for the troops in second line on both sides. The best places for the construction of bridges were naturally just where the bridges destroyed by the Germans had existed, nor was it generally possible to choose other sites, without constructing a prohibitive amount of roadway, and thus it happened that the bridges had to be placed near the villages, which resulted in their being exposed, like the villages themselves and the roads leading to and from

them, to the fire, either direct or high angle, of the German guns.

The question arises, what were the weak points of this position ? It was undoubtedly one of great strength, and if the defenders were in good heart and well supplied, a frontal assault must necessarily be very costly and of doubtful success. Had the Allies been pressed for time and had there been no " way round," they would have been constrained to undertake the venture, cost what it might. But since time was, or seemed to be, on their side, their procedure must obviously be to deliver only such frontal attacks as would be sufficient to hold the enemy to his ground while endeavouring to turn one or other of his flanks. To try to turn his east flank through Alsace would entail moving a very large body of men on a narrow front between the Vosges and the Rhine, liable to attack in flank by troops from across the Rhine, and separated by the Vosges from the main body of the Allied Army. Moreover, this turning movement must needs go such a long " way round " that the enemy would have ample time to head it off. Such a manœuvre seemed foredoomed to failure. There remained only the enemy's west flank. The vulnerable point about this flank was that the German right depended for its supplies upon the railways which ran from Tergnier through Namur and Liége to Aachen, and that

PONTOON BRIDGE AT COMPIÈGNE.
Convoy of Algerian soldiers crossing with their horses.

[*Topical.*

17—2

von Kluck's right barely covered his communications. It is true that the German flank was covered by the Oise in much the same way as it had been covered by the Ourcq in the Battle of the Marne, but it is also true that the Oise was no very formidable barrier.

On **Friday, September 11,** the Allies' Left was in full pursuit of the Germans retreating from the basin of the Marne. At dawn the British Army broke up from its billets and bivouacs, which extended along the Ourcq from La Ferté Milon eastwards with the 6th French Army abreast of it to its left and the 5th and 9th French Armies following in echelon to its right rear. The British Cavalry reached the line of the Aisne that day and found the enemy in occupation of the heights south of the river. The 1st Cavalry Division (1st, 2nd, and 4th Brigades) passed the night on the high ground about Couvrelles and Cirseuil and the 2nd Cavalry Division (3rd and 5th Brigades) south of Soissons.

On **Saturday, September 12,** it was officially announced that the German 3rd, 4th, and 5th Armies had given way in front of Vitry-le-François, along the Saulx, and in the Argonne ; and that the Belgians from Antwerp had embarked on a vigorous sortie against the German communications east of Brussels. At the same time the Russians claimed that they had inflicted a signal defeat on von Auffenburg's Austrian Army at Rawaruska in Galicia.

The retreat of the 4th and 5th German Armies must have been received with intense relief by the French General Headquarters. Both these armies had missions of special importance, and the success of either must have had very serious consequences for the Allies. The former was commissioned to break the French battle-line in the Plain of Châlons, the latter to pierce the Verdun-Toul fortress-barrier at Troyon. The fracture of the French front must have had results plain to view. The western half would have been hunted away, while the eastern half would probably have been driven into the frontier fortresses, interned, and captured in due course. The piercing of the fortress-barrier would not have had such serious consequences, but it would have permitted the investment of Verdun with its garrisons and such portions of the French 2nd and 3rd Armies as might be caught north of Troyon, and the fall of Verdun would have opened up very much better railway communications with the Fatherland. The reverse suffered by the 1st German Army east of Paris and its

BRITISH ARTILLERY AND FRENCH DRAGOONS.

A FRENCH 75-MM. GUN, SHOWING BREECH MECHANISM AND
AMMUNITION LIMBER.

enforced retreat had necessitated the retirement of the 2nd, 3rd, 4th, and 5th Armies in succession and had obliged the German Headquarters to abandon *for the time* its designs on the French centre and fortresses.

On Saturday morning the reconnaissances of the 1st British Cavalry Division discovered that strong hostile detachments, supported by guns and machine guns, were holding the town and bridge of Braine and the heights beyond. General Allenby set to work immediately to drive the enemy out of his positions. In these operations, in which the Queen's Bays were conspicuous, effective support was received from the advance guards of the 3rd (Infantry) Division. By midday the enemy had been driven north, a hundred prisoners had been captured around Braine, and a large amount of field-gun ammunition had been found in the River Vesle, where it was visible in two feet of water. On the British left the 6th French Army was approaching the heights to the south of the Aisne, and on its right the 5th French Army had reached the line of the Vesle. On Saturday afternoon and all through the night heavy rain fell, which severely handicapped the transport.

In the afternoon the 1st British Division had arrived at Vauxcéré, the 2nd at Vauxtin, and the 3rd at Brenelle without encountering any opposition other than that already mentioned. The 5th Division approached Missy, but was brought to a standstill by the enemy's fire. The 4th* reached the neighbourhood of Buzancy, where it found the right of the 6th French Army endeavouring to dislodge a German advanced post on the Mont de Paris, south of Soissons, and immediately brought its guns into action in co-operation with the French, with the result that the enemy was driven across the river at Soissons, where, however, they destroyed the bridges. The 10th Brigade captured a ridge overlooking the valley of the Aisne. From a spur here the Germans could be seen retiring along the Maubeuge road to the north-east. Their last files were scarcely over the river when the bridge at the little town of Venizel was blown up with a loud explosion. The British Field Artillery was

---

* Official reports are accustomed to describe the operations by "Army Corps," but this is confusing to the lay mind, since French and German 1st Line Corps consisted of 3 Divisions each, 2nd Line Corps and British 1st and 2nd Corps of 2 Divisions each, while the British so-called "3rd Army Corps" consisted of the Fourth Division with an attached Brigade—the 19th—and was, therefore, merely a strong Division. To avoid confusion the operations are here described by Divisions, which in the French, German and British services consisted of 12 battalions, one or more squadrons, a dozen or more batteries, and some subsidiary services, the whole totalling nearly 20,000, of whom perhaps some 15,000 were combatants.

FRENCH INFANTRY WATCH BRITISH GUNNERS BRING UP ONE OF
THEIR HEAVY GUNS.

able to shell the enemy all the afternoon and
evening at a range of 2,700 yards with such
accuracy that it forced some of them to evacuate
their trenches. Night fell in torrents of rain.

For several miles west of Soissons the French
found themselves under infantry and artillery
fire from points on the hither bank, as well as
from heavy guns on the plateau across the
river. The heavy battery of the 4th British
Division now occupied high ground on the
south bank just east of Soissons, and from here

supported the French guns on their left in a
long-range artillery duel with the enemy's
artillery on the opposite heights, which continued throughout the remainder of the day
and until nearly midnight. The opposition
encountered by the British and 6th French
Armies east and west of Soissons suggested
that the passage of the Aisne might be disputed
by something more formidable than mere
rearguards. As Sir John French says, " The
Battle of the Marne, which lasted from the

BRITISH GUNNERS PLACING A HEAVY GUN IN POSITION.

morning of the 6th to the evening of the 10th, had hardly ended in the precipitate flight of the enemy when we were brought face to face with a position of extraordinary strength, carefully entrenched, and prepared for defence by an Army and a Staff which are thorough adepts in such work."

In spite of the exceeding strength of the enemy's position, an attempt to force the passage must be made. Yet the task was no light one. The river was swollen with rain, bridges must be built and crossed—and repaired whenever necessary—under a devastating fire at ranges carefully measured by the enemy from every point of vantage on the opposite bank.

It does not appear from official reports that the Aisne was crossed by any troops on the 12th, but from private letters received it seems certain that a detachment of the 1st Division got across this evening near Bourg and that the 11th Brigade (4th Division) crossed near Venizel at night in pouring rain, and gained the line Crouy (exclusive) to Missy (exclusive). Their officers claim that the brigade maintained this position unshaken until the whole British Army was relieved by French troops more than three weeks later.

On **Sunday, September 13,** it was officially announced that French troops had crossed the Marne between Epernay and Vitry-le-François, and had occupied Revigny, Brabant-le-roi, St. Dié, Lunéville, Raon l'Etape, Baccarat, Remereville, Nomeny and Pont-à-Mousson; that the enemy's retreat had been so precipitate that he had abandoned maps and papers, official and private, and letters and parcels just received or about to be dispatched; and that the Russians had defeated the Germans on the Niemen.

In front of the 6th French and British Armies the situation was obscure. "The tract of country," says Sir John French, "which lies north of the Aisne is well adapted to conceal-ment, and was so skilfully turned to account by the enemy as to render it impossible to judge the real nature of his opposition to our passage of the river, or to gauge accurately his strength; but I have reason to conclude that strong rearguards of at least three army corps* were holding the passages on the early morning of the 13th. On that morning I ordered the British Forces to advance and make good the Aisne."

---

* Eight or nine Divisions.

GERMAN GUNS DESTROYED BY THE FRENCH.

The British artillery, which had got into position overnight, opened on the enemy's positions and particularly on his guns, as far as they could be located, for until their fire could be subdued a little the passage must be ex-tremely costly, if not impossible. Hour after hour the shells wailed and shrieked across the valley from both sides; and hour after hour the engineers toiled at getting up their pontoons and launching them. The labour was immense, the danger imminent, and yet the bridges steadily grew under cover of the tremendous fire of the British guns, and under that same cover the infantry advanced to the passage of the Aisne under storms of shrapnel and high-explosive shell and in squalls of cold and driving rain.

The lines of advance for the British Divisions were, practically speaking, Troyon* for the 1st Division, Braye for the 2nd, Aizy for the 3rd, Sancy for the 5th, and Margival for the 4th.

On the right the 1st Division and the 1st Cavalry Division were directed on the canal bridge at Bourg. To the east of this bridge a small pontoon bridge had been constructed, and a body of infantry belonging to the 1st Division was pushed across it. A brigade of Cavalry began to follow them, and two regiments had crossed when the Germans opened fire with guns and rifles from all sides. High-explosive

---

* This, of course, is not the same Troyon as the fort of that name in the fortress-barrier from Verdun to Toul.

shells pitted the approaches to the bridge with holes three feet deep, and shrapnel from the flanks burst around it. The horsemen, however, reached the town on the far bank, and endeavoured to make ground up the heights, but found it impossible either to advance or to get to the flanks. The town was now subjected to a bombardment by high-explosive shells; houses collapsed as though made of cardboard, and part of the town took fire. A message was sent to the infantry to ask if they wanted any help, and, a negative reply being received, the cavalry, after three hours' sojourn on the north bank, undertook the apparently suicidal task of retiring by the bridge, which was now swept by the enemy's fire. Marvellous to relate, they reached the south bank with the loss of a few wounded and none killed. The whole movement—advance and retirement—was an example of the finest courage and discipline. The main body of the 1st Division met with slight opposition. It crossed by means of the aqueduct which carries the canal across the river, and pushed on, supported by the Cavalry Division on its outer flank, driving small parties of the enemy before it. By nightfall the 1st Brigade had occupied Paissy, the 2nd was in billets and bivouacs at Moulins, with an advanced post in Vendresse, and the 3rd was in Geny.

The 2nd Division advanced on the left of the 1st Division. Its leading troops reached the river by 9 a.m. The 5th Brigade found that the only means of passage consisted of the broken and partially-submerged girders of the demolished road-bridge at Pont-Arcy, which were crossed in single file under considerable shell fire. The construction of a pontoon bridge was commenced at once and was completed by 5 p.m. The 4th (Guards) Brigade attempted to cross the canal and river at Cys and Chavonne, but encountered such vigorous opposition at the latter place that it was not till nightfall that one of its battalions managed to cross in boats and effect a lodgment on the far bank. Thus the 6th Brigade and three battalions of the Guards Brigade were obliged to bivouac on the southern shore.

The 3rd Division advanced on the left of the 2nd. The 8th Brigade got across at Vailly and established itself on the north bank before nightfall, but the 9th and 7th Brigades had to bivouac on the hither side.

The 5th Division advanced on the left of the 3rd. The only bridge which had not been destroyed in the whole British front was that at Condé, which, however, was found to be covered by such a murderous fire as to be quite unapproachable. The 13th Brigade, therefore, essayed the passage opposite Missy. The

STRETCHER PARTY WORKING BY SEARCHLIGHT.   [*Photopress.*

BRITISH GUNS COVERED WITH BRUSHWOOD TO CONCEAL THEM FROM THE GERMAN AIRMEN.

southern heights here stand back from the stream, leaving an open space which was under a close and accurate fire from the slopes above Missy, the 13th Brigade was therefore obliged to convert its advance into a demonstration while the 14th Brigade moved upon a less exposed point between Missy and Venizel, and by rafting managed to reach the opposite side and secure itself on the steeps above with its left in Ste. Marguerite. The 15th Brigade followed the 14th and later on cooperated with it in repelling a heavy counter-attack delivered upon the 4th Division.

The 4th Division advanced on the left of the 5th. The 11th Brigade had established itself overnight on the heights above Bucy-le-Long and found that a strong force of the enemy was securely entrenched upon the Vregny plateau. The road bridge at Venizel had not been completely demolished, and was repaired during the morning to an extent which allowed field guns to be man-handled across it, while an attempt was made to throw a pontoon bridge across near Soissons. The 12th Brigade crossed at Venizel and was massed in Bucy by 1 p.m. An hour later it advanced between the 14th and 11th Brigades with the object of securing the heights west of Chivres as a base for a further advance against the plateau above Vregny. By 5.30 p.m. it was astride the Chivres brook, but found that a very heavy artillery and machine-gun fire from the north forbade further advance.

About this time a pontoon bridge had been completed at Venizel and the 10th Brigade advanced to Bucy; but the attempt of the Bridging Train of the 3rd Corps to throw a heavy pontoon bridge across the river east of Soissons had to be abandoned owing to the fire of the enemy's siege howitzers. Before nightfall the whole 4th Division was across the river, with the exception of one Brigade of Field Artillery and the heavy battery, while the 19th Brigade remained at Billy, south-east of Soissons.

At nightfall the enemy withdrew to his main position on the ridge along which runs the Chemin-des-Dames, about two miles north of the river, but retained strong detachments of infantry and machine guns, heavily entrenched, on commanding points on the spurs in front. During the night the positions gained by the 12th Brigade (4th Division) east of the Chivres brook were handed over to the 14th Brigade (5th Division).

During the crossing, a German aeroplane attempted to reconnoitre the British lines from an altitude beyond the reach of rifle fire, but a British airman shot up to the attack, tracing a wide circle in the endeavour to get above his adversary. The German tried to close on him from above and there quickly ensued a giddy circling of machines like two gigantic birds in combat, punctuated by the exchange of shots between the aviators. Suddenly the

BRITISH SOLDIERS DISMANTLING A MAXIM.

German reeled. Wounded in mid-air, he yet retained sufficient strength to get his machine slowly to the ground, but it was within the British lines.

The passage of the Aisne, effected in the face of an enemy heavily entrenched in a carefully selected and prepared position, was one of the most remarkable river crossings in military history. During the climax of the conflict the valley of the river had become a perfect inferno, filled with a pandemonium of sound. From height to height the rival artillery discharged a never-ceasing flood of projectiles across the valley. At the selected crossing points the engineers laboured to construct the bridges. Successive lines of khaki-clad figures, in extended formation, advancing from cover to cover, sought to reach their objectives. The air above was filled with the buzzing of aeroplanes and the bursting of shrapnel. The rattle of riflery, the insistent rat-rat-rat of machine-guns, the explosions of shells in the air and on the ground, and the thunder of the artillery produced an indescribable medley of tremendous sound. The meadows by the river side became a hell of fire in which it seemed impossible that anything could live. But foot by foot the unmoved engineers built their bridges, and foot by foot the dauntless infantry won their way to the river, across it and up the further steeps. All night long the enemy's searchlights swept the southern shores, seeking insistently to discover any attempts to move troops down to the stream. It was not till morning that comparative silence fell upon the valley of the Aisne.

The French 6th Army had advanced to the attack on the left of the British. There was a fierce interchange of artillery fire between the guns posted on the opposite sides of the stream. The German artillery greatly overmatched their rivals in number, range, and power, and their heavy howitzer shells detonated with tremendous violence all along the southern heights, but were not causing as many casualties as one would have expected from the noise and number of the explosions. The French had seized the upper half of Soissons, but the lower half was in flames. Volumes of black smoke mixed with the dust of collapsing walls rose to meet the fleecy white puffs of bursting shrapnel ; the thunder of the guns shook the houses, and yet some of the population, among them women and children, remained stupefied but calm. Above all this smoke and flame and ruin arose the twin towers of the doomed Cathedral, which had dominated the old town for seven long centuries. A large body of French Reserves was formed up behind some high ground 600 yards south of Soissons. Further to the left the 8th Army Corps crossed the river under cover of a furious cannonade from the southern heights, and further west still a body of Zouaves, who had won their way across at Vic-sur-Aisne, was endeavouring to turn the German right.

On **Monday, September 14,** it was officially announced that the German centre had taken up a position behind Reims ; that the Germans had fallen back in the Argonne beyond the Forest of Belnoue and Triaucourt ; and that, in the direction of Nancy and the Vosges, they had completely evacuated French territory.

For some days and nights after the passage of the Aisne the engineers laboured incessantly to improve and add to the bridges constructed on the 13th. In the British section nine pontoon bridges—one of them only a footbridge—were laid across the river under heavy artillery fire ; the road bridges at Venizel, Missy, and Vailly, and the railway bridge east of the latter were sufficiently repaired to take road traffic, and the bridge at Œuilly strengthened to bear weights up to six tons ; and preparations were made for the strengthening of the road bridges already mentioned and that at Bourg to bear heavy motor lorries. At the same time the continuous rain made the already indifferent approaches to the bridges soft and easily cut up, which entailed a great deal of work to repair and improve them. Altogether, it would be difficult

to realize the amount of labour thrown on the Engineer Field Companies or to overpraise their devotion and skill.

The partial passage of the Aisne on Sunday, the 13th, had left it still in doubt whether the enemy was fighting a delaying action to cover a further retreat or whether he proposed to definitely check the Allies on the line they had now reached. With a view to clearing up the situation Sir John French ordered a general advance. He reports that :—

" The action of the 1st Corps on this day " [September 14] " under the direction and command of Sir Douglas Haig was of so skilful, bold, and decisive a character that he gained positions which alone have enabled me to maintain my position for more than three weeks of very severe fighting on the north bank of the river.

" The corps was directed to cross the line Moulins-Moussy by 7 a.m."

The 2nd Brigade from Moulins and the 25th Artillery Brigade (less one battery) under General Bulfin, pushed northwards to cover the advance of the rest of the Division up the Vendresse valley. An officer's patrol from this

GERMAN TRENCH, SHOWING THE ZIGZAG FORMATION AND TRAVERSES.

Brigade having reported a considerable hostile force near a factory on the north side of Troyon, the Brigadier directed the King's Royal Rifles and the Royal Sussex Regiment to advance against it at 3 a.m. The Northamptonshire Regiment was to move an hour later and occupy a spur east of Troyon, while the Loyal North Lancashire Regiment was to move at 5.30 a.m. straight upon Vendresse. The enemy at the factory was found to be in such strength that the North Lancashire Regiment was ordered up to support the King's Royal Rifles and the Sussex. Even with this support, however, it was found impossible to advance, and it became necessary to reinforce the Brigade by moving the Cold-stream Guards (1st Brigade) to the right of the three battalions, while the remainder of the 1st Brigade moved to their left. All these battalions became hotly engaged, and a thick mist which shrouded the slopes prevented their artillery affording them effective support till after 9 a.m. An hour later the 3rd Brigade reached the hollow south of Vendresse, and was directed to move up on the left of the battalions engaged in order to prolong their line and to connect up with the 2nd Division. This

GERMAN OFFICER DISTRIBUTING
IRON CROSSES.

Brigade was just in time to deliver a vigorous counterstroke with two of its battalions against a strong German force advancing upon the right of the 2nd Division. By noon a party of the North Lancashire Regiment had secured the factory at Troyon, and the whole of the eight battalions comprising the 1st and 2nd Brigades were extended upon a line immediately north of Troyon, confronting a strong German force securely entrenched along the Chemin-des-Dames. Repeated attempts to advance against the Germans were driven back by tempests of shrapnel and machine-gun fire, and for the rest of the day the combat resolved itself into a series of attacks and counter-attacks, in which those delivered by the enemy gradually decreased in vigour and were finally repulsed with heavy loss.

The 2nd Division was to have cooperated by sending the 6th Brigade through the line held by the 5th Brigade to occupy the ridge of the Chemin-des-Dames south of Courtecon, while the 4th (Guards) Brigade and the 36th Brigade R.F.A., under Brigadier-General Perceval, were detached to secure the heights east of Ostel. The 6th Brigade crossed at Pont-Arcy, pushed up the Braye ravine, and by 9 a.m. had reached a line south of Braye, where it was checked by heavy shrapnel and rifle fire. The General Officer Commanding 2nd Division, therefore, sent up the 34th and 44th (Howitzer) Brigades, R.F.A. and the Heavy Battery to support the 6th Brigade.

The 4th (Guards) Brigade crossed at Chavonne at 10 a.m., and immediately encountered severe opposition. It had to fight its way through dense woods, which made it very difficult to afford it any supporting artillery fire, but a section (2 guns) of field artillery was eventually pushed right into its firing line, and by 1 p.m. the left of the Brigade was south of the Ostel ridge. By this time the enemy, who had passed around the left flank of the Guards Brigade, had penetrated between the 2nd and 3rd Divisions and threatened to cut the communications of the latter.* Sir Douglas

* An Irish Guardsman relates the following incident connected with the advance of the Guards Brigade :

" There were several regiments involved in this affair : a company of the Coldstream Guards, half a company of the Irish Guards, and a lot of Connaughts and Grenadiers. While the fight was going on the Germans in front of us hoisted the white flag and we all went forward to take them prisoners. As soon as we got into the open there burst out a ring of fire from concealed artillery, and then the Germans seized their rifles and joined in the slaughter. It was awful. We were helpless ; caught in a trap ; the whole lot of us were practically done in."

SOISSONS.   [*Topical.*

**Entrance to the Quarries where the Germans imagined they were impregnable,
but which were taken by the French.**

Haig, commanding the 1st Army Corps, was very hard pressed and had no Reserves in hand, but Sir John French was unable to do more than place the 1st Cavalry Division at his disposal. Fortunately the British Cavalry had long been trained in dismounted work and could use the rifle just as efficiently as the infantry. Part of the Division was sent to prolong the left flank of the Guards Brigade and, after some severe fighting, assisted in driving back the enemy with heavy loss. About four in the afternoon the enemy's attacks began to weaken—the crisis had passed—and Sir Douglas Haig took the bold resolution of ordering a general advance. Although the 1st Army Corps encountered considerable opposition and a heavy fire of all sorts, it had secured by nightfall a position which ran from a point on the Chemin-des-Dames north-east of Troyon through Troyon and Chivy to La Cour des Soupirs. This line was extended by the 1st Cavalry Brigade down the valley to the Chavonne-Soissons road ; and the right of the Corps was secured by the arrival of the Moroccan troops of the 18th

Corps (5th French Army), who entrenched themselves in echelon to its right rear. During the night the 1st Army Corps dug themselves in along the positions they had gained and held them unshaken throughout the subsequent operations, day and night, for three weeks. During the 14th the 1st Corps took 12 field guns, several machine guns, and 600 prisoners,* besides those taken by the Cavalry. The prisoners belonged to the Reserve and Landwehr as well as to the Active Army, which suggests that the enemy was already using the older classes to meet the wastage of war. The casualties in the British 1st Army Corps were very severe and included three out of the four Colonels in one Brigade.

The 3rd Division attempted an advance on the left of the 2nd and had almost attained the high ground east of Aizy when it encountered a very superior force of the enemy and fell back in good order to a position north of Vailly, which it entrenched, effectively protecting the

---

* During the past week the British had captured about 60 guns, 30 machine-guns, and 40 wagons, besides a considerable quantity of ammunition and several thousand prisoners.

GERMAN GUNS CAPTURED BY THE BRITISH.

bridge to the south. The 5th and 4th Divisions found themselves unable to do more than maintain their ground. They were mercilessly shelled all day with practically no opportunity to reply. For instance, an officer of the Seaforth Highlanders writes, " They fairly shelled (our) trenches in the afternoon. Evening put an end to the show, fifteen hours of real hard shelling, and yet . . . the regiment's . . . total casualties were (only) 3 officers killed and 1 wounded, and between 60 and 70 men killed and wounded. It was a hard ordeal for the men, but they were quite splendid, cool and confident all day."

On **Tuesday, September 15,** it was officially announced that the Germans had taken up the front Noyon, Vic-sur-Aisne, Soissons, the Mount of Laon, the heights north and east of Reims, a line north of Ville-sur-Tourbe and Varennes, and thence towards Le Bois de Fourges on the Meuse north of Verdun.

Tuesday dawned damp and dismal. A careful examination of the position and reports from the French Armies right and left of him, served to assure Sir John French that it was no mere rearguard opposition, but a deter-

mined stand with which the Allies had to deal. The enemy had evidently been strongly reinforced, and the fall of Maubeuge had enabled him to bring up a quantity of siege artillery, for during the 15th many shells fell in the British positions which must have been thrown by 8-inch siege guns with a range of at least 10,000 yards. Throughout the whole course of the fighting on the Aisne the Allies suffered severely from the fire of heavy artillery, to which, as yet, they could make no adequate reply. Not till bridges in the rear had been built of sufficient strength would the Allies be able to bring up siege artillery. Everything possible was done by way of concealment and entrenchment to protect the troops from the devastating fire of the enemy's heavy artillery, and the countryside around was searched for digging implements, of which a large number was collected.

In the afternoon the Germans subjected the 4th Division and the right of the 6th French Army to a tremendous bombardment from heavy guns, preparatory to delivering a furious counter-attack upon them, supported by the fire of machine guns and field artillery

The Allies, however, held their ground with splendid tenacity, poured a murderous fire into their assailants and repulsed them everywhere, in some cases at the point of the bayonet. These counter-attacks were accompanied by others on the 1st and 2nd Divisions, and though repeated six times were driven back with heavy loss, particularly one made on the 4th (Guards) Brigade. Meanwhile the 3rd Division advanced from Vailly with great vigour and regained all the ground it had lost on the 14th, thus securing positions which effectively covered the river passages to its rear. The 5th Division, however, was not so fortunate. It could not stay where it was, since its trenches along the southern edge of the Chivre plateau were rendered untenable by enfilade fire from the enemy's position about Vregny, neither could it advance, since the ground to its front was not only swept by fire from the north, but was also enfiladed from the high ground east and west of it. The Division was, therefore, obliged to withdraw to a line which ran from a point on the river immediately east of Missy through the northern edge of that village to Ste. Marguerite. Even here its position was not an enviable one, as its trenches could be fired into from above by the enemy about Fort de Condé, at a range of only 400 yards.

During the closing hours of Tuesday it came on to rain more heavily than ever, soaking the fighting men and flooding the trenches, while the continuous roar of the artillery and detonations of bursting shells made one thunderous and monotonous noise in which individual explosions became indistinguishable. Above all this turmoil and bloodshed hung the airmen, driven at times to descend dangerously close to earth in their efforts to locate the enemy's positions in the faulty light.

During the night ten more counter-attacks were delivered upon the British front, those on the left wing being particularly vigorous, but all were defeated with great slaughter.

While the British and the right of the 6th French Army were subjected to these furious assaults the battle spread westwards, and an enormous number of guns were in action on both sides, so that the roar of their fire became like monstrously magnified musketry. At nightfall the French left began to drive the enemy back towards Noyon, but their right, north of Soissons, could make no progress. In this direction the enemy held a number of quarries, which apparently had been owned by Germans for some years before the war and had been turned into veritable fortresses. The slopes around them were simply shambles. Soissons itself had been subjected to a regular daily bombardment, in which the cathedral and the churches suffered as much as the humble dwellings around.

On Saturday the 6th French Army had

BRIDGE DESTROYED BY THE GERMANS IN THEIR FLIGHT.

GERMAN ENCAMPMENT ON THE AISNE.

crossed the Aisne at Vic and Fontenoy. On Monday they had thrown pontoon bridges across the river at those places under heavy gun fire, had driven the German rearguards through St. Christophe, and had established themselves in Nouvron, Autrèches, and the valley of Morsain. On Tuesday night a furious German counter-stroke from the neighbourhood of Nampcel drove the French out of all their advanced positions and back to the edges of the plateaux where they overhung the stream. All Wednesday and Wednesday night these French positions were pitilessly shelled.

On **Wednesday, September 16,** the 6th (British) Division* arrived from England. Sir John French had proposed to use the 1st, 2nd and 6th Divisions to drive the enemy from their position on the Chemin-des-Dames, so that from this point a fire could be brought to bear across the front of the 3rd Division to enable that Division to advance and thus relieve the pressure on the 5th and 4th Divisions in succession; but he found that the forward movement of the British right could not be

supported by the left of the 5th French Army, and that, therefore, the former would be dangerously exposed. He also heard from General Joffre that since the Germans obviously intended a serious defence of their position, he proposed to turn their west flank rather than attempt to break their line, and had begun to strengthen his own left accordingly. The 6th Division, therefore, was sent to the south side of the river behind the British left, to serve as a General Reserve.

The Germans continued to bombard the British positions throughout the day, but their counter-attacks were rather in the nature of demonstrations than of serious efforts. Indeed, the extreme accuracy of the British artillery fire obliged them to evacuate some of their trenches for the time, but as they reoccupied them at night, the situation remained unchanged at the close of the day.

On **Thursday, September 17,** the Russian official report recorded the utter rout of the Austrian Army in Galicia, with losses of 250,000 killed and wounded, 100,000 prisoners, 400 guns, and flags and stores. The 6th French Army, which had been heavily reinforced, retook all the positions it had lost on Tuesday night and even drove the Germans beyond Nampcel itself.

This day the German heavy artillery bom-

---

* 6th DIVISION.—16th *Brigade*: 1st E. Kent, 1st Leicester, 1st Shropshire, 2nd Yorks and Lancs. 17th *Brigade*: 1st Royal Fusiliers, 1st N. Staffs, 2nd Leicester, 3rd Rifle Brigade. 18th *Brigade*: 1st W. Yorks, 1st E. Yorks, 2nd Notts and Derby, 2nd Durham. *Artillery Brigades*: 2nd, 24th, 38th, eighteen pounders, and 12th Howitzer.

barded the whole British position more vigorously than on the previous day, but their infantry was quiescent except in front of the British right. Here a number of attacks were made and, as usual, repulsed with heavy loss—on this occasion mainly by the field artillery. Nevertheless the 1st Division was in action the whole day.

It has already been related how, on Monday, the 14th, the right of the 2nd Brigade had won very advanced positions on the Chemin-des-Dames, near Troyon. The Northamptonshire Regiment was on the right, which was the most advanced and the most exposed portion of the British line. One of its companies—a captain, two subalterns, and 160 men—held a trench along the road. It had poured with rain for a week, the water draining in from the road stood knee-deep in the trench, the men had lost their great-coats in the retreat from Mons, they had now held their position under a continuous bombardment for four days with scarcely any rest or sleep the whole time, and they had in front of them, across a turnip field only 250 yards wide, trenches held by an enemy three times their strength. Picked shots on both sides made it certain death to show above the parapet. Sentries peeping through their look-outs had been shot through the mouth, the captain had been shot through the head, a lieutenant had been mortally wounded, and

food and water could only be brought up at night by men who crawled out and back on their stomachs. The best shot in the company had been accustomed to adorn his "balaclava helmet" with turnip leaves and to crawl out towards the enemy's trench after nightfall. Here he would lie patiently amid the turnips and in the soaking rain until a foeman's head showed above the "sky-line"—a press of the trigger, and a gasp or a cry announced that a German had gone to his last account. In rear of the trench was a haystack known as "the hospital," because behind it the British had collected some 70 Germans who had been severely wounded in Monday's fight. These men were fed and attended to at night, but the enemy's fire made it impossible to reach them during daylight. On Wednesday a German shell set fire to the haystack. The more severely wounded were burnt alive and, of course, the "cover" which had so far protected the others from their countrymen's fire was destroyed. The cries of the wounded were horrible to hear, but the deadly nature of the enemy's fire made it impossible to afford them any assistance. On Thursday the Germans in the trench opposite made two or three ineffectual attempts to advance, and then put up their arms or their rifles and made other signals of surrender. The British signed for them to come out and the Germans streamed

GERMAN ROLL CALL AFTER AN ENGAGEMENT.

THE FOREST OF COMPIÈGNE.
Motor omnibuses bringing up supplies for the troops.

across the intervening space. The only sur-
viving British officer—a second lieutenant of
less than a year's service—advanced and called
for an officer to come forward. A private
hastened out. The subaltern told him to retire
and again shouted for an officer. The private
withdrew and another private advanced. The
subaltern ordered him back and again shouted
for an officer to come forward. All this time the
Germans were moving on and had nearly
reached the trench. At last a German officer
with a sergeant and a private came forward.
"You surrender—you are my prisoner," said
the British officer. Whether the German
officer now perceived how small was the force
opposed to him and changed his mind about
surrendering, or whether the act of treachery

had been intended from the outset, is not
known, but certain it is that the German officer
replied, " No, you are mine," waved his men on
and made for the British officer. The latter
raised his revolver and shot both the German
officer and the sergeant, but the private closed
with him and the Germans began to shoot.
One shot went through the subaltern's cap and
another through his shoulder, and he was
knocked down and stunned at the same time.
Further away some of the Northamptons had
left their trench and were taking over rifles or
shaking hands with their prospective prisoners,
but far the greater number of the Germans had
pressed forward to the parapet, where they
started firing point blank at the men in the
trenches. A scrimmage ensued between the

BRITISH TRAVELLING REPAIR SHOPS.

leading Germans and the Northamptons, and the remaining Germans began running up to reinforce those on the parapet. It so happened that the Northampton's trench was flanked at a range of 400 yards by a machine-gun detachment in a neighbouring trench held by the Queen's Regiment. The latter had been very interested observers of the supposed surrender, but they immediately grasped the situation, switched on the machine gun and cut down the Germans. Out of 400 Germans 300 were killed by bayonet and bullet and 100 surrendered to a detachment of Coldstreamers who had doubled up to the scene. Of the Northamptons only 12 men were left on their legs, and of these 4 were wounded.*

---

* "Eyewitness" gives a brief account of this incident as happening to a platoon of the Northamptons. He remarks of the German behaviour in general :

"The Germans are a formidable enemy, well trained, long prepared and brave, their soldiers are carrying on the contest with skill and valour. Nevertheless they are fighting to win anyhow, regardless of all the rules of fair-play, and there is evidence that they do not hesitate at anything in order to gain victory. A large number of the tales of their misbehaviour are exaggerations, and some of the stringent precautions they have taken to guard themselves against the inhabitants of the areas traversed are possibly justifiable measures of war. But at the same time it has been definitely established that they have committed atrocities on many occasions and they have been guilty of brutal conduct.

" Further evidence has now been collected of the misuse of the white flag and other signs of surrender during the action of the 17th, when, owing to this, one officer was shot. During the recent fighting also some German ambulance wagons advanced in order to collect the wounded. An order to cease fire was consequently given to our guns which were firing on this particular section of ground. The German battery commanders at once took advantage of the lull in the action to climb up their observation ladders and on to a haystack to locate our guns, which soon afterwards came under a far more accurate fire than any to which they had been subjected up to that time.

"A British officer who was captured by the Germans and has since escaped reports that while a prisoner he saw men who had been fighting subsequently put on Red Cross brassards. That the irregular use of the protection afforded by the Geneva Convention is not uncommon is confirmed by the fact that on one occasion men in the uniform of combatant units have been captured wearing the Red Cross brassard hastily slipped over the arm. The excuse given has been that they had been detailed after a fight to look after the wounded. It is reported by a cavalry officer that the driver of a motor-car with a machine-gun mounted on it, which he captured, was wearing the Red Cross."

Mr. H. W. Forster, M.P. for the Sevenoaks Division, has received a letter from an officer at the front, in which he refers to the death of his son, Second Lieutenant Forster, who was killed in action. The following is an extract from the letter : "It was a terrible day for our battalion. By midday there were only six company officers left. We lost fifteen officers out of twenty-four, and 283 men. These heavy losses were mostly caused by those dirty Germans holding up their hands in token of surrender, and then opening fire on us when we got within twenty yards of their trenches."

WITH THE FRENCH RED CROSS.
Entraining a wounded soldier at the rear of the fighting line.

Later in the afternoon the German 53rd Regiment (three battalions) advanced against the trenches held by the Northamptons and Queen's, but was driven back. The two British battalions were then reinforced by the King's Royal Rifles from the divisional reserve and directed to counter-attack the enemy. Under cover of a mist the Northamptonshire Regiment crept close up to the enemy's trenches undiscovered, charged with the bayonet and drove the enemy up the hill. They then found that the crest itself was held by a very strong force of German infantry, but the Queen's on the left managed to reach a point from which they could enfilade the enemy's line, and the King's Royal Rifles on the right, wheeling up to their left and supported by a squadron of cavalry, promptly joined in a concerted attack which drove the enemy back with heavy loss.

All night long a gale raged and the rain poured, flooding out the trenches and drenching the unfortunate soldiers that held them. The men were soaked to the skin, covered with mud, their faces caked with greyish clay, chilled to

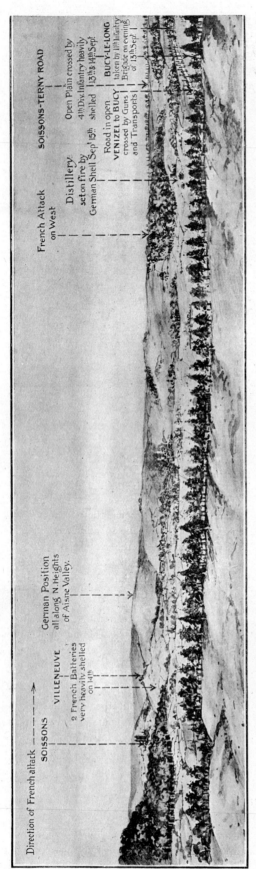

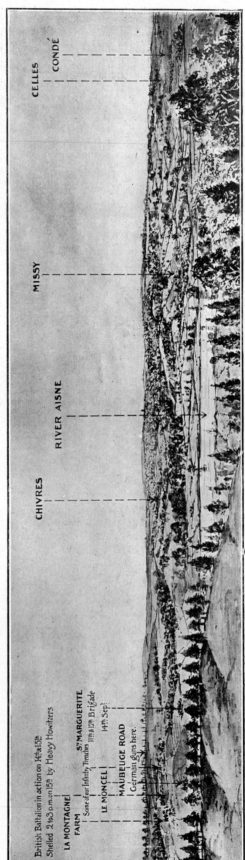

PANORAMIC VIEW OF THE AISNE VALLEY.

the marrow by the wind and wet, and shaking with cold. Said one man : " It is absolute hell in the trenches, and the rain and the cold are worse than the shrapnel."*

During the day fire was opened upon a German aeroplane which attempted to fly over the British lines, and a sudden rocking of the machine showed that a bullet had found its billet. The aviator, however, managed to turn northwards, began to descend very gradually, and it seemed for the moment as if he would succeed in reaching his own lines, but when within a few hundred feet of the ground the machine suddenly dived head-first downwards, and though the result was not visible from the British trenches, it was afterwards ascertained that the machine had been smashed to pieces and the aviator injured, if not killed.

The following, given by "Eyewitness" and published by the Press Bureau, are interesting as giving some idea of the condition of the German Army at this time :

The following is an epistle from a German soldier of the 74th Infantry Regiment (Xth Corps) to his wife :

" My dear Wife,—I have just been living through days that defy imagination. I should never have thought that men could stand it. It was horrible, it was ghastly. But I have been saved for our happiness and I take heart again, although I am still terribly unnerved. God grant that I may see you again soon and that this

* A doctor with the R.A.M.C. at the front writes :

" We speak of brave men. Yes, these men are brave ! If the people of the United Kingdom could see the conditions under which our fellows fight and how they die, I swear that every head would uncover to the colours of any regiment bearing the name of a battle, because that name had been won through the blood of real heroes. For example, some colours will have ' Marne ' upon them. I know what deeds were done, what lives were given, what wounds were received to have that one name so inscribed. Believe me, the Victoria Cross is won over and over again in a single day. They are brave. What if you were to see how the wounded act after the excitement of battle ? They suffer their wounds, great and small, without a murmur ; they get their wounds dressed and take chloroform, give consent to have their limbs amputated just as if they were going to have their hair cut. They are gloriously brave. Men who have been in the thick of the fight all day, seen their chums wounded and killed, their own lives not worth a second's insurance, still these men cook their food and go off to sleep, and. most wonderful of all, go back to the thick of it next day.

" It is Sunday and we have had Holy Communion administered in a cowshed, and very impressive it was in the circumstances. In the evening we had another service in a barn, conducted by the Chaplain and a Wesleyan minister. A great crowd of the officers and men collected. The scene was very impressive, with the room only lit with camp candles, the soldiers rough and dirty with the work of war, some of them just returned from the trenches and others going there the same night—some who in all probability would be dead before another night came along. The men sang heartily, but when the prayer for dear ones at home was being offered there were few dry eyes among those brave men who faced death daily."

MOTOR AMBULANCE WRECKED BY GERMAN SHELLS.

horror may soon be over. None of us can do any more, human strength is at an end.

" I will try to tell you about it :

" On September 5 the enemy were reported to be taking up a position near St. Prix (N.E. of Paris). The Xth Corps, which had made an astonishingly rapid advance, of course attacked on the Sunday. We were met with shell fire and a violent fusillade from the enemy's infantry. Our Colonel was badly wounded—he is the third we have had. Fourteen men were killed round me. . . . We got away in a lull without being hit.

" The 7th, 8th, and 9th of September we were constantly under shell and shrapnel fire and suffered terrible losses. The fear of a death of agony which is in every man's heart, and naturally so, is a terrible feeling.

" How often I thought of you, my darling, and what I suffered in that terrifying battle which extended along a front of many miles near Montmirail, you cannot possibly imagine. For four days I was under artillery fire. It is like Hell, but a thousand times worse. On the night of the 9th the order was given to retreat. The First and Third Armies had not been able to attack with us, as we had advanced too rapidly.

" Our *moral* was absolutely broken.

" They say nothing has been lost. We hear that three armies are going to get into line, entrench, rest, and then start afresh our victorious march on Paris. It was not a defeat, but only a strategic retreat. I have confidence in our chiefs that everything will be successful. Our first battalion, which has fought with unparalleled bravery, is reduced from 1,200 to 194 men. These numbers speak for themselves. . . . "

The prisoners recently captured appreciate the fact that the march on Paris has failed, but state that the object of this movement is explained by the officers as being to withdraw into closer touch with supports which have stayed too far in rear. The officers are also endeavouring to encourage the troops by telling them that they will be at home by Christmas. A large number of the men, however, believe that they are beaten. The following is an extract from one document :—

" With the English troops we have great difficulties. They have a queer way of causing losses to the enemy.

FRENCH HEAVY HOWITZER AT THE MOMENT OF FIRING, AND SHELLS.

They make good trenches, in which they wait patiently. They carefully measure the ranges for their rifle fire, and they then open a truly hellish fire on the unsuspecting cavalry. This was the reason that we had such heavy losses. . . . According to our officers, the English striking forces are exhausted. The English people never really wanted war."

From another source :—

" The English are very brave, and fight to the last man. . . . One of our companies has lost 130 men out of 240."

The following letter, found on an officer, has been printed and circulated to the troops :—

" My dear parents, . . . Our Corps has the task of holding the heights south of Cerny in all circumstances till the XV. Corps on our left flank can grip the enemy's flank. On our right are other corps. We are fighting with the English Guards, Highlanders, and Zouaves. The losses on both sides have been enormous. For the most part this is due to the too brilliant French Artillery. The English are marvellously trained in making use of the ground. One never sees them, and one is constantly under fire. The French airmen perform wonderful feats. We cannot get rid of them. As soon as an airman has flown over us, ten minutes later we get their shrapnel fire in our position.

" Three days ago our division took possession of these heights, dug itself in, etc. Two days ago, early in the morning, we were attacked by immensely superior English forces (one brigade and two battalions),* and were turned out of our positions ; the fellows took five guns from us. It was a tremendous hand-to-hand fight. How I escaped myself I am not clear. I then had to bring up supports on foot (my horse was wounded, and the others were too far in rear). Then came up the Guard Jäger Battalion, 4th Jäger, 65th Regiment, Reserve Regiment 13, Landwehr Regiments 13 and 16,† and with the help of the artillery drove back the fellows out of the position again.

" Our machine guns did excellent work. The English fell in heaps.

" During the first two days of the battle I had only one piece of bread and no water, spent the night in the rain without my great coat. The rest of my kit was on the horses, which have been left miles behind with the baggage (which cannot come up into the battle), because

* An English " brigade and two battalions " would be 6 battalions.
† A German " Regiment " consists of 3 battalions. This reinforcement apparently consisted of 14 battalions.

as soon as you put your nose out from behind cover the bullets whistle. The war is terrible. We are all hoping that the decisive battle will end the war, as our troops have already got round Paris.

" If we first beat the English, the French resistance will soon be broken. Russia will be very quickly dealt with, of this there is no doubt."

By **Friday, September 18,** the situation had become much clearer. The Germans' defences, long prepared, were of an extremely formidable character. They were retired just behind the crests of the ridges or followed the edges of the woods. They were protected against direct attack by barbed-wire entanglements and rabbit fencing, and every avenue of approach was covered by a cross fire. The Germans boasted that they could hold their positions for three months, if necessary, and indeed their positions constituted a series of natural fortresses of hills, woods and quarries, which in some places were backed by eight or nine successive lines of trenches. Considering that neither side had a great preponderance of force, it was not likely that either could attain definite results until heavily reinforced or greatly weakened by the necessity for making considerable detachments. It was, therefore, apparent that the operations might drag on for an indefinite period, and Sir John French considered it necessary to establish a regular system of relief, by which one brigade in each Division could be brought back in turn to some place out of reach of the enemy's fire. The arrival of the 6th Division and the employment of the cavalry in the trenches enabled this to be carried out.

At night the scene was magnificent. A number of German searchlights continually moved like ghostly fingers up and down and along the opposite landscape, pausing with minatory glare upon suspicious localities and objects. It was only during these hours of darkness that the relief of the trenches and the portage of food and ammunition to the men in them could be effected. The use of searchlights and large numbers of siege guns by the Germans suggests that this *matériel* had been destined for the siege of Paris.

All day an intermittent artillery fire was kept up by both sides. In the course of the day General French and the officers commanding the 2nd Army Corps and the 3rd and 5th Divisions discussed the possibility of capturing Condé, which lay between the two Divisions, and securing the bridge, which had remained in the enemy's possession throughout. They concluded, however, that the bridge being commanded at close range from many points on the south side, the enemy would be unable to make any use of it, and that as a further advance of the 3rd and 5th Divisions would threaten to cut off the enemy's troops in Condé, it was not advisable to incur the heavy losses of a direct attack.

During the day anti-aircraft guns, belonging to the 4th Division, accounted for a German aeroplane. After nightfall the Queen's, on the extreme right, were heavily attacked. About midnight the 1st Division as a whole was attacked, and shortly afterwards the 2nd Division had their turn. In every case the attack was supported by an artillery bombardment, and in every case it was repulsed with heavy loss. Before dawn the Gloucester Regiment had advanced from their position near Chivy and had captured the enemy's trenches opposite to them and two Maxims, and had filled in the trenches. On the whole the Germans had succeeded in maintaining their positions, but the uniforms of the prisoners taken from them revealed the fact that they were mixing together units of the Active Army, the Reserve and the Landwehr, which suggested that their losses had been extremely severe. Prisoners' reports of terrible losses among the Germans are corroborated by such entries in the diaries of captured German officers as the following :

1. "Modern war is the greatest folly of peoples. In the 10th Corps companies of 250 men have been as a rule reduced to 70. There are companies of the Guard which are now commanded by *einjährige*, all the officers having disappeared."

2. "For tactical reasons the Guard had to retreat. abandoning 10 officers and 800 wounded. The 1st Battalion of the 1st Regiment of the Guard has not a single officer left."

3. "On the 16th we advanced, and, after about one hour, during which time the company lost about 25 men, we were forced to retire. This brought our total strength down to 80 (we started with 251 men). We had no officers left. . . .

GERMAN HEAVY GUN IN POSITION.
The men are bringing up baskets containing shells.

A FRENCH FIELD AMBULANCE CORPS AT WORK.

"On the 18th, at 4.30 a.m., we reached a village where we expected to be able to rest. Before half an hour had passed, however, the shrapnel again found us out. . . . Our condition is now really awful, for we have to lie out in all weathers ; and we are all looking forward to a speedy end. We are very badly off as regards food. . . . Some of our regiments * can only muster three to four companies."

4. Another letter written during the retreat in front of the French from Montmirail contains the following :

"After a 36 hours' march we had a rest, and arrived just in time for the fight. For three days we did not have a hot meal, because our field kitchens were lost. We got a hot meal yesterday evening. Though we are all just ready to drop, we must march on. . . .

"We found great quantities of food, but for fear of poison did not take possession of it until we had got hold of the proprietor of the house and forced him to taste it.

"We are near Reims, after having gone through hard, bloody, and most horrible days. Thank God I am still alive. Of our regiment of 3,000 men there are now only 1,600. Let us hope that this battle—which ought to be one of the greatest in history—will leave me safe and well, and give us peace. I am absolutely done, but we must not despair."

For six days and nights this tremendous artillery duel had continued, varied only by repeated attacks. In the British section a score of attacks and counter-attacks had been delivered in the last twenty-four hours. No sooner had one German line been decimated and driven back than another had come on, to be mown down in its turn and to be followed by others like it in endless succession. But if the Germans failed utterly against the section held by

* A German infantry regiment consists of 3 battalions.

the British, they had better fortune further east. During Thursday and Friday they carried out a series of furious attacks upon the French in the neighbourhood of Reims, securely established themselves in the heights crowned by the forts of Brimont, Nogent l'Abesse and Berru, commenced a sustained bombardment of the Cathedral town* and seriously prejudiced the defence of this part of the French front. If they could break that front at any time it would have all those far-reaching consequences that would have ensued from a similar success at Vitry-le-François.

On **Saturday, September 19,** the German bombardment of the British lines was resumed at daylight and was answered intermittently by the British artillery. At different times and at different places during the day the German infantry advanced as though to attack, but retired on coming under fire. The object of these advances was not very clear unless it was to make certain that none of the British had been withdrawn for employment elsewhere.

* "Eyewitness" says : "The Germans bombarded the Cathedral twice with their heavy artillery. There was no justification on military grounds for this act of vandalism, which seems to have been caused by the exasperation born of failure. It is noteworthy that a well-known hotel not far from the Cathedral which was kept by a German was not touched."

A strong wind and driving rain made the conditions very unfavourable for aerial work, which perhaps accounts for the fact that a German airman ventured rather too close to earth and was brought down within the British lines. A British airman was more successful, for he managed to drop a certain number of bombs in the German trenches and landed an incendiary bomb upon a German transport park near La Fère, which was set on fire. A cache of German war stores, consisting of 10 wagon loads of shell and 2 of cable, were dug up near the river, and signs were found that they had burned large quantities of stores which they had been unable to remove.

It was not till one o'clock in the afternoon that the Germans made any serious effort. They then directed a strong attack, supported by artillery fire, upon the 2nd Division, which repulsed them with heavy loss. The attempt was renewed at dusk with a like fate.*

---

* The following appeared in *The Times* of September 19 :

" And in the trenches too, the tale of heroism unfolds itself hour by hour. Here is an example, one among

The following extracts give some idea of the general character of the fighting in which the French were engaged :

A British officer on the staff of General Joffre wrote home as follows :

" I have been here for over a week, during the whole of which a fierce battle has been raging and still continues. The Germans had evidently fortified their present position very strongly in case they were obliged to retreat after their dash on Paris. This, of course, they had to do after their defeat a fortnight ago. The English and

ten thousand, the story of a wounded private : ' We lay together, my friend and I . . the order to fire came. We shot and shot till our rifles burned us. Still they swarmed on towards us. We took careful aim all the while. " Ah, good, did you see that." I turned to my friend, and as I did so, heard a terrible dull sound, like a spade striking upon newly turned earth. His head was fallen forward. I spoke, I called him by name. He was moaning a little. Then I turned to my work again. They are advancing quickly now. Ah ! how cool I was. I shot so slowly . . . so very slowly.

" ' And then, do you know what it feels like to be wounded ? I rose just a little too high on my elbow. A sting that pierces my arm like a hot wire—too sharp almost to be sore. I felt my arm go away from me—it seemed like that—and then my rifle fell. I believe I was a little dazed. I looked at my friend presently. He was dead.' "

An officer in the Army Service Corps writes :

" Lately I have had to transport wounded on my lorries, and pending the arrival of a medico I was

LOADING UP SUPPLIES FOR THE FIGHTING LINE.

SOISSONS.
Removing harness from wounded horses.
A shell exploded in this street a few minutes before the photograph was taken.

French Armies pursued them closely, taking numbers of prisoners, guns, ammunition, &c., but when we got to this place we found the Germans so strongly entrenched in the position they had prudently fortified against such an eventuality that it has so far proved impossible to dislodge them. There have been fierce attacks and counter-attacks all the time, and the losses on both sides have been enormous. Most of the fighting has been in the nature of a violent artillery duel. The pandemonium has been indescribable ; indeed, as I write, the guns are still thundering all round. The effect of the big shells is simply tremendous. Wherever they fall great clouds of earth and rock are blown up, and if they happen to fall at all near the shock is terrific. I was with the French General and his Staff the other day in a little town about three kilometres behind our firing line when the Germans evidently got to know that the French Staff was there, and began to shell the place with their big guns from a distance of about nine kilometres. Since then they have bombarded this poor little town at odd moments of the day and night, though the French Staff left it after a few hours.

"I was there the day before yesterday, and the whole place was quite calm, though full of reserve

virtually medical man. It is extraordinary how cheerful these wounded men are—indeed, the general cheerfulness and adaptability of the British soldier is wonderful. Nothing disturbs him, and in this way they have suffered as no other troops could have stood without a complete collapse of their *moral*. I am glad our troops are still the British soldier of history, taking everything that comes in a most philosophical and courageous manner. Lying in rain-soaked trenches for three days under a murderous and hellish fire, wet, hungry, merely provokes him to song and laughter. Give him a comfortable camp and plenty of food and comfort and he never ceases 'grousing.' Curious fellow. We are unable to get any matches or cigarettes now, and a match is the rarest thing imaginable. I lost my pipe three weeks ago, and have been disconsolate."

troops, transport, etc., when suddenly one heard the familiar singing noise of a big shell coming. Everyone craned their necks and some ran for shelter, while the singing came nearer and nearer, and then with the most terrific bang the shell landed, followed a few seconds later by a second and third. A singing and bang, one more in the same place, and the third a little further off. Then all was quiet again. It was evidently a case of 'Good morning' from our friendly Germans. These big shells are very unlikely to do you much harm at a distance of more than 15 yards, but up to that they smash everything to bits. The shrapnel is far worse. Apparently the German infantry are very poor, and the cavalry not much better, but their generals are evidently very good and their organization extraordinarily perfect. As to their artillery, I can vouch for its excellence after watching it closely for nearly a week. Whenever the French infantry advance out of their shelters to charge, their whole front is at once regularly covered with shrapnel, and the unfortunate men are knocked over like rabbits. They are very brave, and advance time after time to the charge through an appalling fire, but so far it has been of no avail. No one could live through the fire that is concentrated on them the moment they leave their shelter. I have seen some wonderful acts of bravery the last few days. The officers are splendid ; they advance about 20 yards ahead of their men as calmly as though on parade, but so far I have not seen one of them get more than 50 yards without being knocked over. The French artillery is also splendid—much better than the Germans in a way—but they cannot tell exactly where the Germans are, and the latter are so strongly entrenched that gun fire cannot make much impression on them. However, of course they cover the infantry to a certain extent ; otherwise the latter would all be wiped out pretty quick. Still, the Germans must have lost pretty heavily, in spite of their strong trenches, as the fire of the French guns has been incessant, and whatever they try to hit they do. At the same time it can only be largely guesswork to know where to aim. I was with a French battery for about five hours the other day, and was much impressed by their very rapid firing and wonderful coolness. They laughed at the German shells and played cards during the lulls in the fight."

The following is an extract from the letter of an officer in a Highland regiment at the front :

" These Zouaves are priceless fellows ; about 30 of them go off every night to the enemy's trenches, and stand about 200 yards in front and start hooting and booing, calling forth a perfect fusillade of musketry, which always goes over their heads, and then they return, and as regularly as clockwork the 30 always come back. This was told me by one of our own officers in the —— who are up in the trenches quite near me."

An inkling of the mental, moral and physical condition of the German Army at this time is to be obtained from statements of prisoners, diaries found on German officers, and other documents. The following extracts are from the diary of a German found dead in a trench captured by the French and published in *Le Temps* :

September 5 : Yesterday we received the news of great victories. It appears that in Russia, after a ten days' battle, we have gained a brilliant victory. Our first Army is before Paris. The French have been thrown back on Paris and an English cavalry division defeated.

September 6 : The enemy occupies the heights near Vitry. We approach the French. We are met with so fierce an artillery fire that we retreat. It is not precisely a defeat, merely a retreat. Our losses are heavy, but not as heavy as the enemy's.

September 7 : The troops occupying the bridge of the Marne Canal have suffered terribly. Of sixty men only twenty-five remain. We leave the trenches at 11 o'clock and look for potatoes to stay our hunger after a day of fasting.*

---

* Almost all the German prisoners admitted that their food supplies had been irregular and scanty. They had subsisted largely on vegetables torn from the fields. A

September 9 : We have been four days in the trenches. We have time for reading, and one would soon get used to this mode of existence if the corpses of men and horses did not smell so badly and the flies multiply so rapidly.

September 10 : We have been in the trenches all night under torrential rains. We are soaked to the bones. There has been heavy fighting on the right wing. It appears that the French army is in a bad way.

September 11 : At two o'clock we got orders to retire. We thought we were going to attack. They say that two French army corps have pierced our lines. We fly without eating anything. We march with great speed. Our first and only meal is taken at ten o'clock at night, and after it we walk the whole night through.

September 12 : We are worn out. They tell us that we are executing a turning movement, and not a retreat at all. It looks more like a flight. We halt at four kilometres from Souain and entrench the heights. We are still hungry, and find nothing to eat. It is raining in torrents. We are soaked. War is a plague. At half-past four we have to turn out again to the trenches. Suddenly French shells burst over us, and we are compelled to retire, as our trenches are not yet complete.

September 14 : We have eaten nothing all day, and are terribly hungry. I don't know when it will end. It has never stopped raining.

September 15 : All our killed and wounded are " on the conscience " of the artillery. At nine o'clock we go for our one meal—a little meat and rice, coffee, and little biscuits which ought to have been kept for to-morrow. It is a dog's life. Soon we shall have a long sick list.

September 16 : We are always hungry, hungry, hungry. We dare not lift our heads above the trenches. That would mean death.

September 17 : Raining in torrents. We have no fires. We are still in trenches. Since we have been suffering so terribly from hunger our mentality and enthusiasm are no longer what they were. At eleven o'clock at night we at last have a meal, but not enough

---

letter found on one man says : " How long is this misery to continue ? We have only seen bread thrice since the war began." All such letters agree as to companies being reduced from 250 to 40 or 50 men.

FUNERAL OF A GERMAN OFFICER PASSING THROUGH A FRENCH VILLAGE.

RETHEL.
The Germans spared the Church, the clock tower of which is conspicuous among the ruins.

to satisfy us. The night is cold and damp, with a terrible north wind.

September 18 : Rain has stopped, but there is a fierce storm of wind. Still hungry as usual. It seems as if we are always to be hungry.

Here the diary comes to an end.

An entry in a captured field note-book runs thus :

September 16 : At dawn the shelling began. We retired with the prisoners. My two prisoners work hard at digging trenches. At midday I got the order to rejoin at the village with them. I was very glad, as I had been ordered to shoot them as soon as the enemy advanced. Thank God it was not necessary. . . .

On **Sunday, September 20,** it was officially announced that in spite of the most violent attacks the Germans had failed to gain any ground in front of Reims, except that part of Mont Brimont which had been captured by the French and was now recaptured by the Germans ; that without the least military reasons they had bombarded and set on fire the Cathedral at Reims, and that the French had captured the Fort de la Pompelle, the village of Souain and the district of Avricourt.

During the night of the 19th-20th there was a recrudescence of activity on the part of the Germans. Shortly after nightfall they launched a severe attack upon the 3rd Division. From dawn on Sunday they directed a number of similar attempts on various points held by the 1st Division ; later on they made a more

serious effort upon the 2nd Division ; in the course of the afternoon they made a number of desperate attempts against all the points held by the 1st and 2nd Divisions ; and after nightfall made yet another assault upon the 2nd Division. All these attacks were repulsed with fearful losses to the enemy, whose killed and wounded were left lying in front of the British trenches. But the 1st Army Corps, whose positions had been the chief objectives of the enemy's efforts, incurred considerable losses and were, naturally, much exhausted by the continuous fighting, and it became necessary during the day to reinforce them by a Brigade from the Reserve and by the 1st Cavalry Division.

During the afternoon there was a brief but welcome break in the weather, and a little sunshine served to cheer the troops, though not to dry their clothes. But in spite of hostile attacks and inclement weather, of living and sleeping in the trenches deep in liquid mud, of continuous bombardment and incessant night alarms, the British infantry remained unshaken and were invariably able to beat back the superior numbers of the enemy's masses.[*]

[*] " Eyewitness " says, " The British soldier is a difficult person to impress or depress even by immense

On **Monday, September 21,** it was officially announced that the French had occupied the heights of Lassigny (west of Noyon) also Mesnilles-Hurlus and Massiges in the centre ; and that the Germans had bombarded Hatton-châtel in the Woevre.

Before nightfall on Sunday the look-outs in the advanced British positions had observed the signs of an impending attack, and some hours later sounds of fierce firing were heard to the front, though no bullets fell about the British trenches. The solution of the mystery was forthcoming on Monday morning, when evidence accumulated to the effect that in the German attacks of the preceding night their columns had fired into one another as the result of the notoriously dangerous attempt to bring off a converging advance in the dark.

On Monday morning the weather improved, but little beyond an artillery bombardment was attempted by the Germans. At one point they commenced the construction of a redoubt, but

---

shells filled with high explosives which detonate with terrific violence and form craters large enough to act as graves for five horses. The German howitzer shells are 8 to 9 inches in calibre, and on impact they send up columns of greasy black smoke. On account of this they are irreverently dubbed 'Coal boxes,' 'Black Marias,' or 'Jack Johnsons' by the soldiers. Men who take things in this spirit are, it seems, likely to throw out the calculations based on loss of *moral* so carefully framed by the German military philosophers."

were shelled out of it by the British guns. The only serious attack made by the Germans this day was directed after nightfall against the 3rd Division, with the usual result.

Up to this date it was calculated that the air mileage made by British airmen since the beginning of the war amounted to 87,000 miles, an average of 2,000 miles per day, and that the total time spent in the air was 1,400 hours.

The net results of the fighting up to this time went to show that the operations on the Aisne could no longer be regarded as a battle in the general acceptance of the term. The fighting obviously approximated more nearly to that of the trenches before Sebastopol or the protracted engagements of Manchuria. The really serious point revealed by the fighting was that the enemy had received considerable reinforcements, and that it was rather he who attacked the Allies than the Allies who attacked him—that is to say the initiative was gradually passing into his hands. Even on the west flank, where General Joffre had proposed to make his principal effort, the Germans were successfully engaged in heading off the French attempts to envelop their right ; only on the east flank were the Germans failing to stop the French attacks pushed into Southern Alsace and the valleys of the Vosges.

The development of the action on the flanks

SENLIS.
A demolished portion of the business quarter.

had now brought the Allied positions to a line which ran from the extreme south of Alsace through St. Dié (in the Vosges), Lunéville (on the Meurthe), Point-a-Mousson (on the Moselle), Consenvoye (on the Meuse), Montfauçon, Grand Pré (in the Argonne), Souain, Fort de la Pompelle, a line west and south of Berru, Brimont and Craonne, Noyon, Lassigny, Roisel to Le Catelet ; while strong German forces were in possession of St. Quentin. The extension of the French flank to Péronne and towards St. Quentin was, of course, made by fresh troops. We now know that these had been brought up from the extreme right flank and that they were commanded by General de Castlenau.

On the left of the British contingent the 6th French Army had been heavily engaged during the past week. Reinforcements received by the Germans had enabled them to drive the French back, but the French declined to accept defeat, and, coming on again, recaptured their positions and even took a German Colour.

On **Tuesday, September 22,** the weather was fine and the wind had dropped. During the previous night British patrols discovered that

FRENCH MILITARY POSTMEN DELIVERING LETTERS.

the Germans had abandoned their advanced trenches, together with over 100 dead and wounded and a quantity of rifles, ammunition and equipment. The day was uneventful along most of the British front, but, as usual, the 1st Army Corps was given no rest. In front of the trenches throughout the British lines, but more particularly in front of those held by the 1st Army Corps, the bodies of the Germans killed in their repeated counter-attacks were lying in rows where they had fallen. Neither would the enemy remove them himself nor would he permit the British to do so. Some of the bodies had lain in this " No Man's Land " for several days, and each German attack as it swept across this deadly zone had added its quota of dead and wounded to those who already lay there.

A prolonged stalemate had now set in all along the British front, and the effort to attain a decision was transferred to other parts of the field, chiefly to the west flank.

No detailed accounts of the French operations are available, but the severity of the fighting may be guessed from the following letter which appeared in the Norwegian newspaper, *Oesterdaeles Avis*, and was published in the *Globe* of October 30 :

BERLIN : October 9 (Friday), 1914.
HERR EDITOR,—I had yesterday the opportunity of seeing a letter from a twenty-one year old " Jaeger " soldier who has been given the Iron Cross. With his mother's kind permission I have translated the letter. As it will certainly not be passed by the German Censor, I am sending it with a Swede who is returning to-morrow to Sweden.—Yours, etc.,

Then follows a translation of the German soldier's letter referred to :
Written on the battlefield of Nouvron,* September 22, 1914.
MY DEAR MOTHER,—I received yesterday your first letter, dated August 24. That is to say, nearly a month on the way. We are at present in the tenth day of battle with the Frenchmen, and have suffered frightful losses. Of my earlier 4th Company there were yesterday still 39 men remaining, and yet we were 250 men when we moved out. The dear God has always conducted me in the most wonderful manner unscathed through a rain of shell and bullets. To the right and left I saw my dear comrades fall, and I, as by a miracle, escaped. We will thank our dear God and beg Him also in the future graciously to aid us.
Our Army Corps, owing to its enormous losses and sickness—the result of the eternal rainy weather—is to be withdrawn from the fighting line. This will be splendid, because we shall then, possibly for some time, not have to fight. It is also inhuman what we have had to do and suffer. Last Sunday we made a storming attack on the French position. It was simply a blood bath. French as well as German corpses lay in heaps upon one another. Should I ever return, I shall always

---

* Nouvron is on the heights north of the Aisne five miles west of Soissons, opposite the centre of the 6th French Army.

TEAM OF HORSES KILLED BY A BURSTING SHELL.

remember for the rest of my life, and with terror, these days. Fancy ! Of our battalion there are only four officers left, and of 1,200 men only about 370 remaining. And yet we are only a reserve battalion, consisting entirely of married reservists and Landwehr, which should rather have been taken care of. How, then, must the active troops of the line have fared ?

What want and nameless misery must occur in such a frightful war. Would to God it were soon at an end.

Live well, dear mother. Until our next meeting. With hearty greetings.—Your faithful son,

FRITZ.

On **Wednesday, September 23,** there was a marked diminution in the enemy's efforts, which suggested that he had been obliged to withdraw forces from all along his line to cope with General Castlenau's enveloping operations on his west flank.

Sir John French had been so much impressed with the work of the enemy's heavy artillery during the earlier part of the campaign that he had asked for four 6-inch howitzer batteries to be sent out from home. These batteries arrived to-day and were equally divided between the 1st and 2nd Army Corps. These weapons are not very mobile and are, consequently, difficult to get away in a retreat or to bring up in a pursuit, especially when the enemy has broken down the bridges behind him, but they possess tremendous power and are indispensable in protracted operations of a more or less stationary character in which both sides are able to entrench themselves

heavily. The past ten days of wet and cold had been exceedingly trying to the troops, who had been obliged to fight day and night, drenched and shivering, in trenches deep in mud and water. The roads in all directions were quagmires, and it was really wonderful that the Army Service Corps should have been able to bring up everything that the Army required with certainty and in sufficient quantity.

On **Thursday, September 24,** the weather still remained fine, and the heavy guns which had arrived the day before were brought into action with excellent effect. The statements of prisoners taken during the last fortnight made it clear that the German soldiers had been systematically deluded by their officers. One prisoner said that when his battalion was mobilized the commanding officer informed them that they were going to cooperate with the English in repelling a French invasion of Belgium. They had all been seriously informed that Germany had achieved an unbroken series of successes by land and sea, and that the retreat of their own particular units had not extended to the rest of the army—it was part of a successful strategic movement. They were all quite convinced of the eventual triumph of German arms and simply could not envisage the possibility of final defeat. They were

BRITISH IN THE TRENCHES.

evidently sore and astonished at the prowess
of the British Army, which they had been
taught to believe was very inefficient in leading
and in quality, as well as in numbers. They
were particularly struck by the invisibility of
British troops, the accuracy of their shooting,
and the disconcerting manner in which they
appeared in positions from which it was thought
every living thing must long before have been
driven by the fearful deluge of shell fire poured
upon them.

The corpses which littered "No Man's
Land" between the British and Germans had
been lying there for many days and the smell in
the advanced trenches was almost unbearable,
but no sickness had as yet appeared among the
British troops. The latter took advantage
of the lull in the fighting to improve their
cover and to construct or improve underground
shelters in which men, after duty, could rest
in security from the enemy's fire. All the
steeper parts of the slopes in this part of the
terrain were honeycombed with caves cut out
of the soft sandstone, which in times of peace
had been the dwellings of a considerable
population. The soil on which the advanced
trenches were situated was a sticky white
clay, which, on being turned up, was very
visible from the front and from aircraft.
Therefore the trenches themselves, as well

as guns and all other objects within range of the
enemy's artillery, were assimilated to their surroundings by pine branches and facings of sods.

It is very hard for anybody, impossible for
most of us, to realise what life in the trenches
on the Aisne was like, and yet the effort must be
made if one is to appreciate at all what the
soldiery on both sides had to endure. Let the
reader imagine himself a soldier in one of the
British trenches near the Chemin des Dames
about this time. For days a gale has roared
through the forests of Compiègne and de
l'Aigle, tearing the yellow autumn leaves from
the trees and hurling them with sheets of cold
rain across the sodden downs, howling around
the chateaux and farmsteads, flooding the
trenches and drenching the soldiers in them.
The small hours of a September morning are
growing towards dawn ; the men in the trench
are lying on bundles of hay and straw, through
which the liquid mud has percolated into their
clothes. Every here and there along the
trench a worn-out sentry is straining his
hearing and his sight in the darkness to detect
the approach of the enemy. The men are got
under arms before the dawn comes. Gradually
the light grows, and presently a slight rustling
to the front falls upon the sentry's hearing.
"Halt, who goes there ? " he hisses. "Friend,"
comes a whisper from the front, and the private

signal, and out of the darkness crawls a figure, his " balaclava helmet," his shoulder straps and his khaki jacket decorated with turnip-tops, his clothes, his face, his hands, caked with whitish clay. Numbed and chattering with wet and cold, worn out, utterly exhausted with his long vigil among the turnips in front of the enemy's lines, he half stumbles, half slides into the trench. It is a sniper returned. He catches the officer's eye, and a feeble smile of good comradeship is exchanged. " What luck ? " says the officer. " Three, I think, sir," says he ; " two for certain. I think I killed one so dead he had no time to make any sound at all ; one of them moaned, so he was number one, and another cried : " Ach Gott, ach du lieber Gott " once or twice, so he was number two. But they nearly got me," he adds, as he points to the tip of his ear which has been flayed by a bullet. " Well, you had better turn in," says the officer, who marks the strained, white face and the red-rimmed eyes of the draggled figure, and, nothing loathe, the sniper moves off to his well-earned rest.

The daylight broadens. Suddenly a shot rings out from the front, and a sentry who has been looking through a " look-out " in the parapet staggers back and subsides in the bottom of the trench, shot through the face. A moment later is heard that peculiar singing, shrieking, wailing sound which announces the approach of a " Black Maria," and presently the huge shell lands just beyond the trench with a terrific thud, bursts with a truly appalling crash, shoots a fountain of mud and greasy black smoke into the air, and shakes the earth with a concussion like an earthquake. In a moment or two a second, and then a third arrives, one after the other and, from that on, through the rest of the day, there rages a deluge of these monstrous projectiles, each of which tears a crater out of the ground large enough to bury a motor-car. Presently one lands beside the trench, blows the edge of it in and buries three men alive. The nearest men crawl up with shovels and commence feverishly to exhume their comrades. Here a foot protrudes, there an arm and hand. Gradually the men are uncovered. The first is unhurt, the second is dazed, almost unconscious ; a third is simply a mangled mass of humanity. The earth around him is carefully cleared away. He is moaning slightly, with the blood oozing out of the corner of his mouth. The problem is how to move

PONTOON BRIDGE.   [*Central Press.*
This bridge was built in less than three hours to facilitate the pursuit of the Germans.
The wrecked permanent bridge is seen in the background.

BRITISH CAMP IN FRANCE.

him without causing him the most exquisite pain. He is just a khaki uniform full of smashed humanity. But why move him ? His case is obviously hopeless. In any case, he cannot be carried from the trench till nightfall, and by that time he will be beyond all help. Suddenly the shelling stops ; a sentry says, "Here they come, sir ; here they come " ; and out of the driving rain and mist, over the gently swelling rise in front, comes a German attack—mobs and mobs of men shouting as they come to encourage themselves and each other, and ever above all other sounds can be heard, " Vorwärts, vorwärts," from the officers. A whistle goes in the trench and the order rings out, " *Rapid fire,*" and immediately sheets of bullets fly from the trench into the packed mass in front. A machine gun on the flank opens with that metallic, jarring rat-rat-rat which is so startling to young soldiers. The mass in front reels like a fainting man. Men from behind rush up. The mass pulls itself together and comes on again. Once more it wavers under the terrible tempest of lead. More men rush up. The officers shout, " Vorwärts, vorwärts," and the mass comes on. Still the flood of shrapnel, rifle and machine-gun fire pours into it, and still it comes on. But 30 yards from the trench it has had enough. The mass breaks. Those who have survived the holocaust flee, panic-stricken, for the other side of the crest, and one more of the innumerable German attacks has been repulsed with terrible slaughter. The shelling recommences. Here and there a few brave German snipers from the crest fire into the trench as a target offers. Now and then bursts of shrapnel

fire sweep the trench, but the defenders are lying close, and only the sentries put their heads up occasionally to look through the protected "lookouts." And so the weary day wears away. The rain and the wind never stop ; the shelling only does so just before an attack, and recommences immediately it is repulsed. The ground in front of the trench is covered with dead and wounded men in grey. Most of the dead seem to have pitched on their faces with their heads towards the trench ; some of them seem to have fallen with their knees doubled under them. There are hundreds of wounded : some try to crawl away, others try to crawl towards the trench. Of those who are too badly hurt to move, some are silent, some moan, and some shriek aloud in agony. Many of the dead have been there for days, and the air is charged with the foetid odours of the charnel-house. Night comes, but not yet any respite from the dreadful shelling, nor any respite from the drenching rain and howling wind. The wounded are collected and carried away by stretcher parties. Food and water are brought up from the rear. The enemy's snipers crawl as near as they dare, and prevent any free movement in the neighbourhood of the trenches. It needs a great effort of the imagination to realize the mental and physical strain on these men, ceaselessly exposed to the rain and cold, incessantly shelled, constantly attacked, always outnumbered, their strength worn away with much watching and fighting, their nerves racked by the imminence of a dreadful death, by the unending difficulty of maintaining their positions (so necessary to the safety of the

whole army), by the constant loss of comrades
to whom death and wounds have come in such
dreadful forms, often known to have dear ones
and dependents at "home." But through all
these unspeakable trials they are upheld and
supported by the natural tenacity of their
race, perfected and fortified by military discipline and an unfailing confidence in themselves and their comrades, among whom, be it
noted, the officer is ever a very "guide,
philosopher, and friend."

And so night falls, the darkness deepens,
the shelling ceases. The wind still howls, and
out in the front the wounded moan and wait
for death—otherwise silence reigns and the
worn and weary soldiers huddle down on the
muddy straw. The hours pass. Anon a
sniper crawls back out of the night. "They
are coming," he says, in a tense whisper. The
slumbering men are shaken up. They stand
to arms dazed with sleep and weariness.
There is a period of electric silence broken only
by gusts of wind and driving rain. "Here
they are," runs the whisper through the ranks.
There is a blurred shadow in the darkness, a
deepening of the darkness rather than a
definite shape, but to experienced eyes it
reveals the oncoming of a German night-
attack. Each man experiences the thrill of
intense excitement. "Here they come," runs
down the ranks once more as the mass in front
looms more clearly into view, and the trampling
of many feet and the crackling of breaking
sticks and crumpling leaves falls upon the ear.
"Here they come," runs the whisper. "They
ain't 'arf coming, I don't think," says one man
quite loud, and, indeed, the obscurity in front
is one great, black, trampling mass of humanity.
"Run back, Smith, and warn the supports,"
says the officer, and then loud raps the order,
"Rapid Fire." A sheet of flame blazes along
the trenches, the mass in front staggers and
for one moment seems about to collapse; shouts,
moans, cries of anguish ring out, above all the
inexorable, "Vorwärts, Vorwärts," shouted
insistently, savagely. Some haystacks are
set on fire. They burn with upward flying
columns of smoke and sparks, lighting up the
scene of strife. Strong reinforcements join
the reeling mass and sweep it forward. On
it comes, its weight and momentum make it
irresistible. On it comes, shouting and yelling, trampling its hundreds of dead and dying
under foot. On it comes up to the trenches,

WAR CORRESPONDENTS NEAR THE FRONT.
French Officer examining papers on the road to the fighting line.

Out jumps the slender line of defenders and dashes at the mass with the bayonet. They are thrown down, dashed aside, swept away. The triumphant mob surges over the trenches and beyond them with indescribable tumult and turmoil. But its triumph is short lived— the British supports are upon it, a terrible fire strikes it, stops it, breaks it; and high above the racket of battle peals the terrible " hurrah " of the charging British, and a thousand bayonets glittering in the lurid light of burning haystacks sweeps the assailants back into the darkness from which they so lately burst. Quickly the defenders rally and move to their trenches, desperate efforts are made to hurry the wounded under cover ere the vengeful shelling comes to make impossible all movement in the neighbourhood of the trenches. And so once more to rest for a few hours. Long before dawn the men stand to arms. A rustling and shuffling of many feet behind the trenches betrays the approach of armed men, who file into the trenches. They take the places of the defenders, who are told to file out. They have been here for several days and nights. It seems to them as if they had been here always. Some of them are almost incoherent with their long vigil. All the storms of Nature and man have gone over their heads and now they are told to " file out "—they have been relieved. They shuffle away down the slopes. The light grows stronger. They are plastered with grey mud. Some of them seem to have wallowed in it. The men are mostly young, but their faces seem to have aged, they are pinched with weariness and watching and anxiety, and the eyes are tired and sleepless, but the lips are set and hard. They have been tried very high, higher than British officers, with all their experience of war, would have believed they could stand without breaking, but there is plenty of fight left in them still. Nevertheless, it is time they had a rest and they are on their way to the cave shelters in the steep slopes that overhang the meadows of the Aisne ; and after a sleep and a " wash and brush up " someone will produce a football and they will be running about and playing football as if there weren't any Germans, or any trenches, or any night-attacks on the Aisne. And if the

sufferings and gallantry of the British command our sympathy and our admiration, we may well spare some of these emotions for their Allies and their enemies. The Germans had skilfully chosen and carefully prepared positions, innumerable machine guns, and a monopoly of siege artillery ; but they were half-starved and driven like sheep to the slaughter. The French and the British were worse off in respect of positions and of heavy guns, but they were better fed. The British were also seriously outnumbered, but they were far better found and fed than either the French or the Germans. All through the battles on the Aisne the British artillery had been heavily outnumbered by the German guns and prevented by the ground from affording its infantry close support. The latter had, therefore, been exposed to a heavy artillery fire to which it could make no reply and from which it suffered severely. For this reason the British guns were obliged to devote their fire to keeping down that of the German guns. Thus the German infantry did not have to endure anything like the nerve-racking bombardment which fell to the lot of the British horse and foot, whose courage, intelligence, initiative and wonderful shooting made it possible for them to take up far more widely extended formations than were permissible according to German theory. This, and this alone, accounts for their comparatively small losses. It is obvious that if two trenches of equal length, the one held by 100 rifles and the other by 1,000 rifles, be subjected to bombardments of exactly equal severity the defenders of the latter trench will lose ten times as many men as the defenders of the former. The British suffered far less relative casualties than the Germans, but they had to endure the dreadful shelling by heavy artillery hour after hour and day after day, from which the Germans were practically immune. Indeed, had not the German officers persisted in their futile and foolish attacks their losses would have been very small and their moral unshaken. As it was they shattered their armies to pieces, and broke the moral of their choicest troops against the trenches of the Allies.

(To be continued.)

CHAPTER XXXIV.

THE BATTLES OF THE AISNE.

(*Continued.*)

A FORTNIGHT had passed since the British horsemen heading the pursuit from the Marne were brought to a halt on the banks of the Aisne.

On **Friday, September 25,** it was officially reported that the Germans had pushed along the " Promontory of Hattonchâtel " towards St. Mihiel and were bombarding the forts " des Paroches " and " Camp des Romains " ; and that a French detachment was hard put to it to maintain itself at Péronne.

On the Aisne for the last four days the weather had been fine and there had been comparatively little fighting ; such as there was resulted in little gain and no loss to the British. The enemy's attacks had been isolated and incoherent ; some, indeed, appeared to be indifferently led, and, therefore, to bear out the statements of prisoners as to the great losses in the German corps of officers.

The *moral* of the German Army may be gauged by the following extracts from a diary found on an officer of the 178th German Infantry Regiment published by the Press Bureau on October 17 :

August 9 : Near Gouvy, Belgium (N.E. of Houffalize), 7.30 a.m. We are still without any orders to move.

. . . One of the brigade staff officers came out in the evening and was astonished to find us still here. Our orders must have been lost on the road. . . .

August 15 : I had a look at the little château belonging to one of the King's secretaries (not at home). Our men had behaved like regular vandals. They had looted the cellar first, and then had turned their attention to the bedrooms, and thrown things about all over the place. They had even made fruitless efforts to smash the safe open. Everything was topsy-turvy. Magnificent furniture, silk, and even china. Things that happen when the men are allowed to requisition for themselves. . . . I am sure they must have taken away a heap of useless stuff simply for the pleasure of looting. . . .

August 18 : Late in the evening the train arrived (about fifty vehicles). They had come from Gouvy after doing 60 kilometres, probably the result of a mistake in reading an order. . . .

August 23 : . . . A spy was caught and shot. We marched to Lisogne, but after passing Dorinne the column went astray ; we had to return on our tracks. . . . Our men came back and said . . . we could not get on any further as the villagers were shooting at us from every house. We shot the whole lot, sixteen of them. They were drawn up in three ranks ; the same shot did for three at a time. Two 6-in. howitzers succeeded in getting into position, and in twenty shots reduced the village of Bouvines to ruins. The men were absolutely mad at this sneaking way of fighting. They wanted to burn everything, and they succeeded, too, in setting light to several houses. In the afternoon our artillery fairly sprinkled the principal buildings in the place the whole length of the village with incendiary shells. It was a marvellous sight, the high ground from Dinant to Leppe (?) overlooking the Meuse, all in flames. The division crossed the Meuse ; you never saw such disorder. . . .

BRITISH HEAVY ARTILLERY LEAVING A BASE TOWN.

August 26 : . . . we came to Villers-en-Pagne. The inhabitants had warned the French of the arrival of our troops by a signal from the church tower. The enemy's guns opened on us and killed and wounded quite a few. So in the evening we set fire to the village ; the priest and some of the inhabitants were shot. We passed through Pettigny and Couvin. Couvin had been partially looted. . . . The villages all round were burning. . . . The inhabitants fired on our men again. The division took drastic steps to stop the villages being burnt and the inhabitants shot. The pretty little village of Gué d'Ossus was apparently set on fire without cause. . . . At Leppe apparently 200 men were shot. There must have been some innocent men among them. . . .

August 29 : . . . The other side of Dommery we came on a wood where a hellish fire stopped us. . . . There was a panic ; everybody gave orders and nobody thought of telling us to lie down. . . . There was a shocking mess, shots in every direction. I wouldn't live through those moments again for worlds. At last the captain managed to get a few men together to form a firing line. We were being shot at by friend and foe. It was a grave error on the part of the Staff to start the regiment on a night march after three tiring days. After the fight the night before one might have foreseen that the enemy would take up a strong position and try to surprise us. It was dawn before we could resume our march. Suddenly firing began again. . . . We got on to some high ground about 1,000 metres from Launois, when our own artillery opened fire on us. Some shells burst only forty metres away from us ; it wasn't a bit nice. . . . Our machine-gun company suffered heavily from our own shells, unfortunately. Several officers were wounded. Suddenly we came up against the enemy's artillery, which was in a position on a flank. The men fell back. . . . The whole of Launois was in flames. We advanced again and by means of a very heavy fire forced the Zouave battalion to retire. Launois was the 178th's baptism of fire.

. . . We marched to Villers le Tourneur. The division bivouacked ; all the villages in the neighbourhood were blazing, as our artillery had set them on fire to protect us against attacks.

August 30 : . . . The fight began again. . .

September 3 : Still at Rethel, on guard over prisoners. The houses are charming inside. The middle class in France has magnificent furniture. We found stylish pieces everywhere, and beautiful silk, but in what a state ! . . . Good God ! . . . Every bit of furniture broken, mirrors smashed. The Vandals themselves could not have done more damage. This place is a disgrace to our army. . . . The column commanders are responsible for the greater part of the damage, as they could have prevented the looting and destruction. The damage amounts to millions of marks ; even the safes have been attacked. In a solicitor's house in which, as luck would have it, everything was in excellent taste including a collection of old lace and Eastern works of art, everything was smashed to bits. I couldn't resist taking a little memento myself here and there . . . a splendid aquascutum and a camera for Felix.

September 5 : Les Petites Loges, Tours-sur-Marne : I never want to make such marches again ; simply tests of endurance . . . absolutely exhausted, we waited for the night. In front of us all was still.

September 8 : We went forward again to the attack against an enemy perfectly entrenched. In spite of his artillery fire, which nothing could silence, we passed through the wood again. As soon as we reached the northern edge a perfectly insane fire opened on us, infantry and shell fire with redoubled intensity. We got to the village at last, but were driven out of it again with heavy loss. Our losses were enormous. The 178th Regiment alone had 1,700 men wounded, besides those killed. It was hell itself. There were practically no officers left. . . .

September 9 : We marched to Œuvry. The enemy was apparently two kilometres in front of us. Where was our intelligence branch ? Our artillery arrived half an hour too late, unfortunately. . . .

September 15 : We marched to Pont Givart, Ville-aux-Bois. After marching till we were all absolutely done and our feet knocked to bits, we were sent into the fight again. And they call us Reserve troops ! . . . After a murderous fight we entrenched at Ville-aux-Bois.

September 16 : We were attacked several times by the enemy, but each attack was broken by our machine-gun fire. Our last officer fell, shot through the head. . . .

September 18 : The air is absolutely poisoned. . . . Wounded men keep on coming in. In the evening the enemy made another attack, which was beaten off. . . .

September 22 : Troops of the 18th Corps passed all day. Apparently they are to come up on the right wing. Their infantry has lost as heavily as ours. God knows what the idea of this reinforcement is ! I am convinced that this country will give us all a grave. The 105th Regiment has had a furious fight with the English. . . .

On Saturday, September 26, the Germans in Belgium commenced operations against Antwerp by advancing upon Malines. It was officially announced that " the enemy has crossed the Meuse near St. Mihiel." Thus, laconically, was dismissed an event fraught with the gravest possibilities. It has been already remarked that in the Battle of the Marne the 4th and 5th German armies " had missions of special importance . . . . the former was commissioned to break the French battle-line . . . . the latter to pierce the Verdun-Toul fortress-barrier," and that the German Head-quarters had been obliged " to abandon *for the time* its designs on the French centre and fortresses." We have seen that on Thursday and Friday, September 18 and 19, the Germans had not been so very far off realizing the first of these propositions in the neighbourhood of Reims, and now we find that they had actually succeeded in the second of their plans to the extent of creating the opportunity ; but opportunity and success are not quite the same thing. Success postulates not only opportunity, but the ability to use it. Could they use it ? If the Germans could drive a considerable force through the gap they had broken in the line of French barrier-fortresses they would at least be able to compel the retreat of the French 3rd and 4th Armies, to invest and, in due course, to capture Verdun and all French troops north of St. Mihiel, and to open up new and far better communications with Germany. If at the same time the 5th (Crown Prince) Army could advance again in cooperation with the German columns pushing westward through St. Mihiel, the Germans might be able to meet in the neighbourhood of Revigny and cut off a considerable part of the French 3rd Army. In any case, the retreat of the French in this part of the field, after the recent successes, could scarcely fail to have a most unfavourable effect upon the Allies' *moral*

LEAVING FOR THE TRENCHES BY MOTOR OMNIBUS.

and prestige. At the same time, it was scarcely possible that the Germans could have concentrated in the Woevre a really considerable force, say, 150,000 men, without the knowledge of the French Commander-in-Chief, and therefore it may be assumed that the Germans would not be able to avail themselves of the opportunity they had created until the fortunes of war should once more give them a preponderance of force in the western theatre. Meanwhile, their move against the French fortress-barrier could have only one object, and that was to frighten the French Commander-in-Chief so much for Verdun and the forces in its neighbourhood that he would divert troops to this portion of the field and so slack off his efforts to envelop the German right. Had General Joffre allowed his will to be shaken by this apparently serious threat against his right flank, those vast masses which the Germans were preparing to hurl against the extreme left flank of the Allies would scarcely have failed to break down all opposition in this direction, and it is even conceivable that the Germans might have been able to resume their march on Paris. That the stroke against the fortress-barrier was really a feint was further suggested by the cunning allusions of the German Press to an advance in force from Lorraine.

SERVING OUT BREAD IN THE BRITISH LINES.

During the last four or five days there had been comparative quiet along the fronts on the Aisne. This was apparently due to the fact that the Germans were engaged in reorganizing and refitting their units which had suffered so heavily in the long series of unsuccessful attacks which they had delivered upon the British and 6th French Armies ; and in redistributing the units to meet the developments on the west flank. On the 26th, however, there was renewed activity along the British front. The heavy guns which had arrived from England silenced a German heavy battery which had been located just above Condé and had caused the British much annoyance for nearly a fortnight. At the same time the Germans were busy with a heavy bombardment, maintained steadily throughout the day, and accompanied by attempts to "sap" up to the advanced trenches of the 1st Division. A series of attacks were delivered by the Germans at 8 a.m. and again in the afternoon with the usual result. "The Germans came on in a T-shaped formation, several lines shoulder to shoulder followed almost immediately by a column in support. After a very few minutes

the men had closed up into a mob, which afforded an excellent target for our fire". (Eyewitness.) Later in the afternoon it became apparent that the German efforts to re-establish themselves closer to the British advanced trenches must be checked, and, therefore, the 1st Division delivered a sudden and timely attack which drove them back and stopped their approach operations.

The attacks delivered by the Germans on Saturday the 26th had apparently served to satisfy them as to the dispositions of the Allies in their front, and they utilized the following day to perfect their arrangements for the operations they had in view, and thus it happened that Sunday was one of the most peaceful days known during the past fortnight ; but from nightfall on Sunday, September 27, to nightfall on Monday, September 28, the Germans made a series of most vigorous and most determined attempts along almost the whole line of the Allies.* These desperate attacks succeeded one another like waves of the

* It is difficult to reconcile the following extract from " Eyewitness " report with Sir John French's report (quoted on next page) which is supported by the French

sea which break, recoil and rush on again with greater vigour than ever. "It is certain," says Sir John French, "that the enemy then made one last great effort to establish ascendancy. He was, however, unsuccessful everywhere." It is, perhaps, true to say that his most serious efforts were reserved for the trenches of the 1st Division. The ground in front of these trenches was alive with wave after wave of oncoming Germans. "The same futile attempts," says Sir John French, "were made all along our front up to the evening of the 28th, when they died away, and have not since been renewed."

Along the whole line from the Somme to the Meuse these German efforts persisted with an energy and a desperation which are as astonishing as their costliness. They clearly indicate action on a concerted plan dictated from the German Headquarters Staff, and the Germans fell back at last broken and exhausted after their incredible efforts. They even evacuated some of their natural fortresses among the quarries which had hitherto been impregnable. Rumour has it indeed that they abandoned these positions, not so much under stress of French attacks, as owing to the noisome odour emanating from their own unburied dead. The condition of these quarries when the French came to occupy them was absolutely indescribable, but was only one degree worse than those of many German trenches which have fallen into the hands of the Allies before and since.

The German efforts opposite Reims reached their climax on Monday, the 28th, when the intensity of their bombardment surpassed anything that had hitherto been experienced. The town was set on fire in many places; blocks of buildings were completely demolished and many of the inhabitants were killed. From every part of the line came the same story of attack and counter-attack, of desperate bayonet fighting and of terrific losses, in which the Allies had by no means escaped scatheless. Five weeks' fighting shows a loss of over 1,200 officers killed, wounded and missing in the British Expeditionary Force, to which must be added a certain number of sick. These figures go to show that during this time the

Official *communiqués* and reports from many private sources:

"Monday, the 28th, there was nothing more severe than bombardment and intermittent sniping, and this inactivity continued during Tuesday, the 29th, except for a night attack against our extreme right."

casualties among officers in the first five Divisions amounted to nearly fifty per cent. of those who originally took the field. All that can be said is that the German casualties must have greatly exceeded those of the French and British.

The number of lives that the Germans have squandered in their attacks, most of them purely local attacks, is incredible and cannot but have had an unfavourable effect upon the *moral* of their troops. That this was so is suggested by the fact that when the Allies made their counter-efforts towards the close of the 28th, the Germans were found to have withdrawn for three or four miles in many places. Perhaps the most notable gain of the Allies was the position of La Neuvillette, a couple of miles north-north-west of Reims. The Germans had managed to establish themselves here, whence they threatened to pierce the French line, but a well-timed counter-attack on the evening of the 28th, in which British troops cooperated with great effect, stormed the German position in the face of a murderous fire. In another part of the field the Germans were so shaken that a squadron

DEVASTATING EFFECT OF A GERMAN SHELL.

18—2

MEMBER OF THE RED CROSS TENDING THE WOUNDED ON THE BATTLEFIELD.

of Cuirassiers are reported to have captured the wreck of a battalion of the 3rd Prussian Guard Regiment, of whom the survivors numbered a captain, two lieutenants and 136 rank and file.

From **Tuesday, September 29,** to **Saturday, October 3,** comparative calm prevailed along the British front. The weather, though fine and considerably warmer, was misty and therefore unfavourable for aerial reconnaissance. On the other hand, bright moonlight militated against night attacks. On Tuesday it was officially reported that the Allies' line ran from the plateaux between Albert and Combles, past Chaulnes (held by the Germans), Ribecourt (held by the French), the Forêt de l'Aigle, Soissons, Troyon, the road to Berry-au-Bac and thence to Reims, along the Roman road, to a point north of Souain, Varennes, along the heights of the Meuse (east of the Meuse), to St. Mihiel (held by the Germans), and Pont-a-Mousson (held by the French).

The British were now securely entrenched and were able to regard frontal attacks even by night with perfect equanimity. These night attacks were invariably preceded by an artillery bombardment commenced during

daylight and continued, sometimes, into the darkness. The actual attacks had usually been made from the reverse sides of the hills and presented as they came over the crests a blurred silhouette against the starlight sky behind. They were always allowed to come within a hundred yards or so, when they were decimated by rifle fire from in front and cut down by the scythe-like fire of machine guns from the flanks.

The relief of the men in the British trenches had now been carefully arranged. The sections which were relieved were sent back to places more or less protected from the unceasing flood of projectiles from the German positions.

On **Sunday, October 4,** a military band began to play patriotic airs in one part of the German lines and a number of men collected to enjoy the music, but a few lyddite shells from the British howitzers presently pitched among the assembled soldiery and caused a rapid dispersion of the audience. Later in the day the French and British carried out a successful combined attack upon the German trenches north of Soissons. For some days beforehand they had been gradually working up to the enemy's trenches until they had managed to establish themselves within 200 yards of them. Across this narrow strip a tempest of rifle and machine-gun fire raged all day and practically all night for 48 hours. Attempts on either side to cross the intervening space were unavailing, and it was found necessary to leave the wounded where they lay. At last, on the morning of the 4th, under cover of the misty weather which had lately prevailed, a tremendous rush carried the British and French into and over the German trenches, and thus ended one of the most fiercely contested series of trench fighting in the history of the war.

On **Monday, October 5,** the Germans were thrice repulsed in their attempts to cross the Nèthe near Antwerp, and the British Naval Brigade arrived at that city ; but the place was evacuated by the Allies and occupied by the Germans on the 9th. On Monday an aeroplane duel between German and French airmen was visible from the British trenches. After considerable manœuvring and an interchange of machine-gun fire the German observer and

pilot were killed and their machine brought to earth.

From **Tuesday, October 6,** to **Thursday, October 8,** there was comparative quiet along the British front. On Tuesday afternoon the German guns broke into activity, apparently as a reprisal for the British howitzer fire, which had dropped two high-explosive shells in the enemy's trenches and had killed a number of men. The Germans attempted to sap up to the British lines at one or two points with the idea of gaining points from which their machine guns could bring a cross-fire to bear on the space between their trenches and those of the British, and also to enfilade the latter. These machine guns are mounted on low sledges instead of wheels, which makes them less conspicuous. One of these guns had long been a thorn in the flesh of a French corps recruited mainly from miners, who proceeded to drive a gallery under the gun and blow it up. The British were now suffering very little loss. Firstly because they were well entrenched and had a number of subterranean

[*By permission of "The War Illustrated,"*

A GERMAN SHELL ABOUT TO BURST.

Men and horses alike realise the danger of their position.

shelters,* and secondly because the German bombardment had decreased very considerably in intensity and was now either confined to firing as a target offered or to suddenly dropping

a number of heavy shells on localities which appeared likely to be occupied by Staffs, or resting troops, or transport.

Some of their guns were undoubtedly detailed

* "Eyewitness " writes :

Considerable ingenuity has been exercised in naming the shelters. Amongst other favourites are "the Hotel Cecil," "the Ritz," "Hotel Billet-doux," "Hotel rue Dormir," etc. On the road barricades, also, are to be found boards bearing the notice, "This way to the Prussians." Obstacles of every kind abound, and at night each side can hear the enemy driving in pickets for entanglements, digging trous-de-loup, or working forward by sapping. In some places the obstacles constructed by both sides are so close together that some wag has suggested that each should provide working parties to perform this fatiguing duty alternately, since their work is now almost indistinguishable and serves the same purpose.

And through this pandemonium the inhabitants go about their business as if they had lived within the sound of guns all their lives. A shell bursts in one street. In the next not a soul pays any attention or thinks of turning the corner to see what damage has been done. Those going to the trenches are warned to hurry across some point which the enemy have been shelling and which has already proved a death-trap for others. After running across it some mortification may be felt at the sight of an old woman pulling turnips in the very line of fire. Along certain stretches of road which are obviously "unhealthy" the children continue to play in the gutter, or the old folks pass slowly trundling wheelbarrows. It may be fatalism, for not all these people can be deaf, nor can all be so stupid as not to realize how close they are to death.

It has already been mentioned that, according to information obtained from the enemy, fifteen Germans were killed by a bomb dropped upon an ammunition wagon of a cavalry column. It was thought at the time that this might have been the work of one of our airmen, who reported that he had dropped a hand-grenade on a convoy and had then got a bird's-eye view of the finest firework display that he had ever seen. From the corroborative evidence of locality, it now

appears that this was the case, and that the grenade thrown by him must probably have been the cause of the destruction of a small convoy carrying field gun and howitzer ammunition, which has now been found, a total wreck, on a road passing through the Forêt de Retz, north-east of Villers Cotterets.

Along the road lie fourteen motor-lorries, which are no more than skeletons of twisted iron, bolts, and odd fragments. Everything inflammable on the wagons has been burnt, as have the stripped trees—some with trunks split—on either side of the road. Of the drivers nothing now remains except some tattered boots and charred scraps of clothing, while the ground within a radius of fifty yards of the wagons is littered with pieces of iron, the split brass cases of cartridges which have exploded, and some fixed gun ammunition, with live shell, which has not done so.

It is possible to reconstruct the incident, if it was, in fact, brought about as supposed.

The grenade must have detonated on the leading lorry on one side of the road and caused the cartridges carried by it to explode. The three vehicles immediately in rear must then have been set on fire, with a similar result. Behind these are groups of four and two vehicles, so jammed together as to suggest that they must have collided in a desperate attempt to stop.

On the other side of the road, almost level with the leading wagon, are four more, which were probably fired by the explosion of the first. If this appalling destruction was due to one hand grenade, and there is a considerable amount of presumptive evidence to show that this was the case, it is an illustration of the potentialities of a small amount of high explosive detonated in the right spot ; whilst the nature of the place where it occurred—a narrow forest road, between high trees— is a testimony to the skill of the airman.

It is only fair to add that some of the French newspapers claim that this damage to the enemy was caused by the action of some of their Dragoons.

GERMAN SHELTERS ON THE AISNE.

ROYAL FIELD ARTILLERY FROM INDIA AT THE FRONT.

to watch particular roads. The fire of their artillery was wonderfully accurate and they were very quick in picking up a target, but they had comparatively little success against the carefully-entrenched British. Things were far otherwise at the outbreak of the war, before the British aircraft had been able to take the field. At that time cooperation between the German aeroplanes and their guns gave the latter an enormous superiority over their British rivals. Even now, of course, the German airmen gave their artillery a great deal of assistance by dropping smoke balls or strips of glittering tinsel directly over any suitable targets they might discover. ⁴In addition to the annoyance and losses caused by their artillery, the Germans employed snipers with good effect. That, however, was a line in which the British were by no means behind them.*

---

* An officer at the front writes :

I organized a stout band of five to ten volunteers who used to creep out at dawn down a belt of wood and snipe the blighters whenever they showed themselves, and they used to stay out till dark. In this way they shot eight to twelve Sausages and effectually damped their zeal to snipe us. Our fellows were perfectly splendid—one chap coolly crept up to the enemy's trench and collared the helmet, fur knapsack, and forty-five rounds of ammunition, besides a pair of French patent leather boots (evidently looted) belonging to a German who was asleep in the trench. I wish I could have seen his puzzled face when he awoke and found them gone. . . .

From **Friday, October 9,** to **Tuesday, October 13,** there was again calm along the British front. There was the usual sporadic shelling, resulting in little damage to the British, and on the night of the 10th there was the night attack, which had lately become as rare as it had formerly been common, but the result was that which it had always been.

On **Wednesday, October 14,** the British 7th Division, which had covered the withdrawal of the Allied troops from Antwerp, occupied Ypres.

The operations of the Aisne had now degenerated into an absolute impasse. Nearly a month ago it was the Allies who were the assailants, and it was right to speak of any offensive movements executed by the Germans as counter-attacks, but in the course of a few weeks the Germans first definitely stopped the advance of the Allies and then gradually became rather the assailants of the Allies' positions than the defenders of their own, and it becomes right to speak of German attacks and the Allies' counter-attacks. In the meantime the efforts of the French to out-flank the German west wing had resulted in extending the fighting from the neighbourhood of Lassigny towards Lille. The Germans had at first been hard put to it to head off these efforts, but after a time it was the outflankers rather than the Germans who were in danger

TRENCH ABANDONED BY THE
GERMANS.

of being outflanked. In fact, it only needed
the arrival of those vast numbers of untrained
men, to whom reference has already been
made, to place the initiative very definitely
in the hands of the Germans. The British,
who had started the campaign on the
extreme left of the Allies' line, now found
themselves somewhere about its centre. Their
lines of communication ran back through
Paris to the Biscay coast and, of course,
crossed those of all the French armies on their
left, which was highly inconvenient to both
parties. It is obvious that if the British were
to resume their original place on the left of
the line—which would now be somewhere
immediately east of Dunkirk, Calais and
Boulogne—they would enormously shorten
their lines of communication by transferring
their bases to those ports and to Le Havre,
and would obviate the inconvenient crossing
of communications. Moreover, they had a
particular interest in preventing the ports of
Northern France from falling into the hands of
the Germans, who would assuredly use them
as bases for submarine raids on enemy shipping
in " the narrow seas." And thus it came about
that the British Army on the Aisne was gradually replaced section by section, night after

night, by French troops and railed and marched
to their new scene of activity. The operation
commenced on October 3, when the 2nd Cavalry
Division left for the new theatre.

The relief of the British was a wonderful
piece of Staff work. French troops appeared
out of the darkness and took up the British
positions trench by trench and section by
section night after night. " They had
marched," says an officer, " many miles, but
were quite cheerful and calm, their only desire
seemed to be to get into our ' dug-outs ' and
go to sleep. They cared nothing for the
expected pressure of the enemy." Another
officer says : " No sooner were the French
installed in our places than their look-out
sentries lay down full length on the top of
the parapet. We warned them that this
was a most ' unhealthy ' proceeding, but they
quite cheerfully replied that they liked doing
it that way, with the result that one of them
was shot before we left."

Some, if not all, of the British units were
moved through Paris, but without having an
opportunity for tasting its joys. The troops
were detrained at St. Omer and other places
not far from the English Channel, and once
more had the pleasure of doing a little shopping,
buying bread, cakes and chocolate, and laugh-
ing and chaffing with the cheery French people
of the district.

The question arises, what was the outcome
of the fighting of the past month ? The
general strategical results were important
if not very obvious. Early in October the
Russian Press gave some details as to the
identity of the German Army Corps operating
in the eastern theatre. They claimed that the
German Army defeated on the Niemen was
found to comprise portions of the following
Corps : at Augustowo, 1st, 5th and 17th
Corps ; at Suwalki, 1st, 2nd, 6th, 7th and 8th
Corps ; at Mariampol, 1st, 17th and 20th
Corps ; in Galicia and Western Poland, 3rd,
11th, 12th, 18th, 21st and two Bavarian Corps,
According to this statement there remained
in France only 10 of Germany's 25 1st Line
Corps, but there was obviously confusion
between the " Active " and " Reserve " Corps,
since there were 20, if not 21, German First
Line Corps* in the western theatre as late as
Sunday, November 22. From this we may

* Viz., Guard, 2nd, 3rd, 4th, 5th, 6th, 7th, 8th, 9th,
10th, 12th, 13th, 14th, 15th, 16th, 18th, 19th, 21st, and
the 1st and 2nd Bavarian Corps, perhaps also the 3rd.

conclude that *some* of the First Line Corps had been brought back from the eastern to the western front at the end of September, which goes to show that, though the fighting of the past month had apparently been inconclusive, it had induced the Germans to once more rely on Second Line troops wherewith to check the Russian landslide. The work of the Allies in France was, therefore, of far greater importance to the common cause than is apparent on the surface. Before the war it was estimated that the French would be able to mobilize 80 to 100 Divisions of field troops. Large numbers of untrained men had been called up in France as well as in Germany, and masses of recruits were being hurriedly put together for service in the field. But there was this great difference—the Germans would have to use their new formations earlier and in a less efficient condition than the French, and would have to divide them between the two fronts. Consequently the French new formations would be more numerous than those which the Germans could allot to the western theatre, and General Joffre could wait till his new levies had matured a little, not only as individual fighting men, but as collective fighting masses. From which it followed that these new French formations, together with those others which were gradually growing in numbers and in

efficiency in England, would ultimately give the Allies in the west that numerical preponderance from which alone decisive results might be anticipated.

Even more important are the moral results. These, again, have resulted from the tactical collisions of the belligerents. Eyewitness says :

The following description was given by a Battalion Commander, who has been at the front since the commencement of hostilities, and had fought both in the open and behind entrenchments. It must, however, be borne in mind that it only represents the experiences of a particular unit. It deals with the tactics of the enemy's infantry :

"The important points to watch are the heads of valleys, the ravines, woods—especially those on the side of hollow ground—and all dead ground to the front and flanks. The German officers are skilled in leading troops forward under cover, in closed bodies, but once the latter are deployed and there is no longer direct personal leadership the men will not face heavy fire. Sometimes the advance is made in a series of lines, with the men well opened out at five or six paces interval ; at other times it is made in a line, with the men almost shoulder to shoulder, followed in all cases by supports in close formation. The latter either waver when the front line is checked, or crowd on to it, moving forward under the orders of their officers, and the mass forms a magnificent target. Prisoners have described the fire of our troops as pinning them to the ground, and this is certainly borne out by their action. When the Germans are not heavily entrenched, no great losses are incurred in advancing against them by the methods in which the British Army has been instructed. For instance, in one attack over fairly open ground against about an equal force of infantry sheltered in a sunken road and in ditches, we lost only ten killed and sixty wounded ; while over 400 of the enemy surrendered after about fifty had been killed. Each side had the

FRENCH INFANTRY BRING UP REINFORCEMENTS OF FOOD AND AMMUNITION.

support of a battery, but the fight for superiority from infantry fire took place at about 700 yards and lasted only half an hour. When the Germans were wavering some of them put up the white flag ; but others went on firing, and our men continued to do the same. Eventually a large number of white flags, improvised from handkerchiefs, pieces of shirt, white biscuit bags, &c., were exhibited all along the line ; and many men hoisted their helmets on their rifles.

" In the fighting behind entrenchments the Germans endeavour to gain ground by making advances in line at dusk or just before dawn, and then digging themselves in, in the hope, no doubt, that they may eventually get so near as to be able, as at manœuvres, to reach the hostile trenches in a single rush. They have never succeeded in doing this against us. If by creeping up in dead ground they do succeed in gaining ground by night they are easily driven back by fire in the morning. A few of the braver men sometimes remain behind, at ranges of even 300 or 400 yards, and endeavour to inflict losses by sniping. Sharpshooters, also, are often noticed in trees or wriggling about until they get good cover. The remedy is to take the initiative, and detail men to deal with the enemy's sharpshooters.

" A few night attacks have been made against us. Before one of them a party crept up close to the British line and set alight a hayrick, so that it should form a beacon on which the centre of the attacking line marched. Generally, however, in the night and early morning attacks groups of 40 or 50 men have come on, the groups sometimes widely separated one from another and making every endeavour to obtain any advantage from cover. Light-balls and searchlights have on some occasions been used.

" Latterly the attacks have become more and more half-hearted. Against us the enemy has never closed with the bayonet. The German trenches I have seen were deep enough to shelter a man when firing standing, and had a step down in rear for the supports to sit in. As regards our own men, there was at first considerable

reluctance to entrench, as has always been the case at the commencement of a war. Now, however, having bought experience dearly, their defences are such that they can defy the German artillery fire."*

It seems to be a cardinal point in German theory that the bombardment with which they prepare all their attacks must shatter the nerve of any troops and render them an easy prey to the masses with which they expected to overwhelm all resistance. As examples of blind obedience these German attacks were wonderful, but such discipline seems to be instilled by severity and fear. It has its admirers in many countries, but it is not calculated to appeal to men of the free Anglo-Saxon races. It inspired the legion of Pembe and the impi of Tchaka to sweep like a tropical tornado over every obstacle, but it has broken again and again against the steady front and deadly fire of British battalions.

---

* The following criticism of the German Army appears in a letter from an officer who has had ample experience of it in the past six weeks : " As regards the German Army itself, except for its overwhelming numbers and the undoubted skill of the General Staff, it is no match for our own : on each and every occasion we have met them we have outmarched, outmanœuvred and outfought them. Their artillery is very good, but . . . . their shrapnel does extraordinarily little damage, except against troops in masses, and their H.E. shells none, unless they drop within 20 yards of anyone. I *know* because I have been under fire of each."

SOISSONS.

In the centre of the picture is seen smoke from exploding German shrapnel, and along the back smoke from the French Artillery.

MEN OF THE 1st CAVALRY DIVISION CROSSING THE PONTOON BRIDGE
AT BOURG UNDER TERRIFIC FIRE.
(See page 127.)

The Germans achieved absolutely nothing, in spite of an incredible expenditure of energy and human life. In no direction did they succeed in driving back the British, because they overrated the effect of their artillery fire and underrated the rifle fire of the British infantry. Their devastating bombardments and whirlwind mass-attacks did not demoralize the grandsons of those whose steadfast valour on the field of Waterloo broke every onset of the veteran cavalry and infantry of the finest army France has ever placed in the field. From prisoners' statements it is clear they found it difficult to believe that the concentrated fire of high-explosive shells, with which they had deluged the British trenches, should really have failed to shatter the *moral* of their defenders.

The German practice in the attack was the very antithesis of all that British soldiers had been taught on the subject. It was an article of faith with them that the modern magazine rifle in the hands of good and unshaken infantry had made absolutely impossible the movement of troops in close order over open ground within effective range. They knew that even " Brown Bess " in the hands of their grandsires had never failed to shatter the columns of Napoleon's veteran infantry, and yet at Mons, at Le Cateau, on the Marne,

RED CROSS OFFICERS HAVING A MEAL IN A DUG-OUT.

and here on the Aisne, the Germans came at them in mobs so dense that the ground itself and everything on it was blotted out by a mass of moving humanity slipping towards them like a landslide. That anyone should attempt the thing seemed the height of folly, but to persist in such folly in the face of punishment so bloody and so oft-repeated seemed mere midsummer madness. Again and again these attacks were literally " wiped out " by " rapid " fire. This " practice " had been so assiduously cultivated in peace that the British infantry-man or cavalryman could fire 15 rounds per minute at disappearing targets and make a high percentage of hits without bringing the rifle down from the shoulder. A German mass which found itself in the open and within 600 yards of British infantry was assured of two things, firstly, that it would have dis-charged at it at least 10 rounds per rifle per minute, and, secondly, that the number of hits registered upon such a favourable target as it presented would be considerably in excess of anything ever attained by British troops against the much more difficult vanishing targets of peace practice. It is no exaggera-tion to add that these two things spelt simple annihilation After the first week or ten days on the Aisne it was found that German troops which had faced the British fire a few times

had begun to lose that resolution which is essential to a successful assault. They obvi-ously wavered. That this was so is not at all surprising ; it is only wonderful that they could be got to come on at all. Not till the British encountered new opponents, and particularly the newly raised levies, in Flanders did they again meet an enemy who came at them with the " will to conquer."

The general result of the fighting was that the Germans commenced the operations of mid-Septembe along two lines which met north of Verdun to form a right angle and faced *inwards,* so that all movements behind the line had much further to go than similar movements behind the Allies' lines which faced *outwards* By the end of a month the Germans had managed to reduce operations along their original fronts to a stalemate and to add a new face to their line, which now reversed the situation, as far as it concerned movements behind the fighting fronts. More important still was the recovery of the initiative. One of the chief objects of strategy is to main-tain the initiative, or to regain it if it has been lost, and it must be frankly confessed that it was the Germans who had regained and the Allies who had lost, the initiative. But the advantage was rather apparent than real. The great object which the Allies had always set before themselves was to check the German advance, in order both to wear them down and to gain the time in which they, and especially the Russians, might develop their strength, and in which sea-power might do its slow but deadly work. The Allies in France did not possess sufficient strength to achieve any very decisive results, nor could they hope to push the Germans back very far for the present. It was, therefore, not a matter of very great moment to them whether the Germans were pushed back a little or not. It was really more important to avoid serious defeat than to gain the indecisive victory which was all they could hope for at present. Meanwhile, hundreds of thousands of fresh troops were maturing in every part of the British Empire, the grey legions of the Czar were tramping up in millions from the vasty deeps of Russian and Siberian steppes, and the inexorable pressure of sea-power was gradually choking the life out of the nations of the Duplice. Moreover, the gain of the initiative had cost the Germans very dear in three commodities which they could by no means afford to squander—men, matériel and money. In all three directions the resources of the

Entente Powers were far superior to those of the Central Powers. The German losses in human life were the more serious, inasmuch as they had no reserve of trained men. At the end of the Great Retreat the British losses were officially reported at something over 15,000 men, and it was distinctly stated that these were not a third of the losses inflicted upon the enemy. When we consider that the British losses included between 8,000 and 9,000 prisoners, many of them unwounded, it is obvious that the enemy's losses in killed and wounded were a good deal more than three times the British losses in these categories. Arguing by analogy and remembering that the British on the Aisne suffered none of those losses in wounded or physically exhausted men who fall into an enemy's hands in a retreat, we may confidently reckon that the 13,541 lost by the British on the Aisne in killed, wounded and missing are scarcely a quarter of those lost by the Germans along the same front and at the same time. Curiously enough, this estimate agrees closely with that given by a Staff Correspondent of the *New York World*, who says : " As the Germans were usually the

GERMAN CAVALRY.

GERMANS ERECTING AN IRON BRIDGE IN PLACE OF THE ONE IN THE
BACKGROUND, WHICH WAS DESTROYED.

aggressors their losses must have been between
40,000 and 50,000 and may have been more."
By the time the British came to move from the
Aisne their total losses amounted to less than
33,000 men killed, wounded and captured, but,
in seven weeks, they had put out of action at
least 100,000 Germans, which is a larger number of combatants than the British had ever
had in the field to date.   There can be no doubt
whatever that the German losses, particularly
in officers, had been relatively greater than
those of the French and much greater than those
of the British. They had usually been the
assailants ; they had always been prodigal of
life ; they were unable to replace the wastage of war by trained men, and the vast
losses among German officers obviously told
upon the leading and handling of their
troops. Moreover, the German corps of officers
is mainly recruited from a distinct class of
limited numbers, whereas the French system
has always been to draw something like two-
thirds of their regimental officers from the
ranks, and they therefore have a much larger

reserve to draw upon.   The fact is that the
victory of the Marne was one of those which,
like Gravelotte, results in driving the vanquished
into a fortress.   Subsequent operations are
directed to rivetting the ring of steel more
tightly round the discomfited hosts   Once that
is effected the fate of the interned army is
sealed. Its only hope of escape lies in relief
from *outside*. The victory of the Marne was
decisive because the fighting of the next two
months saw the lines of circumvallation completed round the Powers of the Duplice.
Henceforward their only hope of relief lay in
finding a neutral Power, or group of Powers,
able and willing to raise the siege. No victory
over Russia could save Germany, for Russia
could retreat to the Pacific without exposing
any really vital point and Germany would not
have the strength to follow far. The victory of
the Marne stayed the tide of Teutonic invasion
—the Aisne and Flanders confirmed the
decision. The Allies set out to gain time, to wear
down, to exhaust. in a word to *besiege* the enemy,
and in this they were distinctly successful.

CHAPTER XXXV.

MILITARY AERONAUTICS AND THE BRITISH AIR SERVICE.

NAVIGATION OF THE AIR—AEROPLANE AND AIRSHIP—EARLY BALLOONS—THE "ZEPPELIN"—EVOLUTION OF THE AEROPLANE—SIR GEORGE CAYLEY—CONQUEST OF THE AIR BY THE BROTHERS WRIGHT—NOTABLE EARLY FLIGHTS—THE FRENCH LEAD AND THE PICARDY MANŒUVRES, 1910—THE REIMS MEETING, 1911—FIRST USE OF AEROPLANES IN WAR—THE BRITISH AIR SERVICE—ORIGIN OF MILITARY AERONAUTICS—THE BALLOON SCHOOL AT CHATHAM—THE *NULLI SECUNDUS*—ADVISORY COMMITTEE FOR AERONAUTICS—THE AIR BATTALION—THE ROYAL FLYING CORPS—THE CENTRAL FLYING SCHOOL—THE MILITARY WING, ITS GROWTH AND EXPANSION—ROYAL NAVAL AIR SERVICE—SEAPLANES—NEW ·BRITISH AIRSHIPS AND SHEDS—AEROPLANE EQUIPMENT.

THE great war, unexampled for its magnitude and unprecedented in many of its aspects, will be ever memorable among other things for this, that in it for the first time the recently acquired art of navigating the air was systematically employed by all the principal combatants for purposes of both attack and defence. Military aeronautics had become a new and formidable arm. Its rise had been almost startling in its suddenness. When hostilities began it was little more than ten years and a half since the brothers Wilbur and Orville Wright, in a secluded spot among the sand dunes of North Carolina, had for the first time in the history of man achieved sustained flight against the wind on a power-driven machine rising from the level ground ; it was not quite six years since the elder of these two brothers had given his first public demonstration in France, when, on August 8, 1908, at a race-course near Le Mans, he astonished the world by flying a distance of a mile and a quarter in 1 min. 47 seconds. From that momentous gathering may be dated public recognition of the fact that the air had been "conquered" by man, who was thenceforward free to navigate it at his pleasure, subject to ever-diminishing restrictions, in machines heavier than the medium in which they moved. For these machines the name "aeroplane" was forthwith invented.

But the aeroplane is not the only device by which the air is navigated, and which has been turned in recent years to military account. The airship, or dirigible balloon, inflated with hydrogen so that it rises in the air with a lifting power that can sustain considerable weights, belongs to a wholly different category, and was evolved by a different process of experiment, from an origin that was quite distinct. But these two independent types of aircraft— the heavier than air and the lighter than air— became almost simultaneously available for purposes of war. This was no mere accidental coincidence, but was due mainly to the same cause, the invention and development in connexion with the motor-car of the petrol-driven engine, which combined very high power with remarkably light weight. For the

(Drawn in Germany by Joseph Pennell.

ZEPPELIN LEAVING SHED.

dirigible balloon this combination of qualities was of the utmost importance ; for the aeroplane it was a fundamental necessity.

This is not the place to describe in any detail the steps by which either the airship or the aeroplane has reached its present excellence, but one or two salient facts relating to their development may enable readers unfamiliar with the subject to understand more clearly the position of affairs when the war broke out. Let us take the airship first. The main outlines of its history can be covered in a few sentences. In 1782 the two brothers Montgolfier discovered—half accidentally, it would seem—by experiment at Avignon that a bag of silk when filled with heated air would rise from the ground ; and, proceeding along the line of this discovery, they constructed a large oval balloon, with an open neck at the lower extremity, in the centre of which a brazier was fitted, and round the outer circumference of which ran a wicker gallery whence fuel could be supplied to the brazier. In this balloon a certain M. Pilatre de Rozier made a public ascent in October, 1783. The balloon was then captive ; but the same adventurer made a short free voyage in the following month. Meanwhile experiments with hydrogen had placed at the disposal of balloonists a gas very much lighter than hot air, and in December, 1783, a voyage of over 20 miles was made from Paris in a free balloon inflated with hydrogen. The first successful attempt to propel through the air a hydrogen balloon of elongated shape was made in 1852 by Henri Giffard, who used a light steam engine to turn the propellers, but the speed obtained was unsatisfactory. Electric motors were applied in the 'eighties of the last century with somewhat better results, but nothing really practicable was produced until a German officer, Count Ferdinand von Zeppelin, appeared upon the scene with methods of his own. This remarkable man began in 1897 the construction of an immense airship, designed with great care and forethought to carry a crew of five men. It was to be driven through the air by two 16 h.p. petrol motors, carried singly, each in a separate car, and actuating propellers attached not to the cars but to the body of the ship. This method of attachment was rendered possible by one of the principal distinguishing characteristics of the Zeppelin ship, which was built with a rigid aluminium framework. This was divided into sixteen separate compartments along the length of the

COUNT VON ZEPPELIN.

structure, and each compartment enclosed an independent gasbag, the collective capacity of the bags being nearly 400,000 cubic feet.

This wonderful vessel, the pioneer among dirigibles of the " rigid " type, was tested in June, 1900, when it travelled $3\frac{1}{2}$ miles at a speed of 18 miles an hour, before its journey was cut short by a mishap to the steering gear. It was followed in rapid succession by other Zeppelins of larger size and greatly increased engine power, until by the year 1914 the German army and navy were in possession of Zeppelins of nearly 30 tons displacement and 720 horse-power, with a speed of 50 miles per hour, and an endurance of 30 hours at full speed. The type was adopted in Germany for fighting purposes by army and navy alike, and in spite of its unwieldy bulk and the impossibility of diminishing its size by deflation for purposes of transport or storage, it has many formidable qualities—among them, it is said, the capacity to mount 1-pounder and Maxim guns not only in the cars but on the top of the envelope.

Let us now turn to the evolution of the aeroplane, and briefly note the steps by which man has discovered how to make aerial voyages in machines heavier than air, which, so far from floating above the earth when motionless, must begin to fall the moment their speed is arrested.

From very early times, as the story of Icarus reminds us, the imagination and aspirations of

NAVAL ZEPPELIN "L.1" FLYING OVER HELIGOLAND.

men have been turned, through watching the movements of birds, to the far-off ideal of flight, and much effort has been expended in the endeavour to master its secret; but until our own day the obstacles have been insurmountable. The subject was one of those which occupied the many-sided and penetrating genius of Leonardo da Vinci about the beginning of the sixteenth century; but it was an English man of science, Sir George Cayley, who early in the nineteenth century, after the

PARIS, 1871.
Escape of Gambetta by balloon.

invention of the steam engine, first worked at the problem on really practical scientific lines. His claim to be regarded as the true founder of aerodynamic science is hardly open to dispute. Not only did he declare power-driven flying machines to be theoretically possible, provided that an engine could be produced of sufficient power in proportion to its weight, but he actually invented many of the leading features of the aeroplane as it exists to-day. But the indispensable light and powerful engine was not forthcoming in his time, and the opportunity was therefore denied him of carrying his theories into practice. The subject was pursued experimentally at intervals by, among others, Mr. Horatio Phillips and Sir Hiram Maxim in England, C. Ader in France, and Professor S. P. Langley in America, while the investigations of Otto Lilienthal in Germany in connexion with an apparatus for gliding through the air from heights, with which he assiduously practised from 1891 until 1896, when he met his death, provided much valuable material for the development of the aeroplane. The death of Lilienthal, indeed, which occurred through a mishap to his machine, brings us to the very threshold of the long-desired success. An account of the accident was read by Wilbur and Orville Wright among the ordinary news of the day, and it was not without its influence in starting them upon their career of brilliant achievement. If this were a chronicle of discovery it would be necessary to mention many other names; but we are here concerned only with results, and particularly with those that have a bearing upon war.

It was, as we have seen, the invention of the

petrol engine and its rapid improvement in connexion with the motor-car that provided the one thing postulated by Sir George Cayley a century earlier as indispensable for successful flight. Here at last was an instrument developing immense power in proportion to its remarkably light weight. The Wrights applied it, in a form modified by themselves for their novel purpose, to an aerial glider perfected by prolonged experiment; and independent flight was at once accomplished. The date of this

momentous event was December 17, 1903. They had achieved the conquest of the air; but for reasons of their own they kept their triumph secret. Meanwhile other experimenters, working independently in France— Santos Dumont, Delagrange, Archdeacon, and notably Henry Farman, the Voisins, and Louis Blériot—achieved no small measure of success in the same direction; but it was not until the demonstrations given by Wilbur Wright in the same country, in 1908—first at Le Mans

A GERMAN AIRSHIP IN COURSE OF CONSTRUCTION.

[*Swaine.*

**MAJOR-GENERAL SIR DAVID
HENDERSON, K.C.B., D.S.O.**

and afterwards at Auvour—that the world at large began fully to recognize the new era that had dawned.

Our view is restricted here to the domain of war, and at the outset we must acknowledge the credit due to France for realizing with almost instantaneous promptitude the value of the aeroplane for military purposes. As early as 1905 the French Government endeavoured to buy the Wrights' machine. The attempt came to nothing, but it was characteristic of French alertness, which justly won for France the leading place in this new department of military preparation. Wilbur Wright's performances upon her own soil stimulated her afresh. A French officer took his flying certificate in January, 1909, and after the Reims meeting in the summer of the same year the Government began to buy machines. In this country interest in the science and practice of flying was greatly stimulated by a series of valuable money prizes offered by the *Daily Mail* for the first successful flight over courses then regarded as long and difficult. The first of these, announced as early as 1906, when flying was in its infancy, was a sum of £10,000 for a flight from London to Manchester in twenty-four hours, with not more than two halts on the way. This was won by Louis Paulhan in April, 1910. Other nations more

or less promptly followed the French initiative; for before long all had come to recognize the importance of not being left behind in the new arm. But France, the pioneer, retained the lead, and in order to gain a clear view of the rapid development that followed we must for the moment keep our attention fixed on her.

As already indicated, notable advances had been made in France before the year 1909. The brothers Charles and Gabriel Voisin, working at their factory near Paris, had produced a biplane which was tested for them by Henry Farman, a well-known racing motorist, who, on January 13, 1908, won the Grand Prix d'Aviation of 50,000 francs by a flight of one kilometre in a closed circuit without touching the ground. This he accomplished at Issy-les-Moulineaux on a Voisin biplane, the average height above the ground maintained during the flight being between four and six metres. During the same period another great French pioneer of flying, Louis Blériot, was conducting experiments with a monoplane, on original lines of his own, and a little later he won permanent fame by flying for the first time across the Channel, on July 25, 1909, and thereby winning the prize of £1,000 offered by the *Daily Mail* for the accomplishment of this feat. In the same year, which was marked from beginning to end by wonderful progress, an aviation meeting was held at Reims, where remarkable flights of as much as three

[*Speaight.*

CAPTAIN F. MURRAY SUETER.

[F. N. Birkett, 97, Percy Road, Shepherd's Bush, W.

WRIGHT BIPLANE "BABY."

hours were accomplished by Farman on a biplane of his own construction, fitted with the now famous "Gnome" engine, whose seven cylinders revolved around the crank shaft, cooling themselves automatically in the air. In 1910 flights became ever higher and more daring, and great cross-country journeys, such as that from London to Manchester already recorded, made it plain to military authorities that the aeroplane must be invaluable for reconnoitring. By this time the French Government had provided itself with several biplanes of various makes and a few monoplanes also, and the time had come to give them a serious military trial. The opportunity was afforded by the army manœuvres in Picardy, in the autumn of the same year, and the results were highly favourable. About a dozen machines were employed for scouting. They were

divided between the opposing forces and subjected to tests as complete as possible. Both military pilots and civilian volunteers served as airmen, the latter including M. Hubert Latham and M. Louis Paulhan. It was the first time aeroplanes had ever been employed at manœuvres, and everything was novel and experimental. Most remarkable results were secured by officers already trained in military observation. Two of these, Lieutenant Sido and Adjutant Menard, brought to headquarters information of the utmost importance after two early morning flights, one of which covered 60 kilometres in 65 minutes, while the other established with certainty the fact that the "enemy" was in retreat, a matter of vital consequence for their Commander-in-Chief to know. It was declared on authority at the time that the value of these two reports could

VALKYRIE MONOPLANE.

[F. N. Birkett.

Mr. T. O. M. SOPWITH.

not be overestimated. The Military Correspondent who attended these manœuvres for *The Times* bore emphatic testimony to the same effect. " In my belief," he said, " the aeroplane, given a trained pilot and a skilled observer, must revolutionize the whole service of reconnaissance."

The effect upon the French Government was decisive. They resolved to create an aeroplane fleet, and before the end of 1910 the dozen possessed during the autumn manœuvres had been increased to 32, of which six were monoplanes and the rest biplanes of five different makes. It is interesting to note, as some indication of the attention bestowed upon the subject at this time by the various Powers, that early in December of the same year one of the foremost aeroplane manufacturers in France stated that he had received the following orders for military machines :—from the Government of France 35 aeroplanes, Russia 20, Spain 3, Italy 2, Belgium 1, Japan 1, Britain 1. A German order was received a few months later. The policy embarked upon in France was consistently pursued. Early in the summer of 1911 orders were placed on account of the French army for nearly 150 machines, of which 80 were Blériot monoplanes of two types—one a machine with seats for two, and the other single-seated, but of high speed. Conditions

were imposed as to speed, lifting capacity, rapid climbing power, and the like.

A further impetus was given by the great meeting at Reims in October, 1911, for trials of war aeroplanes, for which more than £50,000 was set aside in prizes and other rewards. Competitors had to fulfil exacting tests, which in themselves supplied clear evidence of the advance that had been made ; for one of the aims was to secure a machine at once swift and " air-worthy," which could fly long distances, carrying both a pilot and a passenger. Among other conditions to be complied with was that of rising with a full load from a ploughed field. The winning machine, a Nieuport monoplane, flew across country, conveying two men and fuel, at a speed of over 70 miles an hour. Some of the flying was accomplished in gusty winds blowing as much as 40 miles an hour, and nothing was more remarkable than the regularity and trustworthiness of the performances. There was an astonishing growth in engine power, some of the aeroplanes being fitted with Gnome engines of fourteen cylinders and developing 100, and even 140, horse power. One biplane weighed, with passengers and load complete, 2,420 lb. The meeting was attended by representatives from all countries, and as a consequence of its success military orders for machines flowed in to all the successful makers. It convinced the British War Office of the necessity for a really decisive move.

But before we turn to British military aeronautics, it may be convenient to summarize the experience obtained in actual warfare before the date of the great European war—an experience confined to nations that did not join in the conflict of August, 1914. The first occasion on which an aeroplane was ever used in war was in February, 1911, when an airman flew over Ciudad Juarez, in Mexico, while fighting was in progress between the rebel troops and the Government forces, and reported the situation to the latter. But the first Power to employ the new weapon systematically in warfare was Italy, between whom and Turkey hostilities began at the end of September, 1911, a few days before the Reims meeting just described. The operations in the air, which were confined to Tripoli, were entirely one-sided, and were not opposed by anything more serious than occasional rifle fire from the Turks and Arabs. Nevertheless much was learned from these Italian operations. They may, in fact, be regarded, from our present

M. LOUIS PAULHAN.
Who flew from London to Manchester, 183 miles, in 1910, winning the "Daily Mail" prize of £10,000.

point of view, as experiments conducted with an immediate practical object and under the influence, at once searching and stimulating, of serious warfare. In the course of six months four officers made an average of 78 flights each, for purposes of survey as well as of reconnaissance, but owing to the low power of the motors available it was never possible to carry a second man as passenger. The lessons deduced from the exploits in Tripoli have been set forth in THE TIMES, and may be briefly epitomized as follows :

1. It was found to be unsafe to fly above an enemy's rifle fire in an unarmoured machine at a height of less than 3,000 feet.

2. Reconnaissance by an untrained observer was worse than useless. A period of continuous training in obser-, vation from a height above the range of fire was indispensable before the airman could be trusted to supply information of any use to his commander.

3. Mere casual dropping from an aeroplane of bombs —or grenades—such as the Italians used was futile.

4. Results of the utmost value were obtainable from aerial photography. By photographing the enemy's positions the Italian air-scouts discovered trenches of which no sign was visible from below, and they were able, further, to make beautifully accurate and detailed maps of the country. By tele-photography these advantages have been much extended.

During the same campaign the Italians employed airships also, for molesting the enemy and for making observations and taking photographs.

Aeroplanes were brought into use again in the Balkan War, which began a year later; but here, again, they were confined to one side— that of the Allies. The only opposition they encountered from the Turks was in the form of shooting from the ground. Many photographs were taken in scouting expeditions, and bombs

TWO-SEATER HENRY FARMAN BIPLANE.   [F. N. Birkett.

AN AVIS MONOPLANE.   [*F. N. Birkett.*

were dropped with little more result than the Italians achieved in Tripoli. Thirty bombs discharged in one day from a Bulgarian aeroplane over Adrianople killed or injured a total of only six persons.

The British Air Service won its laurels within the first six weeks of the war. On September 14 was made public a report from Sir John French's Headquarters in France which contained the following passage, dated three days earlier :

Quite one of the features of the campaign, on our side, has been the success attained by the Royal Flying Corps. In regard to the collection of information it is impossible either to award too much praise to our aviators for the way they have carried out their duties or to overestimate the value of the intelligence collected, more especially during the recent advance. In due course, certain examples of what has been effected may be specified and the far-reaching nature of the results fully explained, but that time has not yet arrived. . . . The constant object of our aviators has been to effect the accurate location of the enemy's forces, and, incidentally—since

the operations cover so large an area—of our own units. Nevertheless, the tactics adopted for dealing with hostile aircraft are to attack them instantly with one or more British machines. This has been so far successful that in five cases German pilots or observers have been shot in the air and their machines brought to the ground. As a consequence, the British Flying Corps has succeeded in establishing an individual ascendancy which is as serviceable to us as it is damaging to the enemy. . . . Something in the direction of the mastery of the air has already been gained.

This emphatic testimony was confirmed by another tribute quite as striking. On the night of September 9, Sir John French tells us, he received the following message from the Commander-in-Chief of the French Armies :

Please express most particularly to Marshal French my thanks for services rendered on every day by the English Flying Corps. The precision, exactitude, and regularity of the news brought in by its members are evidence of their perfect organisation and also of the perfect training of pilots and observers.

DUNNE STABILITY BIPLANE.   [*F. N. Birkett.*

There is special interest in following the history, brief though it be, of a brilliant young corps of which at the very outset of its first trial in war so much could be justly said, and whose later achievements in the field amply confirmed the good opinion thus early put on record. On whatever work engaged—whether some daring raid upon German airsheds at Düsseldorf or Friedrichshaven, or the honourable duty of mounting aerial guard over the person of their Sovereign during his visit to the troops in France and Flanders, or the constant and more ordinary task of observation and direction of artillery fire at the front—the British airmen always proved alike trustworthy and indispensable. The origin of the Flying Corps can be traced back through the airship to the early days of military ballooning, before aeroplanes were thought of or their name was invented ; for, as we have seen, it is the airship, not the aeroplane, that is the true descendant of the simple captive balloon with which military aeronautics was originally associated. The balloon, which in its simplest form was first used in warfare almost exactly 120 years ago, was, at last, after many vain attempts, rendered navigable by the invention of the petrol engine, as already described. The same invention brought into being the aeroplane, which, although itself a startling novelty of the twentieth century, gives embodiment to one of the early aspirations of mankind.

In the first years of the French Revolutionary War a school of aeronautics was founded at Meudon, and the French victory at Fleurus, in 1794, was attributed in great part to the observations made from a captive balloon before the battle. To come down to later times, similar balloons were a good deal used by the Federals in the first two years of the American Civil War (1861–63). McClellan's army had a regular balloon staff, consisting of a captain, an assistant-captain, and about fifty non-commissioned officers and privates. For apparatus they had two balloons, one containing about 13,000 feet of gas and the other twice as large, each drawn by four horses ; two generators, also drawn by four horses apiece ; and an acid cart drawn by two horses. By means of these much useful information was gained on several occasions, but eventually difficulties of transport and unsuitability of locality made ballooning impracticable. In the siege of Paris (1870–71) balloons were the sole means of communication between the city

A WATERPLANE OFF WESTMINSTER.

and the outer world. They were dispatched free, over the heads of the investing force, conveying information and also pigeons, which afterwards returned with news from the provinces to the beleaguered city. Altogether, from September, 1870, to January, 1871, as many as sixty-four balloons were sent out, carrying passengers—among them Gambetta—and dispatches. All these, however, were but interesting episodes of warfare. Military ballooning as a science did not receive anything like general recognition until the early 'eighties of the nineteenth century, when balloon establishments were organized on a regular footing by most of the Powers. It was formally introduced into the British Army in 1879, when a Balloon School was started at Chatham, and in the following year the 24th Company of the Royal Engineers was chosen for special instruction in aeronautics. Later this school was removed to Aldershot, and there it remained with its headquarters at South Farnborough, until, when the great development of aeronautics came, it was expanded, or rather merged in an organization of much wider scope.

The Balloon School did good and useful work, and under the last commandant who held office before its organization was changed,

LATEST PATTERN HENRY FARMAN BIPLANE. [*F. N. Birkett.*

Colonel (afterwards Brigadier-General) J. E. Capper, C.B., an enthusiastic and accomplished balloonist, serious progress was made. A small airship, the Nulli Secundus, was constructed, which in October, 1907, made a voyage with two passengers from Farnborough to London, encircled St. Paul's Cathedral, and then returned as far as Sydenham —a total distance of fifty miles, which was covered in three hours thirty-five minutes. The vessel was anchored at the Crystal Palace, where it was damaged by a high wind before the journey could be resumed, and had to be deflated ; but in the following year it made numerous further experimental trips. Other small, non-rigid dirigibles followed—the Beta, the Gamma, and later on the Delta—useful rather for experiment and instruction than for serious military operations. Meanwhile public opinion was moving faster than the Government, a Parliamentary Aerial Defence Committee was formed to act as a stimulant to the official world, and, as the result of a public subscription organized by the *Morning Post*, a large Lebaudy airship was bought for our army in France, and made a good voyage from Moisson to Aldershot on October 26, 1910. This was a few weeks after the French army manœuvres in Picardy. at which the value of the aeroplane for military purposes was for the first time conclusively demonstrated. It is an interesting coincidence that in the same autumn dirigibles were employed at the manœuvres in Germany. In England we had got as far as erecting six aeroplane sheds on Salisbury Plain, two of which were used by Captain

Dickson and Mr. L. Gibbs while attending manœuvres.

In April, 1909, the Government appointed a permanent Advisory Committee for Aeronautics, composed of eminent scientific and practical men, under the chairmanship of Lord Rayleigh, and charged with the general direction of experimental research work, which was conducted mainly by the engineering department of the National Physical Laboratory. In the same year the Committee of Imperial Defence decided that airships were necessary for military purposes, and after prolonged inquiry the Advisory Committee recommended that the army should be supplied with a small non-rigid type of airship, which could be deflated and conveniently transported, and that a large airship of the rigid type should be provided for the Navy. A great step forward was, therefore, contemplated, though, as far as the naval ship was concerned, it unhappily came to nothing. The ship was ordered, indeed, from Messrs. Vickers, and built in their works at Barrow ; but when launched, in the summer of 1911, it met with an accident and collapsed. In size it was comparable with a Zeppelin, being 512 feet long and 48 feet in diameter. The effect of this disaster was so great upon the official— or political—mind that for two years no effort was made to repair it.

It was at the end of February, 1911, that a Special Army Order was issued describing the peace organization of the new Air Battalion of the Royal Engineers, the formation of which had been announced in Mr. Haldane's

Memorandum on the Army Estimates a few days earlier. It was to supersede the Balloon School, and to come into being from April 1 of the same year. It was explained, rather cumbrously, that to this new battalion was to be entrusted "the duty of creating a body of expert airmen, organized in such a way as to facilitate the formation of units ready to take the field with troops and capable of expansion by any reserve formations which may be formed in the future. In addition, the training and instruction of men in handling kites, balloons, aeroplanes, and other forms of air craft will also devolve upon this battalion." The establishment of the battalion was organized into—(1) headquarters, and (2) two companies, numbering together 14 officers and 176 of other ranks, each company being a separate and self-contained unit. The officers were to be selected from applicants from any regular arm or branch of the Army on the active list, and were to serve in the Air Battalion for a period of four years, of which the first six months were probationary. The rank and file were to be chosen from men in the Corps of Royal Engineers.

The Balloon Factory at Farnborough was reorganized and expanded and renamed the Army Aircraft Factory, and Mr. Mervyn O'Gorman, a civilian engineer, was placed at its head.

The Air Battalion was a transitory and short-lived institution. It was necessary to proceed much farther and create a truly comprehensive organization which should meet the requirements of Navy and Army alike, and by opening the door to civilian talent should be capable of freer and more natural growth. This point was reached in 1912, under the joint auspices of Mr. Winston Churchill at the Admiralty and Lord Haldane at the War Office. On March 4 in that year Colonel Seely, Under-Secretary of State for War, who, like Mr. Churchill, took a strong personal interest in aeronautics, described in the House of Commons the fresh scheme which had been elaborated, and on the 26th he announced that the King had approved of the title "The Royal Flying Corps" for the newly-constituted aeronautical branch of his forces, while the Army Aircraft Factory was in future to be designated "The Royal Aircraft Factory," and to be available for the whole aeronautical service. He added that a standing committee would be appointed, with Brigadier-General Henderson as its first chairman, "to co-ordinate action in dealing with questions that arise in connexion with the Corps." This, which is known as the "Air Committee," has the status of a permanent Sub-Committee of the Committee of Imperial Defence.

The scheme in full was published on April 12, in the form of an official Memorandum, based on the recommendations of a committee which, under Colonel Seely's own chairmanship, had been commissioned by the Government to consider and report upon the whole subject.

It was apparent at the first glance that this War Office Memorandum embodied a scheme

SOPWITH SCOUT, SPEED 114 MILES PER HOUR. [*F. N. Birkett.*

that belonged to a wholly different order of things from the Air Battalion which the new organization was to supersede. It was devised on large, bold and elastic lines. It treated flying as a thing in itself, and not as a mere function of any existing arm. It embraced all the requirements of both Navy and Army and found a place for civilians also. It created for the first time a truly national Air Service.

This fruitful document, starting from the categorical statement that " aeroplanes have now to a great extent passed out of the experimental stage as regards their employment in warfare, and an active and progressive policy has therefore become imperatively urgent," laid down among the general principles adopted as a basis for the new organization that it must both meet present requirements and also be sufficiently elastic to permit of considerable expansion ; that it must be capable of absorbing and utilizing the whole of the aeronautical resources of the country ; that, while supplying the peculiar and different needs of both Navy and Army, the Royal Flying Corps must be available in its entirety for either service if necessary ; that it must encourage private enterprise, and offer inducements to civilians to join ; that experimental work in all branches of the corps must be co-ordinated. In order that it might fulfil these requirements it was laid down that the corps was to embrace a Naval Wing (with headquarters at Eastchurch) ; a Military Wing (Headquarters, South Farnborough) ; a Central Flying School, to be established at Upavon, on Salisbury Plain ; and " The

Royal Aircraft Factory," whose duties would be the higher training of mechanics, the reconstruction of aeroplanes, repair work for the corps, tests with British and foreign engines and aeroplanes, and experimental work. An officer from the Central Flying School and one each from the Naval and Military Wings would be added to the Aeronautical Advisory Committee, which would continue its research work on existing lines. The new " Air Committee " has been mentioned above. The ultimate development of the Naval Wing, it was explained, could not be foreseen, inasmuch as it depended largely upon the result of experiments which were about to be undertaken with hydro-aeroplanes—or, as they have since been named, seaplanes. The Military Wing would consist of a number of Squadrons, of which eight were urgently required to equip the Expeditionary Force—seven being aeroplane squadrons and one consisting of airships and kites. Besides all this, the Royal Flying Corps was to possess a Reserve of unspecified dimensions, capable of absorbing in case of emergency the whole of the resources of the country in this branch of science. The Central Flying School was intended, not to teach officers of the Army or civilians to fly, but to give more advanced instruction to those who had learnt the elements and taken their Royal Aero Club flying certificate at a private aerodrome. The Central School would teach the things which make the difference between the mere airman and the military airman, the scientific as opposed to what has been called the acrobatic

MAURICE FARMAN BIPLANE,
Known as the Gun 'Bus.

[F. N. Birkett.

AEROPLANE USED BY THE RUSSIAN ARMY.

side of the business; and the course of instruction would include "progressive flying," observation and photography from the air, meteorology, flying by compass, signalling, and the like, as well as mechanics and the principles of construction.

After successfully completing a four-months' course and "graduating" at the Central School, officers would be eligible for appointment either (a) for continuous service in the Naval or Military Wing of the Royal Flying Corps, or (b) to the permanent staff of the Flying School, or (c) to the Royal Flying Corps Reserve. The term of continuous service under the conditions (a) and (b) was fixed at four years. Civilians were to pass as a rule direct into the Reserve with the rank of officers. This Reserve was divided into two classes, a First Reserve and a Second Reserve, in which the obligations undertaken in time of peace differed; but both classes were equally liable to be called upon for service in war.

A new and important feature of the scheme was the fact that now, for the first time, was undertaken the training of non-commissioned officers and men as well as of officers. They were either to be transferred from other arms of the service, naval or military, or enlisted specially for a period of four years. The Naval Flying School at Eastchurch, Isle of Sheppey, was to undertake more advanced and specialized training in observation, the transmission of

intelligence and the like, together with experimental work and developments peculiar to the Navy; while similar provision for special training in the Military Wing was made at the flying establishments of the Army.

Officers in the Royal Flying Corps were graded in four ranks—namely, Commanding Officer, carrying the temporary rank of lieutenant-colonel in the Army; Squadron Commander, with rank of major; Flight Commander, captain in the Army; and Flying Officer, with subaltern's rank; and the duties of all carried special rates of pay, terms as to pension, etc.

The Commandant of the Central Flying School—which was the joint property of the Navy and the Army, but was administered by the War Office—might be appointed from either Service, and as a matter of fact at the moment when the War broke out the post was held by a naval officer, Captain Godfrey Paine, R.N. It was estimated at the outset that the total number of flyers required to be passed through the Central School in each year would be 179, made up as follows: For the Navy, 40; for the Army, 91 (half the number being officers and half non-commissioned officers); to make good failures and wastage, 33; civilians, 15.

As far as the Military Wing of the new corps was concerned, attention for the time being was concentrated upon the effort to supply the

NAVY AIRSHIP, THE "ASTRA-TORRES."

requirements of the Expeditionary Force. The purposes for which aeroplanes would be required in land warfare were enumerated as follows : (*a*) Reconnaissance, (*b*) prevention of enemy's reconnaissance, (*c*) intercommunication, (*d*) observation of artillery fire, (*e*) infliction of damage on the enemy. For the Expeditionary Force of 6 divisions and 1 Cavalry Division the following establishments were laid down :

Headquarters.

7 Aeroplane Squadrons, each providing 12 aeroplanes.

1 Airship and Kite Squadron, providing 2 airships and 2 flights of kites.

1 Line of Communication Flying Corps Workshop.

It was reckoned that the minimum number of trained flyers should be two per aeroplane, of whom one should be an officer, though in the case of one-seated machines both should be officers. For purposes of calculation, however, one officer and one non-commissioned officer were allowed. On this basis the flyers required for the 7 squadrons were enumerated as follows : Officers, 7 commanders and 84

THE "GAMMA" LEAVING HER SHED; THE "BETA" IN THE AIR.

others ; non-commissioned officers, 7 sergeants and 84 others. In addition, a Reserve calculated on a basis of 100 per cent. for 6 months' wastage exactly doubled the numbers, making a total of 182 officers and 182 non-commissioned officers, besides a considerable force of " air mechanics " ranking lower. Sheds for the aeroplanes were also to be provided for use in the field. The whole of this computation was regarded as a *war* establishment, to be completed as rapidly as possible. The Memorandum recognized the great advantage of the airship in being able not only to transmit wireless messages, but to receive them also, and to transmit them to greater distances than the aeroplane, but declared that for the purposes of the Expeditionary Force " any immediate extension of the existing equipment of airships is unnecessary." In conclusion it insisted upon the importance of cross-country flights as an essential part of the training of military airmen, and announced certain steps that were to be taken to make provision for these through cooperation with private enterprise, to the encouragement of which, as also of meteorological investigation, attention was being devoted.

The Military Wing came into existence on May 13, 1912, on which date the Air Battalion and its Reserve were absorbed into it.

This great scheme was hailed with welcome in *The Times*, whose Aeronautical Correspondent declared :

It is hardly too much to say that now, for the first time, the Government show that they take flying seriously and that they intend that the British Navy and Army shall be equipped, at the earliest possible moment, with a sufficiency of the human and mechanical instruments of aerial warfare to bring them up to, and, it is hoped, to surpass, the standard in this respect already aimed at by other Great Powers.

The sentences already quoted from Sir John French's dispatches throw into almost startling relief the progress our youngest military corps had made towards the attainment of this ideal within a period of less than two years and a half.

The Royal Flying Corps showed from the very first, in its vigorous capacity for growth, convincing proof of a healthy constitution. Not only did its numbers and its plant increase with rapidity, but the organization itself developed beyond the original limits of the scheme. It had existed little more than a year when it was found necessary to establish at the War Office a separate Department to administer the Military Wing of the Air Service. The new post of Director-General of Military Aeronautics was created, and Brigadier-General David (now Major-General Sir David) Henderson, D.S.O., was selected as its first occupant. He was himself a certificated airman and an officer of the Royal Flying Corps Reserve. Further considerable changes came to pass before long.

A PARSEVAL AIRSHIP.

ZEPPELIN SHED AT DUSSELDORF.
This photograph was taken from a Zeppelin.

On January 1, 1914, the Army airships were turned over to the Navy. It had been found advisable for various reasons to make a clear line of division between the lighter-than-air machines and the heavier-than-air machines, and to administer them separately. The whole of the former were allotted to the Naval Wing, although such airships as were suitable for purposes of land warfare were to be held at the disposal of the Army when required ; while the Army was to devote its whole effort henceforth to the heavier-than-air service. Some of the officers of the Military Wing passed over with the airships into the Naval Wing.

This change was followed a few months later by a development of the Naval Wing itself in the direction of greater independence from the Army and closer incorporation in the structure of the Navy. It did not cease to be the " Naval Wing " of the Royal Flying Corps, but at the same time it acquired the new and more distinctive title of " The Royal Naval Air Service," and became in effect a new branch of the Royal Navy, in some respects analogous to the Royal Marines, although with regulations to suit its own peculiar requirements. Officers and men belonging to it were to be promoted independently of

their rank in the Navy ; and, on the other hand, civilians might enter as officers, on engagements which would enable them if they proved suitable to make a career in the Royal Naval Air Service, while holding a position of entire equality with officers of the Navy and Marines who were of the same grade and seniority. Civilians who so entered were to go to sea for a definite period in each year, in order that they might learn to identify themselves closely with the Navy and might acquire its traditions. They were to be required on entering to sign an engagement to serve four years, with four years more in the Royal Naval Air Reserve.

The administration of the Royal Naval Air Service rested with the Admiralty, and consisted of :

The Air Department, Admiralty.

The Central Air Office at Sheerness.

The Royal Naval Flying School at Eastchurch.

The Royal Naval Air Stations.

All types of aircraft that might from time to time be employed for naval purposes.

A portion of the staff of the Central Flying School was drawn from the Naval Wing.

Officers in the Royal Naval Air Service were

graded in the following ranks. The words within brackets indicate the relative rank in the regular naval service :

Wing Captain (Captain, R.N.) ; Wing Commander (Commander, R.N.) ; Squadron Commander, when in command (Lieutenant-Commander, R.N.) ; Squadron Commander, when not in command, Flight Commander, and Flight Lieutenant (Lieutenant, R.N., of various degrees of seniority) ; Flight Sub-Lieutenant (Sub-Lieutenant, R.N.) ; Warrant Officer, 1st and 2nd Grades.

All promotions were by selection.

As to the men of the Royal Naval Air Service, all classes of ratings on the active list of the Navy were eligible for selection to serve ; and it was expressly laid down that the service embraced employment in connexion with any type of aircraft, in any part of the world, either ashore or afloat.

The Air Department at the Admiralty was placed under a Director, and at the outbreak of the War this post was filled by Captain Murray F. Sueter, R.N., the recently appointed (and first) Director of the Air Department. The Central Air Office was at Sheerness, under the Inspecting Captain of Aircraft. Under him also were the Commanding Officer of the Naval Airship Section, the Commander of the Naval Flying School at Eastchurch—who when the war broke out was the brilliant airman, Wing Commander Charles R. Samson—and the Commanding Officers of the Naval Air Stations round the coast. The Commandant of the Central Flying School, as we have seen, was placed under the Director of Military Aeronautics at the War Office, but was himself a naval officer.

Naval Air Stations existed at various places round the coast, and the number was being steadily increased. By the summer of 1914 there were seven, at the following places : Isle of Grain, Calshot, Felixstowe, Yarmouth, Kingsnorth (on the Medway, a few miles below Chatham), Fort George (Inverness-shire), and Dundee. Of these, Kingsnorth was an airship station, like the Farnborough station inland, which it was to supersede as headquarters of the Airship Section as soon as completed ; the rest were seaplane stations. The men at the seaplane stations occupied the old Coastguard buildings and took over the Coastguard duties.

The term "seaplane" was adopted by the Admiralty in 1913 to denote the naval hydroplane, or hydro-aeroplane, an aeroplane which, in the place of wheels for alighting on the ground, had floats, various in design, for supporting it upon the water. Great progress had been made in this country both in the invention and in the provision of such machines, which could rise from, and alight, travel, or

GERMAN MILITARY AEROPLANE PACKED FOR TRANSPORT ON A MOTOR.

rest upon, the surface of the sea, even when not entirely calm. When the airships were handed over to the Navy at the beginning of 1914, and the aeroplanes were allotted to the Army, this specialized form of aircraft was retained by the Admiralty as a distinctly naval instrument. It was tried with success at the Naval Manœuvres of 1913, when the cruiser Hermes (which was sunk on Oct. 31, 1914, by a German submarine) was fitted with a launching platform and accommodation for several seaplanes on board, in order that these might be submitted to an exhaustive test. A large number of flights were made, and as a result of the experience so gained it was decided to provide for the Navy a special vessel as a seaplane-carrying ship. At the same time advances were made in the designing of the seaplanes themselves, and, although many competing makes had been adopted experimentally in the service, the development of certain standard types for war purposes progressed rapidly. In the great fleet assembled for inspection by the King at Spithead about a fortnight before war was declared an imposing array of aircraft formed the most novel feature, and in the

Solent, off Gilkicker Point, two dozen seaplanes rode at moorings alongside the ships. They had arrived and taken up their stations through the air, and they manœuvred between or over the great lines of battleships and cruisers, sometimes on the surface of the water, sometimes on the wing aloft, like so many gigantic seabirds. One, a Short machine, with a 14-cylinder Gnome engine of 160 horse-power and a speed of about 78 miles per hour, had a total weight—with pilot and passenger, wireless equipment, and fuel and oil for five hours on board—of over 3,000 lb. Another, a Sopwith machine of 200 horse-power, carried and could fire a 1½-pounder gun.

It is impossible to give statistics or anything like full particulars of our equipment in aircraft, anti-aircraft guns, and kindred matters; for details of this kind were, in this country as elsewhere in Europe, sedulously concealed; but some facts had been made public in Ministerial speeches or official publications. The number of airships in our possession was known, and was very few. In this department we had allowed ourselves to be far outstripped, especially, of course, by Germany. We possessed

LATEST TYPE GNOME ENGINE.   [*F. N. Birkett*

FRENCH AEROPLANE ATTACKING A GERMAN TAUBE (ON THE LEFT).

none at all of the larger "battle" class, to which the Zeppelins belonged; but a contract had been made with Messrs. Vickers for a large rigid airship, to be built in England on the same general lines and of the same description as the latest type of Zeppelin, and with about the same displacement. With airships of the second class, for mine-laying and scouting, more progress had been made. An Astra-Torres ship, the most striking peculiarity of which was the shape of her envelope, which looked like three sausages tied in a bunch, giving a cross-section like the ace of clubs, had been delivered early in 1914 by the Astra Company of Paris. She had a displacement of seven tons, was fitted with two 200 h.p. Chenu engines, and had attained the remarkable speed for a vessel of this class of 51·1 miles per hour. A Parseval airship of 8·5 tons—since increased to 10 tons—was delivered from Germany in the summer of 1913. She had two 180 h.p. engines and a speed of 42 miles an hour. Both these were of the non-rigid type. A second Astra-Torres, with a displacement of 12 tons, was under construction for us in France. Messrs. Vickers had contracted to supply three non-rigid ships, and Messrs. Armstrong, who had recently added a department for the building of airships to their extensive business, had undertaken to supply three 15-ton ships of a new Italian

semi-rigid design, known as the Forlanini. The airships taken over from the Army were small, and useful rather for training and experimental work than for purposes of war. They consisted of the Eta of 3·5 tons, the Delta of 5·3 tons, the Gamma of 3·4 tons, and the Beta of 1·2 tons, besides the airship built by Mr. Willows, No. 2, which had been renovated and brought up to date for use in training.

Airships require sheds. Of these Germany had a large supply, which she was rapidly increasing. Great Britain, on the other hand, was only beginning to provide them. The biggest we possessed were the two fixed sheds at Farnborough, built in 1909 and 1911, each 300 feet in length. In place of these, which were ultimately to be removed, the Admiralty were constructing at the new Kingsnorth airship station two sheds 600 feet long and 80 feet high, but of different breadths— 120 feet and 160 feet. The larger of these was of German make, but was being erected by Messrs. Vickers, who were putting up a similar shed at their own works on Walney Island, near Barrow, where they were about to build the rigid airship for which they held the contract. These two German-made sheds would hold four 10-ton ships each, or two rigids. It was in contemplation also to erect another shed in Norfolk. The small canvas portable

BATTERY OF MITRAILLEUSES USED
FOR BRINGING DOWN AEROPLANES.

at which they could drop formidable explosives upon hostile vessels, and could signal 120 miles effectually by wireless telegraphy, and they had even received wireless messages while in the air. At the same date there were 125 officers and 500 men in the Naval Air Service, with a rapid prospective increase of numbers in view. During the year 1913 the Naval Wing had accomplished flights of 131,000 miles, in all weathers and mainly across country.

The Military Wing had been undergoing similar development, and had made great progress in the matter of the aeroplanes to which its efforts were now restricted. In the original scheme, it will be remembered, when the Royal Flying Corps was established in 1912, the provision of eight squadrons was aimed at, of which seven were to be aeroplane squadrons and one an airship squadron. The latter was retained upon the establishment as an additional squadron of aeroplanes when the airships were handed over to the Navy, but by the summer of 1914 it had not been actually formed. Each squadron was to be prepared at any given moment with 12 machines instantly ready for active service in war. These were organized in three "flights" of four aeroplanes apiece, much as a battery of artillery is divided into sections. But experience showed that for every machine required to be always ready for instant service it was necessary to have two machines in hand; consequently the eight squadrons necessitated a stock of, in round numbers, 200 machines. In addition, 50 more

shed at Farnborough and the shed at Wormwood Scrubs—only 300 feet long and destitute of equipment—were the only other things of the kind we had to show.

Of seaplanes the Navy possessed in March, 1914, a total of 62, but this species of craft was undergoing rapid development in both numbers and power. They had already reached a stage

THE ROYAL FLYING CORPS IN FRANCE.

LANDING AN AEROPLANE IN FRANCE FROM A BRITISH TRANSPORT.

were wanted for the Central Flying School, besides a large provision of spare parts, and, of course, a proper equipment of accessories for repairs, etc. This made the establishment of aeroplanes for full equipment of the Expeditionary Force and the Central School 250 in all, when the whole eight squadrons should be complete. Towards this total, according to Colonel Seely's statement in the House of Commons in February, 1914, the Army at that date possessed 161 machines, having struck off 52 from, and added 100 new ones to, the total of 113 that existed at the end of the previous July. No doubt this number had been increased before the beginning of the war. The machines were of various types, but that most approved and comprising the majority in use was a product of the Royal Aircraft Factory, evolved after careful scientific and practical experiment in this country. It is known as the " B.E.," and exists in a variety of somewhat differing designs. In the field aeroplanes are attended by motor-cars conveying

the equipment for supply and repairs upon which their continued efficiency depends.

The excellence of the " B.E." machine probably contributed its share towards securing that " individual ascendancy " over the aircraft of the enemy to which Sir John French has borne such emphatic testimony. It is stated on competent authority to have proved its superiority in two qualities of prime importance, namely, speed and climbing power. The second is hardly, if at all, less valuable than the first ; for to be able to outclimb your enemy is practically to escape him. By getting above him you acquire command of all methods of attack. Climbing power is, indeed, to aircraft much the same as the possession of the weather gauge to line-of-battle ships in the old days of sailing navies. If the position of greater altitude does not in itself secure safety, so that escape by flight after all becomes necessary, you still have the advantage, inasmuch as by diving at the start you can secure an enormous initial speed of flight. The carbine, the revolver, bombs and

METHOD OF DROPPING AIR BOMBS FROM AN AEROPLANE.

multiple darts—the dreaded steel *flèches*—are among the weapons at the disposal of the airman holding the upper position ; moreover, he can head his adversary off by diving into his line of flight. The British " B.E." machine is also declared to be handier in steering than the German " Taube," and much quicker in response to its controls.

Its advantages were at once turned to full account by our brilliant and accomplished airmen, as soon as opportunity was given them in actual warfare.

CHAPTER XXXVI.

THE AUSTRO-HUNGARIAN PROBLEM.

The Anglo-German and Austro-Slav Problems—Their Connexion—Origins of Austria—
The Holy Roman Empire—The 1848 Revolution—Austria and Hungary—The "Compro-
mise "—Francis Joseph's Policies—Position of the Crown—Racial Distribution Analysed
—Germans—Czechs—Slovaks—Poles—Ruthenes—Slovenes—Serbs and Croats—Italians
—Rumanians—Racial Problems—The Austro-German Alliance—The Macedonian Ques-
tion—Serbia—The Annexation Crisis of 1908—The Revolution in Turkey—The Anti-
Serb Campaign—Forged Evidence—Austro-German Relations—Subordination of Austrian
Interests—The Balkan Wars—The Serajevo Murders—The Responsibility of Hungary
—Some Authors of the War.

FEW problems could have seemed at first sight more entirely separate than the rivalry between Germany and Great Britain and the feud between Austria-Hungary and the Slav populations within and without her borders. They were localized in different regions and appeared to involve quite distinct interests. But history shows that when problems of this kind reach a certain state of tension they exercise a fatal attraction upon each other; and these two questions were, as a matter of fact, much less distinct than might have been supposed. Amidst very differing circumstances the same powerful idea was at work—the cause of Germanism. In Germany, the heart of the race, it displayed itself as a deliberate bid for world-dominion, prompted by the new gospel of power. In Austria-Hungary it took the form of an attempted chastisement of the Slav—the last stage of a long warfare which had begun when Austria was a medieval duchy. Whether this policy was primarily inspired by German or by Hungarian feeling, the main-tenance of Austria-Hungary's position in South-Eastern Europe was recognized at Berlin as a German interest. It is this which unites the two cases, and explains why the murder of the

Austrian Heir-Presumptive in a Bosnian town, followed by the Austro-Hungarian ultimatum to Serbia, laid a train of consequence which was to be felt in every town and village of the United Kingdom.

Austria came into existence in the Middle Ages as a southern outpost of the Teuton against the Slav. As she absorbed large Slav populations in her own realm, this side of her policy faded into the background, from which it only emerged again with distinctness in the twentieth century. She soon occupied herself with other tasks and larger ambitions. Rudolf of Habsburg brought her, in the thirteenth century, the imperial title and the grandiose but unsubstantial dignities of the Holy Roman Empire. They gave her the right to supremacy in Germany, and the astuteness of her rulers gave her the power to make it effective. The extraordinary Habsburg talent for match-making enabled her patiently to lay field by field, not only in Germany, but in the Nether-lands, in Spain, and in Italy, and gave rise to the saying that while other nations made wars, Austria had only to make marriages. She long dominated Germany; and for a moment, on the accession of Charles V., the greatest Habs-burg in history, she seemed likely to dominate

[Seebald, Vienna.

THE KAISER AND THE AUSTRIAN EMPEROR.

the world. But a division of the empire—too vast and miscellaneous for a single ruler—inevitably followed ; and in the seventeenth century the ravages of the Thirty Years' War, with the rise of France as a great military monarchy, began to undermine Austria's imperial position in Germany. The aggrandisement of Prussia under Frederick the Great still more decidedly challenged her claim to the control of German interests. In 1806, while the Napoleonic wars were breaking up the map of Europe, Francis II. of Austria recognized in theory what was already becoming a fact, and took the title of hereditary Emperor of Austria, in exchange for that of Holy Roman Emperor, which had descended from Charlemagne. Austria's real position was defined. She had surrendered her patent of German sovereignty. Her power was now definitely localised in the Habsburg dominions and settled there on the dynastic basis of allegiance to the Habsburg House. She was still, as she issued from the struggle against Napoleon, territorially a most imposing State ; for, though she had surrendered the Netherlands and the last Habsburg domains upon the Rhine, she had acquired, in addition to her broad dominions in central Europe, the Illyrian and Dalmatian coastlands, and a great block of territory in Northern Italy which formed the kingdom of Lombardy-Venetia. On the strength of this she still

dominated German politics as long as the old system of disunited German States survived.

The chief political ideas of the nineteenth century were liberty and nationality, and each presented Austria with a crucial problem to solve. For a generation after the battle of Waterloo she was governed on Metternich's principle of iron resistance to change. No doubt it was for this reason that when the fateful " March Days " of 1848 shook the Habsburg throne to its foundations, and Austria was confronted at once with revolt in Italy and revolution in Vienna, in Hungary and in Croatia, she failed disastrously to deal with the constitutional problem, and showed her recognition of nationalities mainly by using one race against another. She turned her composite army against Italy, the Germans against the Czechs, the Croats against the Magyars, called in a Russian army to complete the work, and then lapsed into ten years of repression even more sordid than the era of Metternich. Her best excuse is that the cause of liberty was bound up with nationalist claims which threatened the unity of the empire, but for her ruthless victory a price had to be paid. It was paid in part when France and Piedmont took up arms for Northern Italy in 1859 and Austria found herself powerless to prevent its liberation after the battle of Solferino because reactionary government had left her without any means to go on with the struggle. The rest of the penalty was exacted in 1866, when Prussia compelled Austria to decide by arms the question which State was to control the future of Germany. The minor German kingdoms took Austria's side, but the swift advance of the Prussian armies upset all calculations, and after six weeks' war Austria was decisively beaten and Bismarck had settled once for all that German unity would be established under Prussian leadership. More than this, Austria was by the battle of Sadowa definitely driven outside Germany. What 1806 had foreshadowed, 1866 realized. Her sole link with Germany now was the German population inside her borders, and that was only one element in her strangely miscellaneous empire. Her ambitions could only lie eastwards. Her whole future depended on her adopting a wise internal policy which would satisfy the claims of her mixed populations, and breathe into them the sense of common interests and a common destiny. Perhaps this demanded superhuman statesmanship ; it proved, in any case, far beyond the sagacity of the Emperor Francis Joseph and his advisers.

The great question for Austria when she set her house in order in 1867 was how to deal with Hungary. Hungary, like every other part of the empire, had racial problems of her own, but she had been effectively dominated for centuries by her original conquerors, the Magyars, a high-spirited aristocracy alien in race both to the Germans and the Slavs, filled with a strong sense of their past glories and constitutional privileges, and firmly believing in their mission to govern less distinguished peoples. They roused much sympathy in Western Europe by their brilliant defence of political liberty in 1848, when they were only crushed after Austria had mobilized the rest of her empire against them and called in Russian aid. At the height of the crisis the Emperor Ferdinand had sanctioned laws which made Hungary almost an independent State, and though these were afterwards withdrawn the Hungarians clung to the ideal they embodied and refused to recognize any arrangements for merging them in the rest of the empire.

Hungary's attitude had been a serious weakness to Austria in the war of 1866, and directly this was over it was clear that a settlement must be arrived at. The most hopeful arrangement would have been one giving to the Czechs

GENERAL ALEXANDER KROBATIN,
Austro-Hungarian Minister of War.

of Bohemia and the Slavs in the southern part of the empire approximately equal privileges with those of the Germans and the Magyars, and Belcredi, the Austrian Premier, was in favour of a federalising plan which would have done this. But Francis Joseph, on the morrow of the war with Prussia, cherished the idea of revenge, and his new Foreign Minister, Beust, a Saxon, and a jealous enemy of Bismarck, was willing to give Hungary her independence if he could thereby get a solidarity of feeling in case of war. The settlement of 1867 reflected their state of mind ; it showed every sign of being made in an emergency. Instead of dealing comprehensively with all the races in the empire, it was a purely dual arrangement between Austria and Hungary, after a negotiation in which Hungary held the stronger cards. The two countries came out of it apparently equal partners, and "Austria-Hungary," or the "Dual Monarchy," became recognized names for what had before been only known as "Austria." The first link between them was the person of the Monarch— "Emperor" in Austria and "Apostolic King" in Hungary. The second was their common share in three joint departments of State— Foreign Affairs, War, and Finance. These departments were not directly responsible either to the Austrian or the Hungarian Parliaments, but to two Delegations of sixty members, chosen from each, and meeting in alternate years at Vienna and Budapest to

COUNT VON AERENTHAL,
Late Minister for Foreign Affairs—" The Bismarck
of Austria-Hungary."

discuss joint affairs and estimates. A Customs Alliance, renewable every ten years, settled the commercial relations of Austria and Hungary. This was a matter for direct arrangement between the Ministries and Parliaments of the two countries, and in case it lapsed Hungary retained the right of regulating her own economic interests as she pleased. Such, in outline, was the famous " Compromise " or *Ausgleich*, which governed the internal relations of Austria-Hungary up to 1914.

It was just the sort of arrangement which looks very fair on paper and demands an immense amount of mutual reasonableness in practice. This might be hoped for from Francis Joseph, who had been trained in the school of adversity, and had a strong sense of his duties as a ruler. It might be hoped for and was loyally given by the political leaders who first guided Hungary after the settlement, statesmen of real distinction like Deák and Andrássy, who took a broad and far-sighted view of the settlement they had made. Still, the Hungarians had exposed themselves to temptations to which sooner or later they were bound to yield. They had created a position which overbalanced that of their partners in the Monarchy. Austria was not a thoroughly constitutionalized State like Hungary : her Constitution had been issued for her at the Emperor's pleasure, whereas that

of Hungary had been an equal contract between the Magyar nation and the Crown. Nor did the character of the Austrian-Germans in the least resemble that of the Hungarians. The Hungarians were born leaders, orators, and politicians, and had been trained for centuries in the art of government. The Austrian-Germans were easy-going, pleasure-loving people, accustomed to having their government done for them. They could not even oppose to Hungary the compact racial strength which she possessed. The Magyars of Hungary secured this by the simple expedient of practically shutting out the other nationalities from the franchise, but in the Austrian lands the supremacy of the German element was challenged by the Slavs, who were actually more numerous, and in Bohemia, at least, had a sense of national patriotism and historic unity like that of the Magyars. After 1871, when German victories in France and the foundation of the German Empire robbed Austria-Hungary of any lingering desire she may have had for revenge or interference in German affairs, the Emperor Francis Joseph sought for a few months deliberately to promote the influence of the Austrian Slavs at the expense of the Austrian Germans. His efforts were checked by the combined opposition of Bismarck, Beust, and Andrássy, and, until 1879, Austrian-German influence in Austria was unchallenged. But from 1879 onwards Francis Joseph reverted to his plan of promoting Slav development, and the Austrian-Germans became even less the equals of the Magyars than they had been before.

The real countercheck to Hungarian self-assertion, in point of fact, has always been, not Austria, but the Crown. It was only the immense influence of the Sovereign which kept his ill-assorted empire together, saved apparently impossible situations, and, it must be added, sometimes took liberties which would have been the death-blow of any parliament. This success must not be ascribed to any extraordinary wisdom on the part of Francis Joseph, amiable and devoted as his private character was. His public policy on occasions has been rather aptly compared to that of " a landlord who ignores the petty tyranny exercised by his estate-agent and dismisses the agent only when revenue falls off or disturbances occur." But he knew how to make a constant and tactful use of that remarkable blend of personal authority and dynastic prestige which the

Habsburgs have possessed beyond any other rulers. They gained it, no doubt, because they were the one institution in which all the races of the empire shared, and because they had been in a real sense the makers of their realm. They were the more popular since they had aggrandized it not so much by warfare, like the Hohenzollerns, as by statecraft of a personal kind. Even the heavy-handed policy of their severer moments had not quite robbed them of popularity, and it had certainly paved the way for their unchecked power. In few times or countries has State action been more ruthlessly applied than it was by Ferdinand II. in enforcing the Catholic Counter-Reformation on unwilling subjects, by Joseph II. in laying out his backward dominions on ready-made philosophic principles, or by Metternich and Bach in stifling the soul of a people through official tyranny. The accumulated result of this was an immense fund of personal authority for the Habsburgs. Francis Joseph drew freely on it, and as he and his peoples fared together through the occasional triumphs and the more frequent disasters, public and private, which marked his reign, the feeling grew that, whatever the shortcomings of Austria-Hungary might be, a really paternal relation had been established between the Monarch and his subjects.

Unfortunately, this did not prevent much dangerous friction from arising with Hungary when the patriotic generation of 1867 had passed away. The most serious internal crisis which the Dual Monarchy went through was that which, from 1902–1906, threatened the unity of the Monarchy in its most vital point—the Army—and almost paralysed the working of the whole constitutional machine. The affair showed how inflammable was "Magyar Chauvinism," and how little the Hungarian extremists cared for the common interests of the Monarchy when they had become excited over their own point of view. A quarrel arose because Bills had been presented to the Austrian and Hungarian Parliaments for an increase in the numbers of the army, and the Government had been ill-judged enough to retain several thousand supernumerary recruits with the colours, pending the adoption of the Bills. This was enough for the Hungarian nationalists, who at once came out with the demand that the Magyar language should be used in commands to Hungarian regiments, or else that the Bills

BARON FRIEDRICH VON GEORGI,
Minister for National Defence.

should be withdrawn. The Crown was obliged to withdraw the Bills, though the Austrian Reichsrat had already passed those affecting Austria, and regarded them as a patriotic measure. But the conflict was far from calming down. Ministry succeeded Ministry in Hungary, government was almost brought to a standstill, and the controversy went on raging as to how the extremist demands could be reconciled with the Sovereign's prerogatives as "supreme war-lord" and his unitary direction of the army. It was only ended by the Crown's threatening Hungary with universal suffrage, whereupon the Magyars grew so alarmed at the prospect of losing a political ascendancy that depended on their narrow franchise that they were willing to compromise. But the dispute had strained to the last point of tension both Royal influence and Hungarian policy, and it had placed a deliberate slight on Austria by obliging her to repeal, at Hungary's dictation, Bills which she had already passed.

It was by crises of this kind that the relations of the Austrian-Germans and the Magyars were embittered, and if there had been no counteracting influence it is not very likely that the framework of the Dual Monarchy would have survived up to 1914 without a change. But a common enemy is an excellent political bond ; and the Austrian-Germans and the Magyars were both so apprehensive of the Slavs that they recognized an advantage in keeping together. Finally, the development of Slav States like Serbia and Bulgaria beyond the frontier, and the intense racial feeling among the Slav populations within it, established that real community of policy between Germans and Magyars which was one of the chief causes of the war.

The whole question of the races in the empire which is at once the " Austrian " question and the question of 1914, can only be appreciated if we realize how they are distributed and what is their relative weight.

Taking the Austrian territories first, we find that according to the census of 1910 they contained approximately nine million Germans, nearly six million Czechs and Slovaks, four million Poles, three million Ruthenes, a million Slovenes, 700,000 Serbs and Croats, 700,000 Italians, and 200,000 Rumanians. It will be seen that the Germans thus numbered only about a third of a population which was mainly Slav. The Slav peoples fall, roughly speaking, into three groups. First come the " Northern Slavs," as they may be called, the Czechs, or Slavs of Bohemia, and the Slovaks in Moravia, the contiguous province.

They were isolated from the " Southern Slavs " by the two German-speaking provinces of Upper and Lower Austria. Bohemia, the centre of this group, was a province with a distinct national consciousness and a long history, in which the Hussite struggles and the Thirty Years' War had left an ineffaceable stamp on the people. The ancient Bohemian kingdom dated from the eleventh century, and had passed to the Habsburgs in the sixteenth. Ferdinand II. in the seventeenth century and Joseph II. in the eighteenth had each contributed to extinguish it, Ferdinand by suppressing its free constitution, and Joseph by refusing to be crowned as King of Bohemia in its capital, Prague. None the less, the Bohemians had never really lost their sense of independent existence, and as the smaller nationalities revived in Europe during the nineteenth century under the stimulus of the nationalist movement, the Czech race and Czech language increased until nearly three-quarters of these provinces could be reckoned Slavonic. Their commercial importance—Bohemia stood first among the Austrian provinces as regards industry, and had become a great manufacturing centre—made it impossible for them to be ignored ; and their lively intelligence was sure to make the most of political oppor-

THE ARCHDUKE FRIEDRICH (Commander-in-Chief) and
GENERAL BARON KONRAD VON HÖTZENDORF (Chief of the General Staff).

tunities. In the education of the people they had advanced beyond any other Austrian province.

The next great Slav group after the Czechs and Slovaks was to be found in Austrian Poland, which formed the province of Galicia. Galicia, the north-eastern corner of the empire, was the largest of the Austrian lands. It was dominated, politically speaking, by the Poles, though relatively they were not much more numerous than the Ruthenes. Between these two Slav peoples the relation was that of master and subject. The Poles, like their fellow-countrymen in Germany and Russia, belonged to the hapless race which, after a brilliant if wayward history, had lost their unity and independence through their own factiousness and the greed of their more powerful neighbours. Those of them who had fallen to Austria's share were very much better off than the Poles in Germany or Russia, for Austria had thought it best to conciliate them by giving them a large share of autonomy and confirming their supremacy over the Ruthenes. In fact, if she had not done so she would have found it difficult to induce the Poles to vote for the settlement of 1867. The Ruthenians were racially the same people as the Little Russians, their neighbours across the frontier, who inhabited the wide Ukraine region of the Russian Empire. There was always a potential menace to Austrian rule in Galicia through the presence of this large Russian element, indistinguishable from their 30 million kinsmen in the neighbouring governments of the Czar. They were divided from the Poles not only by race but by religion, the Poles being ardent Roman Catholics, while the Ruthenes belonged either to the Orthodox Church or the " Greek United," which combines Roman Catholic doctrine with Orthodox rites. More recently Austria changed her policy and began to encourage the Ruthenes, aiming apparently at the creation of a new Ruthene border province which might prevent them from hankering after Russia. This was not very agreeable to the Poles, who also had to compete with a large Jewish population, holding most of Galicia's commerce in their hands—a fact of importance in view of the large transit trade with Russia in the east.

The third substantial Slav group in the Austrian Empire were the Slovenes. These were chiefly to be found in the southern provinces of Styria, Carinthia, and Carniola, specially the

GENERAL KONRAD VON HÖTZENDORF.
Chief of the General Staff.

latter. Being a tractable people without an uncomfortably historic past, they had been more liberally treated than most of the Austrian Slavs in the matter of their language, and had preserved their identity without giving political trouble. The Serbs and Croats, the other block of " Southern Slavs," were chiefly of importance in connexion with their brethren under direct Hungarian rule in Croatia, where the racial question, as we shall see, was acute. Finally, the Italians in Tirol and the Trentino and Istria must not be forgotten. They were still another discordant element in the polyglot empire, vociferous out of all proportion to their numbers and importance, but a perpetual anxiety both to Austria and Italy, because they kept alive the old grievance of " Irredentism," recalled the time, not far distant, when Austria had tyrannized over some of the fairest lands of Italy, and prompted the question why Austria should still detain this Italian remnant.

Such was the miscellaneous grouping of races in Austrian territory, without reckoning for the moment the equally crucial questions of the same kind which belonged to Hungary. In the main it was a problem of German and Slav, and the Slavs were in a majority. From the time of the Dual Settlement, save for a brief interlude in 1870, up to the conclusion of the

Austro-German Alliance in 1879, Austrian policy favoured the Germans; but after the conclusion of the Alliance it took a new turn, and proceeded to favour the Slavs at the expense of the Germans. It may have been more than a coincidence indeed, that almost directly after the German victories of 1870 over the French, Francis Joseph held out hopes to Bohemia of a constitution on the Hungarian model. and led the Czechs to believe that he might be crowned as King of Bohemia at Prague. This, of course, would have delighted the Slavs, but it would have upset the Dual basis of the empire, and the Austrian-Germans and the Hungarians alike united to prevent it. Francis Joseph had to recede from his position, and the later developments of his Slav policy were less demonstrative. None the less, it was steadily carried out through the last quarter of the nineteenth century by the Emperor and a Slav-Clerical majority, led first by Count Taaffe and then by Count Badeni. It was the will of the Emperor rather than the will of the people which prevailed, but political conditions were equalized and a surprising sign of confidence in democracy was given in 1906 by the establishment of universal suffrage. The result of this, combined with a redistribution of seats, was that 259 Slav deputies were sent to the Lower House of the Austrian Reichsrat as

against 233 Austrian-Germans. Even with the deputies of " Latin " race the Germans were still in a minority compared with the Slavs, and as the electoral law made parliamentary contests between different races impossible, this meant that the Slavs were placed permanently in a majority, especially as the Italian deputies cooperated with them rather than with the Germans. So far as Austria was concerned, therefore, the Slavs had won their way to a very tolerable position; they predominated in the Reichsrat, even if the administration was still German. The Slav question would probably have solved itself if it had not been for the acute form in which it reappeared in Hungary; and we have now to see what the conditions were in that half of the Dual Monarchy.

In Hungary there were, in 1910, ten million Magyars, including a million Jews, two million Germans, nearly two million Slovaks, nearly three million Rumanians, the same number of Serbs and Croats, and 400,000 Ruthenes. The Magyars chiefly occupied the great central plain of the Danube and the Theiss, and had kindred settlers long established eastwards, in Transylvania. They were neither Germans nor Slavs, and their origin and affinities have always been perplexing. Racially they were akin to the Finns, and had swept into Central Europe among the invading hosts

SWEARING ALLEGIANCE AT THE MILITARY ACADEMY, VIENNA

of the Dark Ages; linguistically they belong, like the Turks and Mongols, to the Turanian family. The Magyar aristocracy of the present day have kept a good deal of the high spirit and gallantry which their ancestors displayed during the fifteenth and sixteenth centuries, when they were the foremost champions of Europe against the Turks. In the fifteenth century Hungary had been one of the strongest and wealthiest of medieval States; but the Turkish attacks and occupation thinned the numbers of the Magyars greatly, and the mixed population of the present day is the result of the immigration which took place afterwards to fill up the land. It will be seen, however, that the position of the Magyars in Hungary was relatively stronger than that of the Germans in Austria, and their numbers were increased by the deliberate " Magyarization " of other races which they carried on in recent times. None the less, they kept, much more decidedly than the Austrian-Germans, the character of an aristocracy dominating over inferiors, and the basis of this was a franchise which has been described as the most illiberal in Europe, which gave votes to only 6 per cent. of the population, and was, in fact, simply an instrument for keeping the Magyars in power. There were two races whose grievance against them was particularly strong. The Rumanians, who were mostly localized in Transylvania, were treated by the Magyar minority practically as a subject population, a condition all the more galling as just across the frontier men of their own race had built up the independent kingdom of Rumania, the earliest of the Balkan kingdoms to reach stability and power. There was always a chance that the cry might be raised of *Rumania Irredenta*, and schemes for the formation of a " Greater Rumania " be formed on both sides of the border.

But a much more critical question was raised by the large population of Croats and Serbs in Croatia-Slavonia, Istria, and Dalmatia—the lands to the south of Hungary and those along the Adriatic coast. Here was the germ of the real " Southern Slav " problem. Croatia, which had belonged to Hungary since the eleventh century, was still ruled from Budapest. It had a one-Chamber assembly which dealt with public worship, education, justice and some provincial affairs; but its important measures had to be countersigned by the Minister who represented Croatia in the Hungarian Government. The effective

PRINCE BISMARCK IN 1894.

administration of the country was in the hands of the Ban or Viceroy, who, though nominated by the Crown, was practically both appointed and removable by the Hungarian Premier. There had been one moment in the nineteenth century when the Croats played an independent part in history, with unfortunate results for themselves. That was in 1848, when Jellatchich, a Croat who held the office of Ban, used the forces of his country on behalf of the Austrian Government against Hungary in the revolution which had torn the empire asunder. It was Kossuth's intolerant Magyarism which led Jellatchich into the field against him, and made the cause of Hungarian liberty odious in Croatian eyes. Between the Croats and the Russians, Hungary was subdued, but the Croats did not escape from her dominion, and the recollection of what Jellatchich had done was not likely to make the Magyars tender to Croatian feelings. The Croats and Serbs were held sternly down and governed by repression or corruption, or a combination of the two. As Fiume, Hungary's one port and outlet to the sea, lay in Croatian territory, she had another reason for not relaxing her grip in this quarter. So the Croats and Serbs remained in political thraldom, which might well have seemed hopeless till the rise of Serbia and the military triumphs of the Balkan States gave a fresh stimulus to Southern Slav feeling. But that belongs to a later phase, which must be dealt with in its place ; here it need only be said that, while the treatment of the Serbs and Croats by Hungary was a serious flaw in the Dual Monarchy, it did not become a pressing danger till the Balkan problem grew acute between 1908–1914. Its gravity was that it illustrated the reckless particularism of the Magyars in dealing with these racial questions— a frame of mind which might one day threaten the whole of Austria-Hungary with ruin. Austria, under pressure of circumstances, had learned to treat her Slav subjects in a fairly comprehensive spirit. But Hungary remained unteachable, and even her virtues seemed to become vices when she had to deal with the Slavs.

On the morrow of the Franco-German War, however, the uncomfortable possibilities of the Slav question were still latent. What Austria-Hungary, like the rest of the world, had to do was to adapt herself to the new situation created by the foundation of the German Empire and the overthrow of France. She frankly recognised the *fait accompli.* Under the guidance of Beust's successor, Andrássy, the last Hungarian statesman who played a really great part on the European stage and refused to limit his vision by the interests of his particular race, she accepted her exclusion from Germany and put away her resentment towards the new German Power. The first form which the cooperation with Germany took was the Three Emperors' League, not a formal alliance, but a more or less personal understanding between the Sovereigns and Ministers of Germany, Austria-Hungary and Russia. This lasted from 1872 to 1877, and during that time it guaranteed Germany the fruits of her victory over France by condemning the latter to isolation, and it established a political *entente* between the Powers of Central and Eastern Europe. But Russia did not remain in league with the central European Powers. In 1879 a new combination was formed between Austria-Hungary and Germany only. This was the Austro-German Alliance which was still in force in 1914 and which, widened afterwards by the inclusion of Italy, was to be known as the Triple Alliance. The terms of its two operative clauses were published in 1888, and in view of their great importance they may be given here :

Clause I.—" Should, contrary to the hope and against the sincere wish of the two high contracting parties, one of the two Empires be attacked by Russia, the high contracting parties are bound to stand by each other with the whole of the armed forces of their Empires, and in consequence thereof, only to conclude peace jointly and in agreement.

Clause II.—Should one of the high contracting parties be attacked by another Power, the other high contracting party hereby binds itself, not only not to stand by the aggressor of its high ally, but to observe at least an attitude of benevolent neutrality towards its high co-contractor.

If, however, in such a case, the attacking Power should be supported by Russia, either in the form of active cooperation or by military measures menacing to the party attacked, the obligation defined in Clause I. of reciprocal help with the entire armed strength, comes immediately into force in this case also, and the war will then also be waged jointly by the two high contracting parties until the joint conclusion of peace."

In form it was a defensive alliance directed against Russia. Germany, foreseeing the possible Franco-Russian combination against her, did not want to have to meet Austria-Hungary also. Austria-Hungary did not want to have to fight Russia single-handed. It was not likely that Germany would join Russia against her, but it was only too probable that if Germany abstained she would put in a claim at the peace for substantial compensations. Looking retrospectively at the alliance, we see that it only reached its full scope when France and Russia formed their counter-alliance afterwards. Its terms and liabilities were in themselves perfectly clear. But Austria-Hungary was not aware that within five years of its conclusion it had been undermined by a secret agreement between Germany and Russia. This was Bismarck's famous " reinsurance treaty." The old Chancellor enlivened his retirement by letting out the secret in 1896, and it threw a curious light on the diplomatic chessboard and particularly on Bismarck's stratagems. It appeared that in 1884 the two Empires had made an agreement that, if one of them was attacked, the other would remain benevolently neutral. Of course there was nothing in this arrangement which expressly contravened the terms of the Austro-German alliance, as that provided simply against an attack by Russia on Austria-Hungary or Germany. The " reinsurance treaty " concerned itself only with the contingency of an aggressive attack on Russia. Bismarck even went so far as to maintain, in the controversy which followed his indiscretion, that it would be

Underwood & Underwood.

VIENNA.
The Schotten-Ring in the Ringstrasse.

a good thing if the whole Triple Alliance concluded similar treaties with Russia. But the
impression was that he had been a little too
clever. If Austria-Hungary and Russia had
gone to war Germany would have had to decide
which was the aggressor—whether, in fact, she
was to grant the Austrian demand for armed
help or the Russian demand for benevolent
neutrality. " Too complicated," was the epithet
applied to this position by Bismarck's successors
in Germany, and they let the reinsurance treaty
lapse. Austria-Hungary received Bismarck's
disclosures calmly, but they were bound to

make her feel uncomfortable, and she gave
signs of having taken them to heart. Without
departing from her obligations under the
German alliance she drew closer to Russia, and
in the next year, 1897, an Austro-Russian
agreement was made for the pursuit of a common
policy in the Balkans. This put an end, for the
time, to the rather dubious relationship of
Austria-Hungary towards Russia during the
last half-century. Russia had saved the Austrian
Empire from disruption in the revolution of
1848–9 by sending in an army to reconquer
Hungary : and Austria, fulfilling Schwarzen-

FELDZEUGMEISTER OSKAR POTIOREK,
In charge of the Transport Department of the
Austro-Hungarian Army.

berg's prediction that she would astonish the
world with her ingratitude, had repaid this
assistance by failing to aid Russia against the
Western Powers during the Crimean War, or
even to assure her of neutrality. The estrange-
ment which naturally followed was checked
when Austria-Hungary and Russia combined
in the Three Emperors' League, an arrangement which satisfied at least the conservative
instincts of both. When the Eastern question
was reopened in 1875 by the rising of Bosnia
and Herzegovina against Turkish rule, and the
Russo-Turkish war followed, Russia purchased
Austria-Hungary's acquiescence in the conquests she expected to make from Turkey by
agreeing to Austrian acquisition of the two
revolted provinces. But Austro-Russian relations seemed fated not to work smoothly, and
here, again, there was a hitch, for ultimately
Russia would not allow Austria-Hungary to
annex Bosnia-Herzegovina, though she consented to an Austrian occupation and administration of the provinces. Russia's own aims
had been thwarted by the Congress of Berlin,
and she probably held that the situation had
been changed since the first agreement. A
similar misunderstanding, though a more
dangerous, and on Austria-Hungary's part a
more deliberate, one, was to put an end eventually to the Balkan agreement of 1897. At first,
however, the relations of the two Powers went

smoothly. Russia was chiefly occupied at the
moment with pursuing her ambitions in the Far
East, and she was quite ready to work in concert
with Austria-Hungary in the question, which
was now coming to the front, of getting reforms
in Macedonia.

It was from the raising of the Macedonian
question at the beginning of the twentieth
century, and the discordant interests involved,
that events led almost continuously on to the
crisis of the great war. We have glanced
already at the complicated race problems of
Austria-Hungary, and seen how the most important of them all was likely to be presented by
the Slavs. We have now to look at the Slav
problem as it had developed itself beyond the
borders of the Dual Monarchy, and trace the
way in which this question and that of the
Austrian Slavs reacted on each other. The
history of South-Eastern Europe in the nineteenth and twentieth centuries is a tale of the
successive liberation of tracts of territory and
the formation of Christian States out of the
dominions of the Turk. Greece, Serbia, and
Rumania had all attained full or modified
independence at the time of the Russo-Turkish
War. After that struggle, which had been provoked by Slav risings in the Bosnian and
Bulgarian provinces, Rumania, Serbia, and
Montenegro became fully independent, Bulgaria
was made an " autonomous vassal State," and
soon after successfully defied the shortsighted
decisions of the Berlin Congress by annexing
Eastern Rumelia—the Southern Bulgaria of
to-day—and Austria-Hungary entered into
occupation of Bosnia and Herzegovina. By
the freeing of Serbia and Bulgaria two powerful
centres of Slav nationality had been created,
or rather revived. When reference is made to
a " Pan-Serb agitation " or " Bulgarian propaganda " it must not be supposed that these
movements appealed to feelings which have
been entirely created since 1878. The semi-
historical, semi-legendary glories of the Serbs
and Bulgars have a considerable basis of fact,
and strike their roots very deeply into the past.
In the tenth century and again in the thirteenth
there had been a Bulgarian Empire which
covered all the modern " Balkans," and left
the Byzantine Cæsars with little except Constantinople and the cities nearest it. In the
fourteenth century Stephen Dushan had founded
a Serbian Empire of even larger dimensions and
led an army of 80,000 men within striking distance of Constantinople. The possession of

Constantinople by a line of vigorous Slavonic princes might have repulsed the Turk and changed the whole history of Eastern Europe. But Stephen died in his camp, and the Balkans lapsed under the crushing weight of Turkish dominion till the nineteenth century. The Turks did their work more thoroughly here than they did when masters of Hungary. While the aristocracy survived among the Magyars, it was crushed out in Serbia and Bulgaria, which emerged when they gained their freedom as peasant States of a democratic type—and perhaps none the weaker for the fact. But the strength which they displayed in the Balkan War was not gained in a day. For a long time Austria-Hungary held Serbia in tutelage. Serbia had no outlet to the sea, and practically no markets for her agricultural produce except that afforded by her powerful neighbour across the Danube. She was also unlucky enough to have, in King Milan, a shiftless and expensive Monarch, who was always out of pocket, and found Vienna the easiest source for replenishing his purse. The part which Austria-Hungary played in these circumstances was anything but creditable. She controlled Serbian commerce, exploited King Milan's vices, and set Serbia on to fight Bulgaria just when the latter was freeing her southern territory from Turkey. As long as the Obrenovitch dynasty sat on the Serbian throne this ascendency of Austria-Hungary continued. The savage murder of King Alexander and his Queen at Belgrade in 1903 enthroned the Karageorgevitch dynasty instead, in the person of King Peter, and was a first step towards Serbian emancipation. Whether the conspirators acted with pro-Russian aims or not, stress of circumstances was to draw Serbia before long away from Austria-Hungary and into the orbit of her more natural protector, Russia. In 1905 she struck a blow for freedom by concluding a Customs Union with Bulgaria. Austria-Hungary, disturbed at this symptom of independence and cooperation among Balkan States, replied by making a tariff war on Serbia—the " Pig War," which was to exclude the large supply of Serbian swine and cattle from the Austro-Hungarian market. The weapon she used recoiled to some extent on herself ; the price of meat rose and her agrarian parties profited freely from the situation at the expense of the people generally. But for Serbia the affair was vital. It drove her to look for markets beyond Austria-Hungary, and she displayed a spirit of

independence in so doing which carried her far on the road to power. It saved her also from falling into military dependence on the Dual Monarchy. Instead of relying on Austrian factories for the purchase of *matériel* to equip her new army, she went westwards, and bought Creuzot guns and ammunition from France.

In the meantime the development of the Macedonian question was leading to a change in the relations of Austria-Hungary with Russia. The two Powers had successfully pressed upon Turkey their " Mürzsteg programme " for the reform of the Macedonian vilayets, and under the eyes of Austrian and Russian Civil Agents and a gendarmerie controlled by foreign officers a great deal of useful work had been done. Very much of the credit for this was due to Lord Lansdowne, who as British Foreign Minister had done his best to internationalize the reforms and disarm

A PIONEER IN MARCHING ORDER.

19—3

Turkey's fears that they would lead to an Austro-Russian partition of Macedonia. Russia, too, chastened by her defeat in the Far East, entered into the work in a more liberal spirit and accepted the principle of European control. But this was not so congenial to Austria-Hungary. She had designs of her own in the Balkans which European supervision might upset. She wanted to enter into formal annexation and possession of the two Bosnian provinces which she had occupied since 1878. She meant to prevent the rise of Serbia, and, if necessary, to annihilate its independence and incorporate it with the rest of her Slav dominions. She also cherished the dream of advancing to the Aegean at Salonika, a project for which a private understanding with Turkey might be necessary, and which an internationalized or liberated Macedonia might upset. The new trend of her policy became visible when Baron von Aehrenthal succeeded Count Goluchowski as her Foreign Minister in 1906. Aehrenthal had been ambassador at St. Petersburg, where his natural conservatism had been deepened by intimacy with the party of reaction. He was devoted to the idea of making his own country great, but his scheme of political greatness was borrowed from the old days of the Three Emperors' League. In the light of later events the idea of reviving that alliance of sovereigns, with Austria-Hungary as the predominant partner, seems a baseless dream. It was she who was in reality far the weakest of the three Powers. But this was not so clear when Aehrenthal came into power, and under

his resolute guidance she entered on a policy which was full of danger, but which, while he lived, might seem to promise success. Aehrenthal's first idea was to tighten the Austro-Russian understanding so as to thwart thoroughgoing reform and international control in Macedonia, both of which he profoundly distrusted. When he found that Russia was inclined to approve the internationalizing of the remaining reforms he had to modify this policy. He proposed, then, an *entente* between Austria-Hungary, Russia, Germany and France on a "conservative" basis. The result of this quadruple *entente* would have been, of course, to upset the understanding between France and Great Britain, and to block the way effectively against the further understanding between Great Britain and Russia which Sir Edward Grey and M. Isvolsky were in process of negotiating. Aehrenthal's plan failed because Russia saw the hand of Germany behind Austria-Hungary, and her experience of Germany's advice at the time of the Japanese war did not incline her to closer combination. If a compact had to be made she preferred to make it with Great Britain, who had warned her steadily that Japan would fight, rather than with Germany, who had encouraged her to believe the contrary. Events thus drew on to the Anglo-Russian understanding, and Aehrenthal had to devise a new line of policy. He took one which disregarded Russia, and pursued simply Austro-Hungarian interests without looking for the cooperation of other Powers. While pretending to work for the

INFANTRY AND MARINES.

accomplishment of the reforms which were still to be carried out in Macedonia, he ceased to give support to Russia and the other Powers and began to negotiate privately with Turkey. He agreed to drop the Macedonian reforms if Turkey would give Austria-Hungary the concession for a railway through the Sanjak of Novi Bazar—the small Turkish *enclave* which ran up into the heart of Bosnian and Serbian territory. Aehrenthal's real objects in demanding this concession are a matter of doubt, for the Austrian General Staff held that from a military point of view the Sanjak was worthless to Austria-Hungary. But whether he was mistaken as to this and other aspects of the Novi Bazar Railway, or whether he simply devised to strike a blow against Russia, the effect of his action was to rouse Russian indignation against such a piece of diplomatic treachery, and to place the Powers of the Triple *Entente* in antagonism to Austria-Hungary.

Such was the position when the revolution in Turkey broke out in the summer of 1908, and the Young Turks came into power. The contradictory elements which composed the movement—Ottomanism, militarism, Jewish finance, and constitutional reform—were not then disentangled, but the view commonly taken was that it would strengthen Turkey. She was pretty certain to assert herself for the salvage of outlying parts of her empire, and so Austria-Hungary had to consider what would be her own position in Bosnia-Herzegovina. These provinces were still nominally Turkish and owned the suzerainty of the Sultan. But Austria-Hungary, as has been explained, had occupied them effectively for thirty years, and had only failed to become their actual possessor through a turn of the diplomatic game. On the whole she had carried out her work very thoroughly. At first she had to go through a lot of hard fighting to subdue the provinces, but afterwards, thanks largely to the genius of a single administrator, de Kállay, she had established an effective, albeit a demoralising, rule. It was not an easy task, and the addition of nearly two million Slavs as virtual subjects of the Dual Monarchy—for the population was almost wholly Serb or Croat—was not regarded as an unmixed blessing either by the Austrian-Germans or the Magyars of Hungary. As the peasantry were exceedingly divided in religion, consisting partly of Serbs who had embraced Mahomedanism, and partly of Christians, who were again opposed as Orthodox or Catholic, the

GENERAL HORSETZKY,
Commanding the cavalry in Poland—a well-known military author.

work of conciliation was all the more difficult. But Austria never let embarrassments of this kind stand in her way when it was a question of acquiring more territory. This is the most persistent feature in the history of the Habsburgs. The reason why Austria-Hungary had displayed so much eagerness to secure the Bosnian provinces in 1878 was, no doubt, because the Emperor Francis Joseph wanted to wipe out the loss of Lombardy and Venetia. He was disappointed that he could not annex them, and he was firmly resolved not to let the last chance slip when it came in 1908. But how should annexation be carried out ? To snatch the provinces just when Turkey seemed to be in the act of reforming herself was not a policy that would commend itself to Europe. The idea of beginning with the grant of a Constitution was rejected, perhaps as too surprising a departure from Habsburg methods. A case had to be got up, and the materials for it were sought in the Hungarian kingdom of Croatia-Slavonia. If it could be shown that

PROFESSOR DR. FRIEDJUNG.

Austrian historian—author of baseless charges
against the Serbo-Croat leaders in 1909.

a deep conspiracy was being carried on by the
Serbo-Croats inside the Dual Monarchy, their
kinsmen in Bosnia-Herzegovina, and the
Serbians themselves outside, to realize the old
dream of a " Greater Serbia," Austria-Hungary
might hold herself politically justified in thwart-
ing a policy that menaced herself. It was true,
in a sense, that the Southern Slav problem transcended all frontiers, and that was why it was
so necessary for Austria-Hungary to treat it
wisely. Her mistake was to put a criminal
interpretation on the stages of a perfectly
natural development. While Serbia was acquiring a keener national sense and laying the
base of economic and military independence,
the Serbs and Croats in Croatia had laid aside
mutual antipathies and combined in a political
coalition. Together they were strong enough to
break down the corrupt Government majority,
and there seemed a chance that Croatia might
be fairly ruled in the interests of the Croatians
at last. It was the time when the conflict
over the Army was raging in Hungary between
the Hungarian political parties and the Crown,
and the Serbo-Croats at Agram managed to
improve their position by making a fighting
alliance with the Hungarian Coalition at
Budapest. For a moment they secured the
political justice which they had sought in vain
since the compact of 1867 placed them in
Hungary's hands. But it was too good to
last, and the Governments of Vienna and
Budapest combined again to check the move-

ment. The Hungarian Government eagerly
accepted " revelations " of a treasonable pan-
Serb movement, which was said to be fomented
among its subjects by the Serbian Government
at Belgrade ; upwards of fifty Serbs—all
innocent—were arrested in Croatia ; and a
huge treason trial began at Agram, the capital,
where it dragged on for months in conditions
that became a public scandal. The charges
trumped up against the victims at Agram were
reinforced on March 25, 1909, by a denunciation
from Dr. Friedjung, the Austrian historian,
in the *Neue Freie Presse*, who, basing his
statements on secret documents supplied to
him by the Foreign Office, accused some of
the leading members of the Serbo-Croat
coalition of treasonable correspondence with
Serbia. When the crisis over the annexation
of Bosnia-Herzegovina had passed, these Serbo-
Croat leaders prosecuted Dr. Friedjung for
libel, and the utter baselessness of his allegations
was revealed. Some of the documents, pur-
porting to be lists of payments by the head of a
Serbian student society to the Croatian leaders,
were exposed by their alleged author, a Serbian
professor, who had been studying at Berlin at
the moment when he was supposed to be making
plots in Belgrade. Others, which Dr. Friedjung
had declared to be official dispatches from the
archives of the Serbian Foreign Office, were
demonstrated by Serbia to be complete inventions ; and, finally, Professor Masaryk, a
distinguished Bohemian savant and politician,
discovered the fact that most of these documents
had been concocted and photographed in the
Austro-Hungarian Legation at Belgrade. The
Minister at Belgrade, Count Forgach, was
transferred by Austria-Hungary to Dresden,
but was afterwards recalled to Vienna, and at
the outbreak of war in 1914 he was in a responsible position of control at the Foreign
Office. The whole affair had shown that the
influences dominant in Austria-Hungary would
stop at nothing to crush the growing feeling of
solidarity among the Serbs. If, as seemed possible at the moment, war with Serbia had broken
out while the Serbo-Croat leaders were under the
shadow of Dr. Friedjung's charges they would
undoubtedly have been shot without scruple.

Fortunately matters were not then carried
to the point of war, though the tension was
extreme. Russia knew that Austria-Hungary
contemplated the annexation of Bosnia-Herzegovina and the declaration of full Bulgarian
independence. She expected to receive suffi-

cient notice of the date for her own arrangements and those of Serbia to be made in view of the changed situation. Aehrenthal, however, sprang the change upon the world in October, 1908, and the astonished Foreign Ministers of Europe found that Austria-Hungary had revised the Treaty of Berlin without consulting anybody. Even Germany had only been told at the last moment (though she may originally have suggested the idea of the annexation) and had scarcely had the option of refusing her support. But "the Austrian Bismarck" was running great risks in his ambitious policy. He had deliberately challenged Russia. He had treated Serbia's attitude with contempt, and assumed that Turkey had nothing to complain of in the loss of her title to the annexed provinces. The Young Turks took a different view and began boycotting Austro-Hungarian trade. Faced by a possible war with Russia, Servia, and Turkey, Aehrenthal was obliged to compensate the late owners of the provinces. He signed a convention by which Austria-Hungary paid a money indemnity, guaranteed the rights of the natives of the two provinces, and agreed to meet various Turkish demands. Meanwhile Russia, as well as Austria-Hungary, had begun to mobilize. But she had not yet reorganized her army, and was far from the state of military preparedness which she showed in 1914. Aehrenthal was confident that she would yield under the threat of war, even

though her surrender would be a blow to Slav prestige. She did yield, as he had expected, only the triumph of compelling the surrender came not to him, but to Prince Bülow. Germany, after a short hesitation as to whether she should back up Austria-Hungary, decided to do so and forestalled her partner by being the first to mention at St. Petersburg her readiness to act in case of war. This was the appearance " in shining armour " to which the Kaiser made his famous allusion eighteen months later. Aehrenthal hardly concealed his mortification that German assistance had taken such a demonstrative form.

It was at this point that the relations of Austria-Hungary with Germany underwent a change, and took the form which they kept until the great war. Up to the annexation crisis Austria-Hungary had played for her own hand. Afterwards she appears more and more as the accomplice, if not the satellite, of Germany. There could not be a better measure of the difference than the coolness and want of combination between Austria-Hungary and Germany in the crisis of 1908 and the complete understanding between the two Powers in the crisis of 1914. Whether the alteration would have been so great if Aehrenthal had not died in 1912 is, perhaps, a question. It was under his direction that Austria-Hungary had made her most distinct and resolute bid for diplomatic independence. But, greatly as per-

DRAGOONS IN FULL DRESS UNIFORM.

GENERAL AUFFENBERG.

sonality still counts in international politics, it is not likely that his survival would have much modified the course of things. The force of circumstances was too strong. The flaw in his policy—and it was one which nothing could very well compensate—was that Austria-Hungary was essaying a task beyond her powers. The Government at Berlin had a much clearer perception of this than the statesmen of Vienna. The idea that Austria-Hungary could ever be the predominant partner, or could be safely allowed a policy which was not inspired from Berlin, must have appeared a singular delusion to the Germans. If it had ever had any basis in fact, that disappeared from the day when the spirit of aggressive Germanism took possession of German statesmanship. A world policy of pan-Germanism could only be directed from one centre. But the supremacy of Berlin was quite consistent with allowing Austria-Hungary to follow, up to a certain point, what she believed to be her interests. She might be permitted, and even encouraged, to cherish the dream of an advance on Salonika, and to frustrate the growth of a strong Slav nucleus in the Balkans, provided these ideas did not encroach on the larger ambitions of Germany in the Near East. For herself Germany needed the command of the roads to Trieste and Constantinople, and an influence in Turkey predominant enough to secure her great political enterprise of the Baghdad Railway and her economic develop-

ments in Asia Minor. For the present all this might be accomplished by peaceful penetration —penetration of Austria-Hungary just as much as of Turkey. On the larger field of European politics Germany found the support of Austria-Hungary also worth retaining. If, as the Emperor William remarked, every Turkish army corps was a corps added to the German Army—every Austro-Hungarian army corps was worth as much, or more, on the same assumption. But for this purpose unity of control was clearly needed. Austria-Hungary could not be allowed to place Germany again in the awkward position of 1908, when the German Government was obliged to support an Austrian challenge to the new Turkish Government from which Germany hoped much. The backing which Germany then gave to Austria-Hungary showed that she was not prepared to sacrifice the Austrian alliance. But it was only worth having on her own terms. Germany was, and intended to remain, the managing partner of the Triple Alliance, and this was made clear to Austria-Hungary when she seemed to be forgetting it. In his last years of office Aehrenthal had reached a clearer knowledge of the limitations to an independent policy, and also of the advisability of cultivating better relations with Italy. The position of the third partner in the alliance was always thankless, and specially so when she was snubbed not only by Berlin but by Vienna. It was really to the interest of Austria-Hungary just as much as of Italy to be on cordial terms, because this was the only way by which the two Powers could attain a certain independence of Berlin. For the very same reason Germany looked with suspicion and disfavour on any improvement in Austro-Italian relations. Nothing could show more clearly the artificial nature of the Triple Alliance as a combination to promote German interests. If there were any two Powers who, it might be supposed, would not work harmoniously together, they were Austria-Hungary and Italy, with the memory of a secular feud between them, its survival in Irredentism, and the clash of counter-interests in the Adriatic and the Balkans. Yet it was only in unison that they could hope to assert a reasonable control of their own policy in the face of Germany. Meanwhile Germany, for her own part, was careful to discourage the idea that they had any such right to mutual consultation and independence.

It may well have occurred to Austria-Hungary to ask herself what she had to gain by the alliance. Were the common interests more than a dream ? The alliance had been founded when the German element in Austria-Hungary was much stronger than it became afterwards, and while Austria-Hungary, though excluded from the German Empire, was more under the influence of German feeling. It was understood by its authors as a pendant to the Dual System of 1867—an arrangement which would guarantee the supremacy of the Germans in Austria and the Magyars in Hungary. But the Dual System worked so decidedly in favour of the Magyars that it was clear the Austrian-Germans lost more than they gained by such an arrangement. They would probably have fared much better under a federalized or centralized system which would have secured fair play all round. Nothing, at any rate, could have been more of a disillusion for them than to be governed, as they were, by Hungary through the Crown, or to be reduced to an instrument for the use of the Crown against Hungary. The Triple Alliance was a monument of this state of things. It perpetuated a false idea and a false direction of the destinies of Austria-Hungary. It meant that her foreign policy was to be governed, not in the interests of the whole Monarchy, not even in those of the Austrian-Germans, but ultimately in those of the Magyars of Hungary and the powerful Jewish financiers who held sway at Vienna and Budapest. Its continuance implied the sacrifice of any claim of Austria-Hungary to be regarded as a whole, or as a unit. That ideal could only have been realized if she had fully accepted the consequences of her expulsion from Germany in 1866, and worked out her salvation as a South-Eastern Power by creating an adequate system for the Slavs. In choosing the opposite policy at the dictation of the Magyars she did, indeed, discover a common interest with Germany, but it was a negative and artificial one. She allowed herself to be used as an advanced guard of *Germanentum* against the Slavs. It was the line of development she had followed in her earliest history, but in the changed world of the twentieth century the resemblance became ironical.

It was this anti-Slav, or rather anti-Serbian, influence which mainly controlled Austro-Hungarian policy from 1908 to 1914. It was repeatedly in evidence during the Balkan War,

which greatly intensified it. The vigorous offensive of the Balkan States and their military successes over the Turks made the anti-Serbian party impatient for action. Everything was done to excite Austrian opinion against Serbia ; the advisability of an immediate attack on her was considered by the Austro-Hungarian War Office. When the terms of peace between the Balkan States and Turkey came to be discussed Austria-Hungary stood firm against Serbia's ambition to get access to the sea. Rather than see a Slav State established on the Adriatic, she invented the plan of an independent Albania and prepared to support it with her full military force. When it was a question of evicting Montenegro—the other Serb State and Serbia's ally—from Skutari in Albania, she risked a joint action with Italy which would almost certainly have landed both Powers in war but for the conciliating influence of the Triple Entente. She did more than any other Power to promote the Second Balkan War by steadily refusing to Serbia and Greece the fruits of their victories in the West, and by the direct instigation of a Bulgarian attack upon them. When the war broke out she gave considerable assistance to Bulgaria, and Count Stephen Tisza, the Hungarian Premier, made a speech openly endorsing Bulgaria's attitude. Meanwhile, her treatment of the Slavs within her borders had become more relentless than ever. The Government of Croatia had improved, indeed, for a time after the exposures of the Friedjung trial, and Baron Rauch, who then held the office of Ban, had been removed. But after a short change for the better the intransigent system was restored. The constitution of Croatia was abolished and the charter of the Serb Orthodox Church suspended. It was a dangerous plan to try repression at the moment when Serbia's victories over Turkey were setting the Serb provinces of Austria-Hungary ablaze with the spirit of enthusiasm for their race. But the successes of the Balkan States threatened the dominance of Germany and Austria-Hungary in South-Eastern Europe. If the result of the war with Turkey had been indecisive they would have had a promising field left open for interference. As it was, all they could try was to break up the Balkan Confederation—which they successfully did in the second Balkan War —and to play off Bulgaria and Turkey against the Slav and Greek confederates. With this policy abroad went the policy of repression at home. In defence of it Austria-Hungary could

ETHNOGRAPHIC MAP

REFERENCE

——•—— International Frontiers
·········· Provincial Boundaries

Scale of Miles
0 10 20 30 40 50   100   150

GERMANS   CZECHS   ITALIANS   SLOVENES   SERBO-CROATS

740

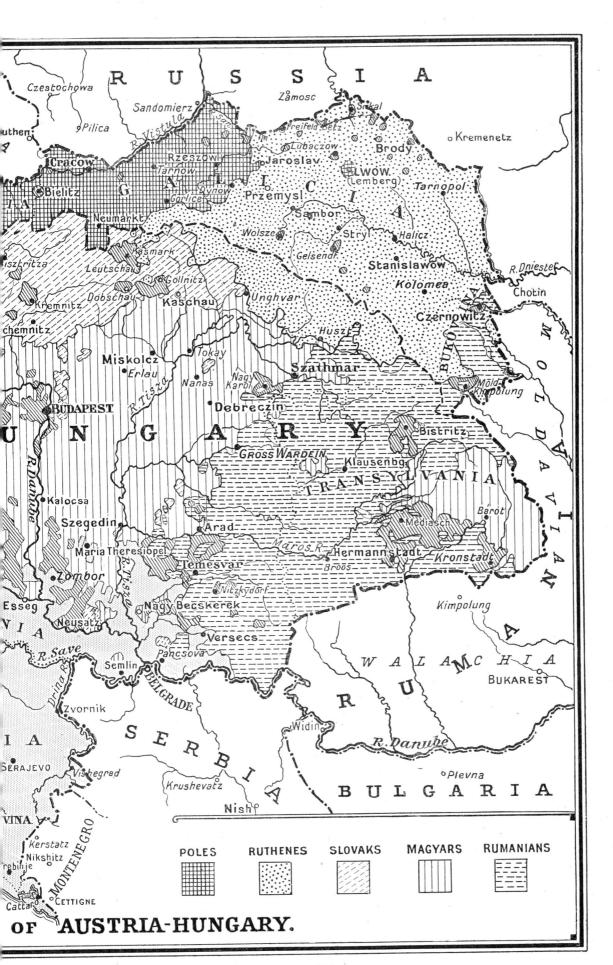

OF **AUSTRIA-HUNGARY.**

Map labels:

RUSSIA

Czestochowa
Sandomierz
Zamosc
Sokal
Pilica
Freifeld Betz
Kremenetz
R. Vistula
Lubaczow
Brody
Cracow
Rzeszow
Jaroslav
LWOW
(Lemberg)
Tarnow
Tarnopol
Bielitz
GALICIA
Dynow
Gorlice
Przemysl
Sambor
Halicz
Neumarkt
Wolsze
Stryi
Gelsendf
Kasmark
Stanislawow
Leutschau
Kolomea
Gollnitz
R. Dniester
Kremnitz
Dobschau
Kaschau
Unghvar
Chotin
chemnitz
Czernowitz
Huszt
BUKOWINA
Miskolcz
Tokay
Szathmar
Mold.
Kimpolung
Erlau
Nanas
Nagy Karol
MOLDAVIAN
BUDAPEST
Debreczin
Bistritz
HUNGARY
Gross Wardein
Klausenbg.
Kalocsa
TRANSYLVANIA
Barot
R. Danube
Szegedin
Arad
Mediasch
Maros R.
Hermannstadt
Kronstadt
Maria Theresiopel
Temesvar
Broos
Zombor
Nitzkydorf
Kimpolung
Esseg
Nagy Becskerek
WALAMCHIA
VIA
Neusatz
RUMANIA
Versecs
BUKAREST
R. Save
Pancsova
Semlin
BELGRADE
Drina R.
Zvornik
Widin
R. Danube
SERAJEVO
SERBIA
Plevna
VINA
BULGARIA
Kerstatt
Krushevatz
Nikshitz
MONTENEGRO
Nish
rebinje
Cattaro
CETTIGNE

POLES RUTHENES SLOVAKS MAGYARS RUMANIANS

THE DANUBE IN WINTER.

Showing the Houses of Parliament and Margaretheuse Bridge at Budapest.

plead that her own unity was threatened by Serbia. Not only had Serbia become an aggressive military State, but by a propaganda encouraged from Belgrade she was tampering with the loyalty of Serb subjects in Austria-Hungary. The existence of this pan-Serb propaganda cannot be denied. It was promoted throughout Bosnia and Herzegovina, the newly-acquired provinces, with their Serb population of nearly two millions, and in Hungary. Serbia was inevitably the focus of the movement, and if it was not encouraged by the Serbian Government it received support, at any rate, in Serbian official circles. The parallel between Serbia's relation to the Serbs and Croats under Austrian rule and the relation of Piedmont to her Italian fellow-countrymen whom Austria held down till 1859, is not merely one which suggests itself in retrospect; it was consciously adopted and developed by Serbian politicians and military officers before 1914. But this was hardly political crime. There would be some inconsistency, at least, in combining an enthusiastic approval of Piedmont and the Italian liberators with a sweeping condemnation of Serbia and the Serb propagandists, because the latter did not appeal so strongly to the Western sense of poetry and culture. And it would be equally undiscriminating to hold the entire Serb movement guilty because of the lamentable murders at Serajevo.

There was nothing, except the bare assertion of the Austro-Hungarian Government, to identify the Serbian Government with the crime. Nothing that could be called evidence was produced in support of the charge, which in itself was inherently unlikely. The murders were committed at a time when Serbia was busy with critical affairs, economic, military and dynastic; the last thing she would be likely to have wanted was trouble with a powerful neighbour. Those who knew the sinister *rôle* played by *agents provocateurs* in Eastern Europe found several mysterious features in the crime which made them all the more unwilling to accept the Austro-Hungarian theory. There was a lack of the most obvious precautions for the Archduke's safety during his Serajevo visit, which was all the more surprising as Bosnia was believed to be seething with treason. If, as there was some reason to think, the existence of a plot against him was known in Vienna, this neglect of police measures was all the more suspicious. Whatever it was that gave a free hand to the Serb fanatics, whether it was negligence or crime, the murder of the Archduke was a deep personal tragedy, and perhaps the gravest of the many calamities which have befallen the Austrian Empire and its dynasty in modern times. Francis Ferdinand was the hope and embodiment of a liberal policy for the races of the Empire. He represented the only programme in the field against Hungarian particularism and the intolerance of the war party. It was believed that if he came to the Throne he would have worked for a drastic change in the Dual System and the raising of the subject races to a position of equality with the Germans and the Magyars. Practically this would have meant the rise of the Slavs and the destruction of Hungarian dominance. Historically—if there can ever be a step backwards in history—it would have meant a return to the conditions before 1867, to the position as it was in 1860-1, when short-lived constitutional experiments were made, only to be sacrificed to the call for an immediate settlement with Hungary. Francis Ferdinand might have followed the federalist lines of the first of these or the centralist lines of the second, but it is fairly safe to assume that his plan would have been a combination of the two, with the modifications suggested by recent history and the great development of the Slavs. There would have been far-reaching questions of principle to settle, whether, for instance, the equalization of races should be recognized by substituting a " triple " or " quadruple " for the " dual " form, or whether it should repose on a broader basis, representing the ten principal nationalities. There would have been almost equally difficult questions of detail, such as the position of Bosnia-Herzegovina, hitherto administered as an Austro-Hungarian Reichsland, and the relations to it of the kindred provinces of Croatia and Dalmatia. Whether any modern ruler could have carried through such a transformation of his empire may be thought doubtful, but there were strong considerations in Francis Ferdinand's favour. First of all, was his own strong, although erratic, will, which had made

him already an outstanding figure in Europe. If an unfavourable picture of his aims and character was drawn at one time in Western countries, that was because it was chiefly inspired from adverse Hungarian sources. As time went on people came more and more to realize that he had devoted himself with singular resolution to what was possibly the one hopeful plan for the future of Austria-Hungary. The mere fact that he was a Habsburg gave him a unique power to further it. The prestige of the Sovereign was still extraordinary, and might have been equal to carrying through a change which would have been scouted in other countries as an impossibility. The Crown was still by far the most living of the political institutions of Austria-Hungary. There could be no instance more striking of the deep-seated authority of the Habsburgs than the way in which it survived the racial hatreds of the empire and the heavy disasters of Francis Joseph's reign. Francis Joseph, too, in one important respect had paved the way for Francis Ferdinand. Quite early after 1867, as we have seen, he had begun to work for the conciliation of the Slavs; later on he had governed with a Slav majority under two Premiers, Taaffe and Badeni; and he had finally endorsed the political predominance of the Slavs in the Austrian Reichsrat by his universal suffrage measure. To this extent he had prepared for a conciliatory policy. If he allowed the opposite party to take control, it was largely from inertia, and

THE LATE ARCHDUKE FRANCIS FERDINAND INSPECTING TROOPS.

[*Topical.*

ARREST OF PRINCEPS,

Assassin of the Archduke Francis Ferdinand and the Duchess of Hohenberg.

because after the Archduke's death the strongest personality was to be found on that side. As the policy of constitutional reform had been embodied in Francis Ferdinand, so the reactionary policy of the Dual System was incarnate in Count Tisza, the Prime Minister of Hungary. He belonged to that Calvinist aristocracy which preserved the traditions of Magyar dominance in their purest form. With a devoted loyalty to his Sovereign he combined a belief in his cause as unyielding as that of the Protestant leaders of Northern Ireland. He was a man of unflinching courage, which he had proved again and again, not only on the duelling ground, but in the not less perilous scene of the Hungarian Chamber. His personality could not be ignored and was bound to win respect ; the pity was that he identified himself wholly with the old ideal of Hungarian self-assertion in the Dual Monarchy and supremacy over the Slav races. It was for this that he clung to "dualism," and was prepared to submit it even to the fiery trial of the great war, as he described it to the Hungarian Parliament. He must, therefore,

rank as one of the chief authors of the conflict. Many and diverse were the influences for war which were brought to bear on the aged Emperor in the fateful days after the Archduke's murder. Herr von Tschirschky, the German Ambassador at Vienna, who was the working agent of *Deutschtum* ; General Konrad von Hötzendorf, the Chief of the Austro-Hungarian General Staff, who was bent on the annihilation of Serbia ; Count Forgach, the Judaeo-Magyar diplomatist, who had been already involved in a sinister plot against Serbia, and was now controlling the threads of anti-Serbian policy in the Foreign Office, all contributed their share. But the chief responsibility for embracing a policy which invited war lay probably with Hungary and her representatives, ancestrally unwilling to see a diminution of their power or to deal fairly with the Slavs.

Illustrations will be found in Volume I., Part 1, of the following : The Emperor Francis Joseph, p. 14 ; the Archduke Francis Ferdinand, p. 12 ; The Duchess of Hohenberg, p. 12 ; Sir Maurice de Bunsen, p. 22 ; King Peter of Serbia, p. 38 ; Serajevo, p. 13 ; Belgrade, p. 17.

CHAPTER XXXVII.

THE ARMY OF AUSTRIA-HUNGARY.

THE ARMY AND ITS UNIFYING EFFECT ON THE EMPIRE—THE OFFICERS, THEIR INFLUENCE—RACIAL FEELING IN THE STATE—THE EMPEROR'S VIEWS—THREEFOLD ORGANIZATION OF THE ARMIES— THE RULES OF UNIVERSAL SERVICE—THE NUMBER OF ARMY CORPS—THE INFANTRY—THE CAVALRY —THE ARTILLERY—THE ENGINEERS—COMMUNICATION TROOPS—HIGHER ORGANIZATIONS—THE DIVISION—THE ARMY CORPS—THE CAVALRY DIVISION—MOUNTAIN BRIGADES—FORTRESSES.

THE Austro-Hungarian Army has always held a position quite unique among the States of Europe. Composed of a number of races differing in varying degrees from one another, and in the case of the Hungarians definitely hostile to the Slavonic elements, it would naturally be thought that, founded on such a basis, it would be a very inefficient instrument of war. Yet its history has told a different tale. It has always fought well, and its troops have displayed a bravery quite equal to that of the soldiers of other countries. It is true that Austria in many campaigns justified the "tradition de défaite" which Napoleon ascribed to her. For this unhappy result there have been many reasons, but among them there cannot be included any lack of warlike energy among the soldiery.

The Austro-Hungarian Army, moreover, was one of the main factors concerned in the preservation of the Empire, inasmuch as it formed a nursery of dynastic feeling; all members of it, no matter what their race, felt a personal allegiance to the Emperor and the House of Habsburg. The chief reason for this was that officers and soldiers alike knew that they were under the Emperor's personal control and received his personal care and attention. He was indeed the father and head of the military forces of the double crown. This feeling tended to make the army a school which inculcated a feeling of trust and reliance on the monarch,

and through him a sentiment of unity and recognition of the country as a whole which counteracted the particularist ambitions of some of its composing elements. The army was for the Empire, and was not Hungarian or Czech, Italian or German, Serbo-Croatian or Polish, Ruthene or Rumane; politics, very properly, had no place in military organization. Another important influence for unity was the corps of officers. Drawn from all classes of society, it formed a microcosm of the State. No longer composed of so-called nobles —though, of course, in a country of universal service many of them were found in it—the bulk came from the middle and lower middle classes, a large portion belonging to families which have for generations found their life's employment in a military career.* Spread over the whole army, no matter from what race they might come, the officers had a unifying influence which brought the various nationalities together in a common devotion to the Emperor-King and to the country he ruled.

Of all armies it is true that this class of hereditary soldiers furnished the best officers, thoroughly imbued with the spirit of the

---

* Germans are in the habit of describing those who bear the particle *von* in front of their names as *noble*. The real equivalent in English is esquire. Frederick the Great always ennobled a man he made captain. In England a captain is called esquire in his commission, junior ranks only gentleman.

service, filled with an honourable regard for the position they and their forbears have held, inspired by their deeds and determined to carry on untarnished the name they hold for the sake of the regiment and for the benefit of the army. This was certainly the case in the British forces, and although this class received no special recognition, politicians of all classes being quite incapable of appreciating its value, we still draw a considerable portion of our officers, and those the very best, from it. It was curious—when every effort was being made to draw candidates from the Universities and Public Schools, because in both cases the education of association was supposed to have some value ; when marks were given in the competitive examinations for entrance to the army to those who had obtained certificates of a certain (no very high) standard of proficiency in military duties at these institutions—that the scion of a race which has for generations devoted itself to the fighting services of the Crown received no consideration whatever, no advantage from the devotion of his forefathers. If half the vacancies of Woolwich and Sandhurst had been confined to them, we should have given some reward to old officers and have obtained a better class than was otherwise to be obtained. This was fully appreciated in Austria, and the consequence was that the Austrian Corps of officers possessed a well-founded reputation for professional knowledge, zeal and devotion, second to no similar body in Europe. They were more intelligent than their Prussian rivals, less hide-bound by the " Réglement," * of easier manners, entirely free from that arrogance which produced the saying, " grob wie ein Preusse " (rude as a Prussian), and, as they were in more intimate and kindlier relationship with their men, they were more likely to get greater efforts out of them, when in difficulties, than their northern neighbours ; they had the devotion of all ; they led them, and did not merely drive them on by fear.

But the Austro-Hungarian Army suffered from one great disadvantage, which was indeed common to the whole Austro-Hungarian administrative system. It was true the Aulic Council had disappeared, but it had left behind it a numerous illegitimate progeny, whose octopus-like grip strangled all the administra-

* The German name for drill-book.

tive offices of State and endeavoured to reduce the whole government of the country to one dead level of red tape, incompetent, dull mediocrity. Initiative was foreign to Austrian bureaucrats, and it was they who directed the entire administration of the country. Their influence was felt with force in the army, and it was doubtful for this reason whether the administration services—*i.e.*, the commissariat and the like—were up to the highest standard required for a modern army, which, to be successful in war, must develop initiative in all branches. A business which pretends to be guided entirely by rules must fail when dealing with men, for it is impossible to devise regulations to meet every possible situation. Administrators who act on the belief that such is feasible, fail entirely when circumstances do not exactly fit in with the hard and fast code. They cannot improvise, and are apt to indulge in the procrustean method and make the circumstances fit the rules, instead of wisely adapting the latter to the former. Officers of the fighting branches who had been well educated in their duties would feel the necessity for acting on their own intelligent conception of the situations arising on the battlefield, but non-commissioned officers, still influenced by the doctrine of passive obedience taught them in the ranks, were not likely to display similar characteristics. Their tendency was to become wooden in movement and in thought, and hence they could not efficiently replace the disabled officer in war. This was recognized by the military authorities, and efforts were made to improve them and induce them to prolong their service by re-engagement, so that they might by longer service become more efficient.

The higher ranks of the army were undoubtedly efficient so far as study could make them. It was no longer the practice to appoint men of high birth to posts for which their only claim was family. A modern Liechtenstein would have to prove his ability, not his quarterings ; a Clam Gallas would be impossible, or if such a man by chance obtained a high position, he would, if he behaved like his namesake in 1866, certainly be tried by court-martial and probably shot, as the latter ought to have been. It was inconceivable that a Benedek would nowadays be made a scapegoat to bear away the sins of his mutinous subordinates and pledged to secrecy to cover the delinquencies of his incompetent superiors. It was incredible

ARMY CORPS COMMANDERS.

1. General Blasius Schemua (2nd) ; 2. Lieut.-General Colerus von Geldern (3rd) ; 3. General Hugo Meixner von Zweienstamm (10th) ; 4. Lieut.-General Otto Meixner von Zweienstamm (7th) ; 5. Major-General the Archduke Joseph of Austria (4th) ; 6. Lieut.-General Edler von Hortstein (9th) ; 7. Lieut.-General Rhemen zu Barensfeld (13th) ; 8. Lieut.-General D. Kolozsváry de Kolozsvár (11th) ; 9. Major-General Giesl von Gieslingen (8th) ; 10. Lieut.-General Wenzel Wurm (16th) ; 11. Major-General the Archduke Ferdinand Karl Ludwig (12th).

VARIOUS TYPES OF THE AUSTRIAN ARMY.

that a future Tegetthoff could win a naval victory and be immediately removed from his command. A better and more rational government existed in Austria-Hungary, but still the bureaucracy remained and prevented reform w ich would cheapen administration and make for reason in the non-combatant branches.

It has been said that the discipline of the regular army formed a common tie which bound the various races together. This was absolutely the case a hundred years ago, before the influence of racial feeling had gained the i nportance it attained in late years. But even in 1866 the Italian regiments had to be largely employed against the Prussians while those of other races were used in Italy against Victor Emmanuel's troops. Since then the individualist feelings of some of the races had grown stronger and shown far greater tendency for segregation under an ethnographical arrangement. Pan-Slavism is a force which must now be recognised. There is no doubt that some of the Slav regiments during the present war expressed their discontent at being led against the Russians. Round Trieste there existed the undoubted desire to see " Italia irredenta " united to the Kingdom of Italy. Transylvania had aspirations, or at least the Rumanian-speaking majority of its inhabitants had, towards a union with Rumania. Whether these particularist ideas had much effect on the actual conduct of the troops in the war of 1914 it is difficult to say, though rumour seems to point to the conclusion that they had.

Doubtless the comparatively small thinking portion of the Monarchy felt that by entering on the war the Government had deliberately thrown the affairs of the Dual Monarchy into the melting-pot, and had some misgivings as to what would be the form the new kingdom would take when the Allies began to remould it. As the struggle progressed, such a feeling assuredly had some effect on the various peoples involved. The Hungarians were not long in showing that they resented the way in which they were sacrificed during the war to Prussian ambition. That the Slavs disliked the war against the great Slav Power was only natural. Certainly, too, some Czech regiments, when they marched out of Prague, openly showed this feeling. In these days of education and the universal spread of news by the papers, soldiers are all more or less thinking bayonets. In Austria-Hungary, as elsewhere, this would be the case, and seeing the nature and origin of the war, sentiment in the ranks, at any rate among the non-German races, was scarcely likely to be favourable to the Government which brought it about.

The percentage of the different nationalities in the army are given below :—

Germans	...	...	...	...	29
Slav races :					
Czechs	...	...	...	...	15
Poles	...	...	...	...	9
Ruthenes	...	...	...	...	8
Slovenes	...	...	...	...	3
Slovaks	...	...	...	...	5
Serbo-Croatians		...	...	7—47
Magyars	...	...	...	...	18
Rumanes	...	...	...	...	5
Italians	...	...	...	...	1
					100

The words of command for the whole army were given in German, but the instructional language varied according to the racial composition of the various regiments. The purely Magyar, Polish, Czech, Ruthene and Serbo-Croatian regiments are taught in their own languages, and in the mixed regiments any percentage above twenty per cent. of the total strength had the right to be instructed in its own language.

In the Honvéd regiments of Hungary proper, Magyar is the official language and the language of command and, as far as possible, the language of instruction. In the Honvéd regiments recruited from Croatia and Slavonia the language is Serbo-Croatian.

There could be no doubt that the use of the German language for command was a powerful instrument acting for unification in addition to the sentiments of loyalty to the cause of the Emperor and the Empire, so sedulously inculcated by the officers. So much was this recognized that the particularists constantly brought the accusation that it was being used for the Germanization of the various races. But although from the force of circumstances German acted as a *lingua franca* for all the different races, it was by no means enforced on them, and it was merely the plain utility of its acquisition which appealed to a recruit who was desirous of acquiring another language in addition to his own. He naturally chose one which not only enabled him to understand his orders better, but which also facilitated his intercourse with those of his countrymen who talked it, and with a large proportion of the inhabitants of Central Europe. Hungarians were permitted to have some slight variations in their uniform,* but these were mere concessions to Magyar national feeling, and the Emperor himself frequently declared he would never allow anything which could interfere with the complete unity of the whole force or sanction a separate Hungarian Army. During the constitutional crisis of 1903 he issued an Army Order, on September 16, which clearly expressed his views :

" The better founded my favourable judgment of the military value, the self-sacrificing delight in service, and the single-minded cooperation of all parts of my whole Defensive Forces, the more I must and will hold fast to their existing and well-tried organization. My Army in particular must know that I will never relinquish the rights and privileges guaranteed

* For instance, the infantry wore their trousers cut tight after Hungarian pattern.

to its supreme War-Lord—my Army whose stout bonds of union are threatened by one-sided aspirations proceeding from misapprehension of the exalted mission the Army has to fulfil for the weal of both States of the Monarchy. Joint and unitary as it is, shall my Army remain, the strong power to defend the Austro-Hungarian Monarchy against every foe. True to its oath, my whole Defensive Force will continue to tread the path of earnest fulfilment of duty, permeated by that spirit of union and harmony which respects every natural characteristic and solves all antagonisms by utilizing the special qualities of each race for the welfare of the whole." Hungary had constantly endeavoured to obtain greater independence for her army, and had at the same time tried by every means to oppress the various non-Magyar elements which were under her rule. The result had been to intensify the latter in their dislike to the bullying rule of Hungary, and make them look for help outside the Empire.

The high spirit breathed forth in the Emperor-King's pronouncement aimed at an ideal, perhaps difficult to obtain, but which nevertheless had been reached in great measure. Of course, the bureaucratic element previously alluded to was not without its bad influence on the military machinery. But the personal supervision of the Emperor-King, or of one of the Archdukes to whom he delegated sometimes this duty, tended to keep this influence within bounds. One typical case of the working of the bureaucratic mind was shown during the occupation of Bosnia and Herzegovina. General Galgotzy, who was in command, undertook the construction of a road. Time was pressing, money was short, but urged on by the General, the troops, who loved him, soon finished the road. He reported : " Road built. Twenty thousand florins received, twenty thousand spent, nothing remains.—Galgotzy." This laconic message was a bad shock to the military auditors, who demanded an exact account with vouchers in continued applications, which grew more and more peremptory in tone. At last Galgotzy replied : " Twenty thousand florins received, twenty thousand expended. Whoever doubts it is an ass." This was too much for the Chief of the Audit Department, who saw the Emperor and drew attention to Galgotzy's want of respect to his high functions and suggested a reprimand. The Emperor

RESERVISTS ON THE MARCH.

blandly inquired : " Do you, then, doubt it ? " The incident closed, not to the discomfiture of the General.

The political organization of the Austro-Hungarian Monarchy was based on the fundamental law of 1867. By taking advantage of the disorganization brought about by the war of 1866, Hungary gained a position of quasi-independence. The difference between the two States was maintained in the armies with this distinction, that the regular, known as the Joint Army, was, as its name implied, common to both States, and was paid and kept on foot by a common fund. But beyond this force two others existed—the one the Austrian Landwehr, with its Landsturm, the other the Hungarian Landwehr (known as the Honvéd), with its Landsturm. These forces in all might be described as Territorial forces in the sense in which these words were used in our country—*i.e.*, forces which had some training but not as much as the regular army, of which they formed no part.

As the armies were divided so were the budgets which keep them on foot. There was the budget for the regular army provided by both Austria and Hungary ; that for the Austrian Landwehr and Landsturm furnished by the State concerned ; that for the Hungarian Honvéd obtained from Hungary and the portions of the Monarchy associated with her. There were also three administrations— viz., that for the Joint Army, that for the Austrian, and that for the Hungarian Landwehr (Honvéd) or National Defence forces.

In Austria-Hungary, as in all countries which felt the necessity for proper military organization, universal service was the law of the land. Only the physically unfit were in theory exempted from this obligation, although in certain cases this rule was, in fact, considerably modified, as will be seen later on. Those excused had to pay a tax in lieu of service. The liability extended from the completed nineteenth to the completed forty-second year—*i.e.*, for twenty-four years altogether. The actual service in the ranks and reserve was twelve years in the Joint Army, but varied slightly with the arm. Thus in the Infantry the time was two years with the colours, eight years in the Reserve, and then two in the Landwehr Reserve. In the Cavalry and Artillery the time was three years in the army and seven in the Reserve. The Reservists who had served two years in the army were liable to trainings not exceeding fourteen weeks in all, each of not more than four weeks during their time in the Reserve, those of three years' army service to three, not exceeding eleven weeks in all. These liabilities were rarely exacted to their full extent, a training period rarely exceeding thirteen days. Those who had served four years in the army were not liable to be recalled during their Reserve service.

After the men had served ten years in the army and its Reserve they were included in the Reserve of the Landwehr (Honvéd) for another two years.

It has been already said that the troops of the Landwehr and Honvéd category resembled, in principle, our Territorial force, for they received only a comparatively short training. Like our Territorial force, the Landwehr is a permanent institution and trains its own men; but before explaining how this was done it is necessary to describe how the allotment of the young men who come up for service was made.

When they presented themselves for enrolment the unfit were eliminated and the rest between the ages of 21 and 24 were divided into various categories by lot.* Those who drew the lowest numbers were told off for the Joint Army until the required contingent had been reached for which the vote of the Delegations had provided. The next highest went to the Landwehr (Honvéd) till its quota was obtained, and the remainder was handed over to the Ersatz Reserve.† The period of service in the Landwehr (Honvéd) was the same as in the common army : but the training (which was conducted by its own regimental cadres) was much more restricted, being only a total of twenty weeks in the Landwehr or twenty-five in the Honvéd, no one period exceeding more than four weeks. The men of the Ersatz Reserve were trained

for ten weeks, and were thereafter liable to three trainings, no one of more than four weeks —*i.e.*, like the Reserve. The total liability of the man, whether for the common army, the Landwehr (Honvéd), or Ersatz Reserve, was therefore twelve years, after which he passed into the Landsturm. In this he served in the first levy up to the end of his thirty-seventh year : in the second levy up to the end of his forty-second year.

In Bosnia and Herzegovina the same law held good, but the Reserve and the first and second levies of the Landsturm were called respectively the first, second, and third Reserve.

The total number of inhabitants of the entire Austro-Hungarian Monarchy was roughly 51,340,000, of whom about 500,000 were available each year, to which must be added those whose entry into military life was adjourned for one cause or another, but the whole of them were not taken. In the first place there were the unfit ; secondly, the exempt who were turned over to the Ersatz Reserve. These included priests, those in training for priestly office (both these classes were practically entirely exempt), then those who fulfilled certain conditions, such as sole supporters of a family. In addition to these, conscripts who had been for a definite period at certain schools, or who had passed certain examinations, served only

---

* The men up to twenty-four are those who have been put back for some reason.

† "Ersatz" is derived from the word "Ersetzen," to replace, and the Ersatz Reserve is intended to replace and fill up vacancies which occur in the other forces.

HUNGARIAN INFANTRY.

COMPARTMENT OF A RED CROSS TRAIN.

one year with the Army and eleven in the Reserve. These furnished the greater part of the medical, veterinary officers and apothecaries, and officers of the Reserve. Men who came under these provisions might adjourn their military service up to their twenty-third year. Any who volunteered for three years' service could choose their regiments.

By the working of the Act of 1912 the following numbers of recruits were embodied in 1913 :

Joint Army	...	...	...	153,500
Austrian Landwehr	...	...	27,000
Tirol	...	...	...	...	1,000
Honvéd	...	...	...	...	25,000
Bosnia and Herzegovina	...	7,800

214,300

(The number of Ersatz Reserve cannot be given.)

When the new law (July 5, 1912) would come into full force it was calculated that

Austria-Hungary would put into the field :

Joint Army	...	...	...1,360,000
Austrian Landwehr	...	...	240,000
Hungarian Honvéd	...	...	220,000
Ersatz Reserve	...	...	500,000
Landsturm	...	...	...2,000,000

4.320,000

It seems improbable that anything like these numbers were embodied, at any rate at the commencement of the war. In the first place the entire available force of the Landsturm was not called out—though within a few months all was probably ordered up. Secondly, there were certainly not enough arms in the country, at any rate of a modern class, to equip them with. It was hardly likely that Austria had at the commencement of hostilities more than 1,200,000 to 1,300,000 at her disposition for war.

Austria-Hungary had in the last three years increased her military establishment very considerably and spent large sums on re-armament.

The organization of the army was based for the Joint Army of Austria and Hungary, the Landwehr and the Honvéd. on the law of July 6, 1912; for the Landsturm on that of 1886. It was regional, regiments being allocated to specific areas. But the requirements of certain special corps prevented this in their case being strictly adhered to. It is impossible to give an exact account of the territorial divisions which furnished the various contingents, because the new arrangements were not completely carried out when the war broke out. But the accompanying map shows generally the divisions into which the country is divided.

The 241,333 sq. miles which compose the Austro-Hungarian Monarchy were divided into sixteen Army Corps Districts, as shown in the following table :

Army Corps and Headquarters.	No. of Divns.		No. of Batteries.				Battalion.		Train.		Corps Cavalry.
	Infantry.	Cav.	Field.	Horse.	Mountain.	Howitzer.	Pioneers.	Sappers.	Divisions.	Squadrons.	
1st Cracow	2	1	18	3	—	2	—	1	1	6	—
2nd Vienna	3	1	18	3	—	2	2	1	1	11	—
3rd Gratz	2	—	18	—	—	2	1	3	1	7	—
4th Budapest ...	2	1	19	3	—	2	1	—	1	8	—
5th Pressburg ...	2	1	19	3	—	2	1	1	1	9	—
6th Kaschau	2	—	19	3	—	2	—	—	1	4	—
7th Temesvar... ...	2	1	19	3	—	2	1	—	1	6	—
8th Prague	2	—	18	—	—	2	—	—	1	5	—
9th Leitmeritz ...	2	—	18	—	—	2	—	—	1	5	—
10th Przemysl ...	2	1	18	3	—	2	1	1	1	7	—
11th Lwow	2	2	18	3	—	2	—	1	1	7	—
12th Hermannstadt ...	2	—	19	—	—	2	—	1	1	5	—
13th Agram	2	—	19	—	—	2	—	1	1	5	—
14th Innsbruck ...	2	—	18	—	12	2	1	1	1	10	—
15th Sarajevo... ...	2	—	—	—	24	—	¼	1	1	9	—
16th Ragusa	2	—	—	—	20	—	—	¼	1	11	—

There were in addition to the Joint Army eight divisions of Austrian Landwehr and eight of the Honvéd. These, too, were organized on the territorial divisions of the country and were analogous in formation to the regular divisions. Altogether Austria-Hungary had forty-nine divisions with which to form the First Line Active Army—viz., thirty-three belonging to the Joint Army and the sixteen furnished by the Landwehr or Honvéd. It was the intention considerably to augment the Land-wehr Divisions, but no more were ready when war broke out. As given above, these were enough to furnish one to each army corps. Eventually the intention of the Government was to double the number so that there would be thirty-two divisions, *i.e.*, two to each army corps.

There were also eight Cavalry Divisions of Regular Cavalry for the Joint Army and two of Honvéd Cavalry.

It is now necessary to describe in detail the various units which went to make up the Army of the Dual Monarchy.

The Infantry of the Joint Army comprised one hundred and two infantry regiments besides twenty-seven battalions of Jaegers, four regiments of Tirolese Jaegers, and four of Bosnia-Herzegovina Infantry.* Each

---

* The name " Jaeger," literally hunter, has no meaning at the present day, as all infantry has the same armament. Formerly the Tyrolese were armed with rifles when the ordinary infantry had smooth bores.

---

infantry regiment had four field battalions and a depôt battalion. The regiments were numbered, and in addition had some permanent title or bore the name of the honorary colonel—*e.g.*, " The 1st Kaiser Franz Infantry Regiment." The companies of the field battalions were numbered throughout, as in Germany, one to sixteen. When mobilized the Depôt Battalion, which was only a skeleton in peace, was expanded into two, one of which was called a Reserve Battalion, the other the Depôt. The duty of these was to furnish reserves to fill up casualties in the others. The former might also be sent into the field.

The strength of a company on war footing was much the same as in Germany or France, viz., four officers and 260 non-commissioned officers and men. The strength of a battalion was 1,064 of all ranks, and of a regiment 4,356. The effective fighting strength of the latter— *i.e.*, rifles in the ranks—was roughly 4,100.

The Jaeger battalions had a similar organization to a battalion of the line. For reserve purposes in war they had a Reserve Company only. Some of the Jaeger battalions had cyclist companies.* The bicycle was of the folding pattern, and in each company there were also two motor-cycles and one motor car.

Every infantry regiment had at least two machine-gun detachments each of two guns,

---

* There were four in 1913, possibly more in 1914.

AUSTRIAN MOUNTED BATTERY

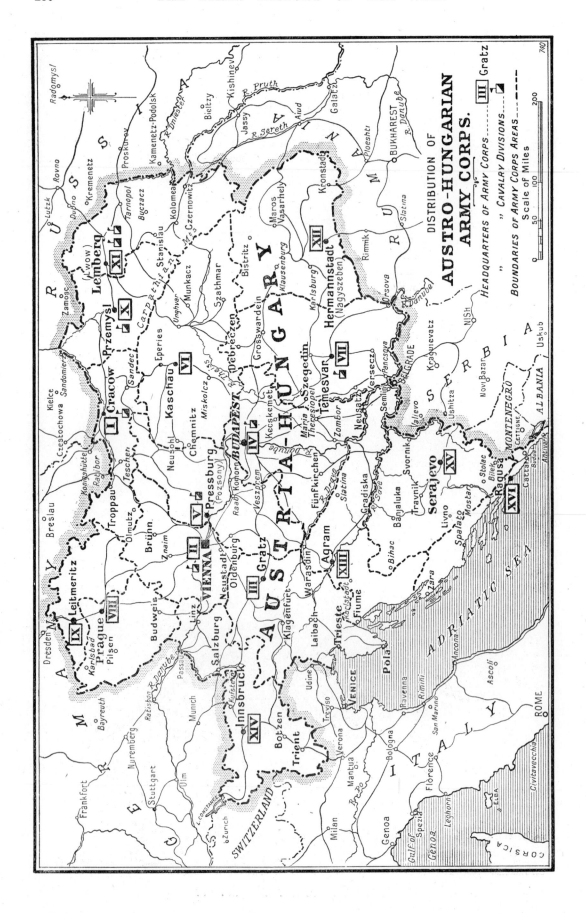

DISTRIBUTION OF
AUSTRO-HUNGARIAN
ARMY CORPS.

HEADQUARTERS OF ARMY CORPS......... III Gratz
"   "   CAVALRY DIVISIONS........
"   "   BOUNDARIES OF ARMY CORPS AREAS..........
Scale of Miles

and probably by the time war broke out there were two guns per battalion. Every battalion in Bosnia and Herzegovina and every Jaeger battalion had four.

The new war uniform of the infantry, as indeed for the rest of the army except the cavalry, was a bluish-grey. Every private in the front ranks carried a Linnemann spade, 1 ft. 8 in. long, weighing 2 lbs. Sixteen men in the rear rank had a small pick. The four pioneers of the company carried certain special tools. These men were usually united into a regimental detachment under a junior officer.

The small-bore magazine rifle had been some years (since 1895) in use in the Austrian Army. It was known, after the name of its inventor, as the Mannlicher. It had a calibre of ·315 in. and had a straight-pull bolt. It fired a pointed bullet with a muzzle velocity of 2,850 ft. It was sighted up to about 2,460 yards and weighed 8 lb. 5 oz. The total length of the weapon with bayonet fixed was 5 ft. The magazine was loaded by means of a charger which held five cart-ridges. The cavalry carbine was much shorter, only 3 ft. 4 in., and weighed only 6 lb. 12 oz., but it took the same cartridge.

The number of rounds carried by the infantry soldier was 120. In addition there were forty rounds in the company ammunition wagon and 160 in the infantry ammunition columns.

The machine gun was that known as the Schwarzlose and was of the same calibre and used the same ammunition as the infantry rifle. It was an extremely simple and efficient weapon, being composed of very few parts.

The Austrian Cavalry, although it still retained various designations—Dragoons, Uhlans, Hussars—was really all of one type, practically light cavalry, uniformly armed with sabre and carbine. Non-commissioned officers and others who did not carry the carbine had an automatic pistol.

There were forty-two regiments, fifteen of which were called Dragoons, eleven Uhlans, sixteen Hussars ; the regiments of each class being numbered among themselves. The last named were recruited in Hungary and Tran-sylvania, as the Hussars originated from the former country.* The dragoon regiments were raised in Austria, eight of the uhlans in Galicia,

two from Croatia and Slavonia, and one from Bohemia. In Bosnia and Herzegovina there were two independent cavalry squadrons. As in the Infantry so in the Cavalry, the regiment bore the name of the honorary colonel or had some other permanent title. A regiment consisted of six squadrons, each of which had a combatant strength of 150 sabres, exclusive of the pioneer troop. Each cavalry regiment had four machine guns, with forty thousand rounds of ammunition. Unlike that of the infantry regiments the gun had no shield.

On mobilization each regiment formed from the Depot Squadron which it had in peace time, a Reserve Squadron and Depot Squadron, which fulfilled the same duties as the battalions bearing these names in the Infantry.

The pioneer troops of the Cavalry, to which allusion has been made above, were particularly well organized—indeed, it was in Austria that they were first introduced. Each consisted of one officer and twenty-five men, who carried the various tools, explosives, etc., which are required by a force like cavalry so constantly used in advance of an army, a position where obstacles have to be removed and where special duties fall on it, such as the destruction of railways, etc. In addition to the pioneer troop eight men per squadron were equipped with tools. Thus, an Austrian cavalry regiment had available seventy-three men trained for pioneer duties, forming a highly efficient body for the purposes required of it. The telegraph section (eight men) carried about seven miles of light wire.

Every squadron had also ten waterproof bags which could be inflated. One sufficed to support two men, and they could be used to construct rafts for crossing water.

The curse of Cavalry on active service is the practice of constantly frittering it away by detailing it for escort and staff duties, such as orderlies to general officers, etc. Wellington found this in the Peninsula, and frequently issued orders to prevent it. The Austrian Cavalry was not allowed to be used for any such minor, and often quite unnecessary, purposes. To provide for them as far as they were really needed, so-called troops of " Staff Cavalry " were employed. Each regiment furnished two sections of these on mobilization (principally from the Reservists), which con-sisted of one officer and fifty men. A similar organization existed in the Infantry. Every regiment provided a " Staff Company " of

---

* The name Hussar is derived from the Magyar word *husz* = (a squadron of) twenty. The uniform is modelled on the Magyar national costume. Similarly the Uhlan uniform is a reproduction of the Polish peasant costume.

two officers and 120 men, who were all attached to the higher tactical units, such as brigades, divisions, army corps, for escort and guard duties connected with these. The sections of both cavalry and infantry were united in pairs and called Staff Squadrons or Staff Companies.

The Austrian Cavalry wore much the same uniform in peace as in war, except that the head-dress had a cover of the same colours as the Infantry uniform.*

The Austro-Hungarian Artillery had undergone great transformations in recent years. In 1866 the cannon employed were brass muzzle-loaders, and they were on the whole superior to the mixed mass of early breech-loading Krupp guns and old smooth-bores that Prussia brought against them. But the Austrian military authorities soon saw that the future lay with the breech-loader. It was considered desirable that the guns should be made in the country, as Austria then had but few and indifferent steel factories. It was decided to construct them on the system proposed by General Uchatius, of his " steel bronze," as these could be turned out from the Royal Arsenal The material was bronze cast under pressure, and with the interior of the barrel hardened by passing a succession of steel cones through it. The method was found to be successful, and is still used for field guns.

The original gun was only a nine-pounder, firing common shell of nine and a half pounds. But as other Powers introduced more powerful weapons Austria-Hungary was obliged to follow suit. The gun used for horse and field batteries was known as M/5—*i.e.*, pattern of 1905. It was a 3-inch calibre gun, a quick firer, throwing a shrapnel shell weighing 14·7 lb., containing 332 bullets of 50 to the lb. The fuse was constructed for use both for time and percussion. High explosive shells were also carried in proportion of two to five shrapnel. The gun had a long recoil on its carriage so that the shock of explosion was absorbed and the gun returned to its place. This rendered rapid fire possible. It had a panoramic sight graduated up to 6,600 yards, and an independent line of sight. It had a shield of chrome steel, affording protection against shrapnel at all ranges, and against pointed rifle bullets beyond 100 yards range. On the whole it was an

* There seems fairly good reason to believe that just before the war some part received a dress not very different in colour from that of the Infantry.

efficient gun, but nothing like so powerful as our own 18-pounder or as the French 75 mm. Both the horse and field artillery were armed with it.

There were six guns in a field battery, only four in a horse battery or in a heavy battery. The number of rounds carried was 126 per gun with the battery and 372 per gun with the divisional ammunition columns. The same amount was carried for the horse battery. Each battery had two miles of wire and four telephonists. It had also a range-finder.

Austria-Hungary, like other Powers, had adopted a howitzer for the heavy batteries. This fired a shell of 38½ lb. There were 123 rounds per gun with the battery, and 204 in ammunition columns. A heavy gun was also in use—viz., a 10·5 cm., equivalent to 4·1 in. The ammunition was similar to that of a howitzer—viz., a shell weighing 38½ lb., containing a high explosive bursting charge, and a shrapnel with 700 bullets, 50 to the lb. When marching the carriage was separated from the gun, and each was drawn by six horses.

Special stress was laid on mountain artillery, as on all the frontiers of the Monarchy mountainous regions are found. There were two varieties of weapon employed, the one a 7 cm. gun, firing a shell of 6 lb. 7 oz., the other a howitzer. The latest idea was to replace these comparatively inefficient weapons by a 10·5 cm., *i.e.*, 4·1 inch quick-firing howitzer throwing a shell of 32 lb. It had a range of over 6,000 yards and was altogether a very powerful weapon for its class.

It may be well here to mention a speciality of the Austrian artillery. In every army corps there were a few 8 cm. guns especially adapted for use on hilly ground when the ordinary gun carriage could not pass. The carriages were so constructed that it was possible to use shorter axle-trees to replace the long ones of the ordinary carriage. The gun carriage and the shield with sighting apparatus was formed into three separate bodies on wheels with a track of only one yard. It took ten minutes to make the alteration and ten to put it back into the ordinary form.

Reference may here be made to the heavy howitzer used by the Germans against Namur and other places. It is quite certain that the majority of these were what is known as the 30·5 cm. (equivalent to 12 in.) Austrian mortar, firing a shell of 858 lb., with bursting charge of 56 lb. of ecrasite. Austria was

PLACING FIELD GUNS IN POSITION.

credited with thirty-four of these, and that some were used in Belgium is proved by the fact that photographs of the weapons used show this piece with Austrian soldiers seated on it. Its extreme range was about 10,500 yards, *i.e.*, roughly six miles. The rate of fire was ten rounds per hour, and it took an hour to get the gun ready for action. Three powerful tractors were required for two guns and their ammunition lorries.

The organization of the engineers in the Austro-Hungarian Army differed considerably from that employed by us, or indeed any other country. In most European forces there were what we call field companies, specially intended for use with the field armies, and fortress companies not associated with the divisions and army corps, but only brought up when required for siege purposes. In Austria a different practice was pursued. Each army corps would eventually have a pioneer and also a sapper battalion. Both were to be equipped for the construction of field defences, road making and field mining, but the pioneers had as their province bridging, with which the sappers had nothing to do. Their special work was fortress warfare. The former had four companies to the battalion, the latter only three.

Experiments were made with bridge trains drawn by motor-wagons, and possibly some of these were employed with the armies in the field. Each army corps had four pontoon troops, each of which could furnish 58 yards of ordinary bridge.

There was to each infantry division a searchlight section, the searchlights being one with a 32-in. and one with a 21-in. reflector. The larger nature was carried on a motor-wagon, which furnished the power to work the dynamo.

In addition to the field organizations already described, there were two other bodies which need notice. These were the Engineer Staff, who constructed fortresses and besieged them, the other a Military Works Department, which constructed and maintained buildings not immediately connected with fortifications.

In aeronautics Austria-Hungary was not so forward as other nations when war broke out. The first beginnings of a service of dirigibles and aeroplanes date from 1909. At Fischamend, about eleven miles south-east of Vienna, a depôt for dirigibles existed, and experiments were made with various types, though there is no reason to suppose that Austria had more than a few of these instruments of war available at first. They were chiefly of the Parseval type. In addition there were a number of captive balloons.

The same was the case with aeroplanes. The organization was not far advanced nor the number very large. The school for teaching aviation was established at Vienna-Neustadt.

Under the name of Communication Troops, especially under the Ministry of War, a number

AUSTRIAN FIELD ARTILLERY.

of troops for miscellaneous purposes were united. These included the Railway Regiment, of three battalions, with a total war strength of 4,383 non-commissioned officers and men with 92 officers. There was also a regiment of Engineer Telegraphists, from which a section was furnished to each army corps ; others went to the fortresses. The wireless telegraphy organization also formed part of this regiment, which further included a detachment of auto-mobilists consisting of 175 officers and men. The school for instructing infantry and cavalry in telegraphy was also under its administration.*

The Train—i.e., the equivalent of the British Army Service Corps—was organized in " divisions," one for each army corps. A division consisted of a variable number of squadrons and had also a skeleton squadron to act as Depôt, and another to furnish the Tool Park. The composition of the squadrons varied with the corps to which they were attached. There were altogether one hundred and fifteen squadrons, of which eighty-nine were field squadrons and twenty mountain squadrons. The larger part of the latter were in Bosnia and Herzegovina, and their transport was done by pack animals.

There was also a division to supply the vehicles necessary for the flying corps.

The Automobile Service—i.e., the corps in

* Every infantry and pioneer company, squadron of cavalry and battery of artillery had a small number of trained signallers, usually three. They used flags by day and lamps by night. The infantry pioneers also carried telephone equipment to be used for various purposes of communication.

charge of mechanical transport—was divided up among the various army corps. In each of these there was an officer whose special duty it was to look after the motors and all matters connected with them. Thus he registered all qualified men within the command and assisted in the mobilization, both of the machines available and the men necessary to work them. Reserve officers and others who had expert knowledge were posted to the mechanical transport. They were required to attend a four-weeks' course annually with the motor cadre of the army corps to which they were posted.

Here it may be remarked as coming under the head of supply duties, which we in England unite with transport in the Army Service Corps, that Austria had gone far in the provision of travelling kitchens. It had been intended to provide one for every company, squadron and battery, other than those specially equipped for mountain warfare. In the latter case and for the smaller units, such as machine gun sections, a cooking chest was allowed. This was of well-known Norwegian cooking-stove construction— i.e., it was a tin box carried in a case surrounded with a thick layer of felt. This kept the food hot for twenty-four hours and, indeed, completed the cooking.

Austria-Hungary, like other properly organized nations, had arranged her troops in higher units instantly available for service on mobilization for war.

To begin with the infantry, two regiments made a brigade of eight battalions. Two of these a division, so that the latter body should have had normally sixteen battalions, or, roughly, 16,000 men; but in some cases rifle battalions were added, and all the regiments had not got four battalions: thus the numbers might be more and sometimes were less. In the case of the 3rd Corps, which had three infantry divisions, this would have given, if the formation of all were normal, six brigades, each of eight battalions—forty-eight battalions; but there were only forty-five, because some of the regiments had not the complete number of battalions. On the whole the sixteen army corps had thirty-three infantry divisions with four hundred and sixty-seven battalions, which worked out at an average of fourteen to the division instead of sixteen. The army before the war was in a state of transition owing to the introduction of the new law of 1912, and in speaking, therefore, of the division as having sixteen battalions it must be looked on as what was aimed at rather than what was really attained.

The division, therefore, was properly two brigades, though in a few cases there were more —*e.g.*, in the 3rd Corps, where there were five brigades instead of four for the two divisions which composed it. The 14th had seven brigades to its two divisions, the 15th six, the 16th eight. But in all the other corps the divisions were normal so far as the brigades were concerned, though the number of regiments and battalions varied.

The distribution of field artillery to the divisions was more regular; the majority had eight field batteries to the division—*i.e.*, forty-eight guns. Only one corps had a horse battery (four guns).

As to the cavalry, the regular proportion was half a regiment to a division—*i.e.*, three squadrons. In some it was more, but in the case of the corps which were stationed in mountainous countries, less.

The division, therefore, theoretically was:

Two brigades of infantry (fifteen to sixteen battalions);

Half regiment of cavalry;

Forty-eight field guns.

It also had one Staff Infantry Company and one Staff Cavalry Troop, and further one Train squadron for transport, besides an Ammunition Park, a Telegraph Detachment, and an Ambulance.

The Army Corps consisted generally of two divisions (three in the case of the 3rd Corps) of regular troops, but in most cases a division of Landwehr (or Honvéd) had been added to it. It had, besides, the Corps Artillery, consisting of three batteries of field artillery and two of heavy howitzers, twenty-six guns in all.* There were, besides, one battalion of Pioneers, in some cases

* There is reason to believe that the artillery of the army corps has been increased by another ten batteries, but this is not quite certain.

PONTOON BRIDGE OVER THE DANUBE.

one of Sappers, a Bridging train, and a Tool Park, an Ammunition Park, a Telegraph and Telephone Detachment, a Field Hospital, and a Supply Column.

There were actually available besides the common army, eight active Austrian Landwehr Divisions, and the same number of Honvéd. Their organization was similar to that of the common army.

Of cavalry besides the regiments attached to the Infantry Divisions, there were eight Cavalry Divisions of the Joint Army and two of the Honvéd Cavalry. These had all a similar organization, viz. :

Two brigades of cavalry of two regiments each—*i.e.*, twenty-four squadrons ;

Three batteries horse artillery, twelve guns ;

Sixteen machine guns with four cavalry regiments ;

Besides an Ammunition Column, a Supply Column, a Field Hospital and Ambulance, and a troop of Staff Cavalry.

As so much of the frontier line of Austria-Hungary is mountainous, there was a special organization to meet the case. Mountain Brigades were formed. These consisted of a variable number of battalions, mostly Jaegers, or in Tirol the Imperial Jaeger Regiment, one or two squadrons of Mounted Rifles, who rode ponies, and the Artillery in the shape of Mountain Batteries—*i.e.*, with the guns carried on packs, as also were the supply and hospital arrangements. These brigades were grouped together in divisions and provided with pioneers and signalling detachments, but from the nature of the country in which they operated their action

was always more or less independent and the brigade therefore was a complete tactical unit.

Austria-Hungary had but few fortresses of modern construction, and it is doubtful if even these were up to the requirements of the present day. In Galicia, Cracow and Przemysl were entrenched camps, while in between them was Jaroslav, a fortress of a similar character to Huy, between Liége and Namur—*i.e.*, of no value. In Tirol there was Trient, an up-to-date entrenched camp, and certain barrier forts which blocked the roads from Italy and Switzerland. On the Adriatic, Pola was a powerful maritime fortress with sea and land defences. Cattaro and Sebenico were defended harbours, the latter being especially intended for torpedo craft.

Austria-Hungary was under one great disadvantage when war broke out : she had not completed the reforms which had been begun in 1912, but nevertheless she chose to place herself in the power of Germany to use her forces as the Northern Power willed. She reaped the consequences of her act. Employed by Germany for purely selfish ends she suffered defeat after defeat. On her southern frontier the Serbians drove back her invading troops. Her ultimate aim of reaching Salonika became a vain dream, and she ran the risk of emerging from the war so wantonly entered on poorer by many millions of money, with the loss of hundreds of thousands of her subjects, and some of her fairest provinces.

[For much of the information contained in Chapters XXXVI and XXXVII we are indebted to Mr. H. W. Steed's valuable work, "The Hapsburg Monarchy."—Ed.]

CHAPTER XXXVIII.

THE RESPONSE OF THE DOMINIONS.

DOMINIONS ILL-PREPARED FOR WAR—LACK OF COMMON MILITARY POLICY—BUT COMPLETE UNITY OF SPIRIT AND RESOLVE—VOLUNTARY OFFER OF ALL RESOURCES—AN UNITED EMPIRE—THE KING'S MESSAGES—FEELING IN CANADA—PARTY DIFFERENCES SUNK—DECLARATIONS OF CANADIAN STATESMEN—POPULAR ENTHUSIASM—ENROLMENT OF VOLUNTEERS—GIFTS TO ENGLAND—AND TO BELGIUM—ECONOMIC SITUATION IN CANADA—ACTION OF DOMINION PARLIAMENT—THE FRENCH CANADIANS—GERMAN COLONISTS—AMERICANS IN CANADA—THE IRISH—THE INDIANS—THE CANADIAN CONTINGENTS—EXPEDITIONARY FORCE INCREASED—THE VOYAGE TO ENGLAND—ARRIVAL AT PLYMOUTH—TRAINING ON SALISBURY PLAIN—AUSTRALIA—UNHESITATING LOYALTY—FEARS ABOUT BRITISH POLICY—DEFEAT OF THE COOK MINISTRY—THE FISHER MINISTRY—AUSTRALIAN DEFENCE AND THE JAPANESE QUESTION—THE EXPEDITIONARY FORCE—TRADE ORGANIZATION—LOYALTY OF GERMAN SETTLERS—COMPOSITION OF THE FORCES—THE COMMANDERS—TRAINING IN EGYPT—NEW ZEALAND—READY FOR ANY CRISIS—IMMEDIATE DECLARATIONS OF SUPPORT—THE CITIZEN ARMY—VOLUNTEERS—THE EXPEDITIONARY FORCE—THE MAORIS—SAMOA—TROOPS IN ENGLAND—AND IN EGYPT—OPERATIONS IN THE PACIFIC—MR. SEDDON'S POLICY—THE AUSTRALIAN FLEET—SEIZURE OF GERMAN POSSESSIONS—DESTRUCTION OF THE "EMDEN"—PURSUIT OF GERMAN PACIFIC SQUADRON—DOMINION GIFTS TO THE EMPIRE.

THE opening of hostilities found the Dominions ill-prepared for war. They were without a common scheme for military or naval defence, and the fundamental principles on which any such scheme must rest were still a matter of acute dispute. There was no central authority that could enforce its directions and demands, for the Committee of Imperial Defence, which sought to unify Imperial military preparations, was an advisory, not an executive body. There was no common naval policy. The Dominions were sharply divided between the principles of local navies and centralized Imperial control. Australia had with great energy adopted the policy of a local navy. New Zealand, after stalwartly upholding centralization, had turned its face towards local development. In Canada a deadlock between the two parties brought about the unfortunate result that nothing was done. Military affairs revealed the same seeming chaos. Canada had a small and totally inadequate permanent force of

about 3,000 men, and a loosely organized and greatly under-manned voluntary militia. Australia, New Zealand and South Africa had accepted the principle of citizen armies, but in Australia the system had been established too recently for its effects to be fully felt on the fighting strength of the Commonwealth. Nothing could be done in any of the Dominions without the voluntary consent of their Governments and of their peoples. Any outside observer, unacquainted with the essential spirit of the two races, who compared in the summer of 1914 the elaborate organization, the centralized control, the automatic precision and uniformity of the German fighting machine with the diversity, the divided councils, and the conflicting methods of the five sister nations of the British Empire, might well have thought the outlook for the latter dark indeed.

Such an estimate would have been a profound miscalculation. At the first sign of danger it was instantly shown that underneath

[Elliott and Fry.

MAJOR-GEN. E. A. H. ALDERSON, C.B.,
Commanding Canadian Expeditionary Force.

the differences of method in the King's Dominions there lay a fundamental unity of spirit and resolve. When it was realized that there was a possibility of war, even before war was declared, the Governments of Canada, Newfoundland, Australia, New Zealand, and South Africa, without waiting to be asked, placed themselves and their entire resources at the service of the Crown. At the earliest possible moment the Government of the Dominion of Canada offered the cruisers Niobe and Rainbow to the Admiralty, and informed the British Government that it would raise an Expeditionary Force of over twenty thousand men to be sent to the United Kingdom, and would supply such further numbers of men as might be required. The Government of the Commonwealth of Australia placed the Royal Australian Navy under the control of the Admiralty, and offered to dispatch an Expeditionary Force of twenty thousand men. The Government of New Zealand placed the New Zealand Naval force under the control of the Admiralty, and promised a force of all arms of eight thousand officers and men, with further drafts to secure the maintenance of the force at strength. The Government of South Africa could not dispatch any considerable Expeditionary Force, for there was every possibility that all its available men would be wanted in its own territories. But it informed the Imperial Government that it was prepared to take all necessary measures

for the defence of the Union and thus to release the Imperial troops in South Africa for work elsewhere. Even Newfoundland, with its sparse population, raised a small Expeditionary Force, and increased the troops in its own territory.

The people of the Dominions, with sure and wide vision, realised the vital import of the struggle ahead. From Toronto and Capetown, from Winnipeg and Johannesburg, from Sydney and Hobart, from Melbourne and Vancouver, there came accounts of one unanimous and spontaneous outburst of public enthusiasm and Imperial devotion, which swept away all party differences and minor disputes, and even made racial issues grow dim. The problems which had seemed to threaten the permanency of our institutions were laid to rest in an hour. The differing nationalities, whose conflicting points of view had time after time caused lesser conflicts, were suddenly fused in the heat of their great emotion into a united Empire. It was not only the men of English descent who rallied to the flag when they heard that the flag was threatened. The French Canadians in Quebec and the newly naturalised American settlers in Alberta and Saskatchewan rivalled in their enthusiasm the Englishmen in Toronto and in Victoria. The Boers in Pretoria and in Bloemfontein were at one with the English in Capetown and Buluwayo. Japanese and Hindus on the Pacific Coast showed that they shared the common spirit. Behind the white men of the five nations of the Empire others stood, less maybe in numbers, but certainly not less in whole-hearted devotion, from the Maori races of New Zealand, who strove, and strove in the end successfully, to put their fighting men alongside of our own against the common foe, to the chiefs of a hundred tribes in Africa and in the Pacific—tribes whose very names were unknown to most Englishmen—who offered their men, their money, their live stock, and themselves to the King. The message of the Basuto chief who indignantly asked why he, the King's servant, should stand idle when his King was fighting his enemies, typified the spirit of all.

It would be incorrect to say that the response of the Empire astonished the people of England. For some years England had been learning more and more of the settled loyalty of the Dominions. But if the response caused no surprise it gave the greatest satisfaction and renewed courage to the Motherland. The King's thanks, in words which we have already quoted,* to the people of Greater Britain, circulated a few days after the war broke out, well said what all felt : " I desire to express to my people of the Oversea Dominions with what appreciation and pride I have received the messages from their respective Governments during the last few days. These spontaneous assurances of their fullest support recall to Me the generous, self-sacrificing help given by them in the past to the Mother Country. I shall be strengthened in the discharge of the great responsibility which rests upon Me by the confident belief that in this time of trial My Empire will stand united, calm, resolute, trusting in God.—GEORGE R.I."

The King shortly afterwards addressed a message to the Governments and peoples of his self-governing Dominions, emphasizing the unity of the Empire in face of this unparalleled assault upon the continuity of civilization and the peace of mankind. The war was not of his seeking. " Had I stood aside when, in defiance of pledges to which my Kingdom was a party, the soil of Belgium was violated and her cities laid desolate, when the very life of the French nation was threatened with extinction, I should have sacrificed My honour and

* Vol. I., p. 161.

given to destruction the liberties of My Empire and of mankind."

The King's personal knowledge of the loyalty and devotion of his Oversea Dominions had led him to expect that they would cheerfully bear the great efforts which the conflict entailed. The full measure in which they had placed their services and resources at his disposal filled him with gratitude. " I am proud to be able to show to the world that My Peoples Oversea are as determined as the People of the United Kingdom to prosecute a just cause to a successful end."

CANADA.

On August 1, the day when war was declared upon Russia by Germany, and when Germany invaded the Duchy of Luxemburg, the Canadian Government showed that it was awake to the dangers of the situation. The Duke of Connaught, who was in the midst of a tour in the West, returned direct from Banff by special train to Ottawa. Sir Robert Borden, the Prime Minister, who had arrived in the Dominion capital that morning, summoned a Cabinet Council, which sat for hours deciding on the lines of national policy. The whole machinery of Canadian defence was quickly set in motion. Steps were taken to guard vulnerable points

H.R.H. THE DUKE OF CONNAUGHT AT VALCARTIER CAMP.
Princess Patricia talking to Sir Robert Borden.

on the Atlantic and Pacific coasts from surprise attacks. The Militia Department was already preparing for mobilization, and it was understood that the different Canadian regiments, small in numbers, would form the nucleus of larger forces to be immediately raised. Within a few hours fifteen Militia regiments volunteered for active service, and many thousands of men flocked around their headquarters, seeking to join them.

The Dominion Prime Minister was debarred for the moment from public speech. Others were not. From political leaders of all parties, and from newspapers of every shade of opinion, came the one expression of sentiment. Party controversy ceased. "Danger unites us," declared one leading Opposition newspaper.

Sir Wilfrid Laurier at the earliest possible moment was able to assure Sir Robert Borden, after conference with his leading adherents, that the Liberal Party would give its support without reserve to all measures deemed necessary by the Government. There was no thought or suggestion of Canada adopting a passive or neutral attitude. The politicians who had talked most in days of peace of Canada taking up a position of conditional neutrality in the event of a European war were now among the first to urge that Canada should throw, if need be, every man and every dollar into the struggle. "I have often declared," said Sir Wilfrid Laurier in a public message, "that if the Mother Country is ever in danger, ever threatened, Canada will render assistance to the full extent of her power. In view of the critical nature of the situation I have cancelled all my meetings. Pending such great questions, there should be a truce to party strife."

Sir Richard McBride, the Premier of British Columbia, voiced the general sentiment :— "Should it unfortunately develop that Great Britain is compelled to engage in hostilities," said he, "Canada will automatically be at war also. That Canada will do her full duty goes without saying ; but if we can now, by a demonstration of our loyal determination to stand by her side, strengthen the position of Great Britain I am sure there will be a universal desire to adopt that course. With Britain supreme in command of the seas the Imperial Government can conceivably in less than a month land in England upwards of 100,000 fresh troops from her far-flung Colonial possessions. These troops might easily be of vital service to the Motherland ; and that they

will be offered from all parts of the Empire if the need be as great as our information would lead us to believe hardly requires to be stated."

The first Monday in August saw the cities of Canada in a white heat of enthusiasm. All day long, crowds gathered around the bulletin boards of the newspapers, waiting for the latest information. Naval reservists, in response to a proclamation, were reporting themselves and leaving for their depôts, and the departure of every man was made the occasion for a great demonstration. The staffs of the Militia were almost overwhelmed by the numbers of volunteers for service.

From every district promises of help and support poured into Ottawa. The Premier of Manitoba, the Hon. R. P. Roblin, offered to raise ten thousand men. The Premier of Ontario declared Canada's plain course was "to exert our whole strength and power at once on behalf of the Empire." Local organizations and individuals proffered men, money and material. The one fear was lest Britain should shrink from her duty and preserve an ignoble peace. The Duke of Connaught crystallized the general sentiment in a sentence :—" Canada stands united from the Pacific to the Atlantic in her determination to uphold the honour and traditions of our Empire."

The demonstrations in the streets, the general enthusiasm, and the spontaneous offers of service did not mean that the Canadian people regarded the situation lightly. Below the surface-current of enthusiasm there ran a quiet, sober, solemn determination. The nation had reckoned the cost, and was willing to pay it. The deeper note of the public temper was most markedly seen when, on the Tuesday, the definite announcement was posted on the newspaper bulletin boards that Britain had declared war. A sudden silence fell on the crowds. Men and women stood gravely still. Then, after a pause, they turned to go. The hour of shouting was over ; the days of work and sacrifice had come.

Within three hours of the declaration of war, the Canadian Government summoned a meeting of Parliament for August 18, and the Militia Department gave instructions for the enrolment of twenty thousand volunteers for service at the front. Before the instructions were issued a hundred thousand men had offered themselves. Canada arranged to take over the garrisoning of Bermuda, to set the

FRENCH CANADIANS. [*By courtesy of "Canada."*]
No. 1 Company of "Le Regiment Royal Canadien."

Imperial troops there free. The Government urged farmers to grow more grain in order to safeguard the Empire food supply. Effective steps were taken to guard the financial and commercial interests of the people.

The public attitude was displayed in a number of gifts to Britain, gifts of a variety and kind unequalled before. One Montreal millionaire provided the entire cost of the raising, equipment, and maintenance of a special regiment, Princess Patricia's Light Infantry, or, as they were soon known from end to end of the Dominion, the "Princess Pat's." A prominent Calgary cattle-dealer offered fifty thousand dollars to equip a Legion of Frontiersmen, and a leading resident in Vancouver expressed his willingness to raise a corps of 500 British Columbians at his own

expense. Word came from England that there was likely to be severe suffering there, owing to lack of employment caused by the war. Within a few days the Dominion Government sent an offer on behalf of the Canadian people of a million bags of flour of 98 lb. each as a gift to the people of the United Kingdom. Following this, the Alberta Government offered England 500,000 bushels of Alberta oats; the Nova Scotia Government sent 100,000 dollars for relief; the Quebec Government asked instruction for shipment of 4,000,000 lb. of cheese; Prince Edward Island gave 100,000 bushels of oats, and the Ontario Government placed a quarter of a million bags of flour at the disposal of the Imperial Government. The Premier of Prince Edward Island asked whether England would like any cheese and hay;

NEWFOUNDLAND CONTINGENT. *"Canada."*
Regimental Drilling at St. John's.

VALCARTIER
Canadian Expeditionary Force

Saskatchewan wanted to know if a gift of 1,500 horses would be acceptable ; Manitoba sent 50,000 bags of flour of 98 lb. each, and British Columbia offered 25,000 cases of canned salmon. The women of Canada raised a fund to provide a naval hospital ship, and on it being suggested that a naval hospital would be more acceptable they sent £57,192, of which £20,000 was to be handed to the War Office for hospital purposes and the balance to the Admiralty for a Canadian Women's Hospital at Haslar. The Canadian Red Cross sent a fully equipped Field Hospital and £10,000 to the British Red Cross Society. The Dominion Government provided £20,000 for a Canadian hospital in France under the French Government. Farmers in different districts gathered vast stocks of flour and of farming produce of many kinds and sent them to England. When stories came through of Belgian distress, Canada, without staying its hand for England, raised further great sums for the Belgian people. To record all the public and private gifts of magnitude to the Imperial cause in the early weeks of the war would be impossible. They ranged from a present of half a million dollars to machine guns. Everyone gave what he could. One Toronto newsboy, having nothing else, gave a street-car ticket costing just over two-pence. The ticket was afterwards sold for a thousand dollars.

In addition to the funds for England, the Canadians had their own Patriotic Relief Fund They took as their first duty the obligation to see that no one dependent on any man from the Dominion who was fighting at the front should suffer want in future. Eighteen cities raised considerably over a million pounds for the Patriotic Fund within ten weeks of the outbreak of the war, Montreal heading the list with £400,000 and Toronto coming second with nearly half as much. In addition, most municipalities made provision for the families of volunteers from their localities, and usually insured the lives of the men for $1,000 each.

All this aid and provision was the more remarkable since Canada in the opening days of the war was in the midst of a period of great financial and industrial difficulty. The long era of prosperity which had been the marvel and envy of the world had apparently drawn to a temporary close. Canada had had her ten years of plenty, with splendid harvests, rapid development, and fast-growing population. Immigrants had arrived by the hundred thousand yearly ; villages had grown to cities, and vast areas of Saskatchewan and Alberta, not long since desolate prairie, were now the centres of active and populous communities. A new industrial system had been built up. Canadian-owned ships yearly spread over wider seas ; Canadian investments were a leading feature of the world's stock exchanges ; Canadian millionaires were beginning to take the place in London occupied previously by South African gold kings and diamond kings ; Canada spelled prosperity. The difficulty of the Dominion had been for some years to obtain

CAMP.
Before Leaving for Europe.

enough men to do the work waiting to be done ; to find sufficient farmers to cultivate the fertile lands freely offered to them ; to bring in enough people willing to step from the struggles and sufferings of the Old World to the prosperity and abundance of the New.

Some months before war broke out this condition of general prosperity had received a decided check. It is hardly within the scope of this history to detail the economic conditions which brought this about. Some of the growth had been too rapid. Capital for Canadian enterprises had been so easily raised that part of it was used without sufficient care. Land values in many districts in the West had been inflated artificially, often at the cost of the foreign investor. A comparatively small amount of unsound business had produced suspicion abroad concerning everything Canadian, and hence outside capital became more and more difficult to obtain. Some foreign monies were withdrawn. At the first suspicion of a bad harvest enterprise began to slacken, and even in the weeks before the war broke out the Canadian people were reckoning on a bad winter. They knew for the first time for years the problem of the unemployed. The war brought the industrial crisis to an acute point. Canada, largely dependent upon England for capital, found that England had now no funds available. Men responsible for great development enterprises—enterprises of necessity largely dependent on borrowed money—learned that borrowing was now impossible.

In the hours when the men of Canada were working most freely and giving most abundantly for Empire they well knew that many of their enterprises were face to face with ruin. The Stock Exchanges were closed. Shares in some of the soundest industrial enterprises were almost unsaleable ; others were offered for little more than half of their market price of a few months before. Thus the shares of the premier railway of the Dominion, the Canadian Pacific, which a little over a year before had reached $254, were now sold for $157½. Many other enterprises showed a much more marked difference. Government and municipal undertakings found it difficult to secure funds for the carrying on of public works, and in consequence had to discharge hundreds of men. A number of establishments closed down altogether, while others ran short time and with reduced staffs. There was a great curtailment of lumbering operations in the woods ; manufacturing was exceedingly quiet, and in a few parts of Saskatchewan and Alberta the crops were a failure.

Some extracts from the official returns from the leading cities in the Dominion for the month of August will show how acute the situation was :

MONTREAL.—The war embroiling Europe in its first effect on employment and industrial conditions in Montreal and district has had a distinctly depressing tendency.

TORONTO.—Owing to the outbreak of the European war, and the resulting financial stringency, the labour situation during August entered upon a more serious phase than at any previous time in the history of Toronto.

All lines of industry were affected, and many thousands of men and women paid off on account of the closing of plants or reduction of staffs. The effect of the enlistment of several thousand men in the Canadian contingent in relieving the congestion of the labour market was inappreciable. The building trade was suddenly paralysed owing to the inability of contractors to obtain advances from the banks and loan companies, and houses built for sale find no market. Some important public works, employing large numbers, have been temporarily discontinued.

PORT ARTHUR AND FORT WILLIAM.—With the beginning of August and news of the commencement of the European war a decided check was felt in all business and commercial affairs, with the result that no new work was started, and as Great Britain became involved matters in the district in the labour market became still worse.

SAULT STE. MARIE.—The inability to get money for public works, such as street and road building, steel mill extensions, and dry dock construction, and a serious falling off in house and public buildings' construction has thrown a great many men out of expected employment, and threatened many hardships during the coming winter, the more especially because of the advancing cost of living in nearly every department excepting rentals.

WINNIPEG.—Industrial conditions were worse than in the month of July. Money was scarce, particularly towards the end of the month. The Provincial Government ordered the stoppage of work on the new law courts and Parliament buildings, owing to financial stringency. Similar action was taken in regard to a goodly number of larger private buildings in the course of erection, thus causing a large number to be added to the unemployed.

REGINA.—August saw an increase of the already large number of unemployed, this being more noticeable among the building trades. Almost simultaneously with the declaration of war all the large contracts in the city were closed down, and the city decided to curtail its programme of improvements. A general depression prevails in all lines of business, and many establishments have found it necessary to reduce their staffs.

CALGARY.—The unemployed situation was more serious than it has been for several years, a large surplus of men of all branches of trades vainly looking for employment. Since war was declared work has closed down on all sides, throwing thousands out of employment. Very few buildings were carrying on operations.

EDMONTON.—Owing to the business depression caused by the European war, the labour market was in such a deplorable state that any comparison with the previous month or the corresponding period a year ago would be unfair. Hundreds of men were thrown out of employment by the stoppage or curtailment of work in all lines.

PRINCE RUPERT.—The outlook from a labour standpoint was very grave. There has been a gradual closing down of all development work since the declaration of war.

VICTORIA.—Owing to the outbreak of war in Europe, labour and business conditions have been very dull and unsettled during the month, with the result that labour of all classes has been very irregularly employed.

The industrial situation was tackled manfully. Distress was relieved; fresh enterprises were begun; wholesale economies were instituted; and vigorous efforts were made to restore financial stability. Soon the result of all these steps began to be markedly felt. Meanwhile, military preparations were carried on without pause.

When the Dominion Parliament met on August 18, two notices of motion were given, one to raise fifty million dollars for the defence

ROYAL GRENADIERS ENTRAINING AT MONTREAL.

TROOPS EMBARKING AT MONTREAL.

and security of Canada, and the other safe-guarding finance. The speeches made in Par-liament quickly proved the reality of the political truce. Not much was said, but what was said was to the point. "The occasion is too great for words," declared one leading Toronto paper. The two parties, recently engaged in prolonged and bitter political con-flict, now joined in a message of loyal devotion to the Motherland, of confidence in the justice of her cause, and of determination to aid in the Empire's war with every resource and to the limit of every sacrifice. "As to our duty," said the Prime Minister, "we are in accord. We stand shoulder to shoulder with Britain and the other British Dominions. With firm hearts we abide the issue." Sir Wilfrid Laurier supported him. "We are British sub-jects," he said, "and to-day we are face to face with the consequences which are involved in that proud fact. Long we have enjoyed the benefits of our British citizenship ; to-day it is our duty and our privilege to accept the responsibility, yes, and the sacrifices. Our answer is 'Ready, aye ready !'" Canada, he declared, had one mind and one heart, to main-tain untarnished the honour and dignity of her name and to save civilization from the un-bridled licence of conquest and power.

Day by day evidence of national unity grew. On one occasion complaints were made that

French-Canadians were backward in recruiting, and that only four hundred of them had joined the first contingent. The defence of the French-Canadians came from the English Press of the Dominion. "There are fifteen hundred of them at Valcartier who have been accepted, and many more volunteered," stated the Toronto Daily Star. "Moreover, there are now at the front—the first of all Canadians to get there—a body of 750 French-Canadians, who, being reservists of France, sailed there direct from Montreal, and are probably by now on the firing line. There is no room for dis-sension and fault-finding. The people of this country will do their duty as they perceive what it is, and will do it as resolutely as any-body could wish."

It was thought that trouble might arise from the large German colonies. The settlers in some of these quickly proved that they shared the common aspirations of the Dominions. The citizens of Berlin, Ontario, for example, sent a cable to Lord Kitchener : "Berlin, Ontario, a city of 18,000 population, of which 12,000 are Germans or of German descent, purposes raising £15,000 or more for the National (Canadian) Patriotic Fund. The German people want to see militarism in Ger-many smashed for good, and the people set free to shape a greater and better Germany. We feel confident that England has appointed the right men in Mr. Churchill and Lord Kitchener to boss the job."

Americans in Canada showed their sympathy in unmistakable fashion. Many of their young men demanded to be enrolled in the ranks of the new Army, and when the first Canadian contingent arrived in England, men of American birth were found in almost every regiment. Some officials who had most to do with the recruiting were emphatic in asserting that, were it necessary, whole regiments could be raised solely composed of volunteers from the United States. The American volunteers proved in many ways that they came not merely for love of excitement and adventure, but from conviction of the justice of the cause of the Allies. One man from Texas wanted to bring 5,000 Texans to Canada to enlist, all of whom, he declared, were of British descent. A major in the American Army offered to resign provided he was given a commission in the Canadian Army, and said he would bring 500 recruits with him. These were typical cases.

The one anxiety of Irish-Canadians was not lest their fellow countrymen in the Dominions should show any weakening, but lest developments in Ireland itself should give encouragement to the foe. They heard with the greatest satisfaction of Mr. Redmond's speeches, and they urged on their compatriots at home by letter and cable the need of prompt aid for the Empire. In Montreal alone one regiment of Irish-Canadians was raised, and the Irish flocked everywhere to the colours.

The attitude of the Red Indians must not be passed over. The Red Indian population of Canada numbers to-day over one hundred thousand. Many of the Indians applied to be allowed to join the Expeditionary Force, and a few were enlisted. One tribe offered to form a corps of guides. Another volunteered the services of their band. Tribes that had fought by the side of England in former struggles now recalled their former exploits—how they had aided us in 1812 or had served as trackers in the Red River Expedition. Eighteen tribes scattered between the Yukon River and Nova Scotia raised among them close on £3,000 as contributions to the different war funds.

The Blood Indians of Alberta passed a resolution in the early days of the war: "The first citizens of Canada, the old allies of warring French and British, the redskins, the devoted wards of Victoria the Good and of her grandson, King George, are no whit behind the Sikhs of India, the men from South Africa, or the British Regulars in testifying to their loyalty

[Chesterfield and McLaren, Montreal.

EMBARKING HORSES AT QUEBEC.

TRANSPORTS WITH CANADIAN TROOPS, ESCORTED BY A BATTLESHIP.

to the Crown or to the unity of the British Empire." Chiefs "Shot Both Sides" and "Ermine Horses," of the Blood Indians, sent £200 from the tribal funds "as a tangible expression of their desire that Great Britain may ever remain the guardian of the weak and the arbiter of the world's peace." The Manitoulin Island Indians sent £400 "toward defraying the enormous expenses of the war in which our great father the King is at present engaged." The Six Nations desired their gift of money to speak for "the alliance existing between the Six Nations Indians and the British Crown."

It was at first intended to raise an Expeditionary Force of 22,000 men, with another 10,000 men in garrison duty or doing patrol work in the Dominion, but it was soon found impossible to keep the forces within these limits. Miners and trappers and pioneers in distant fields abandoned their work at the first word of war and travelled up rivers, over mountains, and through back-wood swamps to the nearest recruiting points. Old members of the Canadian contingent in the South African War demanded as a right that they should again be allowed to serve. Cowboys formed themselves up into regiments in Albertan townships under the shadow of the Rockies,

and asked nothing but to be led in the shortest time to the heart of the fight. "Among the troops from the West just arrived are 200 frontiersmen from Moosejaw," wrote the Ottawa correspondent of *The Times*. "They were refused permission to enlist as they wanted to go as cavalrymen. Nothing daunted, they hired two cars themselves and came to Ottawa at their own expense. They also purchased their own outfits. Nearly all are old Strathcona horsemen who saw service in South Africa. If not accepted for service by the Government they threaten to hire a cattle ship and sail for Europe."

Canada was fortunate in having at this time men of the right type at the head of her military forces. The Duke of Connaught, the Governor-General, himself a trained, experienced, and hard-working Army officer, was able, because of his knowledge of military affairs and his skill in handling men, to stimulate and direct national enthusiasm. The Canadian people, apart from some limited circles in two or three of the great cities of the East, are not over-given to courtly flattery, but the most independent of Canadians would be the first to admit that in the Duke of Connaught the Dominion had in these hours of crisis the right man in the right place. Colonel, afterwards

Major-General, Sam Hughes, the Dominion Minister of Militia, on whose shoulders the main work of organizing the Expeditionary Force fell, had proved before the war broke out that he knew his work and that his heart was in it. A man of great determination, energy and force of character, quick of speech and ready in caustic criticism, he at times aroused by his intensity some enmity. But his hardest opponents did not deny his strenuous enthusiasm. He took part in the South African War, where he won some distinction as a practical fighter. Succeeding Sir Frederick Borden as head of the Department of Militia, he undertook with zeal the task of awakening the Canadian people to the necessity of national defence. He urged in public speeches, in private conferences, and in every way possible, the need for national preparation. He fostered the Cadet Corps movement. He strove for efficiency in the ranks of the very limited battalions which before the war represented Canada's military force.

The first Canadian contingent as finally formed represented the Dominion from end to end. It was built up on the small defence

army, with its permanent force of three thousand men, and its militia. The old Canadian Army had been exposed in former times to scathing criticism, and not without cause, but it gave a skeleton organization, staff machinery, and military traditions which were now found to be of the greatest value. Corps of regulars, such as Lord Strathcona's Horse and the Royal Canadian Dragoons, active militia units such as the different Highland brigades, the Queen's Own Rifles, the Grenadiers, and the artillery, afforded a substantial foundation on which to build. Much benefit was found from improvements in staff organization introduced three years before in consequence of a caustic report on Canadian military unpreparedness from Sir John French.

A selection was made from the vast hosts of volunteers, and the numbers to hand enabled the sifting process to be thorough. Men were mercilessly weeded out for minor physical defects. Sobriety was particularly insisted upon, and while the Expeditionary Force remained in Canada any man who, after enlistment, was found under the influence of drink was dismissed. No married man was taken

PRINCESS PATRICIA'S CANADIAN LIGHT INFANTRY,   [*Central Press.*
At Bustard Camp, Salisbury Plain. The Colours of the Regiment were worked by Princess Patricia.

unless he first obtained the written consent of his wife. The pay of the private soldier was, with allowances, between 4s. 6d. and 5s. a day.

A very large proportion of the men of the first contingent, about 60 per cent., were British or Irish born. There was a strong Scottish element, and the kilted Highland regiments, with their piper bands, were a prominent feature of the contingent. This proportion was not maintained in the contingents formed later. Among the new soldiers were men of every rank of life—undergraduates from McGill, Toronto or Queen's, business men, miners, trappers, cowboys, journalists, railway hands—to name them all would be to name practically every class of Canadian employment. There was an appreciable proportion of townsmen. The common notion in England at the time that the Canadian contingent was made up of cowboys and hunters had only a slender basis in fact. But it must be remembered that the Canadian townsman, or the young English immigrant who has lived for a few years in a Canadian town, is much more self-reliant and more accustomed to open-air life than the average Englishman of the same class. He has learnt to do things for himself, to take greater risks, and to adapt himself to strange surroundings more than the average man accustomed to the set routine of English cities. The atmosphere of New Canada encourages initiative, venturesomeness, and self-reliance—all good qualities in the fighting man.

A monster camp was hastily formed at Valcartier, outside Quebec, and here the regiments were assembled from every part of the Dominion. The original 22,000 grew until the strength of the first Expeditionary Force—including a regiment for Bermuda—was close on 33,000. The avowed aim of the authorities was to make the new army complete in every detail. The personal equipment of the men was as good as money could buy, from the thick under-garments and extra-stout bootlaces to the overcoats. The mounted men were specially proud of their horses. An adequate motor transport ambulance and ammunition train were secured ; 105 fully-trained nurses from the leading Canadian hospitals were sent by the Canadian Red Cross Society to accompany the Army. The generosity of private donors had placed more machine guns at the service of the contingent

FIELD GUN
Being hoisted on board a transport.

than were needed. The contingent had its own aviators, its own medical service, its own intelligence staff. The moral needs of the men were not overlooked, and besides Chaplains, several Y.M.C.A. officials were given military rank that they might accompany the troops. By the end of September all was ready, and 31,250 men, with 7,500 horses and the complete equipment of a fighting army set sail in thirty-two transports for England.

A veil of silence had been thrown over the movements of the new Army. No word was allowed to appear in the Canadian or the British Press concerning their journey until they were safely landed. The troopships, mostly liners of the great Atlantic fleets, were silently assembled in the St. Lawrence, where protecting warships met them. At a given signal the various battalions of Valcartier were summoned to the ranks. The order was given to pack kits, and the men set out. A description of the scene by a western journalist is well worth preserving :

No one who witnessed the departure of the Canadian troops from Valcartier camp, and ultimately from

EXPEDITIONARY FORCE IN ENGLAND.
Canadian Highlanders Marching to Field Church Service.

Quebec on board the transports, will ever forget the sight. The march, for those who did not take the train, was some 18 miles by road to Quebec, and it was mostly made in a drizzling rain, with exceedingly heavy going under foot. As the various battalions at various hours of the day were summoned by the trumpeter to prepare for departure the scene in their lines was one of boisterous activity. Kits were packed, equipment was affixed, and every preparation made to leave the tents behind. On the order to start, the long khaki-coloured lines debouched into the road. As they passed the other battalion lines they were cheered by friends who lined the roadway, and who in many cases provided bands to play the men from camp. "It's a Long Way to Tipperary" was the inevitable song of the soldiers, and the inevitable air played by the bands. The familiar tune could be heard until the last man of the leaving battalion had disappeared from view—slog-slogging it through the heavy sand.

The greater part of the artillery made the march late in the afternoon and at night, arriving in Quebec rain-soaked, mud-bespattered, horses reeking in the rain, but everyone cheerful and content. Even in the drizzling rain the sight of the long lines of guns, ammunition wagons, transports, and horses filing along on the narrow roads, flanked by autumn-tinted trees, fringed by quaint French-Canadian villages and farm-steadings was an inspiring one. Women and children came to the doors to cheer them as they passed. At one point a white-haired old curé of a French village stood for nearly half an hour to his knees in the wet grass of his orchard, plucking apples from the trees and throwing them to the men as they swung along. They cheered him, and a French-Canadian battery which passed sang the Marseillaise.

The scene at Quebec was no less interesting and striking than that on the road from Valcartier. Not since the days of Wolfe in Quebec has the military atmosphere so predominated in the old city. In the Château Frontenac mothers and wives gathered to bid good-bye to sons and husbands. Officers, mud bespattered, were seized upon their arrival from the camp, and openly embraced by wives or sisters, before all the guests in the rotunda of the big hotel. In the café the music played and the last evenings were devoted to an attempt to forget the present, and not to anticipate the future. But all the merriment was hectic in nature, and the underlying minor chords of the violins predominated in the hearts of the majority of the dancers. On the days

of departure hasty farewells were said ; men went away to the transports which were to carry them to England "for the duration of the war." Women went back to their rooms to weep, or prepared to return home to bear the weary waiting of the future with what fortitude they might.

The afternoon the transports sailed to meet their grim convoy at the rendezvous was clear and bright. The Dufferin Terrace overlooking the harbour was black with the thousands which watched them go. From the liners as they passed one by one slowly down the river and past Point Levis came the music of bands, and the singing of the soldiers. Waving handkerchiefs and cheers answered them until the last of the big transports carrying the pride of Canada's soldiery disappeared from view between the Isle of Orleans and the mainland.*

The voyage across the Atlantic took nineteen days, the ships moving in triple line and their pace being regulated by the speed of the slowest. The uneventful journey may well in future form the theme of an imperial epic. Even the least imaginative of the voyagers could not fail to be impressed as he gazed from the decks day after day at the long lines of giant vessels all around, and at the warships convoying them with unceasing vigilance, the gunboats now darting off towards the horizon to hold up some suspicious passing stranger, the cruisers keeping pace front and rear ready for battle.

In England there were days of anxious expectation. The Press had been directed to make no mention of the voyage across the Atlantic, and the authorities even kept back the delivery of every Canadian newspaper in England for some weeks lest anything should become known of it. The absence of information only whetted curiosity. There was a

* Manitoba Free Press.

widespread desire among all classes to give the Canadians a great public reception in order to show the Dominions how England valued the aid of her sister nations. This, for obvious military reasons, was impossible. People of every rank, from Cabinet Ministers to the humblest private citizen, begged permission from the War Office to be on the quay side when the troops arrived. These applications were so numerous that the military authorities were obliged to make a rule that only one outsider should be present at the landing of the men —Lord Roberts. It was expected that Southampton would be the place of arrival, and the municipal authorities there made every preparation to give the Canadians a hearty greeting as they passed out of the dock gates. A false rumour was published one day that the Canadians had arrived in the Solent on the previous night, and people rushed to Southampton to welcome them. The rumour, it afterwards transpired, arose because of the arrival of a limited number of army reservists from Canada.

While the eyes of the country were directed to Southampton, the people of Plymouth were astonished, on the morning of October 15, to find transport after transport arriving in the Sound, forming in line across the harbour, and dropping anchor there. Word went around that the transports had brought the Canadian contingent, and Plymouth and Devonport rose to the occasion. The demonstration that followed, with its spontaneous enthusiasm, will live long in the memories of all who shared it.

The people flocked to the waterside and moved out in row-boats and small steamers to the transports. The Canadians lined the sides of their boats and mounted the riggings. Their bands formed up on the poops and played national airs. The skirl of the Highlanders' pipes, the harsh notes of sirens and hooters from all the British ships in the bay, the cheers, the shouts and the songs of the men of Devon and the men of the Far West filled the air.

The troops were not allowed on shore that day, and the people of the twin towns were not permitted on shipboard. But when in the days that followed the Canadian regiments landed and marched through the streets to the railway *en route* to Salisbury Plain, people of every rank and class showed that they could not do enough for them. " We were snowed under with good things," said one soldier expressively. Workgirls pressed apples and bananas on them ; clerks rushed from their offices with packets of cigarettes ; ladies stood at the stations with great dishes of coffee and piles of sandwiches, offering them to the men as they came in.

Devon has seen many memorable sights in its time, and from the days of Raleigh and before has served as an arena for spectacles of imperial history. It was fitting that the arrival of the

" *Canada.*"

FIRST ROYAL CANADIAN REGIMENT AT SALISBURY PLAIN.

Canadians should be here. The long lines of transports, stretching into the Sound until they vanished in the distant mist, opened up a fresh vision of the union of the sister nations of the Empire.

It had been decided that the Canadian contingent should not proceed at once to the front, but should first go through a course of military training on Salisbury Plain. Four camps were prepared there—the Bustards, West Down North, West Down South, and Pond Farm. It was at first intended that the men should remain for a short space under canvas and then be transferred before winter came on into huts around Larkshill. The transfer to the huts was delayed for some time, however, owing to the difficulty of finding sufficient labour to build them. Hence the majority of the troops remained under canvas until after Christmas.

If it was the intention of the military authorities to put the Canadians through a severe physical test before sending them to the front, they certainly succeeded. The Salisbury Plain camps were placed in very exposed places. Autumn rains came on a few days after the arrival of the contingent, and continued almost daily for many weeks. Soon the countryside was a quagmire. The roads were torn into great holes with the constant traffic of the heavy

Canadian motor transports, and the fields around the tents were some of them little more than seas of mud. The Canadians took their experiences good-humouredly. Chance visitors were inclined to pity them. The men themselves made a jest of the mud. Tent life in the winter days was hard without doubt, but it was soon found that it was exceedingly healthy. A small number broke down under the strain, but the others became hardened. It would be difficult to find a body of men more fit physically than the Canadians at the end of their first two months on Salisbury Plain.

Major-General Alderson took command of the contingent shortly after its arrival on Salisbury Plain, and it was soon evident that the Imperial Government had been happily inspired in choosing him. General Alderson had some of the Canadian troops under his command in the South African War, and gained knowledge of the ways of the men from overseas in Mashonaland and elsewhere. In his first visit to Salisbury Plain he succeeded in capturing the confidence of the Canadians. Meeting some of the battalions on the road, out on a route march, he called the men informally around him and made an impromptu speech, which struck the right note.

The Canadian camps had up to now been

CANADIAN HIGHLANDERS IN LONDON.

CANADIAN AUTOMOBILE MACHINE GUN BATTERY.
Inspection by H.R.H. the Duke of Connaught.

administered on a strict teetotal principle. At Valcartier, on shipboard, and at Salisbury Plain, the troops had been allowed no intoxicants, no alcoholic drinks of any kind being sold in the canteens. The result of this regulation, on Salisbury Plain at least, had not been wholly good. General Alderson told the troops from henceforth they were to be treated as men, not as children. They would be able to purchase beer in the camps, and he placed them on their honour to see that the privilege was not abused. It was the duty of the older and the more responsible men to ensure that the younger and the less-easily controlled observed discipline and kept within bounds of moderation. He trusted them to see that this would be done. Going on from this point General Alderson gave the soldiers a frank and straightforward speech about his plans for their training on Salisbury Plain, and the ideals of military efficiency he was striving for. The speech appealed to the men. It was repeated and emphasized in every tent in the four camps that night, and it infused a new vigour, enthusiasm, and devotion throughout the force.

The main difficulties of the Canadian contingent at the beginning were caused by the isolation of the camps and the difficulty in some of the sections of the men learning the necessity of strict military discipline. The nearest villages were several miles away, and the nearest town of any kind was from 14 to 16 miles, over difficult roads. The troops were consequently largely thrown on their own

resources for recreation and entertainment. Some of the lads from the West found it hard at first to realize that, even in the army of a democracy, rigid obedience is an absolute necessity. Some trouble was experienced in a few regiments over the question of outstaying leave. This quickly righted itself. The great virtues of the Canadian force, physical strength, intelligence, ingenuity, daring and manual skill, became more and more evident, and by the end of December it was clear to all observers that in the first Canadian contingent the Empire had a valuable fighting asset.

While the First contingent was training at Salisbury Plain steps were being taken to raise a Second and a Third Canadian contingent. On October 18 Sir Robert Borden announced that the Government would proceed at once with the organization of the Second Expeditionary Force ; 16,000 to 20,000 men were to be immediately enlisted, and as soon as the necessary arms and equipment were available the Government intended to train a total force of 40,000 men, including some 10,000 needed for garrison and outpost duty in Canada. The response of Canada to this was expressed in the words of a message by the Hon. Walter Scott, the Premier of Saskatchewan : " So long as we are able to raise a man to stand by the guns or a dollar to carry on the fight we shall go on until the oppressor is subdued." In many parts of the country men offered themselves in greater numbers than could be accepted. The Second Expeditionary Force consisted of about 17,000 officers and men, 4,765 horses, 58 field and heavy guns, and 16 machine guns. It included infantry, artillery, engineers, signal and cyclist companies, Army Service Corps, and field ambulances, with ammunition park, a supply column, reserve park, and other line-of-communication units. By early in December the total number of Canadians under arms was 91,000, made up as follows :

Forces already despatched (including regiment garrisoning Bermuda) nearly...	33,000
Forces engaged in garrison and outpost duty in Canada, about	8,000
Forces under training in Canada ...	50,000
	91,000

It was officially announced that as soon as the Second contingent went forward, which would be as early as possible, a further enlistment of 17,000 men would be made, bringing up the total to 108,000. Thereafter the forwarding of further Expeditionary Forces would be followed by the enlistment of men to take their place.

The main difficulty in enrolling the volunteers in Canada was the provision of arms and equipment. Every available factory and mill and arsenal throughout the Empire was working to its utmost capacity. Cooperative arrangements were made by the Imperial Government and the Dominion Governments, so that the resources of all possible parts of the Empire should be utilized in the most efficient manner for the common purpose. " In the western provinces," said an official notice issued in mid-December, " large numbers of men anxious to serve as mounted troops are available. They are excellent riders and good shots ; the Government has made special efforts to arrange that their services can be utilized."

Within a little over four months from the outbreak of the war Canada had provided at its own charge over 90,000 men for the Imperial forces. This response, splendid as it was, did not satisfy the people. Apart from the small local personal following of one politician in the Province of Quebec, the Dominion grew the more determined the more its people knew of the realities and the necessities of the war. Sir Wilfrid Laurier, speaking on the issue in mid-December, when early enthusiasm had had time to cool, voiced the considered judgment of French Canada and of English Canada, of Opposition and of Government alike :

" English Canadians, Irish-Canadians, French-Canadians,—Could we contemplate the possibility of remaining quiescent when the French Armies and the British Army are fighting against the powerful German hosts for the freedom of France, for the freedom of Belgium, and for the civilization of the world ? I do not hesitate to apply to Canada the words of Mr. Asquith, and say that if Canada had remained passive

BUILDING HUTS ON SALISBURY PLAIN.

THE KING AND QUEEN AT SALISBURY PLAIN.
Inspection of Canadian troops.

and quiescent we should have covered ourselves with dishonour."

Sir Robert Borden, the Prime Minister, speaking at the Canadian Club at Montreal in December, predicted that before the war closed, unless the end came sooner than could be reasonably expected, the German armies would find confronting them 250,000 men from the self-governing Dominions. He hinted then at the ultimate effects of this material aid on the future development of the Empire. " Step by step during the past hundred years," said he, " the development of self-government has proceeded in the Overseas Dominions. The enjoyment of these powers is not weakened, but rather strengthened, by the bonds which hold together the Empire. In one respect only has the evolution not attained its full development. The citizens of the self-governing Dominions do not directly participate, through their Ministers or Parliament, in the councils of the Empire which determine the issues of peace and war. It would be rash to predict the method by which the great problem will be solved, but of this I am convinced—that the events of this war will powerfully assist the

hastening of its wise solution. In this great testing time Canada has made known to the Empire and the world her true spirit. It has animated the men who are flocking in thousands to do their part and has equally inspired the women, who in every city, village, and hamlet are busy in manifest activities for the aid and solace of our countrymen wherever needed."

The political truce did not soon die down. The Opposition took up the attitude that its business was not merely to cease to oppose, but actively to help the Premier and the Cabinet. This attitude was clearly stated by the great Liberal newspaper of the East, the Toronto *Daily Star*, in December, on the occasion of a visit from the Premier. " Sir Robert Borden will have a warm welcome in Toronto, as he deserves. In these strenuous days everyone who holds a public position bears a heavy burden of responsibility and anxiety, and should receive all the comfort and support that the people can give. It is said that there is now a truce between the political parties ; but there should be more than a truce. There should be an alliance of all who stand for the common cause."

The people of Canada found that the out-

CAMP KITCHEN ON SALISBURY PLAIN. [F. A. McKenzie.

burst of national enthusiasm over the country helped very materially to overcome the depression which threatened the Dominion so seriously in the early days of August. Trade began to revive ; manufacturers, determined not to give way before threatening ruin, re-doubled their energies and in very many cases secured their own prosperity in doing so ; fresh enterprises were launched ; some firms began to manufacture goods formerly imported from Germany, and found a ready market ; others set out to provide material for the new armies. Enterprise, in August at a standstill, by December had been re-born.

AUSTRALIA.

To Australia, as to Canada, the war came at an unfavourable moment. The country was suffering from a bad drought, and a drought makes its evil effects felt on every section of Australian life. Germany had for some years cultivated Australian trade with special care and success, and the immediate cessation of German demand and the paralysis of German shipping meant much loss in business. But there was no hesitation about the attitude of the people of the Commonwealth, any more than

there was hesitation about the attitude of the people of Kent. The responsible men of Australia prepared quietly and systematically to conserve their means, to strengthen their armies, and to place their entire strength at the service of the Crown. " We must sit tight now and see the thing through at whatever difficulty and whatever cost," said Mr. Cook, the then Federal Prime Minister. " We must be stedfast in our determination. Our resources are great, and British spirit is not dead. We owe it to those who have gone before to preserve the great fabric of British freedom and hand it on to our children. Our duty is quite clear. Remember we are Britons."

Australia understood the vital issues of the war. The national feeling was well expressed by Sir George Reid : " The real inwardness of the struggle between Germany and Great Britain is between two opposite ideals of Imperial power. Are the eyes and ears of humanity to be terrified by ' mailed fists ' and ' shining armour ' and the ' rattle ' of the sabre of Prussian sires, or are they to be attracted by triumphs of peaceful enterprise and political development that leave unlimited scope for the elevation of all the races of mankind ? The answer has already, I think, been given. In every quarter of the globe, in the hands of men of every race, creed and colour, loyal arms have flashed in the sun, saluting the war signal of our Sovereign.''

The only fear before war was declared was lest the British Government, in its desire for peace, should shrink from the great sacrifices demanded. The first cabled reports of Sir Edward Grey's great speech in the House of Commons immediately before the declaration of war conveyed the impression that England had decided to stand on one side. A feeling of disappointment and humiliation swept through the country. "A prominent Labour ex-Minister declared that if Great Britain deserted her friends and allowed Belgium to be invaded in spite of her guarantee, he would never call himself an Englishman again," wrote one man from Sydney at the time. " But the telegrams were very disheartening, and when our declaration of war was announced it was received with a universal feeling of relief—England had not caved in, after all ! Since then Australia has been splendid. No tub-thumping or flag-wagging, but a quiet resolve to do everything and to put up with everything to help the national cause, and, for the rest, to keep cool, and to await the issue as patiently as possible.''

The truce in party politics which prevailed over most parts of the Empire did not remain unbroken in Australia. At the beginning of the war the leaders of the Labour Party expressed their willingness to sink all party controversy for the time and to avoid contests in the forthcoming General Election by an arrangement under which old members would be returned unopposed. They suggested that Mr. Pearce, who had largely created the naval and military policy of Australia in recent years, should co-operate with the then Ministry of Defence. The Government, while welcoming the suggestion that party controversy should cease, declined to accept the definite proposals of the Labour Party. The Prime Minister, at a banquet at Melbourne on August 10, in an important speech on the war, welcomed Mr. Fisher, the Labour leader, who was present, and declared that : " So far as this trouble is concerned all party divisions have been done away with."

Some of the supporters of the Cook Ministry were unable, however, to live up to this declaration, and they attempted, with singular un-wisdom, to represent the General Election as a contest between patriotic Conservatives and a disloyal, anti-war and anti-British Labourite Party. The Cook Ministry was soundly defeated, and, in the opinion of many non-partisan observers, the main cause of its defeat was the attempt to tag the label of disloyalty to the Labour group. Mr. Andrew Fisher, the new Premier, who succeeded to office in September, demonstrated by his actions how baseless the charge was. He sent a message to England on the day of his accession : " At the beginning of the war I said that Australia should support Great Britain with her last man and her last shilling. I am glad to have the opportunity of giving effect if necessary to that declaration." Mr. Pearce now succeeded once more to the Ministry of Defence and his appointment was generally welcomed.

It was difficult for those who knew Australia at the end of the nineteenth century to realize the change that had come over the working

THE MUD OF SALISBURY PLAIN.

THE KING LEAVING BUSTARD CAMP, SALISBURY PLAIN.

classes there on the question of national defence. Even up to the days of the Russo-Japanese War the Australian working man regarded militarism as a form of plutocratic oppression and as an attempt to fleece the workers by making them support an idle and unproductive class. The soldier was the subject of good-natured but contemptuous ridicule. Proposals that Australia should have a fleet of her own or should lend adequate support to the British Admiralty were exceedingly unpopular. The Russo-Japanese War changed the temper of the people. The Commonwealth had already given offence to the Chinese and Japanese Governments by its attitude towards Oriental immigration. The defeat of Russia brought home to the nation the fact that Australia, apart from her Imperial connexion, lay at the mercy of one of the strongest, most daring, and most proud of world Powers. The *Sydney Bulletin,* whose influence as a maker of popular opinion will be denied by none who knows Australia to-day, drove home week by week, by pictures, editorials, comments and verse, the meaning of Great Japan. The visits of some English military leaders, including Lord Kitchener, helped to emphasize in the public mind the need for Australian defence

and the shortcomings of the old military provisions.

The outcome of this was the definite commencement of an Australian Navy and the passing of Defence Acts enforcing compulsory service on all able-bodied males, starting with cadet training from twelve until eighteen years old, and thence onward to service during manhood in the Citizen Defence Force. It necessarily takes time to establish a system of universal service, but at the outbreak of the war the Commonwealth of Australia had 85,000 cadets under training and 50,000 men in the Citizen Forces, well equipped and organized. There were 24 batteries of field artillery of the latest type of 18-pounder guns, artillery of which Sir Ian Hamilton had said when on his visit of inspection to the Commonwealth: " I would not be afraid to take them into action against European troops to-morrow."

The Commonwealth Government at once volunteered to send an Expeditionary Force of 20,000 men to Europe, and the leading newspapers voiced the public decision that this would be followed, if necessary, by five times the number : " Our one anxiety will be to have them placed where they can be of the most service to the Empire as a whole." The call went out for volunteers, and the immediate rush was so great as to cause some embarrassment, for it was difficult to know what men to reject when so much fine material offered. Queensland Bushmen offered to provide a regiment and bring their own horses. The amateur yachtsmen of Australia offered their services for the Royal Naval Reserve. No attempt was made to use compulsion to obtain recruits. This was not necessary and would not have been possible. The Defence Acts made no provision for compulsory service abroad, and even had they done so it would have been needless, for there were twice as many good volunteers as were required, and in many districts the competition to enlist was exceedingly keen.

While recruiting was proceeding, the business men looked to their side of the national struggle. They understood well enough what they had to do. It was to keep Australia going with as little hindrance as possible to sound industry and local development, so that the whole attention of their administrators could be devoted to providing the Mother Country with whatever men or resources she required. Meetings of the Chambers of Manufacturers and other commercial bodies were held, and unanimous resolutions were passed to keep factories open and as far as possible to prevent

[*Elliott & Fry.*

RT. HON. ANDREW FISHER,
Prime Minister of Australia.

unemployment. Much trade had been dislocated by a series of proclamations prohibiting the export to foreign lands of vital articles of food supply likely to be wanted for the Imperial armies. One secondary result of the war in Australia, as in Canada, was to quicken the commercial enterprise of the nation, and before many weeks it became evident that the arrest of German trade would mean, after the temporary dislocation had been overcome, a gain rather than a loss to the Commonwealth generally.

The German settlers in Australia decided to stand by the country of their adoption. The German Lutheran congregations at Rella, Roseberg and Curzo, German-speaking but mostly Australian born, unanimously adopted a resolution soon after the outbreak of the war : " That we, as German-speaking citizens, being British subjects either by birth or naturalization, desire publicly to express our unswerving loyalty and fidelity to His Majesty King George V., and that as citizens of the British Empire, enjoying full civil and religious freedom, we are prepared, if the necessity arises, to sacrifice our property and our lives for the welfare of the British Empire." Australia was one.

The different States of the Commonwealth and the Dominion of New Zealand entered into

HON. JOSEPH COOK,
Late Prime Minister of Australia.

HON. GEORGE F. PEARCE,
Australian Minister for Defence.

different States were : Victoria 7.430, New South Wales 6,420, Queensland 2,380, South Australia 1,770, Tasmania 1,070, West Australia 840. The Force consisted at first of a Light Horse brigade with its own artillery and field train and a division of three infantry brigades, two Light Horse squadrons, heavy artillery, three field artillery brigades, engineers, signal companies, ammunition and transport train, and field ambulances. Apart from the Light Horse brigade of 2,226 officers and men and 10 guns, the Australian Division included 17,553 troops of all ranks, 5,162 horses and 70 guns. The infantry numbered 12,350. The force was dressed in the ordinary Australian khaki uniform, the several branches being distinguished by coloured ribbon on the hat— green for infantry, scarlet for artillery, white for light horse, dark blue for engineers, Royal blue for signalists, blue and white for Army Service, and chocolate for the Army Medical Corps. The actual number of troops sent out with the First Expeditionary Force was slightly in excess of the detailed figures—20,338 men, together with 1,200 Army Reserve. This, however, was only a beginning. By the third

a friendly rivalry in philanthropic war work. By early in November the various war funds in Australia amounted to about half a million pounds, and week after week they rose rapidly. The Commonwealth Government granted £100,000 to the Belgian Relief Fund, the New Zealand Government £20,000, and the Queensland Government £10,000. Other States raised scores of thousands of pounds in money and in food for Belgium. Australia contributed £50,000 before Christmas to the British Red Cross Society. The Pastoralists' Union of New South Wales gave gifts in aid of the war on a princely scale. Up to the end of October these gifts included 40,000 carcases of mutton, 1,500 sheep, a million cartridges, 20 tons of dried fruit, and 1,500 horses. In November it gave a further 7,600 carcases of mutton. The Brisbane Newspaper Co. made itself specially prominent among the many newspapers which raised large war funds. Gifts of tons of flour and of biscuits, of thousands of sheep and of consignments of fruit and clothing were sent from all parts of Australia. One unusual contribution was from the Ministers of Western Australia, who set aside 10 per cent. of their salaries for the National Relief Fund.

It was decided that the First Expeditionary Force of 20,000 men should be drawn from every part of the Commonwealth in proportion to population. The contributions of the

[By courtesy of " The Australasian "
COLONEL F. G. HUGHES,
Commanding the Third Australian Contingent.

week in November over 10,000 more men were being prepared for the front, and three reinforcements, numbering in all about 9,000, were completing their training to be ready to fill up the ranks. Plans were completed to send regularly approximately 2,000 men a month to the front to compensate for the attrition from casualties and sickness.

Late in November Mr. Pearce, the Minister for Defence, was able to announce that on the military side 39,416 troops had been raised for service in Europe and 1,764 naval reservists and infantry had taken part in operations in the Pacific, making a total of 41,180 men. In addition, 56,289 men of the Citizen Forces were armed and equipped, the bulk of them being mobilized under active service conditions for the defence of various parts of the Commonwealth. To these there had to be added 51,153 members of rifle clubs, and 16,000 recruits who had passed from the senior cadets, making a total of 67,153 reservists available for war, or a grand total of 164,631 men under arms. Australia was proud of her record, and with reason. The Government and Opposition were at one in their determination. " We must," said Sir William Irvine, late Attorney-General of the Commonwealth, " send 100,000 or 150,000 men to join shoulders with those fighting in the old land."

The pay of the troops was on the most liberal scale, ranging from 6s. and 1s. a day for a private to 12s. and 2s. for a staff sergeant, 17s. 6d. and 3s. for lieutenant and second lieutenant, and 45s. and 8s. for a colonel and brigadier. Brigadier-General Bridges was in command of the Australian troops at the time of their formation. He was appointed a Major-General in the British Army, and early in December General Birdwood, who served as military secretary to Lord Kitchener in South Africa and in India and who had won distinction in many fields, was appointed to the command of the united Australian and New Zealand troops. Everyone who had opportunity to examine the Australian soldiers while in training was agreed that they were men of magnificent physique, admirably equipped, and that they gave evidence in their conduct and in the details of their organization of good training, high discipline, and real efficiency.

General Bridges, after having inspected the various camps, said : " Physically the troops are very fine indeed, and from what I have observed they are showing a wholly admirable and commendable spirit. They are in the utmost good heart, keen, eager and zealous in all their work. What they lack in technical knowledge and training there is no doubt they make up in adaptability. So far as the *personnel* of the force is concerned, we have practically all the men we require, or we know where we can obtain the troops for a few units."

It was at first intended that the Australian contingent should come to England and complete their training here before proceeding to the front.

No word was allowed to be published about the departure of the Australian contingent for Europe, as the German Fleet in the Pacific under Admiral von Spee was at this time at large, and it was realized that it might attempt to attack the transports. When the Australians were passing the Keeling Cocos Islands a warning was received from the Japanese that the Germans were near, and that they had mined a part of the route. Everything was made ready for any eventualities. One volunteer in the Australian contingent described the scene :—

" That night as we were steaming some ten

[*W. Gregory & Co.*

**SERGEANT-MAJOR,
VICTORIA MOUNTED RIFLES.**

["The Australasian."]

ENROLLING THE AUSTRALIAN EXPEDITIONARY FORCE,
Victoria Barracks, Melbourne.

miles to leeward of the Cocos the orders were given to don lifebelts and fall in at our messes. At 8 o'clock we were all marched up in single file and lined up on deck ready for anything. It was a pitch dark night and lightning playing away in the distance, and as all lights on the ships had disappeared we could not see an inch ahead. The colonel, majors, &c., were all dressed alike—that is, bare to the waist, with trousers rolled up to the knees and lifebelts donned. Not a word was to be spoken except by officers, and there we stood for over an hour until the silence was rudely broken by the muffled roar of a gun some distance astern. Immediately afterwards we saw the dark form of a cruiser jump across our bows and make straight for the starboard horizon, followed by two others. I tell you we held our breaths. We did not get blown up that night after all, and next morning we heard the account of the noise. I'm beggared if it wasn't the Emden, which had evaded the British for so long and tried to get one in on us. She was chased by the Sydney, which easily outstripped all the other boats. Two days afterwards the Sydney passed down our lines, and you bet we gave her a rousing reception."

The rest of the voyage was without incidents of note, until the fleet arrived at the Suez Canal.

There it was learned that owing to the situation in Egypt, due to the attitude of Turkey and the adhesion of the Khedive to the Turkish side, the Australians were to remain for the time in Egypt itself to complete their training there, strengthen the British garrison on the spot, and help to defend the Suez Canal against any possible land attacks.

NEW ZEALAND.

At the end of July, when news came through to New Zealand of the growing seriousness of the situation in Europe, the Government declared its attitude. New Zealand was ready for any crisis. The careful attention that had been paid in recent years to military training was now to bear fruit. Everything was ready for the raising, equipment, and dispatch of an Expeditionary Force on the shortest possible notice. On July 31 the Prime Minister, Mr. Massey, was able to inform the House of Representatives that while, so far as it was possible to judge, there was no occasion for serious alarm, the Government had prepared for possibilities and would ask the Parliament and people of New Zealand, if the occasion arose, to do their duty by offering the services of an Expeditionary Force to the Imperial Government. An understanding had been arrived at with regard to the number and constitution of such a force. "I have no fear," said he, "of volunteers not being forthcoming." The announcement met with a thrilling response. For once the rules and forms of the House were forgotten, and the whole assembly, members and visitors alike, rose to its feet, cheered, and sang the National Anthem. When silence was secured, Sir Joseph Ward, the Leader of the Opposition, rose to support the Premier. "Speaking for the entire Opposition," he said, "we will heartily cooperate with the Government of the day in assisting to defend the interests of this portion of the Empire, and of the Empire as a whole."

On the afternoon of August 5 the Governor appeared on the steps of Parliament House and read to a vast crowd of ten thousand people the cablegram from the King, printed earlier in this chapter, thanking the Dominions for their loyal messages. When he had finished reading the Royal message the Governor added :—"I have yet another message— England and Germany are now at war." The people of New Zealand sent back through the Governor a message to the King :—" New Zealand desires me to acknowledge your Majesty's gracious message and to say that,

come good or ill, she, in company with the Dominions and other dependencies of the Crown, is prepared to make any sacrifice to maintain her heritage and her birthright."

The nation took the news of the declaration of war quietly. It was unanimously felt that England, under the circumstances, could do nothing else, and that New Zealand must of course support England to the utmost of her power. The Dominion was ready financially as well as from a military point of view. The country was prosperous. There were ample funds available, and the temporary unrest of overseas commerce and of finance caused throughout the world by the war soon righted itself. The astonishing feature to every visitor from England at the time was that the war made such seeming small difference to the nation at large. Parliament went on as usual with its customary domestic controversies. The suggestion that party warfare should be suspended and a General Election due in December postponed was not entertained. A chance visitor to New Zealand might well have thought, late in November, that the country was more interested in the electoral fight over the Prohibition question than in the war. This absence of excitement was due, however, not

AUSTRALIANS EMBARKING AT MELBOURNE.

VICTORIA CONTINGENT IN CAMP NEAR MELBOURNE.

to lack of interest, but to the general assurance of victory, and to knowledge that the country was ready for a time such as this. The Prime Minister, speaking at the time of the declaration of war, voiced the national attitude :—" We must stand together, calm, united, resolute, trusting in God, and I am glad to say that not only in New Zealand does this feeling of confidence exist, but it obtains throughout every part of the Empire. My advice at this most trying moment is to keep cool, stand fast, and do your duty to New Zealand and the Empire." The Prime Minister was interrupted by a voice from one of the crowd : " We will do that." " I am sure you will," he responded.

The New Zealand Citizen Army, like the Australian Defence Force, is raised for home defence only, but it supplied a considerable force of trained men from which volunteers could be drawn. Long before it was announced that volunteers were required, the Minister for Defence received letters and telegrams from every part from men anxious to serve anywhere. By eleven o'clock in the morning of August 6 1,000 volunteers had applied in Auckland alone. By evening the number of volunteers was so great that count had been lost. Not only did men offer themselves, but motor cars, horses, and money were placed at the service of the Government from all districts.

On Monday, August 10, six days after the declaration of war, the first part of Auckland's section left for Wellington, ready to the last button. Within three weeks of the declaration of war the contingent was completed, and a message was cabled to the War Office that the Expeditionary Army of 8,000 men could embark at a moment's notice to any part of the world. A few days later a force was despatched to Samoa to capture the German colony there.

The Maori people responded as heartily as the white, and insisted on their right to share in the defence of the Empire against the King's enemies. On behalf of the Maoris in the North, N. P. Kawiti sent a message to the Prime Minister :—" We, the Ngaputi people, wish to convey through you to His Majesty the King, in this most trying epoch in the history of the Empire, an assurance of our loyalty and devotion, and that we are ever ready and willing to assist in any way in the defence of this Dominion against his enemies." The Maoris offered to raise a force of some thousand men, and Kawiti appealed to all his race to be prepared so that they might be able and willing to take their share of the heavy burden that had fallen on the Empire's shoulders. The fact that the British Government had decided to employ Indian troops in the war was at once used as a lever for inducing the New Zealand Government to accept the military service of the Maoris. The argument prevailed, and a camp of 500 Maoris was formed, one half to go off to train in Egypt and the other half to Samoa. It was anticipated that the main services of the Maoris would be as scouts.

The main Expeditionary Force represented the very pick of the young manhood of the Dominion. Plans were made to keep the force up to full strength by the further dispatch of 20 per cent. more men six weeks afterwards and 5 per cent. each subsequent month. " The average young New Zealander," said the *New Zealand Herald* at the time, " is half a soldier before he is enrolled. He is physically strong, intellectually keen, anxious to be led (though being what he is he will not brook being driven a single inch), quick to learn his drill, easily adapting himself to the conditions of living in camp since camping usually is his pastime, and very loyal to his leaders when his leaders know their job. He is an excellent comrade, and anticipates his leader's wish almost before the order is given. He is extraordinarily sensitive to reproof. Where a curse is necessary in some armies to enforce a command, with the New Zealander the slightest stricture is all that is necessary. The organization and equipment of our army are good. Its numbers are increasing every year, its training is proceeding on good lines." This description is not perhaps unbiased, but those who know the character of New Zealand best would generally support it.

The visitor who came to the conclusion in the early days of the war that because of the quiet attitude of the people there was any lack of determination would have wholly misjudged the situation. Whenever anything had to be done it was done promptly. The troops who were required were raised almost without an effort. Necessary supplies were given in a day. The young soldiers were largely drawn from the best professional, business, and farming class. One correspondent who visited the camp of the Canterbury contingent, near Christchurch, gave an example of the class of men in the force, taking at random a single tent containing eight troopers :—" Of these seven were public school men and all were gentlemen. Two were grandsons of a pioneer colonial bishop, another was the son of our most honoured statesmen, five of the eight were farmers of some means ; the others were business men in responsible positions. All of them had played in the fifteen or the eleven of their schools, and five of them had been school prefects. Any one of them, had he chosen the army as a profession, would have made an efficient and probably a distinguished officer. They were men of splendid physique. But all eight were just plain ' Tommies ' with not even a corporal's stripe among them. Men of similar type were common throughout the contingent."

The high quality of the men was specially emphasized by a correspondent of *The Times,*

DRILL IN THE CAMP OF THE VICTORIA CONTINGENT NEAR MELBOURNE.

AUSTRALIAN TROOPS EMBARKING AT MELBOURNE.

who examined the small advance guard of the contingent at Salisbury Plain. The small detachment, he noted, included five members of the " All Black " team, besides one English international player. It could put a team in the field that would do credit to any first class club. " In many ways," he continued, " the little New Zealand contingent is an extraordinary body of men. It contains three Rhodes scholars, besides a regimental poet and an artist of established reputation. The artist has turned his talent to account as scene painter in the regimental theatre ; for the force has no Y.M.C.A. tent at its present camp, and has arranged its own amusement hall. The proscenium is painted in imitation of the entrance to a Maori dwelling, the central ornament being a large and capable Maori god chewing up, with evident relish, a German eagle."

The first intention was to complete the training of the New Zealand contingent in a camp on Salisbury Plain, and a small advance party was sent off to England to undertake the preliminary work of preparation. The date of the departure of the troops was, as with other contingents, kept a profound secret outside the Dominion. The New Zealanders were, like the Australians, stopped at Egypt and landed there

to help for the time, if necessary, in the defence of the Suez Canal route.

OPERATIONS IN THE PACIFIC.

Before the departure of the main New Zealand contingent a small force set out under the direction of the Australian Navy and annexed German Samoa without opposition. This annexation was specially welcome in New Zealand, for the people there had for many years regarded the British consent to the German occupation of Samoa as one of the most serious flaws in our foreign policy. In 1899 the British Government signed an agreement abrogating an older treaty guaranteeing the independence and autonomy of the Samoan group under a native king, withdrew her own claims to the islands and recognized German ownership. The treaty was bitterly resented by Mr. Seddon, the Premier of New Zealand, for it seemed to place an irreparable barrier in the way of the creation of a federation of Pacific Islands, under the British flag, with New Zealand as chief, which the then New Zealand Premier advocated.

Mr. Seddon denounced the surrender to Germany with the utmost emphasis, and although it was impossible then to retract it, he induced the British Government to regularize and ensure her position on some other Pacific groups. Seddon's anger and disappointment was shared by many New Zealanders at the time and afterwards, and the occupation of the Islands by the Expeditionary Force caused the greatest satisfaction throughout the Dominion. By this capture, which has been described at length in a previous chapter,* the British Empire gained possession of a group of islands of considerable size and great fertility. The two leading islands are Savaii, with an area of about 660 sq. miles, and Upolu, of 340 sq. miles. The Australian ships which accompanied the expedition were the Australia and the Melbourne. In addition to helping to capture German Samoa, they destroyed wireless stations in a number of places.

The fact that the New Zealand Expeditionary Force to Samoa had to advance under the protection of the Australian Navy was held by the Australian people to be a justification of their policy in maintaining a local navy rather than in supporting the plan of centralized naval control. The Australian vessels were of undoubted service. The large vessels of the British Fleet were employed in major operations

* Vol. I., p. 37.

in other seas, and the China Squadron was largely engaged in convoying troops. A small fleet of German cruisers was ravaging the Pacific and Indian Oceans. The people of New Zealand had given a battle cruiser, the New Zealand, to the Admiralty with the understanding that this vessel was to be stationed in the Far East. The Admiralty, however, to the great disappointment of the people of the Dominion, determined to use the ship in the general service of the British Navy. The Australian Fleet was on the spot in the Southern Pacific when the war broke out. It was splendidly ready. When the German ships started their raids our naval forces in the Pacific were very small. Had an agreement entered into by the Admiralty with some of the Dominions in 1909 been carried out, we would have had in the Pacific and Indian Oceans in 1914 three Dreadnought cruisers, several ocean destroyers and 10 light cruisers of 25 knot speed. The naval agreement of 1909 fell through, and on Australia lay for a time a large part of the defence of our interests in the southern seas. It was fortunate for England that, as events proved, the Australian Navy had been prepared with a thoroughness that left nothing to be desired, and was well-manned and well-equipped.

Following the advance on Samoa, the

VICTORIA CONTINGENT MARCHING THROUGH MELBOURNE.

TRANSPORTS WITH CANADIANS ARRIVING AT PLYMOUTH.

Australian Fleet, working under the direction of the British Admiralty, co-operated with the China Squadron in searching the Pacific for German cruisers, and took possession of further German colonies. These naval operations have been already outlined in the chapter on the Navy's work in the outer seas.* Early in September the Australian Squadron, carrying with it 1,200 men, advanced on the Bismarck Archipelago. On the morning of September 11 the Squadron arrived at Herbertshöhe Harbour and a party of 25 men was landed to take possession of a wireless station some four miles inland. Apparently no opposition was expected, but a force of Germans and armed natives concealed themselves in cocoanut palm trees and opened fire, killing Captain Pockley, of the Army Medical Corps, and a naval petty officer, and driving the remainder of the party back. Later in the morning Commander Beresford of the Australian Navy landed at a point about a mile from Herbertshöhe with 150 men, and advanced on the wireless station. Snipers impeded their advance, and when they got within a hundred yards of the station they found 40 natives and six Germans entrenched there, and the ground mined and well prepared for resistance. Lieutenant-Commander Elwell

* Vol. I., p. 25.

advanced fearlessly to within 20 yards of the trench, gave his men the order to fix bayonets and charge, and immediately fell with two bullets through the head. Towards the end of the afternoon the defenders of the station came out with a white flag and surrendered. While their arms and ammunition were being collected one of the Germans bolted into the bush and firing broke out again from the trees, where more natives were concealed. Three of the Australians were killed. The natives were promptly dislodged and the wireless station occupied.

While this was going on another party occupied Herbertshöhe without resistance, and a third group took possession of Rabaul, the seat of German Government in the island. The German group was two days later declared a British possession, and after the formal proclamation had been publicly read an address was delivered to the natives by Major Heritage in " pidgin " English and the Union Jack was raised. The address in " pidgin " English was a curiosity well worth recording :—

All boys belongina all place, you savvy. Big feller master, he come now. He new feller master. He strong feller. All ship stop place. He small feller ship belongina him ; plenty more big feller. He stop place belongina him now. He come here. He take him all place. He look out good you feller. He like you feller. Look out good alonga him. Supposing other feller master, he been speak you, " you no work alonga new feller master." He gammon. Supposing you work good with this new feller master, he look out good alonga with you. He look out you get plenty good feller kaikai food. He no fighting black feller boy along nothing. You look him new feller flag. You savvy him, he belong British English. He more better than other feller. Supposing you been making paper before this new feller master come, you finish time belongina him first. You like make him new feller paper. Long man belongina new feller master he look out good along with you. He give you more money, and more good feller kaikai. You no fight other feller black man other feller place. You no kaikai man. You no steal Mary belongina other feller man. Me finish talk along with you now. By and by ship belonging new feller master he come and look out place along with you. Now you give three feller cheers belonging new feller master.

The cheers, it is reported, were given with surprising vigour.

A considerable force of trained Germans, with armed natives, had retired upon Toma, a mountainous district six to eight miles from the coast, and had entrenched themselves there, their trenches extending along the only possible roadway, a road hedged in on either side by impenetrable jungle. A formal attack had to be made upon the place. First the hills beyond Herbertshöhe were shelled by a warship, to drive out the natives. Then the troops under Colonel Watson advanced on Toma itself. The position was shelled with shrapnel and lyddite, and then the troops, after marching some hours under a tropical sun, stormed the trenches. The enemy had, however, already abandoned the position. It was obviously impossible for them to remain long in the tropical forest, and soon afterwards a representative of the Acting-Governor came in under a flag of truce to negotiate. After consideration the Germans surrendered. The Acting-Governor was placed on parole, it being agreed that he should be allowed to return to Germany on the first opportunity. The German officers were deported, and the remainder of the force were allowed to go free, on taking the oath of neutrality.*

Later in September the Australian Squadron advanced on the town of Friedrich Wilhelm, the seat of government of Kaiser Wilhelm's Land, German New Guinea, and occupied it without opposition.

A new task now fell to the Australian Squadron. They aided in the search for the six German cruisers which were ravaging the Pacific, capturing our ships and holding up our trade. It is one of the ironies of history that the Australian Squadron, in its first important naval operations, should find itself working in co-operation with the Japanese Fleet—the Fleet whose supposed menace had

* This account is based on the dispatch of the special correspondent of The Sydney Sun, who accompanied the Squadron.

AUSTRALIAN RESERVISTS DISEMBARKING AT PLYMOUTH.

A SQUADRON OF LIGHT HORSE RECRUITS, AUSTRALIA.

been the main factor in bringing the Australian Squadron into being. Yet so it was.

A large force of British, Australian, Japanese, Russian and French cruisers set out to search the seas for the Germans. The story of the steps taken by the Allied Navies to deal with these German cruisers will be told in a subsequent chapter. It is enough to say here that in the anxious and arduous weeks that followed the Australian Squadron played a splendid part. It was an Australian ship—the cruiser Sydney —that ran the Emden, the most active and destructive of the German Pacific Fleet, to earth in the Keeling Cocos Islands, and, after a short fight, drove her ashore and captured her officers and crew. The warm congratulations sent by Mr. Winston Churchill, as First Lord of the Admiralty, to the Commonwealth Naval Board on the brilliant entry of the Australian Navy into the war, and the signal services rendered to the Allied cause in this fight, were echoed throughout the Empire. It was hoped by the Australians that, working in conjunction with the Japanese Fleet, they might have an opportunity to deal with the remainder of the German Squadron in the Pacific. This was not to be, but the Australians did valuable work in shepherding those vessels south of the Horn, and helping to drive them in the direction where the British Fleet under

Admiral Sturdee was waiting for them and destroyed them. In the operations in the Pacific, the Australian Squadron could claim with justice a long, honourable, prominent and distinguished part.

The following is a list of the principal gifts to the Imperial Government from different parts of the Empire :

CANADA.
Date of offer.

Aug. 7.—The Dominion Government, 1,000,000 bags of flour of 98 lb. each, as a gift to the people of the United Kingdom.

Aug. 7.—Alberta, 500,000 bushels of Alberta oats.

Aug. 19.—£57,192 13s. 3d., gift from the women of Canada, through the Duchess of Connaught ; £20,000 to be handed to the War Office for hospital purposes, and the balance to the Admiralty to build, equip and maintain a Canadian Women's Hospital at Haslar.

Aug. 24.—Quebec, 4,000,000 lb. of cheese.

Aug. 25.—Prince Edward Island, 100,000 bushels of oats, with, on August 28, further offers of cheese and hay.

Aug. 27.—Ontario, 250,000 bags of flour.

Sept. 1.—Saskatchewan, 1,500 horses, costing approximately $250,000.

Sept. 4.—New Brunswick, 100,000 bushels of potatoes.

Sept. 6.—Manitoba, 50,000 bags of flour of 98 lb. each.

Sept. 6.—British Columbia, 25,000 cases British Columbia canned salmon.

Sept. 15.—£20,000 from the Dominion Government to organize, equip and maintain a hospital in France, to be known as the "Hospice Canadien."

Oct. 3.—A gift of provisions and clothing from the people of Nova Scotia for the Belgians.

Oct. 21.—Agricultural produce—viz., oats, potatoes, apples, peas, beans, cheese and flour—from the farmers of various counties of Ontario to the British Government.

Oct. 24.—$100,000 in cash from the Government of Nova Scotia to the Local Government Board for the relief of distress, in lieu of 100,000 tons of coal offered previously to His Majesty's Government.

Nov. 12.—A car of flour from the farmers of the Oaklake District, Manitoba, to the National Relief Fund.

AUSTRALIA.

Aug. 28.—1,000 gallons of port wine from Messrs. Cullen & Wallace, of Rutherglen, Victoria, for sick and wounded soldiers in hospitals.

Sept. 2.—Butter, bacon, beef, condensed milk, and arrowroot suitable for army purposes, together with 50 cases of condensed milk for the benefit of children of the Empire, collected by the *Brisbane Courier.*

Sept. 9.—Frozen meat to the value of £10,000 from the Patriotic Committee, Brisbane, with intimation of further gifts.

Sept. 14.—One ton of butter from Mrs. Hindson and family for use of British soldiers.

Sept. 21.—Second shipment of goods collected by *Brisbane Courier,* foodstuffs valued at £6,200.

Sept. 28.—Third shipment of foodstuffs collected by *Brisbane Courier* valued at £1,950.

Oct. 1.—Gift of sheep for British troops from the Pastoralists' Union of New

H M.A.S. "SYDNEY."

"GOOD-BYE."

South Wales, a part of the gift to be devoted to relief in Belgium.

Oct. 5.—£6,000 from Victoria for Belgian relief.

Oct. 27.—Grant by the Commonwealth Parliament in aid to Belgium of £100,000.

Nov. 11.—Further shipments of frozen mutton from the Pastoralists' Union.

Nov. 12.—£20,000 raised in Sydney for the Belgian Relief Fund, and further sums for the same fund from New South Wales, Queensland, and from Christchurch and Auckland, New Zealand.

New Zealand.

Aug. 15.—Two complete military X-ray apparatus for New Zealand contingent.

Sept. 23.—Bleriot monoplane, Britannia.

Oct. 16.—A quantity of socks and cholera belts in response to Queen's appeal.

Nov. 5.—£20,000 divided between the National Relief Fund and the Belgian Relief Fund.

Union of South Africa.

Sept. 24.—Consignment of invalid port for sick and wounded soldiers from Paarl Wine and Brandy Company.

Oct. 8.—The offer of the services of the South African Field Ambulance to the French Government as a Red Cross unit.

Oct. 16.—A quantity of fruit and eggs from the Bathurst Farmers' Union for distribution among the Red Cross Society and hospitals.

South Africa High Commission.

Sept. 15.—Tobacco and cigarettes from the people of Rhodesia for the Expeditionary Force and the Fleet.

ALEXANDRA PARK,
Section of New Zealand Expeditionary Force

Sept. 16.—Gift from the European inhabitants of Bechuanaland Protectorate of £255 11s. to the National Relief Fund and £54 6s. 6d. to the Red Cross.

Sept. 1.—Offer of maize from the Agricultural Union of Southern Rhodesia.

Oct. 1.—Offer from Griffith, paramount chief of the Basuto, to raise funds for the relief of sufferers in connexion with the war.

Oct. 15.—£1,000 divided between the National Relief Fund and the British Red Cross Society from the Matabeleland Central War Fund Committee, Buluwayo.

Nov. 4.—£200 from Lewanika as war contribution; this sum given to the National Relief Fund.

CEYLON.

Oct. 14 *to Nov.* 18.—£20,500 to the National Relief Fund.

HONG KONG.

Nov. 2.—Donation of $100,000 by Legislative Council to the National Relief Fund, and public subscriptions to same fund, amounting to date to $135,000 donations and $6,000 monthly subscriptions.

MAURITIUS.

Sept. 3.—Offer from planters of 1,000,000 lb. of sugar for the Navy and 1,000,000 lb. for the Army.

Sept. 3.—An increase by 150,000 rupees, voted by the Council of Government, to meet in part the cost of special measures taken for the defence of the island since the outbreak of war.

BARBADOS.

Aug. 25.—Government contribution of £20,000 to His Majesty's Government.

Oct. 14.—Contribution to National Relief Fund.

WINDWARD ISLANDS.

Sept. 11.—£6,000 voted by Legislative Council of Grenada to purchase Grenada cocoa for the use of the Forces, and £4,000 for the National Relief Fund.

Sept. 14.—£2,000 voted by Legislative Council of St. Vincent for purchase of St. Vincent arrowroot for the Forces and contribution to the National Relief Fund; planters also adding 250 barrels of arrowroot with other aid to the National Relief Fund.

Sept. 25.—£2,000 from St. Lucia for the purchase of St. Lucia cocoa for the use of the Forces, and £1,000 to the National Relief Fund.

LEEWARD ISLANDS.

Sept. 4.—Offer from the Legislative Council. St. Kitts, and Nevis, of £5,000 for the National Relief Fund.

NEW ZEALAND.
on review at the Camp.

[*By courtesy of "Brett's Christmas Annual."*]

["Brett's Christmas Annual."
NEW ZEALAND EXPEDITIONARY FORCE
Marching through Palmerston North.

Sept. 26.—£4,000 from Dominica for war
    expenses, and £1,000 for Belgian
    Relief Fund ; £1,000 from Mont-
    serrat for the National Relief
    Fund.

Oct. 27.—£250 from Montserrat for the pur-
    chase of guava jelly for the
    Forces.

TRINIDAD AND TOBAGO.

Sept. 17.—Offer of raw cocoa to the value of
    £40,000 for the use of the Forces.

JAMAICA.

Sept. 19.—Offer of 300,000 Jamaica cigarettes
    by a local firm for the use of the
    British troops at the Front.

Oct. 31.—Offer from Jamaica Agricultural
    Society of oranges for wounded
    soldiers in hospitals.

Sept. 1.—Offer from the people of Jamaica
    of a gift of sugar.

BAHAMAS.

Oct. 8.—£10,000 voted by the Legislature as
    a contribution to the war expenses.

Oct. 8.—First instalment of £2,000 to the
    National Relief Fund.

BRITISH GUIANA.

Sept. 8.—Offer of 1,000 tons of British Guiana
    sugar to His Majesty's Govern-
    ment.

Oct. 16.—Contribution of $12,816 to the
    National Relief Fund, and gifts
    of clothing.

Nov. 17.—Offer of 500,000 lb. of rice for use of
    the British Indian Forces at the
    Front.

["The Graphic."
FIRST TASMANIAN CONTINGENT LEAVING HOBART.

NEW ZEALAND CONTINGENT IN LONDON.

WEST INDIES.

Nov. 13.—Offer from Messrs. S. Davson and
Company, of Demerara sugar,
Demerara rum, and molascuit.

BERMUDA.

Oct. 3.—£40,000 voted by the Colonial Parliament as a contribution towards
the cost of the war.

FALKLAND ISLANDS.

Sept. 9.—£2,250 voted by the Legislative
Council to the National Relief
Fund, and private subscriptions
of £750 for same fund.

Oct. 3.—Further instalment of £500 to the
National Relief Fund.

GAMBIA.

Sept. 19.—£10,000 voted by Legislative Council
as contribution to the National
Relief Fund.

SIERRA LEONE.

Oct. 21.—£5,000 voted by the Legislative
Council as a contribution to
Imperial funds.

NIGERIA.

Nov. 4.—£38,000 from the Emirs of the
Northern Provinces as a contribution to expenses of, and
losses caused by, the war.

Nov. 14.—Contribution of £1,000 from Sarikin
Muslimin to the National Relief
Fund.

GOLD COAST.

Nov. 17.—£60,000 voted by the Legislative
Council for the expenses of the
Togoland Expedition.

["*Brett's Christmas Annual.*"]

NEW ZEALAND TROOPS
Embarking at Wellington.

NEW ZEALAND

"Canterbury Times."

Expeditionary Force disembarking at Wellington.

EAST AFRICA PROTECTORATE.

Sept. 28.—Offer from the Government of 100 tons of local coffee for the use of the British troops at the Front.

Sept. 28.—Gift from the Kavirondo chiefs of the Kisumu District of 3,000 goats for the troops.

Nov. 14.—Gift from the Masai Moran of the Matapatu clan of thirty bullocks for the use of the troops.

NYASALAND.

Oct. 15 *to Nov.* 18.—Contribution of £450 to the National Relief Fund.

FIJI.

Sept. 21 *to Nov.* 7.—£6,700 from the people of Fiji to the National Relief Fund.

Nov. 12.—£10,000 voted by the Legislative Council to the National Relief Fund.

Portraits will be found in Volume I., Part 4, of the following : The Hon. Samuel Hughes, p. 143 ; Sir Robert Borden, p. 145 ; The Hon. T. Allen, p. 146 ; The Hon. E. D. Millen, p. 147 ; The Right Hon. Sir Edward Morris, p. 148.

CHAPTER XXXIX.

THE SERBIAN ARMY.

IN his chapter on "the military virtue of an army," Clausewitz, the greatest of all modern writers on the theory of war, laid down the maxim that an unconquerable military spirit, which makes of courage and endurance a settled habit, can be acquired only by success in war. "This spirit," he wrote, "can be generated only from two sources, and only by these two conjointly: the first is a succession of wars and great victories; the other is an activity of the army carried sometimes to the highest pitch." History is certainly with Clausewitz. This sentence of his epitomizes the secret of the conquests of Alexander and Napoleon, and it explains the preparation of the Prussian victories over France in 1870, by the earlier successes of the Danish and Austrian campaigns. An unconquerable army must have faith in itself, and that faith is commonly a deduction from its own glorious past.

Austria had some considerable advantages on her side. She had the numbers; she had the financial resources; she had the more elaborate organization of roads, railways, and industries behind her, and she had also both in officers and men the more educated human material. She was, in short, a civilized modern Power facing a primitive peasant State. But the "military virtue," if Clause-witz reasoned soundly, was on the side of

Serbia. The Austrian armies went into the field with a secular tradition of defeat to depress them. The Serbians came fresh from their victories over Turkey and Bulgaria. They had the habit of victory. They had confidence in themselves, their comrades, their commanders. What they achieved at Kumanovo and the Bregalnitsa they expected to achieve again. They had behind them not only victory, but a succession of victories. Some of their exploits moreover—the terrific march through the Albanian snows to Durazzo, and the stubborn contest with the Bulgarians—deserved to be counted as "activity carried to the highest pitch." They knew that they could do and dare whatever human flesh is capable of doing and daring. It was much that they were beyond question the most experienced of all the armies in the field. A very few of the senior generals in the French and German armies, who were subalterns in 1870, had seen active service against a civilized enemy, and a considerable proportion of the British and Russian armies were in South Africa and Manchuria. The Serbian Army alone had been through the ordeal as a whole. It had learned how to feed itself over Turkish roads and single-line railways. It had had to improvise substitutes for all the conveniences which wealth and invention lavished on the other armies. It had grown familiar under fire with

COMMANDANTS OF THE SERBIAN REGIMENTS.

all the tactical operations which others had seen only at manœuvres. It had had the opportunity, after the roughest of tests, of weeding out its inferior and promoting its more capable officers. Every man in its ranks had acquired that "second-wind" of courage, which makes even men of a nervous temperament go coolly into their second battle. It started with experience, and that alone is an element of superiority. But it meant even more that its experience was a record of unbroken, but by no means facile, victories.

The military history of the little kingdom was until the last wars uniformly unlucky. King Milan Obrenovitch declared war on Turkey in 1876, as a sequel to the Bosnian popular insurrection, but the campaign was disastrous. Eleven years later, when Eastern Roumelia suddenly threw off its allegiance to Turkey and united itself to the new principality of Bulgaria, the Serbs, by an unlucky impulse of jealousy, sought to prevent the aggrandizement of the neighbouring Slav State. They marched rapidly on Sofia; but though the raw Bulgarian army had been weakened by the withdrawal of its Russian instructors, it inflicted a crushing defeat on the Serbian army at Slivnitsa, and Serbia was saved from invasion only by the veto of Austria. This double defeat at the hands first of the Turks, and then of the Bulgarians, had the natural effect of depressing the nation's self-confidence. It was inevitable, in Serbia's situation, that she should desire to expand. The little

kingdom included the merest fraction of the Serbian race. It was, moreover, land-locked, and, until it could acquire a port, its economic existence depended on the goodwill of Austria. King Milan, a clever but frivolous and dissolute prince, had become the pensioner of the Austrian court. Russia, moreover, had renounced her traditional position of patron and protector, and officially recognized the fact that Serbia belonged to the Austrian sphere of influence. So long as Serbia stood in this dependent relation to Austria, it was futile for her to cherish the dream of reuniting under her crown the vast majority of the Serbian race who were under Austro-Hungarian rule. Nor was it, to all appearances, much more hopeful to pursue political ambitions in Macedonia. Save in "Old Serbia," the historic region of Kossovo along her southern border, the Slavs of Macedonia looked rather to Bulgaria than to Serbia for their eventual liberation. Bulgaria was shepherding them within her schismatic national church. The Serbs, unlike the Bulgarians, had never followed the bold policy of breaking away from the Orthodox Patriarchate, and the result was that they had no recognized national organization in Turkey. Apart from the fact that the Slavs of Macedonia are by race and language more nearly akin to the Bulgarians than to the Serbians, they naturally turned for aid to the more martial and energetic State. Serbia never renounced her ambitions in Macedonia. She subsidized schools and maintained guerilla bands of Serbian *comitadjis* (guerillas) to hold Bulgarian activities in check. But it was hard for any sober-minded Serbian to see his way in the vista of the future. With a disreputable king, wholly subject to Austrian influence, without wealth, without allies, and with a military past that presaged nothing but defeat, it was hard to feel confidence in Serbia's national mission. The little kingdom was condemned to live in a stagnant backwater, and it seemed as probable that it would one day be absorbed by Austria as that it would live to unite the Austrian Serbs or to liberate the Macedonian Slavs. The consequences of this depression were serious for the whole life of the nation. Little was done or attempted to build up a powerful military organization, and education was deplorably neglected. In the latter years of King Milan's son, Alexander, the country lived, moreover, under a reign of terror which stifled its whole public life and terrorized its ablest men.

The new era dated from the return of the Karageorgevitch dynasty in 1903. King Peter showed himself a correct constitutional sovereign, and under the guidance of M. Pashitch and the Radical or Russophil party the country followed both in its internal and in its foreign policy a normal line of development. It re-

covered its hope. It saw its future clearly. It won from the ambition to expand a stimulus which transformed the whole fabric of its public life. It is necessary to dwell on these political changes, for in Serbia, as in all the Balkan States, the army, in an even more literal sense than in the older countries of Europe, is the nation in arms. There is no professional military caste, for there is no class of landed gentry among whom the army is an hereditary profession, with a tradition handed down in families from father to son. The Serbian officer is commonly the son of a farmer, a tradesman, or a lawyer, and he is nearer to the people than the officer in any of the armies of the Great Powers. It was when the whole people began to will a brilliant future that the army transformed itself. The sharp goad of an imminent danger came six years later, during the Bosnian crisis. When Austria definitely annexed Bosnia and Herzegovina, the Serbs were in no temper to acquiesce quietly in the inevitable. They protested and brought on themselves the anger of Austria, and for many weeks war seemed to be probable. The army was hurriedly prepared for the worst; munitions were accumulated, and the whole nation steeled itself for what would have been, if it had come then, a life and death struggle.

KING PETER PRESENTING COLOURS TO AN INFANTRY REGIMENT.

GENERAL RADOMIR PUTNIK.
Chief of the General Staff.

In this hour of peril the modern Serbian army was created, and peace, when it was at length assured, was so manifestly provisional that the stimulus continued to work. It was from this crisis onward that the Serbs began to compare their own case to that of Piedmont. That little kingdom had defied Austria, and had in the end become the nucleus of a united Italy. The Serbs resolved that history should repeat itself, and the younger generation frankly described itself as the Piedmontese party. The first essential was to create an army, and the test of 1912 proved how well these young men had worked. There grew up a military party, with the Crown Prince at its head, and the regicide officers as its leading members, which was able to exert a powerful influence on national policy. Piedmont succeeded in the last round of her struggle because she had Louis Napoleon behind her. Serbia saw in the continual tension between Austria and Russia the guarantee that she would one day be able to reckon on Russian aid. When in the spring of 1912, under the guidance of M. de Hartwig, the Russian Minister in Belgrade, she entered the Balkan League, it is probable that her statesmen saw in the campaign against Turkey only a preliminary to the real struggle with Austria. That, perhaps, is one reason why in the secret treaty of partition she claimed so modest a share in the eventual fruits of victory. Another reason was that she hardly

trusted her own strength. She was far from entering the Balkan War in a mood of over-confidence. The event was to show how profound a change a few short years of peril and ambition had wrought in the *moral* of the army which had been beaten by the same antagonists in 1876 and 1885.

In the first of the two Balkan Wars the Serbian army was not subjected to any particularly severe test. The Turks had disposed their great masses to face the Bulgarian invasion of Thrace. It was, moreover, only to Thrace that Turkish reinforcements could be directed, for the Greek fleet commanded the Ægean and isolated the Turkish armies in Macedonia. The Serbians, after the first battle, had the numerical preponderance, and were dealing with an enemy who could not be reinforced. But the campaign none the less showed their powers of organization and their rapidity of movement. On the material side their work was a triumph of goodwill and intelligence over poverty and inadequate resources. The railways of Serbia were all single lines, and there was only one trunk line, which followed the valley of the Morava from Belgrade to Nish, and thence crossed the old Turkish frontier and entered the valley of the Vardar at Uskub. One of the five divisions of the Serbian army had to mobilize in a region (Zaitchar) which possessed an unfinished railroad serviceable only for local traffic. Over these single lines, most of them built with difficult gradients through mountainous country, the military trains had to crawl at an average of ten miles an hour. The road transport depended partly on pack-horses, but mainly on the light ox-wagons of the country, drawn by patient and indefatigable teams, which travelled at an average of barely two miles an hour. The mobilization was effected within ten days, more rapidly than good observers had thought to be possible, and Serbia placed in the field a much more formidable army than her treaty obligations required from her. The first serious engagement of the war was fought within a week of the establishment of the general headquarters at Nish. It took place on October 23 and 24 at Kumanovo. The Turks, to the number of about 40,000 men, had moved up to strong positions from Uskub, and ought to have been able to bar the Serbian advance for many days. By some incredible piece of muddling, blank cartridge was served out to them, or at least to some of them. A determined bayonet charge was none the less required to dislodge the Turks from their main positions. Though the Serbs captured only twelve guns, the retreat became a rout. The Turkish commander abandoned his men ; many of the officers changed into civilian attire and fled. This one battle gave all the north and centre of Macedonia to the Serbians, and put them in possession of its main railway and of the junction and depot of Uskub. As famous was the fight for Monastir, not so much because the Turks defended this very important town with much obstinacy or skill (it is not a fortified place), but rather because the Serbs had to take it amid the rains and floods of an early winter, wading over plains in which the water stood knee-deep, and fording torrents which swirled breast-high.

Even more remarkable as a test of the *moral* and stamina of the Serbian army was its winter march across Albania to Durazzo. The Serbian march was a triumph over distance and mountains and the winter. The paths which this army traversed were in places mere ledges on the edge of precipices, so narrow that the packs of the baggage ponies could be loaded only on one side. The lower road was so rough that the men had often to pile their greatcoats to fill the ruts for the passage of the guns. Much of the country which the army traversed is practically uninhabited, and all its food was the bread which it carried with it.

The real test on a great scale came only with the ill-omened second war. The Bulgarians were successful in the first stroke which they delivered. They managed to cross the Vardar in superior numbers, and heavily defeated a Serbian force at the bridge of Krivolak, on the Vardar. That first success was, however, retrieved, and the Serbs, returning with reinforcements, recovered this vital position. The real struggle was a prolonged battle of many days for the possession of the lofty plateau of Ovtche Polie, which is the key to Northern Macedonia. This battle of the Bregalnitsa, as it is called, must have been one of the most stubborn in military history. There was probably no serious disparity in numbers, but the Bulgarians were wearied after a nine months' campaign in which they had had to face not only the Turks but cholera. The Serbs had been less heavily engaged, and large contingents had been released from time to time on furlough. The Bulgarian plans were, moreover, disorganized by the conflict between the military chiefs and the civil government,

which at one moment checked the fighting and ordered the evacuation of the positions already won. Their artillery, moreover, was short of ammunition. It was a battle among mountains in a nearly roadless country, which gave little opportunity for any subtle tactics. No authoritative description of the fighting is available from the pen of any neutral eyewitness. The accounts which the writer has received from officers on either side conveyed the impression that the battle consisted of an interminable series of struggles for the possession of obstinately defended positions, which were taken and retaken again and again by bloody bayonet charges. The two armies were well matched and showed the same qualities of dogged endurance and prowess in hand-to-hand fighting. One moral result this fratricidal war had. It may have deepened the hatred of the two kindred but rival races, but at least

[*" The Times" Photograph.*

GENERAL RASHITCH,
Commanding a Serbian Division in the
Battle of the Jadar.

21—2

[" *The Times*" *Photograph.*

COLONEL VASHITCH,
Commanding a Serbian Division.

it implanted mutual respect. Neither of them showed much regard for the modern rules of civilized warfare, and the Carnegie Commission concluded of Serbs and Bulgars as of Greeks and Turks, that each of them broke every one of the rules of The Hague Convention. But Serbs and Bulgars at least ended by recognizing one another's courage and " military virtue." The writer heard again and again from both Serbs and Bulgars the confession that the war had proved the equality of the two armies. The Bregalnitsa was certainly a Serbian victory. It ended in the conquest of the coveted plateau by the Serbian Army. But it was very far from being a decisive and conclusive victory. The Bulgarians lost only about fifteen miles of ground ; and it was the intervention of Rumania which compelled them to make peace. The other operations of the war were unimportant. The Serbs repelled a weak Bulgarian raid on their own territory, and in their turn failed in an excursion against the Bulgarian town of Widin. The Serbian casualty list gives 5,000 killed and 18,000 wounded in the campaign against the Turks, and 7,000

killed and 30,000 wounded in the much shorter and more concentrated struggle with the Bulgarians. Most of these latter casualties occurred at the Bregalnitsa. These figures represent a terribly high proportion of the men engaged. The active army of Serbia, exclusive of the " Third Ban " or Territorial Army, which was seldom under fire, hardly numbers more than 180,000 men. The casualties account for 60,000. Allowing for the men who died of wounds and cholera, the permanent loss was about 19,000 men—a veritable decimation.

This second war did even more than the first to raise the prestige of the Serbian Armies. It displayed their qualities in a struggle with that Bulgarian Army whose victories in Thrace had led qualified observers to rank it as the equal, at least in the primitive soldierly virtues, of good West-European troops. The doubt of themselves which their unlucky military past had left in the minds of the Serbs was dissipated for all time. They had conquered the Turks and defeated the Bulgarians. It was a proud record, and with a new self-confidence and whetted ambitions they thought of themselves

THE CROWN PRINCE OF SERBIA,
With General Youritchitch (commanding the
19th Army) and General Rashitch.

BELGRADE.
As seen from Austrian territory.

as the Piedmontese of the Balkans, destined by their energy and their military qualities to achieve the still greater feat of liberating their Bosnian and Croatian kinsmen from Austrian rule. Such a record makes, in the phrase of Clausewitz, for " military virtue."

ORGANIZATION.

The military system of Serbia was always based upon universal compulsory service. All able-bodied men were liable from 21 to 45 years of age. There was also a liability, which may be regarded as nominal, for service in the militia on youths from 17 to 21 years, and on men from 45 to 50 years. The sacrifices required from a young conscript were much less onerous than in the wealthier countries of the Continent. Serbia was obliged to study economy, and her policy had always been to keep the recruits with the colours only for the minimum period required for training. Before the annexation of Macedonia, in 1913, the number of young men who reached the age of 21 every year was about 25,000. The weeding out of those medically unfit, and the exemption, on a liberal scale, of those excused service on various grounds, used to result, however, in a considerable diminution of this number, so that only about 18,000 recruits went into training each year. The normal period of service with the infantry was eighteen months. But it was thought that at least the better-educated

conscripts could become efficient in six months, and only from one-half to one-third of each year's contingent was ever retained with the colours for the full period. The service in the cavalry and artillery was for two years. For eleven years (21 to 31) young men were liable to service in the first line of the active army, known as the First Ban. As reservists they might be called up for twenty days' training in each year, but this obligation was very rarely imposed.

The Second Ban was a reserve composed of men between 31 and 38 years of age. No permanent cadres existed for the formation of independent units out of this class. It was primarily intended to replace the wastage of war, by reinforcing the First Ban as casualties occurred. But much had been done in recent years to fit it for independent service. Its officers, who were in civil life mainly farmers or professional men, had been encouraged to follow courses of instruction. The men had also been called up occasionally for ten days' training. A large number of battalions were organized from this Second Ban during the Balkan Wars, and did good service in spite of the fact that their officers, including in some cases even the commandants, were not professional soldiers.

The Third Ban was composed of men from 38 to 45 years of age, who corresponded to the French territorial army. They were supposed to be liable only for home defence within the

HEAVY GUNS IN THE TRENCHES.   *[Underwood & Underwood.*

Serbian kingdom. They were, however, used to guard communications in Macedonia during the Balkan Wars. One saw them quartered in little huts of turf and boughs all along the Vardar railway line. They were also used as combatants to meet the Bulgarian raid on Serbian territory, and they even took part in the unsuccessful attempt to besiege and take the Bulgarian town of Widin. They showed, as one would expect, little enterprise in this latter undertaking, but they were invaluable for the tedious but necessary work of securing communications. Peasants age rather rapidly in the Balkans, and these men often looked older than a similar force in Western Europe would do. They wore no uniform, and were clad in their national peasant costumes of brown homespun, with the untidy but serviceable Balkan sandals, tied to the feet with thongs or strings.

The organization of the Serbian Army had the merit of simplicity. The former kingdom (excluding Macedonia) was divided into five territorial divisional districts. The districts were: (1) Nish, (2) Valievo, (3) Belgrade, (4) Kragujevatz, (5) Zaitchar. The names are in each case those of the town in which the divisional headquarters were situated. Nish

had a large but altogether obsolete fortress, and Belgrade a picturesque old Turkish citadel, neither of any military value whatever. Kragujevatz possessed an arsenal of very limited productive capacity. Of these five towns only two, Nish and Belgrade, were situated on the one trunk railway line which Serbia possesses, and even this railway was only a single line. There was, however, a circuitous, narrow-gauge line connecting Belgrade with Valievo, and another running up from Valievo to the river Save. Kragujevatz had also a branch line, which was continued to a point (Ushitza) not far from the Drina and the Bosnian frontier. Zaitchar was almost isolated, and possessed only a line running up to the Danube. The inadequacy of the Serbian railway system was bound to be a serious handicap in time of war. The internal communications were poor, and the two isolated lines which had their termini on the Save and the Danube could be of little use if the Austrian monitors retained command of these rivers. It must also be remembered that the Serbian railway system nowhere gave access to an open port through which munitions and supplies could be introduced. Salonica became by arrangement with Greece a free port for Serbian merchandise, but it could not be used to import munitions without a breach of Greek neutrality. The only available road for this purpose was the long mountain path, practicable only for pack-animals, which led from the Montenegrin port of Antivari through Alpine country to Novi Bazar.

Each territorial division was subdivided into two brigade districts, and each district provided two regiments of four battalions each. The battalion numbered about a thousand men, so that the war-strength of the divisional infantry totalled 16,000 men. Of the battalions in each regiment three existed in time of peace, and the fourth was organized only on mobilization. Attached to each division was a regiment of artillery, consisting of three groups of three six-gun batteries (in all 54 guns). The divisional cavalry was a weak force, non-existent in peace, but raised on mobilization as a regiment of four squadrons (400 sabres), from men and horses previously registered. Each division had also its own technical and administrative units, engineers, and supply column, and its total strength amounted to 23,000 officers and men of First Ban troops.

In addition to these five divisions of the first line, there was also a regiment of mountain artillery, consisting of six batteries, six howitzer batteries, and two battalions of fortress artillery. There was, further, a separate cavalry division composed of two brigades, each of two regiments. Of these a nucleus existed in time of peace, one brigade being quartered at Belgrade and the other at Nish. Its war strength

amounted to 80 officers and 3,200 men. Attached to the cavalry division were two horse artillery batteries (8 guns). This first line army numbered, all told, on a conservative estimate about 125,000 officers and men, with 5,200 sabres and 330 guns.

The Second Ban had a similar organization in five divisions. Each division included, however, only three regiments (instead of four), and the four battalions of each regiment had 800 men apiece (instead of one thousand). There was also with each division a regiment of cavalry, three batteries of artillery, and a company of pioneers. The worth of this Second Ban seemed problematical before the Balkan Wars, and experts who wrote on the Serbian Army were disposed to ignore its existence. It was, indeed, only a militia, but it was a militia of trained men, who had seen much service, and that experience should give it a fighting value superior to that of the corresponding reserve formations of other Continental armies. Its armament, however, was much inferior to that of the First Ban, and only its infantry (say 48,000 men) had to be reckoned as a considerable addition to the strength of the first line. The effective strength of the active army (first two Bans) could not be less than about 180,000, but this would certainly be swollen by large numbers of volunteers gradually incorporated.

It is not easy to estimate the numbers of the Serbian Army with any confidence. The figures given above are an extremely conservative estimate, based mainly on the calculations of experts who had studied its organization before

TROOPS ON PARADE.

the Balkan Wars. It was in those days gravely underestimated ; the tendency to-day is perhaps to rate it rather too high. It is certain, however, that Serbia put into the field a much larger number of men than either her critics or her allies expected her to produce. The Second Ban turned out to be useful material. Volunteers were incorporated in immense numbers. Some of them were Serbians of the kingdom who had been exempted from conscription. Others were men of Serbian race from Austria or from Macedonia. Emigrants came back to fight in their thousands from the United States. The figure of 180,000 as the total of the active army is therefore an under-statement. It is probable that the real total did not fall short of 200,000, and might even have exceeded it considerably. These figures take no account at all of the new population of Mace-donia. It was numerous, and there was no better military material in the Balkans. But it was composed mainly of Bulgarians and Albanians, both hostile elements. There was, indeed, a peasantry of Serbian race and sym-pathies in Kossovo and Novi Bazar, and else-where there was a Serbian party. A con-scription had been held, and the foundations of a permanent territorial military organization had been laid. Some troops of Macedonian origin were used in the Great War, but it might be doubted whether Serbia would ven-ture to employ this Macedonian material without drastic selection in the fighting line. Some addition, perhaps a considerable addition, ought to be made from this source to our

estimate of the strength of the Serbian Army. A high but not impossible figure for its active first line would be 250,000 men. To these must be added about 45,000 Montenegrins. The Third Ban, which would be used in the fighting line only on the gravest emergency, amounted to another 50,000.

The infantry of the First Ban was armed in part with the Mannlicher rifle, but chiefly with a good Mauser rifle (M. 99, calibre ·276 in., weight 9 lbs. 4 oz., with a magazine for five cartridges, a maximum elevation of 2,000 m.—about 2,187 yards—and an initial velocity of about 2,400 ft). The Second Ban carried the much inferior Mauser, M. 80, an old rifle to which a magazine was clumsily fitted in the Serbian arsenals ; while the Third Ban had the old single-loader Berdan rifle. The machine gun was the Maxim of the same calibre as the new Mauser carried on pack animals.

The artillery had a French armament, not, however, of the most recent pattern, and it is uncertain how far Serbia had been able to replace the pieces worn out during the two Balkan campaigns. The field gun was the French piece of 1897. It was a quick firer, calibre 7·5 cm., with panoramic independent sight. Its maximum range for shrapnel was 5,500 m. (6,015 yards). The mountain gun was a Creuzot piece of 7 cm. The Second Ban was armed with old De Bange guns of 8 cm. The heavy guns, which did good service at the siege of Adrianople, came also from Creuzot, and

BLESSING THE COLOURS.

include 24 howitzers of 15 cm. (5·9 inches), and mortars of 24 cm. (9·6 inches). Aviation had not been studied to any useful extent. The cavalry carried swords and carbines, but no lances.

A statistical outline tells in reality comparatively little about any army, and even the conclusions based on its history must be examined in a critical spirit. There are, however, certain general remarks which one may make with confidence about the Serbian Army. It was inspired by a patriotism, a nationalism, which it would be hard to parallel in Western armies. In more advanced countries men dissipate their idealism. They give to countless "movements," social, political, philanthropic, religious, some part of the enthusiasm which the Serbians (and, indeed, all the Balkan peoples) concentrate on their country. A Serbian, in consequence, is much prompter to believe that the interests of his race will best be forwarded by the primitive struggles of war than are the more sophisticated peoples of the West. His mind is seldom embarrassed by any doubt about the moral or political value of war. There are few Socialists in Serbia, and (roughly speaking) no pacifists. If a nation with this old-world mentality had done less than some of its neighbours to prepare for war, the reason was partly that, unlike the Bulgarians, the Serbians were not by temperament a nation of systematic organizers, and partly that their economic resources were limited. The army was emphatically the army of a poor State. It was weak in cavalry, and to a less degree in artillery. It was strong in an infantry, which had both dash and endurance. Its deficiency lay chiefly in all the material adjuncts to warfare—heavy guns, automobiles, flying machines, ambulances and, above all, railways. Its sanitary service in particular was painfully inadequate. Serbia is a simple agricultural community, and she goes into war almost destitute of the mechanical means and the mechanical training which are among the chief assets of Western armies. Another consequence of her poverty was that her supply of professional officers was inadequate even for the First Ban, and altogether wanting for the Second. The training of her officers was undoubtedly less exacting than that of most European armies. A fair proportion of them had, however, studied abroad, chiefly in Russia and in France. About one-third of them had risen from the ranks. Before the two Balkan Wars their education must have

suffered severely from the lack of practical opportunities. Grand manœuvres were, for reasons of economy, unknown in Serbia, and it was only in the years immediately before the war that divisional manœuvres were attempted. The training of the men hardly went beyond drill on the parade ground, and little had been done to prepare them for field-work. The drill, however, was surprisingly smart, and the discipline was good, for the brotherly and democratic relations which prevailed between officers and men seemed in no way to interfere with the elementary duties of respect and obedience. It must be said of the Serbian officers, as of the Young Turks, that they are politicians as well as soldiers. It was the younger officers who carried out the revolution which restored the Obrenovitch dynasty, and the motive which inspired them was primarily the desire to escape from Austrian tutelage. Their thoughts reverted after the Balkan Wars to the much more important question of the predestined struggle with Austria. It is doubtful, however, whether this preoccupation with politics seriously interfered with the efficiency of the army. Feeling within the corps of officers was singularly unanimous, and their interventions in politics were in reality the inevitable consequence of their intense will to carry out the national mission of the army—the achievement of the unity of the Serb race by a successful war against Austria. If they worked for this by agitation and in the Press they worked for it also in the barrack-room and on the parade-ground. They were thoroughly devoted to their chiefs, and believed as implicitly in the handsome white-bearded old veteran, the Voivoda Putnik, as in the young and dashing Crown Prince.

It would not be easy to attempt a serious estimate of the work of the Serbian General Staff during the two Balkan Wars. The Turkish army, demoralized from the very outset of the struggle, hardly put their capacity to a test. Their one big battle against the Bulgarians, on the Bregalnitsa, was in the main a soldiers' victory. It was fought on mountainous ground, and won mainly by bloody and obstinate frontal attacks. But certain conclusions may be drawn with confidence. The mobilization was carried out rapidly and smoothly. The work of the several divisions which operated independently in Macedonia was well planned and well timed, so that the fruits of successes, gained in widely separated portions of the Macedonian theatre, were promptly and fully gathered. The Serbian Staff reacted with skill and spirit against the disconcertingly sudden Bulgarian attack, prepared its own reply with an undeniable talent for improvisation, and showed itself in the end better prepared and better informed than the aggressors. Fuller knowledge than any foreigners were allowed to acquire of that secret fratricidal war might reveal high strategical talent in the Serbian Staff. Of that we cannot decide with assurance. We know only the result, and the result, whatever the explanation, was a victory over very formidable adversaries.

The reader may visualize this Serbian Army as a body of men which was on the whole rather above the physical average of Europe. It marched well. It was clad in serviceable uniforms, tasteful in colour and design. Its equipment was the best in the Balkans. Its carriage was alert, and its smartness in drill pleased the eye. Its professional officers had an elegance and a grace of manner which one would not expect from a peasant race. Its chief handicap was poverty. Its great asset was its passionate sense of a national mission. If it met the Austrians weak in all the resources of modern science and industrial civilization, it confronted their age-long tradition of defeat with that habit of "military virtue" which is based on a record of victory. It entered the war an army of veterans, and it fought for a bigger stake than any other people in the field. Disaster might mean for it the extinction of the Serbian nation. Victory might so expand its territories and add to its population as to make of Serbia a State which would dominate the Balkans, and aspire in time to play a far from negligible part in European affairs.

THE MONTENEGRIN ARMY.

The prowess of the Montenegrins is legendary, and if military history has little to say of their achievements, the poets have done them more than justice. They led for centuries the typical life of wild frontier tribes, on a level of civilization not much above the standard of the Afridis and Pathans. One may doubt, however, whether any tradition unfits a people so hopelessly for modern warfare as this predatory raiding habit. The patient, laborious Bulgarian peasant, and the keen, commercial Greek townsman, each in his own way came

INFANTRY GOING TO THE FRONT.

MONTENEGRIN FORTRESS BATTERY.

out of the Balkan Wars with a better record than these truculent mountaineers. They were brought up to despise the arts and toils of peace. They tended to leave much of the hard work of agriculture to the women, on the plea that they were warriors. Their hard life, the mountain air, and the ruthless process of the weeding out of the unfit made them easily the finest race in Europe from a physical standpoint. The average of height could hardly be less than six feet · the carriage of the men was superb, and their features were regular and handsome. They were bred to arms from boyhood, and no man left his hut without at least a revolver, a dagger, and a belt of cartridges. Along the frontier the ploughmen and the shepherds carried a rifle as an indispensable part of their daily dress. Their mental life was formed by warlike ballads and tales of individual valour. But precisely because they had all been taught to think of war as an occasion for personal prowess, they proved themselves as little fitted for a modern campaign as a legion of medieval knights.

The Montenegrin Army was detained outside Scutari throughout the first Balkan War by a Turco-Albanian force of very modest efficiency, and they entered it at last only with the consent (how won is still a mystery) of the adventurer Essad Pasha. In the second Balkan War they acted as auxiliary troops to the Serbians, who formed a poor opinion of their reliability. The fact is that their traditional mode of warfare

was endless skirmishing behind the cover of rocks on the mountain-side. They were not accustomed to fighting in regular formations, nor had their officers any experience in the handling of large bodies of men. They were, however, aware of their own deficiencies, and accepted before the war was over a certain number of Serbian officers, who may have been able to effect some improvement. But the poverty of this little kingdom was a handicap to its military efficiency which no Serbian aid could remedy. Its armament had been mainly a gift from Russia. The artillery was weak. Cavalry (save for a few mounted scouts) was non-existent. There was no medical service. There was no regular organization of transport and supply. During the campaign before Scutari the transport was mainly effected by the women, who carried out food on their backs, and returned laden with loot. The medical service was left wholly to the charge of kindly foreigners. The Montenegrin Army, in short, was an old-world peasant militia.

It would be a mistake to attempt any elabo rate account of the structure of this primitive force. Its one asset was the indisputable gallantry of its individual soldiers. It was organized in local units, composed of the whole manhood of a district. Youths and old men alike shared in it in some degree. The officers were elected locally, and were typical village captains. In theory a youth became liable for service at eighteen years, and was expected to

21—3

SERBIAN OUTPOST ON THE DANUBE.

undergo forty-eight days' training as a recruit, with two weeks further of what is called on paper "manœuvres." There were usually in training two bodies, each about 250 strong. The active army was composed of the whole manhood of the nation from nineteen to fifty-two years of age. Behind this was a reserve of the older men, from fifty-three to sixty-two years of age, who should be employed in non-combatant work and in guarding the frontiers. The active army underwent in theory an annual training of ten to fifteen days, which did not always amount to much more than a muster and a review. Each man had charge of his own arms, ammunition and equipment.

On a war footing the Montenegrin Army was composed of four divisions, each with its own territorial region, each subdivided into two or three brigades, with a number of battalions varying from twelve to fifteen. The battalion varied from 400 to 800 men. Each division had attached to it a few mounted scouts, a field

battery, and a battery of heavy guns. The total strength of the army might be put at from 40,000 to 45,000 men, with 104 guns and 44 mitrailleuses. The infantry carried the Russian rifle. The reserve had the single-loader Berdan rifle. The mitrailleuses were Maxims and were carried on pack-animals. The artillery had a Krupp field gun and some howitzers and mortars purchased from Italy.

It would be a mistake to think of this Montenegrin Militia as in any sense a regular army. On the other hand it is well to remember that in many respects it was well adapted to the work which it had to do, and to the country in which it was to operate. If it had no modern organized transport, the men were bred to endure privations which no Western army would face. If it had no medical service, the men were not accustomed to depend on doctors in time of peace. If its tradition was the guerilla warfare of the mountains, it was in the mountains of Bosnia that it must fight.

CHAPTER XL.

THE AUSTRIAN INVASION: BATTLE OF THE JADAR.

The Outbreak of War—Text of the Austrian Declaration—Austrian Strategy and the Problem of Invasion—Decision to Cross the Drina—Nature of the Country—Serbian Strategy and the Problem of Defence—The Serbian Concentration—Disposition of the Forces—The Passage of the Drina—Battle of the Jadar—Field-Marshal Putnik—His Strategy—Description of the Operations, August 16-19—Shabatz—Tzer—The Austrian Defeat—End of the First Austrian Invasion of Serbia—Effect of the Serbian Victory.

IF there had existed, in the month of July, 1914, any Serbian in touch with Government circles whose ignorance of the economic and military situation of his country had led him to contemplate any act which might conceivably precipitate a crisis with Austria, he would surely have received a check to his ambitions from the national War Office. Serbia was in the greatest degree unprepared for war: in a state of utter inability to profit from any complication of the ever-threatening situation in Bosnia.

The brief period of peace which followed the signature of the Treaty of Bukarest was all insufficient to permit the Serbians to repair the wastage of war. Orders for cannon, rifles, ammunition, stores, military impedimenta, horses, and clothing were placed with European factories; but, with the exception of an insignificant proportion of the latter, nothing had yet been delivered. Many of the damaged rifles were repaired in the national arsenal at Kragujevatz. There, also, cartridges were manufactured in abundance; but, for the rest, the Serbian army was found in a state of lamentable, if inevitable, unreadiness.

Such, then, was the material condition of the Serbian army upon the declaration of war. One example may be quoted to illustrate the ultimate effect. During the battle on the Tzer mountains many of the regiments, at an effective strength of over 4,000 men, possessed but 2,600 rifles. The armed soldiers went into action, while the unarmed waited in reserve, springing forward as their comrades fell, and taking up the weapons of the fallen to continue the fight.

In the country the brief respite accorded—little more than six months—had been all insufficient. The men had scarce time to rest and repair the wastage to their own homes; the more serious work of restoring the national resources had not yet been commenced. Yet, despite these almost overpowering difficulties, this young, virile nation was able to enter a new war, cruelly thrust upon it by a Great Power, with tremendous energy. All, from young to old, took up the call with enthusiasm, and as the soldiers left their homes once more the women cried, "Strike! and may God strengthen your arm."

Simultaneously with the departure of Baron

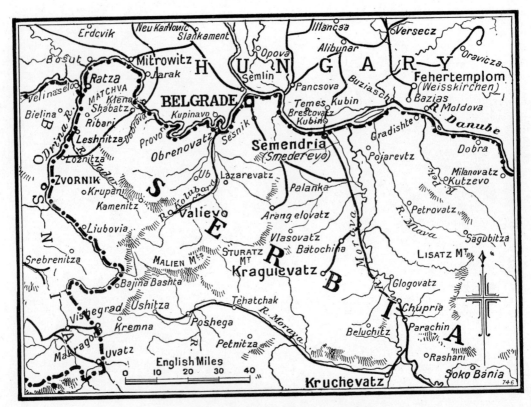

THE AUSTRO-SERBIAN FRONTIER.

Giesl, the Austro-Hungarian Minister, from Belgrade, the Prince Regent Alexander signed a decree ordering the general mobilization of the Serbian army. The operation commenced the following day (July 26).

The Serbian soldiers lacked many important items from their equipment ; but, donning the battle-stained uniforms which had already served through two wars, they abandoned homes, fields and flocks and responded to the new call to arms with an enthusiasm as great as that demonstrated in 1912. Many of them travelled at the risk of their lives, for, finding no place inside the wagons, they clambered on top. To the remonstrances of their officers, they replied only that it was necessary to reach the centre of concentration without delay.

The experience already gained served the military authorities well. The routine followed was precisely similar to that previously adopted, with the consequence that the machine, despite the enormous difficulties by which it was beset, worked with remarkable smoothness.

Two days after the commencement of the general mobilization Austria declared war upon Serbia. The notification was conveyed by a telegraphic communication remarkable in that Count Berchtold, the Austro-Hungarian Foreign Minister, addressed himself on this occasion not to the Serbian Government, but direct to the General Staff. The historic document read as follows :—

Eventuellement, Le Grand Quartier Général,
Kraguévatz.

No. 3523. Handed in at Vienna July 28, 11.10 a.m., received at Kraguévatz 12.50 p.m.

Le gouvernement royal de Serbie n'ayant pas répondu d'une manière satisfaisante à la note qui lui avait été remise par le Ministre d'Autriche-Hongrie à Belgrade à la date du 23 juillet 1914, le gouvernement Imperial et royal se trouve dans la nécéssité de pourvoir lui même à la sauvegarde de ses droits et intérêts et de recourir à cet effet à la force des armes. L'Autriche-Hongrie se considère donc de ce moment en état de guerre avec la Serbie.

Le Ministre des Affaires Etrangères
d'Autriche-Hongrie,
COMTE BERCHTOLD.*

---

* Translation.

The Royal Government of Serbia not having replied in a satisfactory manner to the Note which was sent to them by the Minister of Austria-Hungary at Belgrade under date July 23, 1914, the Imperial and Royal Government finds itself obliged to provide for the safeguarding of its rights and interests, and for this purpose to have recourse to force of arms. Austria-Hungary therefore regards herself from this moment as in a state of war with Serbia.

The Minister for Foreign Affairs of
Austria-Hungary,
COUNT BERCHTOLD.

The declaration of war found Serbia in the midst of her mobilization, and the fact that the Austrians, who had carefully chosen their own time for the opening of hostilities, did not immediately profit by the advantage they thus possessed, seize Belgrade, and penetrate into Serbia was, at the time, the subject of considerable comment. Certain is it that, at the moment of the declaration, the Austrians, with the facilities for transport then at their disposal, should have been in a position to land on Serbian soil and enter the capital with a small force — say, one battalion. But their stay would have been relatively short, for the territorial troops of the Third Ban had been speedily mobilized, the gendarmerie were ready for combat, and a regiment on a peace footing of about 2,000 bayonets, together with a considerable number of volunteers, was concentrated an hour's march from the city.

The difficulties of invasion increased almost hourly. Immediate measures had been taken to prepare a group of 20,000 combatants for the defence of the capital, with the result that, on the evening of the third day of the mobilization —the date of the declaration of war—a force of 10,000 men and 24 cannon was concentrated within striking distance.

According to the information at the disposal of the Serbian Staff, the Austrians had, on July 28, only one division concentrated between Semlin and Pancsova—a force necessarily insufficient for such an operation as the occupation and retention of Belgrade would have entailed. A few days later, thanks to the rapidity with which the Serbian concentration was effected, the enterprise would have necessitated the employment of at least one Army Corps. Even had this been forthcoming, however, the adventure would have been attended with considerable risk to the invaders, in view of the presence, within a two-days' march of Belgrade, of a considerable and ever-augmenting hostile force.

The project would have taken on a different aspect had the Austrians decided to direct their principal offensive against Belgrade. But, in view of the fact that their own concentration was at the time incomplete, and of the increasing tension of Austro-Russian relations, reasons of strategy, which will become clearly evident when the importance of the battle in the Jadar Valley is explained, caused the Austrian Staff to centre their attention upon an invasion across the Drina river, culminating, as they hoped,

SERBIAN OFFICERS ON THE DANUBE.

in the capture of Valievo and Kragujevatz, and the dispersion of the Serbian army.

The Austro-Serbian frontier extends over a length of almost 340 miles, and is formed on the north by the Danube and Save rivers, and on the south by the Drina river. This water barrier is, however, an easily sur-mounted obstacle, for both the Save and Drina are often of shallow depth and abound with convenient places for the passage of a military expedition. To many of these points of vantage on the northern frontier Austria has constructed strategic railways thus permitting her army to threaten the Serbs along the whole front—viz., at Bosut, Mitrovitz, Jarak, Klenak, Semlin, Krevevára (facing Semendria) and Divic (facing Gradishte). Obrenovatz, though in Serbian territory, is at once within a few hours' march of Semlin and the terminus of a Serbian railway, and doubtless also attracted the attention of the prospective invader.

Bosnia and Herzegovina are yet only sparsely served by railway communications, but, for the purposes of an invasion of Serbian territory, the lines running to Tuzla in the north and to Vishegrad and Uvatz in the south are of great strategic importance. Moreover, unlike Hungary and Slavonia, the country is of so mountainous and well-wooded a nature that it can be used effectively to mask the concentra-tion of large bodies of men in close proximity to the frontier.

The problem before the Serbian General Staff was more complicated. A hostile raid was to be feared at one or more of a score of points. To have sprinkled their forces along the whole frontier would have played into the hands of the enemy; to have presumed the probable direction of the chief offensive and massed the armies either at Valievo, Obrenovatz or Pojarevtz, would have disclosed the Serbian concentration and permitted the Austrians, with their superior *réseau* of railways, to pass, almost unchallenged, in another direction.

The Serbians did not, therefore, reckon on opposing any and every attempt of a hostile force to enter their country. On the contrary, strategical considerations led them to the con-clusion that a decisive defeat could only be inflicted upon the Austrians after their penetra-tion into Serbian territory. In pursuance of this idea, it was decided to place fairly strong advance guards at all probable points of Austrian penetration, with orders to oppose any invasion as long as possible—until, in fact, the

tactics of the enemy could be defined and the army moved up to offer battle.

The Serbians, at the outset, did not know where the bulk of the Austrian troops was concentrated. On broad lines, two alternatives presented themselves. The first of these pro-vided for an invasion in force on the line Obrenovatz-Belgrade-Semendria. This line offered the shortest route to the centre of the country—the avowed objective of the enemy— but it would have necessitated a crossing of the Danube, while the Serbs could have moved up their troops by road and rail. The second alternative—an offensive on the front Obreno-vatz - Ratza - Loznitza - Liubovia — entailed a longer journey, but was strategically sounder in that it furnished several bases, all converging on Valievo.

The Serbian concentration was, accordingly, dictated by the necessity of countering either of these projects, and the principal armies were therefore centrally grouped on the line Palanka - Arangelovatz - Lazarevatz. Weaker, though important, forces were massed at Valievo and Uzitze, while the advanced units, to which reference has already been made, were posted in the vicinity of Loznitza, Shabatz, Obrenovatz, Belgrade, Semendria, Pozarevatz and Gradishte.

The choice of positions so central in situation greatly facilitated the operations, and it was found possible to march most of the troops to their allotted posts. The railways were reserved for the transport of material and the conveyance of the advanced units to the frontiers.

On August 6 the Serbian Staff received information to the effect that important Austrian forces were massed in Syrmia, and in North-eastern Bosnia. Simultaneously, considerable military activity was manifested on the Danube. At Belgrade, Semendria, Gradishte, etc., the enemy maintained a vigorous bombardment, elaborately prepared to effect a crossing at many points, and picturesquely played at invasion.* The reports from the outposts,

---

* During a period dating from July 29 to August 11 the Austrians made eighteen attempts to cross the frontier, their object doubtless being to divert the attention of the Serbians from those points where the serious invasion was to be effected. In some cases pontoon bridges were thrown across to small islands situate between the two shores; in others, detachments of infantry were embarked in barges, and an effort made to tow them across the river. On all occasions the attacks were easily repulsed by the troops of the Third Ban, often with serious losses to the invaders.

however, convinced the Serbian Staff that the real danger must be awaited elsewhere. Hostile attempts to cross the Drina at Liubovia and Ratza, and the Save at Shabatz, quickly followed and were repulsed. Nevertheless, the earnestness of these efforts, as compared with the theatrical display on the Danube, suggested that the serious invasion was to be operated from the north-west, and when, on August 8 and 9, Austrian aeroplanes whirred over Krupani, Shabatz and Valievo, the last rays of Serbian doubt and indecision were dispelled.

As was subsequently ascertained, the distribution of the Austrian Army Corps exactly coincided with the conclusions which had been reached by the Serbian General Staff. Retaining but two divisions between Weisskirchen and Semlin, they had flung an imposing military cordon around the fertile Matchva district (north of the line drawn from Shabatz to Leshnitza) and extended other important forces along the left bank of the Drina as far south as Vishegrad.

One and a half divisions of the VII. corps were between Weisskirchen and Pancsova; 1 brigade of the XIII. corps was at Semlin; the IV. corps of 3 divisions spread from Kupi-

navo to Klenak; 1 division of the IX. corps was at Ruma; 2 divisions of the VIII. corps occupied the front Bielina-Janja; 1 division of the XIII. corps was opposite Loznitza; 1½ divisions of the XIII. corps held the line Drinjacha-Zvornik; 2 brigades of the XV. corps were at Srebrenitza; 4 brigades of the XV. corps were between Focha and Vishegrad; 3 brigades of the XVI. corps were at Serajevo. The Landsturm were distributed along the frontier, the 104th brigade of four regiments (25th, 26th, 27th, 28th) being concentrated before Loznitza. Against Montenegro the Austrians sent 3 brigades of the XVI. corps.

The first penetration of Austrian troops into Serbia was signalled from Loznitza on the morning of August 12. Near that town, in fact along the whole length of its lower course, the swift-running Drina river has frequently changed its channel, thus cutting out numerous small islands which serve to facilitate the task of an invading army. It was one of the largest of these islands—that of Kuriachista, between Loznitza and Leshnitza—that the Austrians chose as a base for their enterprise.

The passage was commenced in boats and pontoons. The small Serbian frontier guard of

THE TIMES HISTORY OF THE WAR IN DIFFICULTIES.
The motor car of "The Times" Correspondent with the Serbian Army being dug out of the mud by Austrian prisoners.

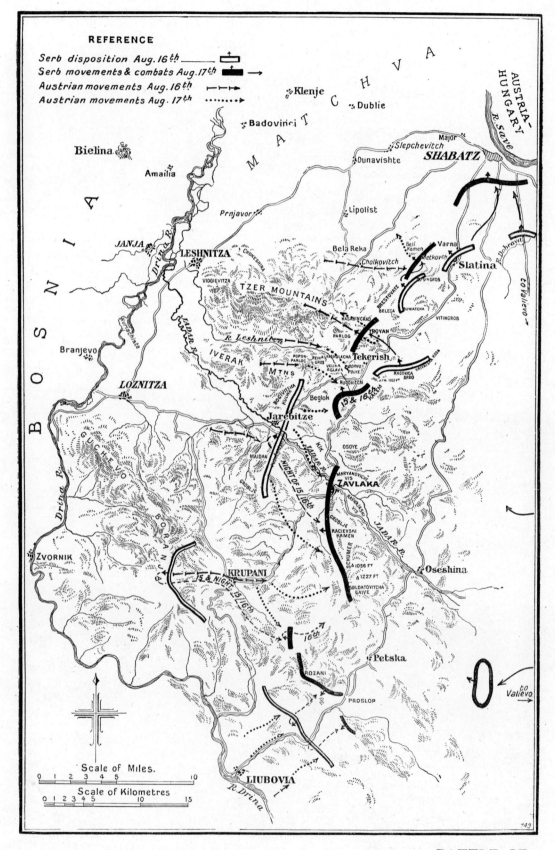

REFERENCE
Serb disposition Aug.16th
Serb movements & combats Aug.17th
Austrian movements Aug.16th
Austrian movements Aug.17th

BATTLE OF

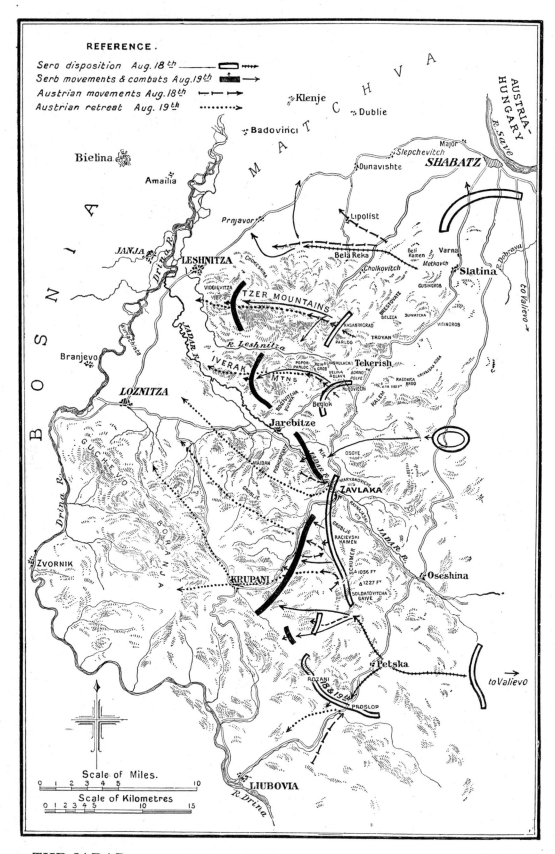

REFERENCE.
Sero disposition Aug. 18th
Serb movements & combats Aug.19th
Austrian movements Aug.18th
Austrian retreat Aug.19th

THE JADAR.

SERBIAN PEASANT WOMEN HELPING TO HAUL THE GUNS.

two battalions of the Third Ban, with two batteries of obsolete " De Bange " artillery, offered what little resistance lay in their power, after which, conforming to their orders, they retired on to the heights of Loznitza. The Austrians then fortified a bridge-head, threw a pontoon bridge over the river, and continued the passage of their troops, representing the entire 13th Army Corps and two divisions of the 8th Army Corps.

The same day an Austrian force crossed the river Save north of Shabatz. Preceding the operation by a heavy bombardment, they first sent detachments across by the south of the island of Drenovatz, and then, fortifying themselves on the Serbian shore, experienced no difficulty in driving back the fraction of the Third Ban there stationed. This feeble defending force retired to the hills lying to the south-east of Shabatz, and the advance guard of the Austrian 4th Army occupied the town, and constructed a pontoon bridge across the river from their railway terminus at Klenak.

Further passages of the Drina were executed by the 42nd division of the 13th Corps and two brigades of the 15th Corps at Zvornik and Liubovia respectively. In addition, the Austrians threw bridges across the river near Amajlia and Branjevo.

It will be observed that the invasion had been carried out in a very thorough and systematic manner. Over a frontier of some

100 to 120 miles in length the Austrians had thrown their troops in at least six great columns, all converging on the military centre of Valievo.

Before proceeding to a description of what, for want of a better name, is known as the " Battle of the Jadar," it will be necessary to sketch briefly the country over which this important engagement—the first great victory registered by the Allies—was fought and won by Serbia.

Shabatz, the north-easterly point of invasion, was a prosperous riverside town of some 15,000 inhabitants. From time immemorial it had been recognized as a centre of great strategical importance. In its vicinity there were many islands to facilitate the passage of the river, and from it many roads leading to the heart of Serbia. On its site the Romans had built a citadel ; through it the Huns had passed on their journeyings north and south and south and north ; in their day, too, the Turks had not only erected a powerful fortress but, at a later date, laid the foundations of a flourishing township. Modern, long-range artillery, however, rendered the town itself indefensible, both from the northern shore of the Save and from the hills lying to the south-east.

North and west of Shabatz lay the great plain of Matchva, bounded on its east and north by the Save and on its west by the river Drina. It was a rich, fertile country, absolutely flat, but much broken up by maize fields and woodland, in such a manner that a good field of fire could nowhere be obtained.

To the south-east, undulating terrain is bisected by the river Dobrava, where excellent defensive positions were available, while due south the great mountain barrier of Tzer rises like a camel's back out of the plain and, if its western extremity of Vidoievitza be included, stretches right across from the Drina to the Dobrava rivers. Even the southbound road, which cuts the range, climbs up and down like some mammoth switchback.

The southern slopes of Tzer are less abrupt than those of the north and descend slowly into the valley of the Leshnitza river, from whence rise the lesser heights of the Iverak mountains. Both Tzer and Iverak are well covered with plantations of maize and prune trees, intersected with patches of woodland.

Descending southward again, the foothills of Iverak are lost in a series of fairly important summits which flank the right bank of the Jadar river—the tributary of the Drina river from which the battle under consideration derived its name.

From the left bank of the Jadar, from its junction with the Drina to Jarebitzé, a great rolling plain stretches south until the giant Guchevo mountains, running in a south-easterly direction, rise abruptly and hide the Bosnian hills from view.

Continuing southward, the country is extremely mountainous, even the main roads being cut out of the hill sides along the innumerable valleys through which run watercourses which, almost dry in summer, are converted into torrential streams by the melted snow of spring.

Of the few existent roads, those which were maintained by the State—such as that from Shabatz to Loznitza—were metalled, of excellent quality and practicable in all weathers. Others, from Shabatz to Jarebitzé, Zavlaka, Oseshina and Valievo respectively, and from Loznitza to Valievo, Loznitza to Krupani, Krupani to Zavlaka, and Liubovia to Oseshina, were merely well-levelled highways of mud, which inevitably became impassable in wet weather for anything other than oxen transport. For the rest, communications consisted of traffic-beaten tracks across the fields or bridle paths over the mountains.

Offensive military operations against Valievo, therefore, called for the possession both of the mountain heights and of the few available roads.

HEAVY CANNON BEING BROUGHT UP BY OXEN.

The Austrians suffered from none of the difficulties which normally confront the invader by reason of his comparative ignorance of the terrain over which he is operating. Serbia had not only been explored time and again by the Austrian surveyors who were responsible for the production of most of the existing maps, but, during that epoch of Serbian history when a King's treaty had reduced her to military dependence upon Austria, the country had been overrun by agents of the Habsburg Government. A highly organised spy-system had doubtless kept the records up to date.

The Austrians planned their chief advance by the valley running down the Jadar to Valievo, and, for the satisfactory fulfilment of this intention, the possession of the heights of Tzer and Iverak was of great strategical importance. The fact that the Serbian Army was thinned down and worn out by two previous wars and, materially speaking, was not in a condition to fight, was well known to them, and they doubtless calculated that the mass of the forces opposed to them, concentrated as they were at Lazarevatz—Arangelovatz—Palanka, would be unable to enter the firing line until the penetration had reached the heart of the country. Here they sadly misjudged the possibilities, for, as we shall afterwards see, the Serbians arrived on the scene of action with truly astonishing rapidity, as the result of a series of long and arduous forced marches.

They wished, no doubt, to finish quickly with Serbia in order to turn their attention to the, for them, more important issues of the great war, and they placed in the field an army which, numerically, vastly outnumbered the forces at the disposal of their antagonist. For the Serbs did not dare to detach their entire military strength towards Shabatz and the Drina. They had need to guard other vulnerable points of their frontier against invasion, and the ambiguous attitude of Bulgaria and the attempts which were being made by Bulgarian bands to destroy the railway line to Salonika, necessitated the retention of fairly important units in Macedonia. Thus, in the vital stages of the battle of the Jadar, Serbia was able to engage only about half her available strength.

Immediately the news of the offensive reached Serbian Headquarters at Kragujevatz, and it was seen that the main operations were being directed against Valievo and not down the Morava valley, the Serbian armies began a general movement westward.

The Serbian strategy was under the direction of the Chief of the General Staff, Voivode (Field Marshal) Putnik.

General Putnik differed from most of his Balkan contemporaries in that he was a purely home-bred soldier, no part of his military education having been received abroad. He sprang, curiously enough, from a Serbo-Austrian stock, for his father was a native of Banat, in Hungary, and emigrated to Serbia in the 'forties. Settling in Kragujevatz, Putnik *père* there followed his vocation of teacher in an elementary school, and in the year 1847 the future generalissimo was born. From early youth the young Putnik was attracted to a martial career, and, having passed through the academy at Belgrade, the war with Turkey in 1876 found him already in commission. In the subsequent campaign against the Ottoman Empire in 1877–8 he served his country as a captain of infantry, and was one of the first officers to penetrate into the historic plain of Kossovo. Throughout the ill-starred Serbo-Bulgarian War of 1885 he held the rank of lieut.-colonel, and was Chief of Staff of the Danube Division First Ban.

On his promotion to colonel, Putnik became at first Chief of the General Staff and then Commander of the Choumadia Division. A reported sympathy with the Radical Party, however, now brought about his downfall, for King Milan was stoutly opposed to his officers mixing in politics. From that time until the accession of King Peter, in 1903, Putnik devoted himself to military studies and writings, and his literary efforts did more, perhaps, to establish his reputation than had his previous work in field or barracks. The restoration of the Karageorgevitch dynasty saw him promoted to the rank of general, and he speedily became the outstanding military figure in the kingdom. When not in command of a division he occupied the portfolio of Minister of War. In this capacity he presided over the re-organization of the army, including the choice and purchase of war material.

At the outbreak of hostilities with Turkey in 1912, Putnik naturally took his place at the head of the army and received the grade of Voivode, being the first Serbian to enjoy that distinction. His confirmation in that position for the Bulgarian War of 1913 followed as a matter of course.

In appearance General Putnik is small of stature, slight of build, and grey-bearded as becomes his years. He enjoys but indifferent

SERBIAN TROOPS CROSSING THE RIVER SAVE, NEAR BELGRADE.

health, is asthmatic, seldom leaves the over-heated room in which he lives, and it has been said of him that he went through the Turkish campaign in his slippers. In character he is inclined to be brusque and painfully outspoken; he excels in the selection of nicknames—usually uncomplimentary—for those about him, but is known as a sound judge of character, and choses his lieutenants with great discretion. A remarkable topographical memory greatly facilitates his task of directing the movements of the armies which he commands. Politics and journalists are his *bêtes noires.* As Minister of War he was most intolerant of criticism, and usually replied to his questioners by asking them what they knew about military matters. He has also remarked that no people with any self-respect write for newspapers or dabble in politics.

The arrest of General Putnik by the Austro-Hungarian authorities before the declaration of war was, at the time, the subject of considerable European comment. He was then returning to Serbia, and had been subjected to several hostile demonstrations *en route.* At length, on nearing Budapest, a number of persons invaded the compartment where he was resting, and, fearing that an attempt was about to be made to lynch him, he attempted to draw his revolver. He was quickly informed, how-

ever, that his disturbers were detectives, and that he was under arrest. He was detained at Budapest under a double guard with fixed bayonets, but was at length informed that he was at liberty and conducted with a great show of respect to the Rumanian frontier, whence he re-entered his own country.

It had already been ascertained that the principal Austrian force had entered by the Jadar valley, and General Putnik therefore despatched the 3rd Army, together with the bulk of the 2nd Army, in that direction; the rest of the 2nd Army being ordered to block the advance of the invaders from Shabatz.

The Austrians proceeded with the work of fortifying their bridge-head, and it was only on August 14 that they delivered an attack upon the Serbian force which had retreated to the heights of Loznitza. It was the first engagement of the campaign, and both sides strove hard for victory. The Austrians, full of yet undamped enthusiasm, attacked vigorously; but the Serbian veterans defended stoutly, and many bayonet charges were driven off with heavy loss. Often enough the defenders were in a critical position, but they held their ground successfully, awaiting the promised reinforcements. These, however, were unable to get up in time, and, having served a useful turn in delaying the enemy for a whole day, the old

ADVANCING UNDER FIRE.

men fell back. Near Jarebitzé they were joined by the tardy reinforcements, and the united forces proceeded to dig themselves in on a front of ten miles, extending from north to south through the town and right across the Jadar valley. The Austrians, it is interesting to note, did not follow up their attack, and the Serbs were thus able to retire and entrench themselves in perfect tranquillity. The next day they were joined by the balance of the 3rd Army.

Having from the outset of hostilities discerned the importance of driving in a wedge between Shabatz and Loznitza, General Putnik had sent his cavalry hot haste towards Matchva to investigate the situation there. The information which they obtained was of a somewhat startling nature, for they reported that hostile forces, coming across the plain, had been seen at points as far apart as Slepchevitch and Belareka. Any idea of attacking Shabatz was, therefore, temporarily abandoned, and the Serbian extreme right, with the Cavalry Division, received orders that, at whatever cost, the Austrians in the north must be prevented from effecting a junction with those in the Jadar valley.

In addition it was now, for the first time, learned that an Austrian column was marching northwards on Krupani. This was, however, according to the initial reports, but a small force, and, in consequence, a company of the Third Ban, together with a detachment of "Komitadji," were deemed amply sufficient to hold it in check.

The designation "Komitadji" as applied to the Serbian fighting man, stands in need of a little explanation, for he should in no sense be confounded with his throat-cutting namesake of Turkish-Macedonian days. The Serbian "Komitadji" were bands of dare-devils under the command of officers of the regular army and were distinguished by their reckless daring on the field of battle.

With the exception of a successful attack on the position of Poporparlok, north of Jarebitzé, and a Serbian movement towards Shabatz, the two armies now occupied themselves with their concentration for the forthcoming struggle. It will have been observed that, up to this point, the Austrian march on Valievo had been practically unopposed ; but, while they were promenading along the Tzer and Iverak mountains, the Serbian Armies, behind the fan-like screen which had been thrown out, were hastening westward by a series of remarkable forced marches.

Into Shabatz the Austrians were pouring their 4th Army Corps of two divisions and the 29th division of the 9th Corps ; a flanking column, coming from the Drina, had arrived at Slepchevitch. Their 8th Corps was marching with its left towards Belareka, centre along the crests of Tzer, and right down the Leshnitza valley. The 36th division of the 13th Corps had its left on Iverak and its right in the Jadar valley. The 42nd division of the same Corps directed its left and centre on Krupani, while its right, with two brigades of the 15th Corps, was moving north from Liubovia.

On the Serbian side the Independent Cavalry Division, with the right wing of the 2nd Army, were developing their mission of cutting off the Austrian forces in the north from a junction with those advancing on Tzer. The centre and left of the 2nd Army were marching to attack the hostile columns on Tzer and Iverak, in liaison with the right of the 3rd Army then north of Jarebitzé. The centre of the 3rd Army held the positions south of Jarebitzé, while its left, now split into several detachments, had been detailed off to deal with the invasion towards Krupani and the advance from Liubovia.

The first real shock of the battle occurred on the morning of August 16. The division on the extreme right of the Serbian armies was working northward in an endeavour to invest Shabatz, when its left flank guard discovered the presence of a strong Austrian column marching across the foothills of Tzer, and presumably destined to clear the ground preparatory to a descent of the 4th Army Corps. This development might well have involved an interference with the plans of the Serbian General Staff but for the initiative and daring of Major Djukitch, of the 4th Artillery regiment. This adventurous spirit asked permission to go out and meet the Austrians with but a single cannon. He might, he submitted, lose his life, and the gun, but he promised meanwhile to inflict considerable damage on the enemy. He was therefore allowed to take one cannon on to the position of Gusingrob. The spectacle which there met his eyes was disconcerting. Austrian columns appeared to be overrunning the country, and he was at a loss to know in which direction to open fire. Then, throwing gunnery etiquette to the winds, he commenced to shell first one section and then another. The effect of this unexpected bombardment upon the Austrians was magical. The troops were thrown into panic and the greatest confusion prevailed.

The first shot had been fired at 8.55 a.m., and half an hour later a messenger arrived ordering Djukitch to return to Slatina. In reply, he sent his Colonel an account of the situation and asked for reinforcements, following upon which he received the balance of his own battery, and a detachment of infantry together with the cavalry division were also sent forward.

CONTINGENT OF RESERVISTS.

The Austrians now hastily reformed and massed on the line Belikamen–Radlovatz, and the Serbs deployed on Slatina–Metkovitch–Gusingrob. From these positions a battle-royal commenced at 11 a.m. on Belikamen and continued, with ever-increasing vigour, throughout the day. Towards 6 p.m. the position of the Serbs, sensibly inferior in point of numbers, was critical in the extreme ; but, upon the timely arrival of assistance, they were able to resume the offensive. This counter-attack resulted in the complete rout of the Austrians, who fled the field, leaving behind them a great quantity of impedimenta, including two field batteries. According to the statements of prisoners, their 102nd regiment was almost destroyed, and the 94th regiment had practically ceased to exist as a fighting unit.

More important than the mere defeat of the enemy or the capture of a certain amount of material was the effect of this first success upon the ultimate result of the great battle, for it immediately and finally cut off the Austrians in Matchva from the chief theatre of operations, definitely freed the right wing of the Serbian army for action against Shabatz and the cavalry for service in any direction which might be dictated by the march of events.

The centre of the Serbian 2nd Army—that directed against Tzer—had arrived before Tekerish towards midnight on August 15.

The country thereabouts is very undulating and richly interspersed with woodland, and it was not until the advance guard had actually arrived on the position that they perceived a strong Austrian column descending from the mountains in the same direction. The two armies, so to speak, fell on top of one another, the Serbs finding themselves in an exposed position on the rolling foothills with the Austrians towering above them, effectively sheltered by the woods. The Serbs deployed on the positions Bornopolye–Parlok–Lisena, with their artillery on Kik, while the Austrians developed an attack from the superior ground then in their possession. Fierce fighting continued without any distinct advantage to one side or the other until 8 a.m. on August 16, when the Austrian artillery got the range of the Serbian left flank and forced the division back on to the line Krivaiska Kosa–Ragonicabrdo–Kik. Here the timely arrival of reserves averted further catastrophe, and the troops were able to dig themselves in. The casualties to both armies were severe. The Serbs had over 1,000 placed *hors de combat,* while the losses suffered by the Austrians included the capture of 300 prisoners and several machine guns.

The left wing of the 2nd Army had, in the meantime, arrived against Iverak. The prompt and, we may assume, unexpected

MOUNTAIN ARTILLERY.

entrance of this division into action was due to its having executed a forced march of fifty-two miles over mountainous country and in a tropical heat during the preceding twenty-four hours. Yet it was ready, at 3 a.m. on the morning of August 16, to continue its route to Poporparlok. At that hour, however, the unfavourable news was received that the Austrians had driven the left wing of the 3rd Army from that position on the previous evening, and the objective was, therefore, in the hands of the enemy.

The situation before this division was, it must be admitted, by no means clear. No news was available from the direction of Shabatz ; the division before Tzer had received a severe mauling during the night ; the 3rd Army had lost Poporparlok ; and the reports of the Austrian advance were of a disquieting nature. A consideration of these facts led the Commander to abandon his projected advance and to devote himself to the task of checking any attempt of the Austrians to push forward from Iverak. The division was accordingly entrenched on the line Begluk–Kik (1,161 ft.), and a strong advance was thrown out towards Kugovitchi. During the morning the advance guard attacked Kugovitchi, carried the positions, and established themselves there.

At 3 p.m. the left flank of the position—at Beglok—was shelled by the Austrian artillery in preparation for an attack in force, which, commencing about 7.30 p.m., was successfully repulsed after one and a half hours' fighting. The enemy then flung fresh forces into the fray, and came on again at midnight. On this occasion the Serbians calmly allowed them to advance in a compact mass close up to their lines and then, after emptying their magazines at them, they charged with bombs and bayonet and hurled them back with heavy loss.

Less encouraging to Serbian arms was the experience of their 3rd Army, charged with the defence of the territory south of Iverak, and the whole line was subjected to a persistent Austrian attack. Poporparlok, as has already been observed, had been lost the night before, and the Austrians now developed a vigorous offensive in an attempt to turn the Serbian left and capture the road to Valievo. The attack on the positions of Jarebitzé commenced at daybreak. Though the hills held by the Serbians were in every way well suited to defensive operations, the approaches almost equally favoured a skilful offensive, for the

summits were restricted and incapable of providing entrenched positions for more than a company or so of infantry, while the interlacing hollows afforded excellent cover under which to develop outflanking movements in comparative security. The field of fire was, further, greatly reduced by the maize and prune trees, which are an ever-present feature of north-western Serbia. It was by deploying around the aforementioned hollows that the Austrians attempted to force the Serbs to withdraw from the coveted position of Jarebitzé.

A frontal attack on the centre and left of the stronghold was simultaneously undertaken by a further hostile column which had advanced across the plain south of the Jadar valley, where the depressions, sunken roads and maize again provided adequate protection. Throughout the day the Austrians made a determined struggle for supremacy in this quarter of the theatre of war. The Serbian positions were, however, exceedingly strong, and the repeated attacks to which they were subjected were all successfully repulsed. The Serbs would, in fact, have been able to make a protracted stand at Jarebitzé but for a disconcerting development farther south, where the Austrian forces moving on Krupani, so far from being limited to the feeble detachments that had at first been imagined, proved to be composed of no less than three brigades of mountaineers. Reinforcements of infantry and mountain artillery were tardily hurried south, but the Austrians were able to continue their advance towards Zavlaka, and the Serbs, seeing Valievo thus threatened, deemed retreat the wiser course, evacuated Jarebitzé and retired on to the line Marianovitche vis–Ravnajaski vis–Groblje–Racievskikamen–Schumer, where a front could be offered to both the hostile columns.

This withdrawal was executed in perfect order and, strangely enough, without interference. That some movement was being effected must have been obvious to the invaders, for the Serbian artillery which had been in position on the right bank of the Jadar was obliged to defile before the Austrian front in order to gain the main road. Yet, fortunately for the Serbians, they were allowed to pursue their retreat unmolested. By 8 a.m. the following morning (August 17) the new line had been occupied and extended to Soldato-vitcha gaive, whence the detachment from Krupani had retreated.

["The Times" Photograph.

HEADQUARTERS AND STAFF OF A DIVISION.

On the day's showing, therefore, we see that although the Austrians had encountered their enemy much sooner than they had probably expected, they had nevertheless temporarily checked the Serbian counter-attack. On the other hand, the attempt to effect a junction of their forces at Shabatz with those on Tzer had been baulked at the outset.

After the engagement on Belikamen on August 16, the Independent Cavalry Division was strengthened by detachments of infantry and artillery, and ordered to pursue its important but perilous mission of penetrating between the Austrian forces at Shabatz and on the Drina. Proceeding in very extended formation, so that its left flank was based on Tzer and its right on the division operating towards Shabatz, it was able not only to penetrate as far as Dublje and Prnjavor in the north, but to assist the column attacking Tzer by a vigorous bombardment of the Austrian position on that mountain at Troyan. In fact, throughout the great battle, the cavalry rendered most noteworthy service by the manner in which, in dismounted action, it co-ordinated its movements with those of the Serbian forces acting on its wings.

The extreme right of the Serbian Armies, having passed the night of August 16–17 at Slatina, now felt the way clear for a resumption of its movement towards Shabatz. The fact that they were proceeding against Austrian forces more than double their own strength served rather to encourage than to damp the ardour of the men, and, deploying in three columns, they set their course northward and pressed lightheartedly on until, on approaching the line of hills Jevremovatz–Prichinovitz–Jelentza, they were suddenly brought up by a heavy musketry and artillery fire coming from well-prepared earthworks.

An investigation of the situation disclosed that Shabatz had been prepared for defence *à l'outrance*. The outskirts of the town had been strongly fortified by solid fieldworks and obstacles—blind trenches, barbed wire, spiked pits—and all the artifices of modern warfare joined hands with heavy artillery to render attack by such a small force as that at the disposal of the Serbian commander a somewhat risky proceeding. It was, therefore, decided to invest the town in such a manner as to counter any attempt to leave it, and await the arrival of reinforcements.

The centre and left of the 2nd Army, now recovered from the gruelling which they had received the previous day, decided to undertake a combined movement against the mountains of Tzer and Iverak respectively. The defeat administered to the Austrians on Belikamen had exercised a salutary influence on the column which had driven back the Serbian centre on the previous day, with the result that, on the morning of August 17 we find them hardly pressed at Troyan, the most easterly and, after Kosaningrad, the most important of the peaks of the Tzer mountain. The Serbians prepared their attack by a well-nourished artillery fire from the south-east and, as has already been noted, from the north, and then, as is their wont, reposing their confidence in bombs and bayonets, they scaled the grassy slopes and rushed the position. This operation was effected by two regiments ; the while a third, advancing along the southern slopes, took the more westerly point of Parlog. The columns made no further progress this day, the time being spent in bringing up cannon and preparing for the attack on the culminating height of Kosaningrad, where the Austrians were found to be concentrating in force.

Although the victories at Troyan and Parlog, coming hot upon the routing of the Austrians at Belikamen, may almost be said to have decided the fate of the first invasion, the enemy, probably hoping to retrieve their position at Kosaningrad, continued to drive home their advance from Iverak. The situation of the Serbian troops in that sector—the left wing of the 2nd Army—was difficult in the extreme,

for their left flank was increasingly exposed by the enforced retirement of the 3rd Army. In point of fact, the only favourable artillery omen for them was the knowledge that the flank of their enemy was, in its turn, being threatened by the advance of the neighbouring Serbian column on Tzer. It was conceivable that the moment Tzer and the Leshnitza valley fell into Serbian hands the pressure on their front would be relieved, but in the meantime the Austrians probably realized that the only strategy now open to them was to drive the forces opposed to them on Iverak rapidly eastward, and by the persistence of their progress towards Zavlaka and Valievo render the possession of Tzer a matter of secondary interest.

Thus from early morning the Swaba—by which name the Austrians were known to the Serbian rank and file—undertook a vigorous onslaught on the line Beglok–Kugovitchi. Half an hour later they had been driven off. The fighting, nevertheless, continued. The Austrians came on in swarms, and by 11 o'clock the engagement had spread to the right wing. Towards noon the 3rd Army again reported its position as critical; and this hardly-pressed division was obliged to send reinforcements to its aid. Thus weakened, and finding its advance guard at Kugovitchi threatened by a cleverly executed turning movement, the division began a strategic withdrawal to the

ROADSIDE SCENE DURING THE BATTLE OF THE JADAR.

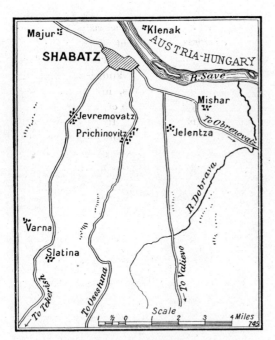

**MAP ILLUSTRATING THE OPERATIONS
ROUND SHABATZ.**

heights of Kalem. The retirement was executed in good order, the Austrians contenting
themselves with the occupation of Kugovitchi
and the hill lying to the south-west. The
Serbs entrenched in strong positions and
awaited the renewal of the Austrian attack
with confidence. Nothing more serious than
artillery fire was sustained, however, and the
good news of the successful advance on Tzer
having been received, preparations were at
once undertaken for a forward movement on
the morrow.

We have already seen that the strength of
the Austrian attack had thrown the Serbian
3rd Army on the defensive and that, in the
early morning of this day (August 17), this
force had retired on to the line Marianovitche
vis–Ravnajaski vis–Groblje–Ragievskikamen–
Schumer–Soldatovitcha gaive, where it could
present a front to the Austrians advancing on
Valievo *via* Jarebitzé and Krupani respectively.
It might have been expected that the Austrians
would have taken Jarebitzé, and then continued
down the main road to Zavlaka, but the disposition of the armies and the stubborn
resistance offered by the division against
Iverak were probably the causes which led the
invaders to concentrate their energies upon
the extreme south of the Serbian line, attempt
to pierce it and come out at Oseshina. The
Austrians therefore remained before Jarebitzé

and hurled their 42nd division of mountain
troops against the Serbian left, doubtless in an
endeavour to turn it up and strike the Petska-
Oseshina road. The defenders were, of course,
greatly outnumbered and, as far as military
equipment went, outmatched, but despite a
decisive hostile effort, they held their ground
all day, and it was only towards evening that
any weakening was observable. The onslaught,
however, had been sufficiently severe to render
a demand for assistance both logical and necessary, and the troops stood their ground the
better for knowing that reinforcements were
hurrying to their aid.

August 17, therefore, had seen both General
Staffs employing the same strategy at different
points. On the extreme north and extreme
south of their line and over a part of their
centre the Serbians were stonewalling, while
prosecuting an exceedingly vigorous advance
on Tzer. The Austrians, for their part, sought
to overwhelm their enemy in the south and to
maintain their positions in other quarters of the
theatre of war. To the military student, as he
looked that night at the respective positions
of the two armies, at the difference in their
strength and equipment, the chances would
inevitably have appeared to favour the triumph
of Austrian arms, but the stamina, courage
and moral of the Serbian soldier were about
to claim a striking and vital victory for the
allied armies.

Just as the dislocation of their plans on
Tzer had caused the Austrians to undertake a
furious onslaught on the 3rd Army and had
almost diverted the projected advance down
the Jadar valley, so it became essential that the
mass of invaders penned up in Shabatz should
break through and endeavour to re-establish
the original situation. It was quite obvious
to the Serbian Staff, however, that, once the
penetration by the centre had failed, the
Austrians would attempt to get home with the
wings. This at once explains a dispatch of
additional reinforcements to the extreme left
and the instructions given to the extreme right
to solidly entrench and prepare to resist any
endeavour of the Shabatz army to descend.

The right had not long to wait, for at 7 a.m.
on August 18—the morning following their
unsuccessful assault on the town—they were
attacked by the Austrians, who doubtless
reckoned on their superior strength to crown
the enterprise with success. An engagement
of a most sanguinary nature at once commenced

with the employment by the Austrians of tactics which are not commonly associated with civilized warfare. Having rounded up some 2,000 of the female inhabitants of Shabatz, including many women dragged from beds of sickness, they forced them to march in advance of the troops as cover against Serbian fire. Two Hungarian regiments were sent ahead in this manner, a Madame Gashitch (wife of a local druggist and a student of the Magyar tongue) being obliged to act as interpreter. Once their opponents came into the open, the Serbs doggedly resisted the effort to pierce their line, but were, nevertheless, forced back step by step, contesting every foot of the way. Finally they succeeded in wearing down the offensive, and the attacks gradually ceased. The division passed the night on the line Leskovitz–Mihana, towards Slatina.

The Independent Cavalry Division, which had intended to continue its pursuit of the Austrians towards Leshnitza, found itself obliged to retire to the line Metkovitch–Brestovatz. The withdrawal from before Shabatz had necessarily affected its plans, but, in addition, the fraction of the enemy which had retreated to Lipolist had been there joined by incoming reinforcements a brigade strong, and was thus able to undertake a counter-offensive. The force then opposed to the Cavalry consisted of the 28th Landwehr division, with two groups of artillery and two howitzer batteries.

The Austrians, however, did not press their advance. Having by this time cultivated a wholesome respect for the Serbian cavalry, and apparently fearing that the retirement was but a ruse to lull them on to destruction, they threw out a strong advance guard and progressed cautiously, showing no disposition to attack. They pushed ahead a little and then retired, and this going and coming continued throughout the day.

Simultaneously with the unsuccessful endeavour to throw troops from Shabatz on to Tzer, the Austrians directed heavy reinforcements to the summit of Kosaningrad in readiness for the Serbian attack on that position. They had, in addition, heavily fortified the height of Rashulatcha, which lay between the crests of Tzer and Iverak, and from whence they could direct their artillery in either direction.

At this stage of the battle the check which the division operating against Iverak had received exercised a delaying influence upon the victorious columns on Tzer, for in marching ahead they not only exposed their left flank, but the assistance which they anticipated would be rendered from the south in the attack on Rashulatcha was not forthcoming. If the division moved more slowly on this account,

THE MARKET PLACE AT KRAGUJEVATZ.   [*"The Times" Photograph.*

it, nevertheless, progressed surely. The aid of oxen was invoked to drag the guns along the crest of the mountain, and after a preliminary shelling a rush was made for the position of Kosaningrad. The Serbians again put their faith in bombs and bayonets, and attacked with their customary vigour, but they failed to get home, and ultimately retired. A second attack was carried out under the same conditions, and although the Austrians flung fresh troops into the fray, the Serbs pressed on and a violent combat developed. Ultimately the blue-grey line wavered, then broke, and the Austrians scattered in all directions, followed by the pursuing Serbians.

The possession of the coveted Kosaningrad paved the way for an offensive against Rashu-latcha, for the position could now be both outflanked and covered by enfilade fire as well as assaulted. This was precisely the tactics adopted by the Serbian commander. He had left a strong reserve on Troyan, and ordering this to join up with a column which had marched along the southern slopes to cover his left wing, he directed the united detachments to storm the height the while he manœuvred on the flank. The movement was not vigorously pressed, for the probabilities were that on the morrow the division on Iverak would be able to threaten the stronghold from the south.

The advance of this latter force had, in fact, already commenced. Forming into two columns, they marched out and attacked the Austrians at Kugovitchi, and after a prolonged and stubbornly contested engagement, drove them from the trenches. Here they were subjected to an intense bombardment from batteries posted on Reingrob and had to dig themselves in under fire. It was not to be expected that the Austrians would tamely acquiesce in this disconcerting upsetting of their plans, and towards midnight they executed a determined counter-offensive. The Swaba were not, however, adepts at night attack. The Serbs allowed them to come within short range and then, after meeting them with point blank magazine fire, drove them off in some confusion. The division continued to be subjected to a more or less desultory rifle fire and accordingly passed the night in battle order.

The same day (August 18) the Austrians renewed the pressure on the 3rd Army, directing their attention also to the line Proslop–Rozani, where the detachment of the Third Ban from Liubovia was concentrated. Soldato-

vicha gaive was the object of the initial attack of the day, and the detachment of divisional cavalry which, following a rearrangement of the defence, had been left in charge of the position, finding themselves overpowered, retired towards the neighbouring summit of 1,227 ft., where they strengthened the troops holding the line between that height and 1,056 ft. Against this line the Austrians massed their entire 42nd division.

The combats over the centre of the front held by the 3rd Army continued without any change in the situation being thereby occasioned, but after a slight transfer of strength the Austrians struck hard at the Serbian right, forced it back, and occupied Marianovitche vis.

During the day the reinforcements to which reference has already been made arrived from the north and, having directed them principally southward, the General Commanding the army ordered his left to undertake a counter-offensive—with such decided effect that towards nightfall Soldatovitcha gaive had been recaptured. All ranks then felt that the moment for the forward movement had at length arrived.

From early morn on August 19 the Austrians at Shabatz, no doubt realizing that the centre of their army had been thrown into retreat and that progress on their left had been effectively barred, renewed their attempt to penetrate southward. The attack was pressed with redoubled energy, so much so that, despite the stubborn resistance offered by the Serbs, they were finally driven over on to the right bank of the Dobrava river. There was strategy in this retreat also, for the Dobrava positions were of acknowledged strength. If the Austrians advanced against them they could, even if in greatly superior force—as they were—be dealt with to the certain advantage of the defenders; whereas had they continued southward towards Tzer, with the object of threatening the Serbian rear on that mountain, the division could have fallen on their flank. The possibility of this last diversion was not lost upon the Austrians, and presumably deeming it prudent completely to wipe out the opposition before proceeding on their way, they advanced against the Dobrava, where the engagement continued until nightfall.

The Austrian success continued, moreover, to act as a brake upon the movements of the Cavalry Division, which had necessarily to lie back in order to guard against any unforeseen

SERBIAN BLÉRIOT MONOPLANE AT SHABATZ.   [*" The Times "* *Photograph.*

movement on Tzer from the north. They were
also, for their part, threatened by the aforementioned enemy force at Lipolist—which,
fortunately, continued its hesitating tactics of
the previous day and made nothing in the
nature of a definite advance—and, later on,
they received fire from the left flank of the
Austrians on Tzer, who were probably reinforced by a part of the troops who had been
driven out of Kosaningrad. Although urged to
continue the pursuit towards Leshnitza, the
division was obliged, therefore, to remain on
the line Belega–Suwatcha–Vitingrob. A further
request for reinforcements met with a ready
response from headquarters, and the division
was so strengthened that it became a combined
but nevertheless very mobile unit.

To the south of the Cavalry Division the
Serbians continued their victorious career along
the crests of Tzer. Towards midday Rashulacha fell after a series of spirited attacks, and
the possibility of danger from the flank having
been removed, a strong advance guard was
thrown out and ordered to pursue the enemy
with all speed.

During the day an Austrian column was
observed to be retreating in the Leshnitza
valley. They were shelled from the heights
above, thrown into disorder, and badly mauled.
In the evening the advance guard of the
division had arrived near Jadranska Leshnitza.

In the early morning of this day the attack
against Iverak commenced in earnest, and a
furious battle raged in which the Serbians
drove their enemy before them over the
mountain with astonishing speed. Hostilities
had opened with an ineffectual counter-attack
by the Austrians on Kugovitchi at 2 a.m. ;
three hours later the Serbian forward movement was inaugurated. The thoroughness of
the victories registered by the neighbouring
division on Tzer of course facilitated the
advance, but the Austrians, realizing that
their position in the north was hopeless, made
a last supreme effort to register some success
in the centre. The Serbians stormed and took
Velika Glava at 11 a.m., but their progress was
there stayed by a nourished gun-fire from the
heights on Iverak to the west of Rashulacha.
A hotly contested artillery duel raged, then a
fusillade spread along the whole line from
Velika Glava to Kik (north of Zavlaka), and by
midday the battle was in full swing. At this
juncture the Serbian left reported that the
Austrians were massing in force near Kik with
intention to outflank, and that the right wing
of the 3rd Army was being hemmed in by a
hostile turning movement. This somewhat
untoward development bade fair to hinder the
general advance, but headquarters came to
the rescue with a reserve division, which was
dispatched in that direction and charged with
the double task of relieving the pressure on the
left of Iverak and the right of the 3rd Army.

The menace from Kik was accordingly
ignored and the right and centre columns

FIELD ARTILLERY.

continued their attack on Iverak. For some time the Austrians defended with partial success. At some points they retired, at others they pushed ahead, but by 4.20 p.m., when Reingrob was captured, the Serbians were masters of the situation. The Austrians, now fighting rearguard actions, delayed the pursuit a little at Poporparlok and again at Vutchiplast, but their defeat was complete and the division passed the night in four groups stretching from Vutchiplast to Kik.

The 3rd Army was again hotly engaged. Its left flank continued its advance from Soldato-vicha gaive ; but the Austrians continued to drive home their success at Marianovitche vis, strove to pierce the centre of the army, and carried out an assault on the Proslop–Rozani line. Both sides exerted themselves on this the critical day of the battle, and the fighting was continuous and intense. As the day wore on and the reinforcements which had been announced failed to arrive (they were delayed by roads so bad that the transport of impedi-menta was rendered almost impossible), a strong detachment was transferred from the left to the right wing, and by a vigorous assault Marianovitche vis was retaken towards evening. The Austrians were driven from the position in great disorder and left a great deal of material, including three hospitals filled with wounded,

on the field. In addition, the Serbs captured a commandant and 500 prisoners.

August 19, therefore, may be set down as the decisive day of the struggle. Though the Austrians had made considerable headway from Shabatz and had checked the advance of the cavalry division, the fact that the Serbians were the undoubted masters of Tzer and Iverak and that the 3rd Army had definitely under-taken the offensive, robbed the invaders of their last hopes of success.

So persistent had been the Austrian attack on the Dobrava river positions that the Serbian force stationed there not unnaturally presumed that it would be resumed with undiminished energy on August 20. The Austrians appeared, however, to have abandoned all thoughts of retrieving the situation on Tzer and Iverak, and even in the Shabatz theatre the idea of a further advance seemed to have been given up. The attack was consequently feeble, and the Serbs were able to cross the Dobrava and establish themselves on the left bank.

The Austrians were certainly in a most unfavourable position. The great battle had, so far as the omens went, been already lost and won. The Serbian advance along Tzer had at length freed the left flank of the cavalry, and that force undertook the pursuit and fell on the rear of a retreating column. Mobile, yet strong in all arms, they threw the enemy troops into disorder, shelled them, charged them, and drove those who escaped slaughter into panic-stricken flight. " This war is a grim business for us," said a Serbian officer who witnessed the spectacle, " but I shook with laughter to see those fellows run." The fugitives retired *via* Belareka and Prnjavor, hurrying through the villages in detached groups and crying out to the peasants as they went, " Where is the Drina ? Where is the Drina ? " They stayed to destroy Prnjavor and to commit sundry atrocities (which will be more fully dealt with in a subsequent chapter) *en route*, but by nightfall there were few of them left in the Matchva district

The Serbian troops on Tzer continued to drive the Austrians off the top of the mountain, and towards noon pushed their advance on to the adjacent summit of Vidieovitza, where they placed a battery in position and shelled another mass of Austrians retreating in the Leshnitza valley and a further contingent going towards Janja, causing great destruction. Some detachments did, indeed, endeavour to make a stand, but they were soon overrun by their own compatriots, who crowded upon them in disordered flight.

Only once did any danger threaten the Serbs, and that was when a hostile column, yet unaffected by the general panic, came up a ravine from the direction of Chokeshina and temporarily isolated the advance guard on Vidoievitza. Though the Austrians proceeded manfully to the attack they were soon overcome, and joined their comrades in the rush for the security of the river.

From early morning the division operating on Iverak had been ordered to direct its attention to the Austrians retreating *via* the Jadar valley, and to act on their flank. The force accordingly split into three sections and advanced westward, sending detachments into the valley and consistently reinforcing them as they descended. The principal masses of Austrians were retreating along the road to Loznitza, and the better to cover their withdrawal, they opened fire with their guns against the pursuing Serbians. This had no other result than to bring the Serbian batteries into action, under protection of which the infantry continued the pursuit. Advance parties of volunteers were sent out to harass the Austrian rear, and the columns followed up what was, in point of fact, nothing but a precipitous flight for safety.

Thanks to the re-occupation of Marianovitche vis the previous evening, the 3rd Army was also able to join in the common chase of the enemy ; the advance continued along the whole line, the Austrians retiring towards the frontier by all available roads with the Serbs hard on their heels.

There remained to be dealt with but the

ARMY TARGET.
Shooting with Quick-Firing Guns.

Austrian forces on Kik, to the north-west of Zavlaka. The Serbian reinforcements which, it will be remembered, had been originally directed towards Marianovitche vis had been afterwards diverted westward, and at dawn on August 20 they approached Kik in two columns. The cross-country going was exceedingly difficult, hills and forests interspersed the land, and even cattle transport proving impracticable, the guns were unyoked and dragged along by the infantry. Osoyé was occupied by the left column without combat, but in descending from that position, the Serbs received fire from Austrian artillery. The greatest difficulty was experienced in bringing their own batteries into action. Indeed, by 8.0 a.m. only one gun was in position, but at this moment the enemy ceased fire.

An hour later two batteries belonging to the right column, which had followed a more northerly route, opened fire, and under cover of the bombardment a Serbian battalion reached the foot of the mountain. The infantry attack which then followed was received exclusively by rifle fire, for the Austrian artillery had already been retired, and, as was subsequently discovered, their maxims had been destroyed by the Serbian guns. In the height of the combat which accompanied the assault the extreme left of the division on Iverak, which had remained to guard against possible attack

from this quarter, moved against the right flank of the Austrians. Seeing this, they did not wait for the bayonet attack which was then in preparation, but at 10.0 a.m. abandoned the position and fled under a cross fire from the two attacking parties. Losses under such conditions are necessarily great. The Serbs buried over 600 Austrian dead on the position. They took 50 prisoners, a field hospital and a mass of impedimenta and rifles. Their own losses were astonishingly low—7 killed and 16 wounded.

The Serbian forces now proceeded to occupy Jarebitzé, after which they joined the Iverak division in its pursuit of the enemy.

Of the events of August on the Drina frontier little need be recorded. The last remnants of the Austrian hosts were chased over the river or captured. Many lost themselves among the mealies or in the forests, whence they from time to time came in to surrender. The Serbian divisions ranged themselves along the banks of the Drina from north to south, and it remained only to drive the Austrian Corps from Shabatz to free Serbian soil from the invader.

After having recrossed the Dobrava river on August 20, the Serbs followed up their advantage and pressed on towards Shabatz. The Austrians had again occupied their old positions before the town, and a fierce engagement at once commenced. All the day of

RESERVISTS PREPARING THEIR MEALS.

ARTILLERY IN ACTION.

August 21 the combat raged with ever-increasing severity, and a part of the long-promised reinforcements arrived and took up a position on the Serbian left. On August 22 a forward movement was undertaken over the whole line. The Austrians, well entrenched on their left and centre and aided by a mass of artillery, resisted stoutly, but they had neglected the western approaches to the town, with the result that the Serb left was able to arrive before the walls before it was stopped. About mid-day the defenders counter-attacked in the direction of the road to Varna, but were well repulsed, and the day's fighting, on the whole, left the situation unchanged.

The next day (August 23) the Austrians returned to the attack with increased energy. As the result of a persistent onslaught they had begun to pierce the Serbian lines between Majur and Jevremovatz, when at a critical moment in the engagement reinforcements in the shape of fresh troops were brought up and thrown into the fray. These men turned the balance, the line was reformed and an advance towards the town at once commenced. Similarly, the violence of the Austrian attack on the front Jevremovatz-Mishar had inflicted very heavy losses on one of the Serbian regiments, and the position there was somewhat grave until, either by good luck or good

management, reinforcements turned up in that direction also. These units were immediately ordered to counter-attack, which they did to such effect that the Austrians were obliged to retire along the whole line, and henceforth to adopt defensive tactics. For the remainder of the day and far into the night a heavy fusilade, combined with machine gun and artillery fire, continued without interruption. The Serbians succeeded in tightening the cordon round the town, and little but the final stroke of victory was left over for the morrow.

During the night a number of siege guns arrived and were placed in position. The following morning (August 24) 98 guns of various calibres simultaneously bombarded the Austrian trenches. The noise and effect of the cannonade was terrific, but, as it so happened, superfluous, for under cover of night the Austrians, deeming further resistance useless, had evacuated Shabatz, leaving only a small covering detachment in the town. The general assault which had been ordered for mid-day was therefore abandoned, and at that hour a detachment of the besieging troops commenced a march towards the walls. At 4 p.m. they arrived on the banks of the Save, and the first Austrian invasion of Serbia had come to its inglorious end.

Following the débacle the Vienna Press

Bureau, with a courage which would have proved invaluable upon the field of battle, issued the following official *communiqué* to an astonished world :

Since, owing to the intervention of Russia into our dispute with Serbia, we find it necessary to concentrate our entire force for the great combat in the north, the war against Serbia must be considered only as a " Straf-expedition " (punitive expedition) which, for the same reason, has become a matter of secondary interest. In spite of that, and both in view of the general situation and of the false news which has been circulated by the enemy, an offensive action had been judged opportune. Yet, also for the above-mentioned reason, this operation was limited to a short incursion into the enemy's terri-tory, after the successful accomplishment of which it was necessary to return to an attitude of expectancy, in adjourning the offensive to a more favourable occasion. The offensive executed by part of our troops was an action replete with bravery and heroism. Its effect was to draw upon us the entire Serbian army, the attacks of which, despite a great numerical superiority, had no result, thanks to the heroism of our troops. The fact that our troops in part suffered heavy losses should not astonish us, for our enemy possessed a numeri-cal superiority and was, in addition, fighting for his existence. Thus when our troops, who had penetrated a long way into Serbian territory, received the order to regain their positions on the Drina and on the Save, they left an enemy completely enfeebled on the field of battle.

In addition to inflicting a tremendous blow upon the military prestige of the Monarchy, the " Strafexpedition " proved to be one of the most expensive punitive campaigns ever undertaken. The estimation of Austrian losses is somewhat difficult as many of the fallen were not discovered until the pene-trating odour of decomposed humanity dis-closed the presence of bodies in wood or unhar vested field. Hundreds of unnamed and un-counted warriors were thus buried where they lay. The Austrian casualties were, however, necessarily heavy. In attack they had made free use of their artillery and then, depending on mass formations to carry the positions, had flung their troops forward in compact masses, only to be mown down like ripened corn by the Serbian infantry. In their disordered retreat they time and again wandered into the valleys, and were there decimated by the Serbian artillery. Their dead numbered not less than six to eight thousand and their wounded 30,000. The Serbs took 4,000 prisoners, 46 cannon, 30 machine guns and 140 ammunition wagons, plus a mass of rifles, field hospitals, transport, engineers' trains, stores, and other impedimenta.

The Serbian losses were inferior, but never-theless heavy. The victory of the Jadar cost them 3,000 dead and 15,000 wounded, but it stemmed the tide of invasion for three precious months, and necessitated the continued con-centration in the southern theatre of the war of five Austrian army corps which the Teutons would fain have transferred to the battlefields of France or Galicia.

In Vol. I. will be found portraits of King Peter, p. 39 ; the Crown Prince, p. 78 ; M. Pashitch, p. 19.

CHAPTER XLI.

THE INDIAN ARMY IN FRANCE.

The Unity of India—Employment of "Coloured Troops"—Precedents—Enthusiastic
Offers—Pathos of the Rusting Sword—Sir Pertab Singh's Speech—Organization of
Imperial Service Troops—Response of the Chiefs—The King-Emperor's Message—
Attitude of the People—German Miscalculations—Fresh Light upon "Indian Unrest"—
The Landing at Marseilles—Welcome to France—Legends of Indian Warfare—Qualities
of the Troops—Their Courage—New Lessons in Scientific War—Failure of the German
"Holy War"—Rally of Moslem India—Wide Sphere of the Indian Army's Operations.

INDIA, the nursery of soldiers, supplied the first Imperial contribution to the Empire in the field. The phenomenon of political unity in the British Isles was repeated in the Dependency.

For the first time in the history of that great continent every class, creed, and community became articulate, and the voice of the three hundred millions was lifted as one. Discontent, it seemed, had only been a phase of "His Majesty's Opposition "—there as here. In the face of stern reality doctrinaire politics went to the wall. The loyal Indian became more loyal ; unsought he showed his loyalty and devotion without stint. The discontented Indian took thought. The unthinking masses stood by the order of things. The military races were filled with a great hope. It seemed that the time had come at last when half the manhood of India might be called upon to unsheathe the sword.

Only for a little while there was great suspense. Indian troops had never before been employed on European soil in a war against white men, and there was fear that the precedent might still hold. The ignorance which prompted the scruple was one of the first illusions which the war swept away. In bringing " coloured troops " to France we opposed to the modern apostles of Culture the descendants of Porus, to whose chivalry Alexander bore witness, sons of an ancient civilization admired of Megasthenes close on twenty centuries ago. To a race guilty of the blood of women and children we opposed the descendants of Jeimul and Putta. It would be difficult to conceive in what terms the bards of Rajput chivalry would celebrate a foe who drove women into the field before his legions to protect them from the fire of the enemy.

Of India's services in Egypt, China, Somaliland, and the Sudan little need be said. As long ago as 1801 in a similar European crisis the mobility of our Indian army served us in good stead when we dispatched troops to Egypt. In Manila, Macao, Java, and Bourbon Indian soldiers have served the purposes of the Empire in conflict with European foes.

South Africa, according to the fiat, was a " white man's war," but we must not forget that the Indian bearers' corps went with the personnel of the Indian hospitals and were supplemented by Indian settlers in Natal. These brave men, who were unarmed under fire, were commended for their coolness, as were the drivers of Danjhibhoy, the Parsee mail contractor's ambulance tonga corps. In a chapter of history the theme of which is the comradeship under arms of East and West these humble camp followers deserve an honoured place.

In 1885, at the time of the Penjdeh incident, India passed through a crisis similar, though in a less degree, to that with which the country was faced in the first week of August, 1914. Then, as now, the Ruling Chiefs and Feudatory Princes came forward with offers of aid. It was the Nizam of Hyderabad who first offered a large sum out of his revenues to Government to swell the war chest. Financial aid naturally suggested a contribution of troops ; but in those days the local corps of the Ruling Chiefs were not trained and equipped on the same lines as the Indian Army. That they should be serviceable on the field this was necessary, and out of the recognition of the need the Imperial Service Corps had its origin.

The suggestion that the States should provide troops rather than gold as their contribution to the maintenance of peace commended itself to the Ruling Chiefs as well as to Government. Not only would these new corps lend added security to our frontiers ; they would also provide an honourable and useful career to men of good family and military antecedents, a class who during long periods of peace and inaction might well deteriorate.

There are races who suffer through suppressed chivalry, who feel the burden of peace. There was tragic pathos in the rust of the sword in States like Hyderabad, Gwalior, Jodhpur, and Jammu. The old military caste had lost its occupation.

At the beginning of the great war the veteran Sir Pertab Singh, Maharaja Regent of Jodhpur, made an affecting speech to his subjects on the eve of his departure for the front. He told them that Englishmen were shedding their blood like water for a great cause. Englishmen had always been ready to do so, and had done so many years ago for the Rajput States, and were ready to do so again. Now was the time for the Rajputs to show their gratitude, and, in turn, be prepared to shed their blood for the King-Emperor. That is the spirit in which the Rajput Chiefs regard the British connexion ; and the same ties unite us and the Sikh and Mahomedan Rulers. More than a century ago we saved the Nizam's dominion from the Mahrattas and other encroaching neighbours.

The Cis-Sutlej Sikh States of Patiala, Nabha, and Jind would have been swallowed up by Ranjit Singh but for the protection of the British Raj. A few years later these same States performed signal service for us during the Mutiny in keeping the road open from the North to Delhi. Mutual services, fidelity to the pledged word, splendid military traditions, bind the British Government and their trusted allies by an indissoluble tie.

The Imperial Service Troops* were organized on the same lines as the Class-Company regiments of the Indian Army, and as far as possible are recruited from the subjects of their respective Rulers, and not as in former days from outside the States. They are trained and inspected by picked British Officers of the Indian Army and commanded when possible by their Chief himself or one of his kin. In war time they are attached to the Regular Army under much the same status as the troops of allies. When the European War broke out they had already seen service in China, Somaliland, in the Relief of Chitral, Tirah, and the Swat and Mohmund Expeditions. Whenever there was trouble on the Frontier the Ruling Princes came forward with offers of military service ; but these were often necessarily disappointed, and the Chiefs might well begin to feel that their soldierly occupation was gone, that their fine troops were to play a spectacular part merely in the Imperial Army.

When war was declared they came forward to a man and put all their troops and the resources of their States at the service of the King-Emperor.† They offered their swords,

---

* Twenty-seven of the larger States in India maintain Imperial Service Troops. The total strength of these forces is : Cavalry, ten regiments of four squadrons each, and one of three squadrons, with eight squadrons in corps of lesser strength than three squadrons. Infantry, six eight-company battalions and six six-company battalions. Artillery, the two Kashmir mountain batteries ; four companies of sappers, five mule or pony transport corps, aggregating 1,650 army carts, two camel transport corps aggregating 1,200 camels, a fighting camel corps of 500 rifles, and three transport escorts for the protection of transport corps, provided by the State.

The services of every corps were immediately placed at the disposal of the Government of India on the outbreak of war. The Viceroy accepted from twelve States contingents of cavalry, infantry, sappers, and transport, besides a camel corps from Bikanir. These troops did not all land in France, details being detached to East Africa, Egypt, and the Persian Gulf.

† From among the many Princes and Nobles who volunteered for active service, the Viceroy selected the Chiefs of Jodhpur, Bikanir, Kishengarh, Rutlam, Sachin, Patiala, Sir Pertab Singh, Regent of Jodhpur, the Heir-Apparent of Bhopal, and a brother of the Maharaja of Cooch Behar, together with other Cadets of noble families.

[*Elliott & Fry.*

LIEUT-GEN. SIR JAMES WILLCOCKS,
K.C.S.I., K.C.M.G., D.S.O.

Commanding Indian Army Corps.

their jewelry, their horses, their troops, their lives. The Nizam of Hyderabad, as in 1885, came forward with a gift of all his horses and sixty lakhs of rupees (£400,000) to meet the expenses of the 1st Hyderabad Imperial Service Lancers, maintained by the State, and the 20th Deccan Horse, of which he is Colonel. The Maharaja of Mysore offered the princely gift of fifty lakhs of rupees. The Maharaja Scindia contributed a Red Cross motor ambulance fleet and, in combination with the Begum of Bhopal and other Chiefs, a hospital ship. All this was in addition to large contributions to patriotic funds. Every Prince gave according to his resources. In the Legislative Council an Indian member stated the desire of the people of India, in addition to the military assistance afforded, to share in the heavy financial burdens imposed by the war. The resolution was supported by representatives of various races and creeds, and was carried without a single dissentient. The people of India, the innumerable millions under the sole control of the Government, were equally lavish in their outpourings and their demonstrations of loyalty.

Hundreds of telegrams were received by the Viceroy every day from communities and associations, religious, social and political, of all classes, castes and creeds, and also from individuals, offering their resources or asking for opportunities to prove their loyalty by personal service.

And from beyond the borders the response was the same. From the grim Khyber, from Las Bela and Kelat in Beluchistan, from the mountain heights of Chitral, promises of assistance and appeals for enrolment were pressed upon the Government of India. The Prime Minister of Nepal, the great Gurkha State, offered the army he controls. The Dalai Lama of Tibet offered a thousand of those brave and kindly men who, in 1904, opposed our advance to Lhasa with their matchlocks and jingalls and bore us no ill-will for the toll they had to pay. The incarnation of Avalokitesvara, who was himself a fugitive at Urga in Mongolia, had since sought asylum with us from a less merciful foe. And now in every *gompa* in Tibet, from holy Kailas by the Mansarowar Lake to the "precipice-encircled" monasteries of the Eastern Tsang-Po, prayers were chanted for the success of our arms and for the happiness of the souls of all victims of war. The monks droned them in litanies to the sound of drums and cymbals and conch shells in the dark halls, dimly lit with butter-lamps, under the images of the impassive Buddha.

[*Elliott & Fry.*

LT.-GENERAL H. B. B. WATKIS, C.B.
Commanding Lahore Division, Indian Army.

The King-Emperor's message* of September 9 to the Princes and Peoples of his Indian Empire, in response to their devoted offers of service, sent a thrill of enthusiastic loyalty throughout the country.

* The King-Emperor's Message was as follows :—
To the Princes and Peoples of My Indian Empire :

During the past few weeks the peoples of my whole Empire at home and Overseas have moved with one mind and purpose to confront and overthrow an unparalleled assault upon the continuity of civilization and the peace of mankind.

The calamitous conflict is not of my seeking. My voice has been cast throughout on the side of peace. My Ministers earnestly strove to allay the causes of strife and to appease differences with which my Empire was not concerned. Had I stood aside when in defiance of pledges to which my Kingdom was a party the soil of Belgium was violated and her cities laid desolate, when the very life of the French nation was threatened with extinction, I should have sacrificed my honour and given to destruction the liberties of my Empire and of mankind. I rejoice that every part of the Empire is with me in this decision.

Paramount regard for treaty faith and the pledged word of rulers and peoples is the common heritage of England and of India.

Among the many incidents that have marked the unanimous uprising of the populations of my Empire in defence of its unity and integrity, nothing has moved me more than the passionate devotion to my Throne expressed both by my Indian subjects and by the Feudatory Princes and the Ruling Chiefs of India, and their prodigal offers of their lives and their resources

In the great wave of sentiment that swept over the country there is no doubt that many who had long imagined themselves hostile to the British connexion were carried off their feet. The loyalty of the Indian Princes had never been questioned ; it was taken for granted that the army would be true to their salt ; the agricultural and industrial classes, the real bone and marrow of the country, it was rightly presumed, would remain stanch to the British cause. But there was another class, whose sympathies had long seemed estranged, a class from which the Government of India might naturally expect embarrassment when the Empire was engaged in a life or death struggle with a foreign Power.

The most extraordinary thing about the

in the cause of the Realm. Their one-voiced demand to be foremost in the conflict has touched my heart, and has inspired to the highest issues the love and devotion which, as I well know, have ever linked my Indian subjects and myself. I recall to mind India's gracious message to the British nation of good-will and fellowship, which greeted my return in February, 1912, after the solemn ceremony of my Coronation Durbar at Delhi, and I find in this hour of trial a full harvest and a noble fulfilment of the assurance given by you that the destinies of Great Britain and India are indissolubly linked.

MOTOR AMBULANCES PRESENTED TO THE BRITISH ARMY BY HIS HIGHNESS THE MAHARAJA SCINDIA OF GWALIOR.

attitude of the Indian people during the war was the suspension of political agitation. In Europe the extreme radicals, anti-militarists, syndicalists, became patriots in their country's hour of need. In India, too, many of those whose whole business had been the fomenting of discontent rallied to the defence of the Empire. But in our Indian Dependency the phenomenon was the more remarkable as the antagonism to the British Government had its seeds in racial animosity.

The prophecies of trouble in India during a European war were not fulfilled. Germany had miscalculated. But it was not Germany alone that was at fault in her reading of the temper of the Indian people. There was surprise in England that the clamour of sedition should be stilled at the moment when the British Empire seemed most vulnerable.

The truth is the disaffected class had made itself articulate out of all proportion to its numerical strength and social influence in the country. When the call to arms came, the millions responded, and the voice of discontent was no longer audible in the outburst of enthusiastic loyalty. The carping critic of Government, the radical Indian doctrinaire, the "political missionary," were silenced, discountenanced or converted. Volunteers from the non-military classes asked to be enrolled in ambulance corps and sent to the front. The twice-deported Tilak, addressing a meeting at Poona, urged them to sink differences and to support Government in every possible way. "The presence of English rulers," he said, "was desirable, even from the point of view of Indian self-interest."

It would, of course, be absurd to pretend that the ghost of political agitation had been laid by the maladroit exorcism of the Kaiser, or that the uncompromising nationalist politician will rest content with the prestige that military achievement has won for his countrymen. Greater claims will be advanced. India, like Ireland, will always present a difficult and thorny problem of administration, and just as Ireland still has her Sinn Fein extremists, so has India still her anarchists and her fanatical bomb-throwers.

At the beginning of the war the German can have been nothing more to the masses of India than a different kind of white man, a sahib of an unknown quantity. No fear of menace to their comfort or liberties, no evil dream of a universal *Kultur*, could have

[*Elliott & Fry.*

HIS HIGHNESS THE AGA KHAN.

inspired their loyalty, which was quite spontaneous and genuine. But in distilling the soul of goodness out of things evil we must recognize our debt to the Kaiser in the rallying of numbers of the disaffected class to the Throne. His officials have carried on the work of reconciliation. On the deeply religious and sensitive soul of India the barbarities of Louvain left an indelible impression. The profaning of sacred places is the unforgivable sin. The Huns who shelled the cathedral of Reims and dropped bombs on Notre Dame would not be likely to spare the mosque of Delhi or the temples of Benares or Trivandrum.

Also it should be remembered that nearly every educated Indian of the middle-class is, through the nature of his circumstances and education, a liberal. Militarism and bureaucracy are his bugbears; the mailed fist and the Prussian heel symbols of Gehenna. A distinguished Bengali politician expressed the feelings of his countrymen when he said: "We cannot expect the same privileges from Prussian militarism or look for political concession at the hands of the hooligans of Potsdam. Hence our abhorrence of any procedure which, by embarrassing the 'Government as by law established,' may weaken the links that bind us to the Empire." The attitude of India at the beginning of the war was even more eloquently expressed by Mr. Malaviya, in his speech in the Viceroy's Legislative Council.

"India recognises her duty at this present moment," he said, "and, God willing, will

22—2

[Vandyk.

HIS HIGHNESS
THE YUVARAJA OF MYSORE.

manfully discharge that duty, that no sacrifice
of men or money will be grudged in order that
the British arms should triumph, in order that
the success of the British arms should establish
the triumph of right over might, of civilization
over the military barbarism of Germany, of
ordered freedom over military slavery."

The arrival of the Indian Corps at Marseilles
was a landmark in history. No episode in
this extraordinary war was more remarkable
or, for Britons, more inspiring than the presence
of Indian troops on the Continent of Europe.
To India, the event was, if possible, of even
greater significance. The march of her sons
through the streets of Marseilles was a kind
of initiation. A phantom had been laid that
shadowed her prestige. Invisible barriers had
been broken down. New vistas of honour were
opened out before her.

That hot September morning when the
interminable line of transports was seen through
telescopes at dawn creeping along by the
Château d'If and the Islands of Pomique and
Ratonneau, will long be remembered in Marseilles. No more romantic landing can have
been witnessed by the old sea-city in all its
varied past. Daily for a couple of months the
streets had echoed to the tread of a medley of
races—Zouaves and Turcos from Algeria, white-
turbanned swarthy Moors from Morocco, coal-
black negroes from Senegal, and a score of
different units from the South of France, but
the welcome the Marseillais gave the Indians
transcended all other demonstrations in spon-
taneity and warmth.

Throughout the forenoon while the troops
were landing excitement had been steadily
rising in the city, and the dispatching of the
British and Indian soldiers through the streets
in the afternoon *en route* to their camps was a
signal for the whole of Marseilles to turn out
en fête. From the Cannebière to the Prado the
gaily-dressed streets were packed with a seething
mass of humanity.

First came a detachment of Sikhs, for the
greater part head and shoulders above the
spectators. They received the plaudits of the
crowd with the imperturbable smiling com-
posure of the Oriental. The police guarding the
road were swept aside, the ranks were rushed,
men and women shook the sepoys by the hand,
and young girls showered flowers upon them,
pinning roses in their tunics and in their turbans.
Tricolours were distributed with prodigal
favour, old ladies with bitter memories of '70
pressed forward the better to admire these
handsome, bearded men, and it would be difficult to conjure up anything more touching than
the sight of those frail women patting the
bronzed giants on the back and calling down
blessings on their heads.

So it proceeded for hours. The troops filed
past to the cries of "*Vive l'Angleterre!*" "*Vivent
les Hindous!*" When the Gurkhas came along
marching to the time of the "Marseillaise"
played on the pipes, the crowd gave the troops

[Vandyk.

HIS HIGHNESS
THE MAHARAJA OF GWALIOR.

the pavement and stood in the cobbled streets, cheering. Men, mountain battery mules, officers on their chargers, marched along under the very awnings of the café *terrasses*, while the spectators stood on chairs and tables waving hats, sticks and handkerchiefs, and crying " *Vive l'Angleterre !* " " *Vivent les Indiens !* " " *Vivent les Hindous !* "

When it was dusk and the last troops had gone by, the crowd followed them to their camps at St. Marcel and La Barrasse and Borély, and watched them cook their evening meal while the camp fires twinkled in the dark, and the smell of wood smoke rose in the air. It was a historic camp this, pitched by the men of Ind on the soil of France between the land-locked harbour and the stately garden of the Borély.

A month later the Indian Cavalry Division arrived. The increasing volume of support was more than physical ; every strange unit was a separate refutation of Bernhardi's " biologically just " war. If the war we were waging had not been as just as the constitution of our Empire, Sikhs, Gurkhas, Rajputs, Jats, Pathans and Punjabi Musulmans would not have been fighting our battles in France. No wonder the Berlin professors counted on disharmony in so complex an organism as ours, of such subtly individualized parts. Our Empire in the East is a piece of creative work of which *Kultur* has not the secret.

[*Vandyk.*

HIS HIGHNESS THE MAHARAJA HOLKAR OF INDORE.

The sight of the troopships in the Quai d'Areng, some of them prizes of war converted to our purposes of transport, brought home to us once more the significance of our command of the sea. For over a century India has been to us another base from which we have been able to pour troops on distant shores when emergency dictated. Earlier European up-heavals had entailed the sending out of expeditionary forces from our Indian Army, though this was the first occasion on which they landed on European soil.

After the disembarcation of the first two Divisions at Marseilles little was heard of the Indian contingent during the next month. The need of acclimatization, the delay in the provision of suitably-warm clothing, the sorry condition of their horses after the sea voyage, held them long in reserve. The continued silence and mystery about their movements may well have led the Germans in the firing line to believe them a myth, or to think that they had been sent over, as one of their journals suggested, for merely spectacular uses—an illusion which was afterwards rudely dispelled. In England the mystification was increased in the last week of October by the appearance of the Indian Mountain Batteries in the New Forest, which drew crowds of motorists and

[*Vandyk.*

HIS HIGHNESS THE MAHARAJA OF BIKANIR.

[*Vanayk.*

**HIS HIGHNESS
THE MAHARAJA OF PATIALA.**

pedestrians to their camp. The throng of
sightseers disgorged from the cars and cabs
gave the scene the appearance of Derby Day.
The impression they took away with them was
of a fine and wiry-looking crowd, lean and hard,
and having a noticeably older air than the men
of an ordinary British regiment. The tales of
prowess that began to pour in from France did
not surprise anyone.

The reader who wishes to sift fact from
fiction will do well to remember that no story
that was current before the end of October,
when the Indian troops were first engaged, has
any foundation. The story of the Gurkhas who
stole through the enemy's lines and blew up the
powder magazine is a fabrication. The eight
German sentries who gave up the ghost on a
still night to eight stealthy Gurkhas with no
more protest than a rattle in the throat ; that

wave of Prussian Guards which was only
checked by Nepalese knives and Sikh bayonets
may live in romance, but not in history.
"Bengali" Lancers do not dismount in hordes
of twenty thousand strong and charge the
enemy with their spears. The Gurkha does not
fling his knife like a boomerang. And there
is no inhibition against his drawing it for
peaceful purposes. It will cut wood at a pinch
and potatoes, and may be honourably un-
sheathed without drawing blood. So the story
of the ladies of Marseilles who offered their
finger tips with Roman fortitude to make good
this sacrificial rite must go with the rest.

The tale of the Gurkhas' murderous knives,
which whistled through the air as the Germans
rose from their cover, seemed at first a palpable
" invention," but the story may have its origin
in honest misconception. The Sikh wears an
iron quoit on his turban—it is one of the five
badges presented by his Guru—and though
now only a symbol it was once a formidable
weapon. The significance of the quoit may
have been explained with other strange Eastern
lore, and the story evolved in some tired brain
in which images of quoit and kukri, Sikhs and
Gurkhas, past and present, danced confusedly
together.

Most of the tales of Sikh and Gurkha prowess
were abroad before the Indian troops were
engaged at all, but the true soldierly qualities
of these men are too well known to suffer
through such fantastic advertisement.

The tall, bearded Sikhs, the sturdy, compact,
little Gurkha, with his Mongol face and his
look of terrier-like tenacity, seem to have
captured the public imagination. One heard
little of the other Indian troops, amongst whom
were to be found the same high qualities. The
Pathan in particular is a fine figure-head. Take
the trans-frontier tribesman. Man to man in
open country, on the hillside or in forest the
German with his two or three years' training
on parade grounds or in manœuvres can be no
match for him. These men are cradled in war.
Tribal vendettas are the breath of life to them.
The young Afridi has been the mark for a
bullet from his infancy. He will glide through
the enemy's lines on a dark night, without a
quickening of the pulse, and lie up like a hare
in its form while the lead splashes against the
rock by his side. He knows nothing of mass
tactics. His every move is instinctive, individual. The Cis-frontier Pathan, who suffers
from protection, being answerable to the penal

code, is almost as good a man. Security, the magistrate, and the police may have taken something off the fine edge of his daring. Still, a fat Prussian the other side of a *nullah* would have small chance against him.

Then there is the Rajput, who with his straw-fire *élan* and unexampled traditions of chivalry is probably as good a man on a horse as any in the world, and whose courage glows in the pages of Indian history.

The Dogra, the Baluchi, the Mahratta, the Jat, the Punjabi Musulman—all come of a hard-bitten fighting stock ; nerves are not in their compositions. A British trooper, who had seen the Indians in the trenches during their baptism of shrapnel fire, said :

" They did not seem to mind. They poked their heads out when a shell went by and stared at the hole it made as if it had been a firework."

That is exactly what one might expect. Indians love a *tomasha*, a museum, a little magic, an entertainment. But it must be remembered that until this war the artillery had always been on our side. Those strange supernatural forces which the Sahibs could command had been their allies. They could count on the Olympians.

No one has ever questioned the courage of the Indian troops. In fighting with naked steel and lead they are " lords of themselves." One has always counted on them in a cavalry charge, or a bayonet rush on foot, or in holding a position against rifle fire. But where the infernal machinery comes in it might well be another matter. To lie up in a trench all day under heavy shrapnel fire directed by an aeroplane with a sixth sense is no part of their tradition. They like to stalk their man and shoot him. But in this war, mines, barbed-wire entanglements, shells, siege guns, mitrailleuses, all the machinery of the " higher civilization," were most palpable phenomena on the other side. The miracles might seem to be against them.

" Sahib, why did you not teach us these things ? " a sepoy said reproachfully to his British officer, unconscious that the same wizardry was being brought into play by his own Sahibs against the enemy.

Yet, with British officers whom they knew and who knew them to lead them and to hearten them, they did not flinch when the parachute flares came rocketing over their trenches and the air was rent with the voice of a thousand

INDIAN LANCER OUTPOST.

devils, and the mitrailleuses poured in their deadly fire as if it were day. The Indians who gave themselves to our cause did so at a greater sacrifice than our own, for the meaning of the struggle did not touch them as nearly as it did us. To them the German was merely a savage with diabolical inspirations, a merely physical menace. The gospel of Treitschke did not trouble their philosophy. Honour—personal, communal and national—was the only reward they looked for. The first advance of the Indians under machine-gun fire was a new spiritual triumph for the East.

From Marseilles the Indian contingent went to Orleans. There was a long period of waiting between their arrival there and their entrainment for the front. The delay must have been especially trying to troops who were anxious to prove themselves in such entirely new condi-

ONE OF GARDNER'S HORSE :
A man of the 2nd Lancers (late 2nd Bengal Lancers.)

tions of warfare. India knew that her ancient chivalry was a household word in Europe, but there were still untried fields to conquer ; other kinds of nerve, resource, and coolness were called for if she were to carry on unbroken her military traditions into the scientific battle-fields of the twentieth century No one knew the temper of his troops better than their General, and it was a stirring appeal that he issued to them in the order of the day, October 10.*

There was still another fortnight to pass before the Indians were to hear the sound of the guns. In the meantime the ancient city of Orleans was invested with a new romance. The ancestors of the Rajputs who filed under the statue of Joan of Arc held the same traditions of chivalrous womanhood as the Maid of Orleans. The women of Chitore fought beside their husbands, or, when all was lost, passed into an underground sepulchre of flame prepared for their ashes. The Jodhpur Lancers rode through the Place du Martroi like men conscious of a past. More than any race the Rajput loves distinction. And they cling to

* Soldiers of the Indian Army Corps,
We have all read with pride the gracious message of his Majesty the King-Emperor to his troops from India.
On the eve of going into the field to join our British comrades, who have covered themselves with glory in this great war, it is our firm resolve to prove ourselves worthy of the honour which has been conferred on us as representatives of the Army of India.
In a few days we shall be fighting as has never been our good fortune to fight before and against enemies who have a long history.
But is their history as long as yours ? You are the descendants of men who have been mighty rulers and great warriors for many centuries. You will never forget this. You will recall the glories of your race. Hindu and Mahomedan will be fighting side by side with British soldiers and our gallant French Allies. You will be helping to make history. You will be the first Indian soldiers of the King-Emperor who will have the honour of showing in Europe that the sons of India have lost none of their ancient martial instincts and are worthy of the confidence reposed in them.
In battle you will remember that your religions enjoin on you that to give your life doing your duty is your highest reward.
The eyes of your co-religionists and your fellow-countrymen are on you. From the Himalayan Mountains, the banks of the Ganges and Indus, and the plains of Hindustan, they are eagerly waiting for the news of how their brethren conduct themselves when they meet the foe. From mosques and temples their prayers are ascending to the God of all, and you will answer their hopes by the proofs of your valour.
You will fight for your King-Emperor and your faith, so that history will record the doings of India's sons and your children will proudly tell of the deeds of their fathers.
JAMES WILLCOCKS,
Lieut.-General
Commg. Indian Army Corps.

a boast of heraldry that ennobles the poorest ; for every true Rajput is in some distant collateral way the kin of the Maharana and can lay claim to unmixed blood for close on two thousand years. Tod, their devoted chronicler, traces their armorial bearings to a date before Troy, and believes that the ancestors of Udaipur carried their Palladium into the field against Alexander. "There is not a village," he says, "that has not had its Thermopylæ, and scarcely a city that has not produced its Leonidas."

The first four Indian Princes to land on the soil of France were Rajputs, all, curiously enough, of the Rathore stock, of the bluest blood in India. These were the Maharajas of Jodhpur, Bikanir, Kishengarh and Sir Pertab Singh of Idar. Next came the young Maharaja of Idar, the adopted son of Sir Pertab Singh, who abdicated to become Regent of Jodhpur. Sir Pertab is one of the most famous of living Indian soldiers, and has rendered conspicuous service to the British Crown. He served on the staff of the Generals commanding both in the Mohmund Expedition of 1897 and in the Tirah Campaign of 1898. In 1900 he went with the British force to China in command of the Jodhpur Lancers. Few would have recognized in that short, well-built soldierly veteran in khaki the brilliant and spectacular figure who led the Imperial Service Corps at Delhi and rode in the Jubilee procession of Queen Victoria, and in the Coronation processions of King Edward and King George. Sir Pertab was over seventy, probably the oldest man in the field, and he came to Europe with the avowed intention of dying a soldier's death. "To die in battle is not to die," he said, and the old Rajput spirit would not be denied— the spirit in which his ancestors put on their saffron robes, the national sign of *combat à l'outrance*, and charged into Ala-ud-Din's host and fell as they clove a path through the foe. His brother's grandson, the Maharaja Soomair Singh of Jodhpur, and his daughter's son, Kanwar Prithi Singh of Bera, came with him, and three of his nephews and several noblemen in his regiment. The Maharaja of Kishengarh also joined his kinsman, and many officers had Indians of high birth in the ranks, as syces, or grooms, and personal servants, as it was impossible for them to go in any other capacity.

The young Maharaja of Jodhpur, a boy of seventeen, brought with him his Lancers, the

INDIAN 2nd LANCERS.

famous Sardar Rissala, lithe men and keen, great horsemen, equally efficient with sword and lance. These were the first Imperial Service Corps to land in Europe. The Patiala Lancers and Jind Infantry were detached for East Africa ; the Bikanir Camel Corps for Egypt, where their high mettle was soon put to the test in an engagement in which they were attacked by superior forces and drove the enemy off.

The Jodhpur contingent were billeted in a seigneurial château on the banks of the Loire. It may be imagined how the Lancers exercising in the park attracted the bourgeois from the city. Through all these weeks Orleans was a strange mixture of East and West. The country people, dressed in black, would be making their way to the Cathedral, there to pray for the safety of their kinsmen at the front, or loitering at the street corners talking over the latest news, when suddenly into the midst of all these would emerge from a side street with all the sudden Indian irrelevancy of a dream, an Indian forage cart, driven by an imperturbably smiling Asiatic, his little mules, all befringed

GROUP OF INDIAN OFFICERS.

and iron-yoked, leaning heavily against each other as if for comfort or support in this strange land. Next a flock of sheep and bearded blunt-faced goats passes down the boulevard, driven by Punjabi Musulmans, who to ring them round safely are almost as numerous as their charge. One of them carries a lamb born in the train. Another calls out instinctively in his own language to an old market woman, who is in danger of being run over by an Indore transport wagon, "*Buddhi, Buddhi, nikal jao*" (old woman! old woman! get out of the way). Next a Pathan sowar canters by on a country-bred, and the traffickers look up and admire his loose and easy seat, wondering perhaps what is the significance of the smart *kula* on his turban and thinking him a prince. A regiment of Dogras comes along, fine upstanding men, not unlike the Pathan in feature. They, too, pass on, while the Place continues its business of buying and selling—but always with apprecia-

tive comments, "*En voilà qui feront danser le Kaiser*," or "*Ils sont joliment solides tout de même*."

Through a gateway visible from the next street there is an Indian bakery, two long rows of domed mud kilns—*lepai-ed*, as they call it in the East, or plastered with mud, but without the concomitant of cowdung, which to the Indian mind is needful for cleanliness. There are a score of them on either side, each with its turbaned cook tending the ash fire. These men carry their atmosphere with them. There is nothing in that yard hooded with fog to remind one that one is not at Jullundur still on a thick November morning. The native soldiers did not frequent the city as a rule unless they were marching through, so the *citoyenne* had to bestow her offerings on the humbler camp-followers. The daughter of the concierge would run out into the street and pin her tri-colour to the coat of a Musulman driver. The *blanchisseuse* would hold out a cigarette bash-fully to a Sikh farrier, who is forbidden by all the laws of his Gurus to smoke. Her child, perhaps, would be honoured by a joy ride in the mule transport wagon as far as the corner of the street.

By no means all the Indian troops which left Karachi and Bombay landed in France. Many were sent to East Africa. Then Turkey's appearance in the struggle, as the vacillating dupe of Germany in her efforts to cut off our communication with the East, made it neces-sary to divert others to the Suez Canal, the Persian Gulf, and the Red Sea.

Nothing during the war illustrated the devotion of our Indian subjects to the Crown more than the detachment of the Moslem element from German intrigue. When Turkey entered on the scene our enemies expected a pan-Islamic upheaval and a demonstration in force against the Allies. They pictured a Mahomedan rising in Northern India in which the Jehad would be preached in all the mosques from Cawnpore to Peshawur, and a fanatical army of the faithful would press over the frontier carrying the torch through the tribal countries into Persia and Afghanistan. Emissaries from Turkey, they believed, had

already prepared the field for the conflagration, and lying notices about the Holy War were hoisted on placards in front of the Indians' trenches or dropped harmlessly from aeroplanes among the British troops. The response of Islam must have been a bitter draught for German aspirations. In every mosque in India prayers were offered for the success of British arms. The King of Afghanistan pro-claimed his neutrality. The frontier tribes remained quiet. The Moslem political associa-tions denounced Turkey's unholy alliance. Mahomedan journals, which in times of peace had been most bitter in their attacks upon the administration, urged their communities to remain loyal to the Crown. The Sheikh-ul-Islam of Egypt and the leading Ulema appealed to all Egyptian Moslems to be calm and peaceful.

In Egypt, too, our Moslem soldiers were greeted by their co-religionists, and sat chatting with the white-bearded mullahs on the steps of the mosques as if it were the most natural thing in the world that they should be called out of the East to fight against the Turk.

Two years before the most sanguine prophet of our Imperial unity could not have believed these things possible. When Italy's suzerainty was recognized in Tripoli, when the seat of

DISEMBARKING FROM TRANSPORTS AT PLYMOUTH.

INDIAN TROOPS MARCHING TO CAMP.

the Caliphate was threatened by the Balkan States, a flame of resentment at the invasion of Turkey and at the supposed sympathy of England with the aggressors spread over Moslem India. The wiseheads understood the necessity of England's detachment in the struggles of the Turkish Empire, but young blood was not so cool, and our non-interference was resented as if it had been an expression of active hostility. Though the movement was anti-British, and illogically so, we cannot altogether withhold our sympathy, as the human nature that prompted it is clear and intelligible— the instinct of the man who is struck wantonly to hit back, if not at the actual aggressor, at the man nearest him.

The rally of Moslem India to the British Throne when we actually engaged in hostilities against the Turks only two years after this crisis might well surprise the wire-pullers in Berlin. The same field hospital which was sent to Turkey during the Balkan War was offered by the Moslems of Delhi for the Indian Expeditionary Force in France. Politicians who bitterly attacked the Raj when it was in no danger hurried to its support when it was assailed and in the throes of a life and death struggle. There is health in such championship and seeds of great hope of a generous understanding in the future.

The best Indian Moslem opinion lost no time in ranging itself. The Nizam of Hyderabad issued a manifesto in which he impressed upon all Mahomedans that it was their bounden duty to adhere firmly to their old and tried loyalty to the British Government.

"I repeat and reiterate," he said, "that in the crisis before us Mahomedan inhabitants of India, especially subjects of this State, should, if they care for their own welfare and prosperity, remain firm and wholehearted in their loyalty and obedience, and swerve not a hair's breadth from their devotion to the British Government, whose cause I am convinced is just and right. They should keep the sacred tie which binds a subject people to their rulers and in no case allow themselves to be beguiled by the wiles of anyone into a course of open or secret sedition against the British Government."

The Begum of Bhopal struck the true note of Mahomedan loyalty when she declared in open durbar before her people that she would always remain loyal to the traditions which exist between the Bhopal State and the British Government, seeing that these traditions were binding on her not only as a ruling chief under the protection of the British Government, but also as a disciple of Islam, which enjoins upon all its followers the sanctity of a promise.

Two resolutions passed by the All-India Moslem League voiced the general feeling of Mahomedans in India:

Firstly, " that the Council of the All-India Moslem League gives expression once more to the deep-rooted loyalty and sincere devotion of Musulmans of India to the British Crown and assures his Excellency the Viceroy that participation of Turkey in the present war does not and cannot affect that loyalty in the least degree, and the Council is confident that no Musulman in India will swerve a hair's breadth from his paramount duty to his Sovereign."

Secondly, " that the Council of the All-India Moslem League expresses its deep gratitude to the British Government for the assurances given to its Muslim subjects as to the immunity of the Holy Places of Islam in Arabia and other places from attack or molestation and for obtaining similar assurances from its Allies."

Responsible Indian Moslems realized as a rule the nature of the intrigue into which the Young Turks had been drawn. They also recognized that Turkey was divided. The specious call of a " Holy War " waged under an infidel standard did not deceive them, and they had no mind to be dragged into the arena on the heels of Germany. The Aga Khan sent messages to his millions of adherents spread over India, the Persian Gulf, the Indian Borderland, Burma, the Straits Settlements, and throughout Africa directing them to place themselves and their resources at the disposal of the local British authorities, and to be prepared for any duty that might be assigned to them. In a speech delivered in London, he expressed his conviction that Germany was the most dangerous enemy of Turkey and other Moslem countries, as she was the Power most anxious to enter by " peaceful penetration " Asia Minor and Southern Persia. She had been passing for years, he said, as a sort of protector of Islam—though Heaven forbid that they should have such an immoral protector. Happily, so far as the Moslem subjects of the King were concerned, these efforts were absolutely futile. They would never break down the strong wall of their loyalty, which was based on the consciousness that their dearest interests, religious as well as civil, were guaranteed to them by British rule more securely than they could be by any other dominion. " All Indians knew," he concluded, " that if Britain was ever weakened, India's aspirations, India's whole future, would go to pieces."

When the last day of the Moharram had passed quietly in the bazaars of India Moslem troops had been engaged against Turks and Beduins in Egypt and the Persian Gulf.

The first Indian troops to be engaged through Turkey's adventure in the war were the Bikanir Camel Corps, Imperial Service troops, who had already seen service in China and Somaliland. On November 20 Captain Chope and Lieutenant Mohammed Anis with twenty of the corps were patrolling between Bir-el-Nuss and Katia to the east of the Canal. They were

INFANTRY CARRYING MAXIM INTO ACTION.

INDIAN MULE CART IN FRANCE.

attacked three times. The first two attacks were repulsed easily. On the third occasion they were attacked heavily on both flanks by a large body of horsemen. Captain Chope retired, dismounting his men, who fired as opportunity offered, while the enemy were firing from horseback. Lieutenant Mohammed Anis was shot during this period, but one of the Bikanir men took him up and carried him behind him on his camel. Unhappily, both were shot. Captain Chope succeeded in getting back to his supports, after beating off the enemy, with the loss of Lieutenant Anis, Subadar Abdu Khan, twelve men killed, and three men wounded.

The wide sphere over which forces of the Indian Army were operating at this time is realizable by the fact that an engagement was fought in Somaliland on the same day as the action of the Bikanir Camel Corps on the east of the Suez Canal, and this was to be followed up almost immediately by the news of a success in Turkish Arabia. At the same time Indian troops were garrisoning East Africa and ports on the Red Sea.

The full narrative of the subsidiary campaigns fought by the Indian Army in the neighbourhood of the Persian Gulf, the Suez Canal, the Red Sea, and in East Africa will provide material for other chapters.

CHAPTER XLII.

THE INDIAN ARMY IN THE TRENCHES.

INDIANS ARRIVE AT THE FRONT—FIRST ACTION AT NEUVE CHAPELLE—SUCCESS AND CONGRATU-
LATIONS—HIGHLANDERS AND GURKHAS—THE FIRST INDIAN V.C.—FUTILE GERMAN EFFORTS TO
SOW SEDITION—LORD ROBERTS IN FRANCE—HIS VISIT TO THE INDIANS—HIS DEATH—COLD
WEATHER—HARDSHIPS OF THE INDIANS—FOOD PROBLEMS—HOSPITAL ORGANIZATION—HEAVY
FIGHTING AT FESTUBERT—CAVALRY IN THE TRENCHES—SAPPERS AND MINERS—GERMAN RECOG-
NITION OF INDIAN PROWESS—THE GARHWALIS—THE KING AT BOULOGNE—VISIT TO THE INDIAN
HOSPITAL—INSPECTION OF THE TROOPS—EAST AND WEST : A NEW PHASE.

THE Lahore Division arrived in its concentration area in rear of the 2nd Corps on October 19 and 20. On the 22nd two battalions were ordered to proceed to Wulverghem in support of the Cavalry Corps.

The Meerut Division arrived shortly afterwards and took up the line of the 2nd Army Corps, operating on the front from Givenchy, west o Neuve Chapelle, to Champigny. The Lahore Division on the left stretched from Champigny northward to a point east of Estaires.

Two and a half battalions of these brigades were returned to the 2nd Corps when the Ferozepore Brigade joined the Indian Corps after its support of the Cavalry further north.

The Secunderabad Cavalry Brigade arrived in the area during November 1 and 2, and the Jodhpur Lancers came about the same time. These were all temporarily attached to the Indian Corps.

The Indian contingent was commanded by General Sir James Willcocks, K.C.S.I., K.C.M.G., D.S.O., whose knowledge of the Indian Army and distinguished record in frontier campaigns

rendered him signally fit for the command. Few living soldiers understood the sepoy better ; and it is perhaps no exaggeration to say that every Indian officer serving in the Force was known to him personally.

From October 25 the Lahore Division, omitting the two battalions which were supporting the Cavalry, were heavily engaged in assisting the 7th Brigade of the 2nd Corps in fighting round Neuve Chapelle. The line held by the Indian Corps was subjected to constant bombardment by the enemy's heavy artillery, followed up by infantry attacks.

October 28 will be a day memorable in the annals of the Indian Army. It was the first occasion on which the Indian troops were called upon to show their mettle on European soil. They were required to take part in an offensive against a strong position held by a force of the regular army of the greatest military Power in Europe. They responded splendidly. The objective was the village of Neuve Chapelle, a position of great tactical importance. Our trenches here presented something of a salient and could be enfiladed. The Seaforths had been particularly exposed and had lost heavily.

333

[*Vandyk.*

HIS HIGHNESS
THE GAEKWAR OF BARODA.

It was necessary to take the village and straighten up the line. The task of storming it was assigned to the 47th Sikhs, the 9th Bhopal Infantry, two companies of the 3rd Bombay Sappers and Miners, in conjunction with the 7th British Brigade. These troops stormed the village, advancing under heavy rifle and machine-gun fire; cleared it and occupied it. Sir John French, in his dispatch of November 20, made special mention of this action and the gallant conduct of the Indian troops, who distinguished themselves in the attack.

It will be remembered that on November 4 the Press Bureau issued a *communiqué* stating that the Indian troops had commenced to take their part in the operations of the British Expeditionary Force. This was the first official reference to the contingent since the landing at Marseilles. The village referred to was Neuve Chapelle. The Indians were described as advancing with a dash and resolution worthy of the highest traditions of the Army. They were also praised for their coolness under artillery fire. One of the first regiments to go into action was heavily shelled while entrenching. An officer who was present particularly observed the indifference of the men throughout this—to them—novel experience. It was noticed that after the first few shells they hardly troubled to look round.

After the action Sir James Willcocks received the following message from the Commander-in-Chief: "Please congratulate your Indian troops on their gallant conduct and express my gratitude to them."

ARRIVING AT CAMP IN FRANCE.

[*Vandyk.*

**HIS HIGHNESS
THE NAWAB OF BAHAWALPUR.**

The Corps Commander under whose orders the first units to be engaged had been temporarily placed also sent a warm message of congratulation and thanks.

The 47th Sikhs mentioned by Sir John French in his dispatch are one of the six Sikh class battalions in the Indian Army. The 14th, 15th, 16th, 35th and 36th make up the complement. In addition to these there are the three Pioneer Battalions, chiefly recruited from the Mazbi Sikhs. In this war the 36th took part in the capture of Tsing-Tau. The 14th Sikhs were one of the regiments that came within the observation of the German Headquarters Staff in China in 1900. Field-Marshal von Waldersee reviewed them on the racecourse at Shanghai and expressed his unbounded admiration for their splendid physique and soldierly bearing. In 1914 the Sikh class regiments were able to persuade the Germans more feelingly of their worth.

The 9th Bhopal Infantry, who also took part in the assault, are not, as is sometimes believed, Imperial Service Corps or local levies of the Bhopal State, but a battalion of the regular Indian Army. When the 9th Bengal Infantry were removed from the general line and included in the separate Gurkha line as the 9th Gurkhas, this battalion, which was originally a local battalion of the Bhopal Durbar, fell into its place. They were one of

the first Indian regiments engaged in the war and lost heavily in officers and men.

In the last week of October the 2nd Battalion of the 8th Gurkha Rifles, of the Bareilly Brigade, arrived in their trenches. They were immediately subjected to a terrific shell fire and found the position untenable. Their initial difficulties were increased by the depth of the trenches, which had been built for taller men. They were enfiladed by machine-gun fire and lost nearly all their British officers. In one of the trenches a havildar got his men together and led them back in the dark to the lines behind. After this heavy pounding the men felt a little lost and uncertain where they would find themselves. By a piece of good fortune they hit on the trenches of a Highland regiment. The Highlanders and Gurkhas are old comrades in arms. The Seaforths, in particular, have a tradition of good fellowship with these Nepalese hill-men which dates back to Mutiny days; they have fought side by side in many a North-West Frontier campaign. In India one often hears picturesque incidents of the entente. The Gurkhas felt themselves at home among their old friends.

No wonder the Indians felt lost at first in these strange conditions of warfare in a far country. Their training and their instincts had accustomed them to quite a different kind of fighting. They must have been in constant doubt. Even to distinguish German soldiers from French was not easy for them in the dark. When their English leaders were killed they had

[*Lafayette.*

**HIS HIGHNESS
THE MAHARAJA OF COOCH BEHAR.**

INFANTRY ADVANCING ACROSS A FIELD.

no language in which they could make themselves understood. Their stragglers were exposed to difficulties in the way of rejoining their units which it is almost impossible to exaggerate, and the Germans were quick to turn their bewilderment to account.

For three days—October 31, November 1 and 2—our lines were subjected to a terrific bombardment and continual infantry attacks. On November 2 a serious attack was developed against a portion of the line west of Neuve Chapelle. In one place the enemy broke through and the line was slightly bent back. The 2nd Gurkhas under Colonel Norie saved the situation in a gallant charge. The losses among officers and men in this affair were distressing. The 2nd Gurkhas are the famous Sirmoor battalion enlisted after the Nepal War. They, with the 60th Rifles, held the exposed flank of the ridge before Delhi from the first day to the last of the siege.

It was on October 31 at Hollebeke that Khudadad, a sepoy of the 129th Duke of Connaught's Own Beluchis, won the Victoria Cross. When the British officer in charge of the detachment had been wounded and the other guns put out of action by a shell, Khudadad, though himself severely wounded, remained working his gun until all the other five men of the machine gun detachment had been killed.

Khudadad was the first Indian to be awarded the Victoria Cross, though not actually the first to receive it. When the King, a month afterwards, presented the decoration on the field of battle the gallant sepoy was lying ill in hospital.

To the uninitiated the titles of Indian regiments are the cause of considerable confusion. It should be explained that Khudadad, though a sepoy in a Beluchi regiment, is not himself a Beluchi. Very few of the tribesmen of Beluchistan, a Mahomedan hill-race of Arab descent, serve in the Indian Army. The pure Beluchis, though a fine fighting stock, do not as a rule accept military service except under the tribal chiefs in their own local levies. The 127th, 129th and 130th Infantry, known as the Beluchi regiments, are recruited from Mahomedans of various tribes within the Indian frontier. They contain few genuine Beluchis.

A similar misconception is prevalent with regard to some of the so-called Sikh regiments. The 51st, 52nd, 53rd, 54th Sikhs are not, as their designation implies, class regiments of Sikhs, but mixed-company regiments composed of Sikhs, Dogras and Punjabi Musulmans.

They derive the title "Sikh" from the fact that they were taken over from the Sikh Durbar and drafted into the Indian Army after the conclusion of the Sikh War.

After the affair of Neuve Chapelle there was a comparative lull in the German offensive along the front held by the Indian contingent. The troops were exposed to a continual bombardment and to isolated night attacks all along the line, which were repulsed without heavy loss to our side ; but for nearly three weeks there was no fighting of the same severe character as the actions in which the 47th Sikhs, the 20th and 21st companies of the 3rd Bombay Sappers and Miners, and the 2nd and 8th Gurkhas lost so heavily.

In his dispatch covering this period Sir John French drew special attention to the initiative and resource of the Indian troops. One story told by the " Observer serving with the Indian Army Contingent in France " offers an unforgettable picture :

Two sepoys were on reconnaissance work over the ground separating our trenches from the Germans when a searchlight was turned on, and exposed one of them to the enemy's fire at short range. Concealment was hopeless, and the Indian was quick-witted enough to realize that no ordinary resource could save him. He immediately rose to his feet, and, in view of our trench, advanced, salaaming to the German trench. Its occupants, disconcerted by so unusual an advance, ceased fire. He still advanced, and approaching quite close to

[*Vandyk.*

HIS HIGHNESS
THE JAM SAHIB OF NAWANAGAR.

the trench, was allowed after some dumb show to enter. A dialogue then followed, which can be imagined more easily than it can be reproduced. The Germans, anxious to define his status, mentioned several Indian nationalities. He shook his head until the word Musulman occurred in the list. Then he nodded most vigorously. A moment later his questioners mentioned the British. He drew his hand across his throat with a lively gesture of disgust, adding, as he re-enacted the scene, a snarl. The Germans, very favourably encouraged by this indication, gave him some rations and a blanket.

He spent the night with them, and the next morning, by the use of his fingers, indicated to a superior officer who had been sent for to deal with so novel a case that there were twenty-five other Musulmans in his trench, whom, if released, he could certainly bring in. The Germans, completely deceived, gave him a final cup of coffee, and sent him on this promising errand. He rejoined his friends, who had long since given him up, with a report of far more than purely local interest, and he has deservedly gained both his promotion and a reputation for wit and presence of mind.

This story, though true, has the appearance of fable, and so is likely to become historical. It embodies as aptly as Æsop the German's psychological limitation, the Indian's subtlety of mind. The German is an adept contriver of wiles, but his sphere is the mechanical world. The Asiatic is a keen reader of men ; he possesses that insight into character and motive which the German lacks. He has also a sense of humour, in which the German is deficient. His diplomacy is as subtle as the Teuton's is crude. The clumsy efforts of the enemy to seduce him from his loyalty to the British Raj must have moved his laughter. Aeroplanes dropped seditious leaflets over the troops ; in these the patient German Professors sought to turn to material account their Oriental research and moral philosophy. Some fell among the British ;

INDIANS AND BRITISH AT A
FRENCH COFFEE STALL.

others addressed to Mahomedans, urging them to revolt, were written in Hindi, a character which few of them understand. They were told that the Sheikh-ul-Islam had on the occasion of the *Am Id* (a festival which does not exist) at Mecca (where he has not been and does not live) declared a Holy War on the Allies and that he had been joined by the Afghans.

The Indians replied by aeroplane in a proper spirit of defiance.

Another hail of sheets marked the descent from heaven of the *Ghadar*, an inflammatory journal published by an Indian revolutionary society in San Francisco. The authors of this poisonous leaflet had long been trying to sow the seeds of sedition in the army in the Punjab. Its arrival in Flanders was sufficient proof of Germany's intrigue with the disaffected Indian community in America, and lent support to the charge that the Kaiser's political missionaries were at the bottom of the Komagata Maru incident. "Ghadar" in Urdu means "Rebellion." The copies that were rained upon our troops urged them to kill their British officers and raise the standard of revolt in Hindustan. The incitement was more subtle and insidious than the appeals sounded in our

enemy's ordinary vehicles for the dissemination of "correct news," since it proceeded from men who understand the nature of the soil in which they are sowing.

One morning from a trench facing the Indians they hoisted up a huge placard on a pole with an inscription in large letters :

HOLY WAR.
INDIANS FIGHT ON OUR SIDE.
WOE TO THE BRITISH.

It at once became a target. The clumsy banner was an expression of the Teuton's political philosophy, concrete enough for the Indians to understand. The shots that riddled it symbolized their contempt.

If the German sedition-mongers could have seen the reception of Lord Roberts on November 12 by the Indians, or afterwards of the King, they might well have been disheartened. The visit of the veteran Field-Marshal to the Indian sepoys was one of the most dramatic incidents of the war. He arrived in Boulogne on November 11, and inspected the Indian Hospital Ship. The effect of his presence in the wards is graphically described in a letter received by the wife of one of the medical

INDIAN CAVALRY IN FRANCE.

THE LATE LORD ROBERTS AND INDIAN OFFICERS.

officers, and published in *The Times* of November 17 :

Lord Roberts came yesterday to inspect the ship and see the wounded. It was wonderful to see them directly he was recognized—they were all trying to get up and salute him. He was very kind to them all and heard all about their wounds, patting their heads and saying, " Poor chap, poor chap ! "

When he left the ward there was a general murmur from them all, blessing him. I have never seen such an affecting sight. The tears ran down the old man's face, but he turned round on me very sharp and said, " Your hospital is as near perfection as any I have seen. I congratulate you, sir." He then saw two native officers, both of whom knew him, wrote his name in my book, shook hands, and went.

He is simply worshipped by these men. Other generals have been round often, but there is never a sound. Yesterday was like a whole church full of men praying. Such is my first official experience of " Bobs," and it brings the water to my eyes. . . . His face is old but his back is as straight as a line, and his signature the large firm writing of a young man.

The next morning Lord Roberts arrived at the headquarters of the Corps, where he was welcomed by the General and inspected a guard of honour of mixed British and Indian troops which was drawn up to receive him. A thousand feet above a British aeroplane almost stationary, battling against a fifty-mile wind, kept guard over the greatest soldier of our Empire, and the continuous roll of guns came from the long line of battle but a few miles away. The Field-Marshal then visited the headquarters of the divisions and of the cavalry behind our lines, pausing here and there and speaking to men from every unit, British and Indian. They came straight up from the trenches to see him, looking hard, keen and soldierly. It was an inspiring moment for the Colonel-in-Chief as well as for the men. If any spirit had been dulled by the hardships of the trenches and the rude weather he must have gone back newly inspired. To the Indians he spoke in Hindustani with an encouraging sympathy that will never be forgotten. No other Englishman has attained to anything near the place which Lord Roberts has won in the heart of the Indian soldier unless it be John Nicholson—" Nikolsain Sahib," who has his niche in the Hindu Pantheon.

LONDON SCOTTISH AND INDIAN SOLDIERS IN CAMP.

It was during this inspection that Lord Roberts greeted for the last time his old friend Sir Pertab Singh, whose guest he had been in the East. No doubt the two veterans spoke of old days when they pursued "the image of war" together, pigsticking in Rajputana— perhaps of that identical boar which Sir Pertab held with his bare hands until Lord Roberts rode up and dispatched it.

On Friday the tour of inspection was continued, but Lord Roberts had overtaxed his strength. His devotion to the Indian Army cost him his life.

On Sunday morning the wounded Indian soldiers awaited him at the hospital of the College of Jesuits, at Boulogne. Word had gone round that the " Lat Sahib " had crossed "the black water " to see them. It was the most moving incident that could befall these loyal and patient men who had left their country to play their part in the great Sahib's war—an honour greater even than the hour of victory, which is common to many. For though Lord Roberts was not known personally to the younger generation of sepoys, he had become a name familiar in the remotest villages.

The day was gloomy—black clouds and drifting rain. It did not seem that a ray of sunshine could enter the long, dark wards. And yet some brightness was due to the fine

men who had left their clear, warm, Indian sky, and with it so many of those simple ties and observances which, with the shock of battle, make up the only happiness they know.

The dark, bandaged figures squatted on their beds, some with their arms in slings, others with their heads wrapped in lint. The most weary of them lay motionless, rolled up from head to foot in their red blankets, which entirely covered their faces. Soon it became known that the Lat Sahib would not come ; he had caught a chill. The depression deepened. Then that he was seriously ill. The weather was too rough for so old a soldier. Then it was whispered that the great leader was dead. He had died in his effort to come to them.

Exposure to the severe weather had brought on a chill. Congestion of one lung and pleurisy set in very quickly. This proved too great a strain on the heart and he gradually grew weaker, relapsed into unconsciousness and succumbed at 8 p.m. on the night of the 14th. He died as he himself would have chosen, in the midst of his old army, within sound of the guns.

It was a thrilling message to India that the last earthly engagement of her old Commander-in-Chief was to have spent an hour comforting the soldiers whom he loved.

Lord Roberts knew well the devotion he had inspired in the Indian Army. " I must go and see the Indian soldiers," he said to a friend a few days before starting. " It is the most useful thing I can do." To realize how useful, one must understand the Indian, his capacity for hero-worship, his quick recognition of an ideal, his responsiveness to sympathy, his fidelity to a cause. An Indian officer in Cureton's Multanis expressed the general feeling of the troops when he said :

" He was truly not only the Colonel-in-Chief of our Army ; he was our father. He was a pattern of the British officer under whom we gladly serve—brave, wise, and above all full of sympathy. It is sad—what parting with one like him is not ?—but, thank God, *we* saw him here at the last, and I, if I live, will be able to tell my children in the Punjab that he shook hands with me and spoke to me in my own language." " And Sahib," he added, " what death could have been more to the choosing of a man like our Colonel-in-Chief than to die amid us—the Army that he loved so well ? "

That is just the epitaph the Happy Warrior would have chosen.

For the next week cold weather worked more havoc than the enemy. On November 12 severe weather set in, rain and hail and a bitterly cold wind, and on the 18th severe frost ; on the 20th there was a heavy snowfall. The Indians suffered considerably. There were a great many cases of frostbite. It was not that the cold was intense ; in Afghanistan and Tibet our Indian troops had endured much harder weather. In January, 1904, when they were encamped on the Tuna plain under Chumalari, the thermometer fell to 25 degrees below zero. The beards of the Sikhs were frozen ; their tent ropes stiff as iron ; digging trenches would have been impossible. Yet there were not more than two or three cases of frostbite during the whole expedition. In France there were sometimes more than thirty cases in a night in a single battalion. The conditions were entirely different. Instead of living in a tent the sepoys had to sleep in the trenches. Often they were standing in mud and water all night in a cramped position in which it was impossible to keep up the circulation, and their wet socks froze in the morning. Happily only a very small proportion of those who suffered from frostbite were permanently injured.

GURKHAS DETRAINING.

During all this severe weather the average health of the Indian troops was higher than that of their British comrades in arms who accompanied them from India. It would be a mistake to think that the native of the Punjab is less inured to cold than the European. Frost is normal on the North-West Frontier in the winter, and though the thermometer does not fall so low, the cold is more trying owing to the great difference of temperature between night and day. One often sees the hardy Sikh or Jat standing naked, save for a loincloth, in icy water, his long hair unbound, performing his leisurely ablutions. The Brahmins from whom two class regiments of the Indian Army are recruited will perform the same prescribed rites in a glacier stream. Their orthodoxy is unaffected by conditions.

The sufferings of the Indian Army from cold, especially from wet cold, were perhaps greater than had been anticipated; but the troops were exposed to no physical hardships which could have been obviated. That the organization of the supply department was almost perfect is generally admitted, and in no campaign have the wheels of the transport run more smoothly. The difficulties in the provision for the Indian troops

were enormous. The mere catalogue of creeds and castes from which the Expeditionary Force was drawn will suggest to anyone who knows the East the most complicated problem of commissariat. The Gurkha, the Jat, the Rajput, and other Hindus will eat goat or mutton, provided the animal has been killed in a special and orthodox way. The disgust which the strict Hindu feels at physical contact with beef is so intense that he will sometimes vomit at the sight of it; the prejudice is so inveterate that Mahomedans who are the descendants of Hindu converts cannot reconcile themselves to the taste. Happily, pork, the Moslem abomination, does not complicate the question of army rations.

But the crucial difficulty is not so much the nature of the meat provided as the manner in which it is killed and cooked. In the case of sheep the Sikh villager's gorge will rise when he sees meat prepared by the Mahomedan butcher, who kills by the *halâl*, or throat-cutting stroke, just as the Mahomedan feels it an outrage that meat should be hung up for sale that has been killed by the *jatka*—the stroke at the back of the neck affected by the Sikhs. In France a certain amount of tinned mutton

PASSING THROUGH CAIRO.

INFANTRY WITH PACK MULES.

was eaten willingly by the troops, but the great bulk of commissariat meat was sent alive to the railhead, and slain there in accordance with prescribed rites. The streets and boulevards on the line of communications were rank with the smell of sheep and goats ; there were goats from all the hills of France, from Corsica and Dauphiné and the Cevennes, from stony Languedoc and Rousillon on the Spanish border, and bearded giants from the Pyrenees, which standing on end might pluck the leaves from the shisham like a young camel, a breed which was likely more than anything else to inspire the Indian with reverence for the virtue of the soil.

That the men might know whether they were eating clean or unclean flesh, units were detached to a point near the railhead, where each man—Mahomedan, Sikh, or Hindu—dispatched his beast by his own peculiar sacrificial stroke, marked it as clean, and sent it on to his comrades in the trenches.

No beef was killed at the front, as the mere proximity of a Mahomedan slaughter-house might carry pollution to the Hindus. For drink, the army ration of the Indian troops was rum, but the Mahomedan, being debarred by the Prophet from all fermented liquor, was given an extra ration of sugar and tea.

The *Huqa* being too cumbrous an article for service equipment, the Indian soldier received two packets of cigarettes a week. Even the transport animals had their ingrained fads, a kind of caste fastidiousness. Indian mules and country-breds, who might have had the time of their lives, nosed suspiciously our sweet English hay, preferring their own chopped straw, the driest of provender. If an English cavalry regiment ever found itself fobbed off with Indian fodder, men and horses showed disgust in their own way.

The Gurkha is proverbially an accommodating person and gives his British officer, with whom he is on the friendliest possible terms, as little difficulty as possible. But in Bombay when a regiment was embarking the question arose as to whether they would eat frozen meat. A conclave of officers decided that it would be better to put the case to the men. The Subadar was called, and, after a little wrinkling of the eyebrow, said : " I think, Sahib, the regiment will be willing to eat the iced sheep, provided one of them is always present to see the animal frozen to death."

There are other complications, but these are typical. The strict law is often aggravated or modified in the case of men of the same denomination by local or regimental influence and tradition. The point is that these men need sympathetic handling ; that they played their proud part in our war is a proof that they have received it. It must be remembered that little more than a hundred years ago the Sikhs were smearing Mahomedan mosques with the blood of swine, and the Mahomedans were fouling the Sikh *Gurudwara* with slain cattle. That

INDIAN CAVALRY.

these races who used to kill each other at sight should have fought side by side for the British Raj against Germany is a phenomenon that should make the disciples of Treitschke look into their political philosophy. What would Germany do with an Eastern empire, one might well ask, if she won it, when her national vanity sanctifies itself in the faith that it is her mission to correct or destroy all humanity that is not German-thinking ? Here is another text for the sermon of Bernhardi's " biologically-just war " and one which the Prussian professors have missed. Germany has certainly not got a " touch." As a student of human nature she is imperfect. The knowledge of the heart of man is perhaps the one lore which she has not reduced to an exact science. In Alsace she has failed in tact ; in Belgium in loving-kindness. It is doubtful if she can make the Oriental love her. If without losing her appalling single-mindedness she could send out a few hundred young men every year of the type that lead our Indian troops she would be a more formidable rival for world-power.

In the hospitals the meticulous care which was taken to respect caste observances was even more noticeable. In the ships at Boulogne visitors might see the East afloat, inhale in the Mahomedan cookhouse the comfortable smell of *dhâl* and rice, or peer into the Hindu kitchen,

the door of which would be profaned by infidel feet. The Indian Medical Service officers made the sepoy literally at home ; nothing was wanting in the vessels for the comfort of body or soul unless it were the holy waters of the Ganges.

Fore and aft there were two kitchens, one Hindu and one Mahomedan, the Hindu on the port side, the Mahomedan on the starboard. From the moment foodstuff or cooking or eating utensils were bought they were kept apart in separate stores duly labelled. The kitchen ranges were specially prepared in accordance with expert Indian advice ; the right kind of urn for the tea, the necessary *chapattie* girdle for cooking flat cakes, the brass pestle and mortar for pounding curry powder. There was no margin for mistake. When the Hindu cook, generally a Brahmin—a caste whose touch cannot defile—had prepared his dish, he brought it into the ward himself, and doled it out to his co-religionists with his own hands. Needless to say, the same precautions with regard to meat were observed as at the rail-head.

The washhouse and lavatory were designed with the same care, for the Hindu is as fastidious in his ablutions as in his diet. The Indians are among the cleanest people on earth, but they must wash in their own way. On the starboard side is the Mahomedan tap, on the port the Hindu, with notice-boards attached in Urdu and Hindi, as in all the railway-stations in India, lest there should be any mistake. The ordinary English baths were regarded with suspicion by the Indians, who squatted on the floor, as in their own country, a bowl in the hand and a tap playing on the small of the back at a foot and a half from the ground. The sanitary requisites were an exact replica of those which obtain in the East. It was the perfection of these more than anything else which moved a venerable Khan Bahadur, who visited one of the ships, to exclaim in admiration: " All India should see this ! "

The hospital fleet at Boulogne comprised the first ships of its kind, if we except the Gwalior and Carthage, which were equipped for the China War. The vessels used for South Africa were transports only, and the wounded did not embark on them until they were more or less convalescent. The Indian contingent consisted of four ships of the Castle Line and two of the Peninsular and Oriental, vessels averaging some 8,000 tons, with provision for from 300 to 500 wounded. The cabins had been gutted on both decks, so that the wards stretched the whole length of the ship. These vessels were

models of finish and were provided with every new accessory, from rocking beds fixed to the floor, which swung with the motion of the ship, to X-ray installations and the most specialized details of modern surgery. From the moment he reached the quay the patient was made to feel that the most careful machinery was being put into motion for his comfort.

When the ship was full the wounded were transferred to England, where they were taken to the hospitals prepared for them at Brighton and in the New Forest. The original plan of subsidiary hospitals at Marseilles and Alexandria was wisely abandoned, and the English people were given the opportunity of showing in a more practical form their appreciation of the sepoys' loyal services. On landing they were received by cheering crowds. Many patriotic Associations worked for their comfort. The Indian Soldiers' Fund, the Red Cross, the St. John Ambulance, sent in a continual supply of warm woollen clothing, cigarettes and chocolate. Later, parties were made up from among the convalescents to visit London, where they were shown " the lions " and enjoyed the hospitality of many houses eager to show their welcome to the Indian soldiers in the

FILLING BELTS WITH CARTRIDGES FOR MACHINE GUNS.

SIKHS AND MACHINE GUN.   [*Record Press.*

heart of the Empire. But it was the provision that had been made for the continuance of his daily rites and observances exactly as in the East that most won the sepoy's gratitude. Also he had been cheered by an English crowd. There was much *izzat* in that. Altogether, the thought of bringing the wounded Indians to England was a happy one, and well calculated to strengthen ties already strong.

In the first week of November the Indian hospitals in France began to fill. The casualties had been very heavy, especially among the 2nd and 8th Gurkhas, who had lost twenty officers, the 6th Jats, the 9th Bhopal Infantry, and the 3rd Bombay Sappers and Miners.

It was then that the British public became familiar for the first time with names of whole classes of the Indian people—men whose achievements in the past in remote lands had not touched them nearly, but who were now fighting beside their own sons on the soil of France, holding the gate with them against the Hun. The Dogra, the Garhwali, the Jat, the Punjabi or Scindi Musulman, at last received their meed of praise. One heard of the Dogra Naik who was very badly hit in the stomach, and who, though dying and in mortal pain, never made a sound, and when carried into hospital tried to rise on his stretcher and salute. He lingered half an hour and never even moaned all that time. Then there was Havildar Gagna Singh, a Dogra of Wilde's

Rifles, who arrived in the ward a bundle of splints and bandages, but full of heart. He had a bullet wound in his leg, another in his chest, and one in each hand from a shot fired point blank. The story was that he and fifteen men of his regiment were attacked in their trench before dawn. The enemy were stopped for some seconds by the barbed wire entanglements and lost heavily before they broke through. In the hand-to-hand struggle that ensued the Havildar shot the German officer, whose bullet grazed his head. He took his sword from him and killed several before he was brought down by the ball in his foot. "Otherwise," he said, "I should have killed more." He was left for dead, the sole survivor of his party. About the same time Khudadad's gallantry became known, and the heroism of the Garhwali, Darwan Negi Sing.

In the meanwhile the Sikh and the Gurkha did not lose their prestige, a prestige which, if swollen sometimes by the collective valour of other races indistinguishable from them by the man in the street, rests none the less on genuine achievement and should not suffer through the reaction of disparagement.

It is no fault of the Sikh's if he fills a disproportionate part in the people's image of the Indian Army : honour accrues to him through a certain natural distinction. And the Gurkha is not given to "additions." In France he did not boast of the Germans he had slain, but complained that he could not get the fingers of both hands around his opponent's throat. "They are not bony men," was his comment—with an inward reflection, perhaps, upon the compensating fact that this would mean less resistance to the *kukri*. The Gurkha, as a rule, is direct and matter-of-fact, more interested in physical than abstract affairs, as when he complains of the thickness of the German's neck. A more Dumasesque type is met with sometimes among the Sikhs and Mahomedans. A Pathan was asked how many of the enemy he had killed.

"A great many," he said; "one cannot count."

"But about how many ?"

After a little consideration he replied in his own expressive *argot*, "So many bullets, so many dead."

Another Mahomedan said, "I killed one, but six ran away."

Certainly fugitives ought to count.

The Sikh often has the Homeric touch. An orderly exclaiming at the devastation of a village near Hazebrouck, asked his British officer :

"Sahib, is it a true word that the German Padishah wishes to make the same ruin in Hindustan ?"

"Perfectly true."

"Then, if he comes to India, it will be over the dead bodies of us all."

A simple and genuine speech, very characteristic. It reminds one of the story of the sepoy who asked the embarcation officer at Bombay how many were coming back.

"Ten thousand, Sahib ?"

"I cannot say."

"A hundred ?"

"I think I can promise you that."

"It is good. They will be enough to carry word to our homes that we have died fighting honourably."

In this phase of the war the Cavalry were not engaged in their proper rôle, but dug themselves in with the Infantry, fought side by side with them in the trenches, and did yeoman service in holding the line against the German advance to Calais.

The unfamiliar uses which the Cavalry served in France demanded of them qualities and resources which are not as a rule included in the widest survey as part of their training. Nevertheless, they responded splendidly. To the English Dragoon or Hussar, parted from his horse, this kind of trench-warfare must have been irksome enough ; to the Asiatic it meant a call for even greater sacrifice ; and one had little reason to think that he would be equally adaptable. The mounted chivalry of the East is not happy on foot. In the old days before Ranjit Singh the Sikhs were all horsemen. The infantry only existed to garrison forts or to follow the cavalry on foot until they succeeded to a horse or looted one. Like the Rajputs and Mahomedans the old Sikh soldiers

A MOUNTAIN BATTERY.

never endured infantry service gladly. They were too proud to go on foot while others rode, and they had not the patience for it. The Sikh ascendancy in the Punjab has been attributed in part to the fact that they adapted themselves to infantry more readily than their neighbours. They were famous for their matchlock men when other races depended on the horse. The traditional contempt for the foot-soldier was stronger among the Mahrattas and died more slowly. In Rajputana the prejudice is still strong. There are classes of Dogras now who, like the Mahomedan clan of Tiwanas in the Punjab, will only enlist in the Cavalry. The defenders of Chitore would no doubt have interned the prophet in the rock who should have dared to tell them that the bluest blood of the Rathores would one day fight on foot, dig with spades and mattocks, lie in their mud-holes all night while the enemy slept secure in theirs, often unchallenged though but fifty or a hundred paces distant. Yet it has been done, and the spirit of the Rajput has conquered more than the enemy.

In the last week of November the Indian troops were again heavily engaged. In this new phase of mole-tactics, in which the combatants were sapping into each other's trenches, visible projectiles at short range began to play an increasing part. The enemy proved resourceful in adapting their machinery to meet these new conditions. One of their deadliest weapons was a revival of the primitive trench-mortar, a kind of miniature howitzer outwardly resembling the clumsy relic which sometimes ornaments the doorsteps of officers' messes and is found in museums of antiquities. Out of this obsolete pattern modern science evolved a formidable machine. In trench warfare it is a weapon to be reckoned with, as it throws a murderous shell at very close range. The heavy casualties in our Indian regiments on November 23 and 24 were caused by this kind of attack and afterwards by clearing the trenches in which the mortars were concealed.

That the Germans were before us with mortars and grenades points to their uncanny preparedness. They had foreseen a development in the campaign which had not been anticipated by the Allies. But it was not long before our own trench-mortars were ready. They were made on the field. The Indian Army sappers at Rurki had long practised with them. They were found useful in the Abor campaign. They were an immediate success. The first

twelve bombs thrown by them exploded in the enemy's trenches.

At nine o'clock on the morning of November 23, in the neighbourhood of Festubert, the enemy in front of the Indian troops made a most determined attack on our position. They had sapped up on the right of our line within a few yards of the trenches held by the 34th Sikh Pioneers. Open ditches running into the position had been used as saps. After shelling us with mortars they pushed the attack home with bombs and hand grenades and captured some of the trenches. A counter-attack delivered by us in the afternoon with the greatest determination was repulsed. At dusk the British and Indian regiments, side by side, again attacked, but could not succeed in breaking through. This was a most desperate struggle in which the issue was long uncertain; the main body of the attack was driven back, but some held their ground, and in the darkness parts of the same trench were held by British, Indians, and Germans. The gallant men who maintained themselves through the night at such close quarters to the enemy contributed to the success of the final assault.

At 10.30 p.m. the Army Corps reserves arrived and the attack was resumed with varied success at different parts of the line. It was a clear night. The assailants were exposed to machine-gun fire, and the snow showed them up as they advanced. A frontal attack would have been too costly, so it was decided to fill up the communication trench and attack the enemy on his right flank. The success was complete. Three officers, more than a hundred of the rank and file, three machine guns and one mortar were captured. A hundred German corpses were counted near the trenches; the number of their wounded was very great. Our own casualties, as was inevitable owing to the nature of the fighting, were considerable.

In this *mêlée* the Garhwalis played a prominent part and did sanguinary execution with their kukris. Another part of the trenches was cleared by a grenade party of the 1st Bengal Sappers and Miners. Some idea of the inextricable confusion in which this hand-to-hand encounter was waged may be gathered from the adventures of the officer who led them. When he was called up from the reserves it was believed that the particular trench which was his objective had been recovered. Nobody was quite sure. He was sent to find out.

TRENCH MORTAR.

He found the Indians in their trench; in the mêlée the three regiments had become mixed. There had been a great deal of bayonet work. It was a long trench, and he knew every inch of it. He found it thinly held. Towards the far end the dead alone were in possession; he had to step over them. There was an unnatural stillness, and the smell of unburied corpses from a neighbouring field poisoned the air. He came to an empty space between two traverses; beyond this he heard men whispering, but could not distinguish whether it was German or Hindustani. At a low pitch of the voice the two intonations are strangely alike. As he stooped and listened a bomb struck the earth at his feet and he was thrown to the ground. He thought he was blinded. A fragment had struck his eyebrow, another his chest; he had wounds in his neck and ribs. But he rolled over and crawled back through the dead bodies again to his men. He directed the attack lying on his side till he was carried away.

Another officer picked up a bag of hand-grenades from a man who had fallen, and accompanied by three Garhwalis crawled along the trench from traverse to traverse, clearing the Germans out as he went along. His little party came away without a scratch. The last of the enemy were driven out of the trenches at dawn.

Sir John French, in his dispatch of November 20, gave special commendation to the work of the Indian Sappers and Miners. They had long enjoyed, he said, a high reputation for skill and resource; and without going into detail he could confidently assert that throughout their work in the campaign they had fully justified that reputation. The action of November 23 and 24, in which they gained new distinction, took place three days after this dispatch.

Two of the three Corps of Indian Sappers and Miners were represented in France. Those engaged at Festubert were the 3rd and 4th companies of the 1st K.G.O. Bengal Sappers and Miners, composed of Sikhs, Pathans, Punjabi Musulmans, Brahmins and Rajputs. The companies engaged at Neuve Chapelle belonged to the 3rd Bombay Sappers and Miners, made up of Mahrattas, Sikhs, and Mahomedans. Each corps has six companies, and in addition to these there is a field troop of the 1st Bengal Sappers attached to the Cavalry Divisions.

The important part that the Sapper played in this stage of the war, when the whole allied front of 250 miles from the Yser to the Argonne was one fortress, his varied and essential rôles, the particular kind of courage and resource demanded of him, have not perhaps been generally recognized. From the last week of October, when the German dash on Calais was foiled, the operations took on the nature of siege warfare and the Sapper came into his own again. Spades were trumps. The Infantry had to do unaccustomed Sappers' work. Even the Cavalry had to dig themselves in like moles, while their horses ate their heads off picketed in a sufficiently extended line far in the rear. They, too, became adept in trench-work, and learnt the art of loopholes and traverses and parapets.

It was a state of affairs in which most of the hard work had to be done at night. To take the offensive against these bristling positions is too costly in daylight ; darkness is needed to cover the attack, and it is in these stealthy operations that Indians of all arms excel— hillmen of Garhwal and Nepal, who can glide through the Himalayan forest with no more rustling than a porcupine or mongoose, trans-frontier Pathans, Afridis, Mahsuds, Orakzais— raiders who know how to slip by the sentries of the Khyber patrols at Landi Kotal without loosening a stone, carrying off their spoil with them into tribal country.

The Sapper is not given trenches to hold under heavy fire. He is seldom called upon to take a position. He carries a rifle, but he seldom uses it. His weapons of attack are bombs and hand-grenades and mortars. He sleeps in the day, when he has time, and is at work all night. It is half-blind, stealthy work in the dark, almost feline, generally over the ground between the enemy's trenches and our own. It requires the least common kind of courage.

Every night there are wire entanglements to be put up which have been broken during the day. However stealthily the Sapper sets to work, it will only be a few seconds before he draws the enemy's fire. Word has been passed to the look-outs in the trenches to expect him, but he does not always get the benefit of the doubt. It is jumpy work for the sentries, too.

Then there are buildings to destroy. The enemy will have occupied some house from which they can snipe our trenches, having sandbagged the windows on the second floor. They are too near to make it safe to shell the building. So the work of destruction falls to the Sappers. This is another night job. If it is a cottage three or four charges will generally suffice, which means only one expedition. But the country is islanded with farmhouses with enclosed courtyards like Arab caravanserais.

These are a more difficult matter. After the first explosion one has to return again and lay more charges. The enemy are thoroughly on the alert. If there is a flashlight it will be turned on, and the proportion of casualties will be heavy.

All this is part of the night's routine— sorties, patrols, reconnaissances, counter-saps, involving the old-fashioned kind of fighting in which a man does good work if he can suppress his nervous system and embody the physical virtues of a terrier and a ferret. It was not Sapper's work only, but work in which, during those long weeks of siege warfare, every Indian regiment of cavalry or foot was called upon to play its part.

The German is terribly afraid of the Pathan, who, he imagines, will cut him up into small bits. And there was a rumour that the brown men would give no quarter. There is no doubt that the Germans who were captured by the Indians expected to be killed by them. The prisoners they took used to put their hands together and ask to be spared.

At the beginning of the war the German did not take the Indian troops seriously, but he soon learnt to respect and fear them. A letter from a German soldier published by the *Frankfurter Zeitung* probably contains an account from the enemy's side of one of those attacks of November 23, in which our troops fought so gallantly and with such heavy loss :

To-day, for the first time, we had to fight against the Indians, and the devil knows those brown rascals are not to be under-rated. At first we spoke with contempt of the Indians. To-day we learned to look at them in a different light—the devil knows what the English had put into those fellows. Anyhow, those who stormed our lines seemed either drunk or possessed with an evil spirit. With fearful shouting, in comparison with which our hurrahs are like the whining of a baby, thousands of those brown forms rushed upon us as suddenly as if they were shot out of a fog, so that at first we were completely taken by surprise.

At a hundred metres we opened a destructive fire which mowed down hundreds, but in spite of that the others advanced, springing forward like cats and sur-mounting obstacles with unexampled agility. In no time they were in our trenches, and truly these brown enemies were not to be despised. With butt ends, bayonets, swords and daggers we fought each other, and we had bitter hard work, which, however, was lightened by reinforcements which arrived quickly, before we drove the fellows out of the trenches.

Earlier in the week the Garhwalis got into the enemy's trenches. The Germans were heard screaming. Their casualties were heavy.

One of the regiments which lost most heavily in the action of November 23 and 24 was the 34th Sikh Pioneers. The twelve battalions of Pioneers in the Indian Army are akin to Sappers.

SIKHS ON THE MARCH.

There is no exact parallel to them in other branches of the Service. Their training combines field engineering with the ordinary routine of the native infantry of the line. Perhaps no troops in the Empire have seen such continued service as the three battalions that are recruited from the Punjab. The 23rd and 32nd were raised during the Mutiny of 1857, when we were in great need of sappers for the siege work at Delhi. A number of Mazbi Sikhs who were employed at the time in the canal works of the Beas were offered military service and volunteered readily. These Mazbis are a race apart, descendants of converts from the despised sweeper caste, who were welcomed by the Sikhs when they were engaged in a life and death struggle with Islam, but rejected of them when they emerged victorious. On the march to Delhi these raw recruits fought like veterans. They were attacked by the rebels, beat them off, and saved the whole of the ammunition and treasure. During the siege Neville Chamberlain wrote of them that "their courage amounted to utter recklessness of life." They might have been engaged on a holy war. Many supernumeraries accompanied the levies, and when a soldier fell "his brother would literally step into his shoes, taking his rifle and all that he possessed, including his name, and even his wife and family." * These Mazbis who fought at

* *Regimental History of the Thirty-Second Sikh Pioneers.* By Colonel H. R. Brander, C.B. Calcutta: Thacker Spink. 1906.

Delhi and Lucknow were the nucleus of the three Sikh Pioneer regiments, one of which has been engaged on nearly every frontier campaign since, from Waziristan in 1860 to the Abor Expedition in 1912. It was the 32nd who carried the guns from Gilgit over the Shandur Pass and relieved the British garrison in Chitral. It was the 34th who helped to regain the trenches at Festubert in an engagement in which half of the officers of the regiment fell.

Reference has been made to the Garhwalis, who played a conspicuous part in the action at Festubert. The King bestowed the Victoria Cross in the field upon a naik of the 1st Battalion of the 39th Garhwal Rifles "for great gallantry on the night of November 23–24, near Festubert, France, when the regiment was engaged in retaking and clearing the enemy out of our trenches, and although wounded in two places in the head and also in the arm, being one of the first to push round each successive traverse, in the face of severe fire from bombs and rifles at the closest range."

The day the Garhwalis took over their trenches they were attacked. The following day they were heavily shelled by siege guns. The shells burst actually in the trenches and the casualties in the battalion were excessive. The men were as cool as veterans, though this was their first experience of shell fire. Every night they were attacked two or three times by the enemy, who had sapped up to within fifty

[Ernest Brooks.

THE KING AND QUEEN VISITING WOUNDED INDIANS.

yards of their trenches. These assaults were always repulsed. Then one night the Garhwalis carried the enemy's trenches, doing bloody execution with their *kukris*. One double company accounted for forty-two Germans. After three weeks in the trenches they were being relieved when the order came on November 23 to "turn about." That was at Festubert. From 8 p.m. to 5 a.m. they were attacking. They first had to build a parapet to shelter the men from a withering fire at close quarters, which was taking them in the flank all down the line.

A subadar of the 1st Battalion who fell shot in the head refused to be carried away, and lay on his back directing the men who were building up the wall. They then took the trench, traverse by traverse, in file.

The Garhwali is often confused with the Gurkha, whom he closely resembles, a mistake not confined to the uninitiated, but shared sometimes by Staff Officers attached to the Indian Army. The confusion is galling to the Garhwalis, officers and men, as it means that their achievements go to swell the traditions of the Gurkha battalions, who, with the Sikhs, have already captured the popular imagination in the East and West to the exclusion of other fighting races. The mistake is natural. The

Garhwali is a hillman and his country lies to the east of Nepal ; the frontiers of the two races are conterminous. Ethnologically he is associated with the Gurkha and resembles him in feature, though he is not, as a rule, so thickset or muscular. Like the Gurkha, he is a born cragsman and scout, and he carries a *kukri* and wears the same rifle uniform with the Kilmarnock cap.

The Garhwalis were originally enlisted among the rank and file of the ordinary Gurkha regiments, but are now separate. The 39th Bengal Infantry became a class battalion, and in 1892 received the title of "The Garhwal Rifles." Later a second battalion was added.

Naik Darwan Sing Negi's gallantry has given these hillmen the distinction they needed. Henceforth the Garhwali will become a household word. He will have his own niche in the temple of fame.

The campaign of the Expeditionary Force in Belgium was the first war, if we except the Abor Expedition, in which it had been possible for an Indian to win the Victoria Cross. Eligibility to the distinction was one of the boons granted by the King-Emperor to his Indian subjects at the Delhi Durbar of 1911. The presentation of the medal by the Sovereign on the field of battle, not far from the spot where it had been earned, was a unique event in the history of the Indian Army.

On December 2 the King arrived in Boulogne, and in the afternoon visited the Indian Hospital. He inspected the wards and spoke to many of the wounded sepoys. His sympathy and solicitude for them were touching and manifest. When he asked them the nature and occasion of their wounds they were astonished to find from the questions he put to them that he knew the details of the actions they had fought in and the dates and the names of the regiments engaged. The pride of a wounded sepoy in the King's personal interest in his regiment may be easily imagined. A sepoy in the 34th Sikh Pioneers discovered that his Majesty knew that it was his regiment, together with men of the 6th Jats, the 9th Bhopal Infantry, and the 39th Garhwalis, who held a part of a certain trench retaken by the bayonet on the night of November 23. The King spent some minutes by the bedside of a man in the same regiment who was paralysed on the right side of the face from a bullet behind the ear. Another young sepoy was a little discomfited to have to confess to his Padishah that he had not been in action ; an artillery horse had trodden on his foot. In the Indian officers' ward, Jemadar Danbir Thapa, of the 2nd

8th Gurkhas, a typical specimen of the thick-set, sturdy recruit from the west of Nepal, gave his Majesty an account of the action in which his regiment had helped in clearing the enemy's trenches after suffering heavy loss on November 2. The tradition of the King's sympathetic interest in their particular regiments is likely to survive long among the sepoys of the Indian Army. The King was impressed by the extraordinary hardihood and patience with which the sepoy bears his wounds. One man had had his leg amputated in the morning. He had borne the pain after the operation stoically, but when the King spoke to him his eyes filled with tears and he could not answer.

It was in the Convalescent Camp, where the soldiers were living in tents under the same conditions as in an Indian cantonment, that a sepoy rose up from his bed and called out " God save the King." It was the only English that he knew, and quite unrehearsed. The spontaneous tribute of the men in that tent must have been more affecting to his Majesty than all the applause of a Royal procession.

On December 3 the King inspected the Indian contingent. It was a wonderful visit— quiet, informal, unexpected. The King strolled up and down the ranks talking to the men and asking them questions. Detachments had been drawn from every company and squadron not

WOUNDED INDIANS AND BRITISH IN ENGLAND.

INTERIOR OF MOTOR FIELD KITCHEN.

actually in the trenches. It was a memorable
and impressive sight. The day was showery
with spells of beautiful weather and blue sky ;
all round the field stood warriors with fixed
bayonets and drawn swords ; in the centre the
King and his suite and the Prince of Wales ;
while up above, against the blue, two British
aeroplanes, hovering watchfully, kept off the
hostile Taubes.

It was a quiet morning in the trenches, and
there had been little firing, except at the
Taubes ; but the troops were drawn up within
range of the German guns. Before he left
the field the King gave General Willcocks his
message to the contingent, and the General
delivered it in Hindustani. The King wished
them to know that both he and the Queen
always kept them in their thoughts, and he
meant to see all of them again with his own eyes
as soon as the war was over.

It would be a mistake to think of the Indians'
tribute merely as a passing wave of emotion
natural in men of quick sensibility. Devotion
to the Sovereign is as deep-set in their hearts
as love of the soil. The sepoy's loyalty is
instinctive and springs from an immemorial
habit of mind. In India, where abstract and
invisible kingship commands fidelity, the
present and visible King stirs unsuspected

depths of loyalty and zeal. The Durbar of 1911
brought this home to the British people, when
the tens of thousands flocked to the vacant
throne at Delhi after the King had left and
prostrated themselves in a fervour of exaltation.
Even in the days of unrest, among the most
bitter opponents of the Government a reference
to the King would often provoke a cheer. During
the South African trouble, in India it was one
of the anomalies of the public indignation
meetings held all-over the country that the
name of the Viceroy or the King was greeted
with almost the same enthusiasm as the most
frantic denunciation of the British Government.
Advanced politicians would explain that they
owed allegiance to the King-Emperor and not
to " the citadel of bureaucratic despotic rule."

The aim of this chapter has been to describe
the Indian Army in France from the time of its
landing at Marseilles to the King's visit in
December ; to give some idea of the various
castes, creeds and communities from which it
is drawn ; to describe the peculiar difficulties
that confronted them in a strange land under
entirely novel conditions of warfare ; and to
record the fine spirit with which they sur-
mounted these, upholding their high traditions,
and proving, as in the past, their fidelity and
devotion to the British Crown.

The part the Indian Cavalry played in
France will be recorded elsewhere. The part
played by the British troops serving in the
Indian contingent—cavalry, artillery and foot
—will fall naturally into those chapters in
which the several stages of the campaign are
recorded. Before we advert to another theatre
of the war a word may be said of some of the
political issues arising from India's participation
in the world struggle.

The dispatch of the Indian contingent to
France marked a new phase in the relations of
East and West. The social and political
influences of the war will be far-reaching. New
bonds will be forged ; old prejudices will be
broken down.

Between British and Indian soldiers there
have always been ties of good comradeship from
the days when the sepoys offered their rations
to Clive at Arcot to the latest *entente* between
the Gurkhas and Highlanders in the bazaars of
the Himalaya. Did not the old 36th Infantry
give up their supplies to the British troops when
the commissariat was destroyed by the earthquake in Jellalabad ?

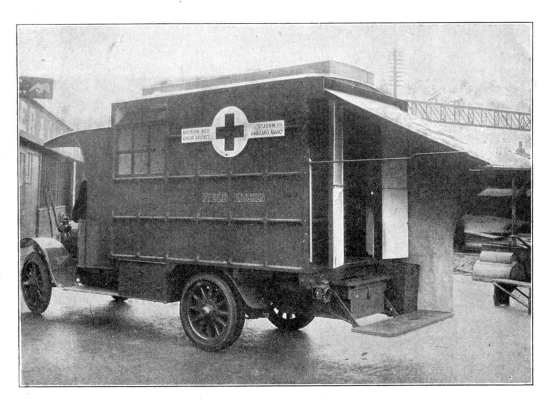

MOTOR FIELD KITCHEN.
Presented to the British Red Cross Society by The Worshipful Company of Leathersellers.

Comradeship in arms, the sharing of danger, the common hardships of a campaign, have, since Clive's days, promoted friendship and respect between our soldiers and the gallant military races of the East, but the participation of the Indian troops in the European war will have a wider effect. When Hindu and Musulman have fought shoulder to shoulder with Canadians and New Zealanders against a common European enemy the differences that have divided the fellow-subjects of the Crown should find an easier settlement. The next chapter in the history of the Empire should record the added strength and union of the component parts drawn together by the threat of *Kultur.* In this the prestige of the East will shine brightly and misunderstandings which have arisen through want of touch or imagination will be modified or swept away.

In the same way Japan's entry into the war removed obstacles to a generous understanding between East and West. The cooperation of the Australian and the Japanese squadrons and the deference to Australian and New Zealand susceptibilities which Japan showed by handing over the Pacific islands she had taken to the keeping of an Australian force must have tended to modify sentiments among our fellow-

subjects in the Dominion that had sometimes threatened to raise delicate problems in the Pacific.

The extraordinary enthusiasm which prevailed in Japan when General Barnardiston landed in Tokio, after the taking of Tsing-Tau by the allied Japanese and British forces, will be memorable in history. The Japanese newspapers described the event as marking a new era in the relationship of East and West and setting the seal for ever on the Anglo-Japanese alliance.

With regard to India and the self-governing colonies happier relations are in sight. In his speech at Simla on September 9 Lord Hardinge outlined proposals for the consideration of the people of India by which the Government proposed to meet the difficulty regarding the emigration of Indians to British Colonies by negotiating for a reciprocal arrangement. By this plan a limited number of passports might be issued, as is already the case between Canada and Japan, and China and the United States, allowing fully for the temporary residence of students and tourists, but strictly limiting their right to permanent settlement. Indians will understand that the Colonies cannot admit classes who they consider, rightly or wrongly,

INDIAN GUARD.

threaten the prosperity of their own people. The economic loss to India through the exclusion of labourers will be faced. Happily the loss of prestige through the exclusion of Indians of all classes is open to remedy. And prestige is the all-important thing. Limited emigration may be accepted by the Colonies, as it is only industrial rivalry that is feared ; and it may be accepted by Indians when it is recognized as an economic precaution and not as an insistence on the racial bar.

The Kaiser's attempt to dismember the Empire proved singularly unsuccessful. His rattling of the sabre in Berlin awakened the same response in India as in Canada and New Zealand. Without loosening one strong tie, he strengthened the weakest. He provided a solution to a problem that seemed insoluble. To the Indian, as to all the rest of the world, the conflagration which he lighted brought suffering, but through it a vision of a wider freedom under the Raj born of the common danger and brotherhood in arms.

The following illustrations will be found in Volume I. : Sir Pertab Singh, p. 164 ; Lord Hardinge, p. 165 ; The Marquess of Crewe, p. 165 ; Gurkha Rifles, p. 155 ; A typical Sowar, p. 157 ; Groups of Officers, pp. 156, 159 ; Subadar-Major of the 45th Rattray's Sikhs, p. 160.

CHAPTER XLIII.

EARLY EAST COAST RAIDS.

Coast Defence—Revolution Caused by the Submarine—The Problem for England—
Possibility of Raids—Raid on Yarmouth—Attack on the Halcyon—A Futile Bombard-
ment—German Mines—A German Description of the Raid—The Second Raid—Three
Contrasting East Coast Towns—Hartlepool and its Industries—The Charm of Scarborough—Whitby and its Abbey—The Fortifications of Hartlepool—Defencelessness of
Scarborough and Whitby—Attack on Hartlepool—Territorials in Action—Attitude
of the Population—Damage to the Port—Churches Injured—Some Examples of Courage
—Scenes in the Hospital—Popular Anger—Report of Hostile Airship's Approach—
Results of the Bombardment—Attack on Scarborough—Bombardment of the Castle
and Town—Some Individual Cases—Tragedy and Humour—The Inquests—How Scar-
borough Suffered—Recruiting and the Raid—The Attack on Whitby—Abbey Struck—
Slight Casualties—Letter from a Resident—Official Reports—Popular Sympathy—The
King's Message—Mr. Churchill's Letter—Foreign Opinion—German Comments—German
Press Views—Some British Criticisms—An Answer to Critics—The Primary Object of the
Royal Navy—Espionage—A Bitter but Salutary Experience—National Resolution.

IN the early days of the war it became evident to all careful observers that the problem of the defence of the British coast had been revolutionized by the coming of the submarine. As far back as 1908, when a fleet of submarines made a non-stop run of five hundred miles and traversed some thousands of miles during the North Sea manœuvres, there were not wanting naval authorities to point out that we were face to face with a change in sea warfare as far reaching as the adoption of steam and the introduction of the ironclad. Up to then submarines had been employed at short distances from their base, when their main value was to protect coasts and harbours. But when it became possible for them to travel and operate many hundreds and even some thousands of miles away from their base they took rank at once among the most powerful weapons of naval offensive war. The war of 1914 brought to a practical demonstration what had hitherto been only a matter of theory. It then became clear that no large fighting ships could remain for long at anchor or on guard in the North Sea without affording the enemy an opportunity of attempting their swift destruction by their small and unseen foe.

The fuller aspects of the development of the submarine in naval warfare are discussed elsewhere in this History. The matter needs only to be referred to here in so far as it affects the defence of the British coast. Formerly it was possible for the stronger fleet to lie outside an enemy's coast, blockade its ships, and wait for them to come out to battle. A fast cruiser might occasionally slip by the guard, but it would almost certainly find the way closed against its return. But in 1914 the containing blockade could no longer be attempted. Had the British Fleet stationed itself in the North Sea waiting for the German ships to emerge into the open, it would have invited its own destruction from German submarines. The North Sea was watched by large numbers of small patrol ships of every kind, whose business was to report any developments of German naval activity.

This changed condition of things obviously gave the fastest German ships much greater opportunity of attempting raids. There are 600 miles of sea-shore on the British East Coast, and it is difficult to place all along this coast adequate fleets sufficient to defend every point against strong attack. The land defences of the British East Coast had, up to the time of the outbreak of the war, been treated as a matter of secondary importance. One dominating principle in our policy was that our coast must rely for protection primarily and mainly not upon fortifications but upon the ships of the Navy. Certain points of special importance—harbours, river mouths and naval and military depôts—were guarded by forts, but in some cases these forts were little more than show places, unfitted for serious conflicts with modern armoured ships. Here and there a military station was to be found, such as Portsmouth, Dover or Sheerness, where adequate defence plans had been carried out, and where the land guns had kept pace with the growth of naval armament. The great majority of our East Coast towns had no land fortifications whatever. We relied on the declaration of The Hague Convention that unfortified towns shall not be subjected to bombardment, and it was accepted as an axiom in many circles that the town certain to receive the least damage was the town which had no defences at all.

Thus England found herself in the late summer and autumn of 1914 in a position involving some obvious risks. The dangers of a German invasion in force were comparatively small, for any attempt to land a force larger than a small raiding party at any point upon the coast would have given the British Navy time to come up and capture or destroy the entire flotilla. But the Germans could attempt to send their swiftest cruisers across the North Sea in the foggy days and long nights of the autumn and winter, to bombard our coast towns at dawn, and to escape in the sea fogs before a British Fleet could close in on them. The distance from Heligoland to such points on the coast as Scarborough and Yarmouth is about 280–340 miles. Scarborough is 385 miles from Wilhelmshaven. The fast German cruisers have a speed of from 25 to 28 knots an hour. They could set out at six in the evening, arrive off our coast at seven in the morning, open fire

as soon as dawn showed them their target, and retire at full speed at the first sign of danger. Such a plan had its very real perils, perils from mines and perils from the possibility of an overwhelming British Fleet being in the neighbourhood. Its very dangers gave it an attraction to the venturesome officers of the new German Navy, anxious to prove the value of their ships and the mettle of their men. It implied and demanded the existence of an intelligence service in England which should keep the Germans informed of the movements of the British Fleet. Events proved that this intelligence department existed.

Many British experts considered that such a venture would be hopeless. Wireless telegraphy would enable the arrival of such ships to be signalled immediately to the British Fleets nearest to hand, and they could not then hope to escape them. These experts were over-confident. The venture was twice tried in the closing weeks of 1914, at Yarmouth on November 3 and at Scarborough, Whitby and the Hartlepools on December 16. In each case a very strong fleet of the fastest German battle cruisers and armoured cruisers was sent out. In each case the German plan was two-fold—first, to ravage our coasts and to irritate the British Fleet into pursuing it, and next to sow the seas with mines so that the attacking British Fleet would be caught on them and suffer serious loss.

THE RAID ON YARMOUTH.

On the afternoon of November 2 eight ships assembled at a point off the German coast. According to unofficial German accounts there were three battle cruisers, the Seydlitz, the Moltke and the Von der Tann, the armoured cruisers Blücher and Yorck, and the protected cruisers the Kolberg, the Graudenz, and the Strassburg. With one exception these were the pick of the cruisers of the German Navy, the one exception being the armoured cruiser Yorck, a comparatively slow boat, which was apparently used as the rearguard of the fleet, and which in the retreat was sunk by striking on a German mine. Two of the vessels, the Moltke and the Graudenz, had a speed of 28 knots, and the slowest—apart from the Yorck—made her 25 knots an hour. The Seydlitz and the Moltke carried each of them 10 11-in. guns and the Von der Tann 8 11-in. guns. The Blücher carried 12 8-in. guns, and the armoured cruisers were powerful fighting vessels.

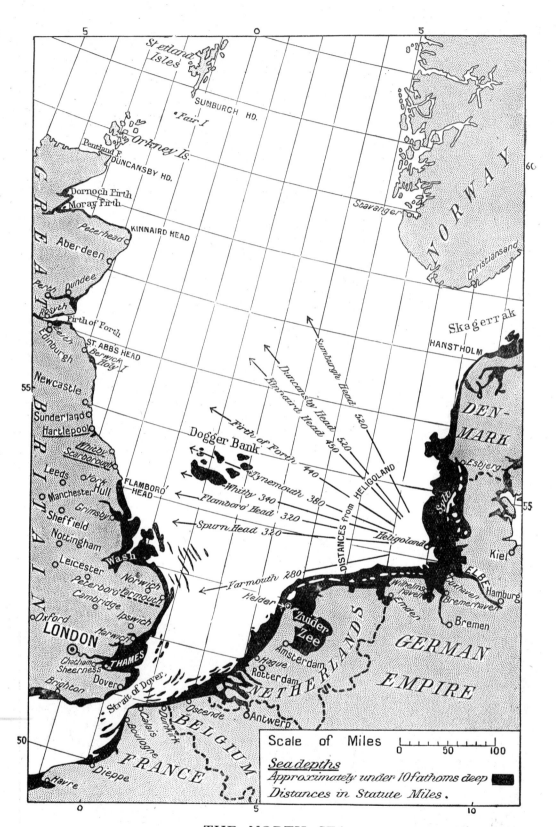

THE NORTH SEA,
Showing distances from Heligoland, and sea depths near coasts.

The ships prepared for action. Kitbags and hammocks were stowed away, to avoid danger from fire, and at six o'clock in the evening they started at full speed for the English coast, lights out, flying no flags, with the crews at their places ready for action. Soon after dawn next morning they passed through a fleet of British fishing boats, about eight miles north-east of Lowestoft. The fishermen at first thought they were British and waved and shouted greetings to them. Some of the sailors in the nearest warship shook their fists in reply. A second glance showed the fishermen that these were no British ships, and abandoning their nets they set off in hasty flight across the water. A few minutes later the German ships sighted the Halcyon, an ancient British gunboat used in coast patrol. They at once opened fire on her, damaged her wireless apparatus with one of the first shots, and struck her bridge and funnel. She attempted to reply but she was hopelessly outranged, and there was obviously nothing for her to do but to escape as quickly as possible. A member of the crew of the Halcyon gave that same evening an account of their experiences :—

We were about 10 miles out when we saw German vessels making towards us. We challenged them, thinking they were our own vessels, as the last things we expected to see were German ships 10 miles off the English coast. The only reply we got was a shot, and in a moment shells were raining around us. The skipper was below, but he ran up to the bridge, and then the fun began. He called out to us, " Keep cool, and remember what flag you are flying." We raised a cheer, and we went to our stations. The ship was put on a course at top speed; the navigation was a wonder. We did not bolt for it. The Germans were firing at us as rapidly as possible. One shot wrecked the wheel-house, seriously injuring the helmsman. Another one went through our aft funnel, and several glanced off the water on to our sides. We were hit about eight times altogether, and, considering that we were covered with spray and going at a good rate, the German gunnery was really good. Our wireless was carried away by their second shot. Just before they cleared off one of our destroyers came up and put up a screen of smoke for us from her funnels.

The German ships then opened fire on Yarmouth, evidently directing their fire on the wireless station, the naval air station, and the town generally. They kept up a very heavy but wholly ineffective bombardment for about twenty minutes. Their shells fell short, many of them dropping into the water between one and two miles out and others merely ploughing the sands. According to German writers, the commander of the fleet had information that an English mine-field had been laid in the waters ahead and he would not go into it.

The people of Yarmouth and Lowestoft were awakened in the early hours of the morning by the heavy thud of the gun fire and by the shaking of their windows from the concussion of the shell explosions. They hurried down to the sea front to learn what had happened,

SCARBOROUGH : THE HARBOUR.   ["Times" Photograph.

BIRD'S-EYE VIEW OF GREAT YARMOUTH SEA FRONT.

and there amid the haze they could see cascades of water rising up in the sea where the shells were falling. Flash after flash was visible on the horizon. Even with the aid of powerful glasses it was only possible to distinguish one of the ships. She was steaming close to the Cross Sands lightship, 10 miles off the coast, and well outside the Yarmouth Roads. The nearest shell went within a few hundred yards of the naval air station. The main firing lasted about a quarter of an hour, and the ships then quickly made eastwards again. As they retired they dropped a large number of floating mines.

Two destroyers and two submarines set out in pursuit. One of the submarines, D5, struck a mine a few miles from the coast and sank in about two minutes, losing all of her crew except two. Two fishing boats were also caught that day on the mines and sunk, fifteen men being drowned. The German ship Yorck struck a mine on the journey back and went down with a loss of 300 lives.

An interesting description of the raid written by a German sailor at Wilhelmshaven to his brother at Basel, appeared afterwards in the Vienna newspaper *Die Zeit* :—

At 4 o'clock in the afternoon of November 2 the order was given to stow away kitbags and hammocks, this being done in order that they cannot be set on fire when the ship is struck by a shell. After this had been done the commander addressed the crew as follows : "At 6 o'clock this evening we shall start at top speed for England, and arrive there at 7 o'clock to-morrow morning, to bombard the English coast and to endeavour to entice the English fleet out of port. You know what you have to do. I will only impress upon you that all bulkheads are to be shut tight and well. Long live his Majesty the Emperor ! "

At 6 o'clock we put to sea. All night we stood at our guns, without any idea of sleep, but we saw nothing of the Englishman. At dawn we were still about 30 nautical miles from the English coast. We saw only a crowd of Dutch and English fishing boats. They were fishing, and we tore through their nets. They must have been not a little surprised to see us steam by. At 8 a.m. on November 3 we came in sight of the lighthouse on the English coast, and soon the command rang out, " Clear for action ! Load ! Distance 10 kilometres." An English coast cruiser and some enemy destroyers came in sight. " Port side fire ! Ten kilometres ! Fire ! " Our heavy and middle artillery thundered at the enemy. Soon came the command, " Starboard fire ! Distance 104 hecto-metres ! At the enemy cruiser ! Fire ! " Once more indescribable noise. The Englishman ran fast. Unfortunately we could not pursue him because of the danger of mines. Nor could we, on account of the enemy's mines, go closer to land. Soon there was no English ship still in sight.

Simultaneously with the bombardment of the English cruiser, which was injured and had some dead and wounded, our heavy artillery (11 in. shells weighing 640 lb.) bombarded the English coast—to be precise the town of Lowestone (sic), near Yarmouth. Unfortunately the distance (15 kilometres) was too great for us to do considerable damage. Some shells fell on the shore, window panes were broken, and so on. If only we had been five kilometres nearer to the coast Yarmouth would have been in flames. The main object of our enterprise had, however, been gained. In the first place our small cruisers, which were packed full with mines, had strewn the local waters with German mines. When the English submarine D 5 tried to attack us it struck a mine and blew up. In the second place we had shown the Englishman,

SCARBOROUGH : THE FORTIFICATIONS.   *["Times" Photograph.*

who is always boasting of his command of the sea, that he cannot even protect his own coast, and that the German Navy is not, like him, afraid to attack. In the third place we have given the inhabitants of England, and especially the people of Yarmouth, a thorough fright. How elegantly (for the English are sportsmen) must they have sprung out of their warm beds when the German guns thundered in front of their town ! The moral effect is also worth much. The noise which the heavy guns make can hardly be described. It is simply gigantic.

To some extent the German raid was a fiasco. Yarmouth and Lowestoft were undamaged. Against the loss of a British submarine there stood the loss of the German armoured cruiser, the Yorck, a 1905 ship of 9,350 tons. But the German vessels had demonstrated the possibility of crossing the North Sea undetected, and of returning before our fleet could catch them. And though they had failed in their effort to bombard the coast, the action was well calculated to encourage the German Navy and the German people. The attempted raid created less concern than might have been anticipated in England. Some surprise was expressed that the ships were not caught by our fleet on their return. The attempt had failed. It would lead to a strengthening of our coast defences, and no great harm had been done. The Germans had not dared to remain more than a few minutes and they had not ventured sufficiently near the shore to do real damage. The prevailing feeling was that it would be a mistake to attach too much significance to the raid or to say too much about it.

THE SECOND RAID.

The second German attempt to raid the British coast was on December 16, and three towns were selected for attack—Hartlepool, Scarborough and Whitby. The second raid was possibly provoked by the destruction of the German Pacific Squadron in the South Atlantic by Sir Doveton Sturdee's Fleet. The British success had been followed by a great outcry in the German Press for revenge. Count Reventlow, the German naval writer, had in particular urged extreme action. "We must see clearly," he declared, "that in order to fight with success we must fight ruthlessly— in the proper meaning of the word." Germany was now to give us an example of her ruth- lessness.

It would be hard to find a greater contrast along the English coast than the three places chosen. Hartlepool—or to be more exact, the Hartlepools, for Hartlepool and West Hartle- pool are separate boroughs—is an important shipbuilding, shipping and industrial centre, of over one hundred thousand people, situated on a south-eastward sweep of the coast. Hartlepool, the parent town, with a population of 25,000, has been largely over- shadowed by the growth of its offshoot West

Hartlepool, whose population is about 75,000. The two towns, which are separated by the docks and a bay, are considered officially one port. Their industries include such important firms as Messrs. William Gray & Co., Messrs. Irvine, Messrs. Furness, Withy & Co., among the shipbuilders ; Messrs. Richardson, Westgarth & Co. and Messrs. J. J. Harvey & Sons among engineering firms ; and various saw-milling, zinc-making and iron and steel works. The Hartlepool Pulp and Paper Works are among the largest in the country. The port itself has a water area of about 200 acres and includes six docks, one basin, two tidal harbours and four timber ponds.

Hartlepool was at the time of the raid at the height of a period of industrial prosperity. Every shipyard was full with orders, and many of them were booked up for eighteen months and two years ahead. Labour was so scarce that more than one firm took the unusual course of publishing day by day large display advertisements to urge skilled men to come to it. Hartlepool, with its shipyards ringing with the sound of the hammers of the riveting squads, with its docks full, with every possible man employed, with its skies lit up at night time by the deep red glare of the blast furnaces, spoke in every street of prosperous industry.

Scarborough presented another picture. Here was a famous seaside resort—the Brighton of the North, as its admirers love to call it—sunny, clean and beautiful, with the hills of fine gardens stretching up behind the town, with a well-kept park coming through a picturesque valley in the centre of the town down to the sea front, with sea cliffs turned into entrancing walks, with a hundred attractions for the temporary visitor or the resident. Scarborough had developed in recent years as the permanent home of many wealthy and retired people, drawn there by its manifold charms. It boasted of its enterprise, its attractions and its amenities of life. Its municipal administrators managed it with all the skill of a great business, advertising its attractions throughout the country, and its catch-names, " Scarborough the Beautiful," " Scarborough the Queen of the North," were familiar to every one. The war, which had brought the Hartlepools increased prosperity, had hit Scarborough somewhat hardly, preventing its summer season and driving out visitors. The hotel proprietors and boarding-house keepers were looking to the Christmas holidays to recoup them. Now their Christmas season was to be killed.

Scarborough's near neighbour, Whitby, was a seaside town of another type. If Scarborough boasted of its modernity, Whitby prided itself on its selectness. A quaint old fishing port and shipping centre, with steep, narrow streets on either side of the mouth of the river Esk,

MINE SWEEPERS OFF SCARBOROUGH, AND CAVALRY ON THE SANDS.

HARTLEPOOL: [*"Times" Photograph.*
FRAGMENTS OF SHELLS PICKED UP IN STREETS AND BUILDINGS.

running sharply up to the East Cliff and the West Cliff, the favourite home of sea captains and pilots and men who love the northern breezes, it was dubbed, by its more modern rivals, old-fashioned and slow. Whitby had succeeded in retaining its ancient character, as few seaside resorts have done. It did not lay itself out for the " tripper " or the chance visitor, but it had a warm place in the affection of thousands who appreciated the fact that it was surrounded by some of the most beautiful country in England and some of the most attractive coast scenery to be found in these islands. Whitby was specially proud of its Abbey, one of the most perfect specimens of Gothic art in the world, now in ruins, but conveying even in its ruin a sense of grandeur, stateliness and dignity hard to exaggerate. To the people of Whitby the Abbey is something sacred. Its great outlines on the cliff top, ever visible, were the symbol of their town.

The only one of these places that could be considered fortified was Hartlepool. There was a small fort on the front, whose armaments at the time of the raid were inadequate against the armoured sides of the German ships that were soon to attack them. Scarborough had no fortifications whatever. Scarborough Castle, atop of a promontory jutting out from the sea, in the centre of the town, has in its time played its part in the history of England, in the Wars of the Roses,

in Wyatt's rebellion, and in the Civil War. It was besieged six times between 1312 and 1648, and was demolished by Cromwell's men. In recent years the ruins of the Castle, three hundred feet above the sea level, have been mainly a show place and have also been used as a look-out post. They were not fortified in any way.

Scarborough was, up to a few years ago, a depôt of the Royal Artillery, and then it had a battery of guns above the Marine Drive at the castle foot. This battery was removed when, under the Haldane scheme of army reform, Scarborough was changed from an artillery to a cavalry depôt. At the time of the raid, and for some time before, there was not a single gun in the place save an ornamental Russian 64 pounder, a relic of the Crimean War, a smooth bore, with its touch hole spiked and a tampion that had not been removed from its muzzle in our time, standing on a fancy carriage and placed alongside of an anchor by the municipal authorities as a decoration on the green lawn of a square in the centre of the town. Were this to excuse bombardment, the presence of a sixteenth century fowling piece in a civic museum would surely also be adequate reason. There was a wireless station to the rear of the town, but the authorities had not considered it necessary to provide any defence for it. There was a barracks where some of Kitchener's Army were in training, and in addition a few hundred Yeomanry were stationed in the place. No attempt whatever had been made to fortify Scarborough. No gun was fired upon the German ships when they drew in close to the shore on the day of the raid, because there was no gun to fire. The statement which appeared in the German Press after the raid, that it was defended by a redoubt containing six 15 cm. guns, was absolutely without foundation. It may be placed alongside of another statement, issued by the German Naval Press Bureau, that it had learned from a trustworthy neutral source that the Scarborough gunners had not replied, because the defenders ran away from their guns when the German ships opened their well-aimed fire !

Whitby, like Scarborough, had no fortifications and no guns. There was not even the excuse of a regimental depôt for the bombardment of this place. The total of soldiers in the Whitby district—a district several miles across—was at the time of the raid 26 men.

The Germans chose the time of their second raid carefully. A heavy mist hung over the North Sea, not a dense fog, but the condition known on the Yorkshire coast as " frosthaigh." There was a moderate sea running, the result of a recent storm, but the air was calm. The

German fleet chosen for the second raid consisted of three battle cruisers and two armoured cruisers, two smaller vessels mainly used for mine-laying, and possibly other minor craft. One battle cruiser and one armoured cruiser, accompanied by the two smaller vessels, bombarded Scarborough and Whitby and laid mines in the waters there. Two battle cruisers and one armoured cruiser attacked Hartlepool.

Owing to the haze over the waters as the ships approached it was impossible for observers to distinguish their names. The ships which attacked the Hartlepools might well have been the Derfflinger, the Von der Tann and the Blücher. It is more difficult to indicate what were the ships which attacked Scarborough and Whitby. They carried lighter armaments. The great number of the shells fired were 5·9 in. or 4 in. It is possible that one of them was the battle cruiser Seydlitz, and the other the protected cruiser Graudenz. If this were so, it is difficult to understand, however, why the heavy batteries of the Seydlitz were not more extensively used.

THE ATTACK ON HARTLEPOOL.

At eight o'clock on the morning of Wednesday, December 16, the people of Hartlepool were

[" *Times*" *Photograph.*

WEST HARTLEPOOL : Nos. 20 and 21, CLEVELAND ROAD.

HARTLEPOOL: VICTORIA PLACE.   [*"Times" Photograph.*
Practically the whole of this street was wrecked.

startled by the sounds of heavy distant firing. At first nothing was visible but flashes of flame far out at sea, but after a time the coastguards could faintly make out through the morning mist the dim outlines of three ships. The watchers on shore believed at first that the ships were part of a British fleet, firing on some approaching Germans, and they tried to exchange signals with them, but could obtain no reply. A number of men and women flocked down to the edge of the Town Moor to witness the spectacle. Proper defence precautions were not neglected. Word was passed to two patrol boats in the harbour and they made ready. A small force of garrison artillery—Territorials, with a few old regulars among them—stood by their guns at the fort. The local force of Durham Light Infantry took up positions at various points ready to resist any attempt at landing.

The three ships gradually drew nearer, until they were a little over two miles from the shore. It has since been said that they approached flying the White Ensign, and that they were firing out to sea to deceive the local garrison. Neither of these charges can be sustained. The morning was too misty to distinguish their flag, but responsible observers declare there was no reason to believe it was the White Ensign.

The German ships came suddenly out of the fog on the British flotilla and immediately started firing. They concentrated their fire on H.M.S. Doon, a destroyer of the " E " class, and H.M.S. Hardy, a more modern boat of the " K " class. Two men were killed, seven wounded, and three slightly wounded on the Doon, and two were killed, one died of wounds, fourteen wounded and one slightly injured on the Hardy. It was obviously impossible for the destroyers to stay and fight the great cruisers. They were, as one sailor picturesquely put it, like little rowing boats alongside of men of war, and all they could do was to attempt to escape, which they did. There is little credit to the German crews that they did not sink them. Evidently they believed they had done so, for in their official report they stated that one destroyer was sunk and the others disappeared in a badly damaged condition.

Suddenly the foremost German ship swung round and fired three shots right at the battery. They were well aimed. One fell to the right of the battery and killed several men, and a second, aimed a little high, struck the upper floors of a house near by. Two maiden ladies lived there. One of them was in the passage making for her sister's bedroom, possibly disturbed by the noise outside. The shot struck one sister, inflicting terrible wounds in the chest and killing her instantly. When neighbours went, after the bombardment, to search for the second sister, they could not at first find her. Careful exploration of the wrecked house showed later that she had been literally blown to bits.

Even as the first shells came tearing through the air the Territorials in the battery opened fire in return. It must be a cause of regret to most Englishmen that in this first battle of modern times between a British battery on British soil and an enemy's fleet at sea, the British soldiers were hopelessly handicapped by inadequate guns.

The men were splendid. Their commander, Colonel Robson, was an old volunteer officer and a local business man. The gun squads were young Territorials, of the Durham Royal Garrison Artillery, called suddenly and unexpectedly for the first time into action. As the first shell fell close to them, almost blinding and deafening them with its roar and fumes, they seemed for a second overcome. A brusque phrase shouted through a megaphone by their Colonel met with a response which showed that they had not lost heart or courage. Veteran regulars near by say that they worked throughout with absolute steadiness and precision. "Nearly all my detachment were Territorials," wrote one old soldier who was in charge of one of the guns. "I had my eye upon them during the action and must say they worked like heroes." The men knew that it was useless to hit the armoured belts of the enemy ships, so they aimed at the upper decks. Onlookers, who watched the whole battle from Redcar, tell how the bridge of one of the German ships was carried right off by one of our shots. The infantrymen occupying positions around never wavered. The 18th Service Battery of the Durham Light Infantry, a "Pals" Company of lads with three months' training, stood their ground under heavy fire at every point. A shell burst at the lighthouse battery, killing two gunners and two infantrymen and wounding seven others. Two infantry sergeants went out of cover, exposed to the full German fire, and rescued a fisherman who had his leg broken in getting out of his boat. When the bombardment ceased the troops led in the highly dangerous work of making their way into the wrecked and falling houses and rescuing the wounded.

The three German ships, skilfully handled, moved rapidly to avoid submarine attack, and kept up an unceasing bombardment on the port with 12 in., 11 in., 8 in., and 6 in. guns. Competent military observers estimate that within fifty minutes about 1,500 shells were fired. A large number of these were directed into the waters of the bay, probably to cripple any approaching submarine. Most of the remainder were fired over the fort into the docks, the gas and the water works. The two leading ships, after bombarding the batteries, passed north, and from a new position fired indiscriminately over West Hartlepool. Some shots fell far out into the country. Others buried themselves in the sand. The marksmanship was not so good as might have been expected. The third ship remained off the main battery and poured in broadside after broadside of 11 in. and 6 in. high explosive shell. The battery should have been quickly wiped out; but even the lighthouse in the centre of it was not demolished. The gunners stuck to their guns till the close of the action, and then fired a parting salvo at the departing ships. Many shells fell in the quiet business

[*"Times" Photograph.*

VICTORIA PLACE, HARTLEPOOL,
Where a Salvation Army Officer was killed.

and residential streets of West Hartlepool on the one side, and in the crowded poor streets of old Hartlepool on the other. These shots covered so wide an area that they cannot be explained by bad marksmanship. The German ships undoubtedly deliberately bombarded the residential part of the two towns, apart from the fort, the docks and the public works.

Some local authorities have considered it necessary to attempt to prove that the population were entirely calm under the rain of gun fire. Were this true, the people in Hartlepool would be either the most callous or the most steel-nerved the world has ever known. The attack came unexpectedly. There were no public instructions about what an individual should do in case of a raid. The first intimation most people had that anything was wrong was the tremendous noise of the firing of the heavy guns, the tearing approach of the shells, the crash and the roar as they burst and scattered. Fragments of shell came hurtling in all directions, varying from monster noses and thick steel bases, weighing from twenty to forty pounds, to jagged, terrible particles weighing only a fraction of an ounce. Windows broke with the concussion. Houses shook until it seemed as though they would fall.

The closely-set streets of old Hartlepool, densely populated, suffered most of all. One street was wrecked; others were badly damaged. The people did not know what to do, whether to remain indoors or to rush out. Many ran to the railway station, and here a dense crowd assembled, women in all stages of undress, some barefooted, some in their night clothes, some with shawl or waterproof hastily thrown over them. Some brought their babies along in perambulators or carried them. The people were rushing into danger in coming to this spot, and the few policemen and officials present who knew it, quietly tried to move them on, and directed them to a road leading out to the country. A shell caught the top of the Carnegie Library near by, and sent great stone corner-pieces and ornaments down among the crowd. Some of those who started out were caught by the shell fire as they stepped on to the pave ments. Others were struck down as they ran along the street. One sad case was that of the wife of a soldier, who sought to make her escape with her six children. A shell burst

WEST HARTLEPOOL: ST. BARNABAS CHURCH.   [*"Times" Photograph.*

HARTLEPOOL: THE BAPTIST CHAPEL.   [*" Times" Photograph.*]

near by, three of the children were killed, a boy of seven, a girl of eight, and a boy of fourteen, two of the other children were injured, and the mother was maimed. She was carried to hospital, where she lay for weeks before she was told of her children's death. A girl, nineteen years old, rushed into the street when the bombardment commenced. She was missed, and her body was found later in the mortuary by her stepfather. One arm and part of her head had been blown off. A poor woman had her body riddled while she was gathering sea coal. A lad of sixteen was killed while he was setting out to bring his mother, sister, and brother to safety. A young woman, twenty-five years old, was blown to pieces by a shell just as the family were sitting down to breakfast. Adjutant William Avery, of the Salvation Army, formerly a Cornish fisherman, was living in one of the most exposed streets. He had already brought his family downstairs and was coming down himself when a shell caught him and killed him instantly. A mission woman living in a house two or three doors off was killed by the same shell.

Perhaps the most tragic part was the deaths of the young children. Two brothers, six and eight years old, were going to school when two fragments of shell struck them; one was

killed outright, the other died later. A little girl of three was killed. The wife of a gunner in the Royal Artillery was taking a perambulator downstairs to convey her children to a place of safety when there came a tremendous explosion and she was plunged into darkness and almost suffocated. When she got free she found that her boy, five years old, was badly injured in the leg; he died later in hospital. Two little girls, four and six years old, the daughters of a naval stoker, were killed by a shell which struck the house where they stayed with their grandfather. The old man said: " I heard the rattling of the guns. I went to the door and saw a lot of people. I turned back to the house and was going to have a cup of tea when, all at once, smash went the corner of the house, and I was thrown to the other side of the room. After recovering myself I went to the door and saw my two poor little grandchildren lying dead among a lot of bricks." As against these deaths of children, place the case of an old lady of eighty-six, who was killed outright in her own home, a piece of shell weighing three pounds being afterwards found in her shoulder. There were some curious escapes. One mother was killed while carrying her child and the child escaped unhurt. In another case a young woman was hurrying along with her little

HARTLEPOOL : THE WORKHOUSE DINING HALL.   ["*Times*" *Photograph*.

brother. The brother was killed, while she was uninjured.

Churches seemed to suffer especially. The old church of St. Hilda, dating back to the late thirteenth century, one of the finest churches in the north, was struck by a shell which fell on the roof, broke it without exploding, and then burst close to the rectory across the way, doing great damage. The stone framework of the figure of the Madonna on St. Mary's Catholic Church was damaged, but the figure itself was unharmed. A shell passed right through the Baptist Church, smashing it front and rear, and it then penetrated into the bedroom of a young lady in a house behind, but did not injure her. The Scandinavian Church was badly splintered, broken and damaged.

The shipyards, the gasworks and the docks were subjected to special fire. At Messrs. Irvine's Middleton shipyard two men were killed, and the electrical and riggers' shops were set alight. A steamer in course of construction was hit by a shell, which pierced her hold, killing a man working there. The well-known works of Messrs. Richardson, Westgarth & Co.

suffered severely, and it was reported that seven men were killed there. Shells struck three great gasometers. The officials in charge had let the gas out of two at the first intimation of danger. The third burst into flames. Several men were injured around the gasworks. The office of the *Northern Daily Mail* was hit.

Invalids rushed from their beds into the street to get away. One woman only two days confined jumped up, wrapped a shawl around her babe, and ran out, away beyond the town, wide-eyed, terror-stricken, thinking of nothing else if she could only save her child. If there were much alarm, there were also many deeds of quiet heroism performed. Even young children displayed courage and helpfulness. One old lady for a long time afterwards tried to discover the name of a little lad who befriended her grandson, a boy of eight. The grandson ran from their home, which was near the gasworks, when shells were dropping all around and the gasometer took fire. As he ran, with nothing on but his shirt and a pair of knickers, another boy, a stranger, drew up alongside of him, asked him if he was not cold, and then took off his own overcoat and put it on him. "That's all right. I have another at home," he declared. In another case a husband was striving to get his family out of the town, the wife being very much alarmed. "I think they've hit me," one boy whispered to his elder brother. "But don't say anything. It'll only make mother more frighten·d." The boy kept on for some time until his father, noticing that he looked ill, took him to a doctor, who discovered a small brown wound in his body, and declared that it was merely a superficial scratch. The boy, still trying to conceal his pain, grew so bad that the father took him to another doctor. The latter examined him with X-rays and found that a particle of shell had penetrated downwards right through the pleura, the lung and the stomach, and was resting then on part of the spine. This story was related at the inquest on the boy.

People were so excited that in several cases they did not realize that they were shot until some time after the event. One man whose left hand was struck off declared that he never knew his hand had gone until he chanced to look down at the stump. Many were struck by splinters and knew nothing of their wounds until the bombardment was over. People made for the country. Large numbers went off by rail. Thousands tramped into Stockton and elsewhere. On the other hand, those who had any public duties kept on with them, disregarding danger. The girls in the Hartlepool telephone exchange continued steadily at their work right through the bombardment. Special constables and the members of a local Citizen Training Force did work beyond praise in keeping the crowds in order, aiding the wounded, and in generally helping the regular police.

A number of shells fell on the workhouse, but no lives were lost. The first fell on the top of the school dining-hall, where only five minutes before about ninety old people had been present at a religious service. Then shell after shell followed in different parts of the building. Apart from the female mental cases, who showed some panic, the inmates acted splendidly, and, in the words of the master, "The officials did their duty like trained soldiers, regardless of personal danger."

["*Times*" *Photograph.*]

HARTLEPOOL : WRECKED CONTAINER AT No. 2 GAS-WORKS.

The two small patrol ships in the harbour set out to attack the enemy. One of these, the Patrol, got under way and prepared for action, but before it was out of the harbour the firing had commenced and a shot caught it, striking the forebridge. The Patrol promptly opened fire, but its small 4-in. guns were of little use against the heavy metal of the enemy. " I don't think our fire reached them at all," said one sailor, writing of the event. Further shots struck the little vessel and then she sheered off, having received some considerable damage, and took refuge in the Tees. The second patrol boat does not seem to have been engaged.

The firing lasted for about fifty minutes, and then the ships retired in a northerly direction, scattering mines broadcast in their wake as they did so. The firing had barely ceased before men were at work everywhere, repairing the damage, calming panic-stricken people, and attending to the wounded. It is said that within half an hour of the battle glaziers were at work in business houses in West Hartlepool mending the broken panes.

A number of buildings were turned into temporary hospitals. Over forty of the wounded were conveyed to the workhouse. The Masonic Hall was used as a refuge. Forty odd cases were taken into Hartlepool Police Station and were laid around the men's billiard room there. All the hospitals were taxed to their utmost capacity. The Hartlepool Hospital, a fine building on the site of the ancient Friarage, which lies behind and quite close to the fort, was in the full line of the fire from the sea. Its beds were all occupied that morning with ordinary cases. When the bombardment began these were immediately transferred from the wards facing the front to the out-patients' department and the basement at the rear, where they were least likely to be hit. Before they were completely removed the wounded began to arrive, some carried along in roughly improvised stretchers by their friends, or brought in by the military or police. They were ghastly spectacles —some horribly torn, some with several great shell wounds, and many minor wounds from splinters. One victim had twenty separate wounds. All were incredibly filthy from the

[" *Times*" *Photograph.*

WEST HARTLEPOOL : THE BACK OF RUGBY TERRACE.

HARTLEPOOL: LILY STREET. ["*Times*" *Photograph.*]

Three people were killed in the house on the left.

black, the slime, and the *débris* that had been torn up in the approach of the shells. They laid them down in lines in the out-patients' department, and, shutting their ears to the apparently unceasing, overwhelming din of the shells flying overhead and around, the doctors and nurses and attendants strove to give some quick first-aid. A dose of morphia was administered to every one of the wounded to ease immediate pain, until opportunity arose to do more for them.

Suddenly there came an almost painful silence. The din of the bombardment ceased as quickly as it had begun. Word came in that the ships were retiring. The patients were taken back again to the ordinary wards, and the doctors began their work in the operating theatre. Close on twenty of the people brought in died before anything could be done for them. Then began a long and dreadful task. Hartlepool doctors are accustomed to tragic cases from the great works around. But those who toiled on hour after hour until midnight in the beautiful operating theatre of Hartlepool Hospital—one of the finest operating theatres in the country—admit that their imagination had scarce conceived such a shattering and tearing and disfiguring of the human frame as

came before them in the fifty cases they dealt with that day.

Apart from the size and number of the wounds made from the pieces of jagged shell, the cases presented many difficulties. In nearly every instance, in addition to the damage directly done by the shell striking a person, there was further damage caused by the splinters of wood and stone and the dirt and wreckage which had been forced into the victims' bodies in the upheaval of the explosions. Then the chemical constituents of the German shells were found to carry a poison in themselves, a poison which blackened the flesh, prevented healing, and afterwards, in spite of every care, made it in many cases impossible to save wounded limbs.

Two further features completed the grimness of the scene. There was one discomfort, minor compared with others, and yet serious enough in itself. The bombardment had injured the gas-works, and all gas supplies were cut off. The hospital employed gas largely for cooking and other purposes. Hot water, fortunately, could be obtained from another source. Then from immediately after the bombardment until late at night the hospital gates were thronged with an eager, anxious crowd of

Reading from left to right:—Top: ALDERMAN T. W. WATSON, Mayor of Hartlepool; LIEUTENANT-COLONEL L. ROBSON, "Fire Commander" of Hartlepool Batteries on December 16, 1914. Centre: C. C. GRAHAM, Esq., Mayor of Scarborough. Bottom: ALDERMAN DAVID McCOWAN, J.P., Mayor of Great Yarmouth; J. EGAN HARMSTON, Esq., Chairman, Whitby Urban District Council.

insistent people, demanding to know if their friends and their relatives were among the wounded and dead there.

In the afternoon a proclamation was issued : " The civil population are requested as far as possible to keep to their houses for the present. The situation is now quiet. The group leaders will advise in case of further damage. Any unexploded shells must not be touched, but information may be given to the police." Committees were immediately formed to care for the wounded and the distressed. The special constables and the Citizen Force worked under direction, clearing up the *débris*. All theatres and places of amusement were closed for some days. Owing to the damage done to the gas-works, no gas could be obtained, and apart from electric light the people had to rely on candles and lamps. The military authorities ordered everyone to be off the streets by seven o'clock at night, and this regulation was strictly enforced.

Hartlepool had been noted before the raid both for its military and non-military temper. It was its boast that it had given more recruits to the new Armies than any place of the size in the country. But in the days before the raid one section of the citizens of Hartlepool

had gravely protested against the guns and the gun practice of the fort. The noise of the practice firing disturbed them and broke their windows. Their fellow-citizens did not forget to remind them of their old complaints after the bombardment was over. The immediate effect was to produce a feeling of bitter resentment among the men of the port and among the men of Durham and of Yorkshire—resentment which took the form in this district of an immediate increase in recruiting. Large numbers of men sent their wives and children away, while remaining themselves at work. They felt, and it is difficult to blame them for it, that while it might be their duty to stay in the town and endure the risks of what might come, they had no right to keep their dependents in a place which the authorities apparently could not adequately protect.

The first estimates of the injured were 22 killed and 50 wounded. It soon became apparent that these figures were wholly inadequate. The authorities in the beginning, for some reason best known to themselves, apparently tried to minimise the death-roll. Within a few days it was known, however, that the killed were close on a hundred, and as one after another of the badly wounded died, the

["*Times*" *Photograph.*

SCARBOROUGH : HOLE MADE BY A SHELL NEAR THE WIRELESS STATION.

[*H. Walker.*

SCARBOROUGH:
INTERIOR OF 24, ROTHBURY STREET.

death-roll rose until early in January it had reached 113. The wounded numbered as nearly as can be told about 300. It is a cause for wonder not that so many were killed and wounded, but so few. When the enormous velocity and destructive power of the great German shells are realized, it is hard to understand how the port escaped so lightly. The German officers and crews might well have believed, as they steamed away, that they had laid the larger part of Hartlepool in ruins and had wiped out many of its population. Had a single shell landed in the dense crowd around the railway station, or in the park, the death-roll would have been enormously increased.

It was only by degrees that the people of Hartlepool realized the full horror of what they had gone through. Later, on Wednesday and on Thursday, they had abundant opportunity to witness the ruin wrought. Then, on Friday morning, when their nerves were taut, an unfortunate incident occurred. A notice was posted up in the Post Office as follows :

" Telegraph message from Staff-Captain Lyons, Headquarters, Hartlepool, 6.30 a.m., December 18, 1914 :

" Received message to look out for hostile airship. Warn all constables to warn all residents on approach of airship to go into basements of their homes and remain till danger is past. Advise them to keep cool, and not congregate in groups in streets. Rumours may be false, but everyone to be prepared."

The special constables were called together and warned. Unfortunately, they or their advisers misunderstood the message, and they hurried from house to house and from works to works, ordering people to their cellars, commanding the workmen in the shipyards to go home, and telling everyone that German aircraft were approaching. The result was what might have been anticipated. The people poured out into the streets. All business ceased. Crowds made for the park. Still greater crowds made for the country, to get away anywhere from the dropping bombs. Some of the women were in a state of high excitement and pathetic scenes were witnessed. Crowds thronged to the railway station and the outgoing trains were packed, mainly with women and children. When the harm had been done the police discovered their mistake, and the mayor issued a proclamation in the afternoon requesting the inhabitants of West Hartlepool to pursue their usual work quietly, as the message sent round in the morning was due to a misunderstanding. " There is no cause for alarm." The message came, however, much too late, and many women and children who had remained after the first bombardment now left the town. The people of West Hartlepool generally agreed, when subsequently surveying the history of the bombardment, that there was much more excitement in the streets on the Friday than on the day when the German ships were shelling them.

The mines scattered by the German vessels when retiring greatly impeded traffic at the port. Three ships were destroyed that night, the South Shields collier Eltwater, the Norwegian steamer Vaaren, and the Glasgow cargo steamer Princess Olga. The Eltwater struck a mine off Flamborough Head and six of her crew were killed. The Vaaren struck a mine off Whitby. She had seventeen men on board and only four escaped. The third ship, the Princess Olga, was blown up after striking a mine off Scarborough. In this case there was no loss of life. One result of the raid was almost to suspend business on the Newcastle

SCARBOROUGH.
DAMAGE DONE TO LIGHTHOUSE, CASTLE WALLS, AND BUILDINGS.

SCARBOROUGH BARRACKS.   [H. Walker.

Exchange for a day or two. Another was to help to stiffen shipping freights.

The German cruisers succeeded in causing a considerable loss of life amongst civilians. Some six hundred houses were damaged more or less. But they did not strike any vital blow at Hartlepool industry. The docks and the railway were uninjured. The gasworks were put right in the course of a few days. The shipyards scarcely stayed their activity for a day. The cruisers were not out of sight before the lorries of the corporation were around mending the broken tramway and other wires in the different streets. Business men whose premises were damaged found plenty of neighbours willing to lend them office room. A certain number of women and children cleared out of the town. But the essential prosperity of the manufacturing capacity and the national utility of the Hartlepools remained unimpaired. The Germans had failed to inflict vital damage; they had succeeded in arousing against themselves bitter and lasting anger that was yet to have far-reaching results.

THE ATTACK ON SCARBOROUGH.

Shortly before 8 o'clock on the same morning the coastguardsman stationed at the look-out point at Scarborough Castle telephoned to the wireless station behind the town: " Some strange ships are approaching from the north. I cannot make out what they are. They do not answer my signals." Then the man's voice could be heard by those listening at the other end in quicker, more agitated tones: " They are Germans. They are firing on us." The voice then ceased. The coastguardsman had scarcely given his warning before a shell from the foremost ship tore over the station, breaking the wires in its flight, and lodged in an empty barracks on the opposite side of the Castle grounds. The coastguardsman and a policeman were in a little wooden house on the cliff top with their telephone and other instruments. As the first shell passed over they made a rush for shelter. They had not got many yards away before a second shell followed, smashing to atoms the building they had just left. Shell after shell, thirty of them in all, poured in rapid succession on the same spot.

The German attacking force, which approached from the direction of Cloughton in the north, consisted of four vessels, two cruisers which carried out the main attack, and two smaller vessels which were mainly engaged in mine-laying. The two larger ships moved past the old Castle, being then about eight hundred yards out at sea, and steamed slowly in front of the town, firing all the time, until they came within little more than five hundred yards of the shore. Old fishermen, gazing at them, could not understand how it was possible for such large ships to come in so close. It was evident that the German pilots had intimate knowledge of Scarborough waters, otherwise they would certainly have run aground. They had learnt a lesson from the Yarmouth fiasco, and did not mean that their shells should fall short again. Their steady and regular progress showed also their confidence that there were no submarines in Scarborough Bay, for as they moved past the town they would have formed an ideal target.

As the ships moved forward they first thoroughly covered the ground in front of the ruins of old Scarborough Castle. They evidently believed that there were guns there and that the old barracks within the grounds was held by troops. Their heavy fire smashed the barracks, made a great gap in the old Castle walls and tore up the ground around. Possibly they considered it incredible that we should have neglected to fortify so ideal a defensive position. Their shell fire on the Castle grounds was merely wasted. The old barrack buildings were unoccupied, and had been unoccupied for some time, although just previous to this a suggestion had been made that women and children should be housed

there. It was fortunate that the suggestion had not been carried out. In various other ways, to which it would be unwise to refer, it could be seen from the direction of the German fire that their intelligence department was seriously at fault concerning the place.

From the Castle, the guns turned their attention to the town. Some of them directed their fire on the Grand Hotel, a large building and prominent landmark on the sea front. The upper floors of this hotel were shattered and the entrance floor from the front and the ground all around broken up. Many of the shells were directed towards Falsgrave, a suburb of Scarborough, where an important wireless station was placed. The wireless station itself was very little injured, but the private houses in the vicinity were badly damaged and many people wounded and killed. Some shells were also sent towards the gasworks and the waterworks, but the German fire was not confined to these spots. The claim that the ships aimed solely at the Castle, the wireless station, and one or two places where they believed troops to be stationed, cannot be sustained. The whole town was fired upon recklessly and indiscriminately, save those streets which were protected by the steep hills between them and the sea. Shells dropped

SCARBOROUGH: GLADSTONE ROAD SCHOOLS. [*"Times" Photograph.*

SCARBOROUGH: No. 2, WYKEHAM STREET,   *["Times" Photograph.*
Where four people were killed.

from very close by Clarence Gardens in the north to the grounds of the Yorkshire Lawn Tennis Club in the south, and from the sea-front eastwards to the small suburban streets on the extreme west side of the town. They landed over St. Oliver's Mount, a high hill to the south. They wrought great destruction in many of the wealthy residential sections, on the Esplanade, and in the Crescent. They killed and wounded people and destroyed houses in the central business portion of the town. They were widely scattered in the small residential streets off Gladstone Road. They went in lesser numbers to the north. It was evidently the purpose of the German commanders to rake the town from end to end, and to some extent they did it.

The people of Scarborough do not keep early hours in winter-time, and large numbers of the inhabitants were in bed when the firing started. At first they thought it thunder, but as the loud continuous explosions kept on, and as the shells burst in street after street, they quickly learned their mistake. One local alderman and magistrate, Mr. John Hall, was dressing in his bedroom when a shell burst in the room, injuring him so that he died as he was being carried up the steps of the infirmary. No. 2, Wykeham Street has since been named the house of tragedy. Four people were killed

here. A young soldier in the Royal Field Artillery, Driver Albert Bennett, was protecting his mother when a shell penetrated the house, killing him, the mother, and two boys, one nine years old, the other five. A tradesman's wife in Columbus Ravine was going down from the house above into the shop when a shell hit her, wounding her in such fashion that she died soon afterwards. Her husband in the shop was almost buried by the *débris.* A young woman picked up a baby to soothe its crying and took it into a bedroom for safety. A shell burst through the roof of the room, killing them both. A hairdresser's wife, on hearing the first shell fire, set out to fetch two neighbours and give them shelter in her cellar. As she was standing near the door of her house a shell glanced off a stone pillar and struck her body, killing her. A servant went upstairs to her mistress when the firing began, and reassured her, telling her that she thought the ships were practising. A few minutes later there was a loud crash and the mistress found her servant dead, struck in the breast by a shell. Mr. J. H. Turner, ex-sheriff of Yorkshire, living in Filey Road, took two of his servants into the boiler-house at the back of the building for safety. The third was missing. He went to look for her when a shell burst near, but left him uninjured. He still kept on with his search, and entering the library he found her there, covered with wreckage dead.

A postman, Alfred Beale, was on his round on the Esplanade when the bombardment began. He continued delivering his letters although he was in a part of the town where house after house was being wrecked. He knocked at the door of one house almost at the end of the town and a maidservant came to take the letters. As he was handing them to her a shell burst at the front of the house, doing considerable damage to the building and killing both of them. The hospital was hit. Public buildings of all kinds were badly damaged. Scarborough people still recall with pride how, when the bombardment began, Morning Communion was being held at St. Martin's Church on South Cliff. A shell passed through the tower and damaged part of the roof. The congregation showed some concern, but Archdeacon Mackarness told them that they were as safe in church as anywhere else, and he quietly carried through the service to the end.

Many of the people in the town were naturally greatly alarmed. Women rushed into the street, not taking time to put anything on.

Great throngs poured down Westborough to the railway station, and soon the station was crowded with people clamouring to get away. The officials carried on their duty as usual, put on extra carriages where possible, and got as many off as they could. Large numbers escaped from the town by road. Men with motors or traps filled them with women and children and drove them out of the town as quickly as possible. Many of the cases of death and of wounded were mainly due to the people being in the streets, as shells exploding in the streets scattered their splinters over a very wide area. But the people did not know what to do. They had received no instructions. The bombardment had come on them as a surprise, and it is not to be wondered at that many thought it well to rush from the shell-stricken houses. In many boarding schools, where the children were starting breakfast, the masters quietly paraded the pupils and marched them into the cellars or out into the shelter of some rising ground. One chauffeur, eighteen years old, in a house on the South Cliff, where the shells were constantly falling, saw another man struck down in the street by

SCARBOROUGH: EXTERIOR OF GRAND HOTEL BUFFET.

a shell. The lad at once rushed out, raised the man on his shoulder and carried him under fire into shelter. There were many incidents of this kind.

Humour was not lacking. A Territorial officer tells how, as he was hurrying down one of the main streets to the front, a typical British workman, with a basket of tools over his shoulder, stopped him : " Aye, sir," said the workman with great emphasis, " this kind of thing would never have happened if we had a Conservative Government in power ! " " I did not want to hear about Governments," the officer added, when telling the story ; " there was too much high explosive shell bursting in the vicinity for one to thrash out political arguments just then." One citizen, much excited, hurried into his garage to tell the driver, an old man, to get ready at once to take the family away. He found the driver quietly polishing a bit of brass. The old man looked up from his task with a face expressing great satisfaction : " Ah ! Master George," he said, " they've coom ! Ah've always said they'd coom, and they've coom ! " One old lady,

living on South Cliff, picked up a gun and hurried out to the sea front, anxious to have a shot at the enemy. Another, called upon to get out of the house, at once looked around to see what she could take with her, and seized upon a Christmas pudding, tucked it under her arm and ran off with it.

The German ships moved on to a point almost opposite the Grand Hotel. Then came a pause in the terrible noise of the shell explosions, and for about three minutes the gun fire ceased. This pause was due to the ships swinging round and reversing their course. They then re-opened fire with their guns on the other side and moved steadily up northwards again. While they were shelling the town the two smaller vessels moved out to sea, dropping long lines of mines from a little way off the shore in an outward direction. The Germans undoubtedly hoped that the bombardment would bring the British fleet up from the south and that in attempting to pursue them as they ran along the coast it would fall foul of the lines of mines. Steaming back, and firing as they retired, the two German cruisers slowly

["Times" Photograph.

SCARBOROUGH: REMAINS OF TWO BEDROOMS IN GRAND HOTEL.

SCARBOROUGH: INTERIOR OF THE GRAND HOTEL BUFFET.

passed their own minefield and then their guns ceased and they started off at full speed for the north.

The bombardment commenced at five minutes past eight and it was over at about half-past eight. During that time about five hundred shells were fired at the town and on the Castle. Quite a number of these shells fell into the sand on the sea front. The only possible explanation of this is that either the guns were too depressed or the Germans believed that some troops were entrenched there. Other shells went many miles out into the country. One struck the lighthouse and injured it so that it had afterwards to be taken down. Seventeen persons were killed, all of them civilians, including eight women and four children, one of the children being a baby of fourteen months. The number of wounded was about five times as great.

When the inquests were held on the victims of the raid, the jury wished to bring in a verdict that they had been murdered. The coroner suggested that the verdict should be that they had met their death through the bombardment of Scarborough by the enemy's ships. The foreman emphasized his demand, but the coroner pointed out that if the jury returned a verdict

of murder he would have to go through the formality of binding the police over to prosecute someone, and as the only persons who could be prosecuted seemed to be the officers of the German ships, such a course would be an absurdity. Nothing could be gained by returning a verdict of wilful murder against the commanders of those vessels, although he agreed with the foreman that it was a murderous attack. In the end the coroner's counsel prevailed.

It would be idle to deny that the Germans succeeded in inflicting very real damage upon Scarborough. One immediate result was that a large number of well-to-do people who had made this place their home left it. It was estimated, a fortnight after the raid, that fully six thousand people had gone away, and many more were going. In some of the wealthy streets only two, three or four families were left. Old people who had come here to end their days in peace naturally felt no call to remain and to expose themselves to unnecessary risks. The loss of so many people told heavily on the tradesmen of the town. The hotels and boarding-houses found themselves faced with a very serious prospect.

Once the first excitement was over, Scar-

borough settled down to take the thing philosophically—maybe too philosophically. It is
somewhat astonishing to read that the places
of amusement were open as usual that same
evening. People went about their work as
before. One shop whose front was blown out
bore a notice on its shutter, "Business as
usual." A new industry sprang up—the selling
of relics of fragments of shell. For a few weeks
large numbers of visitors poured into the town
to see the ruin wrought. The mayor and the
local authorities did their best to meet the
situation. The local evening papers were not
allowed for some time to say anything about
what had happened, not even allowed, until
late in the evening, to describe the scenes in
their own streets. The mayor issued a notice
that day : " I have been asked by many people
what they should do in consequence of the
bombardment of Scarborough this morning.
I have only one piece of advice to give, and
that is : ' Keep calm and help others to do
the same.' "

The local recruiting authorities attempted to
turn the occasion to profit. Special bills were
posted throughout the town and throughout
the county, urging the people to vengeance.
Here is a specimen of the bills :

The response, however, was somewhat dis-
appointing as compared with Hartlepool. The
country districts in Yorkshire responded very
well, but in Scarborough itself the recruiting
did not immediately receive the stimulus which
was anticipated. It must be remembered that
Scarborough, a professional pleasure town, has
a larger proportion of old people and a much
smaller proportion of active young men than
is the average in the great trading centres.

The mines sown by the German ships on
their retirement caused some trouble and some
loss before they were all cleared up. A fleet
of mine-sweepers was put to work under a
naval officer and officers of the Royal Naval
Reserve, and the seas fronting this part of the
coast were patiently swept day by day. There
are few more dangerous tasks on sea than this,
and before the mines were cleared more than
one mine-sweeper was wrecked, several ships
were sunk, and more than one sailor went to
his final rest.

The Attack on Whitby.

The two German ships, after bombarding
Scarborough, made in the direction of Whitby.
Half an hour later the chief officer of the coastguards at the signal station on the East
Cliff, Whitby, noticed through the haze the
ships approaching at great speed, the sea
constantly breaking over their stems and largely
hiding their bodies from view. Within ten
minutes the ships got within easy range and
slowed down, immediately opening fire on the
signal station.

The bombardment began before ten minutes
past nine and lasted only a few minutes. The
ships were two miles from the signal station
when they opened fire. The first broadside
hit the face of the cliff just underneath the
station. Four or five coastguardsmen, a sentry,
and some boy scouts were standing in the signal
station. They at once ran outside for shelter.
As they ran, a second broadside struck the
station, and one large splinter of shell hit a
coastguardsman named Randall, taking a
large part of his head off. His death must
have been instantaneous. One of the boy
scouts, Roy Miller by name, set out from the
station to deliver a message, when he was
caught in the leg by a piece of shell. It was
said at the time that he showed his pluck by
insisting on delivering his message before he
had his wound attended to. The wound
was at first believed to be only slight, but

SCARBOROUGH : ROOF OF THE GRAND HOTEL, *[" Times " Photograph.*
Which was badly damaged at both ends.

complications set in and the leg had to be amputated.

The firing was very heavy while it lasted, the number of shells thrown into the town being variously estimated at from 60 to 200. Probably the smaller was the more correct estimate. The guns were aimed, save for a few chance shots, in the direction of the coastguard station. The ships were so close in to the shore, the cliff immediately in front of them being from 200 to 250 feet high, that they found it difficult to control their angle of fire, and most of the shells went high, passing over the station and alighting in what is known as the Fishburn Park district, immediately behind the railway station. A few shells went wide. Two or three of these

struck the Abbey, doing some damage, more particularly to the west wing, but there is no reason to believe that the Abbey was aimed at. Had the Germans chosen to take this as their mark they could scarcely have failed to demolish it with a few well-placed shells. There is reason for congratulation that more damage was not done, seeing that it lies only two or three hundred yards from the Admiralty buildings. Some of the shells went so high that they fell in the village of Slights, four miles inland. But nearly all the real damage was done within a radius of 300 yards in the district immediately facing the back of East Cliff.

When the firing broke out two men in the Whitby Town railway station started to lead a horse along the line into safety. Just as they passed through a gate a shell exploded in the cattle dock near by and a piece hit an old goods porter, William Tunmore. He died within a few minutes as he was being conveyed to the hospital. The coastguard station itself was repeatedly struck. An invalid lady, Mrs. Miller, was in bed in a house in Springhill Terrace, when a shell struck the front of the house and some of the splinters wounded her. She was conveyed to a convalescent home near by and after lingering some time she died from *tetanus.* A Mrs. Marshall was hit in the leg. The total casualties were three killed and two wounded. One old seaman, 70 years old, was found dead on the day following the raid in one of the alms-houses, and it was believed that his death was brought about by the shock of the bombard-ment. Many people had surprisingly narrow escapes.

Quite a number of houses were badly damaged, the shells bursting in Fishburn Park and scat-tering destruction around for hundreds of yards in every direction. Some of the houses had their roofs torn completely off. Some had their fronts blown in, and some their brickwork dislodged and windows shattered. A pig was wounded, and a dog bled to death. It is sur-prising that two modern warships could fire powerful shells into a town for from eight to ten minutes and accomplish so little.

The people of Whitby scarcely realized what had happened before the whole thing was over. In many parts of the town, out of the line of fire, the people did not com-prehend that the town had been bombarded until the news was brought to them. The story was told in the town how the children in one school were singing the Lord's Prayer when they were startled by the explosion of a shell near at hand, an explosion which smashed the windows of the school. There was no panic and no rush. The mistress drew the children up and quietly marched them to the most protected part of the school building, where they remained until the end of the bombardment. An experience such as this comes as a severe shock to everyone. But Whitby was not nearly so perturbed, and had not so much reason to be, as Scarborough or Hartlepool. Its people, a hardy race of seamen, took their misadventure more as a matter of course and congratulated themselves that it was no worse. A few hundred people left the town, but many of them returned within a few days. The following letter from a lady living in Whitby, written to a friend, without any thought of publication, gives well in its very simplicity the sensations of the people :

I am sure you will be wondering how we fared during our visit from the Huns. I am thankful to tell you we are all alive and well after our terrifying experience. I had just sat down to my breakfast with my little ones when the first bang came, the like of which I had never heard before. I started to my feet to see what it was, when another came, more awful than the first, and still

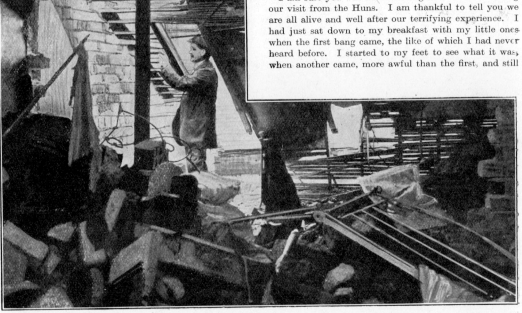

SCARBOROUGH: WRECKED TOP FLOOR OF HOUSE NEAR THE STATION.

more, and I soon realized that we were indeed in the hands of the enemy. I was dumbfounded. I took my children into my next door neighbour, who is an old lady 75 years old, and nearly blind, and lives alone, and there we stayed until the bombardment was over. I was afraid for my children ; Laura trembled like a leaf, and my dear little boy, I thought he would have died in my arms ; he lay with his eyes closed and never moved until the firing ceased. Jack (her husband) had a narrow escape ; he was working on the East Pier with four or five more men, and was watching these two ships, thinking they were English battleships, when they opened fire and shells flew all around them. They scrambled over the Pier side, and fortunately the tide was low and they were able to get on to the concrete ledge which runs along the piers on the harbour side, and there they had to stay until the bombardment was over. He saw every shell that was fired come over the town and explode, and it was agony for him, for he did not know what might be happening to us, yet they dared not move for their lives. You can imagine the joy when he came home and found us all safe : he went back and picked up several pieces of shell. It is impossible for me to try to explain to you what it was like ; the noise of the shells as they whistled and exploded over our heads was terrifying, and much worse than the heaviest peal of thunder I have ever heard, and we live in fear of their return. Three or four hundred people have left the town, and I feel I would like to take my little ones to a place of safety, but one hardly knows what to do for the best. But we thank God we are alive, and pray we may never hear the sound again.

Various official messages were published in London telling of the raid. They are of historic importance :—

" Admiralty, 11.25 a.m., Dec. 16, 1914.

" German movements of some importance are taking place this morning in the North Sea.

" Scarborough and Hartlepool have been shelled, and our flotillas have at various points been engaged.

" The situation is developing."

" War Office, 1.35 p.m.

" The Fortress Commander at West Hartlepool reports that German war vessels engaged that fortress between 8 o'clock and 9 o'clock this morning. The enemy were driven off.

" A small German war vessel also opened fire on Scarborough and Whitby."

" Admiralty, 9.20 p.m.

" This morning a German cruiser force made a demonstration upon the Yorkshire coast, in the course of which they shelled Hartlepool, Whitby and Scarborough.

" A number of their fastest ships were employed for this purpose, and they remained about an hour on the coast. They were engaged by the patrol vessels on the spot.

" As soon as the presence of the enemy was reported a British patrolling squadron endeavoured to cut them off. On being sighted by British vessels the Germans retired at full speed, and, favoured by the mist, succeeded in making good their escape.

THE VEN. ARCHDEACON MACKARNESS,
M.A., D.D., of Scarborough.

" The losses on both sides are small, but full reports have not yet been received.

" The Admiralty take the opportunity of pointing out that demonstrations of this character against unfortified towns or commercial ports, though not difficult to accomplish provided that a certain amount of risk is accepted, are devoid of military significance.

" They may cause some loss of life among the civil population and some damage to private property, which is much to be regretted ; but they must not in any circumstances be allowed to modify the general naval policy which is being pursued."

" War Office, 11.35 p.m.

" At 8 a.m. to-day three enemy ships were sighted off Hartlepool, and at 8.15 they commenced a bombardment.

" The ships appeared to be two battle cruisers and one armoured cruiser. The land batteries replied, and are reported to have hit and damaged the enemy.

" At 8.50 the firing ceased, and the enemy steamed away.

" None of our guns were touched. One shell fell in the R.E. line and several in the lines of

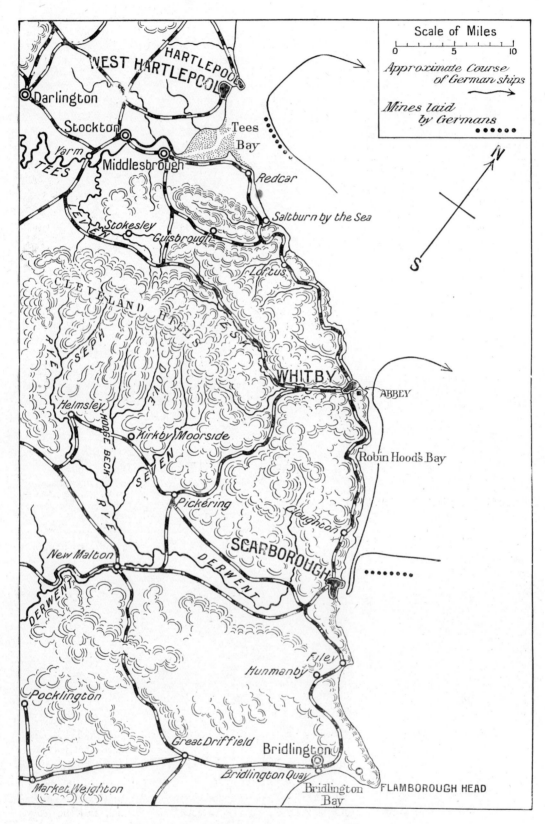

THE SCENE OF THE SECOND RAID.

the 18th (Service) Battalion of the Durham Light Infantry.

" The casualties amongst the troops amounted to seven killed and fourteen wounded.

" Some damage was done to the town, and the gasworks were set on fire.

" During the bombardment, especially in West Hartlepool, the people crowded in the streets, and approximately 22 were killed and 50 wounded.

" At the same time a battle cruiser and an armoured cruiser appeared off Scarborough and fired about 50 shots, which caused considerable damage, and 13 casualties are reported.

" At Whitby two battle cruisers fired some shots, doing damage to buildings, and the following casualties are reported : Two killed and two wounded.

" At all three places there was an entire absence of panic, and the demeanour of the people was everything that could be desired."

The authorities seemed at first anxious to keep back further information of the raid. Thus local newspapers in Scarborough and in Hartlepool were not allowed, until late in the day, to publish any independent descriptions of what had happened. The Leeds Post Office, one of the largest offices in the Provinces, refused to handle any telegraphic messages describing it. It was explained afterwards that this action of the Leeds Post Office was due to a misunderstanding of instructions. But the authorities later relaxed the attempt to suppress details. They were wise to take this course, for the accounts of the raid, circulated throughout the Empire, put a new edge to the temper of the British. Hitherto, in spite of all efforts, it had been difficult to bring home to many of our people the fact that this war was no alien thing, fought in other lands, demanding sacrifices no doubt, but never threatening our shores or the persons of our civil population. Hartlepool and Scarborough, with their shelled streets and wrecked buildings, were a living and actual demonstration that Britain was now engaged in a battle for life. It was not fear that came to the people, but a spirit of indignation and of determination. Some of the daily newspapers printed groups of photographs of the little children murdered by shell fire. Men cut these photographs out of the papers and kept them as reminders of duty. In hundreds of towns and thousands of villages the pictures

SCARBOROUGH : " BUSINESS AS USUAL."
Mr. Merryweather's wife was killed whilst taking some ladies down to the cellar for safety.

of the slain women and children of Scarborough stimulated recruiting and increased effort.

A great wave of sympathy for the people of the towns was manifested. The King voiced it in a message enquiring as to the condition of the wounded and trusting they would have a speedy recovery, when he told how much the people of the bombarded towns had been in his thoughts during the past weeks and how deeply he sympathized with the bereaved families in their districts. Mr. Winston Churchill wrote, as First Lord of the Admiralty, to the Mayor of Scarborough :

ADMIRALTY, S.W., December 20, 1914.

MY DEAR MR. MAYOR,—I send you a message of sympathy, not only on my own account, but on behalf of the Navy, in the losses Scarborough has sustained. We mourn with you the peaceful inhabitants who have been killed or maimed, and particularly the women and children. We admire the dignity and fortitude with which Scarborough, Whitby, and the Hartlepools have confronted outrage. We share your disappointment that the miscreants escaped unpunished. We await with patience the opportunity that will surely come.

But viewed in its larger aspect, the incident is one of the most instructive and encouraging that have happened in the war. Nothing proves more plainly the effectiveness of British naval pressure than the frenzy of hatred aroused against us in the breasts of the enemy. This hatred has already passed the frontiers of reason. It clouds their vision, it darkens their counsels, it convulses their movements. We see a nation of military calculators throwing calculation to the winds ; of strategists who have lost their sense of proportion ; of schemers who have ceased to balance loss and gain.

Practically the whole fast cruiser force of the German Navy, including some great ships vital to their fleet and utterly irreplaceable, has been risked for the passing pleasure of killing as many English people as possible, irrespective of sex, age, or condition, in the limited time

available. To this act of military and political folly they were impelled by the violence of feelings which could find no other vent. This is very satisfactory, and should confirm us in our courses. Their hate is the measure of their fear. Its senseless expression is the proof of their impotence and the seal of their dishonour. Whatever feats of arms the German Navy may hereafter perform, the stigma of the baby-killers of Scarborough will brand its officers and men while sailors sail the seas.

Believe me, dear Mr. Mayor,
Yours faithfully,
WINSTON S. CHURCHILL.

The Mayor of Scarborough's reply indicated the temper of the people of the attacked towns :

It is evident the enemy did not dare to face our Fleet and so attacked an undefended town in this way. Scarborough has taken her part in the great struggle now proceeding. Whilst we deplore the loss of life and property, mourn for our dead and sympathize with our wounded, we are nevertheless as fully determined as ever that the war must be fought to a successful finish.

Our surprise at the attack was greater as we were led to believe from the conduct of the plucky commander of the Emden that German sailors understood something about the glorious old traditions of the sea. It is evident from our experiences of Wednesday that this is not so. Some newcomers into honourable professions first learn the tricks and lastly the traditions. As their commanders get older in the service they will find that an iron cross pinned on their breast even by King Herod will not shield them from the shafts of shame and dishonour.

Neutral countries felt that some explanation was required from Germany as to its reasons for bombarding undefended towns such as Scarborough and Whitby. This feeling found particular expression in the United States, the nation which has strongly and persistently supported the plan of preventing war by inter-

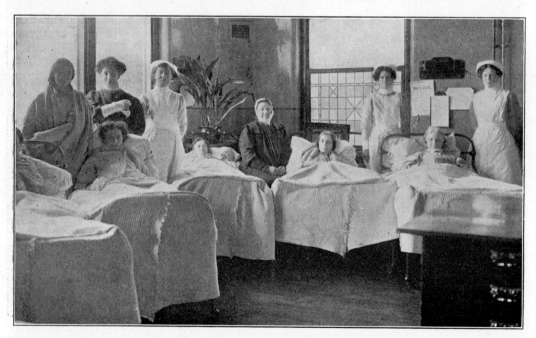

WOMEN'S WARD, SCARBOROUGH HOSPITAL.   ["Times" Photograph.

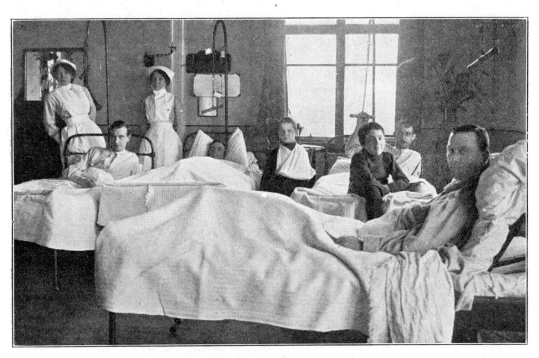

MEN'S WARD, SCARBOROUGH HOSPITAL. [*"Times" Photograph*.

national agreements and by mutual conventions. If conventions are to count for nothing and their stipulations are to be broken at the first period of strain, of what use are they ? This question was raised by many American papers. At the same time the American public recognized that England was likely to gain rather than lose by the incident, mortifying as it was. "The danger has been brought home in the most effective way," said the *New York World*, "and the new knowledge of this danger ought to be worth a million recruits to Kitchener's Army. It may be doubted if those recruits could have been obtained in any other way. In the long run Great Britain stands to gain infinitely more in this daring raid by the German cruisers than the Germans themselves can hope to do." The same feeling found expression in Italy, where the newspapers expressed the conviction of the Italian people, that once more Germany had attempted to terrorize an unarmed and inno- cent population in the hope of distracting the attention of the fighting men from their more important task.

The first note of the German Press was one, not of excuse, but of triumph. "Once more," said the *Berliner Tageblatt*, "our naval forces, braving the danger of scattered mines in the North Sea, have shelled English fortified places." The *Berliner Neueste Nachrichten* said : "This time it is not merely a daring cruiser raid or the

mere throwing of a bomb, but a regular bom- bardment of fortified places. It is a further proof of the gallantry of our navy." Other papers declared the bombardment was the pos- sible herald of greater events to come. Berlin was jubilant. The city was decorated with flags and, in the words of the Copenhagen correspondent of *The Times*: "The Press exults over the opportuneness of the *coup*, which shows that the initiative and the energy of the German Fleet have not been affected by the British victory off the Falklands. It empha- sizes with pride that the Germans traversed both mines and patrols, and greeted British towns while their inhabitants were sound asleep."

Captain Persius, one of the best-known German naval critics, declared in the *Berliner Tageblatt* that Scarborough is "the most important harbour on the East Coast of England between the Thames and the Humber, and is protected by powerful batteries." The chief export from Scarborough, he declared, was corn, and he hoped many shiploads were sent to the bottom. Captain Persius, some time before the war, visited English naval stations, and was even granted special facilities by our authorities. The probable explanation of his statement is that he mistook Scarborough for Harwich. This fable about the defences of Scarborough was persistently repeated in the

WHITBY: THE ABBEY AND THE COASTGUARD STATION ON THE CLIFF.

German Press and in neutral newspapers under German influence. Some of the papers even went so far as to tell the number of the guns, the size of the guns and their position. They failed to explain, however, why, if the guns were there, they did not attempt to reply to the German fire. The bitter regret of old military men at Scarborough was that some of the guns that were there in old days had not been left, for they were confident that even old guns could have raked the decks of the German cruisers, so close were they in to shore. Later on, the more serious defenders of the German action declared that the presence of a wireless station at Scarborough and of a naval signal station at Whitby justified them in bombarding those places.

Underneath the many German comments two things could be observed—one a feeling of satisfaction that English people had been made to suffer, and next, the confident belief that the nerves of the English people and of the British Navy would be shaken. These sentiments were brought out in comments such as the following :

Cologne Gazette : " We think we may say that—the English part of the world apart—people everywhere will

have heard with satisfaction and just *Schadenfreude* of this second punishment of the great sea robber who oppresses the whole world. The punishment has been inflicted with England's own particular weapon, and inflicted in England's very own country, on the soil of the arrogant island upon which John Bull believes himself to be secure and safe from punishment."

Tägliche Rundschau : " Will the overwhelming effect upon English nerves be diminished by the fact that it is from a German source that the people of London hear the painful news of the destruction of two destroyers and of serious injury to a third ? Already the European echo of the thunder of German guns on the English coast rings unpleasantly in English ears. What will it be like when the world learns the news kept back by the English Admiralty of the complete success of the German blow ? The world will learn with new astonishment that England is able to make the North Sea a field of death and destruction for all neutral shipping and even for its own shipping, but that it was not able to make the North Sea unsafe for the German Navy."

Count Reventlow wrote : " The news has created a sensation throughout the whole world. We do not think of drawing the inference that the German blow and the destruction of two English destroyers possess considerable military importance. It would be wrong if people in Germany were to suppose that. The enormous sensation excited everywhere is of all the greater psychological interest because it indictates the superstitious respect which Great Britain was able to procure for herself. The destruction or even the bombardment of a British warship was regarded as something unheard of, but the idea of throwing shells, real shells, which destroy and kill, at the coastworks of Great Britain—that is a crime against the majesty of British supremacy such as no enemy of Great Britain ventured upon. The German people is not disposed to reply to this war of annihilation with a bow and politeness. We hope confidently that this truth will be brought more and more to the consciousness of the English, because it is upon this that our success depends."

In Great Britain itself the raid brought two questions to the front—coast defence and espionage on the East Coast.

The first and the natural question of the average layman was why the Admiralty had not prevented this raid or why, if it was unable to prevent it, it had not succeeded in capturing the German ships before they got back. The paragraph in the Admiralty official announcement of the raid, in which it stated that the bombardments might cause some loss of life among the civil population and some damage to private property, which was much to be regretted, but they must not in any circumstances be allowed to modify the general naval policy which was being pursued, came in for special criticism. It was felt that the authorities had attempted to minimize the bombardment, and the opinion was generally expressed that they ought not to have committed themselves to the early statement that the civilian casualties at the Hartlepools were twenty-two killed and fifty injured. The feeling on the North-East Coast was voiced by two men of position and influence. Sir Walter Runciman, M.P. for Hartlepool, and father of a Cabinet Minister, asked: "How does it come to pass that when German vessels did risk into the open from their hiding-place they were allowed to come to our shores unobserved, unchallenged, and obviously unknown? I think it fair criticism to ask, without casting any reflection on a branch of the national service whose deeds during the present war have thrilled us with pride of race, why it happened that the German ships were first of all allowed to get here without interruption, and, secondly, why they were allowed to escape. What has the Intelligence Department to say to this? Were we caught napping?"

Mr. Samuel Storey declared that, translated into simple language, the Admiralty declaration meant:

"(1) Open towns on the East Coast must expect to be bombarded, and we cannot help it.

"(2) Those who are killed must be killed, and their relatives who mourn must mourn. We are sorry, but this cannot be prevented.

WHITBY: THE ABBEY.   ["*Times*" *Photograph.*]

WHITBY: CORNER OF GEORGE STREET. [*"Times" Photograph.*]

" (3) Though we are supposed to command the North Sea, we cannot scatter our big ships about to prevent bombardments, which, though deplorable, are devoid of military significance.

" I think that nothing more calculated to depress and alarm the public—mind you, not a record of facts, but a prophecy of future misfortunes—could be designed by the most irresponsible alarmist."

The answer to such criticism was given in a leading article in *The Times* :

The protection of these shores is not the primary object of the Royal Navy in war. The safeguarding of England —not necessarily of little bits of England—is a consequence of naval strategy, but not its primary and immediate object. The purpose of the Royal Navy is to engage and destroy the ships of the enemy, and that purpose will be inflexibly pursued in spite of all subtle temptations to abandon it for other objects. Neither raids nor even invasion will deter our Fleet from the aim for which it was created, and for which it keeps the seas. A good many people in this country still think of our warships as stationed like a row of sentinels on a line drawn before the German ports. Whatever their occupation may be, it is not that. The possibility of a German raid upon the English coast has always existed since the war began, and will continue to exist so long as a single German warship of great speed remains afloat ; but the indignant protests we have received whenever we have pointed these matters out show that the first principles of naval strategy are still imperfectly understood even by this maritime race. The duty of repelling invasion, should

it be attempted, rests upon the manhood of the nation. Perhaps it will now be more clearly discerned. The Royal Navy is doing its work, doing it resolutely, and doing it well. It has not failed us yet, and it will not fail us upon that great day for which it longs and waits.

While the Navy could not and must not turn away from this main task, even for the admittedly important work of guarding undefended towns on the coast, there was a general feeling that something should be done to make such raids more difficult, and to ensure that the enemy should meet with some adequate resistance were he again to penetrate our guards. Shortly afterwards satisfactory assurances were given to the people of some of the towns affected that such steps had been taken. At the same time the local authorities in the different districts along the coast recognized the unwisdom of keeping back definite instructions from the public generally about what should be done in case of a raid, lest the people be alarmed. It was frankly recognized and admitted that no absolute guarantee could be given that further raids would not take place, but the authorities at least saw to it that people generally received such elementary instructions of what to do in case of a raid that there should not be, as was the case in Hartlepool and Scarborough, needless loss of life by people rushing into danger through ignorance of how to act.

Much interest was aroused over the question of espionage. For some weeks before the raid there had been a general feeling on the East Coast that the authorities there were too lax in dealing with possible spies. Strangers were allowed to travel freely anywhere they pleased, by motor-car, by rail, or on foot, over almost the whole of the East Coast danger zone. Large numbers of Germans and of naturalized Germans still lived on the coast. Thus at Seaton Carew, just outside West Hartlepool, several dozen Germans were employed by one firm alone. The people were convinced that there were numbers of German agents who, by signalling out to sea and other means, gave the enemy valuable information. Most of the spy stories were wholly groundless. Fevered imaginations twisted the most harmless acts into deadly conspiracies. Innocent people were suspected, and the police were kept busy enquiring into charges which had no foundation whatever. But the attacks on the different ports proved that in some way or another the German authorities kept themselves informed of our naval doings along the coast. It was not by accident that German ships

[*"Times" Photograph.*

WHITBY: CORNER OF ESK TERRACE.

fell on these places when the usual strong naval forces guarding them were absent. It was not by accident that they ran success-

GERMAN CRUISER "YORCK."
She was sunk by a German mine when returning from the Yarmouth Raid.

SCARBOROUGH: THE MONTPELIER HOTEL.   [*"Times" Photograph.*

fully through British mine fields. It was not by accident that the ships before Hartlepool stationed themselves in such a way that our fire should be least effective against them. The task before our authorities was much more difficult than detecting thinly disguised conspirators who flashed lights as signals out to sea. It was evident that along the East Coast careful espionage was being carried out. The raids led to a more determined attempt on the part of the authorities to locate this. As a beginning, many of the Germans resident on the coast were arrested and conducted to detention camps, and others, including naturalized Germans to the second generation, were ordered to leave some of the main points.

The second raid was a bitter but salutary experience for the British people. It taught them the danger of over-confidence. It gave final proof to their conviction that they were face to face with a foe who was restrained by no scruple in his endeavour to carry out his purpose. The long lists of dead and wounded civilians, and the sight of the ruined homes, the broken churches, and the injured hospitals and schools, told us what we as a nation might well expect should the Germans effect any landings here. The nation as a whole did what it could to recoup the bombarded towns for their material loss. The Government announced its intention of paying compensation to those who had suffered. But it was well felt from end to end of the kingdom that the only right answer to the East Coast raid could be an increase of our fighting power, and a renewal of the national determination to conduct the war to a final stage that would make, not for ourselves alone but for generations yet unborn, such attempts in future impossible.

CHAPTER XLIV.

JAPAN'S PART IN THE WAR.

JAPAN DECLARES WAR ON GERMANY—THE EMPEROR'S RESCRIPT—BARON KATO ON THE ALLIANCE
—JAPAN'S MILITARY POSITION—HISTORY OF THE ARMY—RESULTS OF INSULARITY—STRENGTH OF
JAPAN—MILITARY ORGANIZATION—CAVALRY AND HORSES—THE ARMY IN 1914—COMPOSITION OF
TSING-TAU FORCE—NAVAL GROWTH OF JAPAN—EXPENDITURE ON THE FLEET—THE NAVY IN
1914—NAVAL AVIATION—THE BLOCKADE COMMENCED—ARRIVAL OF THE BRITISH FORCE—JAPAN'S
HELP IN EUROPE—PROGRESS OF THE SIEGE—JAPAN AND CHINA—PRINCE HEINRICH HILL TAKEN—
BEGINNING OF THE END—FINAL BOMBARDMENT—GERMANY AND CHINA—THE GENERAL ASSAULT
—SURRENDER OF TSING-TAU—GERMAN HATRED OF ENGLAND—CAPTURE OF GERMAN ISLANDS—
NEUTRAL COUNTRIES AND JAPAN—GERMAN LIES—AMENITIES OF THE ALLIANCE—"THE TIMES"
ON THE SITUATION—CLEARING THE PACIFIC—JAPANESE POLITICS—FINANCIAL DIFFICULTIES—
BARON KATO'S STATEMENT—INTERNATIONAL CRITICISM.

WHEN the great war broke out there was no question of race or colour involved in the invitation of Japan to the arena. The only question was whether, according to the terms of the treaty between Britain and Japan, the latter's duty was to take part in the conflict.

This question was fully and finally answered by the Emperor of Japan in the rescript which announced the declaration of war against Germany. This is a document which demands quotation in full, not only because it clearly defines the cause of war, but also because it indicates the unlimited scope of war which Japan was prepared to carry on in accordance with her treaty obligations.

The following is the text of the Imperial Rescript declaring war on Germany :

" We, by the Grace of Heaven, Emperor of Japan, on the throne occupied by the same Dynasty from time immemorial, do hereby make the following proclamation to all Our loyal and brave subjects :

" We, hereby, declare war against Germany and We command Our Army and Navy to carry on hostilities against that Empire with all their strength, and We also command all Our competent authorities to make every effort in pursuance of their respective duties to attain the national aim within the limit of the law of nations.

" Since the outbreak of the present war in Europe, the calamitous effect of which We view with grave concern, We, on Our part, have entertained hopes of preserving the peace of the Far East by the maintenance of strict neutrality, but the action of Germany has at length compelled Great Britain, Our Ally, to open hostilities against that country, and Germany is at Kiaochau, its leased territory in China, busy with warlike preparations, while her armed vessels, cruising the seas of Eastern Asia, are threatening Our commerce and that of Our Ally. The peace of the Far East is thus in jeopardy.

" Accordingly, Our Government, and that of His Britannic Majesty, after a full and frank communication with each other, agreed to take such measures as may be necessary for the protection of the general interests contemplated

THE EMPEROR OF JAPAN.

in the Agreement of Alliance, and We, on Our part, being desirous to attain that object by peaceful means, commanded Our Government to offer, with sincerity, an advice to the Imperial German Government. By the last day appointed for the purpose, however, Our Government failed to receive an answer accepting their advice.

"It is with profound regret that We, in spite of Our ardent devotion to the cause of peace, are thus compelled to declare war, especially at this early period of Our reign and while We are still in mourning for Our lamented Mother.

"It is Our earnest wish that, by the loyalty and valour of Our faithful subjects, peace may soon be restored and the glory of the Empire be enhanced."

There is no suggestion in the Imperial Rescript that the action of Japan was taken in response to a direct request for assistance from the British Government. If the Emperor of Japan had not been absolutely sure of the devotion of his people it would have been easy and natural for his advisers to have interpolated in this declaration of war a statement that the momentous decision was taken in response to a direct request from an Ally to whom the Empire was bound by treaty, &c., &c. Indeed, in stating the case to the Japanese Diet, Baron Kato, the Foreign Minister, precisely and very properly explained the exact position. After outlining the situation created

by German aggression in Europe and showing that the force of circumstances had compelled Britain to participate in the war, he said:

Early in August the British Government asked the Imperial Government for assistance under the terms of the Anglo-Japanese Alliance. German men-of-war and armed vessels were prowling around the seas of Eastern Asia, menacing our commerce and that of our Ally, while Kiaochau was carrying out operations apparently for the purpose of constituting a base for warlike operations in Eastern Asia. Grave anxiety was thus felt for the maintenance of peace in the Far East.

As all are aware, the agreement and Alliance between Japan and Great Britain has for its object the consolidation and maintenance of general peace in Eastern Asia and the maintenance of the independence and integrity of China, as well as the principle of equal opportunities for commerce and industry for all nations in that country, and the maintenance and defence respectively of territorial rights and special interests of contracting parties in Eastern Asia. Therefore, inasmuch as we were asked by our Ally for assistance at a time when commerce in Eastern Asia, which Japan and Great Britain regard alike as one of their special interests, is subjected to a constant menace, Japan, who regards that Alliance as a guiding principle of her foreign policy could not but comply to the request to do her part.

Germany's possession of a base for powerful activities in one corner of the Far East was not only a serious obstacle to the maintenance of permanent peace, but also threatened the immediate interests of the Japanese Empire. The Japanese Government, therefore, resolved to comply with the British request, and, if necessary, to open hostilities against Germany. After the Imperial sanction had been obtained I communicated this resolution to the British Government, and a full and frank

THE EMPEROR IN NATIVE DRESS.

COUNT OKUMA,
Prime Minister of Japan.

exchange of views between the two Governments followed, and it was finally agreed between them to take such measures as were necessary to protect the general interests contemplated in the agreement and the Alliance.

Japan had no desire or inclination to become involved in the present conflict, but she believed she owed it to herself to be faithful to the Alliance and to strengthen its foundation by ensuring permanent peace in the East and protecting the special interests of the two Allied Powers. Desiring, however, to solve the situation by pacific means, the Imperial Government, on August 15, gave the following advice to the German Government. [Here the Minister quoted the text of the Japanese ultimatum.] Until the last moment of the time allowed—namely, until August 23—the Imperial Government received no answer, and in consequence the Imperial Rescript declaring war was issued the next day.

In this statement before the Diet, where criticism might be expected from every point of view, it was right and proper for the Foreign Minister to state the full facts of the case. From the British point of view it was far better that he should frankly explain that the action of Japan resulted directly from a request by Britain than that this fact should have been elicited by cross-examination in debate.

In the eyes of Europe, America and Australia, Japan occupied a much better position in intervening than would otherwise have been the case when Baron Kato was able to preface his statement of Japan's courageous decision with the words: "inasmuch as we were asked by our Ally for assistance."

The terms of the ultimatum quoted by

Baron Kato were—with intentional sarcasm, no doubt—modelled upon those of the famous German message which compelled Japan to abandon the fruits of victory on a previous occasion. They were to the effect that Germany should withdraw all warships from Chinese and Japanese waters and deliver up by September 15, 1914, the entire leased territory of Kiaochau with a view to the eventual restoration of the same to China. This was presented on August 15 and a reply was requested within a week. The only considerations which might have inclined the Kaiser's advisers to negotiate with Japan would have been connected with the waste of money and blood in defending a hopeless position; but this form of waste does not carry weight with the Berlin Government. They recognized that the ultimatum was in itself a declaration of war, and the actual declaration which followed on August 23, 1914, was only a formality. The purport of Japan's alliance with Britain was to secure the safety of British and Japanese commerce in the Far East. So long as the Far Eastern seas were infested with German

[*Lafayette.*

BARON KATO,
Japanese Minister for Foreign Affairs.

HIS EXCELLENCY Mr. K. INOUYE,
Japanese Ambassador in London.

cruisers and the Germans had a naval base at Tsing-Tau, British commerce would not be safe. The British fleet had a large task to perform nearer home : so the British Government did not hesitate to ask Japan to act up to her alliance. The Japanese Government, acting up to the principle of " faithfulness "— what a contrast to the " frightfulness " of the Germans !—showed no hesitation either. There was only one absolutely necessary condition to the fulfilment of Japan's obligation to secure the safety of British commerce in the Far East, and that was that a clean sweep should be made of German sea-power there. So Japan, confident in her power to enforce her demand, asked the Germans to make a clean sweep of themselves and to promise within a week to do it. The position of Japan was perfectly logical and natural, provided that she was prepared to stand by her pledged word. Fortunately, this was never in doubt, and the fate of Tsing-Tau was a foregone conclusion.

We are not saying, of course, that Japan had no interests of her own to serve in acting loyally towards her British ally. There would be no justification for an alliance from which both sides did not hope to gain advantage ; and in the case of Japan, she was a vigorous, reju-

venated Power in the Far East with the constant aggravation of a mailed fist at Tsing-Tau thrust under her nose. We in Britain now realize the error which we committed in giving Heligoland to the Germans ; but suppose that we had allowed them to establish themselves in the Channel Islands ! Allowing for the more spacious distances of the Far East, this is no worse a supposition than the actual fact involved in the German occupation of Kiaochau.

The actual military position of Japan at the outbreak of the war cannot be completely understood unless we realize the absolute professional detachment of the soldier-man in Japan from all political ideas. In Japan there were at the time of the outbreak of war no party politics, because political " parties " had never existed. Instead, there were only two rival clans. One of these was identified by tradition with the navy, and the other with the army, and both were intensely united in devotion to the Emperor. In the matter of politics, therefore, there was nothing to bar from the conversation in an officers' mess. Nor was it possible for Japanese officers or men, collectively or individually, to be influenced by political " views " —such as might not unreasonably have been

[*Elliott & Fry.*

SIR W. CONYNGHAM GREENE,
British Ambassador at Tokyo

GERMAN SOLDIERS ON THE WALLS OF TSING-TAU.

expected, for instance, in a regiment of Irish Catholics quartered in Belfast before the war, or a regiment of Indian Pathans in Benares—fanatical Mahomedans in the Hindu holy of holies.

Another point which is interesting to note in connexion with the Japanese Army is that although its discipline, equipment and organization may seem to be things of yesterday, our military problems of to-day affected Japan in the seventh century. It was about the year A.D. 690 that the Empress Jito found herself sufficiently strong to be able to provide for national defence by introducing the rudiments of conscription, whereby about a fourth of the population became available for the army. As early as the beginning of the eighth century the army was divided into corps corresponding in command and organization to our modern battalions, and each consisting of 1,000 men. At the same time the cavalry was organized as a separate section, and all the great families were obliged to support the movement. This cavalry, of course, corresponded more nearly to yeomanry than to the strictly trained regular cavalry of to-day, and it is interesting to note that the yeomanry in Britain in modern times was just as closely dependent upon support from the great families in the country as the correspond-

ing force in Japan was eleven centuries before Before the end of the eighth century conscription had taken definite shape, every able-bodied man being obliged to serve his time with the colours, and only the unfit being left untrained upon the farms.

Two results, one good and the other bad, followed from this. Japan was rendered so strong in a military sense that for several centuries the country enjoyed peace, but at the same time the dominant military class gradually gave way to luxury in idleness, internal disorders broke out, until all semblance of military unity in the kingdom was only maintained by the cooperation of the Taira and Minamoto families. Then, as was inevitable, a feud arose between them, ending in the humbling of the Taira family, and leaving the Minamotos in sole possession of the military power for many generations. "The families of the Minamotos," says the historian, "thus conserved the renowned military spirit destined to be transmitted to the nineteenth century" —and after, we may add.

There is no need to describe the various stages by which the fundamental principle of conscription was amended and at the same time the methods of teaching and training were improved. It is sufficient to say that from the

24—2

VICE-ADMIRAL R. YASHIRO,
Minister of Marine.

moment when the Japanese realized that they needed an efficient army for home defence they sedulously set themselves to learn all that foreign nations could teach them, and, as was the case with the navy, for generations they were careful to copy the best European models, defects and all, and were obediently dependent upon foreign instructors in all matters of training and organization.

Side by side with this policy, however, the Japanese aptitude for learning the practical lessons which are taught by troubles and difficulties enabled them in time to understand their own requirements just as well as any foreigner could indicate them, and, as in the case of the navy the time came when Japan decided to build her own ships in future, so in 1882 an Imperial edict was issued which practically closed the period of Japanese tutelage in military affairs. Instruction by foreign officers was superseded by the establishment of the Japanese Staff College, and both the Military Academy and the Medical School were extended and improved. Thenceforward Japan became a law unto herself in military matters, and the events of the war with Russia showed that her self-confidence had not been misplaced.

In spite of the radical difference, based in

the fact that the Japanese forces are composed of an "army of valiant conscripts," while the British Army is filled with voluntary recruits, there is a remarkable similarity in details of organization, discipline and training between the two armies. This is largely due, no doubt, to the fact that in critical periods of transition both freely imitated the German models. The gallantry and high spirits in the field, however, as well as the courteous consideration of non-combatants' interests and even of the enemy's feelings, which are marked characteristics of both, could not have been acquired by imitation of the Teuton. Rather, probably, may we attribute them to the insular position of the two kingdoms, creating seafaring races, careless of danger but careful not to give undue offence to the foreign folk among whom their ventures took them. Also it must be remembered that in insular kingdoms the problems of national defence must always be identical to a great extent. It would be surprising if these resemblances had not created habits of mind in which the British and Japanese find much common ground for sympathetic feeling; but in addition to all this there is something about the Japanese which distinctly appeals to the Briton. We seem to see the same instinctive comradeship in the close friendship which always springs up

VICE-GENERAL OKA,
Minister of War.

between Highlanders and Gurkhas whenever they are quartered together ; for there are many points of likeness between the Japanese and the natives of Nepal. To the European eye they are not dissimilar in physiognomy, and they are alike in stature, courage, strength, and cheeriness in hardship. Both are splendid soldiers ; and in war as in sport the Britisher is never so happy as when he can shout " Go it, little one ! "

At this point we cannot do better than quote a few sentences of the military correspondent of *The Times*, recognized for many years as the best-informed European writer on the military situation in the Far East. He said :

The supreme advantage possessed by Japan as a military power is that, thanks to national service, her home territory is unassailable, not only by any single enemy, but by any reasonable or unreasonable combination of enemies. Her navy is sufficiently formidable to deter any Power except England from the idea of attacking her in her home waters, and her two fighting services in combination, joined with her geographical position, assure to her a predominant position in the Far East. Nothing but the military regeneration of China or the United States seems likely to deprive her of this privileged position—and to talk to a Japanese of such possibilities only provokes a smile.

Japan is already twice as powerful as she was when she challenged Russia in arms. She intends to be thrice as powerful, and nothing but an external cataclysm or some internal convulsion of which there is yet no symptom, or scarcely one, can prevent her from becoming so. The weight of her numbers, the excellence of her organization, the adequacy of her armament, the skill of her staff, the science of her officers, and the splendid spirit which animates, not only the army and navy from

**GENERALS TERAUCHI and HASEGAWA,
with FIELD-MARSHAL YAMAGATA.**

top to bottom, but the whole nation, have no exact counterpart, whether in the New World or the Old.

Were these mighty forces ever employed upon aggressive war, Japan would shake Asia to her foundations. Employed as they are to serve as the guardians and the guarantees of peace, and directed as they are by prudent policy and wise statesmanship, their influence remains beneficent, and they ensure for the Far East the element of stability which it has long lacked.

JAPANESE CAVALRY.

A NEW REGIMENT DRILLING.

The keynote of these sentences—truer, if possible, to-day than when they were written several years before the war—is the pacific strength of Japan; but coupled with her desire for peace is a resolute readiness to face war, if necessary, in pursuit of the objects of peace. The maintenance of peace in the Far East was the purpose of the British alliance, and in loyalty Japan did not hesitate to declare war upon Germany when appealed to. Think what this meant. Supposing that the German calculations had proved accurate and their plans had not miscarried—and, except for the gallant defence of Liége, there was nothing in those early weeks of war to prove that the Kaiser's hosts were not capable of overrunning France and crippling England—what would have been Japan's position with the full weight of the victorious mailed fist descending upon her? But there was no hesitation; and such readiness to face the dire possibilities of war with the most powerful of military empires

JAPANESE SIEGE GUN.

was all the more admirable because the whole trend of the policy of Japan has been to live at peace with all her neighbours, great and small.

From this digression, into which consideration of the similarity between the British and Japanese Armies has led us, we will return to the latter. It is based more closely than the British upon the German model. Thus its constituent factors—apart from the Geneki, or Active Army, and Yobi, or Army Reserve, which have their counterparts in all modern armies—may all be best expressed in German terms. The Kobi is Landwehr, the Kokumin is Landsturm, and the Hoju is Ersatz. The German model is also followed in the rule which makes the liability to military service personal, universal, and obligatory on all able-bodied males between the ages of 17 and 40. This means that there are available 550,000 men per annum, of whom, in practice during the years immediately before the war, 120,000 were taken by ballot, as against 17,000, which was the annual intake before 1888.

One respect in which Japan improved upon the foreign military models which she imitated was the amazing cheapness of the replicas which she produced, having apparently all the strength and durability of the originals. This, of course, is always one of the standing wonders

of the Orient, where, if patent rights do not stand in the way, you can get almost any object reproduced in facsimile, from a pair of trousers to an army corps, at about 10 per cent. of the lowest cost price of the original. Something of this is explained by the fact that a few years ago the pay of the Japanese soldier was under three-farthings a day; but the pay of the men is not everything, and in no detail which directly concerned military efficiency were the Japanese administrators ever unwisely economical. The military results obtained from their scanty resources have been one of the wonders of the age, and apparently they have, after their own admirable fashion, been more frank than is customary with most European nations in publishing all items of expenditure, including even secret service.

A note of criticism is suggested by the fact that we hear so little of the Japanese Cavalry. In the British and other services it is the custom for infantry officers of crack regiments to try to live up to the cavalry standard, especially in the matter of polo and racing ponies. In the whole of India, in fact, there would be very few race meetings but for the patronage and participation of officers of the various garrisons. But in Japan officers were forbidden to attend race meetings and totali-

SIEGE GUN IN ACTION.

THE HARBOUR OF TSING-TAU.

sators were declared illegal. It is possible that Japan obtained an adequate return in economy and thrift on the part of officers from such self-denying ordinances, but without the cult of the horse which race meetings and polo matches signify, Britain would not find it easy to produce the splendid type of cavalry officer capable of leading native sowars, horsemen from infancy, anywhere and doing anything. It must not be supposed, however, that the Japanese Government neglected the supply of horses for cavalry purposes. Like the Government of India, they imported large quantities of Australian horses or "Walers"; and, like the Indian Government, they found the Walers, in spite of their bone and flesh, uncertain, and lacking in endurance of the climate. So—again like the Government of India—they devoted their

attention to the production of stud-bred horses, hybrids between the pure Australian and the country-bred. In Japan these hybrids are known as *zashu*, and are greatly preferred as chargers to the Walers.

No actual returns of the peace strength of the Japanese Army at the time of the outbreak of war had been published, but the total apparently amounted to rather over 250,000 of all ranks. There were 19 divisions (including the guard), 4 independent cavalry brigades, 3 independent field artillery brigades, 6 regiments of heavy field artillery, and a communication brigade. A division consisted of 2 infantry brigades (12 battalions), a cavalry regiment (3 squadrons), a field artillery regiment (6 batteries of 6 guns), a battalion of engineers (3 companies), and a battalion of army

RED CROSS NURSES.

service corps. Some divisions have a battalion of mountain guns. Thus the active army of Japan in peace time might have been summarized as follows : 76 regiments of infantry (228 battalions), 21 regiments of cavalry (89 squadrons), 150 field batteries, 9 mountain batteries, 19 battalions of garrison artillery, and 19 battalions of engineers.

This, however, did not by any means represent the effective military strength of Japan, which was estimated at 1,500,000 trained soldiers, the system of expansion admitting an indefinite increase in the number of battalions per regiment. This force, cooperating, if necessary, with the British-Indian Army and the powerful British and Japanese fleets under the terms of the Anglo-Japanese alliance provided a perfect security of peace in Asia.

Although, of course, the actual details were not made public, the following may be relied upon as an accurate statement of the strength and composition of the Japanese Besieging Force at Tsing-Tau :

Commander-in-Chief, Lieut.-General Mitsuomi Kamio ; Chief of the Staff, Major-General Hanzo Yamanashi.

Troops : 1. The 18th Division, commanded by General Kamio, the 23rd Brigade of Infantry (Major-General B. Horiuchi), the 24th Brigade of Infantry (Major-General Y. Yamada), and other divisional troops.

GERMAN IMPERIAL EAGLE,
Cut in the rocks on the heights of Tsing-Tau.

2. The 29th Brigade of Infantry (Major-General G. Johoji).

3. Siege Artillery Corps (Major-General Y. Watanabe), the Miyama Heavy Artillery Regiment, the Yokosuka Heavy Artillery Regiment, the Shimonoseki Heavy Artillery Batta-

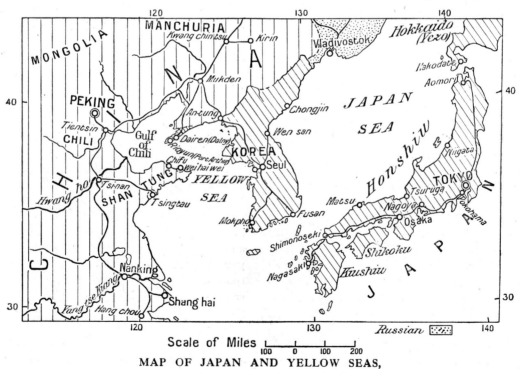

MAP OF JAPAN AND YELLOW SEAS,
Showing position of Tsing-Tau.

THE CAMP AT TSING-TAU.

lion, and the Tadanoumi Heavy Artillery Battalion.

4. Detachments of Engineers and Army Service Corps from the 6th and 12th Divisions.

5. Two Railway Battalions.

6. Railway Guard Troops, the 8th Infantry Regiment.

7. A detachment of Flying Corps.

8. Marine Artillery Detachment.

The entire absence of cavalry, horse artillery, and light field artillery from the composition of the above force may be noted. It was intended for a special work, and was arranged in a businesslike manner. Also, it may be added, it finished its work in a businesslike manner—with promptitude and dispatch.

In the matter of the navy Japan was rather unfortunately situated in the years immediately preceding the war. Political foresight, especially if it involves large new sacrifices, was not to be expected of a heavily burdened people at a time when it was protesting violently against official corruption, and therefore we cannot blame the Japanese for failing to realize the absolute necessity of increased expenditure on the navy. During the years 1907–1910 inclusive there had been no special entries under this head in the annual budgets, and the mere upkeep of a navy, unless it in-

cludes generous provision for the building of new vessels, soon degenerates into idle waste. The effective life of a warship is only fifteen years; and at the beginning of 1910 the naval position of Japan had become disquieting to her patriotic statesmen and her friends. Although at that time there may have been no special reason to apprehend a rupture with Germany, comparison of the shipbuilding programmes of the two Powers showed that whereas at that moment Japan possessed 25 effective battleships and cruisers to 32 flying the German flag, in six years' time she would have only 14 to the German 40. Her own experience in the war with Russia had shown, moreover, that a European Power can, if necessary, dispatch practically the whole of its navy to the Far East. Nor was any consolation to be derived from hoping that the conflict to which German aggression in China steadily tended might be postponed for some years, because a continuance of their respective naval policies to the year 1920 would have resulted in the following contrast of strength in effective battleships and cruisers: Germany, 37; Japan, 8. The friendship of Britain was, of course, a valuable collateral security to the Empire of Japan, but however useful collateral securities may be in the day of reckoning, you cannot trade upon them. So, whether her people liked it or not—whether they could bear it or not—Japan had no alternative but to make generous provision for naval expansion from 1910 onwards, if she hoped to be able to defend her independence. In fact, the problem which faced Japan in the early part of the year 1910 was how to provide the 40 to 45 millions sterling needed to raise her navy to the *minimum* limit demanded by the requirements of national security.

All who know Japan at all, however, are aware that, whenever a serious political necessity becomes imminent it is boldly met, however great may be the patriotic sacrifices demanded of the nation. When, to quote one instance, Japan found herself, in a previous crisis of her history, confronted by Western Powers which had been steadily going ahead while she had been marking time in her self-imposed seclusion, her statesmen realized that a navy on European lines was absolutely necessary for the independence of the Empire—and all that it possessed was a collection of junks, which existed almost in defiance of the edicts which had forbidden maritime enterprise, lest it should bring Japan into contact with the rude foreigner ! Contact, however, had come in spite of Japan's seclusion. Her people had seen the foreign warships masterfully riding in Japanese harbours, and her rulers had been compelled to be civil to the unwelcome visitors, because they had no means of behaving otherwise, even in self-defence.

The lesson was taken to heart, and within fifteen years the antiquated assortment of war-junks was replaced by an up-to-date navy of formidable warships, " manned and officered by warriors who have shaped the destiny of their country, and who have created traditions of which the most valiant kingdoms of the world might well be proud." *

No other navy in the world has had so chequered a history. It was in 1653 that the Tokugawa Government, expressing the national disgust with the uncultured ways of foreigners —German " culture " had not been heard of then—strictly forbade the making of long voyages and the building of large sea-going vessels in Japan. The kingdom of Japan, in fact, deliberately decided to withdraw into its shell, like a snail, and to have nothing to do with those horrid foreign insects. For 200 years the policy of seclusion seemed to have succeeded.

The year of the Indian mutiny, 1857, may be regarded as the birth-year of the modern Japanese navy, and it is pleasant to remember that a ship presented by Queen Victoria in that year was the proudest possession of our Ally's navy in its infancy. Not six years had passed, however, before the whirligig of time brought British warships to bombard Japanese ports, and in the following year, 1864, British, French,

---

* From " The Full Recognition of Japan," by Robert P. Porter (London : Henry Frowde).

JAPANESE AND BRITISH LANDING AT LAO-SHAN BAY.

JAPANESE BLUEJACKETS LANDING NEAR TSING-TAU.

Dutch and American vessels combined for the same purpose. Thus it was a stormy infancy through which the Japanese navy passed, but it grew steadily. In 1871 it consisted of 17 vessels, which only totalled about 6,000 tons between them, but between that year and 1893 the Government spent £24,000,000 on the navy, and at the close of the war with Russia the fleet consisted of 76 vessels, aggregating 264,000 tons. From this time onwards the rate of naval expansion was progressive, and between 1903 and 1910 three separate ship-building programmes had been carried out. One was the inadequate programme provided for in the budget, and the other two were emergency programmes carried out by funds included in the war expenditures, known respectively as " implementing " and " adjustment " funds. The three programmes provided for 13 new ships, which were all completed and launched before the end of 1910. These warships, as well as the Japanese destroyers—of which there were 59, all but two of modern type, in 1909—have the common characteristic of heavy armament for their size. Incidentally, the " third programme " marked the epoch when Japan ceased to go abroad for her warships, and commenced to supply her

own needs almost solely from her own dock-yards, although in 1911 one large cruiser was being completed by the Vickers Company. The reasons for this departure from programme illustrate once more the practical common-sense of the Japanese. In the dangerous position which had been created by their era of national seclusion they had learned a severe lesson regarding the unwisdom of relying upon national resources alone, and in the contracts given to the Vickers Company we see only a wise determination to secure always the best up-to-date models from the West. The astute Bond Street milliner makes his own " creations," but he is never without the latest models from Paris. In 1909 Japan also commenced to build submarines of the Holland type, and the construction of one battleship, six cruisers, several destroyers and six torpedo-boats was arranged.

At the outbreak of war in 1914 the Japanese Navy was truly formidable. It included 2 battleships of the Dreadnought class, the Kawachi and Settsu, both over 21,000 tons, with a speed of 20 knots ; 2 Dreadnought battle-cruisers, each of 27,500 tons, with a speed of 27 knots, the Kongo and Hiyei : 2 semi-Dreadnought battleships, the Aki and Satsuma, between 19,000 and 20,000 tons each, and a speed of 20 and 18¼ knots respectively ; 4 first-class battle-cruisers, with speeds ranging from 20½ to 22¾ knots, and averaging 14,000 tons ; 6 battleships of slightly heavier displacement and slightly lower speed ; 6 first-class coast defence ships, averaging 13,000 tons and 17½ knots ; 9 first-class cruisers, ranging from 7,300 to 9,800 tons, and in speed from 20 to 21¼ knots ; 13 second-class cruisers, some of which had a speed of 26 knots ; 7 second-class coast defence vessels—one of which, the Takachiho, was sunk off Kiaochau ; 9 gunboats ; 2 first-class destroyers of 35 knots, 2 second-class of 33 knots, and 46 others of varying speeds ; 31 torpedo boats, and 13 submarines, besides torpedo depôt ships and dispatch vessels. Thus, without including the 46 minor destroyers or the torpedo-boats and submarines, &c., the Japanese Navy in 1914 had an effective of 459,630 tons. In 1871 6,000 tons, at the end of the war with Russia 264,000 tons, in 1914 459,630 tons—this scale gives a fair idea of the naval progress of Japan ; and although, in addition to the third-class cruiser Takachiho (sunk by a torpedo from the German torpedo boat S. 90 off Tsing-Tau), 1 third-class destroyer, the

Shirotae (wrecked off Tsing-Tau), the torpedo boat No. 33 (sunk by a German mine off Tsing-Tau), and 3 mine-sweepers (sunk by German mines off Tsing-Tau), were lost, the Japanese Navy, like the British, was growing in strength during the war. Even without expediting the work, 1915 would see a gigantic battleship of 30,600 tons, with 22-knot speed, completed, as well as two great battle-cruisers, each of 27 knots and 27,500 tons, and a number of smaller craft ; while other formidable battleships of over 30,000 tons each were in course of construction, which was, of course, greatly expedited as soon as war was decided upon. There was, therefore, little fear of the "attrition" of the Japanese Navy. On the contrary, there was almost certainty that on the declaration of peace Japan would be found with a stronger fleet than she had on the declaration of war.

There were rumours before the war that naval aviation had reached a special and peculiar stage in Japan ; but nothing occurred during the operations against Tsing-Tau to justify these rumours. The Japanese Flying Corps, though small, rendered extremely good service ; but it was service upon exactly the

JAPANESE INFANTRY ADVANCING ACROSS A RIVER
At the taking of Tsing-Tau.

BRITISH INDIAN TROOPS
Transporting ammunition to Tsing-Tau.

same lines as those which the British and French—and, indeed, the German—service rendered in Europe.

Turning now to the actual incidents of the blockade, siege, and storming of Tsing-Tau, we may note that the declaration of war by Japan was dated August 23, 1914, and the real blockade of Tsing-Tau began four days later, when some of the adjacent isles were occupied to serve as a local base. From these systematic mine-sweeping operations were undertaken, and with such success that the loss of the cruiser Takachiho nearly two months later appears to have been the only noteworthy casualty which the blockading fleet suffered from this danger. The actual landing of the Japanese near Tsing-Tau was effected on September 2, 1914, and it was still in the early days of that month that the German garrison had their first practical experience of the fact that they were at war with an up-to-date Power, when two Japanese seaplanes reconnoitered the fortress and dropped bombs with good effect upon the railway station and the barracks. Although one of the seaplanes was hit several times, both returned safely, and thus first blood was recorded to the Japanese.

For a time, however, the campaign stood still. Although the fleet maintained a spasmodic bombardment of the harbour and forts, torrential rains had caused floods which effectively barred all advance upon Tsing-Tau by land, making swollen streams impassable. In these circumstances the Japanese artillery was compelled to return to Lungkow; while the only exploit on the German side was the accidental killing of a number of Chinese who persisted in going out to work in the fields in spite of warnings and the weather, and were all blown up by a mine which had been laid for the Japanese.

Although, during the heavy rains, Tsing-Tau was so surrounded by floods as to be accessible only by boat, the Japanese were not idle, and on September 13 the railway station at Kiao-chau was captured by their advance guards. Some confusion usually exists between Kiao-chau and Tsing-Tau, because, although the whole of the territory leased by China to Germany, on which the fortified naval and military stronghold of Tsing-Tau was built, is known as Kiaochau, there is also a town of that name about 22 miles distant and connected with Tsing-Tau by railway. It was the Kiao-chau terminus of this railway which the Japanese captured on September 13. On the same day a Japanese aeroplane paid another unwelcome visit to Tsing-Tau, dropping more bombs on the German barracks. During the next few days still more bombs were dropped on the ships in the harbour, the wireless station and the electric power station. One large ship was seen to take fire; and the powerlessness of the garrison to repel these attacks must have given to the Germans some premonition of the inevitable end. Probably this feeling of helplessness had something to do with the surrender of the fortress later, before the assailants expected it. At any rate the incidents showed that the Japanese were by no means backward in aviation in war.

It was not until September 23 that a British force arrived to cooperate with the Japanese, under Brigadier-General Barnardiston, commanding the British forces in North China, including Wei-hai-Wei ; but the distance which separated Laoshan Bay, where the British forces landed (on the original leased territory, thus avoiding the breach of neutrality alleged by the Chinese against the Japanese), from Tsing-Tau was so much shorter, and presented so much less of difficulty than the Japanese had to encounter in their preliminary advances, that the British really arrived on the scene just as the Japanese were finishing their first engagement in force on September 28.

And, incidentally, it is worth noting, for several reasons, that when we speak of the "cooperation" of the two forces, we necessarily imply that Brigadier-General Barnardiston, with the British and Indian troops which he commanded, came automatically under the supreme command of Lieut.-General Mitsuomi Kamio, the Japanese Commander-in-Chief of the besieging force. This does not mean that the British General's independent authority over his own troops was in any way impaired or interfered with, but only that the Japanese commander, by virtue of his higher rank. automatically exercised supreme command over the allied forces, in the same way that Field Marshal Joffre exercises supreme command over the allied forces in the West. The fact, however, of a British General acting under Japanese orders in the war against Germany is worthy of passing note, as illustrating the complete recognition of Japan as a first-class Power.

And even at this early date of the war the services which Japan had rendered to the cause of civilization had been great. As *The Times* stated in a leading article of September 28, 1914 : "She has cooped up two or three cruisers which would have seriously interfered with the vast trade that centres at Hong-kong, and she has foiled the German design of turning Kiaochau into a base for hostile operations against British commerce. That in itself is an immense service which we owe to our Ally. When she shall have driven the Germans from the territory which they extorted from China, and shall have restored it to its rightful owners, she will have extirpated a constant source of disturbance in Eastern Asia." The same leading article of *The Times* went on to emphasize the amazing disinterestedness of Japan in

JAPANESE SIEGE GUN.
Receiving orders by telephone to fire.

OIL TANKS DESTROYED AT TSING-TAU.

fulfilling her treaty obligations ; but this is not the place to deal with that matter. For the moment we are only concerned with the actual course of the war ; and among the other ways in which Japan was fortunately able to assist the Allies was in the supply of munitions of war. As has been shown previously, the outbreak of this war found Japan in an absolute state of military readiness for all eventualities ; and the deliberate limitation of the scope of her intervention left her with a surplus of the necessaries of war, which she was able to place at the service of the Western nations, whom the outbreak of war had found unprepared for the full scope and intensity of the German onrush. An instance of this was afforded in the telegram of *The Times* correspondent at Petrograd on September 13, 1914 : " I am permitted to state that heavy siege guns purchased from Japan at the outset of the war are already at the front." This—the possibility that German forces operating against Poland would,

TSING-TAU WIRELESS STATION DESTROYED.

within six weeks of the outbreak of war, find themselves in front of heavy Japanese siege guns—was one of those unexpected details which played so large a part in this war in upsetting the German plans and calculations of forty years.

Meanwhile, of course, the Germans were not behindhand with their " resources of civilization " at Tsing-Tau. Every night their aeroplanes ascended—they did not ascend in the daytime, out of respect for the Japanese cruisers' guns—but every night they found that, under cover of the darkness, the wary Japanese fleet had changed its moorings, and they never had the good luck to discover where it was.

By September 26 the floods had sufficiently abated to permit active operations to be resumed by land, and on the afternoon of that day the Japanese succeeded by a dashing assault in driving the Germans from the high ground between the two rivers Pai-sha and Li-tsun, and on the following day they advanced to the high ground between the Li-tsun and the Chang-tsun, about seven miles north-east of Tsing-Tau. They did not rest here, and the following morning found them in possession of positions within five miles of the fortress, which was then almost completely invested. During this development of the operations, German warships had actively bombarded the right wing of the Japanese force, but were compelled to withdraw by Japanese aeroplanes—a sufficiently striking contrast to the victorious persistence of British warships in bombarding the German forces on the Belgian coast, as showing how great an advantage superior aviation confers in modern warfare. The Japanese success with this arm was repeated on September 29, when three aeroplanes succeeded in dropping bombs upon German ships at close quarters and getting safely away, although the wings of the machines were riddled with bullets.

Meanwhile the Japanese were steadily working their way and consolidating their positions as they advanced up to Tsinanfu, and their fleet landed a force which successfully occupied Laoshan harbour in the immediate vicinity of Tsing-Tau. Here they made their first capture of German field-guns, and with them a large quantity of ammunition. On the following day (September 30, 1914) they succeeded in sinking a German destroyer, but lost two mine-sweepers, one of which was sunk and the other badly damaged by exploding mines.

[*Garrett Portsmouth.*

JAPANESE BATTLE CRUISER "IKOMA."

On the same day the Germans made their great effort to repel the Japanese attack, their warships and aeroplanes cooperating with the land batteries ; but the Japanese casualties were not severe, and, taking this experience as a sample of the worst that the enemy could do, General Kamio seems at once to have taken the decision not to proceed with preparations for a slow siege, but to take the place with as little delay as possible by assault. Possibly he was influenced in this decision by the fact that the Chinese Government, taking wise note of the weakening of the German defence, was no longer raising strong objections to the proceedings of the Japanese. When, for instance, on October 3, 1914, the Japanese took over the Shantung Railway from Tsinanfu to Weihsien, the Chinese Government made no serious attempt to controvert the Japanese argument that the line was essentially a German railway, and that it was strategically impossible to allow the Germans to continue to control a line of communication in the rear of their invested fortress. With the proviso

BRITISH SOLDIERS AT TSING-TAU.

that the ultimate ownership of the railway should be settled after the war, the Chinese Government agreed that the Japanese should control the administration temporarily, the traffic being worked by Chinese. This was, of course, an arrangement which suited Japan admirably, and she could afford to ignore the bombast of some of the Chinese State Councillors, whose object was to satisfy public opinion at home without risking conflict with Japan. Subsequently, however, when the Japanese found it necessary to send troops to Tsinanfu in order to counteract the mischief of pro-German agents there, and also to occupy Weihsien, because German land-mines had been discovered outside the zone of hostilities, the Chinese Government stated that the amicable arrangement for working the railway until the

JAPANESE HYDROPLANE,
Used to direct the fire of the Battleships.

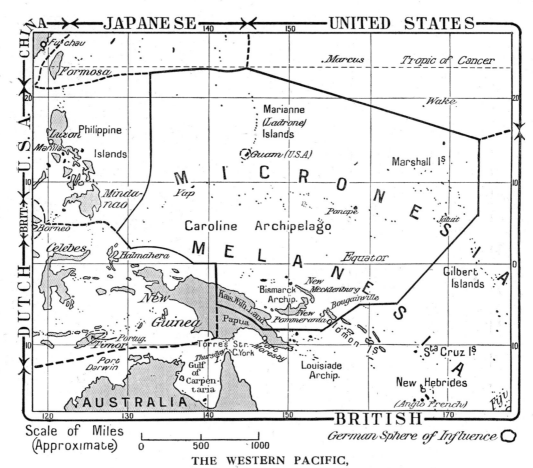

THE WESTERN PACIFIC,
Showing German Possessions at the beginning of the War.

end of the war had been rendered abortive, and that it only submitted to the Japanese occupation of Tsinanfu under strong protest. This, however, did not seem to produce any effect upon the minds of the Japanese, who at the time were busy with deeds, not words. Kid-glove methods were inappropriate for dealing with the German system of espionage, which seems to have been as perfectly developed in Kiaochau as in Belgium or on the East Coast of England, coloured lights being regularly used after nightfall to indicate the positions of the Japanese and British troops or vessels to the German gunners. About the same time as the Shantung Railway was seized, the Japanese torpedo flotilla performed good service in destroying the Tsing-Tau barracks by bombardment, while their heavy siege guns ashore succeeded in putting the gunboat Iltis out of action.

The beginning of the end became apparent on October 8, when the German artillery fire, hitherto conspicuous for its extravagance of ammunition, was perceptibly slackening, but at the time this was attributed to other reasons, because the Commander-in-Chief of the Japanese forces, General Kamio, had expected to meet with a prolonged resistance in which, according to the German Emperor's orders, the last breath of the last man and horse of the garrison would have been expended. He had, therefore, calculated that it would take him at least three days to capture his first objective. This was Prince Heinrich Hill, a dominant position from which all the forts around Tsing-Tau could be bombarded. It was, therefore, a surprise when this position was taken without serious loss on the first day of assault. It scarcely seems possible that this result could have been achieved if the Germans had been really determined to carry out the no-surrender policy so grandiloquently impressed upon them from Berlin at the commencement of the campaign. Rather, it seems to confirm the Chinese report that a long cipher message, received by the German representative at Peking as soon as the landing of the Japanese had been announced, consisted of instructions regarding the surrender of the fortress. Confidential communications, even in cipher, have

TSING-TAU.
Set on fire by Japanese and British shells.

a marvellous way of leaking out in the East, and although one's first impulse on learning that a report has emanated from Peking is to think that it cannot be true, one may modify that opinion on learning that the information might have been obtained by making surreptitious notes of confidential correspondence. No suspicion, however, was aroused in the minds of the Japanese that the Germans did not really intend to put up such a desperate fight as they had proclaimed even by the amazing waste of ammunition in which the fort batteries indulged, as many as 1,000 to 1,500 shells being fired off daily without any adequate objective.

The Japanese were not disposed to be misled into forming any premature conclusions, and after their easy capture of Prince Heinrich Hill they proceeded to mount their siege guns there on the positions selected for them while the troops sapped closer and closer to the fortress, having now and then slight encounters with the Germans. As their preparations for the assault became complete, the Japanese—still believing, of course, that the Germans were determined to defend themselves to the last breath—decided to give all non-combatants in

Tsing-Tau an opportunity to leave the fortress. Consequently on October 15 a party of European ladies and children with the American Consul and a number of Chinese were given safe conducts through the Japanese lines.

Thus it was not until October 16 that the combined Japanese and British forces considered themselves to be in a position to commence a general bombardment from the sea. This was chiefly directed against the Kaiser and the Iltis forts, and was assisted by aeroplanes. Considerable damage was done, and there were only three casualties, all British, among the assailants. Three days later, however, the Japanese fleet suffered a mishap in the sinking of the 3,000-ton cruiser Takachiho through striking a mine. Only ten of the crew were saved, 243 being drowned. This, however, was a small offset to the success of the same day when the Kaiser and Iltis forts were seriously damaged by the heavy guns of the warships cooperating with the artillery of the land forces, and aeroplanes succeeded in dropping bombs upon many parts of the fortress.

The general and final bombardment of Tsing-Tau commenced at dawn on the last day of

October, 1914. This day had been chosen because it was the anniversary of the birthday of the Emperor of Japan; and as the first account to reach England picturesquely stated, " daylight saw the royal salute being fired with live shell at Tsing-Tau." The Iltis fort was again the subject of special attention, but the fort of Siao Chau Shan almost equally shared the same unpleasant favour, while neither the harbour nor the shipping had reason to think themselves neglected. Most of the forts were silenced during the day, and on the morning of November 1 only two were replying regularly to the Allies' guns. A conflagration was then raging near the harbour and an oil-tank had exploded. The Siao Chau Shan fort was in flames and the German gunboat, whose funnel had been shot away on the previous day, was out of sight under the water.

At this crisis it was interesting to read, as part of the same cablegram which announced the effect of the bombardment of Tsing-Tau, that " after to-morrow no British newspaper will be published in Peking, the Germans having bought up the *Peking Gazette*. . . . In addition the Germans are taking over the financial control of the entire native press in Peking." One cannot help admiring the assiduity with which the Germans must have secretly prepared for this war; because wherever they

have been defeated the ragged threads of their previous intrigues have been left apparent. It is certainly a lesson in preparation for war which they have taught to the world. What they overlooked was the fact that to be successful a world-war must be righteous. And so we come back to the " Imperial Precepts " of Japan, which inculcate " faithfulness and righteousness " as the virtues which soldiers and sailors of all ranks should cultivate. Perhaps we have something to learn from a civilization which is twenty-five centuries old.

To continue the story of the bombardment of Tsing-Tau on November 1, the British battleship Triumph established a record in silencing the powerful Bismarck forts with seven shots; and this left only one fort, Huichuan, still replying to the Japanese cannonade. The bombardment from the sea continued, practically without intermission, from day to day, and meanwhile the land forces were not idle. On November 3 they destroyed 26 German guns and captured 800 prisoners—a considerable percentage, about one-sixth in fact, of the force of nearly 5,000 men which constituted the garrison. On the same date it was discovered that the Austrian cruiser Kaiserin Elisabeth, which was at Tsing-Tau when the siege began, had disappeared—having apparently been blown up—and also that the

FIRST BREAKFAST OF RICE BALLS
After the general night attack on Tsing-Tau.

floating dock in Tsing-Tau harbour no longer presented a mark for the Japanese gunners, because it had been sunk. It is curious that from these details the conclusion should not have been drawn that the fortress was on the point of surrendering; but the fact remains that no suspicion of this was entertained when, on November 6, the Allies' infantry commenced a general attack, the Japanese commander having concluded that the havoc wrought upon the forts by his heavy artillery had sufficiently prepared the way. It was by acting upon this principle that the Germans had succeeded in making such short work of the strong defences of Namur, after neglect of it had caused them such heavy losses in men, prestige, and all-important time at Liége. In the case of Tsing-Tau, however, the chances of resistance had been over estimated, and no one could have been more surprised than were the various commanders of the Japanese troops on the morning of November 7, 1914, to see white flags fluttering from the German defences. Believing that the Kaiser's command to hold out to the last

would be obeyed, and estimating the resources of the garrison in food and ammunition, the Japanese had calculated upon spending at least another month before Tsing-Tau.

During the whole of the previous night, November 6, the guns had roared at intervals, and the following account of an eye-witness may be accepted as a correct version of the finale, since it is confirmed by other accounts in every detail:

The infantry, pushing up, occupied the central positions on the main line of defence, and a fortress on the west, by 1.40 a.m. on the 7th. At 5.10 a.m. the north battery of Shaotan hill was captured, and 25 minutes later the east battery of Tahtungchin was taken, as well as Chungchiawa fort on the west.

This gave the besiegers the opportunity to advance in mass. Shortly after daylight it was decided to charge the remaining forts, and the troops were tensely waiting the order to storm the positions when, between 6 and 7.30 a.m., white flags were run up on the various forts. The first white flag appeared on the observatory at 6 o'clock, but this was not seen by the bulk of the troops, who were unaware that their fighting had ceased until they saw the flags flying on the positions in front of them.

At 7.50 p.m. on the evening of the 7th representatives of the two forces had signed the terms of capitulation, the Germans accepting those imposed by the Japanese

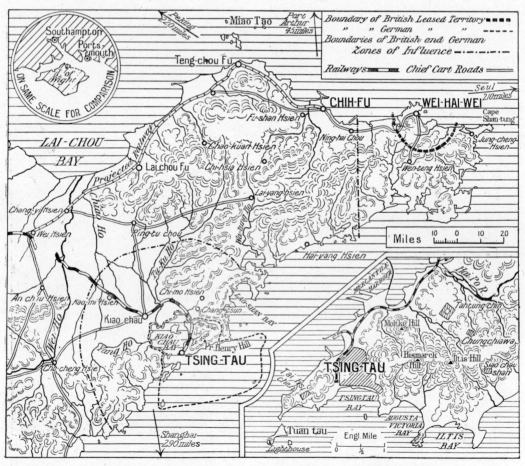

SHANTUNG PENINSULA, WITH INSET OF TSING-TAU.

DESERTED "BISMARCK FORTRESS."
Silenced by H.M.S. "Triumph" in seven shots.

unconditionally. Honours of war were accorded the garrison, and on the 9th the representatives arranged that the actual transfer of the garrison should take place on the following day. At 10 a.m. on the 10th, therefore, Governor Meyer-Waldeck formally transferred the garrison to General Kamio, and Germany's possession of territory in China ended. The Governor and 201 German officers and 3,841 non-commissioned officers and men, in addition to a number of non-combatants, remained with the Japanese as prisoners of war.

The Japanese land forces engaged in the operations numbered 22,980 officers and men and 142 guns.

The British force, under the command of General Barnardiston, consisted of nine staff officers, 910 non-commissioned officers and men of the 2nd Battalion South Wales Borderers, and 450 non-commissioned officers and men of the 36th Sikhs.

At this point of the story it is well to note that, in the whole of the operations preceding the final assault upon the fortress, the British force had 12 killed and 61 wounded; the Japanese, in those operations and the final assault, had 236 killed and 1,282 wounded. These figures may not, of course, accurately represent the proportionate work done by the British-Indian and Japanese forces, although they are not disproportionate to the numbers engaged; but they show at least, that the siege was essentially a Japanese affair, and that the enthusiastic welcome subsequently given to General Barnardiston in Tokyo was rather a token of friendship for a gallant ally than a national tribute to a deliverer.

After the surrender of the fortress, the Japanese Commander-in-Chief, General Kamio, was formally appointed Governor-General of Kiaochau, and work was at once undertaken in removing dangerous mines on land and sea and clearing away the *débris* of the battered fortifications. The prisoners, now numbering about 3,000, were drafted off to concentration camps in Japan; but the Emperor, with the tactful generosity which always distinguishes the international actions of Japan, permitted the late German Governor and all his officers to retain their swords.

On November 16, 1914, the Allied troops made formal occupation of Tsing-Tau, and their first act was to hold a memorial service for the dead, among whom were, unfortunately, numbered two officers and eight men killed, several days after the surrender of the fortress by the explosion of German land mines. Fifty-six other Japanese were wounded at the same time.

Upon General Kamio's return to Tokyo on December 18 the city was *en fête*. The General was welcomed by the highest officials and escorted by them to the Palace.

INSPECTING ONE OF THE FALLEN GERMAN FORTS.
Piles of shells are seen on the right.

One pleasant detail—for in the days of war every detail was pleasant which suggested a victorious end to bloodshed—of the fighting around Tsing-Tau was the fact that the British troops employed there were able to assert the same " moral ascendancy " over the Germans which Field-Marshal French claimed in his despatches for the British troops in Flanders. Many letters received from British soldiers at Tsing-Tau showed that the almost invariable result of their " getting to grips " with the Germans was that the latter asked for an armistice to bury their dead. This was as invariably refused, and—says one report of many—" the British troops literally chased the Germans right up to their innermost barbed wire defences."

Although the British and Sikhs did not get into the final assault, it was not their fault, and according to Mr. A. M. Brace, who was the only Press correspondent in Tsing-Tau during the siege, the part which they played was interesting and illuminating in bringing out the bitter feeling of the Germans for the British.   He wrote (*The Times*, December 17) :

The British did good work considering their numbers, working in trenches of their own along a small section of the German front and advancing very near to the German trenches through the barbed wire entanglements. Their losses were large in proportion to their numbers. If they did not get into the final assault it was because the Japanese left them behind.

The Germans were anxious for a chance at the British troops. The hitting of the British ship Triumph by a shell from Huitchienhuk caused rejoicing in Tsing-Tau that would not have been equalled by the sinking of a Japanese Dreadnought. The German airman, after locating the British camp by its white tents, singled it out for his bombs. The German artillery tried particularly to hit the British camp ; and when the British entered the city and camped at the artillery depôt their name was anathema, and German prisoners showed their hatred in various ways.

This special hatred of the Germans for the British was not only apparent in the behaviour of the prisoners after the surrender.   Early in November a British naval officer, writing from " off Tsing-Tau," said : " I think the German hates us more than the Japanese, for he always fires his 12-inch at us. So far, twenty-five projectiles, all short except one hit, but one is quite enough.   The Japanese have repaired our mast splendidly, and are behaving splendidly over the whole campaign. The Japanese Crown Prince sent us a message, encouraging us to ' Press the enemy, braving all hardships ' : so now we call bombardment ' Pressing the enemy.' "

Another letter from a British officer at Tsing-Tau contains some sentences which are worth quoting. Describing the bombardment, he said : " It really was a wonderful sight, and the Japanese shooting was magnificent. With one of the first shells they set fire to enormous oil tanks, which made a tremendous blaze, and then they started on the forts and redoubts. Every shell seemed to find the mark, and now that one can actually see the shell marks (this was written after the surrender of the fortress) most people think that the shooting was probably the best that has ever been seen. There is hardly a stick left in the forts and redoubts—concrete platforms, trenches, guns, and barbed-wire entanglements. . . . There is no doubt the Japanese are wonderful soldiers. . . . Our small force, consisting of the South Wales Borderers and 36th Sikhs and the usual details, did their full share."

The successful Japanese method of dealing with the German Islands in the Pacific deserves separate notice, not only on account of the ultimate importance of the results which were so easily achieved, but also as an illustration of the quality of " correctitude " which has been described as the guiding principle of the foreign policy of Japan. Modest and intensely sensible of the feelings of others, she nevertheless exhibited, whenever the

occasion demanded it, an unflinchnig self-possession which commanded universal respect, coupled with an innate tact which enabled her to do whatever needed to be done in the way which would give least offence to the most captious critic. This is the keynote of Japan's successful foreign policy : and if we are inclined to be surprised that a " yellow race " which has only lately adopted modern civilization should behave so well, we must remember that the Japanese character is the outcome of a civilization far more ancient than ours.

This inborn talent to avoid offence was admirably exhibited in the successful raid upon the Marshall Islands. These are a group of the islets in the Western Pacific collectively known as Micronesia. A map of this part of the ocean has much the appearance of a sky-chart, so thickly studded is it with constellations of small islands : and it was here that the comet of German aggression blazed with an almost more disturbing influence than anywhere else. Taking advantage of the pre-occupation of Britain—who was then isolated and almost friendless among the nations, with the imminent danger of a Russian war in 1885-6—Germany practically seized upon every island on which the flag of some other Power was not already flying. More than this, she claimed the northern part of New Guinea : and

DISMANTLED GUN AND CUPOLA.

the connection between Australasia and the Mother Country was never more severely strained than when in 1889 the British Government formally conceded all the German demands. Of the islands which thus definitely passed into German possession the Marshall group is the most easterly, and Jaluit, the chief of these, was made the seat of the German Imperial Commissioner. As such it was considered to form a part of the basis of Germany's naval forces in the Pacific Ocean; and on October 6, 1914, we learned that a part of the Japanese Fleet had visited the island, the Germans surrendering without resistance. Japanese marines were landed and "destroyed all establishments of a military nature and seized all munitions of war: a British merchant vessel which had been held there was set free and one Japanese who was imprisoned in the port was released." To this the Navy Department at Tokyo added that the landing had been made for military purposes and not for permanent occupation. This assurance was also specially conveyed at the same time to the Government of the United States, which, as the owners of Guam to the east and Wake to the north of the Marshall group, were naturally suspicious of Japan's intentions in that quarter.

On the following day the seizure of the Island of Yap was announced. This island was also a local German headquarters, being situated at the western end of the Caroline group and thus only a short distance south of Guam (or Guahan), which the United States took from Spain in the late war. Within the fortnight, on October 20, 1914, we were informed that Japan had taken all the Marshall Islands, as well as the Marianne (Ladrones) group and the East and West Caroline Archipelagos. Thus by a bloodless display of force and promptitude Japan had undone in fourteen days all the masterful work upon which Germany had been engaged for years.

Although, however, the Germans, bottled up in Tsing-Tau, were unable to strike a blow in defence of their island empire in the Pacific, it was not without risk that Japan undertook the bold course of action which the effective execution of her compact with Britain seemed to demand. This Far-Eastern Archipelago was a very hotbed of political complications, as may be understood by a glance at the map, which shows that the sphere from which German influence was thus summarily expelled occupied roughly the triangular centre of an area which had Japanese possessions on the north-west, American possessions on the north and north-west, British on the south and south-east, French on the south-east, and Dutch on the south-west, while due south the vital interests

WIRE ENTANGLEMENTS OUTSIDE THE WALLS OF TSING-TAU.

DISMANTLED AND DESTROYED GUN.

of Australasia were directly concerned. If Japan had entered upon possession of this very debatable region with a truculent flourish of the " mailed fist," many serious difficulties might have arisen : but the unsolicited and repeated assurances from Tokyo that the occupation was only temporary and for purely military purposes went far to allay international jealousies. It was, moreover, a complete guarantee to France and Australasia of the honest intentions of Japan that in these proceedings she was acting only as the ally of Britain : and even in the United States this consideration went a long way in inducing frank acceptance of the Japanese assurances. Germans and pro-German politicians in New York strained every nerve of course in the effort to persuade President Wilson that American interests were menaced and the dignity of the United States flouted by this extension of Japanese dominion.

In this Far-Eastern campaign of course the Germans did not neglect the machinery which they worked so assiduously in Europe and America with a view to perverting public opinion in neutral countries to their side. In addition to purchasing the *Peking Gazette* and the entire native press of Peking, German

agents were indefatigable in spreading reports, which purported to be authentic news, of fictitious events calculated to disturb the equanimity of neutrals.

One large and mischievous lie circulated to the world through German agency from America was that the northern half of the Island of Saghalien (Sakhalin) had been ceded by Russia to Japan in return for heavy guns sent for use with the Russian Army. On the face of it, such a bargain seemed curious : but a little knowledge is dangerous, and those who recollected that by the Treaty of Portsmouth, which ended the Russo-Japanese war, half of the island was ceded to Japan, and who had sufficient geographical knowledge to be aware that the arbitrary frontier thus created across the island will certainly need modification, were not disinclined to accept the report. It was the turn of the Russian Foreign Office to issue a categorical denial of the reported cession of territory : but it was not possible that the contradiction should ever completely overtake the lie.

Nevertheless the Japanese disclaimer, which closely followed that of Russia, is worth reproducing in its entirety as an example of the way in which the diplomats of Japan succeed in

CENTRAL RAILWAY STATION, TOKYO.
Departure of Troops.

enunciating the principles which govern their policy, while ostensibly dealing only with details. It runs :—

"The report emanating from the United States in regard to the cession by Russia of part of the island of Sakhalin to Japan is not to be regarded as serious. Whatever assistance Japan may have given, or may propose to give, to Russia is an outcome of the cordial relations existing between Russia and Japan, and especially of the fact that both are fighting a common enemy. Assistance of this sort can never form the basis of political bargaining or territorial acquisition. Such bargaining would not be in conformity with the relations of special amity which have long subsisted between the two Empires, and would be entirely foreign to the national spirit of both Powers."

Although, in the earlier stages of the war, the Germans gained distinct temporary advantage by their adroit dissemination of false reports, they must soon have discovered that the work was expensive in other ways than the mere distribution of money as bribes. The campaign of lies had not continued for many months before all truly neutral countries began to realize that statements " made in Germany " were not to be taken at their face value : and to an impartial critic—if there were such a

person in the whole world during this war—it must have been interesting to note how the Japanese, British, French, or Russian statements of successes or reverses were accepted as statements of fact, and the German statements circulated by wireless were invariably printed in smaller type and usually headed with some such phrase as " The German Version." Thus the Germans were being taught by the inexorable logic of facts that, even in the dissemination of war news for the consumption of neutrals, honesty is the best policy, after all.

General Barnardiston's reception at Tokyo was probably one of the events which will live in history as setting the seal upon the charter of Japan, entitling her to enter the ring of the World Powers upon equal terms. For General Barnardiston was the commander of the comparatively small force of British and Indian troops which cooperated with the Japanese Army and Navy in the reduction of Tsing-Tau, the German stronghold in the Far East. The investment, blockade, and capture of Tsing-Tau, involving the extirpation of the German disease from the Far East, was the work of Japan ; and the visit of General Barnardiston to Tokyo afterwards—as the commander of allied troops which had had some share in the victory—was an advertisement to the world that from the British point of view Japan had done her work in the cause of civilization nobly and well, and that the British Empire, as represented by the officer commanding British-Indian troops in the Far East, was glad to congratulate her upon the achievement. That was the real significance of General Barnardiston's visit to Tokyo ; and in his welcome by parades of troops and thousands of cheering school-children we heard Japan's full-hearted acknowledgment of our recognition of her service. Never has the loyalty of a nation to its obligations been more fully shown. Never has it been more fully realised.

Upon General Barnardiston the Emperor conferred the Order of the Rising Sun, second class, and upon Major Pringle and Captain Moore, his Chief of Staff and D.A.A.G. respectively, the Fourth and Fifth Classes of the same Order.

The actual announcement of the fall of Tsing-Tau had come as a welcome surprise on November 7 to the public at Tokyo, where the event was not expected until at least the end of the month ; but by mid-day the British and Japanese flags were flying everywhere, and at night the main streets were illuminated and there were general rejoicings. The Emperor of Japan promptly sent a message to the British forces, in which he said that he " deeply appre-

ciated the brilliant deeds of the British Army and Navy which, cooperating with the Japanese, had fought for and bravely achieved one of the objects of the war."

On the same day felicitations were exchanged between the British Board of Admiralty and the Japanese Ministry of Marine. The British telegram was :—

" The Board of Admiralty send their heartiest congratulations to the gallant Army and Navy of Japan on the prosperous and brilliant issue of the operations which have resulted in the fall of Tsing-Tau."

To this the Japanese Minister of Marine replied :—

" I fully share with you in the felicitations on the fall of Tsing-Tau. It affords me great pleasure to assure you that the outcome of the efforts of the Navy of our Ally in cooperation with ours during the investment of Tsing-Tau was splendid.—Minister of Marine, Tokyo."

We have noticed elsewhere the graceful tact of the Emperor of Japan in allowing all the German officers who surrendered at Tsing-Tau to retain their swords ; and this kindly spirit was reflected in the behaviour of the people of Tokyo when the batches of prisoners arrived. To each one Japanese ladies presented a chrysanthemum bearing a friendly greeting in

BOYS' BAND AT TOKOROZAWA.   [*By courtesy of " Asahi Shimbun."*]
Welcoming the Flying Corps there.

LIEUT.-GENERAL KAMIO and MAJOR-GENERAL BARNARDISTON,
Commanding the Allied Armies.

German. The prisoners, according to a telegram of November 22, " appeared to be touched by the attention " ; and well they might be, if they knew anything of the reception which was accorded to British prisoners in Germany. Here, at Tokyo, they were detrained in the suburbs, so that there should be no incidents ; and from first to last there was not a single instance of any kind of offensive conduct towards a German.

Most people supposed that the *rôle* of Japan in the war came to an end with the fall of Tsing-Tau and the seizure of the German islands of the Pacific. They were partially disillusioned by the British Admiralty's generous acknowledgment of the service which the Japanese fleet was rendering throughout the war and, still more by the Emperor's speech at the opening of the Japanese Diet on December 7, just one month after the capture of Tsing-Tau. After noting that the crisis had had the result of uniting Japan in closer bonds of amity with Britain and also with France and Russia, his Majesty went on to say :—" Peace in the Orient is gradually being restored, but the great war is not yet ended. We rely upon the loyalty and bravery of our subjects in our wish

to obtain the final object as quickly as possible." This measured utterance from the Throne, a whole month after Tsing-Tau had fallen, was significant ; but the fact remained that the reduction of Tsing-Tau was a solid achievement in itself. Its effect and meaning can hardly be better expressed than in the following extracts from the leading article in *The Times* of November 9, 1914. It said :—

" The surrender of Tsing-Tau by the Germans is an event of great importance in the history of the Far East. We heartily congratulate our Japanese Allies upon the attainment of an object on which their hearts have been set ever since Prince Henry of Prussia's visit to China in 1898, and we rejoice that British and Indian troops have worked with them to achieve it. The gracious message in which His Majesty the Emperor of Japan acknowledges their services speaks of the fall of the German fortress as ' one of the objects of the war.' The phrase shows what great weight is attached in Japan to this victory. . . . The chief incidents in the siege which has terminated by the expulsion of the Germans from the Far East show that the garrison made a good defence, though the ultimate issue was never in doubt. At a cost which is relatively small, the Allies have undone the work of seventeen years of intrigue and of labour. Kiaochau, of which Tsing-Tau is the capital, was in the first instance seized by Germany on the plea that a temporary occupation of the site was requisite to exact reparation from China for the murder of two German missionaries. Reparation was made, but the occupation was not discontinued. On the contrary, a long lease of the territory was obtained from China, and Germany proceeded to settle down comfortably in her ' place in the sun.' She exerted her ' influence ' far beyond the boundaries of the leased territory, and arbitrarily extended her authority into the province of Shantung. Money was lavished on her new possession. It is said that so much as £20,000,000 has been devoted to it by the German State, and that last year the expenditure, partly paid by the German taxpayer, amounted to £877,000. The fine harbour was developed by the erection of a massive breakwater nearly three miles long, and by the construction of piers, docks, and jetties, until it greatly surpassed in accommodation the Russian port at Dalny. Government offices, barracks, hospitals, schools, and waterworks were built in the town, a considerable garrison was maintained there, and the works mounted no fewer than 600 Krupp guns of one calibre or

another. Everything showed that the Germans had ' come to stay,' and that they intended Kiaochau to be the centre of their future dominions in the Far East and the base of their future adventures there.

" They have been driven out, and their expulsion will not only shatter their prestige in Peking, but it will lessen their credit throughout Asia. . . . They have ' lost face,' and that loss is very serious in the East, especially for a Power which has but lately appeared there. To our Japanese Allies in particular the capture of Tsing-Tau is of the utmost moment. They have always regarded the establishment of this German fortress, administered directly by the German Navy Department, as a standing menace to themselves. They have never mistaken the extent of German ambitions. They have never forgotten how it was Germany who was the principal in defrauding them of the legitimate fruits of their victories over China in 1905. Kiaochau, as it grew in riches, in trade, and in strength, became year by year a more formidable threat. But it is not only the Japanese who have special reasons to be gratified by the defeat of German designs in the Far East. The Russians had discovered the advantages of Kiaochau long before the murder of the missionaries gave German diplomacy an excuse for seizing it, and they can hardly forget

ADMIRAL MEYER-WALDECK,
Commander at Tsing-Tau, a prisoner of war.

["*Asahi Shimbun.*"]

VICE-ADMIRAL TOCHINAI.

the way in which they were duped by the German occupation. We, too, have our reasons for satisfaction at the obliteration of the fruits of Prince Henry's adventure. The circumstances in which it was made were sorry to look upon. When he sailed from Kiel, 'to declare,' as he told his brother and Emperor, 'the gospel of your Majesty's hallowed person,' he started on his lofty mission with a couple of old ships, the Gefion and the Deutschland, which constantly broke down in the most deplorable manner on the voyage. The Emperor, as we pointed out at the time, wanted to increase his Fleet, and his subjects did not want to pay for the increase. The shameful plight of the ships dispatched with the exalted aim of shaking the German 'mailed fist' in the face of the Son of Heaven, and the solid, practical results which even these unsatisfactory craft achieved, were deftly used as unanswerable arguments for the establishment of a formidable German Navy. It is from the year of Kiaochau that the growth of that Navy really dates. The Navy Act of 1898 has been the prolific parent of the numerous progeny which has created the present German Navy. All the Allies, and indeed all the neutral States which trade with China, may look forward with complacency to a share in the extensive commerce which has grown up in the

German port. Both the exports and the imports of Kiaochau appear to exceed very largely those of any other German possession, the former amounting to £2,746,000 and the latter to £4,015,000 in 1912. China, for her part, must be gratified at getting rid of the particularly grasping and obnoxious tenant, who had thrust herself upon her, and must welcome the prospect of recovering her property, in a greatly improved condition, after the war."

Most of the problems which would confront Japan after the war were prematurely raised in the newspapers of various countries immediately after the fall of Tsing-Tau, under the mistaken impression that the *rôle* of Japan in the war came to an end with the reduction of that fortress. Of course this was not the case, as the Japanese frankly stated. Tsing-Tau was necessarily their first and main objective ; but, as has been shown, there were other directions in which they found useful work to do within the scope of their treaty obligation to Britain. And the Japanese, as business-like in their amity as in their hostility, did not believe in complicating the fulfilment of a plain undertaking with premature side issues. So long as Germany retained the power and the wish to disturb British or Japanese commerce in the Pacific the dominant duty of Japan under the terms of her alliance was to remain actively on guard : and the transference of the entire Baltic fleet of Russia to the Far East during the previous war had taught Japan that so long as a hostile Power retained a warship anywhere that warship had to be regarded as a menace in the Pacific.

The immediate question which, of course, occupied the minds of all Japanese after the fall of Tsing-Tau was as to the future of the territory taken from Germany. It had never been a German freehold, it is true ; but there were so many years of the lease still to run that this did not much matter. It is also important to note that the general opinion in Britain and probably in other countries, that Japan had "promised" to hand over Kiaochau to China, was not the general opinion in Japan. The foreign opinion was based upon the terms of the Japanese ultimatum to Germany ; but, as the ultimatum was not accepted, its terms were nugatory. The circumstances of war had greatly altered the case as it existed at the time when the ultimatum was launched. Owing to its rejection by Germany, Japan had been forced into great expenditure of money and considerable expenditure of lives. Success had crowned her arms; but that welcome fact placed her under no compulsion to fulfil the offer which she had made previously. The acceptance of that offer would have saved the waste of money and blood and would not have involved Japan in the danger of possible defeat. She had faced that danger and had resolutely incurred the inevitable losses: she had won; and how should she recoup herself? This was the question upon every Japanese tongue; and the reply of the Government was contained in the statement that the future of Kiaochau would be settled by negotiation after the war. Meanwhile it would be retained by Japan, as a useful asset for the purpose of negotiation.

Japan's political difficulties appear to arise chiefly from two causes—the immense strategic importance of the position of the island kingdom and the lack of developed industries.

The former necessitates military and naval expenditure and the latter keeps the country too poor to bear such expenditure.

The political troubles arising from this difficult financial position of Japan culminated in the spring of 1914 in the downfall of Admiral Yamamoto's Government; and thus Japan, like Belgium and Britain, was taken at a disadvantage—as it appeared—when the Kaiser decided to launch the thunderbolt of war. But in Japan, as in Britain and Belgium, as

[" Asahi Shimbun."
VICE-ADMIRAL KATO,
Commander-in-Chief of the Tsing-Tau Expeditionary Fleet, and his Adjutant,
LIEUT.-COMMANDER YAMAMOTO.

well as Russia and France, cooperation in a righteous and successful war proved to have been a rare political tonic.

In order to understand the difficulties of Japanese politics, we must realize that previously to 1914 party government was unknown. In theory the Government of the day existed only by favour of the Throne; but in practice no Government was able to survive defeats in both Houses, backed by popular

TSING-TAU.
March past of Japanese Army on the day of triumphal entry.

demonstrations of disfavour. Especially since the successful issues of the Chinese and Russian wars had the spirit of the Japanese people risen too high to submit to permanent dominance by a Government of which they disapproved. They were painfully aware that it was on their shoulders that the burden of war expenditure fell. They were sadly but proudly conscious that it was their blood which had paid the price of victory. So when Count Yamamoto's Government—foreseeing, no doubt, the danger of the coming war-storm—strove to insist upon heavy naval expenditure at the moment when widespread naval scandals were revealed, the Government had to go.

But this meant more than a mere change of party government. Not only were there no parties in Japan, but the fall of this Ministry involved an even more decisive condemnation of its recognised opponents. In order to understand this, one must realize that political power in Japan was the bone of contention between two opposing clans of hereditary aristocrats— one of which was supreme in the navy, and the other dominated the army. In the previous year the Ministry of the latter, under Prince Katsura, had been thrown out and the army

expenditure had been drastically cut down. So, although the downfall of Admiral Yamamoto was in a sense a triumph for his military rivals, it did not rehabilitate the latter in public opinion.

In ordinary times a possible alternative might have been a stop-gap Government of officials merely : but the nation, having realized its own strength in war, whereby it definitely took its place among the great nations, needed a national government. This, of course, means party government ; because a Ministry can only claim to be carrying out a national policy when this commands the approval of the majority of the nation. So soon as election results show that the majority has passed to the opponents of the Government, the latter becomes, *ipso facto*, the national party. The significance, therefore, of the political disturbances which emphasised the unpopularity of Admiral Yamamoto's Ministry lay in their expression of the nation's demand for a new system of government.

Curiously enough, the change had already been provided for by the previously-defeated Premier, Prince Katsura, who formed just before his death a new political party known as the

WELCOME TO GENERAL BARNARDISTON   [*"Asahi Shimbun."*]
At Tokyo, Shimbashi Station, December 12, 1914.

Doshikai. Incidentally the formation of this party signified a radical change in Prince Katsura's own views. From being an uncompromising bureaucrat and acknowledged leader of one of the opposing clans, he became a progressive politician, equally opposed to both of the great clans ; and Count Okuma, over 75 years of age, was accepted as the political mentor of the new party. So when Prince Katsura was dead and further tenure of power by his opponents was rendered impossible through popular disfavour, Count Okuma seemed the only possible Premier. It was with great reluctance, no doubt, that the elder statesmen— the lingering power which still stood behind the throne in Japan—sanctioned his selection, and it was with his courage in both hands that he accepted it. He was disliked by the elder statesmen on account of his Liberal views as to party government ; he was avowedly opposed to the domination of the two great clans ; and, worst of all perhaps, he was distrusted by the progressive party, which had no faith in the professed Liberalism of the Doshikai men of the party formed by Prince Katsura. In all these circumstances it is not surprising that Count Okuma had no majority in the Diet. But he was able to select efficient colleagues. Baron Kato, leader of the Doshikai, became Foreign Minister ; Mr. Wakatsuki, the disciple of Katsura both before and after his conversion, took charge of finance ; and Mr. Ozaki, perhaps the most popular progressive orator in Japan, was made Minister of Justice and brought to the support of the Cabinet his small following in the Diet known as the Chuseikai. This left in the cold and in Opposition all the powerful sections which had hitherto shared the loaves and fishes of office between themselves. It was, therefore, a foregone conclusion that on the occasion of the first political crisis the aged but wise Premier would be in a minority. This duly happened at Christmas, 1914, when the Government was defeated in the Diet on the Army Estimates.

This did not necessarily, and certainly not immediately, involve a change in the government of Japan or even an appeal to the people. Following precedent, it was open to Count Okuma to ignore his defeat and open negotiations with the Opposition for a compromise. The Throne might even have been invoked to procure a settlement. Failing this, the Diet might have been prorogued and then adjourned, the Government being carried on meanwhile by

**GENERAL BARNARDISTON ACKNOW-
LEDGING THE GREETING OF THE
PEOPLE OF TOKYO.**

the automatic repetition of the annual Budget. Count Okuma was, however, a man with principles. It was as a " party " man—the first ' party " man who had ever held office in Japan as such—that he took the Premiership, and it was as a " party " man that, when he was outvoted, he decided to dissolve the Diet and appeal to the country. Thus party government began in Japan, and none too soon : because, although the system had not been politically recognized, the brief summary of events given above shows that modern Japan was simply seething with " party." It only needed coordinating.

And Count Okuma was wise, as always, in the issues which he selected for submission to the nation. He had behind him the successful issue of the operations at Tsing-Tau, the new status which Japan had attained as a World-Power, and the formulation of a definite and well-devised financial policy, besides other domestic measures calculated to win popular favour ; and in the long run the party which has deserved well of the State never misses its reward. But in this case the interesting fact of the situation at the close of 1914 was not that this or that party had good prospect of dominance, but that at last there really was the beginning of party government in Japan.

This fact, however, did not dispose of the immediate, practical difficulties of the situation Nominally the only ground for dissension

GENERAL BARNARDISTON AT TOKYO. ["*Asahi Shimbun.*"]

among the political parties in the Japanese Diet was the Government project for the expansion of the Army ; but behind this was the uncomfortable fact that, while the Government was proposing to incur a larger war expenditure, finance and commerce had suffered heavily on account of the war. But, of course, the pressing fact of the political situation was that the Seiyukai party, who were opposed to Count Okuma's Government, commanded a majority in the Diet. They had, indeed, been defeated in a frontal attack upon the foreign policy of the Government, imputing political subjection to Britain ; but in the side issue concerning increased expenditure, estimated at £55,600,000, at a time when revenue was failing and finance was shaky, causing an estimated loss of revenue to the extent of £8,100,000, they were in a stronger position. Little surprise, therefore, was felt when the news came that the Government had been defeated on the Army Estimates ; nor in the case of a European country would any surprise at all have been aroused by the announcement on the following (Christmas) day that the Diet had been dissolved. In countries which are under party government the dissolution of parliament almost automatically follows the defeat of the Government of the day ; but in Japan the system had hitherto been unknown

and a majority in the Diet had by no means been necessary for the continuance of a Government in power. Count Okuma was, however, a convert to the party principle, and he took this opportunity to put the principle into practice. The political manœuvres and the elections which followed do not belong to a History of the War. This is fitly concluded by the statement that, so far as the war was concerned, Japan fulfilled her obligations nobly.

In this connection the statement of Baron Kato, Japanese Minister for Foreign Affairs, to the Diet on December 8 was admirably lucid and straightforward. After deploring the growing magnitude of the war, but claiming that relations between Japan and the other Allies had " grown more intimate than ever " and that all were perfectly frank with one another in their exchange of views, he continued :—

" Our relations with neutral Powers are also in an excellent condition. Various questions which were raised between Japan and China in connexion with the attack on Kiaochau have been on the whole satisfactorily settled, the Chinese Government being fully alive to the general situation. Complete success has attended the efforts of our Army and Navy at Tsing-Tau, and in this respect I wish highly to appreciate the loyal assistance rendered by the British land and naval forces.

" With regard to our action in the Pacific, the Imperial Government dispatched a squadron to the German South Sea Islands—namely, the Marshall, the Caroline, the Mariana (Ladrones), and the Palao (Pelew) Islands—which islands are now under military occupation and are being guarded.

" Previous to the rupture of our diplomatic relations with Germany the German Government, on the pretext that they were protecting the Japanese, detained many of them in different parts of the country, and even in some cases incarcerated them. The German Government ignored the protest of our representative in Berlin against such treatment, and they flatly refused his repeated request to be allowed to visit the places where Japanese subjects were interned. The Imperial Government having requested the United States Government to protect the Imperial Embassy in Berlin and Japanese interests in Germany, the United States Government willingly consented, and as the result of the kindly and timely action taken by them the great majority of the Japanese in detention were released. It is believed that there are some still detained, for whose release we shall have to rely upon the further good

offices of the United States Government. We deeply appreciate and are sincerely grateful to the United States Government for their goodwill.

" With regard to China, the Imperial Government most earnestly hope that nothing will arise there to disturb peace and order, as their maintenance is of the greatest importance."

Nothing could have been better than this as a statement of resolute, successful and conciliatory foreign policy in time of war; and, although the opponents of Count Okuma's Government commanded a majority in the Diet, they were quite unable to carry home their attacks upon this policy. The vulnerable point of the Government, however, as has been shown, was on the side of finance.

One circumstance which undoubtedly added to the difficulties of the Japanese Government was the partial success of the characteristic German campaign of lies which was actively conducted in Tokyo and the provinces. Many agencies were at work in this; but one commonly successful trick was worked by the visits of men who were obviously Americans to the various Japanese newspaper offices with letters or cablegrams, which they had apparently just received from New York, stating that the United States was hurriedly strengthening her garrisons in the Pacific

VICE-ADMIRAL S. KATO,   [" *Asahi Shimbun.*"
Who completed the attack on Tsing-Tau, being photographed in Tokyo.

and was sending out her fleet, and that war might be regarded as inevitable. The Japanese newspapers published these statements, apparently in all good faith, and, of course, their comments thereon tended in two directions. One was to deplore that Japan had been dragged by Britain into war with the United States, and the other to resent the national humiliation implied in the Government's very friendly references to the United States at a time when the hostility of the latter was so manifest. The authorities described the publications as too ridiculous for contradiction, and many of the lies were exposed as such by internal evidence ; but their effect undoubtedly was to create a dangerous uneasiness in the public mind, just when the Government stood most in need of calm and confident support.

The comments of the German newspapers upon the fall of Tsing-Tau were practically unanimous, and the following extract from the *Lokalanzeiger* may be accepted as expressing all that the Germans had to say :—

"The inevitable has happened—Tsing-Tau has fallen. The history of the German leased territory is henceforth at an end. It was short but glorious. From a decayed Chinese fishing village had been made a shining testimony to German culture. That the most beautiful, the cleanest, and the most progressive town in the Far East had sprung in a couple of years from the soil was calculated to awake the jealousy of the slit-eyed island people of the East. . . . Never shall we forget the bold deed of violence of the yellow robbers or of England that set them on to do it. We know that we cannot yet settle with Japan for years to come. Perhaps she will rejoice over her cowardly robbery. Here our mills can grind but slowly. Even if the years pass, however, we shall certainly not often speak of it, but as certainly always think of it. And if eventually the time of reckoning arrives, then as unanimously as what is now a cry of pain will a great shout of rejoicing ring through Germany, ' Woe to Nippon.' " *

* From the time of the Japanese ultimatum to Germany the German Press had nothing bad enough to say about Japan, and made a special point, in its campaign against England, of the iniquity of bringing Japan into the " war between white men." In reality only German diplomacy had been disappointed. Indeed, on August 2, 1914, the Berlin *Lokalanzeiger* announced in a special edition that Japan had declared war against Russia. This did not produce any anxiety about the " Yellow Peril," but there was a demonstration of enthusiastic approval by an enormous crowd before the Japanese Embassy in Berlin.

In Germany at large the news of the fall of Tsing-Tau was received with feelings which were admirably concealed for the most part under an exterior of confident calmness, which was well expressed in the telegram of condolence sent by the President of the Reichstag to the Kaiser, stating his belief that " the day would come when German civilization would reoccupy its place in the Far East."

The feeling in Britain was equally well expressed in the telegram which Lord Kitchener, as Secretary of State for War, sent to the Japanese Minister of War :—

" Please accept my warmest congratulations on the success of the operations against Tsing-Tau. Will you be so kind as to express my felicitations to the Japanese Forces engaged ? The British Army is proud to have been associated with its gallant Japanese comrades in this enterprise."   " KITCHENER."

In China the predominant feeling on the fall of Tsing-Tau was one of amazement. The German campaign of bluster had been so efficiently conducted by means of the suborned Chinese Press that the very least that was expected was that Tsing-Tau would be another Port Arthur for the Japanese. That the German garrison, after only a short artillery duel, and without a single serious infantry battle, should have surrendered seemed scarcely credible, and caused the Chinese to wonder whether all the vainglorious things which the Germans were telling them of victories in Europe were really true. Perhaps, indeed, it was in its effect upon public opinion in China that the greatest importance of the Japanese success at Tsing-Tau lay.

In Japan itself, it is needless to say, the news caused wild rejoicings. A procession of five thousand members of various guilds, carrying lanterns illuminated with designs in celebration of the victory, paraded the streets of Tokyo, first visiting the British Embassy, then those of France and Russia, and finally halting before the Belgian Legation, where the multitude remained, cheering vociferously, for two hours. It is pleasant to realize that the set-piece of the demonstrative fireworks—the toast of the evening, so to speak—was for Belgium, because Japan and Belgium are no less widely sundered politically than geographically. But this was a war which drew all the " faithfulness and righteousness " of the four corners of the earth together, and Tsing-Tau was the first definite answer to Louvain.

CHAPTER XLV.

PARIS UNDER THE GERMAN MENACE.

PARIS ON THE EVE OF WAR—THE CAILLAUX TRIAL—SUDDENNESS OF THE INTERNATIONAL CRISIS—
PANIC ON THE BOURSE—NATIONAL UNITY—MOBILIZATION—THE PRESIDENT'S PROCLAMATION—
CHANGES IN PARIS LIFE—PROBLEMS OF SUPPLY—DEMONSTRATIONS OF PATRIOTISM—MEETING
OF THE CHAMBER—SIR JOHN FRENCH IN PARIS—THE GERMAN ADVANCE—DEFENCES OF PARIS—
GENERAL GALLIENI APPOINTED GOVERNOR—BOMBS DROPPED FROM AEROPLANES—DEPARTURE
OF THE GOVERNMENT TO BORDEAUX—EXODUS FROM PARIS—THE VICTORY OF THE MARNE—
LIFE IN BORDEAUX—RETURN OF THE GOVERNMENT—REOPENING OF PARLIAMENT—CHRISTMAS
IN PARIS.

PARIS in July, 1914, differed from the Paris of ordinary years only by reason of the Caillaux trial. Towards the middle of the month *tout Paris*, instead of preparing for its usual exodus to the watering places of Normandy and abroad, settled down with all the joy of expectation to the spectacle offered by the Seine Assizes, where the wife of M. Joseph Caillaux, former Prime Minister and Minister of Finance, leader of the Radical-Socialist Party and of a turbulent, erratic, but nevertheless formidable coalition in the Chamber, was being tried for the murder of her husband's bitterest political opponent, Gaston Calmette, editor of the *Figaro*. The tragedy in the *Figaro* office on March 16 was the culminating episode in a political campaign of a virulent violence rare even in the annals of French political life. The negotiations of M. Caillaux with the traditional enemy, Germany, during the Agadir crisis of 1911 had laid him open to charges of treason ; he had nevertheless succeeded by a cleverness which amounted almost to genius in re-establishing his hold upon the more extreme sections of the Radical Party. At

their head throughout the summer of 1913, he had combatted with every political weapon the proposal for a return to the Three Years' military service, and, when that measure of national defence had been finally adopted, at the head of his Socialist-Radical combination he fought with determination for the introduction of an income tax—a wide-reaching reform in the French fiscal system—in order to meet the increased military expenditure required of the country.

Chief among the opponents of the income tax were the conservative interests represented by the *Figaro*, the editor of which did not scruple to publish documents of a more or less intimate nature concerning M. Caillaux. Alarmed by these publications and dreading the revelation of still more intimate facts, Mme. Caillaux called at the *Figaro* office and without any preliminary discussion emptied the contents of an automatic revolver into the body of the editor. The crime, involving as it did every section of French political life, promising as it did the washing of much dirty linen in public, yielding as it did a wide field to the activity of the café gossiper, containing as it

Vol. II.—Part 25.

THE CAILLAUX TRIAL.
M. Caillaux in Court—he is seen standing on the right.

did the elements of the two things which most appeal to Parisians — passion and politics—absorbed attention throughout the month of July to the exclusion of every other topic. The funeral of Calmette was attended by riotous scenes, and the trial opened in an atmosphere of great political excitement, which was turned to the best possible effect by the extremist parties in French life that refuse to recognise the Republic —the Socialists and the Royalists. Day after day the Palais de Justice was besieged by anxious crowds, hoping by favour or by influence to obtain even standing room within the court ; night after night the boulevards were invaded by gangs of Royalist or Syndicalist hotheads clamouring for or against Caillaux, and giving much occupation to the police and municipal guard.

In the midst of all this internal commotion the appearance of a tiny cloud on the eastern horizon of Europe passed almost unnoticed save by the specialists in foreign affairs. Even the news of the Austrian ultimatum to Serbia failed to arouse any widespread alarm. Socialist Deputies bewailed the fact that if war broke out between Austria and Serbia it would

be impossible to hold the International Socialist Congress in Vienna. Esperantists and dental surgeons, who were to hold their annual international congresses in Paris, felt that perhaps their gatherings might be inopportune. It was not until July 26, when the news of the rupture of diplomatic relations between Austria and Serbia became known, that Paris appeared to realize the imminent possibility of international conflict involving France. Then, for the first time in the growing crisis, it appeared to come home to the Parisian that the day which had been so long prophesied, so long discussed, and so little expected—the day of Armageddon—was at last within measurable distance. Unusual animation reigned throughout the boulevards and the customary military tattoos gave rise to frequent demonstrations. A band of young men gathered in front of the Austrian Embassy, and, after much shouting and singing, managed to burn the Austrian flag before they were dispersed by the police. Nevertheless, once the growing danger had been brought forcibly to their notice, Parisians with their quick political appreciation realized to the full what lay ahead of them, and accepted in cheerful silence the various preliminary and precautionary steps taken by the military authorities for the defence of the country. The fact that they realized the danger was evident in the anxious questions which Frenchmen addressed to all their English acquaintances, with a view to ascertaining what would be the attitude of Great Britain in the struggle which was in prospect. It was further made clear by scenes in the Paris Bourse, when an operator of Austrian nationality named Rosenberg, who had rendered himself conspicuous by "bearing" French Bank securities and French Rentes throughout the year, was driven from the building by a shower of eggs and other unpleasant missiles.

In spite of all the gathering of black clouds and the ominous rumble of thunder in the East, the Caillaux trial retained its hold upon the public attention up to the end of July 28, when the acquittal of the prisoner gave rise to turbulent scenes in the centre of the city. It was not until the return of the President of the Republic, M. Poincaré, and the Prime Minister, M. Viviani, from a visit to the Emperor Nicholas of Russia that the demonstrations with which Paris had been seething for ten days or so acquired a purely patriotic note. There were

shouts of "Vive Poincaré!" and "Vive l'Armée!" as the President of the Republic, accompanied by M. Viviani and General Joffre, drove from the Gare du Nord to the Elysée. An occasional shout of "Vive la Guerre!" was raised, but the demonstration as a whole was patriotic rather than jingo. On the same day, as though the curtain had been rung down on the Caillaux tragi-comedy and raised upon this fresh drama of world-wide interest, the whole of Paris turned its attention to the development of the situation with absorbed interest. The boulevards, that great index of Parisian life, became long lines of fluttering newspapers, as edition after edition poured from the presses in the Montmartre quarter.

The French in every international crisis of recent years have shown a pronounced tendency to hoard their gold. This defect produced situations which, but for their actual gravity, would have been entirely amusing. The financial panic on the Bourse was followed by a credit panic, which led to a famine of cash and a general refusal to give change for the notes of the Bank of France. All the usual credit machinery collapsed, as has been explained

BIRD'S-EYE VIEW OF PARIS.
Taken from the top of the Eiffel Tower.

in a previous volume of this History ; English and American millionaires were wandering round Paris with their pocket-books full of bank notes, unable to purchase a meal at any restaurant. At the banks long lines of depositors began to collect, and at the Bank of France, during the days before war was actually declared, there was a daily crowd of four or five thousand persons anxious to obtain gold for notes.

It is curious to note that while in England crowds assembled to watch the arrival and departure of Ministers and Ambassadors in Downing Street, the feverish activity which prevailed at the Quai d'Orsay throughout the last days of the crisis aroused not the faintest interest among Parisians. Yet in the Quai d'Orsay, in the dying days of July, history was being made with every circumstance of drama. On July 31 *The Times* correspondent was closeted with the Under-Secretary of State for Foreign Affairs, M. Abel Ferry. He was speaking of all that France had done to prove her desire for peace. Although a state of war had been proclaimed in Germany, although the 16th, 8th, and 15th German army corps had been moved up to battle positions upon the French frontier France, in order to minimise the chances of accidental conflict, in order to show to the world the intensity of her wish to avoid war, had kept at a distance of ten kilometres from the frontier her first line of defence. M. Abel Ferry was saying what great personal sacrifice this decision had meant for him, since all his family was in the strip of territory thus abandoned to a possible enemy, when the telephone bell rang and the Minister of War gave him news of the first acts of aggression, of the tearing up of the railway line on the frontier, of the posting of mitrailleuses along the frontier, of the seizure of French rolling stock.

The time had come and the people of Paris, from Syndicalist to Monarchist, knew that the hour was past for any display of political dissension. That night Jaurès, the beloved leader of the French Socialist Party, was assassinated at the dinner-table, and as his body was borne along the boulevard men of every party uncovered to a son of France. The crime, in time of peace, would have aroused the most tremendous political conflict ; in the darkening hours of the moment it came as a grief even to the most bitter opponent of the Socialist leader.

As it was, the crime only served to emphasize the union of all parties in France in the face of the imminent danger of war. On that day,

CROWD READING MOBILIZATION ORDERS.

PLACE DE LA CONCORDE.
Searchlights watching for Aeroplanes.

July 31, the covering troops of France were mobilized and the reservists called to the colours. On August 1 the following proclamation was addressed to the people of Paris by the Prime Minister, M. Viviani :

An abominable crime has just been committed. M. Jaurès, the great orator, who adorned the French Tribune, has been struck down by a coward. Personally, and on behalf of my colleagues, I uncover myself before the so-quickly opened tomb of the Socialist-Republican who has fought for such noble causes and who in recent difficult days, acting in the interests of peace, has supported with his authority the patriotic action of the Government. In the grave circumstances through which the country is passing the Government counts upon the patriotism of the working class, and, indeed, of all the inhabitants to observe calm and to refrain from adding to public emotion an agitation which would throw the capital into disorder. The assassin has been arrested ; he shall be punished. Let all have confidence in the law and give the example of calm and of union in our present grave dangers.

That same afternoon the German Ambassador called at the French Foreign Office, when his attitude left in no doubt the determination of Germany to force upon Europe the horrors of a general conflagration. When Baron von Schoen had returned to his Embassy in the Rue de Lille, the general order of mobilization was already posted throughout Paris, and was speeding on its way to every hamlet, village, and city of

France. In the twinkling of an eye the whole aspect of Paris was changed. A fury of speed seemed to have seized upon everybody. Immediately after glancing at the hurriedly scrawled notice at the Post Office which ran " Ministry of War. Order of Mobilization. Extremely Urgent ; first day of mobilization, Sunday, August 2," all the men rushed to their homes to bid farewell to their dear ones before their departure to the regimental depôts. Cab-drivers refused fares and drove off to their homes to prepare for mobilization, and soon the streets of Paris were all but empty of carriage traffic. Cabs and motor-cars conveying to the Gare de l'Est reservists in field kit and their friends were alone to be seen. Here and there the passage of a group of reservists with canvas bags slung over their shoulders aroused some little demonstration. Waving their képis in the air the men marched gaily past the crowded terraced cafés singing the " Marseillaise." Tearful farewells between husbands and wives, sweethearts, mothers and sons changed the aspect of the city as an April shower will sweep across a blue sky. The truly democratic nature of Paris became everywhere apparent. Comfortable bourgeois,

25—2

BUILDING A BARRICADE.

workmen in stained corduroys, élégants in morning coat and top hat, gathered together to discuss the prospects of the struggle, to voice the common determination to fight to the last drop of blood in the defence of France.

To English people in Paris the day brought mingled feelings of admiration for the quiet spirit of gravity with which all Frenchmen, from anti-Militarists to Monarchists, obeyed their country's call, and of anxious regret that the attitude of England did not allow them to participate directly in these scenes or to voice their sympathies with freedom. Everywhere Englishmen went on that throbbing day on August 1 they were questioned by friends, and indeed by complete strangers, as to the intentions of their country. The doubt and anxiety were so great that more than one English business firm established in Paris, fearing an outbreak of anger should England fail in her duty, took steps for the removal from their business premises of anything which might indicate their nationality. No Englishman, whatever his political sympathies may have been, could have failed to be impressed by the attitude of Paris on August 1. The volatile, excitable, inflammable Parisian gave proof of all the virtues of gravity, serenity, and calm which history had up till then denied him.

Here and there a quiet little crowd of people gathered to read the national call to arms issued by the President of the Republic, which ran as follows :

For some days the condition of Europe has become considerably more serious in spite of the efforts of diplomacy. The horizon has become darkened.

At this hour most of the Nations have mobilized their forces.

Some countries, even though protected by neutrality, have thought it right to take this step as a precaution.

Some Powers, whose constitutional and military laws do not resemble our own, have without issuing a decree of mobilization begun and continued preparations which are in reality equivalent to mobilization and which are nothing more or less than an anticipation of it (*qui n'en sont que l'exécution anticipée*).

France, who has always declared her pacific intentions, and who has at the darkest hours (*dans des heures tragiques*) given to Europe counsels of moderation and a living example of prudence (*sagesse*), who has multiplied her efforts for the maintenance of the world's peace has herself prepared for all eventualities and has taken from this moment the first indispensable measures for the safety of her territory.

But our legislation does not allow us to complete these preparations without a decree of mobilization.

Careful of its responsibility and realizing that it would be failing in a sacred task to leave things as they were, the Government has issued the decree which the situation demands.

Mobilization is not war. In the present circumstances it appears, on the contrary, to be the best means of assuring peace with honour.

Strong in its ardent desire to arrive at a peaceful solution of the crisis the Government, protected by such precautions as are necessary, will continue its diplomatic efforts, and it still hopes to succeed.

It relies upon the calm of this noble nation not to give rein to emotions which are not justified. It relies upon the patriotism of all Frenchmen, and it knows that there is not one who is not ready to do his duty.

At this moment parties no longer exist ; there remains only France, the eternal, the pacific, the resolute. There remains only the fatherland of right and of justice, entirely united in calm vigilance and dignity.

Very different, indeed, were the scenes in Paris at the beginning of the great war of 1914 from those which marked the departure of French troops from Paris in 1870. All the feverish delirium of the madly excited mob, which devoured German Army corps with the ease of a man eating an egg, was conspicuously absent. There were no theatrical scenes with women of questionable morality figuring as France, with play-actors gaining the applause of heroes ; the whole life of Paris was diverted to the frontier. In the evening, it is true, a crowd of three or four hundred youths paraded the boulevards, waving the flags of France and Russia, and in anticipatory gratitude those of all the Powers thought to be friendly to the cause of France. These demonstrations were, however, entirely superficial, and it was over a more than usually tranquil city that the new constellations of war, the anti-aircraft search-lights of the Eiffel Tower and the Place de la Concorde, cut their arabesques of light on the eve of the first day of mobilization.

On the Sunday, August 2, mobilization throughout France was proceeding with rapidity and method. Paris, except at the railway stations, resembled an English provincial town on Sunday. At the Gare du Nord and at the Gare de l'Est there were busy and pathetic scenes. Around the station there were great crowds of the relatives and friends of departing soldiers, come to see the last of their sons, lovers, or husbands. The final farewells were made at the gates of the station, and then the men marched out of sight shouting " Vive la France ! " and chanting the " Marseillaise."

Although the effects of the mobilization order were immediately experienced in Paris, it took some time to persuade the tourist that his place at this critical hour was at home, and not wandering round Paris, Baedeker in hand, admiring the Arc de Triomphe or endeavouring to obtain admission to the Louvre. The stoppage of ordinary life, and above all of all forms of amusement and of credit, finally persuaded the travelling foreigner that Paris was no longer a city of pleasure. Cafés and restaurants were closed by order of the military authorities at 8 p.m. All theatres, music halls, and cafés-chantants were forbidden to open. Every motor-omnibus left the streets of the capital for the high road to the East, to act as meat carrier to the armies. The underground railway system ceased to work. Travel facili-ties between Paris and London became slow and restricted.

Provisions of every sort rose in price during these days and the grocers' shops were besieged with crowds of housewives laying in stocks of preserved food of every sort. The feeding of Paris during war-time was a

RESERVISTS LEAVING FOR THE FRONT.

problem which had long exercised the authorities. The difficulty to be surmounted was not so much that of supply as that of transporting the supply from the provinces to the capital during the nineteen days when every railway in France was crowded to the utmost of its capacity by trains bearing troops towards the frontier. The supply for the capital had for some months before the outbreak of war formed the subject of negotiations between the town of Paris and the military authorities. The Municipal Council from patriotic motives decided to contribute 400,000 francs towards the formation of a stock of flour amounting to 100,000 quintals (9,842 tons), to be used between the eighth and twentieth days of mobilization, that is to say, after the normal bakers' supplies of flour had been exhausted, and before the release of the railways by the completion of mobilization had allowed fresh supplies to enter the capital from the provinces.

This agreement was not entirely observed, but nevertheless, thanks to the cooperation of the municipal services and the *Intendance*, the capital was spared any appreciable shortage of food supplies. The military authorities furnished the millers with wheat and fixed the price at which the flour was to be sold. Further, in order to meet the difficulties caused among the Parisian bakeries by reason of the drain upon their labour entailed by general mobilization, it was decreed that no fancy bread should be baked in Paris.

The military authorities also had to come to the assistance of the town of Paris with regard to meat supply. The *Intendance* had, in fact, two duties to perform : first, to provide the entrenched camp of Paris with resources of all kinds which would enable it to withstand the pressure of investment ; and, secondly, quite apart from all question of investment, to ensure during the period of mobilization a regular supply of flour, sugar, butter and groceries of all sorts, fresh meat and coal, shortage of which might be occasioned by lack of railway facilities. The activity of the *Intendance*, although prices rose to some extent, was soon made evident in all the big open spaces in and around Paris. Thus large areas of the Bois de Boulogne, the famous Auteuil and Longchamp racecourses, became covered with wire pens for thousands of heads of sheep and cattle destined mainly to feed the army of Paris, but a good deal of which had to be placed upon the ordinary Paris market in order to keep down the price of fresh meat.

Another matter deeply affecting the welfare of the capital was the milk supply. In this,

PREPARING FOR THE SIEGE.
A Queue outside a Provision Shop.

RESERVISTS FROM THE OUTLYING COUNTRY ENTERING PARIS.

as, indeed, in all questions concerning the feeding of Paris during the war, the Municipal Council gave proof of clear-sighted patriotism and energetic action. A large stock of milk was secured by the Municipal Council at the very outset of the war, and 100,000 kilos (98 tons) of powdered milk and 1,000,000 litres (220,000 gallons) of milk in condensed form were purchased. Thanks to these and similar precautions taken with regard to other articles of food the Paris population in the first six months of war had experienced practically none of the effects of shortage of food.

The shortage of cash was extremely serious, but it was met by the issue of the 20 franc and 5 franc notes of the Bank of France, which, printed several years before, had been kept in the vaults of the bank. These were the problems which beset the rulers of Paris the very first day of the mobilization. They were specifically Parisian difficulties.

On the third day of mobilization Paris was the scene of a solemn and impressive demonstration of the national union and patriotic resolve. There are few parliamentary buildings better suited for the display of national feeling than the Palais Bourbon, in which the French

Deputies are housed. In ordinary times the red-covered benches which fill the vast hemicycle are crowded with gesticulating, shouting men, whose sole apparent object in life is to prevent any of the orators from taking their stand at the tribune opposite and making themselves heard. On August 4 only the unusual crowd which pressed behind the double row of the guard of honour and saluted the President of the Chamber as he passed through the square indicated that a sitting of unusual importance was to be begun. The usual eager hum of the Salle des Pas Perdus was hushed. In the crowded galleries inside the House there was an unwonted silence, and the roll of the drums from the outer corridor, the traditional salute to the President of the Chamber on taking the chair, had a new significance. The Deputies, as they streamed into their places, did not exchange the usual greetings with their friends ; the customary gossip was forgotten ; and it was amid a self-imposed silence that M. Deschanel, President of the Chamber of Deputies, read the decree convoking the assembly for an extraordinary session. M. Deschanel, a distinguished and eloquent speaker, struck the note of complete

A FRENCH CATTLE CONVOY.

harmony which had been formed among the most bitterly opposed political parties by the challenge flung down by Germany in alluding at the outset of his speech to the death of M. Jaurès. The name of the great Socialist leader had hardly left his mouth when, as one man, Monarchists, Socialists, Republicans, and Conservatives rose to their feet and listened in silence to his tribute.

The same wonderfully impressive unanimity marked a cry of " Vive la France," which rose from everybody in the House, actor and spectator, when M. Deschanel declared that it was for the welfare of civilization, for the liberty of France and the whole of Europe, that the country was fighting. At the conclusion of his speech M. Deschanel announced that the Prime Minister, M. Viviani, would be with the House in a moment. The Prime Minister's entry was rendered impressive by the unbroken silence with which it had been awaited. His first act when the tumult and the shouting died down was to read the following message from the President of the Republic, which was listened to standing :

France has just been the object of a brutal and premeditated aggression which is an insolent challenge to the rights of humanity. Before a declaration of war had been addressed to us, even before the German Ambassador

had demanded his passports, our territory has been violated. Not until last night did the German Empire give the true name to a situation which it had already created. For more than forty years the French in their sincere love of peace had repressed in their breasts their desire for legitimate reparation. They had given to the world the example of a great nation which, definitely rehabilitated from its defeat by good will, patience, and industry, has used its renewed and rejuvenated energy only in the interests of progress and for the good of humanity. When the Austrian ultimatum opened a crisis which threatened the whole of Europe, France decided to follow and to recommend to all a policy of prudence, of wisdom, and of moderation. No one can impute to her any act, any gesture, any word, which was not pacific and conciliatory. At the moment of the first encounters she has the right solemnly to make this claim for herself—that she made up to the last moment the strongest efforts to avert the war which has just broken out and of which the German Empire will have to take the crushing responsibility throughout history.

On the morrow of the day in which our allies and ourselves expressed publicly the hope of seeing the negotiations begun under the auspices of the Cabinet of London peacefully carried on, Germany suddenly declared war upon Russia. She has invaded the territory of Luxemburg, she has outrageously insulted the noble Belgian nation, our neighbour and our friend, and she has endeavoured treacherously to surprise us in the midst of diplomatic conversations. But France was watching, as alert as pacific. She was prepared, and our enemies will meet on their path our brave covering troops who are at their posts, and under whose shelter the mobilization of all our national forces will be methodically completed. Our fine and brave Army, which France to-day accompanies with motherly thought, has arisen eager to defend the honour of the flag and the soil of the country.

The President of the Republic, who voices the unanimity of the country, expresses to our troops who will fight by land and sea the admiration and confidence of all Frenchmen. Closely united in one feeling the nation will maintain the *sang-froid* of the possession of which she has given daily proof since the beginning of the crisis. France will, as ever, combine the most generous impulses and the most enthusiastic spirit with that self-command which betokens lasting energy and the best guarantee of victory. In the war upon which she is entering France will have on her side that right which no peoples, any more than individuals, may despise with impunity—the eternal moral power. She will be heroically defended by all her sons, whose sacred union in face of the enemy nothing can destroy, and who to-day are fraternally bound together by the same indignation against the aggressor, and by the same patriotic faith. She is faithfully supported by Russia, her ally, she is upheld by the loyal friendship of England, and already from all parts of the civilized world come to her sympathy and good wishes, for she represents once more to-day before the world, Liberty, Justice, and Reason. *Haut les cœurs, et vive la France ! ! !*

The final phrase led to a splendid demonstration of patriotism, and it was some time before quiet was restored and the Prime Minister was enabled to justify to the House the manner in which the Government had discharged its heavy responsibilities during the critical negotiations.

His clear statement of the preceding few days' history, his burning condemnation of German aims and German methods having been brought to an end in a thunder of applause,

18 Bills rendered necessary by the state of war were laid before the House and passed into law without discussion. The Chamber emptied, and those Deputies affected by the order of mobilization left Paris for their posts.

That evening Baron von Schoen, the German Ambassador, was escorted out of Paris with every respect due to his rank as Ambassador, and provided with a special train to take him to the frontier. His departure passed absolutely unnoticed by the inhabitants of the capital, and none of the disgraceful incidents which marked the return of the French Ambassador from Berlin found an echo in France.

Before leaving Paris the German Ambassador handed the following declaration of war to M. Rene Viviani, French Prime Minister :

M. LE PRÉSIDENT,—The German administrative and military authorities have remarked a certain number of definitely hostile acts committed on German territory by French military airmen. Several of these latter have manifestly violated the neutrality of Belgium by flying over the territory of that country. One has endeavoured to destroy buildings near Wesel ; others have been seen in the Eifel region ; another has thrown bombs on the railway line near Carlsruhe and Nuremberg. I am ordered, and I have the honour, to inform your Excellency that in view of these aggressions the German Empire considers itself to be in a state of war with France by the act of this latter Power.

At the same time I have the honour to inform your Excellency that the German authorities will retain French

AMERICAN VOLUNTEERS FOR THE FRENCH ARMY.

merchant ships in German ports, but that they will release them if, within 48 hours, complete reciprocity be assured.

My diplomatic mission having come to an end, I have but to ask your Excellency to be good enough to furnish me with my passports and to take the steps which may seem necessary to your Excellency to assure my return to Germany with the staff of the Embassy, as well as with the staff of the Bavarian Legation and of the German Consulate-General in Paris. Pray accept Monsieur le Président, the expression of my very high consideration.

(Signed) SCHOEN.

That night there was the first outbreak of rioting upon the boulevards of Paris. All the Austrian and German establishments, dealers in imitation jewels, in Viennese statuary, and in German provisions, received the visit of the mob ; their establishments were wrecked, and every now and then upon the boulevard one came across a heap of German sausages, bottles of Rhine wine, broken *débris* of some sculptured manifestation of the new art of Vienna, or the contents of one of the innumerable Maggi milkshops. The rioting, such as it was, could not be described as general, nor did Parisians as a whole participate in it. The undesirable element to be found in every big city hoped to find in the outbreak of war some licence for rowdiness. Stern action by the police quickly brought them to their senses. With the exception of about three hours' pillaging, from the

first day of war no single disorderly action was committed in Paris up to the end of 1914. The gangs of hooligans were rapidly cleared from the streets, and Paris was reminded sternly that demonstrations of every kind, even those in favour of France, would be suppressed by the authorities. Even the display of the French flag was forbidden, lest it might lead to any chauvinistic outbreak. The main streets of the capital were occupied by strong forces of police, while at the big centres, such as the Place de l'Opéra and Place de la République, bodies of mounted municipal guards were stationed. Proclamations were issued reminding the inhabitants of Paris that they were under martial law, and that any offences would be punished with the utmost rigour. All this display of police severity was somewhat excessive. It was based apparently upon the mentality and attitude of Paris during 1870, and in no way took into account the changed spirit of La France Nouvelle. Never did a people or a city more quickly realize the absolute necessity for concentration upon the one aim, the defeat of Germany, than did the French and Paris.

Parisians were far too busy wondering what was happening in Belgium and along the eastern frontier to have time to indulge in the

PALAIS BOURBON,
Where the Chamber of Deputies sits.

SOLDIER GUARDING A BRIDGE AT ST. DENIS.

bombastic and pathetic demonstrations of jingoism which marked the opening days of 1870. The whole soul of France was on the frontier during those first dark days of August, and by a terrific effort of self-discipline Parisians succeeded in abstaining from the rumour-mongering which had so disastrous an effect upon the morale of France in the previous struggle with Germany.

The idea of a new France had been ridiculed by writers and by events. It had been argued three years before the outbreak of war that the attitude of the country at the time of the Agadir crisis marked the arrival of a new generation of Frenchmen, more northern than Latin in character, which placed more value upon reality than upon theory. M. Lavisse, who for many years had directed the training of the French educational corps at the Ecole Normale, was acclaimed as the main author of this new France, which was conscious of its power but disciplined to self-restraint, eager to serve, and not impatient under control, arrogant and eager for personal distinction, as was the generation of sorrow in 1870. Never was the existence of this new France more clearly demonstrated than in the opening days of August, 1914. The assassination of Gaston Calmette, the Rochette scandal, the intrigues of the minis-

terial crises which followed it, were interpreted in Germany as a sign that the old canker still existed. With the declaration of war France, as apart from her politicians, showed how completely erroneous was this idea. A city which some forty years before swung from the heights of delirium to the depths of despair on the mere circulation of a rumour through the café or the boulevard, refused to be shaken in its confidence by the successive bulletins of defeat and of danger published by the War Office, as the Germans steadily battered their way through Liége, flooded Belgium, captured Namur, and began what appeared to be an irresistible rush through the north of France.

Parisians by their attitude in August claimed a place of greater honour, if of less dramatic importance, in history than did their fathers in the siege of Paris in 1870. They had every excuse for panic. The military authorities, that the mistakes of 1870 might not be repeated, enforced upon the Press of Paris a censorship iron in its silence. Only the barest outline of events was given out, but it was enough at the very outset, while the war still had as its main theatre the stricken kingdom of Belgium, to prove that the concentrated effort of every Frenchman and every Frenchwoman would be required if the invader was to be beaten back and rendered harmless for future generations. With the fervour of the Latin and the calm method of the northerner, Parisians of every class set themselves to discover how best they could contribute their aid to the troops in the field. Innumerable committees were formed to look after the interests of the extremely varied classes of Paris. Hospital work claimed the attention of most. The big shops of the Rue de la Paix, deserted by their customers, became vast workshops for the manufacture of bandages and medical stores. Hotels, emptied of their customers, were converted into hospitals. In every quarter centres were established for the instruction of the women of Paris in nursing and elementary medicine. The big organisations, such as the Croix Rouge, Les Dames de France, naturally absorbed most of the voluntary workers who at once came forward. Others found a fruitful field for their activities in numbers of charitable and patriotic organizations which were at once started to deal with requirements which were unknown to England, owing to the absence of universal service.

Paris to the foreigner is mainly a city of light and of pleasure. The British visitor knows the Grands Boulevards between the Rue Drouot and the Madeleine. He may know the Montmartre of the Moulin Rouge; he knows nothing of the vast popular quarters of industry of Belleville, Clignancourt and Clichy. The Rue de Rivoli ends for him at the Louvre, and the workman's quarter of Saint-Antoine is a land he does not visit. Paris is almost as much an industrial city as our Manchester and London. The lot of its inhabitants is just as grey, and the barrier which separates them from starvation just as slender, as anywhere in industrial England. The departure of the breadwinner from all the small households of Paris brought about in every one of them an economic crisis, which Parisians as a body by their Municipal Council and as individuals through organized channels did their best to solve. The list of the various war charities started in Paris during 1914 filled eight printed pages. There were dispensaries for children, orphanages, maternal relief funds, soup kitchens, workshops, canteens, shelters, clothing depôts, literally by the hundred. Relief funds were opened for soldiers' families, for musical composers, for

AUSTRIAN SHOP WRECKED BY THE PARIS MOB.

PREPARING FOR THE SIEGE.
Felling Trees at Porte Maillet.

artists, actors, journalists, whose means of livelihood had been taken from them at the outbreak of war. At the various Mairies committees of every kind were organized; men who were too old to serve in the firing line gave up their time to the tracing of missing soldiers, to breaking the news to wives who had lost their husbands, children their fathers, mothers their sons.

From the very outbreak of war it became apparent that special measures would be required to deal with the large colony of British subjects employed as servants, stablemen, coachmen, chauffeurs, and in the workshops of the capital, who with but a day or two of warning were thrown out of employment. The various English bodies in Paris—the Church, the Chamber of Commerce, members of the Embassy, all combined—grappled with the problems of the hour. At the main railway stations of Paris a delegate of the British colony was always to be found, to whom perplexed British travellers overtaken by the storm of war while returning from their travels could turn for advice or assistance. Under the lead of the British doctors in Paris, organized preparations were made for the accommodation and reception of British wounded, and with the scanty means at its disposal the British Colony Aid Fund endeavoured to relieve the distress

among the British poor, for whose requirements about £500 a week was needed. The other foreign colonies, and especially the American, were not behindhand with their generous preparations; and foreign volunteers came forward from all the foreign colonies to offer their services to the French Army.

The position of many foreigners was extremely difficult; the majority of them tried in vain for days to get away from the country, but the railways were congested with military traffic, and the police stations were besieged by thousands of foreigners in search of the papers required before they would be allowed to leave the country. The completeness of the demand made upon the country's manhood by universal service brought about a complete stoppage of work in many of the Paris industries, and all the various funds started to relieve distress soon found plenty of work to do. Many of the unemployed found occupation in the great industry of newspaper selling. The scenes in the newspaper-land of Paris all day long, as special edition after special edition poured from the presses, were extraordinary. Outside each office large crowds of men, women and children of all ages and of all sections of life waited for hours and then sped through the city to sell the very sparse news contained in the official communiqués. Their greatest day was

CARRYING FRENCH AND BRITISH FLAGS THROUGH THE STREETS OF PARIS.

Saturday, August 8, when the news of the capture of Altkirch in Alsace first reached Paris. It was spread like wildfire through the city and received in a silence which would have appeared strange to one unacquainted with the development of French character during the few previous years.

The newspapers themselves were perhaps the strangest sight in Paris. Nearly all of them, fearing a paper famine or lacking labour in their editorial staffs and composing rooms, were forced to reduce the size of their papers to such an extent that some of them were little larger than handbills.

While business people were coping with all these difficulties the police were gradually strengthening their hold over the inhabitants of the city. The enemy aliens were drafted out into big concentration camps in the provinces. Neutral and allied aliens were slowly supplied with all the necessary papers to enable them to reside in Paris during the war. It was a vast work accomplished with much patience and efficiency by the Paris police, who at that time were an extremely able body of men. All the continental machinery of papers of identity which the travelling Briton found so irksome proved of highest importance in the days of mobilization. Belated passers-by—and belated then for Paris meant half-past ten in the evening—were stopped and called upon for their papers. Anyone not possessing the valuable

BRITISH VOLUNTEERS FOR THE FRENCH ARMY DRILLING.

documents was at once arrested and detained pending inquiry. The police during the first two months of the war arrested in Paris over 500 deserters, innumerable spies, discovered much illegal wireless apparatus, instituted special motor patrols throughout Paris and its suburbs, seized large stocks of material suitable for the army belonging to alien enemies, and displayed great activity in preventing food frauds, which were to be expected in view of the high price of provisions. Thus during the war period of 1914 over 8,000 grocers' shops were visited by the food inspectors. All this extra work was accomplished at the increased cost of only £4,000 a month, and the strain upon the service was not so great as might have been imagined, since crime became almost extinct.

Paris, which up to the outbreak of war had been known as the city of Apaches, the home of the revolver tragedy, did not produce a single shooting crime throughout the first five months of the war. Cases of theft, which in July amounted to 203, fell in September to 80.

Thanks to the splendid spirit of Parisians, to the smooth working of all the municipal services, the whole process of mobilization interfered but little with any of the essential things of life. Every day brought forth some fresh change in conditions, or some interesting sign of the vastness of the struggle upon which Germany had entered. The walls of public buildings became hidden under a mass of proclamations to the population, all of them businesslike, all of them dealing with something which was to contribute to the efficiency of the nation in some way or other—vaccination orders, the prohibition of absinthe, the destruction of house refuse, the use of disinfectants.

All these regulations proved extremely effective, and the mortality statistics of Paris during the five months of war in 1914 were lower than they had been in peace. By the time all these preparations had been finished the Parisian, who had been too busy and too much occupied to think of more than his personal share in the conflict, was able to settle down to the state of war and to accept it as likely to be normal for some long time to come.

It was on the 15th day of mobilization that Paris had its first real personal knowledge of British participation in the war and its first glimpse of the khaki uniforms which became so familiar to them in succeeding months.

It had been the intention of the British military authorities to maintain complete secrecy with regard to Sir John French's visit to Paris, but the desire of Parisians to do honour to the leader of the Allied Army proved too much for their discretion, and on August 15 a short paragraph in the Paris papers announcing his arrival for that day sent crowds of people up to the Gare du Nord, there to await his arrival. In spite of bad weather, for more than an hour before the train reached the station the big square in front of the Gare du Nord was packed with people representing every class of the population of Paris. The Field-Marshal was met at the station by M. Malvy, Minister of the Interior, representing the French Government, and by Sir Francis Bertie, the British Ambassador at Paris. As soon as he emerged from the station the enthusiastic crowd broke into applause. Some English volunteers who were present started to sing " God Save the King." The cheering stopped and the crowd listened bareheaded until the National Anthem was over. As Sir John French's motor-car passed down the crowded Rue Lafayette to the Embassy the cheering was continuous ; later in the day Sir John French, accompanied by the British Ambassador and the British Military Attaché, Colonel Yarde-Buller, was received at the Elysée by the President of the Republic. M. Viviani, the Prime Minister, M. Doumergue, Minister of Foreign Affairs, and M. Messimy, Minister of War, were also present.

It was not until the dark days which preceded the battle of the Marne that Parisians again had an opportunity of cheering representatives of our expeditionary corps. The latter end of August was passed in conditions of great secrecy and suspense. News was allowed to trickle out very slowly, and it was only in a very gradual manner that it became known to Parisians that the Germans after their rush through Belgium had swept on across the French frontier, scattered the plucky resistance offered to their advance by the French and British armies along the Mons-Charleroi front, had overcome with but little trouble the defences of the fortresses of Namur, Maubeuge and Longwy, and had driven back the French invader from Alsace. The great dash on Paris had begun.

Paris, as the widening circle of her boulevards testifies, has a long record of defence. The war of 1914 found it in conditions very different from those which prevailed in 1870-71, but it was defended by a ring of detached forts which, beginning in the north at Saint Denis, forts de

CROWD OUTSIDE THE BANK OF FRANCE DURING THE EUROPEAN CRISIS.

la Briche, du Nord and de l'Est, continued through the forts of Aubervilliers, Romanville, Noisy, Rosny, Nogent, Vincennes, Charenton, Ivry, Bicetre, Montrouge, Vanves and Issy to Mont Valerien. The perimeter of these forts was about 34 miles. In 1914 they had become almost merged in suburban Paris. Since 1870 the whole defensive scheme of the capital had been altered and the girdle of forts flung far out into the country, so that in the north the line began at Daumont, continued west to Montlignon, Cormeilles, Saint Cyr, Buc, Villeras, Palaiseau, Villeneuve, Sucy, Villiers, Chelles, Vaujours, Stains and Ecouen. The area defended by these forts and by the batteries and redoubts included Enghien and Argenteuil, Saint Germain, Versailles and Bondy. The perimeter was eighty miles, and for a successful investment and siege operations such as those conducted in the Franco-Prussian war a force of some 500,000 men would be required.

The value of these forts was completely uncertain. The success with which the German heavy artillery had demolished the defences of Liége, Namur and Maubeuge had shown fairly conclusively that the science of attack had been developed beyond that of defence, and in Paris it was generally held that, although the Germans would probably not attempt or, indeed,

need to tie up vast numbers of their armies in a regular investment of the city, they would endeavour to batter their way through one section of the fortified line. Those latter days of August were filled with feverish activity in placing the outer line of defences in a condition which would at least give them some chance of stemming the tide of invasion, if only for a while. Most energetic measures were adopted. To a country possessing so highly centralized a form of government as that given to France by Napoleon, to a country which had concentrated in its capital so much of its material and intellectual activity as France had in Paris, the capture of the capital would have been a blow of tremendous effect. To the world Paris was pre-eminent among cities, perhaps because it typified as did no other capital the achievements and aspirations of the whole nation. And though great would have been the material loss entailed by the capture of the city by the Germans, it would have been as nothing when compared with the moral disaster and effect, not only throughout France and the allied countries, but throughout the whole neutral world.

The situation was grave in the extreme. The French plan of campaign and the whole of its army organization had been conceived in the spirit of offensive. That offensive, after some success in Upper Alsace, had been more than checked ; it had been broken under the sledge-hammer blows of Germany's millions. In spite of the dogged resistance of the newly arrived British troops, of the fine fighting of the French armies, what was to have been an attack seemed to be degenerating into a retreat. It was felt that in the face of these grave events it was necessary to give to the Government a character more definitely representative of every section of national opinion. On August 26 the Prime Minister tendered his resignation to the President of the Republic, and was immediately entrusted by M. Poincaré with the task of forming a new Ministry. The most important change was in the Ministry of War. M. Messimy was replaced in this portfolio by M. Millerand, who when previously an occupant of this office had done much to eradicate the old spirit of political distrust and agitation arising out of the Dreyfus trial. Perhaps the most significant alteration in the Ministry was the inclusion, for the first time with the consent of their party, of Socialists ; M. Marcel Sembat, who succeeded Jaurès in the leadership of the Socialist Party,

became Minister of Public Works, and M. Jules Guesde, a doctrinaire Socialist with a small following in Parliament, joined the Ministry without portfolio. M. Delcassé came back to his old post as Minister of Foreign Affairs, from which he had been made to withdraw by German menaces over the Moroccan affair. M. Augagneur, a Socialist-Radical, took charge of the Navy ; M. Ribot, of Finances. This was a Ministry of National Defence formed to pursue no policy save that of victory. It was well received by Parisians, to whom the composition of the Government had always been a peculiarly Parisian affair, and in its first proclamation to France it laid down as follows its conception of the task before it :

FRENCHMEN,—The New Government has just taken possession of its post of honour and of battle. The country knows she may count upon its vigilance and upon its energy, and that it is devoting itself with all its soul to her defence. The Government knows that it can rely upon the country ; the sons of France are shedding their blood for their country and for freedom. At the side of the heroic Belgian and British armies they are withstanding without trembling the most terrible storm of iron and of fire which has ever been let loose upon a people, and all bear themselves worthily. Honour to them ! Honour to the living and to the dead ! The men fall, but the nation goes on. Thanks to so much heroism the final victory is assured. A battle is now in progress. It is important undoubtedly, but not decisive.

MOBILIZATION SCENE.

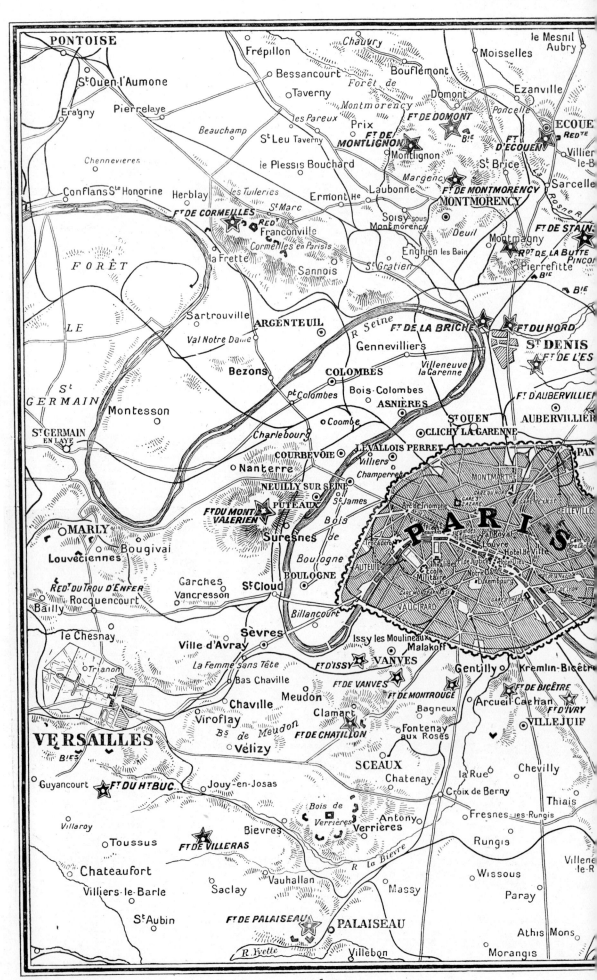

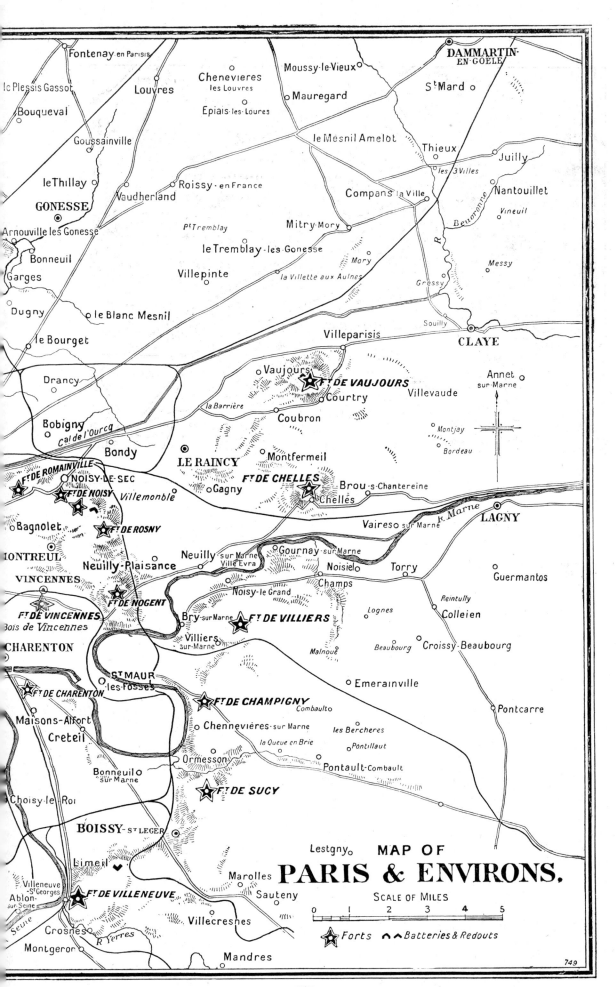

MAP OF PARIS & ENVIRONS.

SCALE OF MILES

0   1   2   3   4   5

⭐ Forts   ⋀⋀ Batteries & Redouts

Fontenay en Parisis

Ic Plessis Gassot

Bouqueval

Goussainville

le Thillay

Vaudherland

GONESSE

Arnouville les Gonesse

Bonneuil

Garges

Dugny

le Blanc Mesnil

le Bourget

Drancy

Bobigny

Cal de l'Ourcq

Bondy

Ft DE ROMAINVILLE

NOISY-LE-SEC

Ft DE NOISY

Villemonble

Bagnolet

Ft DE ROSNY

MONTREUL

Neuilly-Plaisance

VINCENNES

Ft DE NOGENT

Ft DE VINCENNES

Bois de Vincennes

CHARENTON

Ft DE CHARENTON

St MAUR les fosses

Maisons-Alfort

Creteil

Bonneuil sur Marne

Choisy-le-Roi

Villeneuve St Georges

Ablon sur Seine

Ft DE VILLENEUVE

Crosnes

Montgeror

R Yerres

Mandres

Villecresnes

Sauteny

Marolles

Lestgny

Limeil

BOISSY-St LEGER

Ft DE SUCY

Ormesson

la Queue en Brie

Pontillaut

Pontault-Combault

les Bercheres

Chennevieres-sur Marne

Ft DE CHAMPIGNY

Combaulto

Emerainville

Pontcarre

Malnoué

Beaubourg

Croissy-Beaubourg

Villiers sur-Marne

Bry-sur Marne

Ft DE VILLIERS

Noisy-le-Grand

Lognes

Reintully

Colleien

Champs

Noisiel

Torry

Guermantos

Neuilly sur Marne

Ville Evra

Gournay sur Marne

Vaireso sur Marne

R Marne

LAGNY

Chelles

Brou-s-Chantereine

Ft DE CHELLES

Gagny

LE RAINCY

Montfermeil

Coubron

la Barrière

Courtry

Ft DE VAUJOURS

Vaujours

Villevaude

Annet sur-Marne

Montjay

Bordeau

CLAYE

Villeparisis

Souilly

Gressy

la Villette aux Aulnes

Villepinte

le Tremblay-les-Gonesse

Pt Tremblay

Mory

Messy

Mitry-Mory

Compans la Ville

Vineuil

Nantouillet

Bevoronne R

les 3 Villes

Juilly

Thieux

le Mesnil Amelot

St Mard

DAMMARTIN-EN-GOELE

Maurgard

Moussy-le-Vieux

Chenevieres les Louvres

Epiais-les-Loures

Louvres

Roissy-en France

749

THE OUTSKIRTS OF PARIS.
Barricades erected on the roads.

Whatever may be its issue, the struggle will continue. France is not the easy prey she was held to be by the insolence of the enemy. Our duty is tragic, but it is simple : to repulse the invader, pursue him, save our soil from his contamination and liberty from his clutches, to endure as much as need be to the end, to keep up our spirits and our souls above the thought of danger, to remain the masters of our destiny. Meanwhile, our Russian allies are marching with decisive gait towards the capital of Germany, where anxiety begins, and are inflicting many reverses upon retiring troops. We shall ask of the country every sacrifice and every resource which it can give in men and energy. Therefore be firm and resolute. See to it that national life, helped by appropriate financial and administrative measures, is not suspended. Let us have confidence in ourselves and forget everything which is not our country. Look to the frontier. We have the method and the will ; we shall have the victory.

That same day it was announced that General Michel, the Governor of Paris, had been replaced by General Gallieni. This change, while it threw no slur upon the character or professional ability of General Michel, nevertheless indicated that the hour for decisions had struck, that measures for the defence of the capital had become a matter of urgent importance, and were to be pushed forward with the utmost rapidity and vigour. Born in 1849, General Gallieni, in spite of his age, was one of the most active-minded officers on the army list.

Throughout his career, which began in the war of 1870, he distinguished himself not only as an artillery officer of great value, but as a soldier possessed of political and administrative ability of no mean order. He found a wide field for the exercise of his talent in the pacification and organization of French colonial possessions in Senegal, the Sudan, Martinique and Indo-China. His fame before the war rested chiefly on the order he made out of the chaos existing at Madagascar after the campaign of 1895. He was an ideal officer to whom to confide the task of the defence of Paris, the ruling of its population with firmness and yet with tact, with the control of the vast amount of work which had to be done in very little time. His appointment was a clear indication of the imminence of the German approach. A more striking, because a more widespread, impression was made upon Paris by the thousands of refugees who poured into the city at about the same time. Earlier in August Belgian refugees had arrived in some numbers. Then had come a small stream of refugees from the north of France, and finally the roads to the north and east of Paris were dotted with the hurrying processions of fleeing peasants from the neighbourhood of Amiens and Compiègne. These refugees dotted the "i's" and crossed the "t's" of much that had not been appreciated at its full value by the man in the street. The significance of the military and administrative changes that had taken place was made very clear to all. The arrival of the first German aeroplane confirmed the popular impression. It flew over Paris in the afternoon of August 30, dropping five bombs. One fell at the corner of the Rue Albouy, two burst on the Quay Valmy, and two others fell harmlessly in the same district. Very little damage was done and but one life was lost. An oriflamme entwined with German colours attached to a sandbag was also dropped, with the following message in French, signed by Lieutenant von Heidessen : "The German Army is at the gates of Paris ; there is nothing left to you but to surrender."

If the gates of Paris had been north of Compiègne the statement might have been regarded as accurate. On that day only the most imaginative ear could hear the faint rumble of the guns from the north-east, but Paris nevertheless realised the truth of the impression

conveyed by the first portion of the German airman's message. Those who could afford it began to send away into the provinces their wives and children, so that Paris should have as few " useless mouths " as possible in the event of a siege. The visits of German aircraft were repeated daily. The tide of battle rolled slowly nearer and nearer towards the capital. In the concluding days of August preparations were pushed forward for the removal of the various Government offices and embassies to Bordeaux.

Paris, as a whole, was not taken into the confidence of the Government as to its plans, and the vast work of packing up the archives of the various Government offices and embassies, of removing the gold from the Bank of France, was conducted with the utmost secrecy. Indeed, Paris did not hear of the departure of the Government until it had arrived in Bordeaux, when the following proclamation was issued :

FRENCHMEN,—

For several weeks past our heroic troops have been engaged in desperate conflicts with the enemy's army. The bravery of our soldiers has given them at several points marked advantages. Up in the north the pressure of German forces has compelled us to retire. This situation obliges the President of the Republic and the Government to take a sorrowful

AVENUE PHILIPPE AUGUSTE,
Where a bomb was thrown from a German aeroplane.

RUE DES VINAIGRIERS.
Damage done by bomb from German aeroplane.

decision. It is the duty of the public authorities, in order to guard the national safety, to leave Paris for the moment. Under the command of an eminent leader the French Army, full of courage and of dash, will defend the capital and its patriotic population to the utmost vigour. But the war must be prosecuted at the same time on the rest of the territory. Without peace or truce, without ceasing or faltering, the sacred struggle for the honour of the nation and the reparation of violated rights will be continued. None of our armies has been broken through. If some of them have suffered heavy losses the gaps have been immediately filled up from the depots, and the summoning of troops assures us for the morrow fresh resources in men and in energy. To last and to fight, such must be the *mot d'ordre* of the allied British, Russian, Belgian, and French Armies ; to last and to fight while upon the sea the British help us to cut the communications of our enemies with the world ; to last and to fight while the Russians continue to advance in order to strike the decisive blow at the heart of the German Empire. It is the duty of the Government of the Republic to direct this obstinate resistance. Frenchmen will rise up everywhere for independence, but if this formidable struggle is to be given all its dash and efficacy, the Government must remain free to act. At the request of the military authorities the Government, therefore, transfers its residence to a spot where it can remain in constant communication with the whole country. It calls upon members of Parliament to rally round it, so as to form with the Government and their colleagues in the face of the enemy a rampart of national unity. The Government only leaves Paris after having taken all precautions in its power for the defence of the town and of the entrenched camp. It knows that it need not recommend calm and resolution to the admirable Parisian population, which shows every day that it is equal to its greatest duties.

Frenchmen, let us all be worthy of these tragic circumstances. We shall obtain the final victory ; we shall obtain it by untiring will, by endurance and by tenacity.

A nation which does not wish to perish, and which in order that it may live shrinks neither from suffering nor from sacrifice, is sure of victory.

The swiftness of the German invasion took Paris by surprise. On August 25 the French were still attacking the Germans on Belgian soil. Eight days later the Allies had retreated to the Marne, and the pursuing Germans were within thirty miles of Paris. Few Parisians had contemplated during the first weeks of the war the necessity of leaving their homes, but the arrival of the refugees from the big northern towns towards the end of August brought the question of the safety of Paris home to everyone, and families began to pack their trunks and trickle away to relations in the south and west of France. Few people, however, realized how close the danger had already come when on Sunday, August 30, the new governor of Paris began to take the measures which precede the beginning of a siege by ordering all proprietors of buildings within the field of fire of the Paris forts to leave them in order that they might be destroyed. On the same day a German aeroplane appeared over Paris and dropped several bombs, together with a message announcing the defeat of the French and Russian Armies, and declaring that the Germans were at the gates of Paris. Then began the exodus of the population, and for a week roads, railways and rivers bore thousands and thousands of people of all classes toward the south. The humbler sort, to whom Paris meant a livelihood, thought of 1870 and the hardships of the siege, and without reasoning much whether history was likely to repeat itself, took what valuables and necessities they could carry in their hands and transported themselves as best they could to parents or relations in the country; the wealthy bourgeois retired *en villégiature* with less dignity and comfort than usual. The departure of the Government carried all the official classes in a flood to Bordeaux.

The railway stations were crowded. The companies sold only a limited number of tickets each day. Yet from morning till night there was always a long line of people waiting to take their turn at the booking-office. The trains were packed, and in the hot September weather the sufferings of the refugees, wedged by the dozen in the crowded carriages and deprived for many hours of all food or drink, were often considerable. Those who could find horses or motor-cars left the city by road, but the advantage of the rich in this respect was minimized by the difficulty of obtaining petrol and by a decree which allowed no motors to leave Paris without a special pass. Many English residents

took advantage of a river steamboat plying on the Seine to reach Havre by river.

For a day or two it must have seemed as if everybody in Paris was leaving the capital, such was the rush to escape to the country before the attack on the city began. As a matter of fact, it was calculated that by September 8 out of the normal population of 2,800,000 over a million had departed. Besides these, many thousands of refugees from the towns and villages to the north swelled the crowds that poured into the railway stations and out of the gates.

Those that were left found themselves in a Paris which they could hardly recognize. Most of the population which remained consisted of working-class people whose labours were essential to the life of the city, but whose presence did not make itself felt in the streets except at certain times of the day. The boulevards in the middle of the morning came to be more like the streets of a country town than those of the capital of France; in the evening, after 10 o'clock, they were as deserted as at the most lonely hours of the night. More shops were shut than ever; there was little buying and selling, the shopgirls in the big stores sat together sewing behind their

BELGIAN REFUGEES IN PARIS.

THE EXODUS FROM PARIS.
Scene at the Gare de Lyon.

counters, and there were few customers to interrupt their work. Most of the Paris newspapers had moved their offices with the Government to Bordeaux, or to one of the other chief provincial cities. Some of them appeared simultaneously at Paris and Bordeaux. The *Journal des Débats*, the oldest newspaper in France, announced that it would continue to be published in Paris "so long as it is materially possible," and M. Arthur Meyer, the veteran editor of the *Gaulois*, declared his intention of remaining in Paris in 1914 as he had done in 1870.

But newspapers had ceased for the moment to count for much in the life of Paris. People had begun to look elsewhere for news than in the Press. Was not the cannon audible daily from the height of Montmartre ? Did not German aeroplanes fly over the houses and drop death-dealing bombs from day to day ? The news was in the air of Paris itself and not in the papers. Stragglers from the battles in the north, with tales of the fighting, were to be met anywhere in the chief streets ; dusty and sunburnt figures in khaki wandered in, tasted for a few hours of the lavish hospitality which the people of Paris meted out to the chance-met British soldier, then reported themselves at the military headquarters, and were sent westward

to Le Mans, whither the British base had been moved from Havre.

From the tales of these stragglers, however garbled and fragmentary, Paris could gain much comfort. It learned that the Allies were far from having been defeated and crushed. There was not a soldier who came into Paris from the front who would not assure his anxious questioners that the armies, in spite of their hurried retreat from the frontier, were full of fight, and that the Germans were being drawn into a trap and would meet disaster before long. How near these assertions were to the truth was to be shown. For the moment, however, reassuring as they sounded, they were difficult to harmonize with the very evident advance of the German armies nearer and nearer to Paris. On the day the Government left the capital for Bordeaux, German troops had reached the line Chantilly-Senlis, roughly 25 miles from the gates of Paris, and an engagement had taken place just to the north of these two towns which had resulted in a further retreat of the French. The news was brought into Paris on Thursday morning by the streams of refugees, who had seen columns of smoke rising over the trees behind them as they trudged southward along the dusty roads. The minds of the people of Paris were torn with anxiety. Was an attempt to be made to defend the city, or was it to be abandoned to the enemy, to feel, like Brussels, the ignominy of a German force of occupation ? Their doubts were soon settled by a stirring proclamation of General Gallieni, declaring his intention to resist to the last :

" To the Army of Paris and the Population of Paris !

" The members of the Government of the Republic have left Paris in order to give a new impulse to the national defence.

" I have received the order to defend Paris against the invader.

" This order I shall fulfil to the end.
" Gallieni."

" The Military Governor of Paris Commanding the Army of Paris.

" Paris, September 3, 1914.

A great battle seemed imminent on the northern fringe of Paris. The average Parisian had gleaned little idea of the actual position of the armies from the scanty information communicated in the official bulletins. It was imagined that the whole of the German army of invasion was marching straight upon Paris, and that the left wing of the Allies would withdraw within the entrenched camp to defend it. As a matter of fact, General Joffre had decided to divert the whole of the Allied army which

had faced the Germans on the frontier to the east of Paris, and to retire successively on the Marne, the Aube, the Seine, and if necessary the Loire, and to draw on the enemy till his position had been rendered so precarious by the lengthening of his lines of communication that he could be attacked with a certainty of success. A new army, the Sixth, had been formed to the north-west of Paris, partly of first, partly of second, line troops. It was placed under the command of General Manoury, and its rôle was to protect the capital and to operate on the flank of the Germans. It was a portion of this army which had engaged the right wing of the Germans at Senlis. As the left of the main Allied army drew south through Meaux and Coulommiers Manoury's divisions spread in a screen eastwards round Paris waiting for the attack on the capital to begin. To their amazement the French scouts found the Germans leaving the acknowledged goal of their invasion on their right, and pushing across the Marne to smash the army which was retreating before them. On September 6, when the bulk of the pursuing Germans had crossed the Marne, General Manoury's army, which had been designated the Army of Defence of Paris, advanced out of the entrenched camp and fell upon their right flank on the Ourcq.

All this, however, was unknown to the people

AT THE GARE DU NORD.
Orphan children in the Customs Officers' Rooms.

A LITTLE FRENCH SOLDIER.

of Paris. They pictured the German Army trying to force a way through the outer ring of forts, battles bloodier than those of 1870 being fought in the northern suburbs and howitzer shells raining into the streets. The preparations for the defence were watched with eager interest. In this direction the vigorous personality of General Gallieni and his strong grasp of essentials made themselves felt from the beginning.

Signs were at once forthcoming to show that the defence and protection of Paris had been thought out in its smallest details. The activities of the foremost scouts of the German Army, the aeroplanes, were soon checked by the organization of a squadron of Allied machines which patrolled the air, and gave chase to the intruders whenever they appeared. Steps were taken to ensure that other hostile emissaries did not spy upon the city by simpler means. A number of the gates were closed, and the passage of persons in and out of the others was

carefully checked; none except soldiers were allowed in at night. The fortifications, from the old ramparts to the outermost forts, were extended and improved. Naval guns were hurried up from Brest to replace the older cannon. Minefields were laid and barbed-wire entanglements erected. New outworks were constructed. Nearer home the approaches to the gates were barricaded, and an army of volunteer workers was set clearing the field of fire round the inner forts and digging vast entrenchments. Stores were assembled in case of an investment. The working people of Paris watched these preparations intently, fascinated by the possibilities which loomed before them. The clear summer weather encouraged cheerfulness. They jested as they stooped to the spade in the new trenches outside the ramparts, wondering the while in the bottom of their hearts what was going to come of it all.

The communiqué of September 4 had announced that the armies outside Paris were no longer in contact, and as yet no details of fresh fighting had come in from the direction from which the cannon had been heard. The Tunis division of Colonial troops had been rushed up from Marseilles on the 3rd to reinforce the Paris army, but for the present they were known to be still quartered in the north-eastern suburbs.

There were two days of suspense. Nothing happened, or rather nobody knew what was happening. The refugee-trains still steamed southward day and night packed with stifled Parisians. A Taube or two tried again to show themselves over Paris and were brought down in the suburbs. It was reported that the fort of Chelles, to the east, had opened fire on a party of Germans which had come within range. That was all. At last, on September 6, came a little piece of news. To the population of Paris it conveyed little, yet it was welcome, if only as indicating that the danger which they had been fearing from moment to moment was, for a few days at any rate, postponed. It was announced that the Army of Paris had advanced to the Ourcq, and had come into contact with the forces covering the German left wing.

If they had only known it, it was the beginning of the victory of the Marne. The time had come to strike. The blow was being delivered which was to arrest the Germans in full advance. For the next three days General Manoury's army pounded the German flank. General von Kluck transferred a division from his centre to stave off this attack on his left. The attack continued : the German flank was again reinforced. The issue of the whole battle from Paris to Verdun began to depend upon the ability of the Germans to maintain their front beyond the Marne while warding off the attack of the Army of Paris on the Ourcq. General Manoury began to be very hard pressed. He appealed to General Gallieni to send him any reinforcements he possibly could. General Gallieni had at his disposal the newly arrived Tunis division. A requisition order was issued by telephone to the taxicab companies of Paris. In a few hours between two and three thousand taxicabs had been withdrawn from the streets ; the Zouaves from Tunis were packed into them and whirled off to the battlefield. Thus it came about that on Tuesday, September 8, those battalions which five days before had marched so gaily through the streets of Paris, were clinging to the villages on the downs above Meaux in the face of a diabolical fire and un-supported by artillery, while the weakened German centre was driven by the British across the Petit Morin, and rolled back farther still by the French Fifth Army at Esternay and Mont-mirail.

The reports of the fighting which drifted into Paris were fragmentary and confused. It was only gradually, as Joffre's dispatches spoke in fuller and fuller detail of the enemy's hurried retreat and the losses which had been inflicted on him, that the people began to realize the greatness of the victory. The news even then was received with remarkably little excitement. The victory was accepted with pride and thankfulness, but there was as little emotion over the advance as there had been over the retreat. The French nation had changed much since 1870 : a stouter generation and a graver spirit had arisen. Perhaps, too, there was some foreboding of the hard and bitter struggles still to come.

When the victory of the Marne was complete and the trains of prisoners and captured war material began to roll into Paris, those among the population who had elected to stay at home and risk the coming of the Germans had good reason to congratulate themselves on the sagacity of their choice. During the period of ten days in which the issue of the battle was uncertain, residence in Paris had entailed none of the discomforts and inconveniences which the refugees had pictured as they crowded into the trains for Marseilles, Nantes and Bordeaux. Communications with the north and east of France were, of course, cut off. A somewhat precarious train service was maintained by a devious route to Dieppe and Havre, whence boats sailed for England. The Germans had blown up a bridge at Pontoise and their patrols had pushed as far as the Lower Seine, so a guard of soldiers was placed on every train which went out of St. Lazare station, and there was always the possibility of a surprise attack. However, in spite of the difficulty of communi-

BORDEAUX.
The Prefecture.

GERMAN PRISONERS WORKING IN THE STREETS.

cations, Paris continued to be supplied regularly with all that she needed in the way of provisions from the country, and the prices of food hardly rose at all. As the days passed by and the possibility of a siege disappeared, the population began to plume itself on its *sang-froid*, and make a positive parade of it.

Enterprising merchants hired out chairs and opera-glasses at points of vantage when the German warplanes paid their occasional visits to the city, and the picture postcards, which had succeeded the comic papers as the organs of popular humour, began to poke fun at those whose exodus from Paris had been too hurried to be dignified.

Business men came back to their shops and offices, and it was not long before the city began to fill again. There was plenty of work for the women to do in the hospitals and at the public relief centres. Previous to the battle of the Marne all the wounded had been sent as far west and south as possible, but now that the capital was safe, thousands of cases from the Marne were poured into the innumerable hospitals that had been prepared for them in the schools and hotels there. All the charitable and public-spirited energy which the mobilization had called forth among those who did not go to the front broke out again after the victory of the Marne.

Paris society, whether at home or at Bordeaux, forgot its usual preoccupations and threw itself heart and soul into work for the war. The theatres were still closed. There was no autumn salon, and the Grand Palais became a hospital. The fashionable dressmakers' shops became centres where ladies met together to work at supplying warm garments and underclothing to the army in view of the approaching winter. These *ouvroirs*, which were established all over Paris, served the double object of supplying the articles necessary for the soldiers and of giving work to countless poor women who would otherwise have been without employment.

There were two armies of sufferers to be thought of, those in the hospitals and on the field of battle, and those who, owing to the dislocation of business, were left without the means of gaining a living. A Commission was appointed by the Government to consider how business could best be stimulated and what could be done to mitigate unemployment. Gradually trade began to revive and settle down into an approximately normal course ; the demand for labour slowly reduced the supply available ; many shops reopened, and Paris resumed a more usual aspect. Even so, the amount of suffering and misery among the poorer classes was very large. Many families, all the males of which were at the front, were left entirely without income, and the wives and mothers had to shift as best they could. The situation was faced by the women of France with a courage and cheerfulness which equalled if not surpassed the fortitude of their husbands and sons before the grim ordeal of the trenches. A spirit of comradeship and sympathy sprang up between rich and poor, which was one of the noblest outcomes of the war. Bereavement proved to be a bond which drew women of all classes close together ; the lady of fashion took her dressmaker and her concierge into her confidence, and the difficulties and the crises which the hour brought forth were faced together.

The thousands of artists and artists' models who inhabited the Quartier Latin were as hard hit as any section of the population. Poor and improvident as a class even in ordinary times, the altered conditions of wartime bore peculiarly heavily upon them. The way in which the trials of the situation were met was characteristically picturesque. Studio canteens were established by a confederation of artists, where members of their trade could get meals at the smallest possible cost, or for nothing at all if necessary. The funds were originally supplied by some wealthy American art students and patrons, but the canteens in time practically supported themselves. Certain artists and their wives visited the markets with a handcart and bought up meat and vegetables in quantity, others prepared the meals, and yet others served them. The charity and energy of all were combined for the common good, and penniless painters, art students, and models, all gathered together to share it in studios converted for the time into dining-rooms.

So Paris lived on, adapting itself as best it might to war conditions ; very different, indeed, from its normal self in time of peace, but struggling always to preserve some of its characteristic gaiety. To those who had known it at other times, there were many unusual sights. Officers and soldiers in English and Belgian uniforms came to be among the familiar features of the street. Particularly popular with the Parisians were the London Scottish, part of whose 1st battalion was for some time quartered in Paris. They arrived soon after the battle of the Marne, and were given the unpleasant duty of burying the dead, who for weeks after the fighting was finished still lay thick on the field of battle. Later the London Scottish were employed as military police, and every evening their patrols used to go the rounds of the cafés and music halls on the look-out for British soldiers.

It was not long before the life of the capital was resumed in Paris. Ten days or so after the German retreat to the Aisne, President Poincaré left Bordeaux for a motor tour on the front of the armies. In the course of this tour he came to Paris, and though his return was without any ceremony, it prepared the way for the gradual transfer of the chief elements of the Government back to their ordinary homes. The Ministries themselves were the last to move, but long before the Chamber assembled for an extraordinary session just before Christmas, all that counted in the official and political society of Paris had already come back from Bordeaux. The severity of the war regime was relaxed. Although until the beginning of 1915 Paris was still nominally in the zone of the armies, the regulations with regard to passports for going in and out of the gates were not strictly observed, and the cafés and restaurants were allowed to remain open later than at the beginning of the war. Some of the theatres were opened, and efforts were made in different

WOMAN WORKING TRAMWAY POINTS.

GERMAN RESERVISTS LEAVING
POTSDAM IN A TRAIN THAT
DID NOT GET TO PARIS.

directions as Christmas drew near to give the
capital something of its normal appearance.

PARIS—BORDEAUX.

In September, 44 years before, the seat of

the French Government had been removed
from Paris to Tours, and later on, in December,
from Tours to Bordeaux. Different, indeed,
were the conditions when President Poincaré
and his Ministers decided to withdraw from the
capital, where their presence could but serve to
hamper military operations, by forcing the
Generalissimo to detach from the main armies
a force for the protection of the chief of the
State, which might have found more useful
occupation in the prosecution of the main
object of the operations—the defeat of the
German armies in the field. The Government's
decision to leave the capital was criticised with
some bitterness when after the victory of the
Marne it became apparent that Paris had been
in no danger. This wisdom after the event
does not, however, alter the facts of the situation,
which was undoubtedly serious. It was felt
that in the comparatively calm atmosphere of
Bordeaux, far from the menace of German
occupation, the Government, supported by the
Deputies who gathered to its call, would be
able more tranquilly to continue the work of
organization, more efficiently to do all that was
really asked of it at that moment—to give the
army in the field everything it required; in
fact to organize victory.

The President of the Republic and Mme.
Poincaré, accompanied by Ministers, left Paris
on September 2, at 11 o'clock in the evening,
from the Gare d'Auteuil, and did not arrive

WOUNDED TURCOS.

GERMAN FLAGS CAPTURED BY THE FRENCH.

until noon the following day at Bordeaux; the special train having taken 23 hours on a journey usually accomplished in 10 or 11 hours, so great was the block of military and Red Cross traffic on the line. He was greeted on his arrival by General Ourdard, commanding the 18th region, the Prefect, the Mayor, and the chief civil authorities of the town and the province. The Girondin capital formed in many ways an ideal site for a temporary seat of government. Most of it was built at a time when the great merchants of Bordeaux were at the height of their power and their wealth. It possesses an unusually large number of fine public buildings and magnificent private houses. The public buildings were by the time the Ministry arrived already in possession of the removal people; huge furniture vans disgorged bale after bale of official documents, and the spectacle of Paris arriving at Bordeaux, tragic though was the hour, was not without its incongruous humour. The President of the Republic was given dignified lodging in the residence of the Prefect. But the Ministry of War, which required a vast amount of space, was accommodated in the Faculty of Letters, where, in a mingled smell of zoology and chemistry, amid plastered casts of antiquity,

blackboards, and all the paraphernalia of higher education, bewildered officers endeavoured for some days to get their services running smoothly again. The embassies and legations, with the exception of those of the United States, Spain, Denmark and Norway, went to Bordeaux with the Government with which they were accredited. Thus the British ambassador, Sir Francis Bertie, and the whole of his staff, travelled down in the diplomatic train which followed the Presidential special to Bordeaux. M. Geusttier placed his magnificent house in the Cour d'Albret at the ambassador's disposal. The Consulate in Paris was left so that British subjects in need of assistance could obtain it. Unfortunately it was hurriedly closed a day or two afterwards, and eventually Sir Henry Austin Lee, the British commercial attaché, returned to Paris to look after British interests.

The journey down to Bordeaux was no comfortable business. The diplomatic train took about 24 hours to reach its destination, and for a long time after its arrival terrible stories were told of Excellencies sitting five a-side, and fighting with third secretaries at wayside refreshment rooms for a scrap of something to eat. Following the lead given by the Government, thousands of Parisians and foreigners crowded down to Bordeaux. As the train service was extremely faulty, the journey in some cases taking no less than 36 hours, all who could possibly afford it travelled by road. It was a strange journey. Every imaginable kind of motor-car was whirling along under a blazing sun towards the Atlantic. The road to Bordeaux took these hurried travellers through Versailles, where they had to run the gauntlet of much good-humoured and some bitter chaff from the troops of the army of Paris, which were later on to free Paris from the threat of occupation. " Bon jour, les froussards," " Ah, les riches fuyards ! " When motor-cars slowed up at guarded level crossings, the occupants had to enter into somewhat painful conversation with the reservists on duty. The road was marked every now and again by some tragic breakdown. Families of seven or eight crowded into a Paris taxicab, which in those days was only nominally built to accommodate four, were to be seen seated by the side of the road some two hundred miles from their destination, with the taxicab they had chartered put completely out of action by the mishap of collision. The heat was tremendous, and burst tyres were of such frequency that after the first four days of the flight not another tyre was to be found along the whole road from Paris to Bordeaux. All the towns along the route, Orleans, Tours, Poitiers and

Angoulême, were so crowded that in many a private house there were five or six people sleeping in a room. Bordeaux itself rose nobly to the occasion. Most of the hotel accommodation had already been booked by the Ministers, officials, Deputies and Senators, and diplomatic people before the departure of the Government had been announced. The thousands of private individuals, business men, and minor Government officials, who were, or thought themselves, obliged to follow the Government in its retreat were accommodated by private individuals and boarding-house keepers. The restaurants opened up new rooms, the cafés extended their terraces, and after the first few days all the material discomfort of life had disappeared. It did not take the Parisians very long to make of Bordeaux another Paris. Many of the newspapers, whose circulation to the provinces from Paris had been stopped by reason of the removal of one of the big distributing firms, transferred their whole staff to Bordeaux, where there were two or three printing works of unusual size. Local newspapers, *La Gironde*, *La France* and *La Liberté du Sud Ouest*, tendered their hospitality to their wandering Parisian confrères, which included *Le Temps*, *Le Figaro*, *Le Matin*, the *Echo de Paris*, and the Paris *Daily Mail*.

The people of Bordeaux live well. They have a generous open-hearted hospitality, which goes

RESERVISTS LEAVING PARIS.

THE HOSPITAL AT VAL DE GRAS.

with the growing of good wine. Bordelais cooking fills a large chapter in the French cuisine. It is an agreeable and a beautiful city, with fine squares and graceful gardens, and the comments of the Parisians of Paris on the Parisians of Bordeaux were not lacking in a certain cheerful malice. Superficially, there certainly was in the first three or four days of Paris at Bordeaux an air of unusual gaiety. At the Chapon Fin, the restaurant patronized by the Government and diplomats, the crowded terrace of the Café de Bordeaux resounded with gossip and chatter. It would have formed a fine subject for the pencil of the famous French cartoonist Sem. He would have found there all the types and persons whom he caricatured in Paris ; the dandy, politician, the actors and actresses of the Comèdie Française and of less recognized theatres, Deputies and Senators, journalists ; in fact a small edition of *tout Paris.* After the first few days, however, when people had settled down and were no longer overwhelmed with surprise at the sight of a familiar face and impelled by the desire to exchange the most confidential conversations with persons whose acquaintance in Paris they had not wished to cultivate, this fever of excitement died away and the thoughts of the exiled Parisians turned to their immediate concerns.

The first act of the Government on reaching Bordeaux was to close by decrees the sitting of Parliament, which had technically remained open since August 4. This was a measure which took some Deputies by surprise and caused a certain amount of indignation. Why, they asked, were we invited to follow the Government here, and immediately told upon our arrival that we are no longer wanted ? Some members of Parliament decided that since they were not wanted at Bordeaux they could employ themselves usefully in their constituencies, all of which had their own special problem arising out of the war, due either to an inrush of refugees, the menace of occupation, or the care for the wounded. A few, however, determined to stay on in Bordeaux and to form there some kind of Parliamentary existence. The personnel of the Chamber and of the Senate had, of course, accompanied the Government. They obtained the use of two music halls, the Alhambre and the Apollo, and there they proceeded to make a few changes, so as to be ready for any formal sittings of Parliament.

The opinion of the whole country viewed with some dismay the prospect of the resumption of Parliamentary proceedings while the decisive battle, which was to free Paris from

OUTSIDE THE AMERICAN HOSPITAL.
M. Poincaré (left) being welcomed by Mr. Herrick, the American Ambassador (extreme right).

the invader, was still in progress. Most of the Deputies themselves, aware of the fact that it was not a time for talking, were either fighting in the field or were active in helping their constituents in their many difficulties. After some talk the whole project for holding a Parliamentary session at Bordeaux was abandoned in favour of a lecture tour by Deputies, an idea which in its turn was also given up. Bordeaux, far from the scenes of operations, after the first bustle of the move, dropped into its usual pleasant lethargy and ceased to occupy any prominent position in the chronicles of the war save as the seat of government.

Almost as quietly as Ministers had left for Bordeaux they returned to the capital. The Ministries returned in straggling formation in the latter half of December, and all were present in Paris in time for the opening of Parliament on December 22, which was again the scene of a memorable sitting, which afforded the French Government as truly representative of the French people an opportunity of showing to the world its resolution to press on to the final victory, its confidence in itself and in its Allies in the prosecution of the same. There was a slight and subtle change in the atmosphere of the House. At the previous sitting on August 4, on the outbreak of hostilities, there was a

solemnity in the atmosphere due to the fact that every man and woman present was still under the impression of the first shock of events. The hour which everyone had discussed, but which none in France had felt to be in his individual fate, had come at last, and confident though the French were in the justice of their cause and in its ultimate triumph, none knew then the nature and the magnitude of the sacrifices which would be demanded of them ; nor, it may be said, the strength with which they would be borne. By the end of the year every man felt that he knew the worst. Even under the heaviest blows from the German sledgehammer the spirit of France had not faltered. The rush upon Paris had been stemmed, the legend of German infallibility for ever shattered on the Marne, the Germans' staying power had been proved to be no greater than that of the French in the long drawn out and furious fighting on the Yser, the enemy's offensive had been broken, and to use General Joffre's phrase, his defences were being " nibbled away " bit by bit. The dead silence which marked the assembling of Deputies for the sitting of August 4 was replaced by the cheerful exchange of news from the front, brought by many Deputies who returned from the trenches to take part in the session. On every hand there was reason for confidence. In the vacant seats of the three Deputies who had fallen in battle the Chamber saw a more tangible sign than it usually was given of its personal participation in the affairs of the nation. Those three vacant seats gave to the opening address of the President of the Chamber, M. Deschanel, a realistic note of sincerity. While mourning their loss he gloried in their end. To the Prime Minister, M. Viviani, one of the finest Parliamentary orators of his day, fell the duty of stating again the aim and policy of France and of her Allies. He did so in language which by its similarity to that used by Mr. Asquith, in an earlier declaration at Guildhall, constituted a most striking proof that five months of bitter warfare, with its constant opportunities of friction between Allies, especially under the stress of retreat, had but consolidated the purpose of Great Britain and France. Mr. Asquith, speaking at the Guildhall, on November 9, declared :

" We shall never sheath the sword which we have not lightly drawn until Belgium recovers in full measure all and more than all that she has sacrificed, until France is adequately secured against the menace of aggression, until the rights of the smaller nationalities of Europe are placed upon an unassailable foundation, and until the military domination of Prussia is wholly and finally destroyed."

The parallel passage in M. Viviani's speech was as follows :

" France, in accord with her Allies, will not lay down her arms until she has avenged outraged right, regained for ever the provinces ravished from her by force, restored to heroic Belgium the fullness of her material prosperity and her political independence, and broken Prussian militarism."

The following are the principal passages of the speech :

This communication is not the customary declaration in which a Government, presenting itself to Parliament for the first time, defines its policy. For the moment there is but one policy—a relentless fight until Europe attains definite liberation guaranteed by a completely victorious peace. That was the cry uttered by all when, in the sitting of August 4, a sacred union arose, as the President of the Republic has so well said, which will throughout history remain an honour to the country. It is the cry which all Frenchmen repeat after having put an end to the disagreements which have so often embittered our hearts and which a blind enemy took for irremediable division. It is the cry that rises from the glorious trenches into which France has thrown all her youth, all her manhood.

Before this unexpected uprising of national feeling, Germany has been troubled in the intoxication of her

THE STRASBURG STATUE.
Patriotic demonstration when French troops entered Alsace.

dream of victory. On the first day of the conflict she denied right, appealed to force, flouted history, and, in order to violate the neutrality of Belgium and to invade France, invoked the law of self-interest alone. Since then her Government, learning that it had to reckon with the opinion of the world, has recently attempted to put her conduct in a better light by trying to throw the responsibility for the war upon the Allies. But through all the gross falsehoods, which fail to deceive even the most credulous, the truth has become apparent. All the documents published by the nations interested, and the remarkable speech made the other day at Rome by one of the most illustrious representatives of the noble Italian nation, demonstrate that for a long time our enemy has intended a *coup de force*. If it were necessary, a single one of these documents would suffice to enlighten the world. When, at the suggestion of the English Government, all the nations concerned were asked to suspend their military preparations and enter into negotiations in London, France and Russia on July 31, 1914, adhered to this proposal. Peace would have been saved even at this last moment, if Germany had conformed to this proposal. But Germany precipitated matters. She declared war on Russia on August 1 and made an appeal to arms inevitable. And if Germany by her diplomacy killed the germ of peace, it is because for more than 40 years she had untiringly pursued her aim, which was to crush France in order to achieve the enslavement of the world.

Since, in spite of their attachment to peace, France and her Allies have been obliged to endure war, they will wage it to the end. Faithful to the signature which she set to the treaty of September 4 last, in which she engaged her honour—that is to say, her life—France, in accord with her Allies, will not lay down her arms until she has avenged outraged right, regained for ever the provinces torn from her by force, restored to heroic Belgium the fullness of her material prosperity and her political independence, and broken Prussian militarism, so that on the basis of justice she may rebuild a regenerated Europe.

This plan of war and this plan of peace are not inspired by any presumptuous hope. We have the certainty of success. We owe this certainty to the whole army, to the navy which in conjunction with the English navy gives us the mastery of the sea, to the troops which have repulsed in Morocco attacks that will not be repeated. We owe it to the soldiers who are defending our flag in those distant colonies of France, who, on the first day that war broke out, turned with patriotic affection towards the mother country ; we owe it to our army, whose heroism in numerous combats has been guided by their incomparable chiefs from the victory on the Marne to the victory in Flanders ; we owe it to the nation, which has equalled that heroism with union in silence and quiet trust in critical hours.

Thus we have shown to the world that an organized democracy can serve by its vigorous action the ideal of liberty and equality which constitute its greatness. Thus we have shown to the world—to use the words of our Commander-in-Chief, who is both a great soldier and a noble citizen—that " the Republic may well be proud of the army that she has prepared." And thus this impious war has brought out all the virtues of our race, both those with which we were credited, of initiative, *élan*, bravery and fearlessness, and those which we were not supposed to possess—endurance, patience, and stoicism. Let us do honour to all these heroes. Glory to those who have fallen before the victory, and to those also who through it will avenge them to-morrow ! A nation which can arouse such enthusiasm can never perish.

Everything serves to demonstrate the vitality of France, the security of her credit, the confidence which

FRENCH CUIRASSIERS IN PARIS.

she inspires in all, despite the war which is shaking and impoverishing the world. The state of her finances is such that she can continue the war until the day when the necessary reparation has been obtained.

We should honour also those innocent civilian victims who hitherto had been safe from the ravages of war, and whom the enemy, in the effort to terrify the nation, which remains and will continue immovable, has captured or massacred. The Government hereby takes a solemn engagement, which it has already partly discharged, in asking you to open a credit of 300 million francs (£12,000,000). France will rebuild the ruins, anticipating the indemnities that we shall exact and the help of a contribution which the entire nation will pay. proud to fulfil its duty of national solidarity in the hour of distress for a portion of its sons.

Gentlemen, the day of final victory has not yet come. Till that day our task will be a severe one, and it may be long drawn out. Let us stiffen our will and our courage for that task. Destined to uphold the heaviest burden of glory that a people can carry, this country is prepared beforehand for every sacrifice.

Our Allies know it. Those nations who have no immediate interest in the fight know it too, and it is in vain that an unbridled campaign of false news has attempted to rouse in them the sympathy which has been won by us. If Germany, at the beginning of the war, made pretence to doubt it, she doubts no longer. Let her recognize once more that on this day the French Parliament, after more than four months of battle, has renewed before the world the spectacle that it gave on the day on which our nation took up the challenge.

In order to conquer, heroism on the frontier does not suffice. There must be union within. Let us continue to preserve this sacred union intact from every attempt made upon it. To-day, as it was yesterday, and as it will be to-morrow, let us have only one cry—Victory; only one vision before our eyes—" La Patrie " ; only one ideal—Right. It is for Right that we are striving, for which Belgium has poured out her blood, for which unshakeable England. faithful Russia. intrepid Serbia, and the gallant Japanese Navy are still striving.

If this is the most gigantic war that history has ever known, it is not because nations are in arms to conquer new lands, to obtain material advantage or political and economic rights ; it is because they are fighting to

GENERAL JOFFRE SPEAKING TO AN OFFICER.

settle the fate of the world. Nothing more grand has ever appeared before the eyes of men. Against barbarism and despotism, against a system of provocation and methodical menace which Germany called peace, against the system of murder and universal pillage which Germany calls war, against the insolent hegemony of a military caste which has unchained this scourge, France, the liberator and avenger, with her Allies, has raised herself at one bound.

A FAMOUS PICTURE.
The Soldier, with Death as his companion, pursuing the figure of Ambition, might well represent the German advance on Paris.

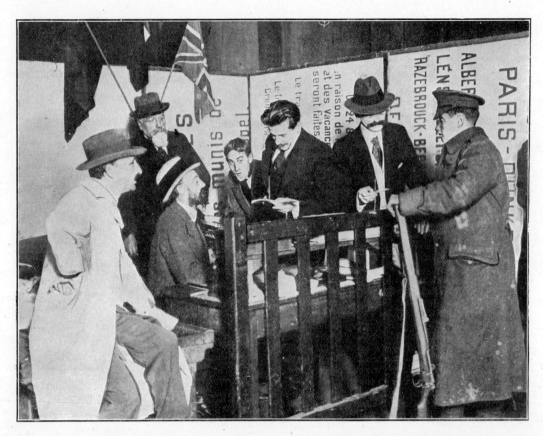

BILLETING TICKETS FOR BRITISH SOLDIERS BEING DISTRIBUTED.

The stakes are more than our own lives. Let us continue, then, to work with a single mind, and to-morrow, in the peace of victory, when politics have been freed from the restraints which we have voluntarily placed upon them, we shall recall with pride these tragic days, for they will have made us more valiant and better.

With these stirring words Paris began to prepare for spending as merry a Christmas as it could in all the circumstances. The French do not as a rule make very much of a festival at Christmas, but this year they seized upon it as a splendid opportunity for sending to their dear ones in the trenches a multitude of presents and of cheering up the wounded in the various Paris hospitals. The usual stalls which are set up along the boulevards for Christmas and New Year were present in almost

the usual numbers and apparently did almost the usual trade. The boulevards were thronged throughout the day and evening by crowds which differed from those of past years only by reason of the diminished number of French soldiers to be seen. The Christmas night suppers were, however, abandoned. The restaurants were still closed by order of the military authorities at ten o'clock. It was in the great churches that Paris kept Christmas and prepared in prayer for the trials and sacrifices of the coming year.

Illustrations will be found in Vol. I. of M. Poincaré, 28; M. Viviani, 37; M. Delcassé, 63; M. Ribot, 174; General Joffre, 82, 83, 399; General Gallieni, 242, 399 M. Messimy, 256; and in Vol. II. of General Foch, 45; General Manoury, 47.

CHAPTER XLVI.

THE FRENCH OFFENSIVE FROM THE AISNE TO YPRES.

Causes of Joffre Retaking the Offensive—Importance of Lille and Antwerp—An Advance Against the Germans North of the Aisne and a Reinvasion of Lorraine and Alsace Inadvisable—Danger of Sending a Separate Army to Antwerp—Movement between the Somme and the Oise Preferable—General Castelnau's New Army Formed—Battles Round Lassigny, Roye, and Péronne—Germans Check Castelnau's Advance—Formation of General Maud'huy's Army, North of Castelnau's—Battles Round Arras, Lens, and Lille—First Bombardment of Arras—The French Line Extended from Lens to Dunkirk—Formation of General d'Urbal's Army, and Transfer of the British Expeditionary Force to the Plain of the Scheldt—Command of the Allied Left Wing Given to General Foch—Meeting of Foch and Sir John French at Doullens—The Germans Cross the Lys, Occupy Ypres, and Threaten Calais—Considerations on General Joffre's Strategy.

IN Chapter XXXIII. were described the defence and fall of Antwerp, in Chapter XXXIV. the phases of the Battles of the Aisne up to the moment of the departure of the British Army, and—slightly anticipating the narrative of the fighting in the Western Theatre of War—the composition of the Indian Expeditionary Force transported to the plains of Belgium and Northern France and the influence exerted by it during the months of October and November, 1914, were explained in Chapters XLI. and XLII. In the present chapter the vast battle fought between September 20 and October 10 by the left wing of the Allies against that portion of the German Force which had invaded Luxemburg, Belgium and Northern France will be described.

The line of this battle stretched from Dunkirk (25 miles east of Calais) to Compiègne, where the Oise from the north joins the Aisne in its westward flow from the wooded hill country of the Argonne. As the crow flies, Compiègne is some 120 miles from Dunkirk—roughly the space between London and Yarmouth.

While this battle was in progress we must not forget that, almost at right angles to it, another struggle was going on, also over a length of 120 miles, from Compiègne to Verdun, and that from Verdun to Belfort on the edge of Switzerland the conflict was continued in a south-easterly direction for yet another 120 miles.

The total length of the fighting line from Dunkirk to Belfort, therefore, measured 360 miles, and along the whole of this immense front the fighting was almost incessant. Imagine that the fighting from Belfort to Verdun occurred from Ben Nevis to Stirling, the struggle between Verdun and Compiègne from Stirling to York, and the combats now to be described between York and King's Lynn; one has then an idea of the magnitude of the battle and the character of the ground over which it was fought. The loftiest summit of the Vosges is near Belfort; it is 260 ft. higher than Ben Nevis; and the latter mountain is 360 miles from King's Lynn.

For the benefit of American readers we may mention that the distance from Cleveland on the southern shore of Lake Erie to Richmond at the mouth of the James River is approximately 360 miles, while students of the Russo-Japanese War will remember that the length of the battle line at Mukden was only a little over 100 miles.

The Allied front may be considered in three sections—viz., from the sea to Compiègne ; from Compiègne to Verdun ; from Verdun to Belfort. Along the last two the French Generalissimo during the closing days of September and the whole of October was, to use his own expression, content with " nibbling " at the German lines which faced him, but in the section Dunkirk-Compiègne he directed a turning movement towards the outer flank of the German main army calculated to threaten its communications backwards from the Aisne, and incidentally to save Antwerp. If that movement had been successful the enemy's force engaged against the Belgian Bristol must either have retreated or risked annihilation.

So long as Verdun remained in French hands there was no possibility of the Germans using the railways from Thionville and Metz through that town, and the main communications of the huge German armies must perforce continue to pass through Belgium. Verdun was not likely to fall, for the perimeter of its defences had been so extended by field works that the enemy could not reach its permanent fortifications with their heavy howitzers, as in the case of

Maubeuge at the beginning of September. Moreover, the fortifications of Verdun had before the War been brought up to date. As was explained in Chapter XXVI., pp. 443–4, when the French Government had to choose between spending money on the Eastern or North-Western frontiers of France, they naturally selected for fortification the former as being the more directly threatened by their hereditary enemy. Lille, Maubeuge, Laon, La Fère, Reims, were, comparatively speaking, neglected and consequently overrun with ease

Nevertheless, the frontier defences on the North-West which had yielded with little effort to the desperate onslaughts of the Kaiser's armies, might be of material use for defensive purposes when in German hands. That the enemy were busily restoring and adding to the defences of Maubeuge, Namur and Liége, perhaps completing those of La Fère and Laon, and certainly digging lines of trenches in the neighbourhood of Brussels, rendered it imperative that the offensive which had been taken at the Battle of the Marne, but checked at the Battle of the Aisne, should again be resumed. If time were granted them, the Germans—who forced the civilians in the conquered districts to construct works designed to keep back their liberators—could cover the country between the Aisne and Antwerp with a series of obstructions. The rapidity with

A BRITISH FIELD BATTERY GOING TO THE FRONT.

which they had entrenched themselves behind the Aisne was a warning not likely to be lost on the illustrious French leader, who had entered the Army as an Engineer and had helped to design the principal fortifications of his country.

There were other reasons why Joffre wished with the least possible delay to attack the Germans. Lille, the chief manufacturing centre of Northern France, whose works supplied so many of the French railway engines and motor cars, had been evacuated by the Germans. The importance of locomotives and automobiles had in this war been brought forcibly home to the French. At any moment the Germans might reoccupy Lille, and its shops would be available for the repair of their traction material. On September 20 the enemy from Cambrai and Valenciennes were threatening Douai, twenty miles to the south of Lille. The ruin of the Manchester of France, which the barbarian foe would, if its destruction seemed desirable, not scruple to carry out would be a heavy blow to the finances of France.* It was the programme of the Germans, as M. Chevrillon, the nephew of the philosopher-historian, Taine, and himself a distinguished writer, points out, to ruin the sources of wealth in foreign provinces which they might have to abandon. For example, they destroyed the coal pits and took to pieces and sent to Germany all the looms in the factories. "My brother," said M. Chevrillon, writing after the enemy had entered Douai, "is interested in a big petroleum refinery at Douai. When the Germans approached, the stock of petroleum was sent within the French lines. On reaching Douai at the end of September the *Bosches* made at once for the factory to seize the petroleum for their motors and, finding none, forthwith burnt the factory. War," added M. Chevrillon, "has never before been waged quite in this spirit."

Then there was the danger that the Germans from the Scheldt would strike at Calais and Boulogne and so deprive the British of valuable subsidiary lines of connexion with the Mother Country. The seizure of these two towns by the Germans might alarm the British. If the Germans reached the coast, Lord Kitchener might be hampered in his arrangements for the offensive on the Continent and be confined to measures limited to the immediate defence of the home country. The hesitations of the

* The value attached to the possession of this manu-facturing centre may be gathered from Sir John French's despatches.

GENERAL MAUD'HUY.

British Cabinet at the opening of the war had not inspired the French with an exaggerated opinion of the courage and capacity of our Government, and it was even believed that certain British Ministers had desired to keep our Expeditionary Force at home for purely defensive purposes, rather than use it on the Continent in accordance with the principles of sound strategy.

Finally, the Germans were preparing to attack Antwerp, and it was not to be expected that the Brialmont forts there would offer any lengthy resistance to the modern weapons which had proved so destructive at Liége, Namur and Maubeuge. So long as Antwerp was in Belgian hands it would be possible to strike at the German communications between Namur and Liége and even, by air raids, to attack the German arsenals and depôts on the Rhine. On September 23 the British Admiralty announced that the Zeppelin airsheds at Düssel-dorf had been successfully attacked by airmen.

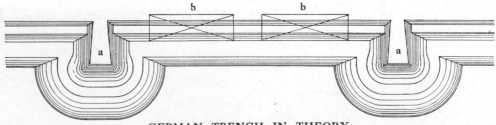

GERMAN TRENCH IN THEORY.
a a Traverses.   b b Overhead shelters.

Düsseldorf was about twenty miles from Essen, the seat of Krupp's colossal cannon foundry. Krupp's, it may be mentioned, had undertaken to furnish weapons to Belgium, but, although paid for them, had deliberately delayed their delivery, while, at the same time, they had secretly prepared the huge weapons destined to work havoc with the forts of Belgium and France.

Such were the cogent reasons why the offensive should be resumed by the French. Letters found on dead, wounded or captured Germans suggested that doubt and despondency were becoming prevalent in the German Armies. A Saxon officer of the 177th Foot wrote in his diary on September 15: "We were told to-day that 125,000 French had been taken prisoners; I wonder if it is true." The same officer on the 19th made the following note: "Our troops," he said, "are starved and are suffering dreadfully from hunger, cold, and continuous fighting. Nearly all our officers are dead." All this was significant.

In which direction, then, should the Allied offensive be made?

Except at a price which Joffre and French—both humane commanders—were not prepared to pay, the Germans could not be driven by frontal attacks from their entrenchments on the north bank of the Aisne; and, while the invaders held the difficult country of the Northern Argonne and the Woëvre, the left wing of the Germans could not be severed north of Verdun from their centre. Behind the northern end of that wing were the powerful fortresses of Metz and Thionville.

GERMAN TRENCH IN PRACTICE,
Showing the traverses.

Nor did an offensive from the region of Nancy against the centre of the German left wing promise to lead to decisive results. In the first three weeks of the War, it is true, the French advance from the Moselle and the Meurthe to the railway connecting Metz with Strassburg had for a time been successful. By August 18 the French had gained the crest of the Vosges from the Donon southward to the Ballon d'Alsace, and at that date the line of forts from Verdun to Toul had not yet been attacked. Now, with the Germans west of the Vosges and butting at the Verdun-Toul barrier near St. Mihiel,* a blow at the Metz-Strassburg railway, a re-invasion of German Lorraine would be a hazardous operation. Until, too, the French blockaded or reduced Metz and Thionville, not a single line of communication of the German Armies on the Aisne and Oise would be affected.

The chief object of the French invasion of Alsace and Lorraine in August had been to keep as many of the enemy's army corps as possible from joining in the march through Belgium on Paris.† During the month which had passed, from August 18 to September 20, the problem had changed entirely. From the environs of Verdun to Liége the whole line of the Meuse was in German hands. So was the Sambre from its sources to Namur. Both banks of the Oise almost down to Compiègne, the heights behind the Aisne from Compiègne to the hills of the Argonne west of Verdun were all occupied by the enemy. From Brussels the Germans were threatening Antwerp, and had established themselves on and beyond the Scheldt from Cambrai northwards. South of Cambrai and west of the Oise they were in possession of St. Quentin and the banks of the Somme to Péronne, only some 30 miles distant from Amiens.

The German armies disposed between the Aisne and the Lower Scheldt, between the Upper Scheldt and the Upper Somme and the Meuse, were supplied by the roads and railroads crossing the political frontier from Aix-la-Chapelle to Metz. The most important of these communications ran through Liége, and consequently an offensive against Metz might be disregarded by the German leaders. Needless to say, the turning of the southern end of

[*H. Walter Barnett.*

GENERAL SIR HENRY RAWLINSON.

the German left wing by reoccupying Mülhausen and moving up the west bank of the Rhine to the fortress of Neu Breisach, or even to Strassburg, would be little likely to lead the invaders to retire from Belgium and Northern France. To gain this end a more direct line of attack was needed.

Joffre had, in fact, only two possible solutions to the problem set him.

One was to transport by sea or along the coast a large army to Ostend, to reinforce the Belgians north of the Scheldt and in Antwerp, then to debouch from Antwerp, cross the Scheldt between Ghent and Antwerp, recover Brussels, and strike at the German communications on the Meuse.

The other was to work round the German right wing north of Compiègne, and by moving eastwards oblige the enemy to evacuate the Somme, Scheldt and the Oise, and, ultimately, the Aisne, the Sambre, the Dendre, and the Meuse.

The objections to the first of the two plans were numerous. If the transport of the Army were effected by sea, the process would be a long one owing to the lack of facilities for disembarkation.

If, however, the transfer took place by land, it could not be concealed from the enemy, and the Germans moving along interior—*i.e.,*

* The loss of the forts protecting St. Mihiel was officially announced on the morning of September 26.

† See the official explanation in the Bulletin des Armées of December 4, 1914.

26—2

A BRITISH DUG-OUT.

shorter—lines, might concentrate overwhelming forces at any point of the arc Amiens-Ypres-Ghent-Antwerp on which the French Army would be moving. In addition, the first part of the march would be round a coast with few and poor ports, two of which alone—Calais and Dunkirk—had permanent fortifications, and those of a more or less obsolete character. During the traject from Amiens to Ostend or Bruges the army might, if defeated, be driven into the sea ; and, even assuming it reached Bruges in safety, its march would have to be continued over the narrow strip of land between the Ostend-Ghent Canal and the Scheldt to the south and the Dutch frontier to the north. Its commander might find himself in a position analogous to that of MacMahon at Sedan !

Further, to detach any considerable body from the French theatre of war to Antwerp would probably cause the Kaiser to bring huge reinforcements from Eastern Prussia or Silesia to the Aisne with a view to recommencing his march on Paris. The magnificent railway system of Germany permitted William II. to move his " travelling army " from one theatre to the other in a manner hitherto undreamt of in war. It was claimed by the Germans that only 48 hours were needed for the transit of each unit. The trains were said to move with only five minutes' interval between them ; but, be that as it may, the Kaiser could, and cer-

tainly did, shift army corps from the Rhine to the Vistula and from the Vistula to the Rhine with amazing celerity.

The second plan commended itself more to Joffre. He determined first to aim a blow at the railways from St. Quentin, La Fère and Laon to or beyond the Sambre, and thence to Liége. These were the conduits through which the Germans on the Oise and Aisne were being supplied with food and munitions.

Accordingly, about September 20, an army was formed west of Compiègne—to the left of General Manoury's force, which had turned Kluck's right flank at the Battle of the Marne. The command of the new force was entrusted to Joffre's " brilliant junior," * General Castelnau, one of Joffre's most trusted lieutenants.

Joffre himself, as Lord Kitchener was to observe at the Guildhall on November 9, was " not only a great military leader, but a great man," and he chose his subordinates solely for their capabilities. Castelnau had an excellent record. He and General Dubail on August 25 had saved Nancy after the retreat of the French Army which had penetrated between Metz and

* General von Heeringen in December was interviewed by a reporter of the *New York Times.* He spoke generously of Sir John French's leadership. General Joffre, he said, was " doing his hard job in a creditable, soldierly fashion," ably seconded by his " brilliant junior General Castelnau." To their credit be it said, the Germans, if not the Kaiser, were, as a rule, ready to acknowledge the technical abilities of their adversaries.

Strassburg. At the critical moments of the Battle of the Marne these two Generals had held the Gap of Nancy. General Castelnau's character was stoical. His mental processes had not been disturbed by the news that his sons had died on the battlefield. This cool and intelligent officer, supported by the Territorial Divisions of General Brugère on his left, was ordered to fill with his troops the space between the Somme and the Oise and to extend his line north of the Somme to the region of Albert on the Ancre. His immediate task was to advance north-east on St. Quentin and La Fère.

To appreciate Castelnau's movements we must have a clear idea of the features, natural and artificial, of the district in which he was to operate.

From the Oise at Compiègne to the Somme extends a plain practically on the same level as the great plain which is bounded by the Scheldt from Cambrai to its southern mouth, and by the sea from that mouth to the low hills that run from the south of Calais round the west of St. Omer, Béthune and Arras to the south of Cambrai. These hills or heights, which, between Albert and Péronne, approach the north bank of the Somme, divide the plain of the Scheldt from the plain of the former river. Along the eastern edge of the plain of the

Somme flows the Oise and, on the left bank, between Compiègne and La Fère to its north, the ground rises near Lassigny and Noyon.

The Somme, rising a little to the north of St. Quentin, flows south-west to Ham, turns north-west to Péronne, and then flows westward to Amiens, which had been evacuated by the Germans on September 13. From Amiens the Somme proceeds through Abbeville to the English Channel ; a few miles above Amiens it receives the waters of the Ancre. The sources of this tributary of the Somme are near Bapaume, a town on the high road from Amiens to Cambrai. In August the French had been beaten at Bapaume during the march of the Germans on Paris. Between Amiens and Bapaume is the town of Albert.

High roads join Bapaume to Arras, to Cambrai and to Péronne on the Somme. From Péronne a road and railway run southwards to Compiègne ; halfway on them is Roye, and to the east of the railway, between Roye and Compiègne, Lassigny. At Compiègne the Oise receives the Aisne, and, skirting the Forest of Compiègne, flows south-west, finally entering the Seine a few miles below Paris.

In a direct line Compiègne is about 40 miles from the capital and the same distance from Amiens. Twenty miles from Compiègne stands

GERMAN AVIATORS PREPARING FOR AN ASCENT.

Roye, in the middle of the plain of the Somme, half-way between Compiègne and Péronne. The latter town is 15 miles to the south-east of Albert, some 30 miles from Arras, and 23 miles from Cambrai.

The army of Castelnau by filling the gap between the Somme and the Oise, besides threatening the German communications, blocked any advance of the enemy to Amiens, or down the western bank of the Oise to the vicinity of Paris.

The feelings of Joffre and Castelnau when coming to their decision must have been somewhat mixed. On the one hand, they were eager to attack the invader, on the other, they felt that the advance must lead to the injury, if not the destruction, of some of the most celebrated and beautiful towns and buildings in France which, lying between Compiègne and Lille, would be in the theatre of operations. Their sacrifice might be necessary to save the French nation. "It is of no consequence," wrote Major-General von Ditfurth in the *Hamburger Nachrichten* in November, "if all the monuments ever created, all the pictures ever painted, and all the buildings ever erected by the great architects of the world were destroyed, if by their destruction we promote Germany's victory over her enemies, who have vowed her complete annihilation. The

commonest, ugliest stone placed to mark the burial place of a German Grenadier is a more glorious and perfect monument than all the cathedrals in Europe put together. . . . Let neutral peoples and our enemies," continues this strange, but in Germany by no manner of means unique, being, "cease their empty chatter, which may well be compared to the twitter of birds. Let them cease their talk about the cathedral at Reims and about all the churches and all the castles in France which have shared its fate. These things do not interest us."*

This German Mummius expressed the sentiments of the invaders. To save the life of one of their petroleum-laden incendiaries, the German officers would not scruple to demolish the Hôtel de Ville at Arras or the Cathedral at Noyon. It is true the district of Arras was associated with the Gallic chieftain Commius who, with Vercingetorix, had endeavoured to drive Cæsar from Gaul, and whose gallant struggles have formed the theme of many a striking romance. Close by at Noyon the Protestant Calvin had been born, Charlemagne had been crowned, and Hugh Capet elected king; Douai was the birthplace of

* It will repay psychologists to study the whole of the passage and the similar effusions reprinted by Mr. J. J. Chapman, in " Deutschland über Alles " (Putnam's).

.OUR VETERINARY CORPS AT WORK.

GERMAN PRISONERS CAPTURED BY THE BELGIANS.

Giovanni da Bologna, the celebrated sculptor ; the kindly and eloquent Fénélon had been Archbishop of Cambrai ; as readers of Scott's "Quentin Durward" will remember, Péronne was the spot where Charles the Bold had imprisoned Louis XI. for inciting the inhabitants of Liége to rebel against him. Facts such as these no longer interested the race which had produced Niebuhr, Schiller, Goethe, Ranke and Mommsen. The masters of the science of destruction agreed with General Ditfurth. "Our troops must achieve victory," he wrote, "what else matters ? "

By September 21 Castelnau's right wing had pushed up the west of the Oise to the neighbourhood of Noyon. Violent encounters ensued in the region of Lassigny. A château near Lassigny had belonged to a German diplomatist. It was visited by some French officers, who discovered that the numerous lawn-tennis courts concealed concrete platforms for the support of heavy artillery. From Lassigny the French moved towards Roye while their left wing seized Péronne. The Germans, alarmed at the menace to their communications through St. Quentin, which is some 20 miles from Péronne, promptly concentrated a large army in the district. The corps forming it were drawn, some from the centre on the Aisne, others from Lorraine and the Vosges. Those from Lorraine and Alsace were railed to Liége and thence *viâ* Valenciennes to Cambrai, a convenient centre for attacking any French troops to the north of the Somme and for reinforcing the army in front of St. Quentin, which is 25 miles south of Cambrai. The news of the passage of the Germans through Liége to Cambrai reached or was notified to the Belgians on the Scheldt. At once 150 soldiers volunteered to cross the German lines and cut the railway from Liége to Cambrai. Starting at night, the little band made a dash for Mons. They were discovered by the German patrols, attacked and chased. Some, however, succeeded in destroying the railway line in several places. Of the 150 only 43 escaped.* But the efforts of these brave and adventurous men failed to divert the torrent of troops pouring westwards. For such eventualities the German engineers were fully prepared.

On the morning of the 25th the French near Noyon began to be pushed back. Castelnau hurried up fresh troops and the offensive was resumed. During the 25th, 26th, 27th there was a desperate battle from Péronne to the Vosges. The German assaults were everywhere repulsed, and a standard, guns, and prisoners captured. Judging from documents found on dead Germans this battle may be regarded as a great French victory, and, though the impressions of individual soldiers are, of course,

---

* This reminds one of the gallant exploit of Major-General Hunter-Western, who cut the railway from Bloemfontein to Pretoria behind the Boers.

GOING TO HELP THE WOUNDED.

no very certain index to the temper of a large army, it is interesting to contrast the following passages from letters written by Germans in France at the time. The first is dated September 22 ; the second September 27, which was the last day of the battle from Péronne to the Vosges :

September 22. . . . My best comrades are killed or wounded. One company has dwindled to two-thirds of its original strength. We want peace quickly. We have been driven to exhaustion and have marched for entire weeks, even through the nights. We have not even had bread every day, have not washed for a fortnight, nor shaved since the commencement of the war. But all this is nothing, and we shall soon be home, for it will all soon be over. We have just been under the enemy's artillery fire for eight days.

We get no letters. We have passed thousands of full mail bags on the road, but there are no officers to deal out the letters.

After a 36 hours' march without halting we arrived just in time for the fight. For three days we did not have a hot meal because our field kitchens went astray. We had a hot meal yesterday evening. We are all ready to drop, but must march on.

In this letter the writer, though exhausted, seems confident that he will " soon be home, for," he adds, " it will soon be all over."

The second letter, dated September 27, strikes a different note :

We are very anxious about the result of the fighting. We have nothing but reports of great successes, but don't now put much faith in them. To-day we got some papers of the 1st to 5th September, and it is really painful to read the boastful announcements of the march on Paris, for we are no nearer to Paris now than we were then. I don't know whether you realize this, but there is no use in trying to hide it.

After a day's rest the battle was renewed by the Germans, but this time chiefly against Castelnau's Army. As a result of the fighting Castelnau had been driven from Lassigny. His line now ran through Ribécourt on the Oise to Roye, then to the west of Chaulnes, and ended on the plateau north of the Somme between Combles and Albert. On October 1 the Germans made a desperate effort in the region of Roye to break Castelnau's centre. The forces on the Aisne had been weakened to provide the necessary " cannon-fodder." Success did not crown the German attempts. Two divisions supported by Death's Head Hussars were decoyed by French Dragoons to a wood in which French infantry and four batteries of quick-firers lay in ambush. The batteries opened with murderous effect, and the infantry charged the Germans and secured 800 prisoners, including a colonel and ten officers. Near Lassigny on October 5 the Germans again failed to dislodge the French and, two days later, the latter advanced between Chaulnes and Roye ; in an action near Roye they took 1,600 prisoners, and on the 11th near Lassigny a standard belonging to the Pomeranian Army Corps was captured.

It should here be observed that unless treated in minute detail, which would cause this History to run to an inordinate length, the modern battle, packed as it is with incident and lasting for more weeks than the encounters of a hundred years ago did hours, does not admit of the same dramatic treatment that the latter did. The struggle consists mostly of long, protracted artillery duels, the throwing up of innumerable trenches covered by lengthy and complex obstacles, and interminable skirmishing varied by occasional rushes of charging men from concealed positions. The fighting is round towns and villages rather than in them, and the change which has come over the Art of War is aptly indicated by the phraseology of the French communiqués, which, for example, speak of violent attacks in " the region," and not in " the town," of Roye.

A rigid censorship was wisely imposed by the Allied Governments. They fully appreciated that France was struggling for her very life as an independent nation against a people greatly exceeding the French in numbers, and organized, not for the purposes of defence, but with the deliberate intention of waging a war of conquest. This rendered the greatest precautions necessary to keep all details of the opera-

FROM THE AISNE TO THE NORTH SEA.

A GERMAN FIRING LINE.

tions and composition of the forces from the
enemy, which has given to the battles in which
the troops were engaged an anonymous character, hiding from the reader the heroism of the
French troops and the extraordinary skill of
their officers.   When "la bête immonde et
hideuse" ("the foul and hideous beast"), as
a French gentleman, speaking of Germany,
wrote*, leapt at the throat of France, the
French were not as prepared as they might
have been.   The tactics of the new warfare
(the "guerre d'Apaches," so it appeared to
them) were repugnant to chivalrous soldiers
remembering that they were the descendants
of warriors who had followed Napoleon, Hoche,
Villars, Turenne, Condé, Henri IV., Bayard,
Jeanne d'Arc, Du Guesclin, Godefroi de Bouillon
and Charlemagne.   But with a coolness and
sagacity seldom if ever rivalled the French had
adapted themselves to the circumstances.

We now return to the consideration of Joffre's
strategy.   The discovery made by him in the
last week of September that the Germans had
shifted very large forces from the Vosges, from
Lorraine, and from their centre on the Aisne to
their right wing, could mean but one thing.
Plainly the Germans would meet the outflanking manœuvre by a counter-stroke which

* We quote textually the words of this gentleman,
whose father had seen Napoleon in 1808 on the way to
Spain.   "Nos vaillantes armées," he writes, "si étroite-
ment unies, ne se reposeront pas avant que l'œuvre
soit terminée et que la bête immonde et hideuse soit
morte et bien morte."   The proper policy of the Allies
could not be more clearly and pithily expressed !

in its turn would outflank the outflanker.   To
deal with this the French Generalissimo, in
his turn, decided to extend his left northward
to Arras, Lens and Lille, and thus threaten
again the enemy's flank by moving through
Arras on Cambrai and, behind Cambrai, on
Le Cateau, and from Lens on Valenciennes and,
behind it, the lost fortress of Maubeuge.   If
the French occupied the area in the parallelo-
gram Cambrai - Valenciennes - Maubeuge - Le
Cateau the Germans on the Upper Somme, the
Oise and the Aisne would have lost control over
the two main railways to Liége.

Whether that would lead to the abandon-
ment of the siege of Antwerp and the retreat
of the Germans to the Sambre and Meuse would
be another question.   Motor traction had converted every high road into a fair equivalent for a railroad.   There would besides be
several railways still open to the Germans—e.g.,
the line Laon-Vervins-Hirson-Charleroi-Namur-
Liége, and that from Laon by Mezières and
Montmédy to either Luxemburg and Treves or
to Thionville and Metz.

Yet, if Antwerp was to be saved, there could
be no delay.   On September 26 the Germans
had advanced to the ruined Termonde, situated
at the junction of the Dendre and Scheldt, and,
though they had been defeated by the Belgians
at the actions of Audegem (September 28) and
Lebbekke (the 29th), it was clear that an
attempt was being made by them to isolate
Antwerp by crossing the Scheldt and occupying
the country that stretches north from that river

to the Dutch frontier. To cover that movement and to menace Ghent they bombarded and captured Alost on the Dendre, south of Termonde (September 29–30). Belgian peasants and children had been forced in front of the attacking columns, and when the cowardly victors occupied the town they wreaked their vengeance on its inhabitants.

To carry out Joffre's new plan, on September 30 an Army (the 10th), commanded by General Maud'huy, assembled north of General Brugère's Territorials, which were beyond the left of Castelnau's Army. The latter in its entrenchments would henceforth play a defensive rôle, preventing the Germans penetrating further between the Somme and the Oise and guarding the communications of the 10th Army, which passed through Amiens.

Maud'huy had been a Professor of Strategy at the Ecole de Guerre, and when the great war broke out was only a Brigadier. For his gallant deeds he had been decorated on the field of battle with the cross of Commander of the Legion of Honour and for his clever leading he had now secured the important position of an army leader. His forces were concentrated round Arras and Lens, on the hills between the plains of the Somme and Scheldt. A portion of his cavalry was north of Lens, in touch with

Territorial Divisions moved south from Dunkirk. In the vast plain which stretches from the Scheldt between Cambrai and Ghent to the sea between Calais and Ostend the city of Lille was occupied by French Territorials. North of Lens and Lille the River Lys, rising in the high ground south of St. Omer, divides the plain into two sections. Flowing through Armentières and Courtrai the Lys joins the Scheldt at Ghent. From Ghent the Scheldt goes eastward to Antwerp. A canal—the Canal de Ghent—connects Ghent with Bruges and Ostend. Ypres, north of the Lys between Lille and Ostend, was not yet in German hands. A canal joined Béthune to Lille, and Béthune, like Lens ten miles south-east, was on the edge of the plain. East of, and opposite to, Béthune was La Bassée.

Looking north and east from Béthune a forest of mill chimneys and collieries met the eye. Lens, with its population of nearly 30,000, was the centre of the coalfields of the Pas de Calais and the site of a victory of Condé over the Spaniards in 1648. The "Black Country" of France began at Lens, and on the south side of the Lys miles of houses—"the street of the Lys"—extended to Armentières (population over 30,000) on the Lys, eight miles west of Lille. North of the Lys the inland country

A FIELD GUN COVERED FROM VIEW.

26—3

resembled parts of Essex, and, nearer the coast, the Fens.

Arras, the centre of the battle about to begin, was an old-world city of 25,000 inhabitants, with a semi-circle of low hills to the west of it. At its northern fringe flows the Scarpe, a tributary of the Scheldt. The ramparts designed by the celebrated Vauban were still standing. The capital of the Atrebates, and famous for its woollen cloth as early as the fourth century, Arras had been sacked by the Vandals in 407 A.D. In the Middle Ages it had been renowned for its tapestries. Towards the end of the Hundred Years' War, in 1435, a Peace Congress had been held there. It was a town which delighted the artist as well as the historian and antiquary. Its Grande Place and Petite Place were surrounded by beautiful gabled houses with arcades below supported by huge sandstone pillars. The Cathedral Church of St. Vaast stood on the site of an earlier church.

But it was not the Cathedral so much as the Hôtel de Ville, with its belfry, that drew art-lovers to the city. The Hôtel de Ville, begun in 1501, was a magnificent specimen of Hispano-Flemish architecture. The belfry, nearly 250 ft. high, had been completed in 1554. It possessed a famous peal of bells and a remarkable clock. Arras had been the birthplace of

Robespierre, whose idealism the Germans despised but whose methods of terrorism they emulated and surpassed.

About September 15 the Germans had entered Arras and they had remained in the quiet little city for several days. They had fed and drunk of the best and after their departure no less than 4,000 empty wine bottles were counted in a single lumber room. The only person who, it is recorded, paid for what he consumed was a member of the Hohenzollern family, who, by a curious coincidence, stayed at the Hôtel de l'Univers. Whether, however, he paid with his own or requisitioned money is uncertain.

The approach of Maud'huy's Army cleared the town of its unwelcome guests. There had been wonted scenes of revolting debauchery, and many houses had been ransacked, though none demolished.

The right of Maud'huy's Army rested on the Ancre; his left extended from Arras through Lens to Lille; his centre was at Arras. From Arras railways and high roads radiate in all directions, northwards to the Lys, westwards to the coast of the English Channel between Abbeville and Boulogne, southwards to the Somme. Looking eastward, the city is the apex of a triangle of which the base line is Lille-Cambrai. In front of that line, nearer Cambrai than

GERMAN BARBED WIRE ENTANGLEMENTS.

BRITISH SOLDIERS ERECTING BARRICADE ON THE OUTSKIRTS OF A FRENCH TOWN.

Lille, stood Douai, with a population of over 30,000 souls, famed for its college of English Benedictines founded in 1560, and also for the Roman Catholic translation of the Holy Scriptures into English, known as the Douai Bible.

The Germans were in force between Douai and Cambrai, and from Cambrai west to the region of Bapaume. Lens is on the road from Arras to Lille. Douai was garrisoned by French Territorials. The plan of Maud'huy appears to have been to move the mass of his Army through Arras and Douai on Valenciennes ; that of the Germans to capture Lille and advance from Tourcoing down both banks of the Lys on Béthune and St. Pol, and, while this turning movement was in progress, to capture Douai and Lens, and, seizing the heights north-west of Arras, cut the roads between that city and St. Pol. They would then roll back Maud'huy's Army to the Somme, while an army from the Lys proceeded to Boulogne, Calais, Dunkirk and Ostend.

The outposts of the opposing armies were soon in contact. On Wednesday, September 30, at Vitry-en-Artois, a village twelve miles or so up the Arras-Douai road, a patrol of Death's Head Hussars were ambushed by French Cavalry,

supported by armoured motor-cars. Similar skirmishes took place at Etaing, Eterpigny, Croisilles, Boisleux and Boyelles. Soldiers of every description—cavalry, infantry, artillery and engineers, Moroccan auxiliaries—were traversing Arras and moving along the Douai road. Sixteen batteries of French 75 cm. guns took up a position a few miles south-south-east and east of the town.

The next day (October 1) the battle began. By nightfall the German artillery appeared to have had the worst of the duel, while the French Infantry had driven the Germans from a wood between the guns of the two armies. At 6 p.m. a haze was settling over the country, but a French aeroplane could be seen from Arras descending in wide circles over the German positions. Smoke-balls, as it were, surrounded the gallant pilot. They were the visible evidences of bursting shells, and seemed " apparently coming into being from nowhere all around the machine." During the night an almost endless stream of reinforcements passed through Arras. The French were attempting to retake Douai which, attacked from Valenciennes and Cambrai, had been lost. No fewer than forty houses in Douai had been burnt as a ".chastisement," on the pretext that the inhabitants had fired at the

FRENCH INFANTRY IN THE FIRST LINE OF TRENCHES.

German troops from the houses. All the small villages round Douai were destroyed. A prominent resident who left Douai on October 2 informed a *Times* Correspondent that "the last time he gazed at Douai from a considerable distance he saw a great column of flame mounting to the sky."

The battle was resumed in the morning (October 2) and by Saturday (October 3) an

CLIP OF BRITISH CARTRIDGES,
Transfixed by a German bullet.

enormous German force was gathered on the plain to the east of Arras. During Monday (October 4) the Germans pushed the centre of the French left wing back west of Lens and Maud'huy commenced withdrawing his troops to the hills behind Arras. Civilians began to stream out on the road to Doullens, through which they could reach either Amiens or Abbeville, or on that to St. Pol, which led to Etaples and Boulogne. The latter avenue of escape was threatened by the German advance from Lens. In the small hours of the night Mr. Atherton Fleming, a War Correspondent of the *Daily Chronicle*, who—with his Burberry waterproof strapped tightly round him—had fallen asleep by a strawstack off the road from Arras to St. Pol before Aubigny is reached, was awakened by mitrailleuse and rifle firing.

We leave *The Times* correspondent who left Arras on October 4 to tell the tale of the migration of the inhabitants of that city. The Germans were not bursting into a country of wandering savages, but one peopled by men and women accustomed to a quiet life and to the security afforded by police and courts of justice. The story may bring home to those who live in neutral countries a too-forgotten aspect of the nature of the conflict raging in Europe :

About three miles out on the road to St. Pol we settled down into a leisurely measured step, as men do who have far to go. Stretching away in the distance the long straight road, lined with tall trees—a seemingly endless avenue ; hedgeless, open, undulating country rising on each side of us ; farmsteads and woods standing out sharply in the clear moonlight. A dark moving mass in front of us ; a dark moving mass behind as far as the eye could reach. All sorts and conditions of men hurrying from their homes, leaving behind them wives, sisters, daughters, whom they were powerless to defend. Their very helplessness was a pang that tears at the heart-strings. Exaggerated fears of the fate that might overtake their dear ones haunted them. They are fears to which they gave an understanding, but no name.

They were expressed in gesticulation, in ejaculation. "Les barbares, Mon Dieu." Some have brought their wives and children with them.

On we marched. The lengthening line thinned out. Many had gone ahead of us. Many had dropped behind ; some fell out by the roadside and camped for the night under the corn stacks. We reached a village. The *estaminets* were open, but so crowded with refugees that we could not enter So we began to realize that we had missed our dinner. Refugees with whom we had had friendly talk shared their small stock of sand-wiches with us, and we ate by the roadside.

On again. Another village ; the *estaminets* open and full of tired men and weary women. We found a place in the low, evil-smelling room, but there was nothing to eat, not even bread, and only poor coffee and worse cognac to drink.

Beyond Aubigny we passed a convoy, a long line of wagons and cavalry blocking the road, cavalry stretched across the fields, motionless. The horsemen were wrapped in their long cloaks, muffled to their eyes. Some were asleep in the saddle. Away on a distant hill a twinkling light, signalling. At St. Michel, a little village outside St. Pol, we obtained basins of milk and coffee, steaming hot, and bread and butter. We ate and drank, thankfully, and started out again, refreshed.

Approaching St. Pol we passed soldiers marching silently in the shadows of the night. It was a weird, impressive spectacle. Officers stopped us and asked us for news from the front. We told them all we knew of the situation. We passed under a railway bridge hastily repaired—girders resting on piles of timber cleverly arranged—and so into St. Pol.

The town was silent and asleep. It was 4 a.m. on Monday, October 5. We knocked roundly at the door of the Hôtel de France and a military officer appeared in the doorway, obstructing us. We could not enter. All the hotels in the town were requisitioned by the military authorities. So we sat on a bench in front of a café and, chilled by the keen morning air, slept fitfully

GENERAL DUBAIL.

until daylight. Having returned to the hotel we asked for coffee, were allowed to enter, and were supplied with a welcome meal of hot coffee and bread and butter. We nodded over it and slept. Officers eyed us over their *petit déjeuner*, and one of them came over to us to examine our papers. He spoke English perfectly. We told him we wished to go on to Boulogne, and he was willing to help us. He took us to the Etat Major to obtain permission for us to leave the town, but the military authorities were too busy to attend to us and

AFTER A BATTLE.
The German Dead.

we had to wait. We appealed to the civil authorities, but they had no power to aid us. We must stay in the town. There was no help for it.

The streets were packed with refugees, hindering the movements of the troops. We had nowhere to rest, every lodging was full. We stumbled across our good friends of the road. They had found a lodging in a small inn on the outskirts of the town. They were five, and they had two small bedrooms, one of which they gave up to us. The accommodation was meagre, the food unsavoury, but we were overwhelmed with kindness, and we were grateful. Hundreds of less fortunate people slept in the streets that night.

Arras was bombarded by the Germans on Tuesday (October 6). Dr. Francq Celse, the editor of *L'Avenir d'Arras*, who was reading proofs for his paper, noted that the first shell fell into the town at five minutes after 9 a.m. It was followed by others. This gentleman dismissed his printers and returned home. On the way he met a woman in the Rue Gambetta. "Stand back," she shrieked, her eyes mad with terror, "my child, my poor child!" Little incidents like this enable one to appreciate at its right value the boasted German Kultur. Multiply them a millionfold and one has a faint idea of the mental anguish caused by the tyrant whose "table was earth, whose dice were human bones." Mlle. Suzanne Le Gentil, a young lady—the daughter of a lawyer of Arras—who, with her parents and eight brothers and sisters ultimately took refuge in England, jotted down in her diary her impressions of the bombardment. The entries under

October 6, 7, 8, and 9 are here quoted. To understand the horrors of modern warfare one must study it in detail :

October 6.—The Germans commence to bombard Arras. The shells fly over our roof. We set the fowls and rabbits at liberty, with some food, and install ourselves in the cellar. What a bombardment ! What noise ! . . . 2 o'clock.—The stables of M. Cabuil and the house of M. Prévost catch fire. . . . We look out to see if we must fly. . . . Papa returns from the St. Sacrement. When the bombardment commenced he was with Dr. Carpentier at the Hôtel de Ville. 5 o'clock.—The shells recommence. . . . We hear the pealing of the cannon. 6.30.—The house of Franqueville is burning ; the sparks come over us. Another fire near the Hôtel de Ville. More water ! The Hôtel de Ville is silent, and is said to be burning. . . . 8 o'clock. —"Installation" of mattresses for the night. Papa and Simone, André, Renée, and Albert on mattresses in the wine-cellar ; Ivy and Emma, Robert, Joseph. Bernard in the beer-cellar ; Mama, M——, and myself on two mattresses in the coal-cellar ; and Marie in a blanket on the ground. No further bombardment taking advantage of the calm, the *Arrageois* come out and chat. During the night Mama goes to get some provisions from the storeroom.

October 7.—About 2 a.m. we hear the distant sound of cannon. . . . At 7 o'clock the bombardment recommences, but less violent than yesterday. But soon there appear two German aeroplanes, which throw bombs on Arras. . . . 2.30 p.m.—*Grande joie !* M. Ducroc tells us that the noise we have heard is that of the French guns. General Pau has arrived : he has been expected for two days, and he is repulsing the Germans. . . . We come out of the cellar, delighted. Papa makes a tour ; the Hôtel de Ville is destroyed, save the tower. . . . all the *quartier* near to the Hôtel de Ville is destroyed up to Planqué's, the pastrycook's. . . . Papa goes as far as Segaud's. People come out, they open the little shops. There is no further danger. Then all at once a bomb bursts over Papa, who has only just time to run into Segaud's. He is hurrying

FRENCH SPAHIS.

GERMAN LANDWEHR IN A VILLAGE,

back when another bursts in the Place du Théâtre. Happily he is not hurt, and comes in just as we are making haste down to the cellar.

4.35 p.m.—A great report, a red glow, and heat we can feel in the cellar ; a bomb has fallen in the little yard, breaking the telegraph wires, the kitchen windows, the verandah, and some bottles. Happily there is no fire. But the fire at M. Acrement's is gaining hold, so we hesitate whether to leave. . . . We go to sleep *chez* M. Wartelle, who has the kindness to lodge us all. So we leave, *toute la bande,* and forget to have our supper. . . . We instal ourselves at M. Wartelle's, along with a number of other refugees.

October 8.—During the night an interminable procession of people who are seeking safety. . . . About 5 o'clock Papa and M. Wartelle go to our house and visit the town. What havoc ! The town in ruins ! Our house is not burning. At 9 o'clock Papa and Mama return to the house to fetch some provisions. He does not return until half-past 12 ; *nous étions si inquiets !* An aeroplane had thrown a quantity of bombs on the Rue du Bloc, the Cathedral, the Petite Place, and the Grande Place. At 4 o'clock the Chanoine H——— brings us some good news. The Germans are retreating. . . . Their centre still holds, however, so we may still have some bombs. . . . The Chapelle de St. Sacrement is damaged, and a nurse and two wounded have been killed. The Hospice badly damaged, and a nun and 17 soldiers killed. A baby which a nun held in her arms was killed, but she was not hurt ! . . . Pauvre Hôtel de Ville, adieu !

October 9.—The news is not so good. The Germans are behind Beauvais . . . the bombardment may recommence. . . . We ascend and have our meals upstairs. People come out of their houses. Papa takes us out to see the town. . . . *Quelle horreur !* One would say there had been an earthquake. Rue St. Géry is impassable ; *débris* blocking the street. The Church of St. Jean Baptiste is so badly damaged

that it will not be possible to hold the Office there any more. By the direction of the bombs we see that the Alboches directed their fire on the beautiful monuments of Arras—the Hôtel de Ville, St. Jean Baptiste, the Cathedral. At the Ecole Normale a bomb falls, kills two French wounded, and spares a German who is by their side. . . . The horror of horrors is the Hôtel de Ville—an irreparable disaster. . . .

A German of the 9th Jaeger Battalion, which had formed part of a column that reached Lens on October 5, gives us in a letter of October 21 a glimpse of the sensations felt by the Kaiser's troops :

On October 5 we reached Lens, and on the 7th took up a position at Jeuer. The enemy shelled us so heavily all day that Lieut. B——— gave the order to retire at 4 p.m., and we lost touch of the other companies. We retreated under terrible rifle and shell fire, and had hardly arrived under cover when our captain drove us out again to our old position. The fire was so heavy on our return that I was surprised that we got there at all ; it was so terrible that one could imagine hell had opened up, and was pouring fire out of a thousand craters. I spent the most terrible hours of my life that day. The awful bombardment continued, our artillery not being able to give us any protection. At noon the next day we were forced to retire. This movement took place under still heavier artillery and machine-gun fire. How I survived is a wonder.

The next day a Bavarian non-commissioned officer was making in his diary the following entry : " We are now near the town of Arras. I am now leader (as sergeant) of my company, as all our officers have either been killed or

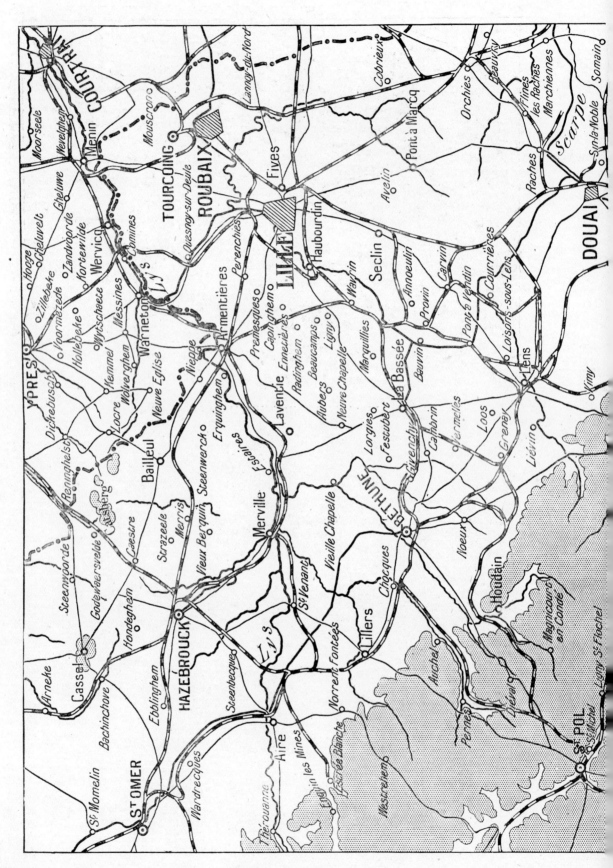

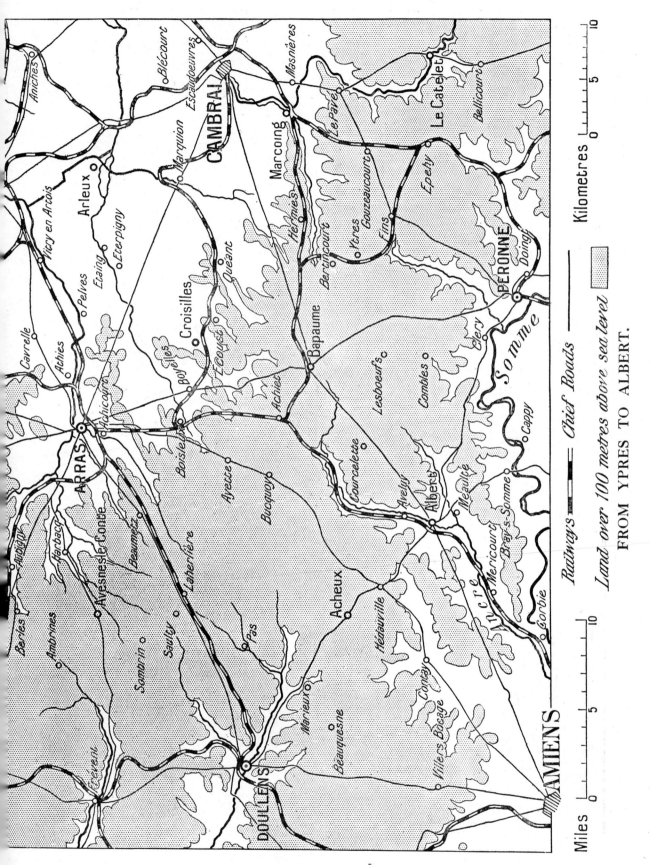

FROM YPRES TO ALBERT.

Miles

Railways ▬ Chief Roads ▬

Land over 100 metres above sea level

Kilometres

wounded. We have suffered terrible losses during the last few days. Yesterday I was nearly killed, a bullet hitting my belt-buckle."

Into Arras itself the Germans attempted to penetrate. After a fierce struggle they gained a footing inside the Vauban ramparts, but French reinforcements arrived through the Porte d'Amiens and the Germans were expelled. Arras itself remained in the possession of the French; it was destined later in the month to suffer still worse experiences.

Away to the north-east, on the road from Arras to Lille, the battle continued to rage. Douai and Lens, as has been mentioned, had been captured by the Germans, but their attacks in the direction of St. Pol had been repulsed. On October 7 French artillery approached Lens, and firing over it battered the German position near the village of Loison.

The German line, therefore, extended by October 7 from Cambrai through Douai to the east of Lens. They had been throwing shells into Lille since the 4th. A strong force was moving up the right bank of the Lys from Tourcoing to Armentières. An armoured train arrived at Fives, on the east of Lille, and fierce encounters took place in the suburbs during the 4th and 5th. From the chimneys of a large factory owned by Germans fifteen spies were dislodged. Covered from head to foot with soot they lay on the ground, said an eye-witness, "screaming their allegiance to France." The French Territorials did not give way and the enemy were driven back, but large numbers of the inhabitants fled on foot

ARRAS.
The Hotel de Ville after the first bombardment.

ARRAS AFTER THE SECOND BOMBARDMENT.

or in trains to Calais and Boulogne. Tuesday (the 6th) the Germans assaulted the eastern, northern and north-western suburbs, but the Territorials and the French artillery mowed them down. The Germans appear to have had few guns, and the batteries of *Soixante-quinze* wrought terrible execution among the enemy's masses. If ever any man may be regarded as the saviour of a nation it is the inventor of those deadly instruments.

Maud'huy's offensive, like Castelnau's, had been brought to a standstill by October 4. His troops had fought with conspicuous gallantry, he had handled them with remarkable skill, but he had not been able to turn the flank of the German Army, and for a frontal attack he had not sufficient force. In modern warfare frontal attacks involve enormous losses and consequently require great numerical superiority. Against the powerful German artillery, their innumerable machine guns, and their vastly greater strength it was impossible to make headway. The Germans held the inner arc of the two curves on which the forces were disputing, and the line they held was naturally strong. On their extreme left in the Vosges and at their centre the Germans, owing to the position of stalemate which for the time existed, required no more men than was needed to hold their own, and all available troops were therefore hurried hastily up to support their right wing, and everything in the shape of reserve formations which could be obtained

brought with the utmost celerity to the decisive point.

It was a critical moment for Joffre, and, when examining his strategy, we must always remember that Paris was the heart of France; and the Germans on the Aisne were not 50 miles from it. It speaks worlds for Joffre's self-reliance and his confidence in the superior quality of the Allied Army that he did not now refuse his consent to Sir John French's proposal to transfer the British Expeditionary Force from the Aisne to the left of Maud'huy's Army, which, like Castelnau's, would have to remain mostly on the defensive.

Antwerp was *in extremis*, the Lys had been crossed by the enemy, and Ypres occupied by them on the 3rd. It followed that Calais, Boulogne, Ostend, Zeebrugge, Bruges and Ghent, as well as Lille, were in danger. To assist in the relief of Antwerp, if it were still possible, to prevent the enemy either gaining Ghent, Bruges, Zeebrugge, Ostend, and intercepting the Belgian Army if it had to retreat to the coast, or taking Lille or enveloping the left wing of Maud'huy's Army, Joffre decided to concentrate still another army between Lens and Dunkirk. The command of it was given to General d'Urbal. This army and the British Expeditionary Force were to form the extreme left of the Allied Forces, while the right of their vast line extended to the borders of Switzerland. General Foch was selected by Joffre to co-ordinate the movements of Castelnau's,

REFRESHMENTS FOR THE BRITISH TROOPS.

Maud'huy's, Sir John French's and d'Urbal's armies.

Foch had been born at Metz. He was of the same age as Joffre. He had been educated at the Ecole Polytechnique. Like Maud'huy, he had been a Professor of Strategy at the Ecole de Guerre, and he had published two important works on the Art of War which showed he was a lucid observer and profound thinker, thoroughly alive to the new conditions introduced by the progress of science, as applied to war. In July he had commanded a corps, but Joffre had speedily perceived that in Foch he possessed a soldier of rare merit. On August 20 the French Generalissimo had formed a 9th Army, and it was to Foch that the command of it had been given. He had at the Battle of the Marne amply justified Joffre's choice. From September 6 to 9 Foch had held with his troops the position between Sezanne and Mailly and prevented the Germans from piercing the centre of the French line. On September 9, by an audacious manœuvre, he had swung the left of his army on the flank of the Prussian Guard, which was supported by certain corps of Saxons. The Germans retired precipitately and, on the morning of the 11th, Foch entered Châlons-sur-Marne.

The headquarters of General Foch were fixed at Doullens, a town of 6,000 inhabitants north of Amiens and half way between Arras and Abbeville. Here this "short, quick-moving, clear-glanced man," marshalled the forces arrayed between Dunkirk and Compiègne. Those forces were smaller than the armies being hurled by the Kaiser against them, but, judged by the standards of the nineteenth century, they were an enormous body of armed men. Let us try to realize how General Foch co-ordinated the armies under his direction.

In the twentieth century a Commander-in-Chief could not base his movements on personal observation. The extent of country over which his troops operated was far too great. By telegraph, wireless, telephone, motor-car, motor-cycle, bicycle and aeroplane he received reports from his subordinates in the fighting line, who sent to him the information which the eyes of the army had seen. This information was laid down for him by members of his staff on maps spread out on large tables. Movements of his own or the enemy's forces were recorded with the aid of flags or coloured chalk. Facts not capable of being presented pictorially were analysed by the staff, and thus the Commander obtained a complete presentment of the situation. He might perhaps seek to clear up some point by reading a message in the form in which it was delivered at headquarters, but rarely would this be needed. Moreover, he had at his side the heads of the services which ministered to the men actually engaged in the fighting: the directors of supplies, transport and the like.

Nearer the fighting line but outside it were the Corps Headquarters. Between these and the General Headquarters were certain Report Centres where the Commander-in-Chief could meet his subordinates for consultation. Special officers passed to and fro daily from the General to the Corps' Headquarters to convey verbal or written orders or wishes. Others moved from the Headquarters of one Corps to that of another. The Corps' Headquarters were a reproduction *in petto* of the Headquarters of the Supreme Commander.

Still nearer the front were the Divisional Headquarters, which were within range of the enemy's heavy artillery. Beyond—probably in an underground dwelling—were the Brigadier-General and his staff, and, 400 or 500 yards further on, the Colonels commanding battalions. There were intermediate posts between each of these centres and officers moved from one to the other. A telephone wire from the firing line to General Headquarters kept the Commander-in-Chief, as a rule, almost immediately in touch with the line of battle. The importance of telegraphs and telephones may be judged from the following extract from a British officer's letter:

I am very much surprised to see in the English Press so little mention made of the field telegraphs, or signal service, as it is now known. In time of war the signal companies of the Royal Engineers are one of the most important and necessary arms of the service. They are the nerves of the Army.

Most of the important towns in the north of France and also London and Paris are in direct touch with General Headquarters. These are called the main lines of communication, and over their wires day and night pass a continuous flood of traffic for the hospital bases, ordnance, remount, and store depôts. From General Headquarters radiate wires to the various army corps headquarters, and, again, each army has its communications to the divisions, which, further, have wires right up to the brigades. It will thus be seen that in the space of a few minutes the War Office is fully and clearly informed of what is going on in the firing line. In fact, were the lines joined straight through it would be possible to hear the roar of artillery and the bursting of shrapnel in Martin's-le-Grand.

As the tide of battle turns this way and the other and headquarters are constantly moving, some means have to be provided to keep in constant touch with General Headquarters during the movement. This emergency is met by cable detachments. Each detachment consists of two cable wagons, which usually work in conjunction with one another, one section laying the line whilst the other remains behind to reel up when the line is finished with. A division is ordered to move quickly to a more tactical position. The end of the cable is connected with the permanent line, which communicates to Army Headquarters, and the cable detachment moves off at the trot; across country, along roads, through villages, and past columns of troops, the white and blue badge of the signal service clears the way. Behind the wagon rides a horseman, who deftly lays the cable in

BELGIAN CAVALRY RETIRING FROM ACTION.

the ditches and hedges out of danger from heavy transport and the feet of tramping infantry with the aid of a crooked stick. Other horsemen are in the rear tying back and making the line safe. On the box of the wagon sits a telegraphist, who is constantly in touch with headquarters as the cable runs swiftly out. An orderly dashes up with an important message; the wagon is stopped, the message dispatched, and on they go again.

At Le Cateau the situation was so desperate that signal companies were sent to the trenches to assist the infantry in repelling a heavy attack. For this piece of work we were highly complimented by General Smith-Dorrien, who at the same time expressed his great satisfaction at the way in which his communications had been established throughout the campaign.

Telegraphists are often left on duty in the trenches and lonely farm houses, châteaux, etc., close to the firing line, and I leave it to your imagination to picture how difficult it is to concentrate one's mind on the signalling and reception of important messages while the air is filled with the deafening roar of artillery and the screaming and bursting of shells. An experience of this kind happened to me a short time ago in a lonely château on the Ypres-Menin road. The château was the centre of a perfect hell of German shrapnel for nearly a week, until it become almost untenable, and was abandoned by the Headquarters Staff. The General gave instructions that a telegraphist was to remain behind to transmit important dispatches from the brigades, and I was left in charge of the instruments in this shell-swept château for a day and a night. On the second day the Germans broke through our trenches, and the wires were cut up by shell fire. I was given orders to evacuate the building and smash up my instruments. These I saved by burying in a shell-proof trench, and then had to escape between our own fire and that of the enemy's across a field under a terrible tornado of shrapnel. On the early morning of the same day one of our cable detachments was cut up and another captured by the Germans, only to be retaken by our sappers and drivers after a desperate and glorious fight.

In the region of the Aisne, where the hilly and wooded nature of the country admitted of much cover, spies often took advantage of this to tap our wires. The lines are constantly patrolled by mounted linemen, whose duty is attended with much risk. On one occasion a lineman, in passing along his patrol, noticed that there was a quantity of slack cable lying on the side of the road. Dismounting to coil it up out of the reach of traffic, he found to his surprise that a piece of spare wire had been tied into the main line, and upon investigating discovered that it led to the top of a haystack, the wire being cunningly hidden in the straw. Going further down the line he tapped it and reported the matter to headquarters, then, mounting guard over the haystack, he awaited the arrival of an armed escort, who discovered the spy, together with several days' supply of food, hidden in the depth of the hay.

Telegraphists of experience can often detect if anyone is tampering with the line. An operator on duty at Bavai; near Mons, was listening attentively to the buzz of the various stations in circuit on an important line when his attention was arrested by a very faint drone, which he knew immediately was caused by induction from another cable. He amused himself by writing down on a scrap of paper the signals as they faintly echoed in his receiver. Some French telegraphist, he thought, sending a cipher message. An officer looked over his shoulder. " Hello," he said. " so you understand German." When the excitement had subsided after the telegraphist's explanation, a scouting party was dispatched from ends of the wire, and succeeded in making a very neat capture. Wireless telegraphy, of course, plays an important part in this war, most of the larger aeroplanes being equipped with apparatus, by which means they swiftly communicate important observations to headquarters. The Germans also make elaborate use of this system.

How different was the position of the modern Generalissimo from that of one a hundred years ago, when Napoleon could survey the whole field of battle with his small telescope scarcely larger than one barrel of an opera glass !

FRENCH SOLDIERS TAKING THEIR HORSES TO BE WATERED.

DUNKIRK.
Headquarters of General Dubail's Army, and British Air Corps.

As early as 1866, at Königgrätz, it had been found impossible for a Generalissimo to command the whole line of battle. In 1870, at Gravelotte, the Prussian king on the right wing of his army was unaware of the progress on its left, till an officer of his Staff, observing the red glint through the trees about St. Privat, and knowing this must come from the famed *pantalons garances* of the French, deduced the fact that they were in full retreat. In 1914 a General within range of modern weapons would not command a view of one-fiftieth of the fighting, nor could he, in the days of smokeless powder, obtain anything more than a very imperfect impression of the progress of the conflict. Battles are now fought by the many subordinate leaders ; the Generalissimo can only direct their efforts generally, and cannot personally influence them by his presence.

At Doullens on October 8 Sir John French was received by General Foch. Arrangements for the withdrawal of the British Army from the trenches on the Aisne had been already made by the French General Staff, and the operation had commenced on October 3, when there was perhaps still a faint hope that Antwerp could hold out until it was relieved. The 2nd Cavalry Division, commanded by General Gough, had led the way. Under cover of darkness the units silently left the trenches, often not a hundred yards away from the enemy, whom they had so long and gallantly held at bay. They were replaced by French soldiers. Next they descended—frequently down steep slopes and difficult paths—to the northern bank of the Aisne, groped their way, often under fire of the enemy's artillery, across the plank roadways of floating bridges or of other bridges but imperfectly repaired, and then ascended slowly to the top of the heights which bordered the southern side of the river.

The diary of a non-commissioned officer in the 1st North Staffordshire Regiment—a Wolverhampton man—contributed to the *Daily Chronicle*, and the letter of an officer published in *The Times* of November 7, enable us to catch glimpses of the rapid transfer of the British Expeditionary Force from the Aisne to the confines of Flanders. On October 9 the Staffordshire man was at Compiègne ; the next day he travelled by train to "Blendiques." where he was billeted in a large paper-mill. On October 11 he was at Arques, three miles or so from St. Omer, which is about 23 miles from Calais. There he lodged at a glass-works. On the 12th he moved to Hazebrouck, and on the 13th he was under shell fire three miles out of the latter town.*

From the officer's letter is extracted the following :

We left the River Aisne, and now we are a long way north of that position. It was a wonderful move.

---

* Hazebrouck is the junction of the railway lines from Lille and Lens to Calais.

COMPIÈGNE.
Divers clearing the River Oise where a pontoon bridge was sunk.

French troops appeared out of the darkness and took our places. They had marched many miles but were quite cheerful and calm, their only desire being to get into our " dug-outs " and go to sleep, they cared nothing for the expected pressure of the enemy. Then we marched down the hill into a comparative peace. and. joy of joys, were allowed to smoke and talk. It was a bitterly cold night, and we were dreadfully sleepy, so that we nodded as we trudged along, and saw visions of the men in front of us, as it were of trees walking ! Mine were geraniums and palm branches—omens of victory.

And so we entrained, and slept, closely packed, indeed, but on beautiful soft cushions instead of the mud of a trench ; the men were comfortable, being wedged by forties in covered trucks with clean straw for a bed. But we awoke in Paris ! There it was, with the church of the Sacré Cœur on Montmartre, all the same as ever. All was peace. But it was not for us ; and we passed slowly through and slept again until we stopped for water at Amiens. . . .

Our journey continued as fast as a train holding 1,000 men and their transport wagons can travel, and we were at Calais by evening. But a murrain on the foggy weather which prevented us catching a glimpse of the heights of Dover town ! However, at another stopping place there was a charming English girl giving the soldiers cigarettes, and the sight of her and a word or two made us doubly brave.

Not all the soldiers travelled by train. Some in auto-buses, taxicabs, motor-cars, were hurried by high road and by-road to the new theatre of operations. So great was the throng of vehicles that many roads resembled the highway to Epsom on an old-fashioned Derby Day. Overhead the noisy, throbbing aeroplanes flew like a flock of migrating birds.

As the British Forces passed northward they met trains and motor-omnibuses crammed with the French reinforcements being moved to the support of Castelnau's and Maud'huy's hardpressed armies and the units of the new Army which under d'Urbal was to fill with the British Expeditionary Force the wide gap (50 miles) between Lens and Dunkirk. The skill and precision with which the French General Staff transported the British and d'Urbal's troops across the lines of communication of Castelnau's and Maud'huy's Armies were worthy of all praise. It must have been a surprise to the Germans.

In 1913 the old Prince Henckel von Donnersmarck, in a conversation with a member of the French Embassy at Berlin, had expressed an opinion that the French in a war with the Germans would be beaten because they were not " precise." The Frenchman, according to the Prince, had a great facility for work, but was not as punctilious as the Germans in the accomplishment of his duties. In the coming war, he had added, the victorious nation would be that nation whose servants, from the top to the bottom of the ladder, were exact in the accomplishment of their duty, however important or however trivial it might be. That the

French, inspired by the noblest patriotism, would rise to the standard of execution observed by the Kaiser's troops had not entered into the Prince's calculations.

While the British were being carried towards the Straits of Dover, Sir John French, at Doullens, on October 8, was, as has been said, arranging the plan of operations with General Foch. The weak spot in the line from Compiègne to Dunkirk was the 50 miles of country from Lens to Dunkirk and Nieuport. On October 3 German Dragoons had appeared at Ypres and bullied the inhabitants. The next day (October 4) another party of Dragoons fired on a train at Comines on the Lys. This village was about half way from Ypres to Lille. The whole country round Poperinghe and Ypres was swarming with Uhlans, who (October 5) shot the rural policeman of Westoutre and lashed the Mayor of that town and his two assistants across the face. On October 5 the German artillery near Bailleul blew up the railway line which connected Lille and Courtrai with Hazebrouck, St. Omer and Calais, while the sound of cannon was heard to the north of Hazebrouck. German prisoners reported that two Army Corps were advancing to attack the Allies' left wing. The day that French met Foch at Doullens (the 8th) a patrol of 22 Dragoons rode to the little Flemish town of Cassel, situated on a hill overlooking the surrounding plain, and burnt the station and inn of a neighbouring village. Cassel was only 20 miles south of Dunkirk. That night 40 Bavarians at 9 p.m. stormed the station of Hazebrouck. They killed the sentry at the level crossing and two guards of trains at rest in the station. A brave young French motor-cyclist shot one of the Germans and, almost single-handed, captured four others ; an old woman and a child flying in terror were killed. After this brave exploit the German patrol withdrew in haste.

It was in these circumstances that French and Foch drew up their plans. Antwerp was falling and the Belgian and British Forces were retiring from the doomed city to Ghent, Bruges and Ostend. The 7th Infantry Division and the 3rd Cavalry Division, under Sir Henry Rawlinson, had landed at Ostend and Zeebrugge. They would assist and cover the retreat of the Belgians and the British from Antwerp. The presence of the Germans in the region between Hazebrouck and Ypres implied either that an attempt was being made to encircle from the south and west the retreating British and Belgians, and that the Kaiser was bent on capturing Dunkirk and Calais, or that an effort would be made to turn the left wing of the Army of Maud'huy in the region of Lens. That Lille, which had been occupied, ransomed, and abandoned in August would be retaken, admitted of little doubt.

The following decisions were come to. The road running from Béthune to Lille was to be the dividing line between Maud'huy's and French's force. The British Army was to be posted north of this line, and its right wing, composed of the 2nd Corps (Smith-Dorrien's),

BRITISH AEROPLANES AT THE BASE IN FLANDERS.

was to attack from the north in flank the enemy opposing Maud'huy's left wing west of La Bassée. In the course of this manœuvre the British would move between the Lys and the Aire-Béthune-La Bassée-Lille Canal, and would also attempt to defend or recover Lille.

The 2nd Corps was to arrive on the line Aire-Béthune by the 11th. The Cavalry Corps (Allenby's) was to be stationed on its northern —*i.e.*, left flank, until replaced by the 3rd Corps (Pulteney's) which was to detrain at St. Omer on the 12th. After the arrival of the 3rd Corps the cavalry were to move to Pulteney's northern flank and remain there until relieved by the 1st Corps (Haig's), which was not expected to be concentrated between St. Omer and Hazebrouck before the 19th. Rawlinson's Corps (the 4th) had been now placed by telegraphic instructions from Lord Kitchener under Sir John French's orders. It was to continue to help the Belgians and eventually to form the left wing of the British Army, which would be reinforced in the course of ten days or so by the Lahore Division of the Indian Expeditionary Force, and by units of the Territorial Army. The Army of D'Urbal was to act in conjunction with the British Army, and it was hoped that the whole of the Allied

Forces sweeping the Germans through Ypres and Lille would be able to join hands with the Belgians and Rawlinson's Corps and drive the enemy back on Brussels.

Antwerp was on the point of falling ; the Belgian Army and the British auxiliary force under General Paris were retreating, the Germans were crossing the Scheldt between Antwerp and Ghent. As the bombardment of Antwerp ceased the bombardment of Lille began. A tremendous battle was about to open from Nieuport to Lens. But first we must narrate the events which occurred in Belgium from the fall of Antwerp to the arrival of the Belgian Army on the banks of the Yser ; but before doing this we will exhibit another and more pleasing aspect of the war.

A medical correspondent of *The Times*, writing on October 11, explains how the waterways which played so important a part in the fighting between Dunkirk and Compiègne were being utilized for the conveyance of the wounded to the base hospitals :

I have had an opportunity to-day of inspecting one of the large hospital barges which, under the auspices of the Union des Femmes de France, are being fitted up for service between Paris and the battle-front. This visit has impressed me very much. The use of barges is nothing less than an inspiration, because the barges

GERMAN TRENCHES.

BRITISH SOLDIERS WRITING HOME.

render possible what is impossible by any other means—treatment while in course of transport.

The north of France, as is well known, is exceedingly rich in waterways—rivers and canals. The four great rivers, the Oise, the Somme, the Sambre, and the Escaut (Scheldt), are connected by a network of canals—quiet and comfortable waterways, at present almost free of traffic. So far as the reaching of any particular spot is concerned these waterways may be said to be ubiquitous. They extend, too, right into Belgium and have connexions with the coast at various points—for example, Ostend. Here, then, is a third system of "roads" for the removal of the wounded—a system which, if properly used, can be made to relieve greatly the stress of work imposed upon the ambulance motor-cars and trains. Here also is the ideal method of removal, as I realized during my visit this morning.

The Ile de France is lying at present at the Quai de Grenelle, near the Eiffel Tower. This is a Seine barge of the usual size and type, blunt-nosed, heavily and roomily built. You enter the hold by a step-ladder, which is part of the hospital equipment. This is a large chamber not much less high from floor to ceiling than an ordinary room, well lit and ventilated by means of skylights. The walls of the hold have been painted white, the floor has been thoroughly scrubbed out for the reception of beds, of which, it is hoped, some 40–50 will be accommodated. At the after-end of the chamber there is a little apartment which will form an excellent retiring room. Amidships, and built in such a manner that entry can be made either from outside by a short flight of steps leading downwards or from the hold itself by a flight leading upwards, is the barge-master's cabin, now converted into a living-room for two surgeons.

The forward portion of the barge can accommodate more beds, and there is no reason why a portion of it should not be walled in and used as an operating-room—more especially since in the bow a useful washing appara-

tus is fitted. The barge is heated by stoves, and a small electric plant could easily be installed. It is calculated that for £100 a barge can be completely transformed into a floating hospital, furnished, and put into commission. The cost of the hire of each barge is, roughly, about 9s. per day. The barges are used in groups of four, and a small tug supplies the motive power. In favourable circumstances about 50 kilometres a day can be travelled.

The great advantage of a floating hospital is, of course, that treatment can begin immediately the patient is brought aboard. Moreover, thanks to the presence of a small crane, a stretcher can be lifted into the hold without disturbing the wounded man in the least, and, of course, lifted out again in the same manner. I witnessed a demonstration of this lifting, and it left nothing to be desired. If we suppose that our barge has been brought up to, say, a distance of ten miles from the front (this it would appear is perfectly possible in most instances), it will be clear that the lot of a severely wounded man who is carried to it and immediately attended by a competent surgeon is happier even than that of the soldier who must travel sixty miles by road. It is, of course, not to be compared with the lot of a man who has a train journey of a couple of days to endure before competent treatment is possible.

There is thus very clearly a place for these ambulance barges in a comprehensive scheme of ambulance work. It must not, however, be forgotten that certain drawbacks are likely to be encountered. For example, locks and bridges may have been broken, and progress thus impeded—though the very rich network of canals ensures to some extent against this—or again floods may occur and so render it difficult to manipulate the barges. These difficulties will be faced. The barges are simply too good to lose. To some extent they may take the place of "immediate case hospitals," to which I referred in a previous article; in any event they will provide another much-needed means of transport.

It is not for a moment to be supposed that the employment of these barges can supersede the use either of ambulance cars, of which still more are needed, or of trains. All agencies are necessary in this great and difficult work; all must be used to the full. But the barge does afford a new hope to the unfortunate with broken bones, who must experience a twinge of agony at each bump of the road, and to the case where stillness is necessary to control bleeding. Of this particular problem it is, in my opinion, the best solution yet offered.

To conclude with a few remarks on General Joffre's strategy : his attempt by indirect pressure to save Antwerp from the invaders had failed and the Germans had successfully protected their lines of communication from the advance, first of Castelnau's and next of Maud'huy's Army. The numerical inferiority of the Allies and the fact that the Germans were operating on interior lines had thus rendered nugatory the sane and elaborate calculations of the French leader for the relief of Antwerp. Because of the reasons set out at the beginning of this chapter, Joffre had not been able to remain purely on the defensive. Had he done so, not only would Antwerp have fallen, but the Belgian Army might have been rapidly and suddenly overwhelmed by the Germans. Now the march of Castelnau on St. Quentin, of Maud'huy on Cambrai and Valenciennes, had forced the enemy to keep the mass of his reserves south and east of the Scheldt. But for this the whole, or a portion, of those reserves could have been directed on Ghent and Ostend while the Belgian Army was being attacked by the troops under Beseler in the neighbourhood of Antwerp. Though Antwerp itself was not saved, the Belgian Army (and its British auxiliaries) was unquestionably protected by Joffre's offensive, which, to that extent may be unhesitatingly pronounced to have been successful.

Nor was that all. The French movements on St. Quentin, Cambrai and Valenciennes had paralysed the menacing advance of the German left wing through the gap made towards the end of September at St. Mihiel in the Verdun-Toul line of permanent fortifications. If that advance had been continued, Verdun might have been isolated and the French defences in the Argonne region turned at their southern extremity. As it happened, the presence of Castelnau's Army in the plain of the Somme and of Maud'huy's Army on the high ground between the plain of the Somme and the plain of the Scheldt had obliged the German Staff to transport large and ever larger bodies of troops from Alsace, from Lorraine, and from the entrenchments north of the Aisne, to the banks of the Oise, Somme, Scheldt and Lys. Joffre's prudent offensive had again scored. The Germans, to counterbalance the dislocation of their plans to reduce Verdun and crumple up the French right wing, had nothing to set but a succession of drawn battles between Compiègne and Lens.

Lastly, it must not be forgotten that it was the existence of Castelnau's and Maud'huy's Armies in their entrenchments between Compiègne and Béthune that permitted Sir John French safely to move the British Expeditionary Force from the Aisne to the region of Ypres and General Foch to reinforce without serious risks the, at first, scanty forces under General d'Urbal stationed between Béthune and Dunkirk. And, if Sir John French and General d'Urbal had been unable to concentrate their armies on the plain of the Scheldt, the Belgian and British forces retiring from Antwerp would probably have been either destroyed, captured, or driven on to Dutch soil, while the enemy would most certainly have occupied Dunkirk and Calais, with results disastrous to the Allies.

END OF VOLUME TWO.

INDEX TO VOLUME II.

P

Pacific, operations of New Zealand Contingent, 266–270

Paine, Captain Godfrey, 187

Pallada, Russian cruiser, sunk, 24

Papeeta shelled, 35

Paris under the German Menace, 437–476

Paris : Aliens, treatment of, 452 ; bombs dropped on, 459, 460 ; charitable organizations, 450 ; exodus of population, 461 ; financial panic, 439 ; fortifications, 453 ; German advance on, 460 ; Government transferred to Bordeaux, 49, 459 ; returns to Paris, 467 ; preparations for defence of, 50 ; press censorship, 449 ; reception of Field-Marshal Sir John French, 453 ; rioting in, 448

Paris, General, 93, 94, 506

Pashitch, M., 279

Patey, Admiral Sir George, 37

Pathfinder, H.M.S., loss of, 14

Pau, General, 56, 71

Paulhan, Louis, 178, 179

Pearce, Hon. George F., 257, 261

Pegasus, H.M.S., destroyed, 35, 37

Peking Gazette purchased by Germans, 419

Perceval, Brig.-General, 132

Peronne, 150 ; battle at, 485 ; German accounts of battle, 486 ; Germans in, 481

Petit Morin, 62

Philomel, H.M.S., 37

Pockley, Captain, 268

Poincaré, M. : message to Chamber, 446 ; return from Russia, 439

Pont-Arcy, British cross the Aisne at, 128

Pontoporos, Greek steamer, sunk, 35

Poperinghe, Germans in, 505

Poporparlok, 305

Prince Heinrich Hill, capture of, 417

Prize Court, sitting of, 31

Psyche, H.M.S., 37

Pulteney, Lieut.-General W. P., 58, 506

Putnik, Field-Marshal, 300 ; arrested in Budapest, 301

Pyramus, H.M.S., 37

R

Rawaruska, battle of, 124

Rawlinson, Lieut.-General Sir Henry, lands at Ostend, 505

Refugees, Belgian, from Antwerp, 106–109

Reid, Sir George, 256

Reims, bombardment of, 144 ; operations at, 148, 161, 162

Roberts, Lord : welcomes first Canadian Contingent, 251 ; visits Indian troops in France, 338–341 ; death, 340

Roblin, Hon. R. P., 240

Robson, Colonel, in command at Hartlepool bombardment, 367

Roulers, 82

Royal Engineers, British Officer's letter on work of, 501

Royal Fleet Reserve called out, 4

Royal Flying Corps : mentioned in despatches, 65, 66, 182 ; organization of, 185–190 ; origin of, 183 ; strength, 194, 195

Royal Naval Air Service, organization of, 190–194

Royal Naval Reserve called out, 4 ; mine sweeping by, 7

Royal Naval Volunteer Reserve called out, 4

Roye, 485

Rupel, river, 82, 86

Russian Navy, operations in the Baltic, 24

S

S 115, S 117, S 118, S 119, German destroyers, sunk, 17

Saarburg, 42 ; operations at, 43

St. Mihiel, 481

St. Quentin, 150 ; Germans in, 481

Sakhalin, Island of, German rumour concerning, 425

Sambre, 44

Samoa, 37, 38 ; annexation of, 267

Samson, Commander Charles R., 191

Sarrail, General, 56

Scarborough, bombardment of, 378–384 ; description of, 363

Scharnhorst, German cruiser, in the Pacific, 35, 37

Scheldt, river, 5, 113

Schilde, bombs dropped on, 90

Schoen, Baron von, delivers Declaration of War, 447

Schoonaerde, Germans cross the Scheldt at, 113

Scindia of Gwalior, Maharaja, 319

Scott, Hon. Walter, 253

Serajevo murder, 218

Serbia : military history of, 278 ; railway system, 284

Serbia, King of, 279

Serbian Army : Army Corps distribution, 284 ; Artillery, 286 ; condition at outbreak of war, 291 ; in the Balkan Wars, 277, 280–282, 287 ; mobilization of, 292 ; organization, 283–288 ; spirit of, 287 ; strength, 285

Severn, H.M.S., bombards Belgian coast, 24

Seydlitz, German cruiser, in Yarmouth raid, 358

Shabatz : Austrian occupation and evacuation of, 298, 315 ; Serbian investment of, 306

Shirotae, Japanese destroyer, sunk, 411

Sierra Leone, gifts to Mother Country, 275

Singh, Sir Pertab, 318, 327

Smith-Dorrien, General Sir Horace, 77, 505

Snaeskerke, operations at, 82

Snagge, Commander Arthur L., 24

Soden, German gunboat, captured, 35

Soissons, 64, 78, 124 ; operations at, 125, 126, 129, 130, 135, 162

South Africa, gifts to Mother Country, 272, 273

Speedy, H.M.S., loss of, 14

Spies : see Espionage

Spreewald, German armed liner, captured, 35

Stag, H.M.S., 15

Strassburg, German cruiser, in the Atlantic, 35 ; in Yarmouth raid, 358

Submarines, British : A E 1, lost, 39 ; D 5, mined, 361 ; E 3, lost, 19 ; E 4, E 6, E 8, in Heligoland Bight action, 5, 13 ; E 9, sinks the *Hela*, 15

Sueter, Captain Murray F., 191

Suez Canal, use of by merchant vessels, 23

Sydney, H.M.A.S., destroys the *Emden*, 35, 262, 270

T

Takachiho, Japanese cruiser, sunk, 411, 418

Talbot, Lieut.-Commander Cecil P., 5

Tannenberg, battle of, 46

Termonde : destruction of, 82 ; operations at, 85, 86 ; Germans cross the Scheldt at, 113

ILLUSTRATIONS IN VOLUME II.

PORTRAITS.

PLACES.

MAPS AND PLANS.